GMAT

GRADUATE MANAGEMENT ADMISSION TEST

GMAT

GRADUATE MANAGEMENT ADMISSION TEST

Thomas H. Martinson
David Ellis, M.B.A.

Prentice Hall
New York • London • Toronto • Sydney • Tokyo • Singapore

Fifth Edition

Copyright © 1991, 1989, 1987, 1984, 1983 by Arco Publishing, a division
of Simon & Schuster, Inc.
All rights reserved
including the right of reproduction
in whole or in part in any form

Prentice Hall General Reference
15 Columbus Circle
New York, NY 10023

An Arco Book

Arco, Prentice Hall and colophons are
registered trademarks of Simon & Schuster, Inc.

Manufactured in the United States of America

1 2 3 4 5 6 7 8 9 10

Library of Congress Cataloging-in-Publication Data

Martinson, Thomas H.
   GMAT: graduate management admission test / Thomas H. Martinson,
David Ellis. —5th ed.
    p. cm.
   ISBN 0-13-361783-1
   1.Graduate Management Admission Test. 2. Management—
Examinations, questions, etc. 3. Management—Study and teaching
(Graduate). I. Ellis, David. II. Title.
HD30.413.C75   1991   91-36564
650'.076—dc20   CIP

CONTENTS

Part Four—Full-Length Practice Examinations

HOW THIS BOOK CAN HELP
YOU GET A BETTER GMAT
SCORE

The book you are now holding is different from other preparation books in several ways that can help you get a better GMAT score.

First, it begins with an orientation to the GMAT. This is absolutely indispensable to those who are not thoroughly familiar with this particular exam, and it should also prove valuable as a refresher for those who already know something about the test. The orientation discusses the format of exam, providing examples of the five subject areas, with explanations. Then it describes the procedure for scoring the test. Finally, it addresses the problem of test anxiety and offers suggestions for reducing unnecessary anxiety and tension.

Second, this book contains our exclusive Test-Busters strategies:

TEST BUSTERS

Test Busters takes you inside the GMAT and shows you how to turn the common patterns and multiple-choice format of the test into additional points for a higher score. In all, the book includes over 135 Test Busters plus a comprehensive review of the math you need for the GMAT.

Third, this book contains *six* full-length practice exams that simulate as closely as possible actual GMATs. Each item is written to conform to test specifications such as level of difficulty, appropriateness of wrong as well as right answers, and overall format.

Fourth, following each of the six practice tests is an extensive discussion of every item that appeared on that test. This discussion not only explains why the correct answer is correct, it explains why the wrong answers are wrong and gives suggestions for avoiding future errors.

As you can see, this is a book for serious students who really want the crucial advantage they can get from conscientious study with quality preparation materials.

Part One

About the GMAT and General Test-Taking Information

ORIENTATION

The letters G–M–A–T stand for Graduate Management Admission Test. The GMAT is a service of the Graduate Management Admission Council, an association of graduate business and management schools. The GMAC contracts for the development and administration of the GMAT and distribution of GMAT scores. At present, Educational Testing Service (ETS) has this contract. To obtain registration materials for the GMAT, write to:

Graduate Management Admission Test
Educational Testing Service
CN 6101
Princeton, N.J. 08541-6101

The purpose of the GMAT is to provide a standard measure that will permit admissions decisions to be based, at least in part, on an "objective" comparison of all candidates—no matter what their college or background.

The GMAT generates three different scores: a verbal score, a math score, and a composite score. To learn how your scores will affect your application, you should study the informational bulletins published by the schools to which you are applying. In particular, you should try to determine what weight is given to which scores and what scores you will need to be a competitive applicant.

THE FORMAT OF THE GMAT

The GMAT consists of seven separately timed, 30-minute sections. Each section is devoted to a particular type of question.

VERBAL AREAS

The GMAT uses three different types of verbal questions: reading comprehension, sentence correc-tion, and critical thinking.

Reading Comprehension

Reading comprehension, as the name implies, tests your ability to understand the substance and logical structure of a written selection. A reading comprehension section contains three selections, each about 475 to 525 words long, with eight or nine questions. The total number of questions in the section will be 25. Here is an example of a reading comprehension selection. (To avoid getting mired in a discussion of a particular selection, the passage is shorter than those usually used by the GMAT, and it is followed by only two questions, rather than the usual eight or nine.)

Directions: Below is a reading selection followed by a number of questions. Read the selection. Then, based on your understanding of the selection, select the best answer to each question.

The international software market represents a significant business opportunity for U.S. micro-computer software companies, but illegal copying of programs is limiting the growth of sales abroad. If not dealt with quickly, international piracy of software could become one of the most serious trade problems faced by the United States.

Software piracy is already the biggest barrier to U.S. software companies entering foreign markets. One reason is that software is extremely easy and inexpensive to duplicate compared to the cost of developing and marketing the software. The actual cost of duplicating a software program, which may have a retail value of $400 or more, can be as little as a dollar or two—the main component being the cost of the diskette. The cost of counterfeiting software is substantially less than the cost of duplicating watches, books, or blue jeans. Given that the difference between the true value of the original and the cost of the counterfeit is so great for software, international piracy has become big business. Unfortunately, many foreign governments view software piracy as an industry in and of itself and look the other way.

U.S. firms stand to lose millions of dollars in new business, and diminished U.S. sales not only harm individual firms but also adversely affect the entire U.S. economy.

In this passage, the author is primarily concerned to
(A) criticize foreign governments for stealing U.S. computer secrets
(B) describe the economic hazards software piracy poses to the United States
(C) demand that software pirates immediately cease their illegal operations
(D) present a comprehensive proposal to counteract the effects of international software piracy
(E) disparage the attempts of the U.S. government to control software piracy

The author's attitude toward international software piracy can best be described as
(A) concern
(B) rage
(C) disinterest
(D) pride
(E) condescension

The best answer to the first question is (B). This question, typical of the GMAT, asks about the main point of the selection. (A) is incorrect. Though the author implies criticism of foreign governments, their mistake, so far as we are told, is not stealing secrets but tacitly allowing the operation of a software black market. (C) is incorrect since this is not the main point of the selection. You can infer that the author would approve of such a demand, but issuing the demand is not the main point of the selection you just read. (D) can be eliminated for a similar reason. Though the author might elsewhere offer a specific proposal, he or she does not do so in the selection you just read. (E) also is wrong since no such attempts are ever discussed. Finally notice how well (B) does describe the main point. The author is concerned to identify a problem and discuss its causes.

The best answer to the second question is (A). This asks about the tone of the passage, and *concern* very neatly captures that tone. You can eliminate (B) as an overstatement. Though the author condemns the piracy, the tone is not so violent as to qualify as rage. (C) must surely be incorrect since the author does express concern. The author is not disinterested. (D) also is incorrect since he or she specifically disapproves of the piracy. And finally, (E) is wrong because condescension is not the same thing as disapproval.

Sentence Correction

Sentence corrections test your ability to recognize clear and concise expression by presenting a sentence, part or all of which is underlined, and various ways of rendering the underlined part.

Example: Beautifully sanded and revarnished, Bill proudly displayed the antique desk in his den.
(A) Beautifully sanded and revarnished, Bill proudly displayed the antique desk in his den.
(B) Beautiful, sanded, and revarnished, Bill proudly displayed the antique desk in his den.
(C) An antique, and beautifully sanded and revarnished, in his den Bill proudly displayed the desk.
(D) Bill, beautifully sanded and revarnished in the den, proudly displayed the antique desk.
(E) Bill proudly displayed the antique desk, beautifully sanded and revarnished, in his den.

The correct answer is (E). The sentence as originally written suggests that it was Bill who was sanded and revarnished. Only (E) makes it clear that it was the desk, not Bill, that was refurbished.

Critical Thinking

A critical thinking question presents an argument or an explanation that you are asked to analyze. You may be asked to describe the argument, draw further conclusions from it, attack or defend it, or just find the assumptions of the argument.

Example: Wilfred commented, "Of all the musical instruments I have studied, the trombone is the most difficult instrument to play."
Which of the following statements, if true, would most seriously weaken Wilfred's conclusion?
(A) The trombone is relatively easy for trumpet players to learn to play.
(B) Wilfred has not studied trombone as seriously as he has other instruments.
(C) Wilfred finds he can play the violin and the cello with equal facility.
(D) The trombone is easier to learn as a second instrument than as a first instrument.
(E) There are several instruments which Wilfred has not studied and which are very difficult to play.

The best choice is (B). The question asks you to identify a possible weakness in the argument. The conclusion of the argument is that the trombone is intrinsically more difficult than other instruments. The question asks you to find another explanation for Wilfred's impression. Choice (B) suggests the fault is not in the trombone but in Wilfred. The seeming difficulty of the trombone stems from the fact that Wilfred did not study it as diligently as he has other instruments.

MATH QUESTIONS

The GMAT uses two different kinds of math questions: problem solving and data sufficiency. The math sections test your knowledge of arithmetic, basic algebra, and elementary geometry.

Problem Solving

If you have taken any other standardized exam that included math questions (such as the SAT), then you have probably already seen examples of problem-solving questions. These are your typical word-problem questions. Some test arithmetic.

Example: Betty left home with $60 in her wallet. She spent ⅓ of that amount at the greengrocer's, and she spent ½ of what remained at the pharmacist's. If Betty made no other expenditures, how much money did she have when she returned home?
(A) $10
(B) $15
(C) $20
(D) $40
(E) $50

A quick calculation will show that the correct answer is (C). Betty spent ⅓ of $60, or $20, at the greengrocer's, leaving her with $40. Of the $40, she spend ½ or $20 at the pharmacist's, leaving her with $20 when she returned home.

Other problem-solving items test your knowledge of basic algebra.

Example: If $2x + 3y = 8$ and $y = 2x$, then what is the value of x?
(A) −6
(B) −4
(C) 0
(D) 1
(E) 4

The best answer is (D). To answer the question you need to solve for x. Since $y = 2x$, you can substitute $2x$ for y in the first equation:

	$2x + 3(2x) = 8$
Multiply:	$2x + 6x = 8$
Add:	$8x = 8$
Divide:	$x = 1$

Problem-solving items also test your knowledge of elementary geometry.

Example:

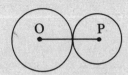

In the figure above, circle O and circle P are tangent to each other. If the circle with center O has a diameter of 8 and the circle with center P has a diameter 6, what is the length of segment OP?
(A) 7
(B) 10
(C) 14
(D) 20
(E) 28

The correct answer is (A). The segment OP is made up of the radius of circle O and the radius of circle P. To find the length of OP, you need to know the lengths of the two radii. Since the length of the radius is one-half that of the diameter, the radius of circle O is ½(8) or 4, and the radius of circle P is ½(6) or 3. So the length of OP is 3 + 4 = 7.

Data Sufficiency

The second type of math question is data sufficiency. Without trying to understand all of the subtleties of the type, you can get the general idea of data sufficiency by reading the instructions.

Directions: Each question below is followed by two numbered facts. You are to determine whether the data given in the statements is sufficient for answering the question. Use the data given, plus your knowledge of math and everyday facts, to choose between the five possible answers.
(A) if statement 1 alone is sufficient to answer the question, but statement 2 alone is not sufficient
(B) if statement 2 alone is sufficient to answer the question, but statement 1 alone is not sufficient
(C) if both statements together are needed to answer the question, but neither statement alone is sufficient
(D) if either statement by itself is sufficient to answer the question
(E) if not enough facts are given to answer the question

Here are some examples of data sufficiency questions:

1. What is the value of x?
   (1) x is 3 more than 5.
   (2) $x^2 = 64$.

2. If n is an integer greater than 5 and less than 10, what is n?
   (1) 2n is less than 18.
   (2) n is a prime number.

3. A flight from New York to Miami, stopping only in Atlanta, left New York carrying 60 passengers. How many passengers were on the flight when it landed in Miami?
   (1) Exactly 15 passengers deplaned in Atlanta and did not reboard.
   (2) 27 new passengers boarded in Atlanta.

4. What is the remainder when the positive integer n is divided by 3?
   (1) n is a multiple of 6.
   (2) n is a multiple of 18.

5. Is Bob older than Sue?
   (1) Bob is younger than Tim.
   (2) Tim is older than Sue.

1. (A) Statement (1) establishes that x is 8. Statement (2) is not sufficient since x might be +8 or −8.
2. (B) Statement (2) establishes that x is 7, since 7 is the only prime number between 5 and 10. (1), however, is not sufficient since 6, 7, and 8 are all less than half of 18 and between 5 and 10.
3. (C) Neither statement alone is sufficient, but both taken together establish that the flight picked up a net gain of 12 passengers in Atlanta. So it was carrying 72 passengers when it landed in Miami.
4. (D) Each statement is by itself sufficient to answer the question. As for (1), since n is a multiple of 6, n is evenly divisible by both 3 and 2. As for (2), since n is a multiple of 18, n is evenly divisible by 3, 2, and 6.
5. (E) The two statements establish:
   (1) B < T
   (2) S < T
   But that is not enough information to answer the question asked.

THE MYSTERY SECTION

Each edition of the GMAT includes three verbal sections and three math sections plus one mystery section. A mystery section can be another math section, another verbal section, or something not even discussed in this book. But the mystery section is a non-counting section. It does not affect your GMAT score.

The mystery section contains questions that are being tested for future use. It's not possible for the test writers to know in advance whether a particular question really fits the design specficiations of the test. They can determine that only by having a large number of responses to a question. Then they can ascertain whether the question is of the correct level of difficulty, whether the right answer and wrong answers are clearly distinguishable, and so on. So they put new questions in the mystery section, testing their validity for future use.

The identity of the mystery section has to remain a mystery. Since the mystery section is not used in computing scores, if test-takers could identify a section as a mystery section, they might just take a 30-minute break. In that case, the test-writers would learn nothing about the validity of the questions being tested.

Can you guess which is the mystery section? Perhaps; perhaps not. And if you think you've found one, what will you do? Put down your pencil and hope that it really is a mystery section? Obviously, you do not want to take a chance that it will turn out to be one of the "live" sections that will determine your score.

The general rule to observe regarding the mystery section is to answer the section to the best of your ability, but if you see something that is a total surprise while answering, don't let the presence of that section interfere with your performance on subsequent sections.

SCORING THE GMAT

Your score report for the GMAT will show three scores: a verbal score, a math score, and a composite score. The verbal and math scores are reported on a scale ranging from 0 to 60 (although scores at the extremes are very rare). The composite score ranges from 200 (the minimum) to 800 (the maximum).

The scoring procedure for the GMAT consists of three steps.

1. Total the number of questions answered correctly. Ignore questions that were omitted, and ignore questions to which more than one response was given.

2. Subtract from the total in step 1 the product of ¼ and the number of questions answered incorrectly. Ignore questions that were omitted, and ignore questions to which more than one response was given. (This is the adjustment for guessing.) The result of this step is called a corrected raw score.

3. Convert the result of step 2 (the corrected raw score) to a scaled score using the tables provided by ETS.

Suppose, for example, that a test-taker correctly answers 100 out of 140 questions on a test, leaving 20 questions unanswered, and answering incorrectly on the remaining 20 questions. The test-taker's composite score would be

1. 100 correct answers
2. $100 - (\frac{1}{4} \times 20) = 100 - 5 = 95$
3. Using the table shown, the composition scaled score is about 590.

Selected Scaled Scores (Composite)

Corrected Raw Score	Scaled Score
140	800
130	780
120	720
110	650
100	610
90	570
80	520
70	480
60	440
50	400
40	360
30	310
20	270
10	230

Part Two

Test Busters

TEST BUSTERS GENERAL METHODS

Even though the GMAT uses several different question types, there are some tactics that are applicable to the test as a whole.

STARTING TO WORK

 TAKE A BRIEF OVERVIEW OF A SECTION BEFORE BEGINNING TO WORK ON IT.

This is just a matter of caution. Some small adjustments in test format are always possible, so do not get caught off guard. When time is announced for you to begin work on a section, take five to ten seconds to look through the pages of that section. If there are unexpected changes, you can readily adjust your plan of attack.

 DON'T STOP TO ASK DIRECTIONS.

Your allotted 30 minutes is all the time you get for a section. No additional time is given for reading instructions. If you spend 30 seconds reading directions each time you begin a new question type, you could lose three or four questions in each section.

The solution to this problem is to be thoroughly familiar with the directions for each question type and the format in which it is presented *before* the exam. Then you will recognize the format and already know what is required without having to review the directions for that part.

COVERING GROUND

The scoring mechanism for the GMAT is the formula "score = correct answers $- \frac{1}{4}$ incorrect answers".

MOVE AS QUICKLY AS POSSIBLE WITHOUT UNNECESSARILY SACRIFICING ACCURACY.

Consider the cases of three test-takers: Peter Goodstudent, Paul Haphazard, and Mary Testwise. On a certain GMAT, of the "live" 140 questions, Peter attempted only 60, but he was very accurate, missing only 4 questions. Paul worked very quickly, too quickly, attempting all 140 questions, missing 60 of them—over half. Mary attempted 120 questions, and she missed 32. Their score reports would show:

Peter:
Corrected Raw Score = $56 - \frac{1}{4}(4) = 55$/Scaled Score: 420

Paul:
Corrected Raw Score = $80 - \frac{1}{4}(60) = 65$/Scaled Score: 460

Mary:
Corrected Raw Score = $88 - \frac{1}{4}(32) = 80$/Scaled Score: 520

The following Test Buster will help you find the right trade-off:

DON'T SPEND TOO MUCH TIME ON ANY QUESTION.

All questions are given equal weight. No extra credit is given for a difficult question. Thus, there is no reason to keep working on a question after you have given it your best shot. Instead, once you realize that you are spinning your wheels, make the decision to guess and move on to the next question.

BRING YOUR OWN WATCH TO THE TEST.

The proctors in charge of administering the test are supposed to keep you advised of the passing time, for example, by writing on a blackboard how many minutes remain. But you should not rely on their diligence. In the first place, it's easy for a proctor to forget to mark the passing time at exactly the right moment. So when you see the proctor write "5 minutes left," you might have only 4 minutes left or as much as 6 minutes left. Further, the proctor might mark the correct time at a moment when you're not looking. When you look up from your work you see "5 minutes left," but when did the proctor write that down?

The solution is to have a watch with you. If you have a digital watch with a stopwatch function, you can use that. If your digital watch does not have a stopwatch function, write down the starting time for the section when you begin. Quickly add 30 minutes to that and write down the time you must finish. Circle that number for easy reference. If you have a watch with hands, adjust the minute hand to half-past any hour (the 6). The hour is irrelevant. If you begin work with the minute hand on the 6, your time will be up when the minute hand reaches the 12.

Keeping track of the time is not an end unto itself. You keep track of the time in order to use it to answer questions.

 CONCENTRATE INTENSELY. IF YOU FIND THAT YOUR MIND BEGINS TO WANDER STOP BRIEFLY AND REGATHER YOUR CONCENTRATION.

The GMAT is an arduous task. There is no way that you can maintain your concentration throughout all seven of the 30-minute sections. There will be times when your attention begins to flag. Learn to recognize this. For example, you find that you are reading and rereading the same line without understanding. At that point, put down your pencil, close your eyes, take a deep breath or two (or rub your eyes or whatever) and then get back to work.

 DON'T BECOME OBSESSED WITH TIME.

Although time is an important part of the test, don't become preoccupied with the passing seconds. There are convenient points in each section to stop and check the remaining time, for example, as you turn a page.

BUSTING THE MULTIPLE-CHOICE FORMAT

Because of the multiple-choice format, you have a real advantage over the GMAT. The correct answer is always right there on the page. To be sure, it's surrounded by wrong choices, but it may be possible to eliminate one or more of those other choices as nonanswers. Look at the following reading comprehension question:

The author argues that the evidence supporting the new theory is

   (A) hypothetical
   (B) biased
   (C) empirical
   (D) speculative
   (E) fragmentary

You might think that it is impossible to make any progress on a reading comprehension question without the reading selection, but you can eliminate three of the five answers in this questions as nonanswers.

Study the question stem. We can infer that the author of the selection has at least implicitly passed judgment on the evidence supporting the new theory. What kind of judgment might someone make about the evidence adduced to support a theory? (A), (C), and (D) all seem extremely unlikely. As for (A), while the theory is itself a hypothesis, the evidence supporting the theory would not be hypothetical. As for (C), evidence is empirical by definition. Therefore it is unlikely that anyone would argue "This evidence is empirical." And (D) can be eliminated for the same reason as (A). Admittedly, this leaves you with a choice of (B) or (E), a choice that depends on the content of the reading selection; but at least you have a 50-50 chance of getting the correct answer—even without reading the selection.

This brings us to the question of guessing.

NEVER GUESS BLINDLY. ALWAYS GUESS WHEN YOU ARE ABLE TO ELIMINATE ONE OR MORE CHOICES.

The so-called "penalty" is designed to eliminate any advantage to random guessing. This can be shown by setting up a situation in which a person guesses blindly at, say, 100 questions. Since there are five choices to pick from, the person should hit on the right answer in one of every five questions. Thus, he or she should answer correctly, by guessing, $\frac{1}{5}$ of the 100 questions, missing the remaining 80. The corrected raw score would be

$$20 - \tfrac{1}{4}(80) = 20 - 20 = 0.$$

Theoretically, over a large enough pool of questions, the net result from guessing blindly should be zero.

The situation is very different when you are able to eliminate even one answer choice. Given a pool of 100 questions, if you are able to eliminate even one choice to each question, your corrected raw score should be

$$25 - \tfrac{1}{4}(75) = 6.25,$$

a net gain. The results are even more favorable when you can eliminate two or more choices; and this may be possible, as we have shown with the preceding reading comprehension question.

You must realize that when you are guessing, you are doing just that.

WHEN THE TIME COMES TO GUESS, GUESS QUICKLY AND DO NOT CHANGE YOUR MIND.

When it is time to guess, go ahead and get it over with. You are guessing because you have exhausted your analytical resources. There is no reason to prefer one choice over another, so make your guess.

STRINGS OF THREE LETTERS ARE USED. STRINGS OF FOUR OR MORE LETTERS ARE NOT USED.

Although strings of four or more of one letter are theoretically possible, they just don't occur. This is because the test-writers break them up. So you should not find a string of four (A)s in a row. If you do, at least one of your four answers is wrong. Which is it? There is no way of knowing for sure without checking your work.

CARE AND FEEDING OF THE ANSWER SHEET

Your test materials come in two parts: a booklet of 30-odd pages containing the test questions and an answer sheet covered with lettered spaces for your responses. The space for marking your answers to a section will look something like this:

17 Ⓐ Ⓑ Ⓒ Ⓓ Ⓔ   24 Ⓐ Ⓑ Ⓒ Ⓓ Ⓔ   31 Ⓐ Ⓑ Ⓒ Ⓓ Ⓔ

18 Ⓐ Ⓑ Ⓒ Ⓓ Ⓔ   25 Ⓐ Ⓑ Ⓒ Ⓓ Ⓔ   32 Ⓐ Ⓑ Ⓒ Ⓓ Ⓔ

19 Ⓐ Ⓑ Ⓒ Ⓓ Ⓔ   26 Ⓐ Ⓑ Ⓒ Ⓓ Ⓔ   33 Ⓐ Ⓑ Ⓒ Ⓓ Ⓔ

Your answer sheet is graded by a machine that "reads" the marks you have made.

 CODE YOUR ANSWERS NEATLY, FILLING COMPLETELY THE ANSWER SPACE WITH A DARK PENCIL MARK. LEAVE NO STRAY MARKS ON THE ANSWER SHEET. ENTER ONE, AND ONLY ONE, ANSWER PER QUESTION. DON'T WORRY IF THE ANSWER SHEET HAS MORE BLANKS THAN YOUR BOOKLET HAS QUESTIONS. LEAVE THE EXTRA SPACES BLANK.

Perhaps a visual aid will help explain the importance of this Test Buster:

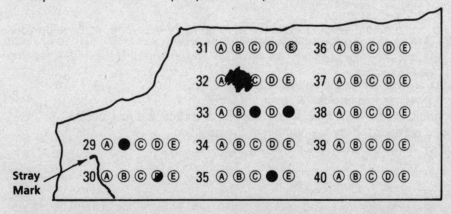

The answers to questions 29 and 35 are correctly entered. The answer to question 30, however, is incomplete; the machine might not see it. The answer to question 31 is too light; again, the machine might miss it. The mark for question 32 is messy; the machine might read (A), (B), or (C) as the intended response. Question 33 will be treated as incorrect since more than one space is darkened (no credit, no penalty). Question 34 will be treated in the same way since it has been left blank.

The most common error in answer sheet management is misplacing an entire block of answers. This occurs when a test-taker skips a question in the test booklet but fails to skip a corresponding space on the answer sheet. The result is that the intended pattern of response is there, but it is displaced by one or more spaces. Unfortunately, the machine that grades the paper reads what is actually on the answer sheet—not what the test-taker intended. Here are some Test Busters to help you avoid this unpleasant problem.

CODE YOUR ANSWERS IN GROUPS.

Most test-takers code their responses to each question just after they have answered the question. They work in the rhythm: solve, code, solve, code, solve, code, and so on. It is this rhythm that can trip them up if they skip a question. Instead, of coding your responses one by one, try coding them in groups.

Work problems for a while (noting your choices). Then find an appropriate moment to enter your responses on your answer sheet. You might just wait until you reach the end of a page. As time for a section draws to a close, you should make sure you are current with your coding, so you will probably want to go to the one-by-one method. You don't want to run out of time on a section without the opportunity to enter answers to every question that you have worked.

Even if you are coding in groups, there is the ever-present danger of an error. If you find that you have made a mistake, what do you do? You erase the wrong responses and enter the correct ones.

IN YOUR TEST BOOKLET KEEP A SEPARATE RECORD OF YOUR PROGRESS, INCLUDING CORRECT RESPONSES, SKIPPED QUESTIONS, AND DOUBTFUL QUESTIONS.

There is no single record-keeping system that is good for everyone, so develop your own. You might consider using some of the following:

Correct answer: Circle the letter of the choice.
Definitely eliminated choice: "X" over the letter.
Changed choice: Fill in circle of first answer, and circle the new choice.
Skipped question: "?" by the number of the question.
Question to recheck: Circle the number.

TEST BUSTERS FOR THE VERBAL SECTIONS

READING COMPREHENSION

The reading selections that you will find on the GMAT are unlike the material you are accustomed to reading in three respects: topic, format, and density. First, the selections are taken from many different disciplines, such as science, medicine, philosophy, psychology, sociology, and literary criticism. Since you took most of your college courses in your major area of interest (with the obligatory survey courses in other areas), you are not likely to be familiar with the topics of the reading selections.

THE GMAT ASSUMES THAT YOU ARE *NOT* FAMILIAR WITH THE CONTENT OF THE READING SELECTIONS.

The test-writers go out of their way to find material that test-takers will not have seen before, since they want to avoid giving anyone an advantage over other candidates. If you do encounter a topic you have studied before, that is an unusual stroke of luck. Rest assured, however, that everything you need to answer the questions is included in the selection itself.

GMAT READING SELECTIONS ALWAYS BEGIN IN THE MIDDLE OF NOWHERE.

When you begin, you will have no advance warning of the topic discussed in the selection. As a result, the selection seems to begin in the middle of nowhere. Imagine that you encounter the following as the opening sentence of a reading comprehension selection on your GMAT:

Of the wide variety of opinions on which evolutionary factors were responsible for the growth of hominid intelligence, a theory currently receiving consideration is that intraspecific warfare played an important role by encouraging strategy sessions requiring a sort of verbal competition.

An appropriate reaction to this might be "What the . . . !" But in reality the topic introduced by the sentence above is not that bizarre. Let's give the sentence a context, say a scholarly journal.

PRIMITIVE BATTLE PLANS: A NEW THEORY ABOUT THE GROWTH OF HUMAN INTELLIGENCE

Of the wide variety of opinions on which evolutionary factors were responsible for the growth of hominid intelligence, a theory currently receiving consideration is that intraspecific warfare played an important role by encouraging strategy sessions requiring a sort of verbal competition.

The title summarizes the main point of the article and alerts you to the topic that will be introduced in the opening sentence. Unfortunately, on the GMAT you will not be shown this courtesy. The selections will start rather abruptly, in the middle of nowhere.

A third factor tends to make GMAT reading selections tiresome:

 THE STYLE OF GMAT READING COMPREHENSION SELECTIONS IS DRY, COMPACT, AND OFTEN TEDIOUS.

To be suitable for the GMAT, the selection must not be too long or too short. So the selections, which are taken from previously published material, are carefully edited. Even when the topic of the selection is itself interesting, the selection that emerges from the editing can be deadly boring.

These three features—unusual topic, abrupt beginning, and dense style—all work together to cause trouble for you.

 DON'T LET THE READING COMPREHENSION SELECTIONS INTIMIDATE YOU.

Many students are simply overawed by the reading selections. They begin to think, "I've never even heard of this; I'll never be able to answer any questions." And when you start thinking like that, you're already beaten. Keep in mind that the passages are chosen so that you will be surprised, but remember that the selections are written so that they contain everything you need to answer the questions.

What about the questions? Every reading comprehension question asked on a GMAT can be put into one of six categories.

Main-Idea Questions

Every reading selection is edited so that it discusses some central theme, that is, it makes a main point. Main-idea questions ask about this central theme or main point. They are most often phrased as follows:

> The primary purpose of the passage is to . . . .
> The author is primarily concerned with . . . .
> Which of the following best describes the main point of the passage?
> Which of the following titles best summarizes the content of the passage?

Supporting-Idea Questions

These questions ask not about the main point of the selection but about details included by the author to support or to develop the main theme of the selection. These questions may be worded as follows:

> According to the passage, . . .
> The author mentions . . . .
> Which of the following does the author discuss?

Implied-Idea Questions

These questions ask about ideas that are not explicitly stated in the selection but are strongly implied. They are often worded as follows:

> It can be inferred from the passage that . . . .
> The author implies . . . .
> Which of the following can be inferred from the passage?

Logical-Structure Questions

These questions ask about the organization of the passage. They may ask about the overall development of the selection, such as:

> The author develops the thesis primarily by . . . .
> Which of the following best describes the author's method?

Or they may ask about the role played by a detail:

> The author mentions . . . in order to . . . .
> The author introduces . . . primarily to . . . .

Further-Application Questions

These questions ask that you take what you have learned from the passage and apply it to a new situation. To answer this type of question you must go beyond what is explicitly stated or even strongly implied and comment on a situation not even discussed in the passage. These questions are phrased as follows:

With which of the following conclusions would the author most likely agree? Which of the following statements, if true, would most weaken the conclusion . . . ?

Attitude Questions

These questions ask you to identify the overall tone of the passage or the author's attitude toward something discussed in the passage:

The tone of the passage can best be described as . . . .
The author's attitude toward . . . is one of . . . .

Later we will study specific examples of each type of question. For the present, you should just realize that reading selections are written in such a way as to be the vehicle for these six types of questions.

How to Read a GMAT Reading Comprehension Selection

Each GMAT reading selection is in a sense an "excuse" to ask the six types of questions just mentioned. So the six types give you a good idea of what the GMAT thinks is good reading.

According to the GMAT, good reading involves three levels of understanding and evaluation. First, you must be able to grasp the overall idea or main point of the selection along with its general organization. Second, you must be able to subject the specific details to greater scrutiny and explain what something means and why it was introduced. Finally, you should be able to evaluate what the author has written, determining what further conclusions might be drawn and judging whether the argument is good or bad.

The first and most general level of understanding is the most important in a sense, since you cannot appreciate the details of a selection unless you understand the overall structure. And the second level must come before the third, because you will not be able to evaluate the selection unless you know exactly what it says. This priority of levels dictates the strategy you should follow in reading the selection.

BEGIN YOUR ATTACK ON A SELECTION BY PREVIEWING THE FIRST SENTENCE OF EACH PARAGRAPH.

Your first task is to grasp the overall point of the selection. The first sentence of a paragraph is often the topic sentence, so a quick preview of first sentences should give you a rough idea of the subject of the selection.

 AS YOU READ, CONSCIOUSLY ASK YOURSELF, "WHAT IS THE MAIN POINT OF THIS DISCUSSION?"

Keeping in mind what you have learned by previewing topic sentences, begin your reading. As you read, try to summarize the main topic of discussion. Once you can articulate the main point of the selection, it will be easier to place the specific details into the overall organization.

 AS YOU READ, CONSCIOUSLY ASK YOURSELF, "WHY HAS THE AUTHOR INTRODUCED THIS IDEA?"

Once you have the main idea in mind, you must try to relate specific details to it, placing them in the overall framework.

 BRACKET, IN WRITING OR MENTALLY, MATERIAL THAT IS VERY TECHNICAL OR OTHERWISE DIFFICULT TO UNDERSTAND.

You don't need to have a full understanding of every single detail to appreciate the organization of the selection and most of its detail. If you encounter material that is overly technical and difficult to understand, draw a box around it with a pencil and leave it. You will already understand what "place" it occupies in the overall argument; having marked its location, you can easily find it if you need to study it more carefully in order to answer a question.

 AT THE END OF YOUR READING, PAUSE AND QUICKLY REVIEW THE STRUCTURE OF THE PASSAGE.

This does not mean try to recall all of the details you have read. You should, however, be able to explain to yourself, at least vaguely, the main point of the selection and the most important features of the argument.

Answering the Questions

Main-Idea questions ask about the author's main point.

 ON A MAIN-IDEA QUESTION, CHOOSE AN ANSWER THAT REFERS TO ALL OF THE IMPORTANT ELEMENTS OF THE PASSAGE WITHOUT GOING BEYOND THE SCOPE OF THE PASSAGE.

The correct answer to a main-idea question will summarize the main point of the passage. The wrong answers are too broad or too narrow. Some will be too broad and will attribute too much to the author. Others will be too narrow and will focus on one small element of the selection, thereby ignoring the overall point.

Some main-idea questions are phrased as sentence completions.

 WITH A MAIN-IDEA QUESTION IN SENTENCE-COMPLETION FORM, BE SURE TO TEST THE SUITABILITY OF THE FIRST WORD OF EACH CHOICE.

Example: *The author's primary purpose is to*

    (A) argue for . . . .
    (B) criticize . . . .
    (C) describe . . . .
    (D) persuade . . . .
    (E) denounce . . . .

Make sure that the first word or phrase is truly descriptive of the passage. In the example just given, if the selection is neutral in tone, providing nothing more than a description of some event or phenomenon, you could safely eliminate (A), (B), (D), and (E).

A Supporting-Idea question asks about something specifically mentioned in the selection.

 ON A SUPPORTING-IDEA QUESTION, FIND THE PART OF THE PASSAGE THAT IS INTENDED TO BE THE BASIS FOR THAT QUESTION.

A supporting-idea question basically asks "What did the author say?" This means that the answer to the question has to be explicitly stated in the passage. The best way to handle such a question is to make sure that you find the correct reference. Watch out! Wrong answers can refer you to other parts of the selection; they cite something specifically mentioned in the selection, but the citation is not an answer to the question asked. Wrong answers can also be things never mentioned in the selection.

ON A SUPPORTING-IDEA QUESTION, ELIMINATE ANSWER CHOICES REFERRING TO SOMETHING NOT MENTIONED IN THE PASSAGE OR GOING BEYOND THE SCOPE OF THE PASSAGE.

One way the test-writers have of preparing wrong answers is to mention things related to the general topic of the selection but not specifically discussed there. An answer to an explicit idea question will appear in the selection.

Sometimes the test-writer will use a thought-reverser; for example:

The author mentions all of the following *EXCEPT:*

IF A SUPPORTING IDEA CONTAINS A THOUGHT-REVERSER, THE WRONG ANSWERS CAN BE FOUND IN THE SELECTION. THE CORRECT ANSWER IS NOT MENTIONED.

This is implicit in what was said above. Sometimes an explicit idea question will include a thought-reverser. In that case, it is asking for what is *not* mentioned in the selection. Out of the five choices, therefore, four will actually appear in the selection. The fifth, and wrong, choice will not.

Some questions ask about what can be inferred from the passage:

THE CORRECT ANSWER TO AN IMPLIED-IDEA QUESTION WILL BE ONLY A SHORT STEP REMOVED FROM WHAT IS EXPLICITLY STATED IN THE TEXT ON THE SELECTION.

A question that asks about what can be inferred from a selection does not require a long chain of deductive reasoning. It is usually a one-step inference. For example, the selection might make a statement to the effect "X only occurs in the presence of Y." Then a question might ask, "In the absence of Y, which should occur?" The correct answer would be "X does not occur."

Some questions ask about the overall logical structure of a passage.

THE CORRECT ANSWER TO A QUESTION THAT ASKS ABOUT THE OVERALL LOGICAL STRUCTURE OF A SELECTION SHOULD CORRECTLY DESCRIBE IN GENERAL TERMS THE OVERALL DEVELOPMENT OF THE SELECTION.

This kind of logical-structure question is very much like a main-idea question. Whereas a main-idea question asks about the *content* of a selection, this type of question asks about the *logical structure* of the selection.

Other questions ask about the logical function of specific details:

ON A QUESTION THAT ASKS ABOUT THE LOGICAL FUNCTION OF A DETAIL, FIND THE APPROPRIATE REFERENCE AND DETERMINE *WHY* THE AUTHOR INTRODUCED THE DETAIL AT JUST THAT POINT.

This kind of question is related to that discussed above about supporting details. Here, however, the question stem states specifically that the detail is mentioned but asks why it was mentioned. What role does it play in the overall argument?

Further application questions are the most difficult of all, for they require you to work in that third and most difficult level of reading comprehension.

ON A FURTHER-APPLICATION QUESTION, FIND THE ANSWER CHOICE THAT HAS THE MOST CONNECTION WITH THE TEXT OF THE SELECTION.

You will see many examples of further applications questions in the practice materials that follow. For the moment, accept the fact that the correct answer will be the one most clearly supported by the text.

ON AN ATTITUDE OR TONE QUESTION, TRY TO CREATE A CONTINUUM OF THE ANSWER CHOICES AND LOCATE THE AUTHOR'S ATTITUDE OR TONE ON THAT CONTINUUM.

Example: *The tone of the passage is best described as one of*

(A) outrage
(B) approval
(C) objectivity
(D) alarm
(E) enthusiasm

You might arrange these attitudes in a line, running from the most negative to the most positive: (−) . . outrage . . alarm . . objectivity . . approval . . enthusiasm . . (+)

A Sample Reading Comprehension

Directions: *Read the passage below, and answer the questions that follow based on your understanding of the passage.*

The need for solar electricity is clear. It is safe, ecologically sound, efficient, continuously available, and it has no moving parts. The basic problem with the use of solar photovoltaic devices is economics, but until recently very little progress had been made toward the development of low-cost photovoltaic devices. The larger part of
5 research funds has been devoted to study of single-crystal silicon solar cells, despite the evidence, including that of the leading manufacturers of crystalline silicon, that this technique holds little promise. The reason for this pattern is understandable and his-

torical. Crystalline silicon is the active element in the very successful semiconductor industry, and virtually all of the solid state devices contain silicon transistors and diodes. Crystalline silicon, however, is particularly unsuitable to terrestrial solar cells.

10 Crystalline silicon solar cells work well and are successfully used in the space program, where cost is not an issue. While single-crystal silicon has been proven in extraterrestrial use with efficiencies as high as 18%, and other more expensive and scarce materials such as gallium arsenide can have even higher efficiencies, costs

15 must be reduced by a factor of more than 100 to make them practical for commercial uses. Besides the fact that the starting crystalline silicon is expensive, 95% of it is wasted and does not appear in the final device. Recently, there have been some imaginative attempts to make polycrystalline and ribbon silicon that are lower in cost than high-quality single crystals; but to date the efficiencies of these apparently lower-

20 cost arrays have been unacceptably small. Moreover, these materials are cheaper only because of the introduction of disordering in crystalline semiconductors, and disorder degrades the efficiency of crystalline solar cells.

This dilemma can be avoided by preparing completely disordered or amorphous materials. Amorphous materials have disordered atomic structure as compared to

25 crystalline materials: that is, they have only short-range order rather than the long-range periodicity of crystals. The advantages of amorphous solar cells are impressive. Whereas crystals can be grown as wafers about 4 inches in diameter, amorphous materials can be grown over large areas in a single process. Whereas crystalline silicon must be made 200 microns thick to absorb a sufficient amount of sunlight for

30 efficient energy conversion, only 1 micron of the proper amorphous materials is necessary. Crystalline silicon solar cells cost in excess of $100 per square foot, but amorphous films can be created at a cost of about 50¢ per square foot.

Although many scientists were aware of the very low cost of amorphous solar cells, they felt that they could never be manufactured with the efficiencies necessary to

35 contribute significantly to the demand for electric power. This was based on a misconception about the feature which determines efficiency. For example, it is not the conductivity of the material in the dark that is relevant but only the photoconductivity, that is, the conductivity in the presence of sunlight. Already, solar cells with efficiencies well above 6% have been developed using amorphous materials, and further research will

40 doubtless find even less costly amorphous materials with higher efficiencies.

1. The author is primarily concerned with

 (A) discussing the importance of solar energy
 (B) explaining the functioning of solar cells
 (C) presenting a history of research on energy sources
 (D) describing a possible solution to the problem of the cost of photovoltaic cells
 (E) advocating increased government funding for research on alternative energy sources

2. According to the passage, which of the following encouraged use of silicon solar cells in the space program?

 I.   the higher cost of materials such as gallium arsenide
 II. the fairly high extraterrestrial efficiency of the cells
 III. the relative lack of cost limitations in the space program

 (A) I only
 (B) II only

(C) I and II only
(D) II and III only
(E) I, II, and III

3. The author mentions recent attempts to make polycrystalline and ribbon silicon (lines 16) primarily in order to

(A) minimize the importance of recent improvements in silicon solar cells
(B) demonstrate the superiority of amorphous materials over crystalline silicon
(C) explain why silicon solar cells have been the center of research
(D) contrast crystalline silicon with polycrystalline and ribbon silicon
(E) inform the reader that an alternative type of solar cell exists

4. Which of the following pairs of terms does the author regard as most nearly synonymous?

(A) solar and extraterrestrial
(B) photovoltaic devices and solar cells
(C) crystalline silicon and amorphous materials
(D) amorphous materials and higher efficiencies
(E) wafers and crystals

5. The material in the passage could best be used in an argument for

(A) discontinuing the space program
(B) increased funding for research on amorphous materials
(C) further study of the history of silicon crystals
(D) increased reliance on solar energy
(E) training more scientists to study energy problems

6. The author mentions which of the following as advantages of amorphous materials for solar cells over silicon crystals?

  I. the relative thinness of amorphous materials
 II. the cost of amorphous material
III. the size of solar cells which can be made of amorphous material

(A) I only
(B) II only
(C) I and II only
(D) II and III only
(E) I, II, and III

7. The tone of the passage can best be described as

(A) analytical and optimistic
(B) biased and unprofessional
(C) critical and discouraged
(D) tentative and inconclusive
(E) concerned and conciliatory

1. **(D)** This is a main idea question. The author begins by noting that solar energy is very important and, further, that the problem of the cost of solar cells, apparently

an important part of solar energy technology, has not yet been solved. The author then discusses research on solar cells and the difficulties with silicon cells. In the third paragraph, the author states that there is a solution to this problem: amorphous materials. So the overall objective of the passage is to present amorphous material as a possible solution to the problem of cost. This is neatly summarized by choice (D). (A) is incorrect since the author discusses the importance of solar energy only by way of introduction. (B) is incorrect because the author never explains how solar cells work. (C) is incorrect because the only reference to history is included to explain the bias in favor of silicon solar cells. (E) is incorrect because the author never mentions such funding. To be sure, the arguments contained in the passage might be very useful in making the further point suggested by (E), but then that is to admit that (E) is not the main point of the passage as written.

2. **(D)** This is an explicit idea question. In the second paragraph, the author discusses why silicon solar cells are used in the space program. The passage states that extraterrestrial efficiency is fairly high, so statement II is part of the correct answer choice. Moreover, the author mentions casually, but explicitly, that cost is not a factor in developing materials for the space program, so statement III is part of the correct choice. The extra cost of scarce materials, however, is not mentioned as a factor encouraging the use of silicon solar cells in the space program. Though it is stated that materials such as gallium arsenide are more efficient and more costly, these factors are not reasons why silicon solar cells are used in the space program. So the correct answer is II and III only.

3. **(A)** This is a logical structure question: Why does the author mention polycrystalline and ribbon silicon? In a way, the mention of these techniques could undermine the case for amorphous materials, since these are recent developments in crystalline substances that improve silicon solar cells. The author surely does not intend to weaken his argument. The logical move is to acknowledge the existence of a possible objection and to attempt to demonstrate that it is not really a very important objection. This is described by (A). (B) is incorrect, for though this is the general idea of the passage, (B) is not a proper response to the question asked. (C) is a point raised in the passage, but this is not the reason for the reference to polycrystalline and ribbon silicon. (D) is incorrect because the author never elaborates on the distinction between crystalline silicon and other forms of silicon. He only mentions that the latter are further developments on crystalline silicon. As for (E), though we infer from the mention of polycrystalline and ribbon silicon that other forms of solar cells exist, this is not the reason the author has introduced them into the discussion.

4. **(B)** This is an inference question. In the first paragraph, the author mentions that the basic problem with solar energy is the economics of solar photovoltaic devices. The rest of the passage discusses solar cells. We may infer from the juxtaposition of these terms that the author uses them synonymously. In any event, none of the other pairs are used interchangeably. As for (A), from the passage we may infer that "extraterrestrial" refers to space and that "solar" refers to the sun. As for (C), these terms are used as opposites. As for (D), though the author claims that amorphous materials are more efficient than silicon materials, he does not equate amorphous materials and efficiency. Finally, (E) is incorrect since a wafer is apprently a big crystal of silicon. But that means the terms are not used interchangeably.

5. **(B)** This is a further application question. We noted earlier, in question 1, that though the author does not specifically advocate greater funding for research on amorphous materials, the passage might be used in such an argument. Since there is a historical bias in favor of silicon cells, and since such cells have been the focus of most research, and amorphous materials offer an alternative, the natural conclusion is that further research should be done on amorphous materials. This is answer choice (B). (A) must be incorrect since the author never condemns the space program. He only notes that silicon cells were appropriate for the space program since cost was no object. (C) must be incorrect since the author advocates amorphous materials as opposed to silicon crystals for solar cells. (D) has some merit. To the extent that the entire passage advocates further research for solar energy, it could be used for the purpose suggested by (D). With an application question, however, the task is to find the answer choice most closely tied to the text, and that is (B). Logically then, there is nothing "wrong" with (D); it is just that it is not so closely related to the passage as (B). Finally, (E) is incorrect for the same reason: one could conceivably use the passage in the service of this goal, but (B) is a more obvious choice.

6. **(E)** This is an explicit idea question. All three statements are mentioned in paragraph 3 as being advantages that amorphous material has over silicon.

7. **(A)** This is a tone question. The tone of the passage is clearly analytical. The final paragraph is the warrant for the "optimistic" part of choice (A). The author implies that the problem of the cost of solar cells can be solved by further research on amorphous materials. (B) is incorrect; although the passage advocates a position, it cannot be termed biased. (C) is correct insofar as the passage is critical, but the author does not seem to be discouraged. (D) is incorrect because the passage is argumentative, and the author seems to be confident. Finally, (E) is correct in that it states that the author is concerned, but there is nothing mentioned in the passage about which the author could be conciliatory.

General Strategies

Here are some points that are generally applicable to the reading comprehension part of the GMAT.

READING COMPREHENSION IS NOT AN EXERCISE IN SPEED READING.

Many people incorrectly think that the key to reading comprehension is speed, but even a fairly slow reading rate is adequate to handle the material on the GMAT. The emphasis is on comprehension, not speed. (Of course, this does not mean you can afford to point at each word in the selection and move your lips as you read.)

It was mentioned above that it can be helpful to preview topic sentences to get an idea of the content of the passage. Here is a related idea:

YOU MAY WANT TO READ THE QUESTION STEMS BEFORE YOU BEGIN READING THE PASSAGE.

This idea is that the question stems will also let you know in advance what the author will be discussing and can also alert you to look for certain key points. Two points of warning. First, this *may* be useful. Some test-takers like this strategy; others find it a waste of time. As you work the practice tests in this book, try both methods and settle on the one that works better for you. Second, don't read the answer choices, just the question stem. The answer choices themselves are so long and involved, it would be a mistake to try to read them before reading the selection. Further, this means that some question stems will not provide any useful information at all. For example, the stem "The author's main purpose is" is meaningless without the answer choices, so you would just skip it. Finally,

READ EVERY ANSWER CHOICE CAREFULLY.

This is something overlooked by most test-takers. If you glance back at the sample reading comprehension exercise you just finished, you will see that many of the questions with their answer choices contain the equivalent of an entire paragraph of words. Reading comprehension does not end with the final sentence of the passage. Your ability to understand exactly what is said in an answer choice and your ability to distinguish choices that are similar are also a part of this reading comprehension test.

SENTENCE CORRECTION

Sentence correction items require that you correct errors in a written sentence. The question stem will be a sentence, all or part of which has been underlined. The answer choices represent different ways of rendering the underlined part.

Answer choice (A) always repeats the original sentence:

CHOICE (A) ALWAYS REPEATS THE ORIGINAL SENTENCE, SO DON'T BOTHER READING IT.

The underlined portion of some sentences contains more than one error:

BE ALERT FOR SENTENCES CONTAINING MULTIPLE ERRORS.

The correct answer choice must correct all of the errors in the underlined part of the original sentence.

Sentence correction items test correct (grammatical and logical) and effective (clear, concise, and idiomatic) expression. They do not test spelling or capitalization:

IGNORE SPELLING AND CAPITALIZATION ENTIRELY.

Additionally, sentence correction is not really a test of punctuation. Occasionally, a question of punctuation will arise, but it will be closely tied with a larger issue of clear and concise expression.

CHECK FOR AGREEMENT BETWEEN SUBJECT AND VERB.

Example: <u>The phenomena of public education is another example of the workings of democracy.</u>

(A) The phenomena of public education is another example of the workings of democracy.

(B) The phenomena of public education is yet another example of democracy at work.

(C) The phenomenon of public education is another example of how the workings of democracy work.

(D) The phenomenon of public education is another example of democracy at work.

(E) Public education, a phenomena, is another working example of democracy.

In this example there is a lack of agreement in number between the subject ("phenomena") and the verb ("is") because "phenomena" is plural ("phenomenon" is singular). The same error eliminates choices (B) and (E) ("a phenomena" is incorrect). Choice (C) is redundant ("the workings of democracy work"). Choice (D) is correct. The general rule is that a singular subject requires a singular verb, and a plural subject requires a plural verb.

Example: Everyone on both sides <u>except the pitcher and me was</u> injured in that game.

(A) except the pitcher and me was
(B) except the pitcher and me were
(C) except the pitcher and I was
(D) accept the pitcher and I were
(E) accept the pitcher and me was

The underlined portion contains no errors. The "was" is correctly used since "Everyone" is always considered to be singular. *Everyone* is an indefinite pronoun, of which there are three types. The pronouns of the first type are always singular: everyone, each, either, neither, someone, somebody, nobody, anyone, anybody, everybody, one, and no one. Those of the second type are always plural: both, few, many, and several. Those of the third type may be singular or plural, depending on whether the noun to which they refer is singular or plural: some, more, most, and all ("some of the cake (singular) is . . ."; "some of the boys (plural) are . . ."). In choice (C), "I" should be "me" because it is the object of "except." Choices (D) and (E) are both incorrect because "accept" is a verb, not a preposition (an error of diction).

Example: His dog, <u>along with his cat and goldfish, prevent</u> him from taking long trips.

    (A) along with his cat and goldfish, prevent
    (B) as well as his cat and goldfish, prevents
    (C) in addition to his cat and goldfish, are preventing
    (D) together with his cat and goldfish, were preventing
    (E) accompanied by his cat and goldfish, prevent

The subject of the sentence is "dog," which is singular; therefore, a singular verb is required. Only choice (B) has a singular verb ("prevents"). The general rule is that the joining of a singular subject with another noun or pronoun, or with several nouns or pronouns, singular or plural, by along with, together with, with, as well as, in addition to, accompanied by, or any similar word or phrase except *and,* does not make the singular subject into a plural one (only *and* will do so). Choice (D) also changes the meaning of the original by making the tense of the verb past instead of present.

Example: <u>Neither the councilmen nor the mayor take</u> responsibility for the passage of the controversial bill.

    (A) Neither the councilmen nor the mayor take
    (B) Neither the councilmen or the mayor takes
    (C) Neither the councilmen take nor the mayor takes
    (D) Neither the mayor nor the councilmen takes
    (E) Neither the councilmen nor the mayor takes

Choice (E) is correct. The general rule is that when two distinct words or phrases are joined by the correlatives either . . . or, neither . . . nor, or not only . . . but also, the number (singular or plural) of the word or phrase nearer to the verb determines the number of the verb. Choices (A) and (D) are wrong for that reason ("mayor take" and "councilmen takes"). Choice (B) is wrong because "Neither" is incorrectly correlated with "or" (rather than "nor"). Choice (C) is wrong because of the insertion of "take"; the *neither . . . nor* correlation must be *directly* between two nouns or pronouns.

 CHECK FOR AGREEMENT BETWEEN PRONOUNS AND THE WORDS TO WHICH THEY REFER.

Example: The preacher said <u>that everyone will burn in eternal damnation for their sins.</u>

    (A) that everyone will burn in eternal damnation for their sins.
    (B) that everyone for his sins in eternal damnation will burn.
    (C) that everyone will burn in eternal damnation for his sins.
    (D) about everyone that they will burn in eternal damnation for their sins.
    (E) that all of us should burn in eternal damnation for their sins.

Everyone is always singular. Therefore, any pronoun that refers to "everyone" must also be singular. Choices (A) and (D) use "their" (plural) instead of "his" (singular) to refer to everyone and are therefore wrong. Choice (B) uses "his" correctly but has its prepositional phrase modifiers placed in an unusual fashion. Choice (E) uses "their" correctly to refer to "all of *us*" (plural "all" because of "us," which is plural), but changes the meaning of the sentence to "should burn" instead of "will burn." Choice (C) is correct.

Example: Of the two leaders, neither Trotsky nor Lenin <u>was most brilliant, but each worked in their sphere</u> for the party.

    (A) was most brilliant, but each worked in their sphere

    (B) was most brilliant, but each worked in their own sphere

    (C) was most brilliant, but each worked in his sphere

    (D) was more brilliant, but each in their own sphere worked

    (E) was more brilliant, but each worked in his sphere

Each is always singular. Therefore, any pronoun that refers back to each must also be singular. Choices (A), (B), and (D) use "their" (plural) instead of "his" (singular) to refer to "each" and are therefore wrong. After the commas in choices (C) and (E), the wording is the same and is correct. In choice (C) "most" is incorrect because only two people are mentioned in the sentence: a comparison between two people or things uses the comparative degree, more (*adjective*) or (*adjective*)er, not the superlative degree most (*adjective*) or (*adjective*)est. Both (D) and (E) use the proper comparative form, but (A), (B), and (C) do not. Therefore choice (E) is the correct answer.

MAKE SURE PRONOUNS ARE IN THE CORRECT CASE

Example: Every conservative candidate <u>except Smith and she</u> was defeated in the primary election.

    (A) except Smith and she

    (B) except Smith and her

    (C) excepting Smith and she

    (D) but not she and Smith

    (E) outside of her and Smith

Since *except* is a preposition, it must take an object (her), not a subject (she). Therefore, choices (A) and (C) are wrong. Choice (C) is also wrong because "excepting" is poor diction as used in this context, as a substitute for "except." In choice (E), "outside of" is also poor diction; either except or other than should be used instead. In choice (D), "but not she and Smith" is an awkward construction, and even if it were used, it should be set off from the rest of the sentence by commas. (B) is correct.

Example: <u>If I were he, I would lay that manuscript</u> on the sofa, and keep it away from the kitchen table.

    (A) If I were he, I would lay that manuscript

    (B) If I were him, I would lay that manuscript

    (C) If I were he, I would lie that manuscript

(D) If I was he, I would lay that manuscript
(E) If I was he, I would lie that manuscript

The various answer choices in this example contain three places where an error may occur: "was" or "were"; "he" or "him"; and "lay" or "lie." The correct choices from the three pairs of alternatives are "were" because the first clause is known as a condition contrary to fact (the "I" is *not* "he") and therefore requires the subjunctive mood of the verb ("I were" rather than the normal, or indicative, mood, "I was"); "he" because whenever a form of the verb to be is used (in this case, "were"), the pronouns on both sides of the verb must be subjects (the "I" is a subject, and the "he" is a predicate nominative); and "lay," which means "to put or place," not "lie," which means "to recline" (an error of diction). Therefore, the correct answer is (A).

Example: The contest judges were told to give the prize to whomever drew the best picture.

(A) to give the prize to whomever drew the best picture.
(B) to give the prize to whoever drew the best picture.
(C) to give whomever drew the best picture the prize.
(D) to give to whoever drew the best picture the prize.
(E) to give the prize to whomever it was who drew the best picture.

In this sentence the preposition to (the second "to" of the sentence) has as its object the rest of the sentence, not merely the word *whomever*. The part of the sentence after the second "to" is a clause (a group of words containing a subject and a verb) which has "whomever" as its subject ("drew" is its verb, and "picture is the object of "drew"). But *whomever* is an object; the correct word is *whoever*. That eliminates choices (A), (C), and (E). Choice (D) is awkwardly phrased because "the prize" does not immediately follow "give." Therefore, choice (B) is correct. As a comparison, a sentence that would use *whomever* correctly (as the object of the verb liked) would be the following: ". . . to give the price to whomever the audience liked best."

 MAKE SURE EACH PRONOUN REFERS TO SOMETHING.

Example: The coal strike reduced Indiana's energy reserves, which caused unemployment among the workers.

(A) which caused unemployment among the workers.
(B) which caused the workers to unemployed.
(C) a circumstance that resulted in unemployment
(D) a fact that created unemployed workers.
(E) which led many workers to be unemployed.

In this sentence, "which" has no other word in the sentence to which it can logically refer: neither the "reserves" nor the "strike" "caused unemployment," but rather the fact that the energy reserves were reduced "caused unemployment." Therefore, choices (A), (B), and (E) are incorrect. Either "a circumstance" or "a fact" is correct. Since the reduction of energy reserves did not *create workers* (unemployed or otherwise), choice (C) is correct. The "circumstance" resulted in unemployment (and unemployment *of workers* is understood; the context implies that it is workers, and not some other group, who are unemployed). The general rule is that a pronoun in a sentence must unambiguously refer to some other noun or pronoun in the sentence. Otherwise, as here, another word ("circumstance") must be supplied.

Example   In this article they imply that everybody who dislike this philosophy must still accept its principal tenet themselves.

(A) In this article they imply that everybody who dislike this philosophy must still accept its principal tenet themselves.

(B) The author of this article implies that everybody who dislikes this philosophy must still except its principal tenet themselves.

(C) The author of this article implies that everybody who dislikes this philosophy must still accept its principal tenet himself.

(D) The author in this article implies that everybody who dislike this philosophy must himself still except its principle tenet.

(E) The author implies that everybody who dislike this philosophy must themselves still accept its principle tenet.

In this sentence, "they " has no reference, unambiguous or otherwise. Therefore, an appropriate change must be made, as in choices (B), (C), (D), or (E) ("The author"). Choices (A), (D) and (E) contain a second error, namely, "dislike" instead of "dislikes," because "who," which refers to "everybody," must be singular because "everybody" is singular. Choices (B) and (D) contain diction errors (the use of "except" instead of "accept"), so those choices are incorrect. Choices (D) and (E) contain a second diction error, the use of "principle" instead of "principal." Choices (A), (B), and (E) incorrectly use the plural "themselves" instead of the singular "himself," as in choices (C) and (D), to refer to "everybody." Choices (D) and (E) misplace "himself" (or "themselves"); it should appear at the end of the sentence in order to achieve a natural-sounding word order.

MAKE SURE THAT VERB TENSES LOGICALLY REFLECT THE SEQUENCE OF EVENTS DESCRIBED.

Example: When I opened the hood and saw smoke pouring from the engine, I realized that I forgot to add oil.

(A) I realized that I forgot to add oil.
(B) I had realized that I forgot to add oil.
(C) I had realized that I had forgotten to add oil.
(D) I realized that I would forget to add oil.
(E) I realized that I had forgotten to add oil.

Verb tenses must be in proper sequence. When two or more events have taken place, are taking place, or will take place at the same time, their tenses must be the same. If two events have taken place in the past but one event occurred prior to the other, the later of the two events must be in the past tense, and the earlier of the two must be in the past perfect tense (*had* plus the past tense of the verb). In this sentence, the "opening," the "seeing," and the "realizing" all took place in the past at the same time and therefore should all be in the (simple) past tense. So choices (B) and (C) (with "had realized," which is the past perfect tense) are wrong. The "forgetting" also took place in the past but prior to the other three events and therefore should be in the past perfect tense ("had forgotten"). So choices (A), (B), and (D) are wrong. Only choice (E) contains the proper sequence of tenses.

Example: If they <u>would have paid attention</u>, they would not have had to be told again.

    (A) would have paid attention
    (B) would pay attention
    (C) had paid attention
    (D) paid attention
    (E) were to pay attention

This sentence provides another example of the proper sequence of tenses in a slightly different format. If the two events had actually occurred (neither event did occur), the "paying attention" would have occurred prior to the "having to be told again." Therefore, the earlier event must be in the past perfect tense ("had paid"). Only choice (C) has the correct form of the verb. The *if* clause is known as a condition contrary to fact (in fact, they did not pay attention).

MAKE SURE ELLIPTICAL VERB PHRASES ARE PROPERLY COMPLETED.

Example: <u>She is not and does not intend to run</u> for political office.

    (A) She is not and does not intend to run
    (B) She is not running and does not intend to
    (C) She is not and will not intend to run
    (D) She is not running and does not intend to run
    (E) She has not and does not intend to run

This sentence contains an example of an ellipsis (the omission of a word or words from a sentence) in the omission of some form of "run" after the first "not." In a construction like this one, the verb may properly be omitted only if it is in the same form as another appearance of the same verb. Since "running" is the omitted form and "run" is the form that appears later in the sentence, "running" must appear after the first "not." Choice (B) corrects that error but omits "run" at the end of the underlined portion; therefore, choice (B) is wrong. Choices (C) and (E) also do not correct the error of the original; furthermore, the meaning of the original is changed by the changing of tenses. Only choice (D) is correct.

USE A POSSESSIVE PRONOUN TO MODIFY A GERUND (THE -ING FORM OF A VERB USED AS A NOUN).

Example: <u>He disapproves of you insisting that the rope of pearls were misplaced on purpose.</u>

    (A) He disapproves of you insisting that the rope of pearls were misplaced on purpose.

(B) He disapproves of you insisting that the rope of pearls were purposely mis-placed.

(C) He disapproves of your insisting that the rope of pearls was purposely mis-placed.

(D) He disapproves of you insisting that she misplaced the rope of pearls purposely.

(E) How could you insist she misplaced the rope of pearls on purpose.

In this sentence the object of the preposition "of" is "insisting," not "you." Therefore, "your," not "you," must be used since that word is acting as a modifier of "insisting" (which is a gerund—that is, a form of a verb, ending in -*ing,* which acts as a noun). Choices (B) and (D) contain the same error. Additionally, choices (A) and (B) contain an error of agreement between the subject of a clause ("rope") and its verb ("were misplaced"). The fact that the "rope" is "of pearls" (plural) does not make the subject grammatically plural. Choices (D) and (E) also change the meaning of the original (the reader does not know who misplaced the pearls). Either "on purpose," choices (A) and (E), or "purposely," choices (B), (C) and (D), may be used interchangeably without affecting the grammar or meaning of the sentence. Only choice (C) contains no errors.

ADVERBS ARE USED TO MODIFY VERBS.

Example: The car runs quieter when I add a more heavy transmission fluid.

(A) The car runs quieter when I add a more heavy transmission fluid.
(B) The car runs more quietly when I add a heavier transmission fluid.
(C) The car runs quieter when I add a more heavier transmission fluid.
(D) The car runs more quietly when I add a more heavy transmission fluid.
(E) The car runs quieter when I add a heavier transmission fluid.

The glaring grammatical error in this sentence is the use of "quieter" (the adjective form of quiet) instead of "more quietly." "Quieter" (or "more quietly") modifies "run" (a verb) and therefore should be in its adverb form (adverbs modify verbs, adjectives of other adverbs) rather than its adjective form (adjectives modify nouns and pronouns). The other error in the original is the use of "more heavy" instead of "heavier." As a matter of word choice, it is preferable to use an -*er* ending for a comparative adjective when one is readily available and in common use; such a word choice is more idiomatic (but not "idiomaticer"). Choices (C) and (E) do not correct the "quieter" error; additionally, in choice (C), "more heavier" is incorrect because it joins two comparative forms in one construction. Choice (D) does not correct the "more heavy" error. Therefore, choice (B) is correct.

MAKE SURE THAT COMPARISONS ARE CORRECTLY PHRASED.

Example: John maintained that his scholastic record was better or at least as good as hers.

(A) John maintained that his scholastic record was better or at least as good as hers.

(B) John maintained that his scholastic record at its least was as good as hers.
(C) John maintained that his scholastic record was as good or better than hers.
(D) John maintained that his scholastic record was better or at least as good as her scholastic record.
(E) John maintained that his scholastic record was better than or at least as good as hers.

When two items are being compared and one is stated to be better than the others, the *than* in the comparison is essential. Likewise, when one item is stated to be as good as another, the second *as* is essential. Therefore, the correct construction in the sentence above should be "... better *than* or at least as good *as* hers" or "... at least as good *as* or better *than* hers" (either order is acceptable). Choices (A) and (D) omit "than," and choice (C) omits the second "as." Choice (B) changes the meaning of the sentence slightly and therefore is incorrect. In choice (D), it is unnecessary to replace "hers" (at the end of the sentence) with "her scholastic record." Only choice (E) contains no errors.

WATCH OUT FOR ILLOGICAL COMPARISONS.

Example: A speaker's physical impact—including gestures, facial expression and body carriage—is as important as listening to his message.

(A) A speaker's physical impact—including gestures, facial expression and body carriage—is
(B) A speaker's physical impact—gestures, facial expression and body carriage—are
(C) The examination of a speaker's physical impact—including gestures, facial expression and body carriage—is
(D) Examining a speaker's physical impact—gestures, facial expression and body carriage—are
(E) Examining a speaker's physical impact—including gestures, facial expression and body carriage—is

This question is relatively difficult. The sentence as it stands makes a comparison between "impact" and "listening," which are neither grammatically nor conceptually parallel. Since "listening" is not underlined, the subject of the sentence, "impact," must be changed so as to be parallel with "listening." "Examination" comes close, but "Examining" is even closer to being parallel with "listening." Thus the correct answer is either (D) or (E). Since the subject of the sentence is singular—"impact" in (A) and (B), "examination" in (C), and "Examining" in choices (D) and (E)—the verb must be singular ("is" instead of "are") even though the subject *seems* to be plural ("gestures, facial expression and body carriage" does not make the subject plural). Thus, choices (B) and (D) are incorrect. Furthermore, (B) and (D) are wrong because they eliminate "including" before "gestures" and therefore imply that "gestures, facial expression and body carriage" are the *only* characteristics of a "speaker's physical impact," whereas "including" implies that there may be other characteristics. Therefore, choices (B) and (D) slightly change the meaning of the original underlined portion. Thus, only choice (E) is correct.

Example: Your courage is <u>as great as any other man</u> in defending your country.

    (A) as great as any other man
    (B) so great as any other man
    (C) great like any other man
    (D) as great as that of any other man
    (E) as that of any man

A comparison is being made in this sentence between "Your courage" and "any other man." But "courage" and "man" are not like classes of things. Since "courage" is not underlined, "man" must be altered to make the comparison logical. Only (D) corrects the error, by comparing "courage" to "that of any other man," that is, to the courage of "any other man." The correct construction could be either choice (D) or "as great as the courage of any other man" or "as great as any other man's courage" or "as great as any other man's" (where "courage" after "man's" would be understood).

 CHECK THE SENTENCE FOR PARALLELISM.

Example: The stranger was affable, <u>with good manners and has a keen wit.</u>

    (A) with good manners and has a keen wit.
    (B) with good manners and a keen wit.
    (C) well-mannered and keen-witted.
    (D) good manners as well as keen-witted.
    (E) and has good manners as well as a keen wit.

This sentence contains two illustrations of a lack of parallelism among grammatically equivalent elements of the sentence. "Affable," an adjective, is used to describe the "stranger." Therefore, the other two descriptions of the stranger must agree in form (that is, must be parallel) with "affable." "With good manners" is a prepositional phrase and "has a keen wit" is the predicate portion of a clause; both must be changed into their adjective forms. Only choice (C) makes that correction.

Example: <u>To run for an important political office, to manage a large organization and practicing law effectively</u> all require organizational and problem-solving skills.

    (A) To run for an important political office, to manage a large organization and practicing law effectively
    (B) To run for an important political office and to manage a large organization, practicing law effectively
    (C) Running for an important political office, managing a large organization and to practice law effectively
    (D) To run and manage political offices and large organizations and practicing law effectively
    (E) Running for an important office, managing a large organization and practicing law effectively

This sentence, like the previous example, is a very straightforward example of a lack of parallelism in the subject matter of the sentence: two infinitives ("to run" and "to manage") are used along with a gerund ("practicing"; a gerund is a form of a verb that ends in *-ing* and functions as a noun). Either all three terms must be gerunds. Only choice (E) uniformly uses one construction or the other.

Example: Edward not only resists learning to correlate new facts but also remembering old lessons.

    (A) Edward not only resists learning to correlate new facts but also remembering old lessons.

    (B) Edward not only resists learning to correlate new facts but also to remember old lessons.

    (C) Edward resists not only learning to correlate new facts but also remembering old lessons.

    (D) Edward resists not only learning to correlate new facts but also to remember old lessons.

    (E) Edward resists learning to correlate new facts and remembering old lessons.

The terms *not only* and *but also* (just like *neither* and *nor* and *either* and *or*) must introduce grammatically equivalent, and therefore parallel, sentence elements. In this sentence, "not only" introduces "resists" and "but also" introduces "remembering." "Resists" is the verb of the sentence, and "remembering," along with "learning," is an object of "resists." One way to correct this error would be "Edward not only resists learning . . . but also *resists* remembering. . . ." But the use of "resists" twice is unnecessarily wordy. A better way to correct the error is choice (C), the correct answer. Choice (B) compounds the error of the original underlined portion by using "to remember" instead of "remembering," so that the new term is not parallel with "learning." Choice (D) corrects the original error, but makes the same mistake as choice B. Choice (E) slightly changes the meaning of the original sentence by eliminating the comparative emphasis between "learning" and "remembering."

BEWARE OF MISPLACED MODIFIERS

Example: By leading trump the contract was defeated resoundingly by the defenders.

    (A) By leading trump the contract was defeated resoundingly by the defenders.
    (B) By leading trump the defenders defeated the contract resoundingly.
    (C) The defenders resounded the defeat of the contract by leading trump.
    (D) The contract, by leading trump, was defeated resoundingly by the defenders.
    (E) Resoundingly, the contract was defeated by the defenders by leading trump.

An introductory modifier of a noun or pronoun, in this case the prepositional phrase "By leading trump," must modify the subject of the main clause, in this case "the contract." But clearly the "contract" did not lead trump; rather, the "defenders" led trump and "defeated the contract resoundingly." Therefore, the subject of the main clause must be "defenders," if "By leading trump" is to remain as the introductory modifier. The error here is known as a dangling, or misplaced, modifier because it does not *logically* modify the noun or pronoun that it *grammatically* modifies. Choice (B) corrects the error and is the correct answer. Choice (C) changes the meaning of the original by stating that

"The defenders resounded the defeat . . ." (D) and (E) still imply, grammatically, that the contract led trump. An additional point concerning the construction of these answer choices is that, as a matter of writing style (but not as a matter of grammar or usage), the active voice ("the defenders defeated the contract") is preferable to the passive voice ("the contract was defeated by the defenders").

Example: In addition to those specified for professions, <u>the corporations maintained endowments in purely academic fields, especially in the physical sciences.</u>

- **(A)** the corporations maintained endowments in purely academic fields, especially in the physical sciences.
- **(B)** the corporations had maintained purely academic endowments like those of the physical sciences.
- **(C)** in purely academic fields, endowments, especially in the physical sciences, were maintained by the corporations.
- **(D)** endowments were maintained in purely academic fields, especially in the physical sciences, by the corporations.
- **(E)** purely academic endowments, especially for those fields like the physical sciences, were maintained by the corporations.

Grammatically, this sentence states that "the corporations" are "In addition to those specified for professions," whereas it is the "endowments" that are "In addition to those specified for professions." One way to classify this error is to say that the nonunderlined portion of the sentence is a dangling, or misplaced, modifier because it grammatically modifies "the corporations" but logically should modify the "endowments." Another way to classify the error is to say that the reference of the pronoun "those" is ambiguous because "those" grammatically refers to "corporations" (the general rule is that a pronoun should refer, whenever possible, to the noun or other pronoun closest to it in the sentence) but logically should refer to "endowments." In either case, the subject of the main clause must be "endowments" rather than "corporations." (C), (D) and (E) all use "endowments" as the subject of the main clause. In choice (C) the prepositional-phrase modifiers "in purely academic fields" and "especially in the physical sciences" are misplaced so that the sentence is awkwardly constructed, causing the reader to slow down when he reads it in order to put the pieces (of the sentence) back together. Choice (D) corrects the awkwardness and misplacement of modifiers of choice (C) and is therefore the correct answer. Choice (E) is more brief in its use of "purely academic endowments" rather than "endowments in purely academic fields" (making the sentence more concise and therefore better, probably without changing the meaning), but changes the meaning of the next expression by using "especially for those fields like the physical sciences": the endowments were maintained "especially in the physical sciences," not "especially for those fields *like* the physical sciences."

WATCH OUT FOR SENTENCE FRAGMENTS.

Example: The lovestruck boy was sad because <u>the girl who he loved and who had left him for another.</u>

- **(A)** the girl who he loved and who had left him for another.
- **(B)** the girl whom he loved and whom had left him for another.

(C) the girl whom he loved and who had left him for.
(D) the girl whom he loved had left him for another.
(E) the girl who he loved had left him for another.

The underlined portion of this sentence is a fragment because it contains a subject ("girl") but no verb to act as a predicate for the subject (the two clauses that begin with "who" act as modifiers of "girl"). Removing "and who" after "loved" will correct this error, as in choices (D) and (E); "had left" then becomes the verb that acts as the predicate for "girl.". Another error in the original underlined portion is the first "who," which is in the form of a subject but which should be in the form of an object ("whom") since it acts as the object of "loved" ("he" is the subject of "loved"). The second "who" is correct since it is the subject of "had left" ("him" is the object). Therefore, choice (D) is correct.

WATCH OUT FOR RUN-ON SENTENCES.

Example: Initially Bob was the group's spokesman, <u>afterwards it occurred to them that</u> Jane was more articulate and more diplomatic.

(A) afterwards it occurred to them that
(B) that wasn't the best thing to do since
(C) but they came to realize that
(D) they concluded, however, that
(E) then they decided that

This sentence is an example of a run-on sentence, that is, a sentence which contains two independent clauses that are not properly joined together. The portion of this sentence before the comma is an independent clause (which means a clause that can act as a sentence all by itself), and the portion of the sentence after the comma is also an independent clause. A comma by itself is not sufficient to separate two independent clauses; rather, a coordinating conjunction like *and, but, yet, for, or,* or *nor* must be used between the comma and the second independent clause. Only choice (C) provides such a conjunction at the beginning of the second clause. Since "they came to realize" has virtually the same meaning as "it occurred to them," choice (C) is the correct answer. The main consideration here is that choices (A), (B), (D) and (E) are run-on sentences.

WATCH OUT FOR ILLOGICAL SUBORDINATION.

Example: The Beatles were to be honored <u>on account they bolstered the sagging British economy.</u>

(A) on account they bolstered the sagging British economy.
(B) being that they bolstered the sagging British economy.
(C) when they bolstered the sagging British economy.
(D) the reason being on account of their bolstering the sagging British economy.
(E) since they bolstered the sagging British economy.

The underlined portion of this sentence is a subordinate (or dependent) clause, that is, one that cannot stand by itself as a complete sentence but which must be joined to an independent or other dependent clause by a subordinate conjunction. Both (C) and (E) introduce the clause by a subordinate conjunction ("when" and "since"). Since the relationship between the two clauses of the sentence is one of cause and effect, *since* is a better word than *when*. *On account,* if used at all, should be in the form *on account of;* furthermore, since *of* is a preposition, it must take an object, for example, "their bolstering of the sagging British economy." *Being that* is poor diction (because it is not acceptable in Standard Written English, that is, it is a slang expression, as is *being as*) if used as a substitute for *since* or *because*. Choice (D) is redundant ("the reason being" and "on account of" say the same thing).

 "BECAUSE" CANNOT INTRODUCE A NOUN CLAUSE.

Example: <u>Because he agrees with you</u> does not signify that his reasons are the same as yours.

    (A) Because he agrees with you
    (B) If he agrees with you
    (C) When he agrees with you
    (D) Because you and he agree
    (E) That he agrees with you

The underlined portion of the sentence acts as the subject of the sentence, that is, the underlined portion "does not signify . . ." The correct answer is choice (E) because "That" is short for "The fact that," and "fact" is the true subject of the sentence. The ommission of "The fact" from choice (E) is another example of an ellipsis (the omission of a word or words from a sentence). None of the other choices can act as the subject of the sentence.

 WATCH OUT FOR ERRORS OF DICTION (INCORRECT CHOICE OF WORDS).

Example: <u>The prisoner was expedited from California to Florida.</u>

    (A) The prisoner was expedited from California to Florida.
    (B) From California to Florida, the prisoner was expedited.
    (C) The prisoner from California was extradited to Florida.
    (D) The prisoner was extradited from California to Florida.
    (E) From California, the prisoner was expedited to Florida.

In this example, "expedited" (meaning "speeded up, hastened or accomplished promptly") is used incorrectly; therefore, answer choices (A), (B), and (E) should be eliminated. The proper word to use in this context is *extradited* (meaning "surrendered by one state or authority to another"), which appears in choices (C) and (D). The meaning of the original is changed in (C): "The prisoner from California" seems to mean that the prisoner is a person from the state of California, not necessarily that the state of California is extraditing him. The error in choice (C) is an example of a misplaced modifier (in this instance, the prepositional phrase "from California").

Choices (B) and (E) also contain misplaced modifiers—"From California to Florida" in choice (B); "From California" in choice (E). Therefore, (D) is the best choice.

 AVOID ANSWER CHOICES THAT ARE UNNECESSARILY WORDY.

Example: If one begins to smoke at an early age, *it is likely that he will go on smoking further.*

  (A) it is likely that he will go on smoking further.
  (B) he will probably keep smoking more and more.
  (C) it is hard to stop him from smoking more.
  (D) he is likely to continue smoking.
  (E) he will have a tendency to continue smoking.

This example illustrates a lack of brevity of expression in the original underlined portion. In shortening a wordy expression such as the above (and, in fact, any time you select an answer choice that changes the original wording), you need to make sure that the meaning of the original is preserved. Choice (C) changes the meaning of the original and therefore should be eliminated. Choice (E) changes the meaning slightly but is a possibility. Choices (A) and (B) are quite wordy in comparison with the correct answer, choice (D). Choice (D) expresses the meaning of the original clearly and concisely. None of the answer choices in this question contains any grammatical mistakes, which is rare. Also, you should not blindly choose the shortest answer choice.

Example: After being in school for sixteen years, Jack couldn't wait to get out to get a job.

  (A) Jack couldn't wait to get out to get a job.
  (B) there was great desire in Jack to get out and get a job.
  (C) Jack was eager to get a job.
  (D) Jack wanted out and a job badly.
  (E) Jack arranged to look for a job.

This example also illustrates a lack of brevity of expression, as well as poor diction in answer choice (D). Choice (C) expresses the idea of the underlined portion clearly and concisely. In choice (D) "out" used without "to get" is poor diction. Choice (E) changes the meaning of the original by using "arranged to look" (the reader of the sentence does not know what steps, if any, Jack has taken in pursuit of a job). Both choices (A) and (B) are wordy.

Example: The scholar's reluctance over committing himself as to judging the authenticity of the manuscript may be caused as a result of his uncertainty of its recent history.

  (A) over committing himself as to judging the authenticity of the manuscript may be caused as a result of
  (B) to judge the authenticity of the manuscript may be caused as a result of
  (C) to judge the authenticity of the manuscript may be a result of
  (D) over committing himself as to judgment of the authenticity of the manuscript may be caused by
  (E) over committing himself as to judging of the authenticity of the manuscript may be a result of

The underlined portion of this sentence uses too many words to express two ideas and also uses poor diction. "Over committing himself as to judging" should be either "to commit himself to judge" ("reluctance over committing" uses poor diction; "reluctance" in this context should be followed by an infinitive) or merely "to judge," which is even better. "Caused as a result of" is redundant. his "reluctance" either "is caused by his uncertainty" or "is a result of his uncertainty," not both. Therefore, the correct answer is (C).

CRITICAL THINKING

Critical thinking questions ask you to evaluate arguments. An argument is a group of statements or assertions, one of which—the conclusion—is supposed to follow from the others, the premises. For example:

> All men are mortal.
> Socrates is a man.
> Therefore, Socrates is mortal.

The third statement is the conclusion of the argument, and the first two statements are its premises. The movement of thought that joins the conclusion to the premises is called the inference.

The argument above is called a deductive argument, and it is the kind of reasoning we associate with college logic courses. The most striking feature of a deductive argument is that the conclusion follows from the premises "automatically."

Most of the arguments we use on a daily basis, however, have a different form. For example:

> My car will not start; the fuel guage reads "empty."
> Therefore, the car is (probably) out of gas.

Here the conclusion does not follow with certainty; it is not guaranteed. It is possible, for example, that the fuel gauge is broken and that the car won't start for any number of other reasons (the battery is dead, the distributor cap is wet, someone stole the engine). This kind of argument is called an inductive argument.

In evaluating an argument, you must be concerned with the interrelationship of all three parts: the conclusion, the premises, and the inference.

Finding the Conclusion

Locating the conclusion of an argument and defining its exact scope is the first step in evaluating the strength of any argument. You cannot begin to look for fallacies or other weaknesses in a line of reasoning or even find the line of reasoning until you have clearly identified the point the author wishes to prove. Any attempt to skip over this important step can only result in misunderstanding and confusion. We have all had the experience of discussing a point for some length of time only to say finally, "Oh, now I see what you were saying, and I agree with you." Of course, sometimes such misunderstandings are the fault of the speaker, who perhaps did not clearly state his position in the first place. This is particularly true in less formal discourse, such as conversation, where we have not carefully prepared our remarks before the discussion begins; but it can also occur in writing, though in the case of writing the proponent of a claim generally has the opportunity to consider his words carefully and is therefore, one would hope, less likely to misstate his point. Often, however, the misunderstanding cannot be charged to the speaker or writer, and the blame must be placed on the listener or the reader.

Careful thinkers will obviously want to know precisely what is being claimed in an argument they are examining. They know it is a waste of their mental energy to attack a point that has not been advanced by their opponents but is only the product of their own failure to pay careful attention. In order to help you become more sensitive to the importance of finding the exact point of an argument, we will discuss conclusions in two steps: (1) locating the main point of an argument and (2) defining exactly the main point of any argument.

Locating the Main Point

SOMETIMES THE MAIN POINT OF AN ARGUMENT IS THE LAST STATEMENT IN THE PARAGRAPH.

Example: Since this watch was manufactured in Switzerland, and all Swiss watches are reliable, <u>this watch must be reliable.</u>

Here the conclusion or the point of the line of reasoning is the part that is underlined. The argument also contains two premises: "this watch was manufactured in Switzerland" and "all Swiss watches are reliable." The same argument could be made, however, with the statements presented in a different order:

<u>This watch must be reliable</u> since it was manufactured in Switzerland and all Swiss watches are reliable.

or

<u>This watch must be reliable</u> since all Swiss watches are reliable and it was manufactured in Switzerland.

or

Since this watch was manufactured in Switzerland, <u>it must be reliable</u> because all Swiss watches are reliable.

So we cannot always count on the conclusion of the argument being the last sentence of the paragraph even though sometimes it is.

IF THE CONCLUSION IS NOT THE LAST STATEMENT IN A PASSAGE, IT MAY BE *SIGNALED* BY INDICATOR WORDS.

We often use transitional words or phrases such as *therefore, hence, thus, so, it follows that, as a result,* and *consequently* to announce to the reader or listener that we are making an inference, that is, that we are moving from our premise(s) to our conclusion. For example:

Ms. Slote has a Masters in Education, and she has 20 years of teaching experience, therefore (hence, thus, etc.) she is a good teacher.

Here the conclusion is "she is a good teacher," and the premises are "Ms. Slote has a Masters in Education" and "she has 20 years of teaching experience."

IN SOME ARGUMENTS THE PREMISES RATHER THAN THE CONCLUSION ARE SIGNALED.

Words that signal premises include *since, because, for,* and others that normally connect a dependent clause to an independent one. For example:

> Since Rex has been with the company 20 years and does such a good job, <u>he will probably receive a promotion.</u>
>
> or
>
> <u>Rex will probably receive a promotion because</u> he has been with the company 20 years and he does such a good job.
>
> or
>
> If Rex has been with the company 20 years and has done a good job, <u>he will probably receive a promotion.</u>

In each of the three examples just presented, the conclusion is "Rex will probably receive a promotion" and the premise is that "he has been with the company 20 years and does a good job."

Not all arguments, however, are broken down by the numbers, so to speak. Sometimes inattention on the part of the author or speaker, or sometimes matters of style, result in an argument that does not include a prominent signal of any sort.

ASK YOURSELF "WHAT IS THE AUTHOR OR SPEAKER TRYING TO PROVE?"

For example:

> We must reduce the amount of money we spend on space exploration. Right now, the Soviet Union is launching a massive military buildup, and we need the additional money to purchase military equipment to match the anticipated increase in Soviet strength.

In this argument there are no key words to announce the conclusion, nor is the conclusion the last sentence or statement made in the passage. Instead, the reader must ask, "What is the author trying to prove?" Is the author trying to *prove* that the Soviet Union is beginning a military buildup? No, because that statement is used as a premise in the larger argument, so it cannot be the conclusion. Is the main point that we must match the Soviet buildup? Again the answer is "no," because that, too, is an intermediate step on the way to some other conclusion. Is the author trying to prove that we must cut back on the budget for space exploration? The answer is "yes, that is the author's point." The other two statements are premises that lead the author to conclude that a cutback in space exploration is necessary.

AN ARGUMENT MAY CONTAIN ARGUMENTS WITHIN THE MAIN ARGUMENT.

Thus, the argument about the need for military expenditures might have included this subargument:

The Soviets are now stockpiling titanium, a metal that is used in building airplanes. And each time the Soviet Union has stockpiled titanium it has launched a massive military buildup. So, right now, the Soviet Union is launching a massive military buildup.

Notice that now one of the premises of an earlier argument is the conclusion of a subargument. The conclusion of the subargument is "the Soviet Union . . . buildup," which has two explicit premises: "The Soviets are now stockpiling titanium" and "a stockpiling of titanium means a military buildup." So in trying to find the main point of an argument, one must also be alert to the possibility that an intermediate conclusion may also function as a premise in the main argument.

Defining the Main Point

Once the main point of the argument has been isolated, it is necessary to take the second step of exactly defining that point.

DEFINE THE MAIN POINT OF THE ARGUMENT BY ASKING:

(1) HOW GREAT A CLAIM (OR LIMITED A CLAIM) IS THE AUTHOR MAKING? (2) PRECISELY WHAT IS THE AUTHOR TALKING ABOUT? AND (3) WHAT IS THE AUTHOR'S INTENTION IN MAKING THE CLAIM?

The first of these questions reminds us that authors will frequently qualify their claims.

PAY CAREFUL ATTENTION TO WORDS SUCH AS *SOME, ALL, NONE, NEVER, ALWAYS, EVERYWHERE,* AND *SOMETIMES.*

Thus, there is a big difference in the claims:

> All mammals live on land.
> <u>Most</u> mammals live on land.

The first is false; the second is true. Compare also:

> The United States and Russia have <u>always</u> been enemies.
> <u>For the past 30 years,</u> the United States and Russia have been enemies.

Again, the first statement is false and the second is true. Finally, compare:

> It is raining and the temperature is predicted to drop below 32°F, therefore it will surely snow.
> It is raining and the temperature is predicted to drop below 32°F, therefore it will probably snow.

The first is a much less cautious claim than the second, and if it failed to snow the first claim would have been proved false, though not the second. The second statement claims only that it is probable that snow will follow, not that it definitely will. So someone could make the second claim and defend it when the snow failed to materialize by saying, "Well, I allowed for that in my original statement."

PAY CAREFUL ATTENTION TO DESCRIPTIVE WORDS USED IN A PASSAGE.

Here we cannot even hope to provide a list, so the best we can do is present some examples.

> In nations that have a bicameral legislature, the speed with which legislation is passed is largely a function of the strength of executive leadership.

Notice here that the author makes a claim about "nations," so (at least without further information to license such an extension) it would be wrong to apply the author's reasoning to *states* (such as New York) that also have bicameral legislatures. Further, we would not want to conclude that the author believes that bicameral legislatures pass different laws from those passed by unicameral legislatures. The author mentions only the "speed" with which the laws are passed—not their content. Let us take another example:

All of the passenger automobiles manufactured by Detroit automakers since 1975 have been equipped with seat belts.

We would not want to conclude from this statement that all *trucks* have also been equipped with seat belts since the author makes a claim only about "passenger automobiles," nor would we want to conclude that *imported cars* have seat belts, for the author mentions Detroit-made cars only. Finally, here is yet another example in which the descriptive terms in the claim are intended to restrict the claim:

> No other major department store offers you a low price and a 75-day warranty on parts and labor on this special edition of the XL-30 color television.

The tone of the ad is designed to create a very large impression on the hearer, but the precise claim made is fairly limited. First, the ad's claim is specifically restricted to a comparison of "department" stores, and "major" department stores at that. It is possible that some non-major department store offers a similar warranty and price; also it may be that another type of retail store, say, an electronics store, makes a similar offer. Second, other stores, department or otherwise, may offer a better deal on the product, say, a low price with a three-month warranty, and still the claim would stand—so long as no one else offered exactly a "75-day" warranty. Finally, the ad is restricted to a "special edition" of the television, so, depending on what that means, the ad may be even more restrictive in its claim.

BE CAREFUL TO DISTINGUISH BETWEEN CLAIMS OF FACT AND PROPOSALS OF CHANGE.

Do not assume that if an author claims to have found a problem, he also knows how to solve it. An author can make a claim about the cause of some event without believing that the event can be prevented or even that it ought to be prevented. For example, from the argument:

> Since the fifth ward vote is crucial to Gordon's campaign, if Gordon fails to win over the ward leaders he wil be defeated in the election.

You cannot conclude that the author believes Gordon should or should not be elected. The author gives only a factual analysis without endorsing or condemning either possible outcome. Also, from the argument:

> Each year the rotation of the Earth slows a few tenths of a second. In several million years, it wil have stopped altogether, and life as we know it will no longer be able to survive on Earth.

You cannot conclude that the author wants to find a solution for the slowing of Earth's rotation. For all we know, the author thinks the process is inevitable, or even desirable.

To summarize this discussion of conclusions, remember that you must find the conclusion the author is aiming at by uncovering the structure of the argument. (Did the author try to prove this, and if so, did he use this as a premise of a further argument?) Then pay careful attention to the precise claim made by the conclusion.

Finding the Premises

In our discussion of conclusions, we implicitly treated the problem of finding the premises of an argument, for in separating the conclusion from the remainder of the paragraph, we also isolated those premises explicitly used by the author in constructing his chain of reasoning. In this section, we do not need to redo that analysis, but it will be useful if we describe three important kinds of assumptions an author might make—value judgments, factual assumptions, and definitional assumptions. Then we will discuss the significance of assumptions.

One very important kind of assumption is the *value judgment.* For example, if we argue that the city government should spend money to hire a crossing guard to protect schoolchildren walking to school, we have implicitly assumed that the lives of schoolchildren are important and, further, that protecting these lives is a proper function of city government. Another kind of assumption is the *factual assumption.* For example, "The ball struck the window and the glass shattered. So the person who threw the ball broke the window." Here the explanation uses the factual assumption that it was the ball that broke the glass—and not some super-ray fired by a Martian at the same time. Finally, a third group of assumptions, *definitional assumptions,* are those called into play when we use vague terms. For example, the person who threw the ball is to blame for the broken window because a person is responsible for his misdeeds. Here the conclusion rests on the assumption that throwing the ball is, by definition (at least under the circumstances), a misdeed.

With this in mind, we can turn to a discussion of the importance of assumptions in evaluating an argument. In our discussion of conclusions, we noticed that the conclusion of one argument may function as a premise of yet a further argument. With a little imagination, we could construct an argument in which there might be 20, 30, or even more intermediate links in the chain of reasoning joining the initial premise and the final conclusion. Of course, in practice our arguments are hardly ever so complicated. Usually, we require only three or four steps. For example, we may reason:

> Since there is snow on the ground, it must have snowed last night. If it snowed last night, then the temperature must have dropped below 32°F. The temperature drops below 32°F only in the winter. So, since there is snow on the ground, it must be winter here.

We can easily imagine also extending this string of situational assumptions in either direction. Instead of starting with "there is snow on the ground," we might have backed up one further step and reasoned, "If there is a snowman on the front lawn, it must be because there is snow on the ground"; and from the presence of the snowman on the front lawn we could have reached the conclusion that it is winter here. Or we might extend the argument to yet another conclusion. Using the additional premise "If it is winter here, it is summer in Australia," we could reason from "there is a snowman on the front lawn" to "it is summer in Australia."

In practice, however, we do not extend our arguments indefinitely in either direction. We stop at the conclusion we had hoped to prove, and we begin from what seems to us to be a convenient and secure starting point: "If there is snow on the ground, then it must have snowed last night." Now it is obvious that the strength of an argument depends on the legitimacy of its assumptions.

DEFEATING AN ASSUMPTION IS THE MOST EFFECTIVE WAY OF ATTACKING ANY ARGUMENT.

Let us consider examples of arguments using our three types of assumptions.
A very simple factual assumption is the following:

Premises: If there is gasoline in the tank, my car will start.
I checked and there is gasoline in the tank.

Conclusion: Therefore, my car will start.

A very effective attack on this argument can be aimed at the first premise. One would want to object that the situational premise "if gas, then car starts" is unacceptable because it ignores the fact that there are other reasons the car may fail to start, e.g., the battery is dead, the distributor cap is wet, the engine was stolen. Now the conclusion "my car will start" no longer has any support. Of course it is possible that the car will start, but whether it does or not will not be determinable from the specific argument we have just defeated.

An example of a value judgment is the following:

Premises: The government should help people who might hurt themselves.
Cigarette smoking is harmful to people.

Conclusion: Therefore, the government ought to prevent people from smoking.

One way of attacking this argument is to attack the value judgment that the government ought to protect people from themselves. That might be done by talking about freedom or individual rights, and it will not be possible to clearly *defeat* the assumption of value. In our first argument, the assumption was a question of fact—causal laws in the physical universe—and could be resolved by empirical evidence. In arguments resting on value judgments, it may never be possible to get final agreement. But for purposes of evaluating the strength of an argument, one way of *pursuing the issue,* which is to say, one way of objecting to the argument, is to reject the value judgment on which it rests.

Finally, a definitional assumption is similar to a valuational one:

Premises: An inexperienced person will not make an effective Supreme Court justice.
A person with only ten years of legal practice is inexperienced.

Conclusion: Therefore, a person with only ten years of legal practice will not make an effective Supreme Court Justice.

This argument is a valid deductive argument, but that does not mean it is unassailable as it applies to the real world. One way of attacking the argument is to question its second premise by insisting that ten years is long enough to make a person experienced. Of course, that might be disputed, but at least that is a possible line of attack on the argument. After all, if it could be *proved* that ten years of practice makes one experienced, then the conclusion of the argument must be considered to have been defeated.

Hidden Premises

In each of our three examples, the attack on the argument was fairly easy to find. To be sure, there were others available to us; but at the very least we knew one way of attacking the argument would be to question the assumptions on which it rested. Unfortunately, the attack is not always this easy to find because many times arguments are built on hidden or concealed assumptions, and this is not necessarily because the proponent of the argument in intentionally hiding something that he knows will weaken his argument. Since an argument could be extended backward indefinitely (But why do you believe that? So why do you think that? What is your reason for that?), the starting point of an argument is always a bit arbitrary. Even someone who is giving what he thinks to be a correct and honest argument will make some assumptions that he does not explicitly acknowledge.

ATTACK AN ARGUMENT BY FINDING ITS HIDDEN ASSUMPTIONS.

Argument: The ground is damp, so it must have rained last night.

Hidden premise: Rain is the only thing that causes the ground to become damp.

Argument: Homosexuality is a sin; therefore, there should be laws against such practices.

Hidden premise: The government ought to enforce morality.

Argument: John is the perfect husband; he never cheats on his wife.

Hidden premise: Any husband who does not cheat on his wife is a perfect husband.

So, in evaluating an argument, it is always important to be aware of the possibility of hidden assumptions that might be open to attack. This is particularly true if one finds an argument that on the surface appears to be logically correct but reaches a conclusion that seems factually impossible, or one that seems valuationally or judgmentally absurd. In such a situation, it is a good idea to look for a hidden assumption that makes the argument work. Of course, even though the conclusion seems strange, it might just be correct, in which case careful thinkers admit that their initial reactions to the argument were wrong, and they change their minds. Similarly, a reasonable-appearing conclusion can be based on inadequate or wrong argumentation.

With regard to premises, then, we have learned that every argument rests on them. An explanation of events usually rests on factual premises, and a proposal for action rests on value judgments. And both kinds of arguments will make definitional assumptions. It should also be kept in mind that since a complex argument is made of subarguments, a final factual conclusion may ultimately have a value judgment somewhere in the argument supporting it and by the same token a final value judgment may have a factual premise somewhere in the argument supporting it. Many times the assumptions of an argument will not be explicitly mentioned by the author; they may be hidden. But whether an assumption is explicit or just implicit, it is of critical importance to the argument, and for this reason attacks on premises can be very powerful.

Evaluating Inferences

In the preceding two sections, we describe the importance of finding the conclusion and the premises of an argument. We now turn our attention to techniques for evaluating the inference that is supposed to link the conclusion to the premises. Our discussion of inductive inferences is a checklist of the most important kinds of fallacies. You should not, however, allow yourself to think that you can memorize the list and apply it mechanically to logical reasoning problems. The classification we present is somewhat artificial, and discretion is required in using it. We will discuss seven fallacies: The ad hominen attack, circular reasoning, appeals to irrelevant considerations, false cause, hasty generalization, ambiguity, and false analogy.

 AN *AD HOMINEN* ATTACK IS AN ARGUMENT THAT IS DIRECTED AGAINST THE SOURCE OF THE CLAIM RATHER THAN THE CLAIM ITSELF.

Since there are times when such attacks are useful, as when the credibility of the speaker is at issue, we must be careful to distinguish the illegimate ad hominem attack from the legitimate attack on a person's credibility. An illegitimate ad hominem argument is one that ignores the merits of the issue in favor of an attempt to discredit the source of the argument where the credibility of the speaker is not at issue. For example:

> We should not accept Professor Smith's analysis of the causes of traffic accidents because we know that she has been unfaithful to her husband.

Setting aside such outlandish speculations as the possibility that Professor Smith has killed her husband in a fake accident, we can see that there is no connection between Smith's analysis of accidents and her infidelity to her husband. So this is an illegitimate attack. A student who wants to see further examples of such attacks need only read the daily newspaper with particular attention to any political campaign or other political struggle. On the other hand, there are attacks on the credibility of speakers that are legitimate. We are all suspicious of the claims made by salespersons, and rightly so! More generally, it is legitimate to take account of any possible self-interest in making a statement. For example:

General: The army needs more and bigger tanks. Even though they are expensive, they are vital to the nation's security.

Politician: And if I am elected governor, I will cut taxes and put an end to crime.

In these cases it is not wrong to point out that the speaker's vision may be clouded by his own interest in the outcome of the matter.

AN ARGUMENT THAT INCLUDES THE CONCLUSION IT HOPES TO PROVE AS ONE OF ITS PREMISES IS FALLACIOUS BECAUSE IT IS CIRCULAR.

For example:

Beethoven was the greatest composer of all time, because he wrote the great-est music of any composer, and he who composes the greatest music must be the greatest composer.

The conclusion of this argument is that Beethoven was the greatest composer of all time, but one of the premises of the argument is that he composed the greatest music, and the other premise states that that is the measure of greatness. The argument is fallacious, for there is really no argument for the conclusion at all, just a restatement of the conclusion.

There are two common argument forms that involve an appeal to an irrelevant consideration as proof of the conclusion.

AN ARGUMENT THAT APPEALS TO THE POPULARITY OF A POSITION TO PROVE THE POSITION IS FALLACIOUS.

For example:

Frederick must be the best choice for chairman because most people believe that he is the best person for the job.

That many people hold an opinion obviously does not guarantee its correctness—after all, many people once thought airplanes couldn't fly.

BE CAREFUL TO DISTINGUISH LEGITIMATE FROM ILLEGITIMATE USES OF AUTHORITY.

Another appeal to an irrelevant consideration might be an illegitimate appeal to author-ity. For example:

The theory of evolution is only so much hogwash, and this is clearly proved by the fact that Professor Edwards, who got an M.A. in French Literature from Yale University, says so.

In this case, the authority is not an authority on the topic for which authority is needed. For example:

Inflation erodes the standard of living of those person who are retired and have fixed incomes such as savings or pensions; and Professor Jones, an economist who did a study on the harms of inflation, concluded that over 75% of retired people live on fixed incomes.

In this case, the appeal to authority is legitimate. We often must defer to the expertise of others, but we must be careful to select our sources of authority so that we find ones that are unbiased and truly expert.

 AN ARGUMENT THAT ATTRIBUTES A CAUSAL RELATIONSHIP BETWEEN TWO EVENTS WHERE NONE EXISTS (OR THAT INCORRECTLY IDENTIFIES THE TRUE CAUSE OF AN EVENT) COMMITS THE FALLACY OF THE FALSE CAUSE.

For example:

Every time the doorbell rings I find there is someone at the door. Therefore, it must be the case that the doorbell calls these people to my door.

Obviously, the causal link suggested here is backwards. It is the presence of the person at the door that then leads to the ringing of the bell, not vice versa. A more serious example of the fallacy of the false cause is:

There were more air traffic fatalities in 1979 than there were in 1969; therefore, the airways are more dangerous today than they were ten years ago.

The difficulty with this argument is that it attributes the increase to a lack of safety when, in fact, it is probably attributable to an increase in air travel generally.

 A COMMON WEAKNESS IN AN INDUCTIVE ARGUMENT IS THE HASTY GENERALIZATION, THAT IS, BASING A LARGE CONCLUSION ON TOO LITTLE DATA.

In our discussion about the structure of an argument, where we distinguished inductive from deductive arguments, we remarked that the best one can hope for in an inductive argument is that it will *probably* be true. We pointed out that some arguments are very strong, while some are weak. For example:

All four times I have visited Chicago it has rained; therefore, Chicago probably gets very little sunshine.

The rather obvious difficulty with the argument is that it moves from a small sample—four visits—to a very broad conclusion, Chicago gets little sunshine. Of course, generalizing on the basis of a sample or limited experience can be legitimate:

All five of the buses manufactured by Gutmann that we inspected have defective wheel mounts; therefore, some other buses manufactured by Gutmann probably have similar defects.

Admittedly this argument is not airtight. Perhaps the other uninspected buses do not have the same defect, but this second argument is much stronger than the first.

ANYTIME THERE IS A SHIFTING IN THE MEANING OF TERMS USED IN AN ARGUMENT, THE ARGUMENT HAS COMMITTED A FALLACY OF AMBIGUITY.

For example:

Man is only 1 million years old. John is a man. Therefore, John is only 1 million years old.

The error of the argument is that it uses the word *man* as two different meanings. In the first occurrence *man* is used as a group; in the second occurrence *man* designates a particular individual. Another, less playful example:

Sin occurs only when man fails to follow the will of God. But since God is all-powerful, what He wills must actually be. Therefore, it is impossible to deviate from the will of God, so there can be no sin in the world.

The equivocation here is in the word *will.* The first time it is used, the author intends that the will of God is God's wish and implies that it *is* possible to fail to comply with those wishes. In the second instance, the author uses the word *will* in a way that implies that such deviation is *not* possible. The argument reaches the conclusion that there is no sin in the world only by playing on these two senses of "will of God."

THE STRENGTH OF AN ARGUMENT FROM ANALOGY DEPENDS UPON THE SIMILARITY OF THE SITUATIONS COMPARED.

We do sometimes present legitimate arguments from analogy. For example:

The government should pay more to its diplomats who work in countries with unstable governments. The work is more dangerous there than in stable countries. This is very similar to paying soldiers combat premiums if they are stationed in a war zone.

The argument here relies on an analogy between diplomats in a potentially dangerous country and soldiers in combat areas. Of course, the analogy is not perfect—no analogy can be more than an analogy. But some analogies are clearly so imperfect that they have no persuasive force. For example:

People should have to be licensed before they are allowed to have children. After all, we require people who operate automobiles to be licensed.

In this case, the two situations—driving and having children—are so dissimilar that we would probably want to say they are not analogous at all—having children has nothing to do with driving.

While the ingenuity of the test-makers can result in problems that do not precisely fit these fallacies of induction, there will be very few problems on the test that have any other sort of inductive reasoning errors. The practice tests in this book contain many illustrations of each kind of problem, with full explanations. There are also problems that show how these different errors can be combined in one problem.

Critical Thinking Test Strategy

PREVIEW THE QUESTION STEM.

The first point of attack in the Critical Thinking section is to read the question stem (the part to which the question mark is attached) before reading the paragraph or sample argument. The reason for this suggestion is easily explained. There are many different questions that one might ask about an argument: "How can it be strengthened?" "How can it be weakened?" "What are its assumptions?" "How is the argument developed?" and so on. If you read an argument without focusing your attention on some aspect of it, all of these aspects of argumentation (and even more) are likely to come to mind. Unfortunately, this is distracting. The most efficient way to handle the critical thinking questions is to read the stem of the question first. Let that guide you in what to look for as you read.

FIND THE CONCLUSION OF THE ARGUMENT.

This is always helpful, even when it is merely a descriptive statement. Keep in mind the importance of finding the exact conclusion for structuring the argument and assessing its strengths or weaknesses.

ATTACK THE ANSWER CHOICES.

The differences between the answer choices often help you isolate the issues in the problem. Attack the answer choices by:

1. always reading all of the answer choices
2. eliminating obviously incorrect choices
3. contrasting remaining choices to isolate the relevant issues

Remember that you are only trying to choose the best answer. The best is often not perfect, and the less than best—and thus incorrect—answers often have some merit.

TEST BUSTERS FOR THE MATH SECTIONS

NOTE: The math sections of the GMAT test arithmetic, basic algebra, and elementary geometry—all material usually covered in high school courses. On page 97, you will find the start of a comprehensive review of these topics.

Don't automatically assume you need to spend hours in a lengthy review. Start by reading the Test Busters for math and refer to the math review only when you need a refresher on some point.

If, after a few pages, you find you really do need to review basic math before tackling the Test Busters, then do the comprehensive math review first.

PROBLEM SOLVING

Each problem-solving section of the GMAT contains 25 items. For purposes of attacking this kind of question, we can divide problem-solving items into three groups: manipulation problems, practical word problems, and geometry problems.

Manipulation problems, as the name implies, test your knowledge of arithmetic or algebraic manipulations.

Example: $0.2 \times 0.005 =$

    (A) 0.0001
    (B) 0.001

(C) 0.01

(D) 0.1

(E) 1.0

The correct answer is (B). The item just tests whether you remember how to keep track of the decimal point in multiplication. Other manipulation problems involve algebra:

If x + 5 = 8, then 2x − 1 =

(A) 25

(B) 12

-**(C)** 5

(D) 4

(E) 0

The correct answer is (C). Since x + 5 = 8, x = 3. Then substitute 3 for x in the expression 2x − 1: 2(3) − 1 = 5.

Practical word problems go beyond simple manipulations. They require that you use your knowledge of manipulations in practical situations.

Example: *Joe works two part-time jobs. One week Joe worked 8 hours at one job, earning $150, and 4.5 hours at the other job, earning $90. What were his average hourly earnings for the week?*

(A) $8.00

(B) $9.60

(C) $16.00

(D) $19.20

(E) $32.00

The correct choice is (D). To find Joe's average hourly earnings, we divide the total earnings by the number of hours worked:

$$\frac{\text{Earnings}}{\text{Hours}} = \frac{\$150 + \$90}{8 + 4.5} = \frac{\$240}{12.5} = \$19.20$$

Geometry problems involve the use of basic principles of geometry.

Example:

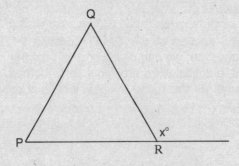

In the figure at the bottom of page 62, PQ = QR = PR. What is the value of x?

(A) 30

(B) 45

(C) 60

(D) 90

(E) 120

The correct answer is (E). This is an equilateral triangle (one having three equal sides), and equilateral triangles also have three equal angles, each 60°. Then PR, as extended, forms a straight line. So x + 60 = 180, and x = 120.

Some of the problems you will encounter will be fairly simple, others will be more complex—particularly, practical word problems and more difficult geometry problems. The more complex the question, the easier it is to misread it and to set off down a wrong track.

READ THE QUESTIONS VERY CAREFULLY.

The importance of this point is illustrated by the following very difficult practical-word problem:

The people eating in a certain cafeteria are either faculty members or students, and the number of faculty members is 15 percent of the total number of people in the çafeteria. After some of the students leave, the total number of persons remaining in the cafeteria is 50 percent of the original total. The number of students who left is what fractional part of the original number of students?

(A) $\frac{17}{20}$

(B) $\frac{10}{17}$

(C) $\frac{1}{2}$

(D) $\frac{7}{17}$

(E) $\frac{7}{20}$

The correct answer is (B). Let T be the total number of people originally in the cafeteria. Faculty account for 15% of T, or .15T, and students account for the remaining 85% of T, or .85T. Then some students leave, reducing the total number of people in the cafeteria to half of what it was originally, or .5T. The number of faculty, however, does not change. So the difference between .5T and .15T must be students: .5T − .15T = .35T. But this is not yet the answer to the question. The question asks "The number of students who *left* is what fraction of the original number of students?" Originally, there were .85T students; now there are only .35T students, so .50T students left. Now, to complete the solution we set up a fraction: .50T/.85T = $\frac{10}{17}$.

By this point, you can appreciate that there are several ways to miss the question. Someone might just put .35T over .85T (.35T/.85T = $\frac{7}{17}$) and choose (D). But this answers the question "The remaining students are what fraction of the original number of students?" And that is not what the question asked.

Someone might also put .35T over T (.35T/T = $\frac{7}{20}$) and select choice (E). But this too answers a different question: "The number of students who remain is what fractional part of the original number of people in the cafeteria?".

There are probably hundreds of other ways to miss the question, but it would be a shame to know how to answer the question and still miss it just because you did not read the question carefully.

A related error is answering in the wrong units.

BE SURE TO EXPRESS YOUR ANSWER CHOICES IN THE UNITS SPECIFIED IN THE QUESTION.

Example: *A certain copy machine produces 13 copies every 10 seconds. If the machine operates without interruption, how many copies will it produce in an hour?*

- **(A)** 78
- **(B)** 468
- **(C)** 1800
- **(D)** 2808
- **(E)** 4680

The correct answer is (E). The question stem gives information about copies per 10 seconds, but you must answer in terms of copies per hour. To solve the problem, first convert copies per 10 seconds to copies per minute. This can be done with a proportion:

$$\frac{13 \text{ copies}}{10 \text{ seconds}} = \frac{x \text{ copies}}{60 \text{ seconds}}$$

Solve by cross-multiplication: $13 \times 60 = 10x$
Solve for x: $x = 78$

78, however, is not the correct answer. A machine that produces 78 copies per minute will produce 60 times that in an hour: $60 \times 78 = 4680$. The correct answer is (E).

IF THE QUESTION REQUIRES AN ANSWER TO BE EXPRESSED IN CERTAIN UNITS, DRAW A CIRCLE AROUND THAT PART OF THE QUESTION STEM.

The circle will help you remember what units you must finally have.

A related problem is the presence of thought-reversers in a question stem:

CIRCLE ANY THOUGHT-REVERSERS IN THE QUESTION STEM.

A thought-reverser is any word, such as *not, except,* or *but,* that turns a question inside out.

Example: *A survey of 100 persons revealed that 72 of them had eaten at restaurant P and that 52 of them had eaten at restaurant Q. Which of the following could not be the number of persons in the surveyed group who had eaten at both P and Q?*

- **(A)** 20
- **(B)** 24

(C) 30
(D) 50
(E) 52

The correct answer is (A). Since there are only 100 people in the group, some of them must have eaten at both P and Q. The combined responses for P and Q equal 124, and 124 − 100 = 24. So 24 is the smallest possible number of people who could have eaten at both P and Q. (The largest possible number would be 52, which is possible if all of those who ate at Q had also eaten at P.)

Thus far we have been concentrating on the question stem, but the answer choices too deserve special mention.

ANSWER CHOICES TO PROBLEM-SOLVING ITEMS ARE ALWAYS ARRANGED IN A LOGICAL ORDER.

(There are some exceptions to this, such as questions asking you to find the largest or smallest of five expressions.)

Example: *Xxxx xxxxxxx xxxxxx xxxxxx xxxxxxxxxxxx xxxxxx. Xxxxxx xxxxxxx xxxxxx xx xxxxxx xxxx xxx xxxxxxxxxxxx?*

    (A) 3200
    (B) 4800
    (C) 12,000
    (D) 16,000
    (E) 20,000

Notice that the choices in this dummy question are arranged from least to greatest. In other questions, choices are arranged from greatest to least. And in algebra questions, the choices are arranged logically according to powers and coefficients of variables.

Additionally, the wrong choices are not just picked at random. They are usually written to correspond to possible mistakes, such as misreading. This actually helps you.

IN A PROBLEM REQUIRING SOME CALCULATION, LET THE ANSWER CHOICES CHECK YOUR MATH.

To illustrate this technique, look at the dummy answers. Suppose that you worked a problem, and your solution came out exactly to be choice (B) 4800—not 3200 and not 12,000, nor anything else. In that case, you could be confident that your math was correct. To be sure, you might have a wrong answer because you set the solution up incorrectly. But there is no real possibility that you made a mistake in your number-pushing.

You can also turn this feature of the answer choices to your advantage in another way:

ELIMINATE ANY ANSWER CHOICE THAT CANNOT POSSIBLY BE CORRECT.

To illustrate this, here is an actual question to go with the dummy answers:

In a certain population, 40% of all people have biological characteristic X; the others do not. If 8000 people have characteristic X, how many people do not have X?

    (A) 3200
    (B) 4800
    (C) 12,000
    (D) 16,000
    (E) 20,000

The correct choice is (C). You can arrive at this conclusion by setting up a proportion:

$$\frac{\text{Percent with X}}{\text{Number with X}} = \frac{\text{Percent without X}}{\text{Number without X}}$$

Supplying the appropriate numbers:

$$\frac{40\%}{8000} = \frac{60\%}{x}$$

Cross-multiply: $.40x = .60(8000)$
Solve for x: $x = 12,000$

But you can avoid even this little bit of work. A little common sense, when applied to the answer choices, would have eliminated all but (C). In the first place, 40% of the people have X, so more people don't have X. If 8000 have X, the correct choice has to be *greater* than 8000. This eliminates both (A) and (B). Next, we reason that if the correct answer were (D), 16,000, then exactly 50% of the people would have X. But we know only 40% have X. This allows us to eliminate (D) and with it (E).

Manipulation Problems

Your approach to a manipulation problem depends on the degree of difficulty of the manipulation.

FOR AN EASY ARITHMETIC MANIPULATION, PERFORM THE OPERATIONS AS INDICATED.

Example: *0.04 × 0.25 =*

    (A) 0.0001
    (B) 0.001

(C) 0.01

(D) 0.1

(E) 1.0

The correct answer is (C). The manipulation is very simple, so you should just do the indicated multiplication (keeping careful track of the decimal).

 FOR A DIFFICULT ARITHMETIC MANIPULATION, LOOK FOR A WAY TO SIMPLIFY, SUCH AS CANCELING, FACTORING, OR APPROXIMATING.

Example: $\frac{2}{3} \times \frac{3}{4} \times \frac{4}{5} \times \frac{5}{6} \times \frac{6}{7} \times \frac{7}{8} =$

(A) $\frac{2}{33}$

(B) $\frac{1}{4}$

(C) $\frac{3}{8}$

(D) $\frac{1}{2}$

(E) $\frac{27}{33}$

The correct choice is (B). Given enough time, you could work the problem out by multiplying the numerators, multiplying all of the denominators, and then reducing. But the very fact that this would be time-consuming should prompt you to look for an alternative. Try canceling:

$$\frac{2}{\cancel{3}} \times \frac{\cancel{3}}{\cancel{4}} \times \frac{\cancel{4}}{\cancel{5}} \times \frac{\cancel{5}}{\cancel{6}} \times \frac{\cancel{6}}{\cancel{7}} \times \frac{\cancel{7}}{8} = \frac{2}{8} = \frac{1}{4}$$

Example: $(27 \times 34) - (33 \times 27) =$

(A) -1

(B) 1

(C) 27

(D) 33

(E) 918

The correct answer is (C). Again, given the time, you could do the multiplication by hand; but that is not the point of the question. The question is included to see whether or not you understand that you can simplify matters considerably by factoring:

$$(27 \times 34) - (33 \times 27) = 27(34 - 33) = 27(1) = 27$$

Similarly, your approach to an algebraic manipulation will depend on the manipulation to be performed.

 IF THE MANIPULATION CONSISTS OF A SINGLE EQUATION WITH JUST ONE VARIABLE, SOLVE FOR THE UNKNOWN.

Example: *If 3x − 5 = x + 11, then x =*

    (A) 16
    (B) 8
    (C) 3
    (D) 2
    (E) 1

The correct answer is (B), and the appropriate method is to solve for x:

$$3x - 5 = x + 11$$

Combine terms: $2x = 16$
Solve for x: $x = 8$

IF A MANIPULATION INCLUDES TWO EQUATIONS AND TWO VARIABLES, SOLVE BY USING THE TECHNIQUE OF SIMULTANEOUS EQUATIONS.

Example: *If x + y = 8 and 2x − y = 10, then x =*

    (A) 16
    (B) 8
    (C) 6
    (D) 4
    (E) 2

The correct answer is (C), and the correct technique is to treat the two equations simultaneously. First, isolate y from the first equation:

$$x + y = 8$$

So: $y = 8 - x$

Next, substitute 8 − x into the second equation in place of y:

$$2x - (8 - x) = 10$$

Combine terms: $3x = 18$
Solve for x: $x = 6$

FOR A QUESTION THAT ASKS YOU TO FIND AN ANSWER CHOICE THAT MEETS CERTAIN CONDITIONS, TEST EACH CHOICE UNTIL YOU FIND THE ONE THAT SATISFIES THE CONDITIONS.

Example: $5^3 \cdot 9$

    (A) $5 \cdot 27$
    (B) $15 \cdot 9$
    (C) $15 \cdot 15 \cdot 5$

(D) 25 · 27

(E) 125 · 27

The correct choice is (C), and you learn this by testing each choice to see which one is equivalent to $5^3 \times 9$. The expression $5^3 \cdot 9 = (5 \cdot 5 \cdot 5)(3 \cdot 3) = 15 \cdot 15 \cdot 5$.

Practical Word Problems

Some practical word problems are fairly easy.

Example: *$2000 is deposited into a savings account that earns interest at the rate of 10% per year, compounded semiannually. How much money will there be in the account at the end of one year?*

    (A) $2105

    (B) $2200

    (C) $2205

    (D) $2400

    (E) $2600

The best answer is (C), and a simple calculation gets you the answer. First, calculate the interest earned on the first six months:

FIRST SIX MONTHS

Principal × Rate × Time = Interest Earned
$2000 × 10% × 0.5 = $100

This $100 is then paid into the account. The new balance is $2,100. Now you would calculate the interest earned during the second six months.

SECOND SIX MONTHS

Principal × Rate × Time = Interest Earned
$2100 × 10% × 0.5 = $105

This is then paid into the account. So the final balance is:

$2100 + $105 = $2205

Other practical word problems are not so easy. For a difficult one, it will be necessary to break the solution into steps.

FOR A DIFFICULT MANIPULATION PROBLEM, BREAK THE SOLUTION PROCESS DOWN INTO STEPS. FIRST, FORMULATE A STATEMENT OF WHAT IS NEEDED; SECOND, FIND THE NUMBERS YOU NEED; AND THIRD, PERFORM THE REQUIRED ARITHMETIC.

Example: *The enrollments at College X and College Y both grew by 8% from 1980 to 1985. If the enrollment at College X grew by 800 and the enrollment at College Y grew by 840, the enrollment at College Y was how much greater than the enrollment at College X in 1985?*

 (A) 400
 (B) 460
 (C) 500
 (D) 540
 (E) 580

The correct choice is (D), but the solution is a good deal more involved than the one we used for the preceding problem. So take the solution step by step.

First, begin by isolating the simple question that must be answered:

The enrollments at College X and College Y both grew by 8% from 1980 to 1985. If the enrollment at College X grew by 800 and the enrollment at College Y grew by 840, the enrollment at College Y was how much greater the enrollment at College X in 1985?

This can be summarized as follows:

College Y in 1985 − College X in 1985

So you know you must find the enrollments at both colleges in 1985. How can you do that? The numbers are there in the question; you just have to figure out how to use them. Take College Y first. You know that enrollments grew by 840 and that this represents an increase of 8%. These numbers will allow you to find the enrollment in 1980:

$$8\% \text{ of } 1980 \text{ Total} = 840$$
$$0.08 \times T = 840$$
Solve for T: $$T = 10{,}500$$

This was the enrollment at College Y in 1980, but you need to know enrollment at College Y in 1985. To do that, just add the increase:

$$1980 + \text{Increase} = 1985$$
$$10{,}500 + 840 = 11{,}340$$

Now do the same thing for College X:

$$8\% \text{ of } 1980 \text{ Total} = 800$$
$$0.08 \times T = 800$$
$$T = 10{,}000$$
$$1980 + \text{Increase} = 1985$$
$$10{,}000 + 800 = 10{,}800$$

Now you have the numbers you were looking for. Substitute them back into your original solution statement:

College Y in 1985 − College X in 1985 = Final Answer
11,340 − 10,800 = 540

This is not the only way of reaching the correct solution, but it is the one most people would be likely to use. And it is very complex. A problem such as this would be one of the last ones in a math section. It does nicely illustrate what you should do when you encounter a complex practical word problem.

Sometimes, however, you can avoid the necessity of going through the process above by using the answer choices.

SOMETIMES YOU CAN WORK BACKWARDS FROM THE ANSWER CHOICES.

Example: *A car dealer gives a customer a 20% discount on the list price of a car, and he still realizes a net profit of 25 percent on his cost. If the dealer's cost is $4800, what is the usual list price of the car?*

(A) $6000
(B) $6180
(C) $7200
(D) $7500
(E) $8001

You know that one of these five choices must be correct, so all you have to do is test each one until you find the correct one. Start with (C).

If the usual list price is $7200, what will be the actual selling price after the 20% discount?

Usual List Price − 20% of Usual List Price = Final Selling Price
$7200 − 20% of $7200 = Final Selling Price
$7200 − $1440 = $5760

On that assumption, the dealer's profit would be:

Final Selling Price − Cost = Profit
$5760 − $4800 = $960

Is that a profit of 25%?

$960/$4800 is less than $\frac{1}{4}$ and so less than 25%

This proves that (C) is wrong.

Now you need to test another choice, logically either (B) or (D). But which one? Apply a little reasoning to the situation. Assuming a usual cost of $7200, the numbers worked out to a profit that was too small. Therefore, we need a larger price to generate a large profit. So try (D).

$$\$7500 - (.20)\ (\$7500) = \$6000$$

If the final selling price is $6000, that means a profit for the dealer of $1200. And $1200/$4800 = 25%. So (D) must be the correct answer.

You might think this was a lucky guess. What if the answer choices had been arranged differently?

(A) $4000
(B) $6000
(C) $6180
(D) $7200
(E) $7500

In this case, you test (C) first and learn that it is incorrect. Then you go to (D) as above. Again, another wrong choice. Does this mean you have to do a third calculation? No! Since the choices are arranged in order, once you have eliminated (C) and (D), you *know* that (E) must be correct.

Some practical word problems give data in algebraic form rather than number form and then ask for an algebraic formula as an answer.

IF THE ANSWER CHOICES ARE ALGEBRAIC FORMULAS USING UNKNOWNS FROM THE QUESTION, SUBSTITUTE VALUES TO FIND THE CORRECT ONE.

Example: *At a certain printing plant, each of m machines prints 6 newspapers every s seconds. If all machines work together but independently without interruption, how many min-utes will it take to print an entire run of 18,000 newspapers?*

(A) 180s/m
(B) 50s/m
(C) 50ms
(D) ms/50
(E) 300m/s

Since the information is given algebraically, the letters could stand for any numbers (so long as you don't divide by 0). Pick some values for m and s and see which answer choice works. For purpose of discussion, assume that the plant has two machines, so m = 2. Also assume that s = 1, that is, that each machine produces 6 newspapers each second. On this assumption, each machine prints 360 papers per minute; and with two such machines working, the plant capacity is 720 papers per minute. To find how long it will take the plant to do the work, divide 18,000 by 720.

$$18,000/720 = 25 \text{ minutes}$$

On the assumption that m = 2 and s = 1, the correct formula should produce the number 25. Test the choices:

(A) 180s/m = 180(1)/2 is not equal to 25 (WRONG!)
(B) 50s/m = 50(1)/2 is equal to 25 (CORRECT!)
(C) 50ms = 50(2)(1) is not equal to 25 (WRONG!)
(D) ms/50 = (2)(1)/50 is not equal to 25 (WRONG!)
(E) 300m/s = 300(2)/(1) is not equal to 25 (WRONG!)

A similar technique can be used when no numbers or variables are supplied:

FOR QUESTIONS WITH UNDEFINED QUANTITIES, ASSUME ARBITRARY VALUES.

Example: *If the value of a piece of property decreases by 10% while the tax rate on the property increases by 10%, what is the effect on the taxes?*

    (A) Taxes increase by 10%
    (B) Taxes increase by 1%
    (C) There is no change in taxes
    (D) Taxes decrease by 1%
    (E) Taxes decrease by 10%

The correct answer is (D). Since no numbers are supplied, you are free to supply your own. Assume the piece of property has a value of $1000, and assume further that the original tax rate is 10%. On those assumptions, the tax bill is originally 10% of $1000 or $100. Now make the specified adjustments. The value of the property drops by 10%, from $1000 to $900, but the tax rate goes up by 10%, from 10% to 11%. The new tax bill is 11% of $900, or $99. The original tax bill was $100; the new tax bill is $99; the net result is a decrease of $1 out of $100, or a 1% decrease.

Geometry Problems

Geometry problems do require a knowledge of elementary geometry. You will need to know how to do things such as how to find the area of a triangle, a rectangle, and a circle. But this does not mean that you need to review the formal proofs that you had to go through when you first studied the subject. In fact, you probably remember what you need to know.

TRUST YOUR SPATIAL INTUITION.

There is a difference between having an important piece of knowledge about geometry and being able to present a formal explanation of that knowledge. For example:

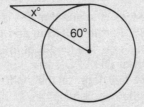

In the figure at the bottom of page 73 what is x?

(A) 15
(B) 30
(C) 45
(D) 60
(E) 90

The correct answer is (B). To solve the problem you need to know that angle P is a right angle. Then you have a triangle with angles 60, 90, and x. Since there are 180 degrees in a triangle, x must be 30.

You probably did realize that angle P must be a right angle—and not just by looking at it and seeing that it seems to be 90°. Rather, your mind's eye probably told you that for one reason or another, angle P had to be 90°.

In fact, angle P must be 90 degrees. PQ is a tangent, and PO is a radius. A tangent intersects a radius at 90°. But you do not need to know the "official" justification to answer correctly. Just trust your spatial intuition.

Most geometry problems involve figures that are made up of two or more simple figures.

IN A FIGURE COMPOSED OF TWO OR MORE SIMPLE FIGURES, A FEATURE OF ONE FIGURE CAN BE REDEFINED AS A FEATURE OF ANOTHER FIGURE.

Example:

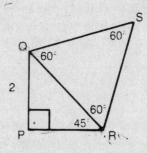

In the figure above, what is the perimeter of triangle QRS?

(A) 12
(B) $6\sqrt{2}$
(C) 6
(D) $3\sqrt{2}$
(E) $2\sqrt{3}$

The correct answer is (B). The trick is to see that QR is not only a side of triangle PQR, it is also a side of triangle QRS. Further, QRS is an equilaterial triangle; so if you can find the length of one side, you know the length of the other sides as well.

How can you find the length of QR? PQR is a 45°-45°-90° triangle. Since QP is 2, PR is also 2. Now you know two legs of the right triangle, and you can use the Pythagorean Theorem to find the hypotenuse:

$$QP^2 + PR^2 = QR^2$$
$$2^2 + 2^2 = QR^2$$
$$4 + 4 = QR^2$$
$$QR^2 = 8$$
$$QR = \sqrt{8}$$
$$QR = 2\sqrt{2}$$

Each of the three sides of QRS is equal to $2\sqrt{2}$, so the perimeter of QRS = 3 times $2\sqrt{2} = 6\sqrt{2}$.

Another common kind of geometry problem is the shaded area problem.

 IF A GEOMETRY QUESTION ASKS FOR THE AREA OF AN IRREGULAR FIGURE, THE SHADED AREA CAN BE REGARDED AS THE DIFFERENCE BETWEEN THE AREAS OF TWO COMMON, REGULAR FIGURES.

Example:

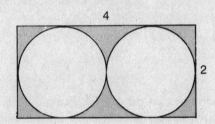

What is the area of the shaded portion of the figure above?

   (A) $8 - 8\pi$
   (B) $8 - 4\pi$
   (C) $8 - 2\pi$
   (D) $8 - \pi$
   (E) π

The correct answer is (C). The shaded area is what's left over if you take the area of the two circles away from the area of the rectangle:

Rectangle − Two Circles = Shaded Area

First, the area of the rectangle is just $2 \times 4 = 8$. Then, the diameter of the circles is equal to the width of the rectangle. So the diameter of the circles is 2, and the radius is 1. The formula for the area of a circle is πr^2, so each circle has an area of $\pi(1^2) = \pi$. Now we know the area of the shaded part of the diagram:

$$8 - 2(\pi) = 8 - 2\pi$$

Most of the figures in this part of the GMAT are drawn as accurately as possible. (*Note:* This is not true in the Data Sufficiency section. See below.) If a figure is not drawn to scale, it will include a warning: Note: Figure not drawn to scale.

FOR PROBLEM-SOLVING ITEMS, IF A FIGURE IS DRAWN TO SCALE, ESTIMATE QUANTITIES.

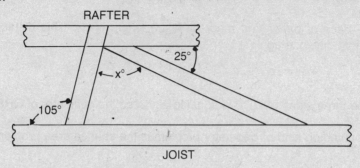

The figure above shows a cross-section of a building. If the rafter is parallel to the joist, what is x?

(A) 45
(B) 60
(C) 80
(D) 90
(E) 105

The correct choice is (C), and you can get that without a calculation. Look at the size of x. It is not quite a right angle, so you can eliminate both (D) and (E). Is it as small as 60°? No, so you eliminate (B) and (A) as well. This means that (C) must be the correct answer.

You can even refine this technique:

IN PROBLEM SOLVING, WHEN A FIGURE IS DRAWN TO SCALE, YOU CAN MEASURE LENGTHS WITH THE EDGE OF YOUR ANSWER SHEET.

Example:

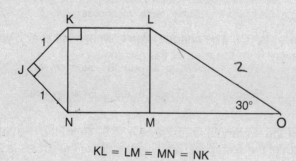

KL = LM = MN = NK

In the figure above, what is the length of LO?

(A) 2
(B) $2\sqrt{2}$
(C) $2\sqrt{3}$
(D) 4
(E) $4\sqrt{2}$

The correct choice is (B). Since there is no warning note to the contrary, the figure must be drawn to scale. Now you can get the correct answer to the problem just by measuring.

Take a piece of paper and mark on it the length of JK. This distance is 1. Now measure that distance against LO.

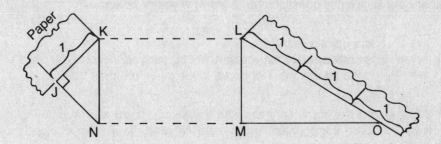

It appears that LO is slightly more than 2.5; make it about 2.8. Which answer is closest? The best approximation for the $\sqrt{2}$ is 1.4, so (B) is 2 (1.4) = 2.8

DATA SUFFICIENCY

Data Sufficiency is the "other" math section on the GMAT, the one with the peculiar instructions:

Directions: *Each question below is followed by two numbered facts. You are to determine whether the data given in the statements is sufficient for answering the question. Use the data given, plus your knowledge of math and everyday facts, to choose among the five possible answers.*

(A) if statement 1 alone is sufficient to answer the question, but statement 2 alone is not sufficient

(B) if statement 2 alone is sufficient to answer the question, but statement 1 alone is not sufficient

(C) if both statements together are needed to answer the question, but neither statement alone is sufficient

(D) if either statement by itself is sufficient to answer the question

(E) if not enough facts are given to answer the question

The Data Sufficiency section contains 25 questions.

What Do the Choices Mean?

Data sufficiency questions are different from the other math questions we have studied because you are not really expected to solve math problems as such. Rather, you are asked to determine whether or not a problem *could* be solved, given certain information.

Some data sufficiency questions ask whether it is possible to arrive at an exact numerical solution given certain information:

What is the value of x?
What is Joan's salary?
How many bricks are there in a pile?

Each of these questions can be answered only with a number.
Other data sufficiency questions require only a yes or no answer:

Is x greater than 1?
Is Joan's salary more than $10,000 per year?
Is the total number of bricks in the pile more than 300?

The first kind is the more common, but the second form also appears with some frequency. Here are some examples to illustrate what the answer choices mean for each of the two types.

FOR A QUESTION THAT REQUIRES A NUMERICAL VALUE AS AN ANSWER, MARK (A) IF (1) ALONE PROVIDES THE EXACT VALUE ASKED FOR (AND (2) DOES NOT).

Example: *What is x?*

(1) $x + 2 = 4$
(2) $x^2 = 4$

(A) (1) alone is sufficient to establish the exact value of x as 2. (2), however, is not sufficient. If $x^2 = 4$, x can be either $+2$ or -2, and that is not sufficient to answer a question that asks "What is x?"

FOR A QUESTION THAT REQUIRES A NUMERICAL VALUE AS AN ANSWER, MARK (B) IF (2) ALONE PROVIDES THE *EXACT* VALUE ASKED FOR (AND [1] DOES NOT).

Example: *What is x?*

(1) $x^2 - 1 = 0$
(2) $x = (10)^0$

(B) (2) is sufficient to peg the exact value of x. Since any number to the zero power equals 1, $10^0 = 1$, and x must be 1. (1) is not sufficient. (1) establishes that either $x + 1 = 0$ or $x - 1 = 0$, so that $x = \pm 1$. But knowing that x is one of two possible values is not sufficient to answer a question that asks for *the* value of x.

FOR A QUESTION THAT REQUIRES A NUMERICAL VALUE FOR AN ANSWER, MARK (C) IF NEITHER (1) NOR (2) ALONE PROVIDES THE EXACT VALUE NEEDED BUT (1) and (2) TOGETHER PROVIDE THE EXACT VALUE.

Example: *How many cubic blocks of wood will fit into a box?*

(1) The edge of each block is 2 inches long.
(2) The box has the shape of a rectangular solid with inner dimensions 20 inches by 40 inches by 16 inches.

(C) To determine exactly how many blocks the box will hold, we need both the size and shape of both the blocks and the box. Neither (1) nor (2) alone will give us all of the information we need. (1) gives us the size and shape of the blocks. (2) gives us the size and shape of the box. Both taken together give all of the information we need.

 FOR A QUESTION THAT REQUIRES A NUMERICAL VALUE FOR AN ANSWER, MARK **(D)** IF BOTH (1) AND (2) ALONE PROVIDE THE EXACT VALUE.

Example: *What is the area of Circle O?*

(1) The diameter of Circle O is 4.
(2) The circumference of Circle O is 4π.

(D) (1) is sufficient, for knowing the diameter of the circle allows us to determine the radius, and in turn, the radius gives us the area of the circle by the formula Area = πr^2. (2) also is sufficient. The circumference is 4π. Since the formula for the circumference is $C = 2\pi r$, $4\pi = 2\pi r$, and $r = 2$. So (1) alone is sufficient and (2) alone is sufficient to give the exact value of the area of the circle.

 FOR A QUESTION THAT REQUIRES A NUMERICAL VALUE FOR AN ANSWER, MARK **(E)** IF BOTH (1) AND (2), EVEN WHEN TAKEN TOGETHER, DO NOT PROVIDE AN EXACT VALUE.

Example: *The total number of employees on the payroll of Corporation X was what percent greater on June 30 than it was on June 1 of the same year?*

(1) During the month of June, 15 employees were dropped from the payroll.
(2) During the month of June, 37 employees were added to the payroll.

(E) The question asks for the percent increase in the number of employees during June. The two statements together establish that $37 - 15 = 22$ people added to the payroll during June, but that is not sufficient to answer the question asked.

The other form of data sufficiency question is the one that requires either a yes or no answer.

 IF A QUESTION ASKS FOR A YES OR NO RESPONSE, INFORMATION IS SUFFICIENT IF IT ANSWERS THE QUESTION ONE WAY OR THE OTHER. EVEN A DEFINITE NO RESPONSE IS A RESPONSE.

Example: *Is x greater than 0?*

> **(1)** x^3 is less than 0.
> **(2)** $3x = -3$

(D)   Statement (1) establishes that (x)(x)(x) is less than 0, so x itself must be a negative number. Statement (1), therefore, is sufficient to establish that the answer to the question is no: x is not greater than 0. Similarly, statement (2) also establishes that x is negative. Watch out! Some test-takers would call this an (E), reasoning (incorrectly) that since the answer to the question is no, the information is not sufficient. In fact, the information is sufficient to give a definite negative answer to the question.

FOR A QUESTION THAT ELICITS A YES OR NO RESPONSE, MARK (A) IF (1) ALONE PROVIDES A DEFINITE ANSWER TO THE QUESTION (BUT (2) ALONE DOES NOT).

Example: *If the average height of three people is 68 inches, is the shortest person more than 60 inches tall?*

> **(1)**   The height of the tallest person is 72 inches.
> **(2)**   One of the persons is 70 inches tall.

(A)   (1) is sufficient to answer the question with a definite yes. If x, y and z represent the three heights, then

$$\frac{x + y + z}{3} = 68$$
$$x + y + z = 204$$

Then if one of the heights, say z, is 72:

$$x + y = 132$$

This means that the sum of the heights of the other two persons must be 132; but we know that neither of them can be as tall as 72 inches, so the shortest person must be *taller* than 132 − 72 = 60 inches. (2) by itself is not sufficient since it may or may not refer to the tallest person.

FOR A QUESTION THAT ELICITS A YES OR NO RESPONSE, MARK (B) IF (2) ALONE PROVIDES A DEFINITE ANSWER TO THE QUESTION (BUT (1) ALONE DOES NOT).

Example: *Is the product of two numbers greater than 100?*

> **(1)**   The sum of the two numbers is greater than 50.
> **(2)**   Each of the numbers is greater than 10.

(B) That (1) is not sufficient can be proved by examples. If the two numbers are 30 and 31, their sum is greater than 50 and their product is greater than 100; but if the two numbers are 50 and 1, though their sum is greater than 50, their product is only 50, and less than 100. (2) is sufficient. If both of the numbers are greater than 10, then their product must be greater than 10 × 10, or greater than 100.

FOR A QUESTION THAT ELICITS A YES OR NO RESPONSE, MARK (C) IF NEITHER (1) NOR (2) ALONE PROVIDES A DEFINITE ANSWER TO THE QUESTION BUT (1) AND (2) TOGETHER DO PROVIDE AN ANSWER.

Example: *Is x a positive integer?*

   (1) $x > 0$
   (2) $x^2 + 16 = 25$

(C) (1) is not sufficient, for it establishes only that x is positive but has nothing to say as to whether x is an integer. (2) is not sufficient, for it establishes that x is an integer but fails to establish whether x is +3 or −3. Both taken together establish that x = +3, so they answer the question: x is a positive integer.

Example: *Is $a + b > c + d$?*

   (1) $a > c$
   (2) $b > d$

(C) (1) is not sufficient because we lack information about b and d. Similarly, (2) is not sufficient because we lack information about a and c. Both together are sufficient, for if a > c, then adding b to a and d to c will maintain the inequality.

FOR A QUESTION THAT ELICITS A YES OR NO RESPONSE, MARK (D) IF BOTH (1) AND (2) ALONE PROVIDE A DEFINITE ANSWER TO THE QUESTION.

Example: *Is x a positive number?*

   (1) 1,000,001(x) is a positive number.
   (2) −x is a negative number.

(D) (1) establishes that x must be a positive number because 1,000,001, a positive number, multiplied by x is a positive number. (2) also establishes that x is positive, for −1 multiplied by x is negative.

FOR A QUESTION THAT ELICITS A YES OR NO RESPONSE, MARK (E) IF BOTH (1) AND (2), EVEN WHEN TAKEN TOGETHER, DO NOT PROVIDE A DEFINITE ANSWER TO THE QUESTION.

Example: *Is a cubic centimeter of substance S heavier than a cubic centimeter of substance T?*

(1) A cubic centimeter of S weighs more than 0.25 cubic centimeters of T.

(2) 3 cubic centimeters of T weighs less than 5 cubic centimeters of S.

(E) (1) establishes only that a cubic unit of S is heavier than 0.25 cubic units of T, but it does not establish how much heavier. (2) works in the same way. Even taking them together, it is not possible to establish which substance is heavier. For example, S and T might even have equal weights.

A Note About Geometry Figures

In the data sufficiency section, the figures are not necessarily drawn to scale. (So the directions for this section are different from the directions for the problem-solving sections, discussed above.) A figure will conform to the information given in the question stem, but it will not necessarily conform to the additional information provided by the numbered statements.

A FIGURE IS NOT, IN AND OF ITSELF, SUFFICIENT TO ANSWER A QUESTION. DON'T RELY ON "GUESTIMATION" OF THE APPARENT SIZES OF ANGLES OR LENGTHS OF LINES.

To determine whether or not information is sufficient to answer a question based on a figure, you will have to use your knowledge of geometry.

Example:

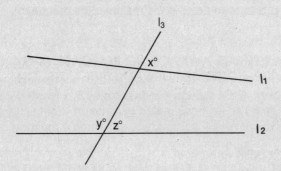

In the figure above, are l_1 and l_2 parallel to each other?

(1) x = z

(2) x + y = 180

(D) Although the lines do not appear to be parallel, you should not conclude on the basis of the figure that they are not parallel. In fact, each statement establishes that they are parallel.

Common Patterns

Now that you understand the meaning of the directions, we can illustrate some of the common patterns used in Data Sufficiency questions.

 IF A QUESTION USES QUANTITIES THAT COME IN INTEGRAL VALUES, BE ALERT FOR THE POSSIBILITY OF A SINGLE INTEGRAL SOLUTION.

Example: *At a clothing store, Fred spent $130. How many of the articles of clothing that Fred purchased were priced at $15?*

  (1) Fred purchased only articles costing $15 and $20.
  (2) Fred purchased more than two $20 articles.

(C) At first glance, you might think that the answer to this item is (E). But you should look a little more closely. Although it is true that (1) alone doesn't provide enough information to answer the question, it does narrow the possibilities to two: two $20 articles plus six $15 articles, or five $20 articles and two $15 articles. And when the information provided in (2) is included, an answer can be obtained. Since the articles of clothing are whole articles (no fractions allowed), Fred purchased exactly two $15 articles.

 IF $\frac{X}{M}$ IS AN INTEGER AND $\frac{X}{N}$ IS AN INTEGER, WHERE BOTH M AND N ARE INTEGERS, THEN X IS A MULTIPLE OF MN.

Example: *Is $\frac{x}{15}$ an integer?*

  (1) $\frac{x}{3}$ is an integer.
  (2) $\frac{x}{5}$ is an integer.

(C) Neither (1) nor (2) is alone sufficient to answer the question. As for (1), even though x is divisible by 3, x might not be divisible by 15. (For example, if x is 9.) Similarly, (2) is not sufficient. Even though x is divisible by 5, x might not be divisible by 15. (For example, if x is 10.) But both statements taken together are sufficient to answer the question. If x is divisible by both 3 and 5, then x must be divisible by 15.

 TO FIND A PARTICULAR TERM IN A SEQUENCE, YOU MUST KNOW THE RULE FOR CONSTRUCTING THE SEQUENCE AND THE VALUE OF SOME TERM IN THE SEQUENCE.

Example: *What is the one-thousandth term in sequence S?*

  (1) The fifth term in S is 47.
  (2) Each term in S following the first term is generated by multiplying the preceding term by 4 and adding 1.

(C) The rule for constructing the sequence is given in (2). And the point of reference is given in (1). There is no need to try to find the value of the thousandth term. You need only recognize that it is possible to do so, so the answer must be (C).

 GIVEN TWO QUANTITIES, X AND Y, KNOWING ANY ONE OF THE FOLLOWING THREE RELATIONSHIPS IS SUFFICIENT TO FIND THE OTHER TWO RELATIONSHIPS: X IS A CERTAIN FRACTION OF Y, X IS CERTAIN PERCENTAGE OF Y, THE RATIO OF X TO Y.

Thus, if you know that x is $\frac{1}{2}$ of y, you also know that x is 50% of y and that the ratio of x to y is 1:2.

Example: *If x and y are positive numbers, what percentage is x of y?*

    (1) The ratio x:y is 5:4.

    (2) y is $\frac{4}{5}$ of x.

(D) Statement (1) is sufficient. Since the ratio of x to y is 5 to 4, $\frac{x}{y} = \frac{5}{4} = 1.25 = 125\%$. Statement (2) is also sufficient. Since $y = \frac{4}{5}x$, $\frac{x}{y} = \frac{4}{5} = 1.25 = 125\%$.

 GIVEN TWO QUANTITIES, X AND Y, IF YOU KNOW WHAT FRACTION ONE IS OF THE OTHER, WHAT PERCENTAGE ONE IS OF THE OTHER, OR THE RATIO BETWEEN THE TWO, YOU HAVE ENOUGH INFORMATION TO FIND THE RECIPROCAL OF THAT RELATIONSHIP.

Thus, if you know that x is 125% of y, you can deduce that y is 80% of x: x = 1.25y, so $x = \frac{5y}{4}$ and $\frac{y}{x} = \frac{4}{5} = 80\%$.

Example: *If x and y are positive numbers, what percentage is x of y?*

    (1) y is 50% of x.

    (2) The ratio y:x is 1:2.

(D) Each statement is sufficient to establish that x is 200% of y.

 FRACTIONS, RATIOS, AND PERCENTAGES DO NOT PROVIDE INFORMATION ABOUT THE ACTUAL QUANTITIES, ONLY ABOUT THE RELATIONSHIP BETWEEN TWO QUANTITIES.

Example: *How much money do Peter and Ed have together?*

    (1) Ed has twice as much money as Peter.

    (2) Peter has $2 less than Ed has.

(C) Statement (1) is not sufficient to answer the question. Although you can infer from (1) that Peter has half as much money as Ed, that is not sufficient to answer the question asked. Neither is statement (2) alone sufficient. But both work together to establish that Ed has $4 and Peter has $2.

 A STATEMENT THAT PROVIDES THE RATIO (OR SIMILAR RELATIONSHIP) BETWEEN TWO QUANTITIES IS SUFFICIENT TO ESTABLISH WHICH IS LARGER.

Example: *Which of three books, X, Y, or Z, costs the least?*

(1) The cost of X is $\frac{2}{3}$ the cost of Y.
(2) The cost of Z is $\frac{5}{4}$ the cost of X.

(C) Neither statement provides the actual cost of the three books, but both statements taken together do establish that X is the least expensive. (1) establishes that X is less than Y, and (2) establishes that X is less than Z.

 A STATEMENT ABOUT PERCENTAGE ALONE DOES NOT PROVIDE INFORMATION ABOUT ACTUAL QUANTITIES.

Example: *Who received the larger bonus, Diane or Claire?*

(1) Diane's bonus was 7% of her annual salary.
(2) Claire's bonus was 8% of her annual salary.

(E) To find the actual size of either bonus, you would need to know the dollar amount for the annual salary. Right now, you know only that Claire's bonus was a larger percentage of her salary than was Diane's, but that is not sufficient to answer the question asked.

Example: *Who received the larger increase in salary, Diane or Claire?*

(1) Diane received a salary increase equal to 7% of her annual salary.
(2) Claire received a salary increase equal to 8% of her annual salary.

(E) This is the same situation described in example 21. Without some information about the dollar amount of the salaries, the question cannot be answered.

INFORMATION ABOUT ONE OF THE FOLLOWING:

 (1) ORIGINAL TOTAL
(2) NEW TOTAL
(3) ACTUAL CHANGE

COUPLED WITH THE PERCENT CHANGE IN A QUANTITY IS SUFFICIENT TO DEDUCE THE OTHER TWO VALUES.

Example: *An item is discounted by 15% from its usual selling price. What is the usual selling price?*

(1) The dollar value of the discount is $45.

(2) The discounted price is $255.

(D) (1) is sufficient, since 15% of the usual selling price is the $45 value of the discount:

$$.15 \text{ Usual Price} = \$45$$
$$\text{Usual Price} = \frac{\$45}{.15} = \$300$$

(2) is also sufficient, for the discounted price is equal to the usual selling price minus the discount; and the discount can be expressed as a percentage of the usual selling price:

$$\text{Discount Price} = \text{Usual Price} - .15 \text{ (Usual Price)}$$
$$\text{Discount} = .85 \text{ Usual Price}$$
$$.85 \text{ Usual Price} = \$255$$
$$\text{Usual Price} = \$300$$

So each statement alone is sufficient.

UNLESS OTHERWISE INDICATED, AN UNKNOWN RANGES OVER THE ENTIRE NUMBER LINE.

Example: *If xy≠0, is x greater than y?*

(1) $4x = 5y$

(2) $x < 0$

(C) Statement (1) is not, by itself, sufficient to answer the question. If x and y are positive numbers, say x = 5 and y = 4, then x is larger than y. But if x and y are negative numbers, say x = −5 and y = −4, then x is smaller than y. Statement (2) is not alone sufficient to answer the question. But both statements together do answer the question. If 4x = 5y and x is less than 0, then x is smaller than y.

WATCH OUT FOR VARIABLES THAT ARE RAISED TO A POWER.

Example: *Is xy > 0?*

(1) $xy^2 > 0$

(2) $x^2 y^3 < 0$

(C) Any quantity raised to the second power (or other positive even power) generates a positive result. But a quantity raised to the third power (or other positive odd power) may be positive or negative depending on the sign of the original quantity. Thus, statement (1) is not sufficient to establish the sign of xy, but it does establish that x is positive. Statement (2) is not sufficient to establish the sign of xy, but it does establish that y^3 and therefore y is negative. So both taken together establish that xy is negative.

 AN EQUATION WITH VARIABLES RAISED TO A POWER MAY HAVE MORE THAN ONE SOLUTION.

Example: *What is the value of x?*

   (1) $x^2 - 9 = 0$
   (2) $x > 0$

(C) Statement (1) is not sufficient to fix the value of x. Since $x^2 - 9 = 0$, $x^2 = 9$, and x = +3 or x = −3. That conclusion coupled with (2), however, is sufficient to answer the question.

 IF EACH STATEMENT CONTAINS A DIFFERENT EQUATION, YOU MAY BE ABLE TO TREAT THEM AS SIMULTANEOUS EQUATIONS.

Example: *What is the value of x?*

   (1) $x + y = 12$
   (2) $2y = 6$

(C) Neither statement alone is sufficient to fix the value of x. But if you solve for y in the second equation (y = 3) and substitute that value for y into the first equation (x + 3 = 12), you can find the value of x.

 IF A DATA SUFFICIENCY ITEM ASKS FOR THE VALUE OF A COMPLEX ALGEBRAIC EXPRESSION, TRY TO SIMPLIFY THE EXPRESSION.

Example: *If x + y≠0, what is the value of $\dfrac{x^2 - y^2}{x + y}$?*

   (1) $x - y = 2$
   (2) $x + y = 2$

(A) Factor the numerator of the expression and simplify:

$$\frac{x^2 - y^2}{x + y} = \frac{(x + y)(x - y)}{x + y} = x - y$$

So statement (1) is alone sufficient to answer the question.

LOOK FOR WAYS TO USE THE PYTHAGOREAN THEOREM.

Example:

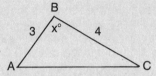

What is the value of x in the figure above?

(1) $AC^2 = AB^2 + BC^2$
(2) $AC = 5$

(D) Statement (1), which is the Pythagorean formula, establishes that the sides of the triangle create a right triangle and that AC is the hypotenuse. So x = 90. Statement (2) also establishes that the triangle is a right triangle. (It has sides of 3, 4, and 5.) so x = 90.

REGULAR (EQUILATERAL) FIGURES HAVE THE SPECIAL FEATURE THAT KNOWING ONE DIMENSION ALLOWS TO DEDUCE EVERYTHING ABOUT THAT FIGURE:

For an equilateral triangle, information about any one of the following—length of side, perimeter, altitude, or area—is sufficient to fix the others.

For a square, information about any one of the following—length of a side, the perimeter, the diagonal, or the area—is sufficient to fix the others.

For a circle, information about any one of the following—length of the radius, length of the diameter, length of the circumference, or the area—is sufficient to fix the others.

Data Sufficiency Strategies

READ EACH QUESTION AND ACCOMPANYING STATEMENTS CAREFULLY.

Example: *How many specially priced boxes of soap powder did a supermarket sell during a day?*

(1) 12% of the customers who came into the supermarket during the day purchased the specially priced soap powder.
(2) The supermarket had 480 customers that day.

(E) Read the question and statements carefully. The question asks for the number of boxes of the soap powder that were sold. Even taking the two statements together, you cannot answer that question. You cannot assume that each person who bought the soap powder purchased exactly one box.

DON'T OVERLOOK THE INFORMATION PROVIDED IN THE QUESTION STEM.

Example: *Paul and Edna have a combined annual income of $40,000. What is Paul's annual income?*

> **(1)** Paul's annual income is $20,000 less than Edna's.
> **(2)** Edna's annual income is 3 times Paul's.

(D) Each statement when coupled with the information given in the question stem is sufficient to establish that Paul's annual income is $10,000.

DO ONLY AS MUCH WORK AS IS REQUIRED TO DETERMINE THE SUFFICIENCY OF THE STATEMENTS TO ANSWER THE QUESTIONS.

The task is to make a judgment about the *sufficiency* of the additional information. Once you know that the information is sufficient to answer the question, the game is over. You don't need to go further and work out an actual numerical solution.

CONSIDER EACH STATEMENT IN ISOLATION OF THE OTHER *BEFORE* **TRYING TO DETERMINE HOW THEY WORK TOGETHER.**

The trickiest answer choices are (C) and (E). But much of the time you don't even have to worry about them. Study each statement in isolation. If you find that either (1) or (2) is alone sufficient, then you can eliminate (C) and (E) as possible answer choices.

ELIMINATE ANSWER CHOICES (IF POSSIBLE) AND MAKE A GUESS.

Even if you are unable to arrive at a complete solution of the problem, you can often eliminate two or three answer choices. And that makes a guess worthwhile. The chart below shows how to eliminate choices. A check mark means you have concluded that the statement is sufficient; an x means you have concluded that it is not sufficient; and a question mark indicates doubt:

(1) ✓

       = (A) or (D)

(2) ?

(1) ?

       = (B) or (D)

(2) ✓

(1) x

       = (B), (C), or (E)

(2) ?

(1) ?

       = (A), (C), or (E)

(2) x

FINANCING YOUR GRADUATE EDUCATION

E ducation is expensive, and the higher the level of education, the greater the cost. As you contemplate going on to graduate or professional school, you must face the awesome question, "How am I going to pay for this?"

With the possible exceptions of a winning lottery ticket, a windfall inheritance or a very wealthy family, no single source of funds will be adequate to cover tuition, other educational costs, and living expenses during your years of graduate study. While the funding task is daunting, it is not impossible. With patience and hard work, you can piece together your own financial package.

CONSIDER DEFERRING YOUR APPLICATION

Y ou might consider putting off applications for a few years while you work at the highest paying job you can find and accumulate some funds. A few years' savings will not cover the entire bill, but they can help. A real effort to earn your own way is a show of sincerity and good faith when you approach funders, too. You are probably better off delaying your applications altogether rather than applying and deferring your entry once you have been accepted. Deferral, if permitted, is generally limited to one year, and one year may not be sufficient to build your tuition fund.

If you cannot find a really high-paying job, you might seek a position or series of positions closely related to your field for the years between undergraduate and graduate or professional school. A year or more of exposure and involvement can help you to focus your interest. Experience in the field shows up as an asset on your graduate admissions applications and on your applications for fellowships. The more crystallized your interests, the better essays and personal statements you can write to support your requests.

Another benefit to deferral is the opportunity to establish residence. As you research the various graduate programs, you are likely to discover that some of the most exciting programs in your field of interest are being offered at state universities. State universities tend to have lower tuition rates than do private universities. Furthermore, the tuition charged to bona fide residents is considerably lower than that charged to out-of-state residents. The requirements for establishing residence vary from state to state; make it a point to inquire about the possibility of in-state tuition at each state university you are considering. The suggestion that you delay application until you are nearly ready to enter graduate school does not hold with regard to delay for purposes of establishing residence. Since you can only establish residence in one state, you want to apply and be accepted before you select your new home state. Most universities will cooperate and will allow you to move to the state, find employment, and defer enrollment until you qualify for in-state tuition.

WORKING PART-TIME

Another possible way to pay—this one hard on you but possible at many, though not at all, institutions—is to be a part-time student and a full- or part-time wage earner. Again, there are a number of options. You might find a totally unrelated but high-paying job. You will have to be creative in your search. Sanitation workers, for instance, tend to have hours like 7 am to 3 pm which leaves afternoon and evening for classes and study. The job of the sanitation worker is physically exhausting but makes no mental demands and in most localities is quite well paid. Another job which does not take too much thought is working for a courier service like United Parcel. Such delivery services operate twenty-four hours a day. During the night, packages are off-loaded from big interstate trucks and from bulk deliveries from individual shippers and are sorted and loaded onto delivery trucks for route drivers the next day. There is usually plenty of turnover among these night workers, and most parcel service employees are unionized, so the hourly rate is attractive. An alternative to physical labor might be seeking a job in a field related to your studies. Such a job could reinforce your learning and contribute to the job experience section of your resume. If you are earning a degree in computer science, you might find computer-related employment. If you are entering law school, you might work as a paralegal.

GETTING HELP FROM YOUR EMPLOYER

If you both defer application and enter a related field, you may be fortunate enough to find an employer who will pay for a part or even all of your graduate education. This option is most viable if the advanced degree is to be in business or law, but some corporations will finance a master's degree or even a doctorate if the further training will make the employee more valuable to them. Employers cannot require that you continue your employment for any specified number of years after earning your degree. Rather they rely on your gratitude and good will.

The programs under which employers help pay for education are as varied as the number of employers and the graduate programs. Many banks, insurance companies, and brokerage houses offer tuition rebates as part of their benefits packages. These companies rebate part or all of the tuition for courses successfully completed by their employees. Sometimes the rate of reimbursement is tied to the grade earned in the course. Some large law firms will advance part of the law school tuition for promising paralegals after a number of years of service. If these students successfully complete law school and return to the firm for summers and a certain number of years afterwards, the balance of the tuition may be reimbursed. And some industrial corporations will cover the cost of part-time study which enhances the skills of employees, thus making them still more useful to the organization. Such corporations may permit these employees to work a shortened work-week at full-time pay while they study. Some companies even give the employee a year's leave, without salary but with tuition paid, and with a guarantee that the employee will have a job at the end of the leave. This guaranteed position at the end of the leave is worth a lot. It offers peace of mind and freedom to concentrate on research and writing and assures that you will immediately begin earning money with which to repay supplementary graduate loans and leftover undergraduate loans.

If you have been working for the same employer for a year or more, you might do well to inquire about a tuition rebate program. If you are a valuable employee, your employer may be willing to make an investment in you.

THE MILITARY OPTION

If you are heavily burdened with loans from your undergraduate years and are willing to serve for three years in the armed forces, the government will pay off a large portion of your college loans for you. Without the undergraduate debt, you will be eligible for larger loans for your graduate study, and you will not have so many years of high repayment bills to face. After your three years of service, you will be eligible for GI Bill benefits so that you will not need to incur such hefty loans for graduate school. While you are actually in the service, you can attend graduate school part time and have 75% of the cost paid for you. Funding for medical school and law school is even more attractive. From the point of view of footing the bill for graduate studies, the military option sounds too good to be true. Of course there are strings attached. You must serve in the armed forces. You are subject to military rules and military discipline. You may find that a transfer of location totally disrupts your studies if you are trying to attend part time. And, in case of war or other military emergency, you must serve and quite possibly face physical danger. This is the trade-off. If the advantages of having the government pay your education bills outweigh the drawbacks in your eyes, by all means explore the military option. Check with more than one branch of the services; programs vary and change frequently. Ask lots of questions. Be certain that you fully understand all of your obligations, and insist that the funding commitment be in writing. You cannot change your mind and just quit the armed forces, so you must be certain that this route is right for you before you sign up.

If full-time military service is out of the question for you, but having the government underwrite your education is still attractive, consider the National Guard or the Reserves. The all-volunteer standing armed forces are not adequate for all national security needs, so efforts are constantly being made to increase the appeal of the Guard and the Reserves. The benefits offered are frequently readjusted, so you must make your own inquiries about loan repayments and funding of ongoing education while you are in service. Life in the Guard or the Reserves is not nearly so restrictive on a daily basis as life in the regular armed forces, but both Guard members and Reservists are subject to call-up in times of need, and if you are called, you must serve. Circumstances of a call-up may include dangerous assignment, severe economic difficulties, or service that you find morally repugnant (such as strike-breaking if you are a member of a Guard unit called by the governor). If these contingencies do not upset you, this form of long-term, part-time military service can relieve you of much of the cost of your advanced degree.

NEED-BASED FUNDING

The need-based funding picture for graduate studies is quite different from its counterpart at the undergraduate level. Most undergraduate funding is need-based; most graduate funding is not. All universities have a mechanism for distributing need-based funding, in grant/loan/self-help packages similar to undergraduate packages, but the funds are more limited. Your application information packet will tell you how to apply for need-based funding.

Basically you will have to fill out a university financial aid application, a U.S. Department of Education approved multi-data entry form (FFS, the family financial statement of American College Testing service; FAF, the financial aid form of the Educational Testing Service; or GAPS-FAS, the graduate and professional school financial aid service of the Educational Testing Service in California), and whatever other forms the university requires. The university will coordinate its need-based package with department sponsored merit funding and with any outside funding you can gather. Plan to look beyond university need-based funding. It will be top-heavy toward loans and will not be adequate for all your needs.

The following information distributed to all graduate school applicants by a leading large state university is specific to that university yet, at the same time, is representative of the need-based funding situation nationwide.

ASSISTANCE THROUGH THE OFFICE OF STUDENT FINANCIAL AID (OSFA)

You may be eligible for financial aid if you are enrolled at least half-time (five semester hours during the academic year, or three semester hours during the summer session) as a graduate student in a program leading to a degree. Students admitted as Special Nondegree Students may also be eligible for some of the programs listed below.

How to Apply

Specific information and application materials may be obtained from OSFA. To determine your eligibility for aid through the OSFA, you must provide information about your financial situation by submitting either the Financial Aid Form (FAF) to the College Scholarship Service (CSS) or the Family Financial Statement (FFS) to American College Testing (ACT). This University does not accept the Graduate and Professional School Financial Aid Service (GAPSFAS) form.

OSFA will process your financial aid application as soon as your file becomes complete. Some financial aid programs are subject to the availability of funds (first-come, first-served) and others are not. To be considered for all limited funds, be sure to submit your materials as soon as possible after January 1 for the upcoming academic year.

Financial need is an eligibility requirement for all of the following sources of assistance except the Supplemental Loans for Students (SLS) program and part-time jobs.

- Graduate Tuition Grants are based on exceptional need. These institutional grant funds are very limited. Approximately 200 students are awarded tuition grants early in the March prior to the academic year in which they plan to enroll.
- Educational Opportunity Program (EOP) Grants are institutional grants for minority students who demonstrate exceptional need.
- The College Work-Study Program is an employment program subsidized by the federal government and the state.
- Perkins Loans are long-term federal loans based on exceptional need.
- Stafford Loans (formerly Guaranteed Student Loans—GSL) are long-term federal loans based on need and arranged with a bank, credit union, or savings and loan.

■ Supplemental Loans for Students (SLS) are arranged with a bank, credit union or savings and loan and are available to students with or without need.

In addition, part-time jobs (not to be confused with College Work-Study jobs) available throughout the campus and community are posted daily on bulletin boards outside of the OSFA.

Special Note to Assistantship/Fellowship Recipients

Since most assistantship income is classified as "wages," it will not affect your academic year financial aid award (which is usually based on your previous year's income, according to the federal formula for determining financial aid eligibility). However, fellowship income classified as "scholarship" rather than "wages" will be treated as "scholarship resources" in your financial aid package, and thus may affect your eligibility for other financial aid programs.

Nonresident financial aid awardees who receive assistantships that allow resident classification for tuition purposes may have their need-based aid decreased due to the decrease in their educational cost.

Outside need-based funding in the form of grants is confined mainly to special populations. Since these grants are limited in number, they too are based on a combination of merit and need, not merely upon demonstrated need. Some of these special population grants are targeted toward bringing minority students into the professions, such as those sponsored by the Black Lawyers' Associations of various states. Others aim to develop academic talent among Native Americans and Hispanics. Others, such as Business and Professional Women's Foundation Scholarships, are earmarked for mature women reentering the academic world in search of advanced degrees. Grant and fellowship directories tend to index grants by specialty, by region of the country, by point in the studies and time span of funding, and by targeted population. When you consult these directories, you must consider your own identity along every possible dimension in order to locate all funding which could apply to you.

Much outside funding comes in the form of loans. Although helpful and often necessary, loans are still a last resort. For this reason, we shall defer our discussion of loans until the end of this chapter.

FELLOWSHIPS AND ASSISTANTSHIPS

By far the greatest source of funding for graduate study is the graduate department or program itself. Most departments dispense a mixed bag of fellowships, teaching assistantships and research assistantships. Some of these may be allocated to the department by the university; still others are foundation fellowships for which the department nominates its most promising candidates. In most cases, the amount of money attached to the various fellowships and assistantships varies greatly—from tuition abatement alone, to tuition abatement plus stipend (also of varying sums), to stipend alone. Some of the fellowships and assistantships are specifically earmarked for only the first year of graduate study. Others are annually renewable upon application and evidence of satisfactory work in the previous year. Still others are guaranteed for a specified number of years—through three years of coursework, for one year of research or fieldwork, or a stipend to pay living costs during the year of writing a dissertation, for example.

The information below describes graduate student funding only at the University of Iowa. It is presented here to open the array of possibilities. The information provided by other universities is similar, but each is unique.

SUPPORT FROM THE GRADUATE COLLEGE AND YOUR DEPARTMENT OR PROGRAM

The following awards and appointments are the primary sources of financial assistance available to graduate students through their department or program.

- Teaching and Research Assistantships available in most departments, offer stipends typically ranging from $9,000 to $10,000 for half-time appointments. In accordance with general University policy, assistantship holders (quarter-time or more) are classified as residents for fee purposes for the terms during which their appointments are held and any adjacent summer sessions in which they are enrolled. Students on an appointment of half-time or more may have to carry a reduced academic load.

- Iowa Fellowships for first-year graduate students entering doctoral programs carry a minimum stipend of $14,500 plus full tuition for four years on a year-round basis (academic year and summer session). For two of the four years and all summers, recipients have no assignments and are free to pursue their own studies, research and writing.

- Graduate College Block Allocation Fellowships carry a stipend of $8,000 for the academic year.

- Graduate Opportunity Fellowships for first-year graduate students from underrepresented ethnic minority groups carry a one-year stipend of $8,000 for the academic year.

- Scholarships, traineeships, and part-time employment are offered by many graduate departments and programs. Funds are received from both public and private agencies, individuals, corporations, and philanthropic organizations. In general, submission of the *Application for Graduate Awards and Appointments* places eligible applicants in consideration for these awards.

How to Apply

Submit your *Application for Graduate Awards and Appointments* to your department or program by February 1 if you wish to be considered for the following fall. These non-need-based awards are made on the basis of academic merit. Only students admitted to a graduate department or program are eligible to apply. Fellowship and assistantship recipients are also eligible to apply for tuition scholarships awarded in amounts up to full-time tuition and fees. Contact your program or department for more specific information.

Surprisingly, the overall wealth of the institution is not necessarily reflected in the graduate funding it offers. Some universities choose to devote the bulk of their discretionary funds to undergraduate need-based aid. Others offer a greater share to graduate students. Some graduate departments in some universities have separate endowments apart from the university endowment as a whole. A department with its own source of funds can dispense these funds as it wishes, within the restrictions of the endowment, of course.

The case of Clark University in Worcester, Massachusetts, is illustrative of the ways a particular department funds its students. Clark is a relatively small, financially strapped institution. University-based funding for undergraduates is severely limited. Yet, every doctoral candidate in the geography department is equally funded; each receives tuition abatement and an equal stipend in return for teaching or research assistance. The funding is guaranteed for three years of course work. How can this be? The geography department at Clark has, over the years, developed an extremely high reputation. It is considered one of the premier geography departments in the United States. The university considers investment in its geography department to be one of its priorities because maintaining the reputation of its flagship department enhances the reputation of the university as a whole. Leading professors are eager to be associated with leading departments, so the Clark geography faculty includes some luminaries in its ranks. These faculty members in turn attract research funds. Research funds are used in part to pay for the services of research assistants. Publication of results of the research attracts further grants. These funds cover a number of graduate students. The reputation of the department also leads it to draw the best and the brightest among its doctoral candidates. These highly qualified students often draw outside fellowships on the basis of their own merit. Students who bring in their own funding release department funds for other students. And because of its reputation and the reputed caliber of its students, the department is often offered the opportunity to nominate its students to compete for private fellowships. Money entering the department in this way releases still more of the limited funds for student support. In a good year, there may even be funds to help some students at the beginning of their dissertation research. The situation at Clark, while it is Clark's alone, indicates that it may be possible to find funding even in a small, struggling school. Graduate aid is not monolithic. You must ask about the special features in each department and in each program. Do not limit your research to the overall university bulletin!

Sometimes a university will offer some departments the opportunity to nominate candidates for outside fellowships open to students of certain specified departments or to students of the university at large. For example, the MacArthur Foundation funds a number of interdisciplinary fellowships in peace studies at a few selected universities. Each participating university is allocated a number of fellowships to dispense at its discretion. The university then opens the competition to appropriate departments, and the departments in turn nominate candidates from among their most promising applicants. The departments choose nominees on the basis of personal statements submitted at the time of application and on the basis of those applicants' credentials and background experiences. They then solicit the nominees to prepare additional application materials and essays and supply additional recommendations to support application for the fellowship. Having MacArthur fellows among its students brings both money and prestige to the department. Each department studies credentials and statements carefully before soliciting applicants. However, the department could overlook someone. If you have not been invited to apply for a fellowship which you think you qualify for, you can suggest to the department— diplomatically, of course—that you consider yourself a likely candidate.

Few individuals are awarded any one fellowship, but each person who does win one is assured a comfortable source of funding. And someone has to win. It might as well be you. Those who win the named fellowships are removed from the competition for other merit-based or need-based funding, thus increasing the chance of other applicants to win any remaining funds.

Most foundation-funded fellowships, especially those for entering graduate students, are channelled through the department or program. To be considered for these fellowships you must be recommended by the department. There are some fellowships out there, however, for which you must apply as an individual. Some of these are regional, and some are targeted at a specific population. Some are tied to a field such as economics or philosophy, and others have a specific purpose in mind such as studies aimed at improving the welfare of the homeless. Of the privately funded fellowships some are for the first year only, some for the full graduate career, some for the last year of course work only, and still others to support the dissertation at a specific stage or throughout research and writing. Some are relatively small awards; others are so generous that they provide total financial security to the student. The sources of these fellowships range from your local Rotary Club to Rotary International, to AAUW (American Association of University Women) fellowships, to the prestigious Rhodes Scholarships.

FUNDING POSSIBILITIES FROM PRIVATE FOUNDATIONS

The names of some of the philanthropic foundations that give grants for graduate study are almost household words—Dana, Mellon, Ford, Sloan, Rockefeller, Guggenheim, MacArthur, Fulbright, Woodrow Wilson are but a few. These foundations, and others like them, offer funding at many levels of study and for a variety of purposes.

The National Science Foundation offers funding for the full graduate program in science and engineering for minority students as well as for the general population. Other National Science Foundation fellowships specifically fund the research and writing of doctoral dissertations. The U.S. Department of Education Jacob K. Javits Fellowships fund full doctoral programs in the arts, humanities and social sciences. The National Research Council Howard Hughes Medical Institute Doctoral Fellowships offer tuition and a $10,000 per year stipend for three to five years of doctoral work in biology or the health sciences. The Eisenhower Memorial Scholarship Foundation offers a number of $3,000 per year scholarships. The Mellon and Ford Foundations both fund ABD (all but dissertation) fellowships for minority Ph.D. candidates. Under the terms of the ABD fellowships, candidates teach one course per term at a liberal arts college and receive a healthy stipend while writing their dissertations. This program has the double-barreled purpose of assisting minority students while developing teaching talent.

The AAUW (American Association of University Women) is very active in disbursing funds to women for graduate study. Local units give small gifts to undergraduates. Larger grants are made by the AAUW through its Educational Foundation Programs office. In some years the AAUW supports as many as fifty women at the dissertation stage. The Business and Professional Women's Foundation gives scholarships to mature women entering graduate programs. Some of these scholarships are earmarked for women over the age of 35. The American Women in Selected Professions Fellowships fund women in their last year of law or graduate studies in sums ranging from $3,500 to $9,000 apiece.

Other funding for doctoral dissertations comes from the Woodrow Wilson National Fellowship Foundation (in social sciences and humanities), from the Social Science Research Council, and the Guggenheim Foundation. Some foundation funding is reserved for study abroad. Rhodes Scholarships, in particular, support students studying at Oxford. Various Fulbrights, Wilsons, Marshalls, and MacArthurs, among others, support research in foreign universities and at field sites.

The above listing is far from exhaustive. In fact, this is only a tiny sampling of the funding possibilities from private foundations. Even so, the number of grants available is far exceeded by the the number of graduate students who would like to have them. You must work hard to identify and to earn the grants for which you qualify.

FINDING SOURCES OF FINANCIAL AID

There are a number of directories that list these prizes, scholarships, and fellowships one by one. The directories give the name of the sponsor, who to contact, addresses, phone numbers, and deadlines. They also tell something of the purpose of the grants, the number of grants awarded, specific qualification requirements, and the dollar amounts. If the grants are awarded to support research, the directories may give representative titles of projects funded. One of the most useful features of the directories is their cross-indexing. When you consult a grants directory you can look up sources under ethnic designations, geographic designations, subject of study, purpose of research, duration of funding, etc. These directories are very useful as a starting point in the search for outside funding.

Consult the list of directories in the bibliography at the end of this chapter. With list in hand, go to a college library, large public library, or the financial aid office of your current institution and sit down with a directory and pad of paper. Give yourself many hours to find all the grants for which you qualify and to photocopy or write down the important details of each. Immediately call or write each sponsor requesting application materials. Do not rely on deadlines printed in the directories and put off requesting materials. Deadlines change. Do not discount grants or prizes with low dollar amounts attached. A small grant may not be adequate to see you through even a semester of study, but it will do much to enhance your resume. The fact that you were able to compete successfully for any prize makes you a more attractive candidate for the higher-tagged fellowships you apply for next year. If a grant cannot be combined, you may have to decline it, but the fact of having won is already in your favor. Most often, small grants can be combined with other sources of funding, so even small ones help.

APPLYING FOR A GRANT

The procedure for applying for grants and fellowships for your coursework years is similar for both university-administered and private foundation sources. The best advice is to start early. Everything takes longer than you expect, and deadlines tend to be inviolate. Everyone with money to give away is besieged by applicants. There is no need to extend deadlines.

Once you receive application material, begin immediately to accumulate the specified documentation. Each sponsor has different requirements, so read carefully. You will probably need official transcripts from every college you ever attended, even if you took only one course over the summer. You are likely to be asked for official copies of test scores, too. Letters of recommendation are always required. Think about them carefully. You want to request letters from people who have known you as a scholar—professors with whom you have worked closely or authors for whom you have done research or fact checking. You want your letters to be written by people whom you believe have admired your work and who express themselves well. And, consider the reliability of the people from whom you request letters of recommendation. Your application can be seriously jeopardized or even torpedoed if your recommendations do not come through on time. Choose carefully. Consider asking for one extra recommendation just in case someone lets you down. Having recommendations sent to you and then forwarding them in their sealed envelopes is the best way to keep track of what has come in if this procedure is permitted by the sponsor. Be aware that you may have to make a pest of yourself to get transcripts and letters in on time.

You are more in control of the other documents you are likely to be asked for in support of your application. The first of these is a "personal goals statement." This is a carefully reasoned, clear statement of your interests, the reasons for your choice of program, personal growth goals, and career goals. Ideally you should prepare this statement on a word processor so that you can retain the basic exposition but tailor each statement to the needs and interests of the specific sponsor. Try to tie in your statement with the special strengths of the program and with the advantages offered by a particular sponsor. Be sincere and enthusiastic. Adhere to the page limits or word count specified in the application instructions. And remember, neatness counts.

You may also be asked for your resume, samples of scholarly writing or summaries of research you have done. If the grant you seek is meant to finance research or dissertation, you may have to go into detail about the scope of your research, methodology, purpose, expected final results and even proposed budget. Give thought before you write. Then follow the sponsor's instructions, providing all the information that is requested, but not so much more as to overwhelm or bore the reader.

One caveat: Read the requirements carefully before you apply. If you do not fully qualify, do not apply. There are ample qualified applicants for every grant. Requirements will not be waived. The application process is an exacting one and requires you to impose upon others. Do not waste their time or your own.

EMPLOYMENT OPPORTUNITIES ON CAMPUS

While your department is clearly the best university-based source for fellowships, teaching assistantships, and research assistantships, do not totally discount the university as a whole. If you have an area of expertise outside of your own graduate department, by all means build upon it. If you are bilingual in a language taught at the university, you may be able to teach in the language department. Your best chance for a teaching assistantship outside of your department is in a university with relatively few graduate programs. Departments must favor their own graduate students, but if a department has no qualified students of its own, it may be delighted to acquire the services of a graduate student from another department. Some universities even have a formalized mechanism for allocating teaching assistants where they are needed. To return to the example of Clark, where all graduate students must serve as research or teaching assistants, often there are not as many openings for assistants in the undergraduate geography department as there are students. Clark has relatively few graduate programs, and geography students tend to have strong backgrounds in political science, economics and ecology. The graduate geography department and the undergraduate deans readily cooperate to place geography students where they are most needed. In universities with less defined needs for teaching assistants, you may have to be your own advocate. Regardless of your current department, if you can document your ability to assist in another department, you should pursue opportunities there. Do not be shy; let your area of special competence be well known.

Another possible source of university employment is as a residence advisor or freshman advisor. At some colleges and universities, residence advisors are undergraduates. At other institutions, older students—graduate students or students in one of the professional schools—are preferred. If you took peer- counseling training while in high school, consider yourself a candidate. If you were successful in a counseling function during your own undergraduate years, you should be a natural. In very large universities with big freshmen dormitories, a few graduate students with experience in residence advising may be taken on to coordinate and supervise the senior undergraduates who serve as floor or wing advisors. Obviously there are not many such coordinator positions available, but if you qualify, you may get the job.

There are a number of possible advantages to being appointed to a major university-based position such as teaching assistant or residence advisor. One is that, at a state university, you will become eligible instantly for in-state tuition. The reduced tuition is a valuable, non-taxable benefit. Another possibility is that you will be classified as an employee of the university. Policies vary, of course, but at many institutions employees of the university are eligible for reduced tuition or even for total remission of tuition. In addition, assistants generally receive a stipend which even if it does not totally cover living expenses is certainly a big help. Residence hall advisors may get free room along with tuition abatement, and residence hall advisors generally get choice accommodations.

If you were a member of a fraternity or sorority as an undergraduate, you may fulfill a role similar to that of residence advisor in your fraternity or sorority house. As an employee of the fraternity or sorority rather than of the university, you will not be eligible for employee-of-the-university benefits, but you will have free housing and, quite possibly, a salary or stipend as well. Fraternity employment will count toward self-help in a need-based package, but it should have no adverse effect on your winning a merit-based fellowship as well. Be aware, though, that if you are holding what is in effect two jobs, you may have to carry a lighter course load.

Students who work part time in the library, equipment and facilities departments, or in food service will probably not qualify for the perquisites of employees of the university (though depending on the institution and the number of hours worked they might). Campus-based hourly work tends not to be very well paid, but it does offer certain advantages such as elimination of travel time and costs and exemption from FICA (social security) deductions from your paycheck. Exemption from FICA is at the option of the institution, but is permitted by the federal tax code. The contribution which is not deducted has the effect of adding more than 7% to your salary.

ALL LOANS ARE NOT ALIKE

Finally loans come in to fill the financing gap. If you are already saddled with loans from your undergraduate education, you may cringe at the prospect of accumulating further debt. Don't panic. Not all loans are alike, and not all repayment schedules are equally onerous.

In particular, members of minority groups find creative financing routes available to them. The Consortium on the Financing of Higher Education (C.O.F.H.E.), a group of thirty-one universities and colleges including the Ivies and Sister colleges, is making a concerted effort to encourage minority students to pursue advanced degrees. The Kluge Foundation program at Columbia University is only one response to the funding problem. Because Columbia University is an expensive private university, its undergraduates often find themselves heavily indebted to the university by commencement. Under the terms of the Kluge grant, minority alumni of Columbia who successfully complete doctoral programs at accredited universities will have their undergraduate indebtedness wiped out by the Kluge funds. The Minority Issues Task Force of the Council of Graduate Schools is working on the funding problems of minority students, many of whom have very few resources. The funding picture is in constant flux. Be sure that you have the most current information at the moment you are ready to begin applying.

The loan forgiveness possibilities for members of the armed forces have already been touched upon. If military service is not for you, there are other loan forgiveness programs you may find attractive. With the shortage of highly-qualified, highly-motivated public school teachers, there has been a concerted effort to attract liberal arts graduates, even without full teaching credentials, into public school teaching. Liberal arts graduates who enter the public school teaching force under certain programs can have their undergraduate loans written off. If you enter public school teaching after receiving a graduate degree, you may still receive considerable help with those undergraduate loans. Paying off your own graduate school loans, then, will not be so overwhelming.

Most of the loan forgiveness programs for graduate loans apply to professional studies—medicine, dentistry, law, social work—rather than to straight academic disciplines. If your graduate studies will lead to a professional degree, you should not discount loan forgiveness programs out of hand.

A doctor who forgoes a lucrative suburban practice in favor of practicing for a number of years in an underserved area, be it poverty-ridden inner city or isolated rural community, may have a good portion of his or her loans paid off by the government or by private foundations or forgiven by the medical school itself. The doctor may find that the challenges of this practice and the gratitude of the population served are so satisfying that he or she will choose to make this practice a lifelong career. If not, the experience will certainly have been valuable as the doctor moves in new directions. Similarly, a number of prestigious law schools will wipe out the loans of their graduates who enter public service law instead of high-paying corporate law firms. And schools of social work or professional associations of social workers may help to pay off the loans of social workers who utilize their advanced degrees in certain aspects of social work or in highly underserved areas. If your ideals encourage using your educational opportunities to help others, you may find this assistance with your loan payments to give you the best of all possible worlds. The time commitment tends to only be a few years, after which you can move into the private sector with excellent experience to further your applications. Or, you may find that you really enjoy the work you have taken on and build a satisfying career in public service.

There are a number of other loan programs which, while they entail repayment, offer attractive features. The Hattie M. Strong Foundation, for instance, offers interest-free loans for the final year of graduate school or law school on the assumption that without money worries the student can earn higher grades in the final year and obtain a better position after graduation.

From your undergraduate days, you are probably aware of Stafford loans, formerly known as GSLs or Guaranteed Student Loans. At the graduate level the annual cap is $7,500 per year up to a borrowing limit of $54,750. The Stafford loan carries a lower rate of interest than most other loans. More important, repayment need not begin until six months after receipt of the degree, and the government pays the interest in the interim. There is a means test attached to the Stafford loan. Not every applicant is automatically eligible. However, many graduate students who are no longer dependent on parental income or assets do qualify for Stafford loans even though they did not as undergraduates.

University sponsored loans tend to be heavily need-based and to come as parts of total financial aid packages with grants, assistantships and jobs. And even need-based loans are often earmarked for specific underrepresented populations. If you think that you qualify, ask for the information and forms.

Everything that has been said about private foundation funding applies equally to loans as to grants and fellowships. The same directories which can lead you to grants and fellowships can lead you to foundation loans. Again, some of these require evidence of need; others are strictly merit-based. Some apply to the early years of graduate study; others are geared to the dissertation years. Some carry no or low rates of interest, and some have forgiveness provisions if certain conditions are met. In general, foundation loans are less painful than commercial loans. Do not limit your search through the grant directories to high-paying grants. Give equal attention to the smaller prizes and to the loan programs.

Most other loan programs are unrestricted as to income or assets but tend to have restrictions related to total debt with which the student is already burdened and to security or cosigners for the loan. The financial aid office of your current institution or the school to which you have been accepted can help you find your way through the maze of acronymic loan programs: SLS, PLUS, ALAS, TERI, Sallie Mae, Nellie Mae, and the Law Access Program administered by the Law School Admission Service. These last four are non-profit loan agencies which allow for greater flexibility than do the first three. In general the rates are tied to prime + 2 which is better than commercial rates. Repayment schedules, loan consolidation arrangements, co-signing requirements, etc. are all considered on a case-by-case basis.

GETTING INTO GRADUATE SCHOOL

Now that you know it is possible to pay for your graduate education, you must move toward securing admission and funding.

You have already taken a step toward graduate school because you have in hand a preparation book for a graduate school admission exam. Presumably you are about to take or have already taken one or more of these exams. A good score on the exam is an important component of the picture of competence and capability that you present to graduate programs and funding sponsors. If your grades and achievements have been impressive, a high score confirms you as an all-around good candidate. If either grades or achievements are mediocre, then high scores are imperative to bolster your cause. If you have not already taken the exam, study hard; prepare well. If you did not achieve a competitive score on a previous administration, it might be worthwhile to prepare further and try again.

The next thing to do is to begin to investigate which schools have the right programs for you. If you are still in college or out only a year or two, consult with professors who know you well, who are familiar not only with your interests but with your style of working. Professors may suggest programs that suit your needs, universities that offer emphasis in your areas of interest, and faculty members with whom you might work especially well. Your professors may have inside information about contemplated changes in program, focus or personnel at various institutions. This information can supplement the information in university bulletins and help you to decide which schools to apply to. If you have been out of school for several years, you may have to rely more on information bulletins. But do not stop there. Ask for advice and suggestions from people in the field, from present employers if your job is related to your career goals, and from the current faculty and advising staff at your undergraduate school. While the current personnel may not be familiar with you and your learning style, they will have up-to-date information on programs and faculties.

Send for university and departmental literature. Read everything you can about programs offered. Then study the statements on aid, both need-based and merit-based. Be sure that you are completely clear as to the process—criteria, forms required, other supporting documents, and deadlines. If any step of the process seems ambiguous, make phone calls. You can't afford to miss out on possible funding because you misinterpreted the application directions.

DON'T MISS DEADLINES

It's a good idea to prepare a master calendar dedicated to graduate school. Note the deadlines for each step of the process for every school, for every foundation, for every possible source of funds. Consult the master calendar daily. Anticipate deadlines, record actions taken by you and by others, follow up, keep on top of it. Do not just let events happen. Be proactive every step of the way.

The university, graduate school, and departmental bulletins will inform you about need-based aid and about any merit-based funding—teaching assistantships, research assistantships, no-strings fellowships, and private foundation fellowships—administered by the university or any of its divisions. This information will be complete for the funding to which it applies. It will include all procedures, documentation required, and deadlines. None of the literature you receive from the university, however, will tell you about fellowships or other funding for which you must apply directly. You must consult grants directories, foundation directories, and other source books to find the prizes, awards, scholarships, grants and fellowships for which you might qualify.

The following bibliography is an eclectic list of directories. The directories are listed by title and publisher without dates of publication. Most directories are updated frequently. Whenever you ask for a directory, look at the copyright date. If the directory appears to be more than a year old, ask the librarian if there is a newer edition available. Consult the most recent edition you can find. No matter how frequently a directory is updated, you should never rely on deadline dates given for grants. Write or call the sponsor of each grant that you are considering, and request the most current literature. Make certain that names and addresses have not changed. Verify dates for each step of the process. The information in the directory is a valuable starting point, but it is just that: a starting point.

Most of the directories listed below apply to more than one population. Use the index and the list of categories to find which portions of the book apply to you. Disregard any categories into which you do not fit. Concentrate in those areas where you do.

Aside from their copious cross-referencing, most directories also include bibliographies listing other information sources. Do not neglect these lists. One may send you to the perfect source for you.

BIBLIOGRAPHY

GENERAL DIRECTORIES

American Legion Education Program. Need a Lift? To Educational Opportunities, Careers, Loans, Scholarships, Employment. American Legion: Indianapolis, IN

Annual Register of Grant Support. Marquis: Chicago, IL

Catalog of Federal Domestic Assistance. U.S. Office of Management and Budget: Washington, D.C.

Chronicle Student Aid Annual. Chronicle Guidance Publication: Moravia, NY

The College Blue Book, Vol entitled *Scholarships, Fellowships, Grants & Loans.* Macmillan, NY

Directory of Financial Aids for Minorities. Reference Service Press: Santa Barbara, CA

Directory of Financial Aids for Women. Reference Service Press: Santa Barbara, CA

DRG: Directory of Research Grants. Oryx Press: Scottsdale, AZ

A Foreign Student's Selected Guide to Financial Assistance for Study and Research in the United States. Adelphi University Press: Garden City, NY

Foundation Directory. The Foundation Center: New York

Foundation Grants to Individuals. The Foundation Center: New York

The Graduate Scholarship Book, by Daniel J. Cassidy. Prentice Hall: New York.

Grants for Graduate Students, edited by John J. Wells and Amy J. Goldstein. Petersons: Princeton, NJ

The Grants Register. St. Martins: New York

Scholarships, Fellowships and Loans, Vols. VI-VIII. Bellman Publishing Co.: Arlington, MA

Selected List of Fellowship Opportunities and Aids to Advanced Education for United States Citizens and Foreign Nationals. National Science Foundation: Washington, D.C.

Taft Corporate Giving Directory: Comprehensive Profiles & Analyses of Major Corporate Philanthropic Programs. The Taft Group

FIELD AND SUBJECT DIRECTORIES

American Art Directory. R.R. Bowker: New York

American Mathematical Society Notices: "Assistantships and Fellowships in the Mathematical Sciences." December issue, each year.

American Philosophical Association. Proceedings and Addresses: "Grants and Fellowships of Interest to Philosophers." June each year.

Graduate Study in Psychology and Associated Fields. American Psychological Association: Washington, D.C.

Grants for the Arts, by Virginia P. White. Plenum Press: New York.

Grants and Awards Available to American Writers. PEN American Center: New York

Grants, Fellowships and Prizes of Interest to Historians. American Historical Association: Washington, D.C.

Grants in the Humanities: A Scholar's Guide to Funding Sources. Neal-Schuman: New York.

Journalism Career and Scholarship Guide. The Newspaper Fund: Princeton, NJ

Money for Artists: A Guide to Grants and Awards for Individual Artists. ACA Books: New York.

Music Industry Directory. Marquis: Chicago

Scholarships and Loans for Nursing Education. National League for Nursing: New York

WHERE TO LOOK

The best bibliography is of no use if you cannot locate the books that you seek. If you are in college, start with your college library and with the library of the office which promotes graduate study. The dean of the college may have a selection of directories on a bookshelf in the Dean's Office. Ask around. Financial aid offices may also have directories of foundation grants on their shelves. If your college is small or if you are no longer affiliated with a college, you might try the libraries of larger colleges and universities in your vicinity. Call before you go. The libraries of some large universities in major cities are restricted to students with ID cards and are closed to the public even for reference purposes. If the library is open to the public, a kind library assistant may tell you which directories are available so that you may make your trip to the most fruitful library.

One of the most helpful organizations in terms of well-stocked library of directories and general assistance in the search for grants is The Foundation Center. The Foundation Center is the publisher of a number of the directories listed. The Center also operates libraries and cooperating collections throughout the country. The center has four full scale libraries. These are at:

79 Fifth Avenue
(at 16th Street)
New York, NY 10003-3050
212-620-4230

312 Sutter St.
San Francisco, CA 94108
415-397-0902

1001 Connecticut Ave., N.W.
Suite 938
Washington, DC 20036
202-331-1400

1442 Hanna Building
1422 Euclid Ave.
Cleveland, OH 44115
216-861-1934

If any of these is convenient for you, call for current hours. The Center also operates a network of over 180 Cooperating Collections located in host nonprofit organizations in all 50 states, Australia, Canada, Mexico, Puerto Rico, the Virgin Islands, Great Britain and Japan. All contain a core collection of the Center's reference works and are staffed by professionals trained to direct grantseekers to appropriate funding information resources. Many host organizations also have other books and reports on funders and private foundations within their state.

Call toll-free 1-800-424-9836 for a complete address list.

If you have exhausted all other funding possibilities—need-based aid; university or department administered merit-based grants, fellowships and assistantships; privately sponsored grants, fellowships and loans; and government guaranteed loans—you may need to look into non-profit lending organizations. Start by contacting:

The Education Resources Institute
   (TERI)
330 Stuart Street
Boston, MA 02116
617-426-0681

New England Educational Loan Marketing Corp.
   (Nellie Mae)
25 Braintree Hill Park
Braintree, MA 02184
617-849-1325

Student Loan Marketing Association
   (Sallie Mae)
1050 Jefferson Street, NW
Washington, DC 20007
202-333-8000

Law School Admission Services
   (for law school loans, only)
P.O. Box 2000
Newtown, PA 18940-0998
215-968-1001

Part Three

Mathematics Review for the GMAT

MATHEMATICS REVIEW FOR THE GMAT

Basic Mathematics Expressions

In order to solve a mathematical problem, it is essential to know the mathematical meaning of the words used. There are many expressions having the same meaning in mathematics. These expressions may indicate a relationship between quantities or an operation (addition, subtraction, multiplication, division) to be performed. This chapter will help you to recognize some of the mathematical synonyms commonly found in word problems.

Equality

The following expressions all indicated that two quantities are equal (=):

> is equal to
> is the same as
> the result is
> yields
> gives

Also, the word "is" is often used to mean "equals," as in "8 *is* 5 more than 3," which translates to "8 = 5 + 3".

Addition

The following expressions all indicate that the numbers A and B are to be added:

A + B	**2 + 3**
the sum of A and B	the sum of 2 and 3
the total of A and B	the total of 2 and 3
A added to B	2 added to 3
A increased by B	2 increased by 3
A more than B	2 more than 3
A greater than B	2 greater than 3

Subtraction

The following expressions all indicate that the number B is to be subtracted from the number A:

A − B	**10 − 3**
A minus B	10 minus 3
A less B	10 less 3
the difference of A and B	the difference of 10 and 3
from A subtract B	from 10 subtract 3
A take away B	10 take away 3
A decreased by B	10 decreased by 3
A diminished by B	10 diminished by 3
B is subtracted from A	3 is subtracted from 10
B less than A	3 less than 10

Multiplication

If the numbers A and B are to be multiplied (A × B), the following expressions may be used.

A × B	**2 × 3**
A multiplied by B	2 multiplied by 3
the product of A and B	the product of 2 and 3

The parts of a multiplication problem are indicated in the example below:

$$
\begin{array}{rl}
15 & \text{(multiplicand)} \\
\times\ 10 & \text{(multiplier)} \\
\hline
150 & \text{(product)}
\end{array}
$$

Other ways of indicating multiplication are:

Parentheses: A × B = (A)(B)
Dots: A × B = A · B
In algebra, letters next to each other: A × B = AB

A **coefficient** is a number that shows how many times to multiply a variable, such as in 3B, where 3 is the coefficient.

Inequalities

When two numbers are not necessarily equal to each other, this idea can be expressed by using the "greater than" symbol (>) or the "less than" symbol (<). The wider part of the wedge is always towards the greater number.

A is greater than B	A is less than B
A > B	A < B
A is greater than or equal to B	A is less than or equal to B
A ≥ B	A ≤ B

An **integer** is a whole number, either positive or negative.

A **prime number** is a whole number (integer) that is evenly divisible only by itself and 1. *Examples:* 1,2,3,5,7,9,11,13,17,19, etc.

Division

Division of the numbers A and B (in the order A ÷ B) may be indicated in the following ways. (See also the discussion of fractions.)

A ÷ B	**14 ÷ 2**
A divided by B	14 divided by 2
the quotient of A and B	the quotient of 14 and 2

The parts of a division problem are indicated in the example below:

$$\text{(divisor)} \quad 7 \overline{)\, 36} \quad \begin{array}{l} 5\frac{1}{7} \quad \text{(quotient)} \\ \quad \text{(dividend)} \end{array}$$

$$\frac{35}{1} \quad \text{(remainder)}$$

Factors and Divisors

The relationship A × B = C, for any whole numbers A, B, and C, may be expressed as:

A × B = C	**2 × 3 = 6**
A and B are factors of C	2 and 3 are factors of 6
A and B are divisors of C	2 and 3 are divisors of 6
C is divisible by A and by B	6 is divisible by 2 and by 3
C is a multiple of A and of B	6 is a multiple of 2 and of 3

Symbols

Common symbols used on the exam are*:

≠	is not equal to
>	is greater than (3 > 2)
<	is less than (2 < 3)
≥	is greater than or equal to
≤	is less than or equal to
: and ::	is to; the ratio to (see also section on ratios)
$\sqrt{}$	radical sign—used without a number, it indicates the square root of ($\sqrt{9} = 3$) or with an index above the sign to indicate the root to be taken if the root is not a square root ($\sqrt[3]{8} = 2$) (see also section on powers and roots).
|x|	absolute value of (in this case x) (see section on basic properties of numbers, item 6).

BASIC PROPERTIES OF NUMBERS

1. A number greater than zero is called a **positive number.**

2. A number smaller than zero is called a **negative number.**

3. When a negative number is added to another number, this is the same as subtracting the equivalent positive number.

   Example: $2 + (-1) = 2 - 1 = 1$

4. When two numbers of the same sign are multiplied together, the result is a positive number.

   Example: $2 \times 2 = 4$

   Example: $(-2)(-3) = +6$

*Geometric symbols are reviewed in the section on geometry.

5. When two numbers of different signs are multiplied together, the result is a negative number.

   Example: $(+5)(-10) = -50$

   Example: $(-6)(+8) = -48$

6. The **absolute value** of a number is the equivalent positive value.

   Example: $|+2| = +2$

   Example: $|-3| = +3$

7. An even number is an integer that is divisible evenly by two. Zero would be considered an even number for practical purposes.

8. An odd number is an integer that is not an even number.

9. An even number times any integer will yield an even number.

10. An odd number times an odd number will yield an odd number.

11. Two even numbers or two odd numbers added together will yield an even number.

12. An odd number added to an even number will yield an odd number.

FRACTIONS

Fractions and Mixed Numbers

1. A **fraction** is part of a unit.

   a. A fraction has a **numerator** and a **denominator.**

   Example: In the fraction $\frac{3}{4}$, 3 is the numerator and 4 is the denominator.

   b. In any fraction, the numerator is being divided by the denominator.

   Example: The fraction $\frac{2}{7}$ indicates that 2 is being divided by 7.

   c. In a fraction problem, the whole quantity is 1, which may be expressed by a fraction in which the numerator and denominator are the same number.

   Example: If the problem involves $\frac{1}{8}$ of a quantity, then the whole quantity is $\frac{8}{8}$, or 1.

2. A **mixed number** is an integer together with a fraction such as $2\frac{3}{5}$, $7\frac{3}{8}$, etc. The integer is the integral part, and the fraction is the fractional part.

3. An **improper fraction** is one in which the numerator is equal to or greater than the denominator, such as $\frac{19}{6}$, $\frac{25}{4}$, or $\frac{10}{10}$.

4. To change a mixed number to an improper fraction:

   a. Multiply the denominator of the fraction by the integer.

   b. Add the numerator to this product.

   c. Place this sum over the denominator of the fraction.

   Illustration: Change $3\frac{4}{7}$ to an improper fraction.

   SOLUTION: $7 \times 3 = 21$
   $$21 + 4 = 25$$
   $$3\frac{4}{7} = \frac{25}{7}$$

   Answer: $\frac{25}{7}$

5. To change an improper fraction to a mixed number:

   a. Divide the numerator by the denominator. The quotient, disregarding the remainder, is the integral part of the mixed number.

   b. Place the remainder, if any, over the denominator. This is the fractional part of the mixed number.

   Illustration: Change $\frac{36}{13}$ to a mixed number.

   SOLUTION:
   $$13 \overline{)\,36} \quad \begin{array}{c} 2 \end{array}$$
   $$\underline{26}$$
   $$10 \text{ remainder}$$
   $$\frac{36}{13} = 2\frac{10}{13}$$

   Answer: $2\frac{10}{13}$

6. The numerator and denominator of a fraction may be changed, without affecting the

value of the fraction, by multiplying both by the same number.

Example: The value of the fraction $\frac{2}{5}$ will not be altered if the numerator and the denominator are multiplied by 2, to result in $\frac{4}{10}$.

7. The numerator and the denominator of a fraction may be changed, without affecting the value of the fraction, by dividing both by the same number. This process is called **reducing the fraction.** A fraction that has been reduced as much as possible is said to be in **lowest terms.**

Example: The value of the fraction $\frac{3}{12}$ will not be altered if the numerator and denominator are divided by 3, to result in $\frac{1}{4}$.

Example: If $\frac{6}{30}$ is reduced to lowest terms (by dividing both numerator and denominator by 6), the result is $\frac{1}{5}$.

8. As a final answer to a problem:

   a. Improper fractions should be changed to mixed numbers.

   b. Fractions should be reduced as far as possible.

Addition of Fractions

9. **Fractions cannot be added unless the denominators are all the same.**

   a. If the denominators are the same, add all the numerators and place this sum over the common denominator. In the case of mixed numbers, follow the above rule for the fractions and then add the integers.

   Example: The sum of $2\frac{3}{8} + 3\frac{1}{8} + \frac{3}{8} = 5\frac{7}{8}$.

   b. If the denominators are not the same, the fractions, in order to be added, must be converted to ones having the same denominator. The lowest common denominator is often the most convenient common denominator to find, but any common denominator will work. You can cancel out the extra numbers after the addition.

10. The lowest common denominator (henceforth called the L.C.D.) is the lowest number that can be divided evenly by all the given denominators. If no two of the given denominators can be divided by the same number, then the L.C.D. is the product of all the denominators.

Example: The L.C.D. of $\frac{1}{2}$, $\frac{1}{3}$, and $\frac{1}{5}$ is $2 \times 3 \times 5 = 30$.

11. To find the L.C.D. when two or more of the given denominators can be divided by the same number:

    a. Write down the denominators, leaving plenty of space between the numbers.

    b. Select the smallest number (other than 1) by which one or more of the denominators can be divided evenly.

    c. Divide the denominators by this number, copying down those that cannot be divided evenly. Place this number to one side.

    d. Repeat this process, placing each divisor to one side until there are no longer any denominators that can be divided evenly by any selected number.

    e. Multiply all the divisors to find the L.C.D.

Illustration: Find the L.C.D. of $\frac{1}{5}$, $\frac{1}{7}$, $\frac{1}{10}$, and $\frac{1}{14}$.

SOLUTION:

$$
\begin{array}{r|cccc}
2 & 5 & 7 & 10 & 14 \\
\hline
5 & 5 & 7 & 5 & 7 \\
\hline
7 & 1 & 7 & 1 & 7 \\
\hline
& 1 & 1 & 1 & 1
\end{array}
$$

$7 \times 5 \times 2 = 70$

Answer: The L.C.D. is 70.

12. To add fractions having different denominators:

    a. Find the L.C.D. of the denominators.

    b. Change each fraction to an equivalent fraction having the L.C.D. as its denominator.

    c. When all of the fractions have the same denominator, they may be added, as in the example following item 9a.

Illustration: Add $\frac{1}{4}$, $\frac{3}{10}$, and $\frac{2}{5}$.

SOLUTION: Find the L.C.D.:

$$2\,)\,4 \qquad 10 \qquad 5$$
$$2\,)\,2 \qquad 5 \qquad 5$$
$$5\,)\,1 \qquad 5 \qquad 5$$
$$\,1 \qquad 1 \qquad 1$$

L.C.D. $= 2 \times 2 \times 5 = 20$

$$\frac{1}{4} = \frac{5}{20}$$
$$\frac{3}{10} = \frac{6}{20}$$
$$+\ \frac{2}{5} = +\ \frac{8}{20}$$
$$\overline{\frac{19}{20}}$$

Answer: $\frac{19}{20}$

13. To add mixed numbers in which the fractions have different denominators, add the fractions by following the rules in item 12 above, then add the integers.

Illustration: Add $2\frac{5}{7}$, $5\frac{1}{2}$, and 8.

SOLUTION: L.C.D. = 14
$$2\frac{5}{7} = 2\frac{10}{14}$$
$$5\frac{1}{2} = 5\frac{7}{14}$$
$$+\ 8 = +\ 8$$
$$\overline{15\frac{17}{14} = 16\frac{3}{14}}$$

Answer: $16\frac{3}{14}$

Subtraction of Fractions

14. a. Unlike addition, which may involve adding more than two numbers at the same time, subtraction involves only two numbers.

b. In subtraction, as in addition, the denominators must be the same.

15. To subtract fractions:

a. Find the L.C.D.

b. Change both fractions so that each has the L.C.D. as the denominator.

c. Subtract the numerator of the second fraction from the numerator of the first, and place this difference over the L.C.D.

d. Reduce, if possible.

Illustration: Find the difference of $\frac{5}{8}$ and $\frac{1}{4}$.

SOLUTION: L.C.D. = 8
$$\frac{5}{8} = \frac{5}{8}$$
$$-\frac{1}{4} = -\frac{2}{8}$$
$$\overline{\frac{3}{8}}$$

Answer: $\frac{3}{8}$

16. To subtract mixed numbers:

a. It may be necessary to "borrow," so that the fractional part of the first term is larger than the fractional part of the second term.

b. Subtract the fractional parts of the mixed numbers and reduce.

c. Subtract the integers.

Illustration: Subtract $16\frac{4}{5}$ from $29\frac{1}{3}$.

SOLUTION: L.C.D. = 15
$$29\frac{1}{3} = 29\frac{5}{15}$$
$$-\ 16\frac{4}{5} = -\ 16\frac{12}{15}$$

Note that $\frac{5}{15}$ is less than $\frac{12}{15}$. Borrow 1 from 29, and change to $\frac{15}{15}$.

$$29\frac{5}{15} = 28\frac{20}{15}$$
$$-\ 16\frac{12}{15} = -\ 16\frac{12}{15}$$
$$\overline{12\frac{8}{15}}$$

Answer: $12\frac{8}{15}$

Multiplication of Fractions

17. a. To be multiplied, fractions need not have the same denominators.

b. A whole number can be thought of as having a denominator of 1: $3 = \frac{3}{1}$.

18. To multiply fractions:

a. Change the mixed numbers, if any, to improper fractions.

b. Multiply all the numerators, and place this product over the product of the denominators.

c. Reduce, if possible.

Illustration: Multiply $\frac{2}{3} \times 2\frac{4}{7} \times \frac{5}{9}$.

SOLUTION: $2\frac{4}{7} = \frac{18}{7}$
$$\frac{2}{3} \times \frac{18}{7} \times \frac{5}{9} = \frac{180}{189}$$
$$= \frac{20}{21}$$

Answer: $\frac{20}{21}$

19. a. **Cancellation** is a device to facilitate multiplication. To cancel means to divide a numerator and a denominator by the same number in a multiplication problem.

    Example: In the problem $\frac{4}{7} \times \frac{5}{6}$, the numerator 4 and the denominator 6 may be divided by 2.

    $$\frac{\overset{2}{\cancel{4}}}{7} \times \frac{5}{\underset{3}{\cancel{6}}} = \frac{10}{21}$$

    b. With fractions (and percentages), the word "of" is often used to mean "multiply."

    Example: $\frac{1}{2}$ of $\frac{1}{2} = \frac{1}{2} \times \frac{1}{2} = \frac{1}{4}$

20. To multiply a whole number by a mixed number:

    a. Multiply the whole number by the fractional part of the mixed number.

    b. Multiply the whole number by the integral part of the mixed number.

    c. Add both products.

    Illustration: Multiply $23\frac{3}{4}$ by 95.

    SOLUTION:
    $$\frac{95}{1} \times \frac{3}{4} = \frac{285}{4}$$
    $$= 71\frac{1}{4}$$
    $$95 \times 23 = 2185$$
    $$2185 + 71\frac{1}{4} = 2256\frac{1}{4}$$

    Answer: $2256\frac{1}{4}$

Division of Fractions

21. The **reciprocal** of a fraction is that fraction inverted.

    a. When a fraction is inverted, the numerator becomes the denominator and the denominator becomes the numerator.

    Example: The reciprocal of $\frac{3}{8}$ is $\frac{8}{3}$.

    Example: The reciprocal of $\frac{1}{3}$ is $\frac{3}{1}$, or simply 3.

    b. Since every whole number has the denominator 1 understood, the reciprocal of a whole number is a fraction having 1

as the numerator and the number itself as the denominator.

Example: The reciprocal of 5 (expressed fractionally as $\frac{5}{1}$) is $\frac{1}{5}$.

22. To divide fractions:

    a. Change all the mixed numbers, if any, to improper fractions.

    b. Invert the second fraction and multiply.

    c. Reduce, if possible.

    Illustration: Divide $\frac{2}{3}$ by $2\frac{1}{4}$.

    SOLUTION:
    $$2\frac{1}{4} = \frac{9}{4}$$
    $$\frac{2}{3} \div \frac{9}{4} = \frac{2}{3} \times \frac{4}{9}$$
    $$= \frac{8}{27}$$

    Answer: $\frac{8}{27}$

23. **A complex fraction** is one that has a fraction as the numerator, or as the denominator, or as both.

    Example: $\frac{\frac{2}{3}}{5}$ is a complex fraction.

24. To clear (simplify) a complex fraction:

    a. Divide the numerator by the denominator.

    b. Reduce, if possible.

    Illustration: Clear $\frac{\frac{3}{7}}{\frac{5}{14}}$.

    SOLUTION: $\frac{3}{7} \div \frac{5}{14} = \frac{3}{7} \times \frac{14}{5} = \frac{42}{35}$
    $$= \frac{6}{5}$$
    $$= 1\frac{1}{5}$$

    Answer: $1\frac{1}{5}$

Comparing Fractions

25. If two fractions have the same denominator, the one having the larger numerator is the greater fraction.

    Example: $\frac{3}{7}$ is greater than $\frac{2}{7}$.

26. If two fractions have the same numerator, the one having the larger denominator is the smaller fraction.

    Example: $\frac{5}{12}$ is smaller than $\frac{5}{11}$.

27. To compare two fractions having different numerators and different denominators:

    a. Change the fractions to equivalent fractions having their L.C.D. as their new denominator.

    b. Compare, as in the example following item 25, for the largest denominator.

Illustration: Compare $\frac{4}{7}$ and $\frac{5}{8}$.

SOLUTION: L.C.D. $= 7 \times 8 = 56$

$$\frac{4}{7} = \frac{32}{56}$$
$$\frac{5}{8} = \frac{35}{56}$$

Answer: Since $\frac{35}{56}$ is larger than $\frac{32}{56}$, $\frac{5}{8}$ is larger than $\frac{4}{7}$.

Note: Actually, any common denominator will work, not only the L.C.D.

28. To compare two fractions, multiply the denominator of the left fraction by the numerator of the right fraction and write the result above the right fraction. Then multiply the denominator of the right fraction by the numerator of the left fraction and write the result over the left fraction. If the number over the left fraction is larger than the number over the right fraction, the left fraction is larger. If the number over the right fraction is larger, the right fraction is larger. If the numbers over the two fractions are equal, the fractions are equal.

Illustration: Compare $\frac{5}{7}$ and $\frac{3}{4}$.

SOLUTION:
$$\overset{20}{\frac{5}{7}} \times \overset{21}{\frac{3}{4}}$$
$$4 \times 5 = 20$$
$$3 \times 7 = 21$$
$$20 < 21$$

Answer: $\frac{5}{7} < \frac{3}{4}$. This method will only determine which fraction is larger. It cannot be used to tell you the size of the difference.

Fraction Problems

29. Most fraction problems can be arranged in the form: "What fraction of a number is another number?" This form contains three important parts:

    • The fractional part
    • The number following "of"
    • The number following "is"

a. If the fraction and the "of" number are given; multiply them to find the "is" number.

Illustration: What is $\frac{3}{4}$ of 20?

SOLUTION: Write the question as "$\frac{3}{4}$ of 20 is what number?" Then multiply the fraction $\frac{3}{4}$ by the "of" number, 20:

$$\frac{3}{4} \times \overset{5}{\underset{1}{20}} = 15$$

Answer: 15

b. If the fractional part and the "is" number are given, divide the "is" number by the fraction to find the "of" number.

Illustration: $\frac{4}{5}$ of what number is 40?

SOLUTION: To find the "of" number, divide 40 by $\frac{4}{5}$:

$$40 \div \frac{4}{5} = \frac{\overset{10}{40}}{1} \times \frac{5}{\underset{1}{4}}$$
$$= 50$$

Answer: 50

c. To find the fractional part when the other two numbers are known, divide the "is" number by the "of" number.

Illustration: What part of 12 is 9?

SOLUTION: $9 \div 12 = \frac{9}{12}$
$$= \frac{3}{4}$$

Answer: $\frac{3}{4}$

Practice Problems Involving Fractions

1. Reduce to lowest terms: $\frac{60}{108}$.
   (A) $\frac{1}{48}$
   (B) $\frac{1}{3}$
   (C) $\frac{5}{9}$
   (D) $\frac{10}{18}$
   (E) $\frac{15}{59}$

2. Change $\frac{27}{7}$ to a mixed number.
   (A) $2\frac{1}{7}$
   (B) $3\frac{9}{7}$
   (C) $6\frac{1}{3}$

(D) $7\frac{1}{2}$
(E) $8\frac{1}{7}$

3. Change $4\frac{2}{3}$ to an improper fraction.
   (A) $\frac{10}{3}$
   (B) $\frac{11}{3}$
   (C) $\frac{14}{3}$
   (D) $\frac{24}{3}$
   (E) $\frac{42}{3}$

4. Find the L.C.D. of $\frac{1}{6}$, $\frac{1}{10}$, $\frac{1}{18}$, and $\frac{1}{21}$.
   (A) 160
   (B) 330
   (C) 630
   (D) 890
   (E) 1260

5. Add $16\frac{3}{8}$, $4\frac{4}{5}$, $12\frac{3}{4}$, and $23\frac{5}{6}$.
   (A) $57\frac{91}{120}$
   (B) $57\frac{1}{4}$
   (C) 58
   (D) 59
   (E) $59\frac{91}{120}$

6. Subtract $27\frac{5}{14}$ from $43\frac{1}{6}$.
   (A) 15
   (B) $15\frac{5}{84}$
   (C) $15\frac{8}{21}$
   (D) $15\frac{15}{20}$
   (E) $15\frac{17}{21}$

7. Multiply $17\frac{5}{8}$ by 128.
   (A) 2256
   (B) 2305
   (C) 2356
   (D) 2368
   (E) 2394

8. Divide $1\frac{2}{3}$ by $1\frac{1}{9}$.
   (A) $\frac{2}{3}$
   (B) $1\frac{1}{2}$
   (C) $1\frac{23}{27}$
   (D) 4
   (E) 6

9. What is the value of $12\frac{1}{6} - 2\frac{3}{8} - 7\frac{2}{3} + 19\frac{3}{4}$?
   (A) 21
   (B) $21\frac{7}{8}$
   (C) $21\frac{1}{8}$
   (D) 22
   (E) $22\frac{7}{8}$

10. Simplify the complex fraction $\dfrac{\frac{4}{9}}{\frac{2}{5}}$
    (A) $\frac{1}{2}$
    (B) $\frac{9}{10}$
    (C) $\frac{2}{5}$
    (D) 1
    (E) $1\frac{1}{9}$

11. Which fraction is largest?
    (A) $\frac{9}{16}$
    (B) $\frac{7}{10}$
    (C) $\frac{5}{8}$
    (D) $\frac{4}{5}$
    (E) $\frac{1}{2}$

12. One brass rod measures $3\frac{5}{16}$ inches long and another brass rod measures $2\frac{3}{4}$ inches long. Together their length is
    (A) $6\frac{9}{16}$ in.
    (B) $6\frac{1}{16}$ in.
    (C) $5\frac{3}{8}$ in.
    (D) $5\frac{1}{16}$ in.
    (E) $5\frac{1}{32}$ in.

13. The number of half-pound packages of tea that can be weighed out of a box that holds $10\frac{1}{2}$ lb. of tea is
    (A) 5
    (B) $10\frac{1}{2}$
    (C) 11
    (D) $20\frac{1}{2}$
    (E) 21

14. If each bag of tokens weighs $5\frac{3}{4}$ pounds, how many pounds do 3 bags weigh?
    (A) $7\frac{1}{4}$
    (B) $15\frac{3}{4}$
    (C) $16\frac{1}{2}$
    (D) $17\frac{1}{4}$
    (E) $17\frac{1}{2}$

15. During one week, a man traveled $3\frac{1}{2}$, $1\frac{1}{4}$, $1\frac{1}{6}$, and $2\frac{3}{8}$ miles. The next week he traveled $\frac{1}{4}$, $\frac{3}{8}$, $\frac{9}{16}$, $3\frac{1}{16}$, $2\frac{5}{8}$, and $3\frac{3}{16}$ miles. How many more miles did he travel the second week than the first week?
    (A) $1\frac{37}{48}$
    (B) $1\frac{1}{2}$
    (C) $1\frac{3}{4}$
    (D) 1
    (E) $\frac{47}{48}$

16. A certain type of board is sold only in lengths of multiples of 2 feet. The shortest board sold is 6 feet and the longest is 24 feet. A builder needs a large quantity of this type of board in 5½-foot lengths. For minimum waste the lengths to be ordered should be
(A) 6 ft
(B) 12 ft
(C) 22 ft
(D) 24 ft
(E) 26 ft

17. A man spent $\frac{15}{16}$ of his entire fortune in buying a car for $7500. How much money did he possess?
(A) $6000
(B) $6500
(C) $7000
(D) $8000
(E) $8500

18. The population of a town was 54,000 in the last census. It has increased $\frac{2}{3}$ since then. Its present population is
(A) 18,000
(B) 36,000
(C) 72,000
(D) 90,000
(E) 108,000

19. If $\frac{1}{3}$ of the liquid contents of a can evaporates on the first day and $\frac{3}{4}$ of the remainder evaporates on the second day, the fractional part of the original contents remaining at the close of the second day is
(A) $\frac{5}{12}$
(B) $\frac{7}{12}$
(C) $\frac{1}{6}$
(D) $\frac{1}{2}$
(E) $\frac{4}{7}$

20. A car is run until the gas tank is $\frac{1}{8}$ full. The tank is then filled to capacity by putting in 14 gallons. The capacity of the gas tank of the car is
(A) 14 gal
(B) 15 gal
(C) 16 gal
(D) 17 gal
(E) 18 gal

Fraction Problems—Correct Answers

1.	**(C)**	6.	**(E)**	11.	**(D)**	16.	**(C)**
2.	**(B)**	7.	**(A)**	12.	**(B)**	17.	**(D)**
3.	**(C)**	8.	**(B)**	13.	**(E)**	18.	**(D)**
4.	**(C)**	9.	**(B)**	14.	**(D)**	19.	**(C)**
5.	**(A)**	10.	**(E)**	15.	**(A)**	20.	**(C)**

Problem Solutions—Fractions

1. Divide the numerator and denominator by 12:

$$\frac{60 \div 12}{108 \div 12} = \frac{5}{9}$$

One alternate method (there are several) is to divide the numerator and denominator by 6 and then by 2:

$$\frac{60 \div 6}{108 \div 6} = \frac{10}{18}$$

$$\frac{10 \div 2}{18 \div 2} = \frac{5}{9}$$

Answer: **(C)** $\frac{5}{9}$

2. Divide the numerator (27) by the denominator (7):

$$7 \overline{)27}$$
$$\underline{21}$$
$$6 \quad \text{remainder}$$
$$\frac{27}{7} = 3\frac{6}{7}$$

Answer: **(B)** $3\frac{6}{7}$

3.
$$4 \times 3 = 12$$
$$12 + 2 = 14$$
$$4\frac{2}{3} = \frac{14}{3}$$

Answer: **(C)** $\frac{14}{3}$

4.

$2 \underline{)\,6 \quad 10 \quad 18 \quad 21}$ (2 is a divisor of 6, 10, and 18)

$3 \underline{)\,3 \quad 5 \quad 9 \quad 21}$ (3 is a divisor of 3, 9, and 21)

$3 \underline{)\,1 \quad 5 \quad 3 \quad 7}$ (3 is a divisor of 3)

$5 \underline{)\,1 \quad 5 \quad 1 \quad 7}$ (5 is a divisor of 5)

$7 \underline{)\,1 \quad 1 \quad 1 \quad 7}$ (7 is a divisor of 7)

$\quad\quad 1 \quad 1 \quad 1 \quad 1$

L.C.D. $= 2 \times 3 \times 3 \times 5 \times 7 = 630$

Answer: **(C)** 630

5. L.C.D. = 120

$$16\tfrac{3}{8} = 16\tfrac{45}{120}$$
$$4\tfrac{4}{5} = 4\tfrac{96}{120}$$
$$12\tfrac{3}{4} = 12\tfrac{90}{120}$$
$$+\ 23\tfrac{5}{6} = +\ 23\tfrac{100}{120}$$
$$55\tfrac{331}{120} = 57\tfrac{91}{120}$$

Answer: **(A)** $57\tfrac{91}{120}$

6. L.C.D. = 42

$$43\tfrac{1}{6} = 43\tfrac{7}{42} = 42\tfrac{49}{42}$$
$$-\ 27\tfrac{5}{14} = -\ 27\tfrac{15}{42} = -\ 27\tfrac{15}{42}$$
$$15\tfrac{34}{42} = 15\tfrac{17}{21}$$

Answer: **(E)** $15\tfrac{17}{21}$

7.
$$17\tfrac{5}{8} = \tfrac{141}{8}$$
$$\tfrac{141}{8}^{\,} \times \overset{16}{\underset{1}{\tfrac{128}{1}}} = 2256$$

Answer: **(A)** 2256

8.
$$1\tfrac{2}{3} \div 1\tfrac{1}{9} = \tfrac{5}{3} \div \tfrac{10}{9}$$
$$= \tfrac{5}{3} \times \tfrac{9}{10}$$
$$= \tfrac{3}{2}$$
$$= 1\tfrac{1}{2}$$

Answer: **(B)** $1\tfrac{1}{2}$

9. L.C.D. = 24

$$12\tfrac{1}{6} = 12\tfrac{4}{24} = 11\tfrac{28}{24}$$
$$-\ 2\tfrac{3}{8} = -\ 2\tfrac{9}{24} = -\ 2\tfrac{9}{24}$$
$$9\tfrac{19}{24} = 9\tfrac{19}{24}$$
$$-\ 7\tfrac{2}{3} = -\ 7\tfrac{16}{24}$$
$$2\tfrac{3}{24} = 2\tfrac{3}{24}$$
$$+19\tfrac{3}{4} = +19\tfrac{18}{24}$$
$$21\tfrac{21}{24}$$
$$21\tfrac{21}{24} = 21\tfrac{7}{8}$$

Answer: **(B)** $21\tfrac{7}{8}$

10. To simplify a complex fraction, divide the numerator by the denominator:

$$\tfrac{4}{9} \div \tfrac{2}{5} = \tfrac{4}{9} \times \tfrac{5}{2}$$
$$= \tfrac{10}{9}$$
$$= 1\tfrac{1}{9}$$

Answer: **(E)** $1\tfrac{1}{9}$

11. Write all of the fractions with the same denominator. L.C.D. = 80

$$\tfrac{9}{16} = \tfrac{45}{80}$$
$$\tfrac{7}{10} = \tfrac{56}{80}$$
$$\tfrac{5}{8} = \tfrac{50}{80}$$
$$\tfrac{4}{5} = \tfrac{64}{80}$$
$$\tfrac{1}{2} = \tfrac{40}{80}$$

Answer: **(D)** $\tfrac{4}{5}$

12.
$$3\tfrac{5}{16} = 3\tfrac{5}{16}$$
$$+\ 2\tfrac{3}{4} = +\ 2\tfrac{12}{16}$$
$$5\tfrac{17}{16}$$
$$= 6\tfrac{1}{16}$$

Answer: **(B)** $6\tfrac{1}{16}$ in.

13.
$$10\tfrac{1}{2} \div \tfrac{1}{2} = \tfrac{21}{2} \div \tfrac{1}{2}$$
$$= \overset{}{\underset{1}{\tfrac{21}{2}}} \times \overset{1}{\underset{1}{\tfrac{2}{1}}}$$
$$= 21$$

Answer: **(E)** 21

14.
$$5\tfrac{3}{4} \times 3 = \tfrac{23}{4} \times \tfrac{3}{1}$$
$$= \tfrac{69}{4}$$
$$= 17\tfrac{1}{4}$$

Answer: **(D)** $17\tfrac{1}{4}$

15. First week:
L.C.D. = 24

$$3\tfrac{1}{2} = 3\tfrac{12}{24} \text{ miles}$$
$$1\tfrac{1}{4} = 1\tfrac{6}{24}$$
$$1\tfrac{1}{6} = 1\tfrac{4}{24}$$
$$+\ 2\tfrac{3}{8} = +\ 2\tfrac{9}{24}$$
$$7\tfrac{31}{24} = 8\tfrac{7}{24} \text{ miles}$$

Second week:
L.C.D. = 16

$$\tfrac{1}{4} = \tfrac{4}{16} \text{ miles}$$
$$\tfrac{3}{8} = \tfrac{6}{16}$$
$$\tfrac{9}{16} = \tfrac{9}{16}$$
$$3\tfrac{1}{16} = 3\tfrac{1}{16}$$
$$2\tfrac{5}{8} = 2\tfrac{10}{16}$$
$$+\ 3\tfrac{3}{16} = +\ 3\tfrac{3}{16}$$
$$8\tfrac{33}{16} = 10\tfrac{1}{16} \text{ miles}$$

L.C.D. = 48

$$10\tfrac{1}{16} = 9\tfrac{51}{48} \text{ miles second week}$$
$$-\ 8\tfrac{7}{24} = -\ 8\tfrac{14}{48} \text{ miles first week}$$
$$1\tfrac{37}{48} \text{ miles more traveled}$$

Answer: **(A)** $1\tfrac{37}{48}$

16. Consider each choice:

Each 6-ft board yields one $5\frac{1}{2}$-ft board with $\frac{1}{2}$ ft waste.

Each 12-ft board yields two $5\frac{1}{2}$-ft boards with 1 ft waste ($2 \times 5\frac{1}{2} = 11$; $12 - 11 = 1$ ft waste).

Each 24-ft board yields four $5\frac{1}{2}$-ft boards with 2 ft waste ($4 \times 5\frac{1}{2} = 22$; $24 - 22 = 2$ ft waste).

Each 22 ft board may be divided into four $5\frac{1}{2}$-ft boards with no waste ($4 \times 5\frac{1}{2} = 22$ exactly).

Answer: **(C)** 22 ft

17. $\frac{15}{16}$ of fortune is $7500.

Therefore, his fortune $= 7500 \div \frac{15}{16}$

$$= \frac{\overset{500}{\cancel{7500}}}{1} \times \frac{16}{\underset{1}{\cancel{15}}}$$

$$= 8000$$

Answer: **(D)** $8000

18. $\frac{2}{3}$ of 54,000 = increase

$$\text{Increase} = \frac{2}{3} \times \overset{18,000}{\cancel{54,000}}$$

$$= 36,000$$

$$\text{Present population} = 54,000 + 36,000$$

$$= 90,000$$

Answer: **(D)** 90,000

19. First day: $\frac{1}{3}$ evaporates

$\frac{2}{3}$ remains

Second day: $\frac{3}{4}$ of $\frac{2}{3}$ evaporates

$\frac{1}{4}$ of $\frac{2}{3}$ remains

The amount remaining is

$$\frac{1}{\underset{2}{\cancel{4}}} \times \overset{1}{\cancel{\frac{2}{3}}} = \frac{1}{6} \text{ of original contents}$$

Answer: **(C)** $\frac{1}{6}$

20. $\frac{7}{8}$ of capacity = 14 gal

Therefore, capacity $= 14 \div \frac{7}{8}$

$$= \frac{\overset{2}{\cancel{14}}}{1} \times \frac{8}{\underset{1}{\cancel{7}}}$$

$$= 16 \text{ gal}$$

Answer: **(C)** 16 gal

DECIMALS

1. A **decimal,** which is a number with a decimal point (.), is actually a fraction, the denominator of which is understood to be 10 or some power of 10.

   a. The number of digits, or places, after a decimal point determines which power of 10 the denominator is. If there is one digit, the denominator is understood to be 10; if there are two digits, the denominator is understood to be 100, etc.

   Example: $.3 = \frac{3}{10}$, $.57 = \frac{57}{100}$, $.643 = \frac{643}{1000}$

   b. The addition of zeros after a decimal point does not change the value of the decimal. The zeros may be removed without changing the value of the decimal.

   Example: $.7 = .70 = .700$ and, vice versa, $.700 = .70 = .7$

   c. Since a decimal point is understood to exist after any whole number, the addition of any number of zeros after such a decimal point does not change the value of the number.

   Example: $2 = 2.0 = 2.00 = 2.000$

Addition of Decimals

2. Decimals are added in the same way that whole numbers are added, with the provision that the decimal points must be kept in a vertical line, one under the other. This determines the place of the decimal point in the answer.

Illustration: Add 2.31, .037, 4, and 5.0017

SOLUTION:

```
    2.3100
     .0370
    4.000
 +  5.0017
   11.3487
```

Answer: 11.3487

Subtraction of Decimals

3. Decimals are subtracted in the same way that whole numbers are subtracted, with the provision that, as in addition, the decimal points must be kept in a vertical line, one under the other. This determines the place of the decimal point in the answer.

Illustration: Subtract 4.0037 from 15.3

SOLUTION:
$$
\begin{array}{r}
15.3000 \\
- \ 4.0037 \\
\hline
11.2963
\end{array}
$$

Answer: 11.2963

Multiplication of Decimals

4. Decimals are multiplied in the same way that whole numbers are multiplied.

    a. The number of decimal places in the product equals the sum of the decimal places in the multiplicand and in the multiplier.

    b. If there are fewer places in the product than this sum, then a sufficient number of zeros must be added in front of the product to equal the number of places required, and a decimal point is written in front of the zeros.

Illustration: Multiply 2.372 by .012

SOLUTION:
$$
\begin{array}{r}
2.372 \quad \text{(3 decimal places)} \\
\times \ \ .012 \quad \text{(3 decimal places)} \\
\hline
4744 \qquad\qquad \\
2372 \qquad\qquad\quad \\
\hline
.028464 \quad \text{(6 decimal places)}
\end{array}
$$

Answer: .028464

5. A decimal can be multiplied by a power of 10 by moving the decimal point to the *right* as many places as indicated by the power. If multiplied by 10, the decimal point is moved one place to the right; if multiplied by 100, the decimal point is moved two places to the right; etc.

Example:
$$
\begin{array}{l}
.235 \times 10 \ = \ \ 2.35 \\
.235 \times 100 \ = \ 23.5 \\
.235 \times 1000 = 235
\end{array}
$$

Division of Decimals

6. There are four types of division involving decimals:

    • When the dividend only is a decimal.
    • When the divisor only is a decimal.
    • When both are decimals.
    • When neither dividend nor divisor is a decimal.

    a. When the dividend only is a decimal, the division is the same as that of whole numbers, except that a decimal point must be placed in the quotient exactly above that in the dividend.

Illustration: Divide 12.864 by 32

SOLUTION:
$$
\begin{array}{r}
.402 \quad\ \\
32 \overline{\smash{)}\ 12.864} \\
\underline{12\ 8\quad\ } \\
64 \\
\underline{64} \\
\end{array}
$$

Answer: .402

    b. When the divisor only is a decimal, the decimal point in the divisor is omitted and as many zeros are placed to the right of the dividend as there were decimal places in the divisor.

Illustration: Divide 211327 by 6.817

SOLUTION:

$$
\begin{array}{l}
6.817 \overline{\smash{)}\ 211327} \\
\text{(3 decimal places)}
\end{array}
$$

$$
\begin{array}{r}
31000 \qquad\qquad\qquad \\
= 6817 \overline{\smash{)}\ 211327000} \quad \text{(3 zeros added)}\\
\underline{20451\quad\ } \\
6817 \\
\underline{6817} \\
\end{array}
$$

Answer: 31000

    c. When both divisor and dividend are decimals, the decimal point in the divisor is omitted and the decimal point in the dividend must be moved to the right as many decimal places as there were in the divisor. If there are not enough places in the dividend, zeros must be added to make up the difference.

Illustration: Divide 2.62 by .131

$$SOLUTION: \quad .131\overline{)2.62} = 131\overline{)2620} = \begin{array}{r} 20 \\ \hline 262 \end{array}$$

Answer: 20

d. In instances when neither the divisor nor the dividend is a decimal, a problem may still involve decimals. This occurs in two cases: when the dividend is a smaller number than the divisor; and when it is required to work out a division to a certain number of .decimal places. In either case, write in a decimal point after the dividend, add as many zeros as necessary, and place a decimal point in the quotient above that in the dividend.

Illustration: Divide 7 by 50.

$$SOLUTION: \quad 50\overline{)7.00} \quad \begin{array}{r} .14 \\ \hline 5\,0 \\ \hline 2\,00 \\ 2\,00 \\ \hline \end{array}$$

Answer: .14

Illustration: How much is 155 divided by 40, carried out to 3 decimal places?

$$SOLUTION: \quad 40\overline{)155.000} \quad \begin{array}{r} 3.875 \\ \hline 120 \\ \hline 35\,0 \\ 32\,0 \\ \hline 3\,00 \\ 2\,80 \\ \hline 200 \end{array}$$

Answer: 3.875

7. A decimal can be divided by a power of 10 by moving the decimal to the *left* as many places as indicated by the power. If divided by 10, the decimal point is moved one place to the left; if divided by 100, the decimal point is moved two places to the left; etc. If there are not enough places, add zeros in front of the number to make up the difference and add a decimal point.

    Example: .4 divided by 10 = .04
    .4 divided by 100 = .004

Rounding Decimals

8. To round a number to a given decimal place:

    a. Locate the given place.

    b. If the digit to the right is less than 5, omit all digits following the given place.

    c. If the digit to the right is 5 or more, raise the given place by 1 and omit all digits following the given place.

    Examples:

    4.27 = 4.3 to the nearest tenth
    .71345 = .713 to the nearest thousandth

9. In problems involving money, answers are usually rounded to the nearest cent.

Conversion of Fractions to Decimals

10. A fraction can be changed to a decimal by dividing the numerator by the denominator and working out the division to as many decimal places as required.

    Illustration: Change $\frac{5}{11}$ to a decimal of 2 places.

$$SOLUTION: \quad \frac{5}{11} = 11\overline{)5.00} \quad \begin{array}{r} .45\frac{5}{11} \\ \hline 4.44 \\ \hline 60 \\ 55 \\ \hline 5 \end{array}$$

    Answer: $.45\frac{5}{11}$

11. To clear fractions containing a decimal in either the numerator or the denominator, or in both, divide the numerator by the denominator.

    Illustration: What is the value of $\frac{2.34}{.6}$?

$$SOLUTION: \quad \frac{2.34}{.6} = .6\overline{)2.34} = 6\overline{)23.4} \quad \begin{array}{r} 3.9 \\ \hline 18 \\ \hline 5\,4 \\ 5\,4 \\ \hline \end{array}$$

    Answer: 3.9

Conversion of Decimals to Fractions

12. Since a decimal point indicates a number having a denominator that is a power of 10, a decimal can be expressed as a fraction, the numerator of which is the number itself and the denominator of which is the power indicated by the number of decimal places in the decimal.

    Example: $.3 = \frac{3}{10}$, $.47 = \frac{47}{100}$

13. When the decimal is a mixed number, divide by the power of 10 indicated by its number of decimal places. The fraction does not count as a decimal place.

    Illustration: Change $.25\frac{1}{3}$ to a fraction.

    SOLUTION: $.25\frac{1}{3} = 25\frac{1}{3} \div 100$
    $$= \frac{76}{3} \times \frac{1}{100}$$
    $$= \frac{76}{300} = \frac{19}{75}$$

    Answer: $\frac{19}{75}$

14. When to change decimals to fractions:

    a. When dealing with whole numbers, do not change the decimal.

    Example: In the problem $12 \times .14$, it is better to keep the decimal:
    $$12 \times .14 = 1.68$$

    b. When dealing with fractions, change the decimal to a fraction.

    Example: In the problem $\frac{3}{5} \times .17$, it is best to change the decimal to a fraction:
    $$\frac{3}{5} \times .17 = \frac{3}{5} \times \frac{17}{100} = \frac{51}{500}$$

15. Because decimal equivalents of fractions are often used, it is helpful to be familiar with the most common conversions.

$\frac{1}{2} = .5$	$\frac{1}{3} = .3333$
$\frac{1}{4} = .25$	$\frac{2}{3} = .6667$
$\frac{3}{4} = .75$	$\frac{1}{6} = .1667$
$\frac{1}{5} = .2$	$\frac{1}{7} = .1429$
$\frac{1}{8} = .125$	$\frac{1}{9} = .1111$
$\frac{1}{16} = .0625$	$\frac{1}{12} = .0833$

    Note that the left column contains exact values. The values in the right column have been rounded to the nearest ten-thousandth.

Practice Problems Involving Decimals

1. Add 37.03, 11.5627, 3.4005, 3423, and 1.141. _____

2. Subtract 4.64324 from 7. _____

3. Multiply 27.34 by 16.943. _____

4. How much is 19.6 divided by 3.2, carried out to 3 decimal places? _____

5. What is $\frac{5}{11}$ in decimal form (to the nearest hundredth)? _____

6. What is $.64\frac{2}{3}$ in fraction form? _____

7. What is the difference between $\frac{3}{5}$ and $\frac{9}{8}$ expressed decimally? _____

8. A boy saved up $4.56 the first month, $3.82 the second month, and $5.06 the third month. How much did he save altogether?

   _____

9. The diameter of a certain rod is required to be $1.51 \pm .015$ inches. The rod's diameter must be between _____ and _____ .

10. After an employer figures out an employee's salary of $190.57, he deducts $3.05 for social security and $5.68 for pension. What is the amount of the check after these deductions?

    _____

11. If the outer radius of a metal pipe is 2.84 inches and the inner radius is 1.94 inches, the thickness of the metal is _____ .

12. A boy earns $20.56 on Monday, $32.90 on Tuesday, $20.78 on Wednesday. He spends half of all that he earned during the three days. How much has he left? _____

13. The total cost of $3\frac{1}{2}$ pounds of meat at $1.69 a pound and 20 lemons at $.60 a dozen will be

    _____ .

14. A reel of cable weighs 1279 lb. If the empty reel weighs 285 lb and the cable weighs 7.1

lb per foot, the number of feet of cable on the reel is _____.

15. 345 fasteners at \$4.15 per hundred will cost _____

Problem Solutions—Decimals

1. Line up all the decimal points one under the other. Then add:

$$
\begin{array}{r}
37.03 \\
11.5627 \\
3.4005 \\
3423.0000 \\
+ \quad 1.141 \\
\hline
3476.1342
\end{array}
$$

Answer: 3476.1342

2. Add a decimal point and five zeros to the 7. Then subtract:

$$
\begin{array}{r}
7.00000 \\
- \ 4.64324 \\
\hline
2.35676
\end{array}
$$

Answer: 2.35676

3. Since there are two decimal places in the multiplicand and three decimal places in the multiplier, there will be 2 + 3 = 5 decimal places in the product.

$$
\begin{array}{r}
27.34 \\
\times \ 16.943 \\
\hline
8202 \\
1\ 0936 \\
24\ 606 \\
164\ 04 \\
273\ 4 \\
\hline
463.22162
\end{array}
$$

Answer: 463.22162

4. Omit the decimal point in the divisor by moving it one place to the right. Move the decimal point in the dividend one place to the right and add three zeros in order to carry your answer out to three decimal places, as instructed in the problem.

$$
\begin{array}{r}
6.125 \\
3.2.\overline{)\ 19.6.000} \\
19\ 2 \\
\hline
4\ 0 \\
3\ 2 \\
\hline
80 \\
64 \\
\hline
160 \\
160 \\
\hline
\end{array}
$$

Answer: 6.125

5. To convert a fraction to a decimal, divide the numerator by the denominator:

$$
\begin{array}{r}
.454 \\
11\ \overline{)\ 5.000} \\
4\ 4 \\
\hline
60 \\
55 \\
\hline
50 \\
44 \\
\hline
6
\end{array}
$$

Answer: .45 to the nearest hundredth

6. To convert a decimal to a fraction, divide by the power of 10 indicated by the number of decimal places. (The fraction does not count as a decimal place.)

$$
\begin{aligned}
64\tfrac{2}{3} \div 100 &= \tfrac{194}{3} \div \tfrac{100}{1} \\
&= \tfrac{194}{3} \times \tfrac{1}{100} \\
&= \tfrac{194}{300} \\
&= \tfrac{97}{150}
\end{aligned}
$$

Answer: $\tfrac{97}{150}$

7. Convert each fraction to a decimal and subtract to find the difference:

$\tfrac{9}{8} = 1.125$ $\qquad$ $\tfrac{3}{5} = .60$ $\qquad$
$$
\begin{array}{r}
1.125 \\
- \ .60 \\
\hline
.525
\end{array}
$$

Answer: .525

8. Add the savings for each month:

$$
\begin{array}{r}
\$4.56 \\
3.82 \\
+ \ 5.06 \\
\hline
\$13.44
\end{array}
$$

Answer: \$13.44

9.

$$
\begin{array}{r} 1.51 \\ +\ .015 \\ \hline 1.525 \end{array}
\qquad
\begin{array}{r} 1.510 \\ -\ .015 \\ \hline 1.495 \end{array}
$$

Answer: The rod may have a diameter of from 1.495 inches to 1.525 inches inclusive.

10. Add to find total deductions:

$$
\begin{array}{r} \$3.05 \\ +\ 5.68 \\ \hline \$8.73 \end{array}
$$

Subtract total deductions from salary to find amount of check:

$$
\begin{array}{r} \$190.57 \\ -\ 8.73 \\ \hline \$181.84 \end{array}
$$

Answer: $181.84

11. Outer radius minus inner radius equals thickness of metal:

$$
\begin{array}{r} 2.84 \\ -\ 1.94 \\ \hline .90 \end{array}
$$

Answer: .90 in

12. Add daily earnings to find total earnings:

$$
\begin{array}{r} \$20.56 \\ 32.90 \\ +\ 20.78 \\ \hline \$74.24 \end{array}
$$

Divide total earnings by 2 to find out what he has left:

$$
\begin{array}{r} \$37.12 \\ 2\ )\ \overline{\$74.24} \end{array}
$$

Answer: $37.12

13. Find cost of $3\frac{1}{2}$ pounds of meat:

$$
\begin{array}{r} \$1.69 \\ \times\ \ 3.5 \\ \hline 845 \\ 5\ 07 \\ \hline \$5.915 \end{array}
$$
= $5.92 to the nearest cent

Find cost of 20 lemons:
$.60 ÷ 12 = $.05 (for 1 lemon)
$.05 × 20 = $1.00 (for 20 lemons)

Add cost of meat and cost of lemons:

$$
\begin{array}{r} \$5.92 \\ +\ 1.00 \\ \hline \$6.92 \end{array}
$$

Answer: $6.92

14. Subtract weight of empty reel from total weight to find weight of cable:

$$
\begin{array}{r} 1279\ \text{lb} \\ -\ 285\ \text{lb} \\ \hline 994\ \text{lb} \end{array}
$$

Each foot of cable weighs 7.1 lb. Therefore, to find the number of feet of cable on the reel, divide 994 by 7.1:

$$
\begin{array}{r} 14\ 0. \\ 7.1\ )\ \overline{994.0.} \\ 71 \\ \hline 284 \\ 284 \\ \hline 0\ 0 \end{array}
$$

Answer: 140

15. Each fastener costs:

$4.15 ÷ 100 = $.0415

345 fasteners cost:

$$
\begin{array}{r} 345 \\ \times\ .0415 \\ \hline 1725 \\ 345 \\ 13\ 80 \\ \hline 14.3175 \end{array}
$$

Answer: $14.32

PERCENTS

1. The **percent symbol** (%) means "parts out of a hundred." Thus a percent is really a fraction—25% is 25 parts out of a hundred, or $\frac{25}{100}$, which reduces or simplifies to $\frac{1}{4}$, or one part out of four. Some problems involve expressing a fraction or a decimal as a percent. In other problems it is necessary to express a percent as a fraction or decimal in order to perform the calculations efficiently. When you have a percent (or decimal) which

converts to a common fraction (25% = .25 = $\frac{1}{4}$), it is usually best to do any multiplying or dividing by first converting the percent or decimal to the common fraction, since the numbers are usually smaller and will work better. For adding and subtracting, percentages and decimals are often easier.

2. To change a whole number or a decimal to a percent:

   a. Multiply the number by 100.

   b. Affix a % sign.

   Illustration: Change 3 to a percent.

   SOLUTION: $3 \times 100 = 300$
   $$3 = 300\%$$

   Answer: 300%

   Illustration: Change .67 to a percent.

   SOLUTION: $.67 \times 100 = 67$
   $$.67 = 67\%$$

   Answer: 67%

3. To change a fraction or a mixed number to a percent:

   a. Multiply the fraction or mixed number by 100.

   b. Reduce, if possible.

   c. Affix a % sign.

   Illustration: Change $\frac{1}{7}$ to a percent.

   SOLUTION: $\frac{1}{7} \times 100 = \frac{100}{7}$
   $$= 14\frac{2}{7}$$
   $$\frac{1}{7} = 14\frac{2}{7}\%$$

   Answer: $14\frac{2}{7}\%$

   Illustration: Change $4\frac{2}{3}$ to a percent.

   SOLUTION: $4\frac{2}{3} \times 100 = \frac{14}{3} \times 100 = \frac{1400}{3}$
   $$= 466\frac{2}{3}$$
   $$4\frac{2}{3} = 466\frac{2}{3}\%$$

   Answer: $466\frac{2}{3}\%$

4. To remove a % sign attached to a decimal, divide the decimal by 100. If necessary, the resulting decimal may then be changed to a fraction.

Illustration: Change .5% to a decimal and to a fraction.

SOLUTION: $.5\% = .5 \div 100 = .005$
$$.005 = \frac{5}{1000} = \frac{1}{200}$$

Answer: $.5\% = .005$
$$.5\% = \frac{1}{200}$$

5. To remove a % sign attached to a fraction or mixed number, divide the fraction or mixed number by 100, and reduce, if possible. If necessary, the resulting fraction may then be changed to a decimal.

Illustration: Change $\frac{3}{4}\%$ to a fraction and to a decimal.

SOLUTION: $\frac{3}{4}\% = \frac{3}{4} \div 100 = \frac{3}{4} \times \frac{1}{100}$
$$= \frac{3}{400}$$

$$\frac{3}{400} = 400 \overline{)3.0000} \quad .0075$$

Answer: $\frac{3}{4}\% = \frac{3}{400}$
$$\frac{3}{4}\% = .0075$$

6. To remove a % sign attached to a decimal that includes a fraction, divide the decimal by 100. If necessary, the resulting number may then be changed to a fraction.

Illustration: Change $.5\frac{1}{3}\%$ to a fraction.

SOLUTION: $.5\frac{1}{3}\% = .005\frac{1}{3}$
$$= \frac{5\frac{1}{3}}{1000}$$
$$= 5\frac{1}{3} \div 1000$$
$$= \frac{16}{3} \times \frac{1}{1000}$$
$$= \frac{16}{3000}$$
$$= \frac{2}{375}$$

Answer: $.5\frac{1}{3}\% = \frac{2}{375}$

7. Some fraction-percent equivalents are used so frequently that it is helpful to be familiar with them.

$\frac{1}{25} = 4\%$	$\frac{1}{5} = 20\%$
$\frac{1}{20} = 5\%$	$\frac{1}{4} = 25\%$
$\frac{1}{12} = 8\frac{1}{3}\%$	$\frac{1}{3} = 33\frac{1}{3}\%$
$\frac{1}{10} = 10\%$	$\frac{1}{2} = 50\%$
$\frac{1}{8} = 12\frac{1}{2}\%$	$\frac{2}{3} = 66\frac{2}{3}\%$
$\frac{1}{6} = 16\frac{2}{3}\%$	$\frac{3}{4} = 75\%$

Solving Percent Problems

8. Most percent problems involve three quantities:

   • The rate, R, which is followed by a % sign.
   • The base, B, which follows the word "of."
   • The amount of percentage, P, which usually follows the word "is."

   a. If the rate (R) and the base (B) are known, then the percentage (P) = R × B.

   Illustration: Find 15% of 50.

   SOLUTION: Rate = 15%
   Base = 50
   P = R × B
   P = 15% × 50
   = .15 × 50
   = 7.5

   Answer: 15% of 50 is 7.5.

   b. If the rate (R) and the percentage (P) are known, then the base (B) = $\frac{P}{R}$.

   Illustration: 7% of what number is 35?

   SOLUTION: Rate = 7%
   Percentage = 35
   $B = \frac{P}{R}$
   $B = \frac{35}{7\%}$
   = 35 ÷ .07
   = 500

   Answer: 7% of 500 is 35.

   c. If the percentage (P) and the base (B) are known, the rate (R) = $\frac{P}{B}$.

   Illustration: There are 96 men in a group of 150 people. What percent of the group are men?

   SOLUTION: Base = 150
   Percentage (amount) = 96
   Rate = $\frac{96}{150}$
   = .64
   = 64%

   Answer: 64% of the group are men.

Illustration: In a tank holding 20 gallons of solution, 1 gallon is alcohol. What is the strength of the solution in percent?

SOLUTION:

   Percentage (amount) = 1 gallon
   Base = 20 gallons
   Rate = $\frac{1}{20}$
   = .05
   = 5%

Answer: The solution is 5% alcohol.

9. In a percent problem, the whole is 100%.

   Example: If a problem involves 10% of a quantity, the rest of the quantity is 90%.

   Example: If a quantity has been increased by 5%, the new amount is 105% of the original quantity.

   Example: If a quantity has been decreased by 15%, the new amount is 85% of the original quantity.

10. Percent change, percent increase, or percent decrease are special types of percent problems in which the difficulty is in making sure to use the right numbers to calculate the percent. The full formula is:

$$\frac{(\text{New Amount}) - (\text{Original Amount})}{(\text{Original Amount})} \times 100 = \text{percent change}$$

Where the new amount is less than the original amount, the number on top will be a negative number and the result will be a **percent decrease.** When a percent decrease is asked for, the negative sign is omitted. Where the new amount is greater than the original amount, the percent change is positive and is called a **percent increase.**

The percent of increase or decrease is found by putting the amount of increase or decrease over the original amount and changing this fraction to a percent by multiplying by 100.

Illustration: The number of automobiles sold by the Cadcoln Dealership increased from 300 one year to 400 the following year. What was the percent of increase?

SOLUTION: There was an increase of 100, which must be compared to the original 300.

$$\frac{100}{300} = \frac{1}{3} = 33\frac{1}{3}\%$$

Answer: $33\frac{1}{3}\%$

Practice Problems Involving Percents

1. 10% written as a decimal is
   (A) 1.0
   (B) 0.1
   (C) 0.01
   (D) 0.010
   (E) 0.001

2. What is 5.37% in fraction form?
   (A) $\frac{537}{10,000}$
   (B) $\frac{537}{1000}$
   (C) $5\frac{37}{10,000}$
   (D) $5\frac{37}{100}$
   (E) $\frac{537}{10}$

3. What percent is $\frac{3}{4}$ of $\frac{5}{6}$?
   (A) 60%
   (B) 75%
   (C) 80%
   (D) 90%
   (E) 111%

4. What percent is 14 of 24?
   (A) $62\frac{1}{4}\%$
   (B) $58\frac{1}{3}\%$
   (C) $41\frac{2}{3}\%$
   (D) $33\frac{3}{5}\%$
   (E) 14%

5. 200% of 800 equals
   (A) 4
   (B) 16
   (C) 200
   (D) 800
   (E) 1600

6. If John must have a mark of 80% to pass a test of 35 items, the number of items he may miss and still pass the test is
   (A) 7
   (B) 8

(C) 11
(D) 28
(E) 35

7. The regular price of a TV set that sold for $118.80 at a 20% reduction sale is
   (A) $158.60
   (B) $148.50
   (C) $138.84
   (D) $95.04
   (E) $29.70

8. A circle graph of a budget shows the expenditure of 26.2% for housing, 28.4% for food, 12% for clothing, 12.7% for taxes, and the balance for miscellaneous items. The percent for miscellaneous items is
   (A) 79.3
   (B) 70.3
   (C) 68.5
   (D) 29.7
   (E) 20.7

9. Two dozen shuttlecocks and four badminton rackets are to be purchased for a playground. The shuttlecocks are priced at $.35 each and the rackets at $2.75 each. The playground receives a discount of 30% from these prices. The total cost of this equipment is
   (A) $7.29
   (B) $11.43
   (C) $13.58
   (D) $18.60
   (E) $19.40

10. A piece of wood weighing 10 ounces is found to have a weight of 8 ounces after drying. The moisture content was
    (A) 80%
    (B) 40%
    (C) $33\frac{1}{3}\%$
    (D) 25%
    (E) 20%

11. A bag contains 800 coins. Of these, 10 percent are dimes, 30 percent are nickels, and the rest are quarters. The amount of money in the bag is
    (A) less than $150
    (B) between $150 and $300

(C) between $301 and $450
(D) between $450 and $800
(E) more than $800

12. Six quarts of a 20% solution of alcohol in water are mixed with 4 quarts of a 60% solution of alcohol in water. The alcoholic strength of the mixture is
(A) 80%
(B) 40%
(C) 36%
(D) $33\frac{1}{3}$%
(E) 10%

13. A man insures 80% of his property and pays a $2\frac{1}{2}$% premium amounting to $348. What is the total value of his property?
(A) $19,000
(B) $18,000
(C) $18,400
(D) $17,400
(E) $13,920

14. A clerk divided his 35-hour work week as follows: $\frac{1}{5}$ of his time was spent in sorting mail; $\frac{1}{2}$ of his time in filing letters; and $\frac{1}{7}$ of his time in reception work. The rest of his time was devoted to messenger work. The percent of time spent on messenger work by the clerk during the week was most nearly
(A) 6%
(B) 10%
(C) 14%
(D) 16%
(E) 20%

15. In a school in which 40% of the enrolled students are boys, 80% of the boys are present on a certain day. If 1152 boys are present, the total school enrollment is
(A) 1440
(B) 2880
(C) 3600
(D) 5400
(E) 5760

16. Mrs. Morris receives a salary raise from $25,000 to $27,500. Find the percent of increase.
(A) 9
(B) 10
(C) 90

(D) 15
(E) $12\frac{1}{2}$

17. The population of Stormville has increased from 80,000 to 100,000 in the last 20 years. Find the percent of increase.
(A) 20
(B) 25
(C) 80
(D) 60
(E) 10

18. The value of Super Company Stock dropped from $25 a share to $21 a share. Find the percent of decrease.
(A) 4
(B) 8
(C) 12
(D) 16
(E) 20

19. The Rubins bought their home for $30,000 and sold it for $60,000. What was the percent of increase?
(A) 100
(B) 50
(C) 200
(D) 300
(E) 150

20. During the pre-holiday rush, Martin's Department Store increased its sales staff from 150 to 200 persons. By what percent must it now decrease its sales staff to return to the usual number of salespersons?
(A) 25
(B) $33\frac{1}{3}$
(C) 20
(D) 40
(E) 75

Percent Problems—Correct Answers

1.	**(B)**	6.	**(A)**	11.	**(A)**	16.	**(B)**
2.	**(A)**	7.	**(B)**	12.	**(C)**	17.	**(B)**
3.	**(D)**	8.	**(E)**	13.	**(D)**	18.	**(D)**
4.	**(B)**	9.	**(C)**	14.	**(D)**	19.	**(A)**
5.	**(E)**	10.	**(E)**	15.	**(C)**	20.	**(A)**

Problem Solutions—Percents

1. $10\% = .10 = .1$

    Answer: **(B)** 0.1

2. $5.37\% = .0537 = \dfrac{537}{10,000}$

    Answer: **(A)** $\dfrac{537}{10,000}$

3. Base (number following "of") $= \frac{5}{6}$
    Percentage (number following "is") $= \frac{3}{4}$

    $\text{Rate} = \dfrac{\text{Percentage}}{\text{Base}}$

    $= \text{Percentage} \div \text{Base}$

    $\text{Rate} = \frac{3}{4} \div \frac{5}{6}$

    $= \frac{3}{4} \times \overset{3}{\underset{2}{\frac{6}{5}}}$

    $= \frac{9}{10}$

    $\frac{9}{10} = .9 = 90\%$

    Answer: **(D)** 90%

4. Base (number following "of") $= 24$
    Percentage (number following "is") $= 14$

    $\text{Rate} = \text{Percentage} \div \text{Base}$
    $\text{Rate} = 14 \div 24$
    $= .58\frac{1}{3}$
    $= 58\frac{1}{3}\%$

    Answer: **(B)** $58\frac{1}{3}\%$

5. 200% of $800 = 2.00 \times 800$
    $= 1600$

    Answer: **(E)** 1600

6. He must answer 80% of 35 correctly. Therefore, he may miss 20% of 35.
    20% of $35 = .20 \times 35$
    $= 7$

    Answer: **(A)** 7

7. Since $118.80 represents a 20% reduction, $118.80 = 80% of the regular price.

    $\text{Regular price} = \dfrac{\$118.80}{80\%}$
    $= \$118.80 \div .80$
    $= \$148.50$

    Answer: **(B)** $148.50

8. All the items in a circle graph total 100%. Add the figures given for housing, food, clothing, and taxes:

    $$\begin{aligned} & 26.2\% \\ & 28.4\% \\ & 12\ \% \\ +\ & 12.7\% \\ \hline & 79.3\% \end{aligned}$$

    Subtract this total from 100% to find the percent for miscellaneous items:

    $$\begin{aligned} & 100.0\% \\ -\ & 79.3\% \\ \hline & 20.7\% \end{aligned}$$

    Answer: **(E)** 20.7%

9. Price of shuttlecocks $= 24 \times \$.35 = \$\ 8.40$
    Price of rackets $= 4 \times \$2.75 = \underline{\$11.00}$
    Total price $= \$19.40$

    Discount is 30%, and $100\% - 30\% = 70\%$

    Actual cost $= 70\%$ of 19.40
    $= .70 \times 19.40$
    $= 13.58$

    Answer: **(C)** $13.58

10. Subtract weight of wood after drying from original weight of wood to find amount of moisture in wood:

    $$\begin{aligned} & 10 \\ -\ & 8 \\ \hline & 2 \text{ ounces of moisture in wood} \end{aligned}$$

    $\text{Moisture content} = \dfrac{2 \text{ ounces}}{10 \text{ ounces}} = .2 = 20\%$

    Answer: **(E)** 20%

11. Find the number of each kind of coin:

    10% of $800 = .10 \times 800 = 80$ dimes
    30% of $800 = .30 \times 800 = 240$ nickels
    60% of $800 = .60 \times 800 = 480$ quarters

    Find the value of the coins:

    $$\begin{aligned} 80 \text{ dimes} &= 80 \times .10 = \$\ \ 8.00 \\ 240 \text{ nickels} &= 240 \times .05 = \ \ 12.00 \\ 480 \text{ quarters} &= 480 \times .25 = \underline{\ 120.00} \\ & \qquad\quad \text{Total}\ \ \ \$140.00 \end{aligned}$$

    Answer: **(A)** less than $150

12. First solution contains 20% of 6 quarts of alcohol.

$$\text{Alcohol content} = .20 \times 6$$
$$= 1.2 \text{ quarts}$$

Second solution contains 60% of 4 quarts of alcohol.

$$\text{Alcohol content} = .60 \times 4$$
$$= 2.4 \text{ quarts}$$

Mixture contains: 1.2 + 2.4 = 3.6 quarts alcohol
6 + 4 = 10 quarts liquid

$$\text{Alcoholic strength of mixture} = \frac{3.6}{10} = 36\%$$

Answer: **(C)** 36%

13. $2\frac{1}{2}\%$ of insured value = $348

$$\text{Insured value} = \frac{348}{2\frac{1}{2}\%}$$
$$= 348 \div .025$$
$$= \$13,920$$

$13,920 is 80% of total value

$$\text{Total value} = \frac{\$13,920}{80\%}$$
$$= \$13,920 \div .80$$
$$= \$17,400$$

Answer: **(D)** $17,400

14. $\frac{1}{5} \times 35 = 7$ hr sorting mail
$\frac{1}{2} \times 35 = 17\frac{1}{2}$ hr filing
$\frac{1}{7} = 35 = 5$ hr reception
$29\frac{1}{2}$ hr accounted for

$35 - 29\frac{1}{2} = 5\frac{1}{2}$ hr left for messenger work

% spent on messenger work:

$$= \frac{5\frac{1}{2}}{35}$$
$$= 5\frac{1}{2} \div 35$$
$$= \frac{11}{2} \times \frac{1}{35}$$
$$= \frac{11}{70}$$
$$= .15\frac{5}{7}$$
$$= 15\frac{5}{7}\%$$

Answer: **(D)** most nearly 16%

15. 80% of the boys = 1152

$$\text{Number of boys} = \frac{1152}{80\%}$$
$$= 1152 \div .80$$
$$= 1440$$

40% of students = 1440

$$\text{Total number of students} = \frac{1440}{40\%}$$
$$= 1440 \div 40$$
$$= 3600$$

Answer: **(C)** 3600

16. Amount of increase = $2500

$$\text{Percent of increase} = \frac{\text{amount of increase}}{\text{original}}$$

$$\frac{2500}{25,000} = \frac{1}{10} = 10\%$$

Answer: **(B)** 10%

17. Amount of increase = 20,000

$$\text{Percent of increase} = \frac{20,000}{80,000} = \frac{1}{4} = 25\%$$

Answer: **(B)** 25%

18. Amount of decrease = $4

$$\text{Percent of decrease} = \frac{4}{25} = \frac{16}{100} = 16\%$$

Answer: **(D)** 16%

19. Amount of increase $30,000

$$\text{Percent of increase} = \frac{30,000}{30,000} = 1 = 100\%$$

Answer: **(A)** 100%

20. Amount of decrease = 50

$$\text{Percent of decrease} = \frac{50}{200} = \frac{1}{4} = 25\%$$

Answer: **(A)** 25%

SHORTCUTS IN MULTIPLICATION AND DIVISION

There are several shortcuts for simplifying multiplication and division. Following the description of each shortcut, practice problems are provided.

Dropping Final Zeros

1. a. A zero in a whole number is considered a "final zero" if it appears in the units column or if all columns to its right are filled with zeros. A final zero may be omitted in certain kinds of problems.

   b. In decimal numbers, a zero appearing in the extreme right column may be dropped with no effect on the solution of a problem.

2. In multiplying whole numbers, the final zero(s) may be dropped during computation and simply transferred to the answer.

Examples:

```
    2310            129
 ×   150         ×  210
   1155            129
   231             258
 346500          27090
```

```
    1760
 ×   205
    880
   352
  360800
```

Practice Problems

Solve the following multiplication problems, dropping the final zeros during computation.

1.　　230
　　× 　12

2.　　175
　　× 130

3.　　203
　　× 　14

4.　　621
　　× 140

5.　　430
　　× 360

6.　　132
　　× 310

7.　　350
　　× 　24

8.　　520
　　× 410

9.　　634
　　× 120

10.　　431
　　× 230

Solutions to Practice Problems

1.　　230
　　× 　12
　　　46
　　　23
　　2760

2.　　175
　　× 130
　　525
　　175
　22750

3.　　203
　　× 　14
　　812
　　203
　　2842
(no final zeros)

4.　　621
　　× 140
　　2484
　　621
　86940

5.　　430
　　× 360
　　258
　129
154800

6.
$$\begin{array}{r} 132 \\ \times\ 310 \\ \hline 132 \\ 396 \\ \hline 40920 \end{array}$$

7.
$$\begin{array}{r} 350 \\ \times\ 24 \\ \hline 140 \\ 70 \\ \hline 8400 \end{array}$$

8.
$$\begin{array}{r} 520 \\ \times\ 410 \\ \hline 52 \\ 208 \\ \hline 213200 \end{array}$$

9.
$$\begin{array}{r} 634 \\ \times\ 120 \\ \hline 1268 \\ 634 \\ \hline 76080 \end{array}$$

10.
$$\begin{array}{r} 431 \\ \times\ 230 \\ \hline 1293 \\ 862 \\ \hline 99130 \end{array}$$

Multiplying Whole Numbers by Decimals

3. In multiplying a whole number by a decimal number, if there are one or more final zeros in the multiplicand, move the decimal point in the multiplier to the right the same number of places as there are final zeros in the multiplicand. Then cross out the final zero(s) in the multiplicand.

Examples:
$$\begin{array}{r} 27500 \\ \times\ .15 \end{array} = \begin{array}{r} 275 \\ \times\ 15 \end{array}$$

$$\begin{array}{r} 1250 \\ \times\ .345 \end{array} = \begin{array}{r} 125 \\ \times\ 3.45 \end{array}$$

Practice Problems

Rewrite the following problems, dropping the final zeros and moving decimal points the appro-

priate number of spaces. Then compute the answers.

1.
$$\begin{array}{r} 2400 \\ \times\ .02 \end{array}$$

2.
$$\begin{array}{r} 620 \\ \times\ .04 \end{array}$$

3.
$$\begin{array}{r} 800 \\ \times\ .005 \end{array}$$

4.
$$\begin{array}{r} 600 \\ \times\ .002 \end{array}$$

5.
$$\begin{array}{r} 340 \\ \times\ .08 \end{array}$$

6.
$$\begin{array}{r} 480 \\ \times\ .4 \end{array}$$

7.
$$\begin{array}{r} 400 \\ \times\ .04 \end{array}$$

8.
$$\begin{array}{r} 5300 \\ \times\ .5 \end{array}$$

9.
$$\begin{array}{r} 930 \\ \times\ .3 \end{array}$$

10.
$$\begin{array}{r} 9000 \\ \times\ .001 \end{array}$$

Solutions to Practice Problems

The rewritten problems are shown, along with the answers.

1.
$$\begin{array}{r} 24 \\ \times\ 2 \\ \hline 48 \end{array}$$

2.
$$\begin{array}{r} 62 \\ \times\ .4 \\ \hline 24.8 \end{array}$$

3.
$$\begin{array}{r} 8 \\ \times\ .5 \\ \hline 4.0 \end{array}$$

4.
$$\begin{array}{r} 6 \\ \times\ .2 \\ \hline 1.2 \end{array}$$

5.
$$\begin{array}{r} 34 \\ \times\ .8 \\ \hline 27.2 \end{array}$$

6.
$$\begin{array}{r} 48 \\ \times\ 4 \\ \hline 192 \end{array}$$

7.
$$\begin{array}{r} 4 \\ \times\ 4 \\ \hline 16 \end{array}$$

8.
$$\begin{array}{r} 530 \\ \times\ 5 \\ \hline 2650 \end{array}$$

9.
$$\begin{array}{r} 93 \\ \times\ 3 \\ \hline 279 \end{array}$$

10.
$$\begin{array}{r} 9 \\ \times\ 1 \\ \hline 9 \end{array}$$

Dividing by Whole Numbers

4. a. When there are final zeros in the divisor but no final zeros in the dividend, move the decimal point in the dividend to the left as many places as there are final zeros in the divisor, then omit the final zeros.

    Example: $2700.\overline{)\ 37523.} = 27.\overline{)\ 375.23}$

    b. When there are fewer final zeros in the divisor than there are in the dividend, drop the same number of final zeros from the dividend as there are final zeros in the divisor.

Example: $250.\overline{)\ 45300.} = 25.\overline{)\ 4530.}$

c. When there are more final zeros in the divisor than there are in the dividend, move the decimal point in the dividend to the left as many places as there are final zeros in the divisor, then omit the final zeros.

Example: $2300.\overline{)\ 690.} = 23.\overline{)\ 6.9}$

d. When there are no final zeros in the divisor, no zeros can be dropped in the dividend.

Example: $23.\overline{)\ 690.} = 23.\overline{)\ 690.}$

Practice Problems

Rewrite the following problems, dropping the final zeros and moving the decimal points the appropriate number of places. Then compute the quotients.

1. $600.\overline{)\ 72.}$

2. $310.\overline{)\ 6200.}$

3. $7600\overline{)\ 1520.}$

4. $46.\overline{)\ 920.}$

5. $11.0\overline{)\ 220.}$

6. $700.\overline{)\ 84.}$

7. $90.\overline{)\ 8100.}$

8. $8100.\overline{)\ 1620.}$

9. $25.\overline{)\ 5250.}$

10. $41.0\overline{)\ 820.}$

11. $800.\overline{)\ 96.}$

12. $650.\overline{)\ 1300.}$

13. $5500.\overline{)\ 110.}$

14. $36.\overline{)\ 720.}$

15. $87.0\overline{)\ 1740.}$

Rewritten Practice Problems

1. 6.) .72

2. 31.) 620.

3. 76.) 15.2

4. 46.) 920.

5. 11.) 220.

6. 7.) .84

7. 9.) 810.

8. 81.) 16.2

9. 25.) 5250.

10. 41.) 820.

11. 8.) .96

12. 65.) 130.

13. 55.) 1.1

14. 36.) 720.

15. 87.) 1740.

Solutions to Practice Problems

1.
$$\begin{array}{r} .12 \\ 6.\overline{)\,.72} \end{array}$$

2.
$$\begin{array}{r} 20 \\ 31.\overline{)\,620.} \\ \underline{62} \\ 00 \end{array}$$

3.
$$\begin{array}{r} .2 \\ 76.\overline{)\,15.2} \\ \underline{15\ 2} \\ 0\ 0 \end{array}$$

4.
$$\begin{array}{r} 20 \\ 46.\overline{)\,920.} \\ \underline{92} \\ 00 \end{array}$$

5.
$$\begin{array}{r} 20 \\ 11.\overline{)\,220.} \\ \underline{22} \\ 00 \end{array}$$

6.
$$\begin{array}{r} .12 \\ 7.\overline{)\,.84} \end{array}$$

7.
$$\begin{array}{r} 90 \\ 9.\overline{)\,810.} \\ \underline{81} \\ 00 \end{array}$$

8.
$$\begin{array}{r} .2 \\ 81.\overline{)\,16.2} \\ \underline{16\ 2} \\ 0\ 0 \end{array}$$

9.
$$\begin{array}{r} 210 \\ 25.\overline{)\,5250.} \\ \underline{50} \\ 25 \\ \underline{25} \\ 00 \end{array}$$

10.
$$\begin{array}{r} 20 \\ 41.\overline{)\,820.} \\ \underline{82} \\ 00 \end{array}$$

11.
$$\begin{array}{r} .12 \\ 8.\overline{)\,.96} \end{array}$$

12.
$$\begin{array}{r} 2 \\ 65.\overline{)\,130.} \\ \underline{130} \\ 00 \end{array}$$

13.
$$\begin{array}{r} .02 \\ 55.\overline{)\,1.10} \\ \underline{1\ 10} \\ 00 \end{array}$$

14.
$$\begin{array}{r} 20 \\ 36.\overline{)\,720.} \\ \underline{72} \\ 00 \end{array}$$

15.
$$\begin{array}{r} 20 \\ 87.\overline{)\,1740.} \\ \underline{174} \\ 00 \end{array}$$

Division by Multiplication

5. Instead of dividing by a particular number, the same answer is obtained by multiplying by the equivalent multiplier.

6. To find the equivalent multiplier of a given divisor, divide 1 by the divisor.

    Example: The equivalent multiplier of $12\frac{1}{2}$ is $1 \div 12\frac{1}{2}$ or .08. The division problem $100 \div 12\frac{1}{2}$ may be more easily solved as the multiplication problem $100 \times .08$. The answer will be the same. This can be helpful when you are estimating answers.

7. Common divisors and their equivalent multipliers are shown below:

Divisor	Equivalent Multiplier
$11\frac{1}{9}$	.09
$12\frac{1}{2}$	.08
$14\frac{2}{7}$	.07
$16\frac{2}{3}$	.06
20	.05
25	.04
$33\frac{1}{3}$	.03
50	.02

8. A divisor may be multiplied or divided by any power of 10, and the only change in its equivalent multiplier will be in the placement of the decimal point, as may be seen in the following table:

Divisor	Equivalent Multiplier
.025	40.
.25	4.
2.5	.4
25.	.04
250.	.004
2500.	.0004

Practice Problems

Rewrite and solve each of the following problems by using equivalent multipliers. Drop the final zeros where appropriate.

1. $100 \div 16\frac{2}{3} =$

2. $200 \div 25 =$

3. $300 \div 33\frac{1}{3} =$

4. $250 \div 50 =$

5. $80 \div 12\frac{1}{2} =$

6. $800 \div 14\frac{2}{7} =$

7. $620 \div 20 =$

8. $500 \div 11\frac{1}{9} =$

9. $420 \div 16\frac{2}{3} =$

10. $1200 \div 33\frac{1}{3} =$

11. $955 \div 50 =$

12. $900 \div 33\frac{1}{3} =$

13. $275 \div 12\frac{1}{2} =$

14. $625 \div 25 =$

15. $244 \div 20 =$

16. $350 \div 16\frac{2}{3} =$

17. $400 \div 33\frac{1}{3} =$

18. $375 \div 25 =$

19. $460 \div 20 =$

20. $250 \div 12\frac{1}{2} =$

Solutions to Practice Problems

The rewritten problems and their solutions appear below:

1. $100 \times .06 = 1 \times 6 = 6$

2. $200 \times .04 = 2 \times 4 = 8$

3. $300 \times .03 = 3 \times 3 = 9$

4. $250 \times .02 = 25 \times .2 = 5$

5. $80 \times .08 = 8 \times .8 = 6.4$

6. $800 \times .07 = 8 \times 7 = 56$

7. $620 \times .05 = 62 \times .5 = 31$

8. $500 \times .09 = 5 \times 9 = 45$

9. $420 \times .06 = 42 \times .6 = 25.2$

10. $1200 \times .03 = 12 \times 3 = 36$

11. $955 \times .02 = 19.1$

12. $900 \times .03 = 9 \times 3 = 27$

13. $275 \times .08 = 22$

14. $625 \times .04 = 25$

15. $244 \times .05 = 12.2$

16. $350 \times .06 = 35 \times .6 = 21$

17. $400 \times .03 = 4 \times 3 = 12$

18. $375 \times .04 = 15$

19. $460 \times .05 = 46 \times .5 = 23$

20. $250 \times .08 = 25 \times .8 = 20$

Multiplication by Division

9. Just as some division problems are made easier by changing them to equivalent multiplication problems, certain multiplication problems are made easier by changing them to equivalent division problems.

10. Instead of arriving at an answer by multiplying by a particular number, the same answer is obtained by dividing by the equivalent divisor.

11. To find the equivalent divisor of a given multiplier, divide 1 by the multiplier.

12. Common multipliers and their equivalent divisors are shown below:

Multiplier	Equivalent Divisor
$11\frac{1}{9}$	.09
$12\frac{1}{2}$	.08
$14\frac{2}{7}$	.07
$16\frac{2}{3}$	.06
20	.05
25	.04
$33\frac{1}{3}$	.03
50	.02

Notice that the multiplier-equivalent divisor pairs are the same as the divisor-equivalent multiplier pairs given earlier.

Practice Problems

Rewrite and solve each of the following problems by using division. Drop the final zeros where appropriate.

1. $77 \times 14\frac{2}{7} =$

2. $81 \times 11\frac{1}{9} =$

3. $475 \times 20 =$

4. $42 \times 50 =$

5. $36 \times 33\frac{1}{3} =$

6. $96 \times 12\frac{1}{2} =$

7. $126 \times 16\frac{2}{3} =$

8. $48 \times 25 =$

9. $33 \times 33\frac{1}{3} =$

10. $84 \times 14\frac{2}{7} =$

11. $99 \times 11\frac{1}{9} =$

12. $126 \times 33\frac{1}{3} =$

13. $168 \times 12\frac{1}{2} =$

14. $654 \times 16\frac{2}{3} =$

15. $154 \times 14\frac{2}{7} =$

16. $5250 \times 50 =$

17. $324 \times 25 =$

18. $625 \times 20 =$

19. $198 \times 11\frac{1}{9} =$

20. $224 \times 14\frac{2}{7} =$

Solutions to Practice Problems

The rewritten problems and their solutions appear below:

1. $.07 \overline{)\ 77.} = 7 \overline{)\ 7700.} \quad \overset{1100.}{}$

2. $.09 \overline{)\ 81.} = 9 \overline{)\ 8100.} \quad \overset{900.}{}$

3. $.05 \overline{)\ 475.} = 5 \overline{)\ 47500.} \quad \overset{9500.}{}$

4. $.02 \overline{)\ 42.} = 2 \overline{)\ 4200.} \quad \overset{2100.}{}$

5. $.03 \overline{)\ 36.} = 3 \overline{)\ 3600.} \quad \overset{1200.}{}$

6. $.08 \overline{)\ 96.} = 8 \overline{)\ 9600.} \quad \overset{1200.}{}$

7. $.06 \overline{)\ 126.} = 6 \overline{)\ 12600.} \quad \overset{2100.}{}$

8. $.04 \overline{)\ 48.} = 4 \overline{)\ 4800.} \quad \overset{1200.}{}$

9. $.03 \overline{)\ 33.} = 3 \overline{)\ 3300.} \quad \overset{1100.}{}$

10. $.07 \overline{)\ 84.} = 7 \overline{)\ 8400.} \quad \overset{1200.}{}$

11. $.09 \overline{)\ 99.} = 9 \overline{)\ 9900.} \quad \overset{1100.}{}$

12. $.03 \overline{)\ 126.} = 3 \overline{)\ 12600.} \quad \overset{4200.}{}$

13. $.08 \overline{)\ 168.} = 8 \overline{)\ 16800.} \quad \overset{2100.}{}$

14. $.06 \overline{)\ 654.} = 6 \overline{)\ 65400.} \quad \overset{10900.}{}$

15. $.07 \overline{)\ 154.} = 7 \overline{)\ 15400.} \quad \overset{2200.}{}$

16. $.02 \overline{)\ 5250.} = 2 \overline{)\ 525000.} \quad \overset{262500.}{}$

17. $.04 \overline{)\ 324.} = 4 \overline{)\ 32400.} \quad \overset{8100.}{}$

18. $.05 \overline{)\ 625.} = 5 \overline{)\ 62500.} \quad \overset{12500.}{}$

19. $.09 \overline{)\ 198.} = 9 \overline{)\ 19800.} \quad \overset{2200.}{}$

20. $.07 \overline{)\ 224.} = 7 \overline{)\ 22400.} \quad \overset{3200.}{}$

AVERAGES

1. a. The term average can technically refer to a variety of mathematical ideas, but on the test it refers to the **arithmetic mean.** It is found by adding the numbers given and then dividing this sum by the number of items being averaged.

Illustration: Find the arithmetic mean of 2, 8, 5, 9, 6, and 12.

SOLUTION: There are 6 numbers.

Arithmetic mean $= \dfrac{2 + 8 + 5 + 9 + 6 + 12}{6}$

$$= \frac{42}{6}$$

$$= 7$$

Answer: The arithmetic mean is 7.

b. If a problem calls for simply the average or the mean, it is referring to the arithmetic mean.

2. If a group of numbers is arranged in order, the middle number is called the **median.** If there is no single middle number (this occurs when there is an even number of items), the median is found by computing the arithmetic mean of the two middle numbers.

Example: The median of 6, 8, 10, 12, and 14 is 10.

Example: The median of 6, 8, 10, 12, 14, and 16 is the arithmetic mean of 10 and 12.

$$\frac{10 + 12}{2} = \frac{22}{2} = 11.$$

3. The **mode** of a group of numbers is the number that appears most often.

Example: The mode of 10, 5, 7, 9, 12, 5, 10, 5 and 9 is 5.

4. When some numbers among terms to be averaged occur more than once, they must be given the appropriate weight. For example, if a student received four grades of 80 and one of 90, his average would not be the average of 80 and 90, but rather the average of 80, 80, 80, 80, and 90.

To obtain the average of quantities that are weighted:

a. Set up a table listing the quantities, their respective weights, and their respective values.

b. Multiply the value of each quantity by its respective weight.

c. Add up these products.

d. Add up the weights.

e. Divide the sum of the products by the sum of the weights.

Illustration: Assume that the weights for the following subjects are: English 3, History 2, Mathematics 2, Foreign Languages 2, and Art 1. What would be the average of a student whose marks are: English 80, History 85, Algebra 84, Spanish 82, and Art 90?

SOLUTION:

Subject	Weight	Mark
English	3	80
History	2	85
Algebra	2	84
Spanish	2	82
Art	1	90

English	3 × 80 =	240
History	2 × 85 =	170
Algebra	2 × 84 =	168
Spanish	2 × 82 =	164
Art	1 × 90 =	90
		832

Sum of the weights: 3 + 2 + 2 + 2 + 1 = 10

832 ÷ 10 = 83.2

Answer: Average = 83.2

Note: On the test, you might go directly to a list of the weighted amounts, here totalling 832, and divide by the number of weights; or you might set up a single equation.

Illustration: Mr. Martin drove for 6 hours at an average rate of 50 miles per hour and for 2 hours at an average rate of 60 miles per hour. Find his average rate for the entire trip.

SOLUTION:

$$\frac{6(50) + 2(60)}{8} = \frac{300 + 120}{8} = \frac{420}{8} = 52\tfrac{1}{2}$$

Answer: $52\tfrac{1}{2}$

Since he drove many more hours at 50 miles per hour than at 60 miles per hour, his average rate should be closer to 50 than to 60, which it is. In general, average rate can always be found by dividing the total distance covered by the time spent traveling.

Practice Problems Involving Averages

1. The arithmetic mean of 73.8, 92.2, 64.7, 43.8, 56.5, and 46.4 is
   (A) 60.6
   (B) 62.9
   (C) 64.48
   (D) 75.48
   (E) 82.9

2. The median of the numbers 8, 5, 7, 5, 9, 9, 1, 8, 10, 5, and 10 is
   (A) 5
   (B) 7
   (C) 8
   (D) 9
   (E) 10

3. The mode of the numbers 16, 15, 17, 12, 15, 15, 18, 19, and 18 is
   (A) 15
   (B) 16
   (C) 17
   (D) 18
   (E) 19

4. A clerk filed 73 forms on Monday, 85 forms on Tuesday, 54 on Wednesday, 92 on Thursday, and 66 on Friday. What was the average number of forms filed per day?
   (A) 60
   (B) 72
   (C) 74
   (D) 92
   (E) 370

5. The grades received on a test by twenty students were: 100, 55, 75, 80, 65, 65, 85, 90, 80, 45, 40, 50, 85, 85, 85, 80, 80, 70, 65, and 60. The average of these grades is
   (A) 70
   (B) 72
   (C) 77
   (D) 80
   (E) 100

6. A buyer purchased 75 six-inch rulers costing 15¢ each, 100 one-foot rulers costing 30¢ each, and 50 one-yard rulers costing 72¢ each. What was the average price per ruler?
   (A) $26\frac{1}{8}$¢
   (B) $34\frac{1}{3}$¢
   (C) 39¢
   (D) 42¢
   (E) $77\frac{1}{4}$¢

7. What is the average of a student who received 90 in English, 84 in Algebra, 75 in French, and 76 in Music, if the subjects have the following weights: English 4, Algebra 3, French 3, and Music 1?
   (A) 81

(B) $81\frac{1}{2}$
(C) 82
(D) $82\frac{1}{2}$
(E) 83

Questions 8–11 refer to the following information:

A census shows that on a certain block the number of children in each family is 3, 4, 4, 0, 1, 2, 0, 2, and 2, respectively.

8. Find the average number of children per family.
   (A) 4
   (B) 3
   (C) $3\frac{1}{2}$
   (D) 2
   (E) $1\frac{1}{2}$

9. Find the median number of children.
   (A) 1
   (B) 2
   (C) 3
   (D) 4
   (E) 5

10. Find the mode of the number of children.
    (A) 0
    (B) 1
    (C) 2
    (D) 3
    (E) 4

Averages Problems—Correct Answers

1.	**(B)**	6.	**(B)**
2.	**(C)**	7.	**(E)**
3.	**(A)**	8.	**(D)**
4.	**(C)**	9.	**(B)**
5.	**(B)**	10.	**(C)**

Problem Solutions—Averages

1. Find the sum of the values:

   73.8 + 92.2 + 64.7 + 43.8 + 56.5 + 46.4 = 377.4

   There are 6 values.

   $$\text{Arithmetic mean} = \frac{377.4}{6} = 62.9$$

   Answer: **(B)** 62.9

2. Arrange the numbers in order:

$$1, 5, 5, 5, 7, 8, 8, 9, 9, 10, 10$$

The middle number, or median, is 8.

Answer: **(C)** 8

3. The mode is that number appearing most frequently. The number 15 appears three times.

Answer: **(A)** 15

4. Average $= \dfrac{73 + 85 + 54 + 92 + 66}{5}$

$= \dfrac{370}{5}$

$= 74$

Answer: **(C)** 74

5. Sum of the grades $= 1440$.

$$\dfrac{1440}{20} = 72$$

Answer: **(B)** 72

6. $75 \times 15¢ = 1125¢$
   $100 \times 30¢ = 3000¢$
   $\underline{50} \times 72¢ = \underline{3600¢}$
   $225 \qquad\qquad 7725¢$

   $\dfrac{7725¢}{225} = 34\frac{1}{3}¢$

Answer: **(B)** $34\frac{1}{3}¢$

7.
Subject	Grade	Weight
English	90	4
Algebra	84	3
French	75	3
Music	76	1

$(90 \times 4) + (84 \times 3) + (75 \times 3) + (76 \times 1)$
$360 + 252 + 225 + 76 = 913$
Weight $= 4 + 3 + 3 + 1 = 11$
$913 \div 11 = 83$ average

Answer: **(E)** 83

8. Average $= \dfrac{3 + 4 + 4 + 0 + 1 + 2 + 0 + 2 + 2}{9}$

$= \dfrac{18}{9}$

$= 2$

Answer: **(D)** 2

9. Arrange the numbers in order:

$$0, 0, 1, 2, 2, 2, 3, 4, 4$$

Of the 9 numbers, the fifth (middle) number is 2.

Answer: **(B)** 2

10. The number appearing most often is 2.

Answer: **(C)** 2

RATIO AND PROPORTION

Ratio

1. A **ratio** expresses the relationship between two (or more) quantities in terms of numbers. The mark used to indicate ratio is the colon (:) and is read "to."

   Example: The ratio 2:3 is read "2 to 3."

2. A ratio also represents division. Therefore, any ratio of two terms may be written as a fraction, and any fraction may be written as a ratio.

   Example: $3:4 = \frac{3}{4}$
   $\frac{5}{6} = 5:6$

3. To simplify any complicated ratio of two terms containing fractions, decimals, or percents:

   a. Divide the first term by the second.

   b. Write as a fraction in lowest terms.

   c. Write the fraction as a ratio.

   Illustration: Simplify the ratio $\frac{5:7}{6:8}$

   SOLUTION: $\frac{5}{6} \div \frac{7}{8} = \frac{5}{6} \times \frac{8}{7} = \frac{20}{21}$
   $\frac{20}{21} = 20:21$

   Answer: 20:21

4. To solve problems in which the ratio is given:

   a. Add the terms in the ratio.

   b. Divide the total amount that is to be put into a ratio by this sum.

c. Multiply each term in the ratio by this quotient.

Illustration: The sum of $360 is to be divided among three people according to the ratio 3:4:5. How much does each one receive?

SOLUTION: $3 + 4 + 5 = 12$
$$\$360 \div 12 = \$30$$
$$\$30 \times 3 = \$90$$
$$\$30 \times 4 = \$120$$
$$\$30 \times 5 = \$150$$

Answer: The money is divided thus: $90, $120, $150.

Proportion

5. a. A **proportion** indicates the equality of two ratios.

   Example: 2:4 = 5:10 is a proportion. This is read "2 is to 4 as 5 is to 10."

   b. In a proportion, the two outside terms are called the **extremes,** and the two inside terms are called the **means.**

   Example: In the proportion 2:4 = 5:10, 2 and 10 are the extremes, and 4 and 5 are the means.

   c. Proportions are often written in fractional form.

   Example: The proportion 2:4 = 5:10 may be written $\frac{2}{4} = \frac{5}{10}$.

   d. In any proportion, the product of the means equals the product of the extremes. If the proportion is a fractional form, the products may be found by cross-multiplication.

   Example: In $\frac{2}{4} = \frac{5}{10}$, $4 \times 5 = 2 \times 10$.

   e. The product of the extremes divided by one mean equals the other mean; the product of the means divided by one extreme equals the other extreme.

6. Many problems in which three terms are given and one term is unknown can be solved by using proportions. To solve such problems:

a. Formulate the proportion very carefully according to the facts given. (If any term is misplaced, the solution will be incorrect.) Any symbol may be written in place of the missing term.

b. Determine by inspection whether the means or the extremes are known. Multiply the pair that has both terms given.

c. Divide this product by the third term given to find the unknown term.

Illustration: The scale on a map shows that 2 cm represents 30 miles of actual length. What is the actual length of a road that is represented by 7 cm on the map?

SOLUTION: The map lengths and the actual lengths are in proportion—that is, they have equal ratios. If m stands for the unknown length, the proportion is:

$$\frac{2}{7} = \frac{30}{m}$$

As the proportion is written, m is an extreme and is equal to the product of the means, divided by the other extreme:

$$m = \frac{7 \times 30}{2}$$
$$m = \frac{210}{2}$$
$$m = 105$$

Answer: 7 cm on the map represents 105 miles.

Illustration: If a money bag containing 500 nickels weighs 6 pounds, how much will a money bag containing 1600 nickels weigh?

SOLUTION: The weights of the bags and the number of coins in them are proportional. Suppose w represents the unknown weight. Then

$$\frac{6}{w} = \frac{500}{1600}$$

The unknown is a mean and is equal to the product of the extremes, divided by the other mean:

$$w = \frac{6 \times 1600}{500}$$
$$w = 19.2$$

Answer: A bag containing 1600 nickels weighs 19.2 pounds.

Practice Problems Involving Ratio and Proportion

1. The ratio of 24 to 64 is
   - (A) 1:64
   - (B) 1:24
   - (C) 20:100
   - (D) 24:100
   - (E) 3:8

2. The Baltimore Colts won 8 games and lost 3. The ratio of games won to games played is
   - (A) 11:8
   - (B) 8:3
   - (C) 8:11
   - (D) 3:8
   - (E) 3:11

3. The ratio of $\frac{1}{4}$ to $\frac{3}{5}$ is
   - (A) 1 to 3
   - (B) 3 to 20
   - (C) 5 to 12
   - (D) 3 to 4
   - (E) 5 to 4

4. If there are 16 boys and 12 girls in a class, the ratio of the number of girls to the number of children in the class is
   - (A) 3 to 4
   - (B) 3 to 7
   - (C) 4 to 7
   - (D) 4 to 3
   - (E) 7 to 4

5. 259 is to 37 as
   - (A) 5 is to 1
   - (B) 63 is to 441
   - (C) 84 is to 12
   - (D) 130 is to 19
   - (E) 25 is to 4

6. 2 dozen cans of dog food at the rate of 3 cans for $1.45 would cost
   - (A) $10.05
   - (B) $10.20
   - (C) $11.20

- (D) $11.60
- (E) $11.75

7. A snapshot measures $2\frac{1}{2}$ inches by $1\frac{7}{8}$ inches. It is to be enlarged so that the longer dimension will be 4 inches. The length of the enlarged shorter dimension will be
   - (A) $2\frac{1}{2}$ in
   - (B) 3 in
   - (C) $3\frac{3}{8}$ in
   - (D) 4 in
   - (E) 5 in

8. Men's white handkerchiefs cost $2.29 for 3. The cost per dozen handkerchiefs is
   - (A) $27.48
   - (B) $13.74
   - (C) $9.16
   - (D) $6.87
   - (E) $4.58

9. A certain pole casts a shadow 24 feet long. At the same time another pole 3 feet high casts a shadow 4 feet long. How high is the first pole, given that the heights and shadows are in proportion?
   - (A) 18 ft
   - (B) 19 ft
   - (C) 20 ft
   - (D) 21 ft
   - (E) 24 ft

10. The actual length represented by $3\frac{1}{2}$ inches on a drawing having a scale of $\frac{1}{8}$ inch to the foot is
    - (A) 3.5 ft
    - (B) 7 ft
    - (C) 21 ft
    - (D) 28 ft
    - (E) 120 ft

11. Aluminum bronze consists of copper and aluminum, usually in the ratio of 10:1 by weight. If an object made of this alloy weighs 77 lb, how many pounds of aluminum does it contain?
    - (A) 0.7
    - (B) 7.0
    - (C) 7.7
    - (D) 70.7
    - (E) 77.0

12. It costs 31 cents a square foot to lay vinyl flooring. To lay 180 square feet of flooring, it will cost
    (A) $16.20
    (B) $18.60
    (C) $55.80
    (D) $62.00
    (E) $180.00

13. If a per diem worker earns $352 in 16 days, the amount that he will earn in 117 days is most nearly
    (A) $3050
    (B) $2575
    (C) $2285
    (D) $2080
    (E) $1170

14. Assuming that on a blueprint $\frac{1}{8}$ inch equals 12 inches of actual length, the actual length in inches of a steel bar represented on the blueprint by a line $3\frac{3}{4}$ inches long is
    (A) $3\frac{3}{4}$
    (B) 30
    (C) 36
    (D) 360
    (E) 450

15. A, B, and C invested $9,000, $7,000 and $6,000, respectively. Their profits were to be divided according to the ratio of their investment. If B uses his share of the firm's profit of $825 to pay a personal debt of $230, how much will he have left?
    (A) $30.50
    (B) $32.50
    (C) $34.50
    (D) $36.50
    (E) $37.50

Ratio and Proportion Problems—Correct Answers

1.	**(E)**	6.	**(D)**	11.	**(B)**
2.	**(C)**	7.	**(B)**	12.	**(C)**
3.	**(C)**	8.	**(C)**	13.	**(B)**
4.	**(B)**	9.	**(A)**	14.	**(D)**
5.	**(C)**	10.	**(D)**	15.	**(B)**

Problem Solutions—Ratio and Proportion

1. The ratio 24 to 64 may be written 24:64 or $\frac{24}{64}$. In fraction form, the ratio can be reduced:

   $$\frac{24}{64} = \frac{3}{8} \quad \text{or} \quad 3:8$$

   Answer: **(E)** 3:8

2. The number of games played was $3 + 8 = 11$. The ratio of games won to games played is 8:11.

   Answer: **(C)** 8:11

3. $\frac{1 \cdot 3}{4 \cdot 5} = \frac{1}{4} \div \frac{3}{5}$
   $= \frac{1}{4} \times \frac{5}{3}$
   $= \frac{5}{12}$
   $= 5:12$

   Answer: **(C)** 5 to 12

4. There are $16 + 12 = 28$ children in the class. The ratio of number of girls to number of children is 12:28.

   $$\frac{12}{28} = \frac{3}{7}$$

   Answer: **(B)** 3 to 7

5. The ratio $\frac{259}{37}$ reduces by 37 to $\frac{7}{1}$. The ratio $\frac{84}{12}$ also reduces to $\frac{7}{1}$. Therefore, $\frac{259}{37} = \frac{84}{12}$ is a proportion.

   Answer: **(C)** 84 is to 12

6. The number of cans are proportional to the price. Let p represent the unknown price:

   Then $\quad \dfrac{3}{24} = \dfrac{1.45}{p}$

   $$p = \frac{1.45 \times 24}{3}$$

   $$p = \frac{34.80}{3}$$

   $$= \$11.60$$

   Answer: **(D)** $11.60

7. Let s represent the unknown shorter dimension:

$$\frac{2\frac{1}{2}}{4} = \frac{1\frac{7}{8}}{s}$$

$$s = \frac{4 \times 1\frac{7}{8}}{2\frac{1}{2}}$$

$$= \frac{\overset{1}{\cancel{4}} \times \frac{15}{8}\,\underset{2}{}}{2\frac{1}{2}}$$

$$= \tfrac{15}{2} \div 2\frac{1}{2}$$
$$= \tfrac{15}{2} \div \tfrac{5}{2}$$
$$= \tfrac{15}{2} \times \tfrac{2}{5}$$
$$= 3$$

Answer: **(B)** 3 in

8. If p is the cost per dozen (12):

$$\frac{3}{12} = \frac{2.29}{p}$$

$$p = \frac{\overset{4}{\cancel{12}} \times 2.29}{\underset{1}{\cancel{3}}}$$

$$= 9.16$$

Answer: **(C)** $9.16

9. If f is the height of the first pole, the proportion is:

$$\frac{f}{24} = \frac{3}{4}$$

$$f = \frac{\overset{6}{\cancel{24}} \times 3}{\underset{1}{\cancel{4}}}$$

$$= 18$$

Answer: **(A)** 18 ft

10. If y is the unknown length:

$$\frac{3\frac{1}{2}}{\frac{1}{8}} = \frac{y}{1}$$

$$y = \frac{3\frac{1}{2} \times 1}{\frac{1}{8}}$$

$$= 3\frac{1}{2} \div \tfrac{1}{8}$$
$$= \tfrac{7}{2} \times \tfrac{8}{1}$$
$$= 28$$

Answer: **(D)** 28 ft

11. Since only two parts of a proportion are known (77 is total weight), the problem must be solved by the ratio method. The ratio 10:1 means that if the alloy were separated into equal parts, 10 of those parts

would be copper and 1 would be alumninum, for a total of 10 + 1 = 11 parts.

$$77 \div 11 = 7 \text{ lb per part}$$

The alloy has 1 part aluminum.

$$7 \times 1 = 7 \text{ lb aluminum}$$

Answer: **(B)** 7.0

12. The cost (c) is proportional to the number of square feet.

$$\frac{\$.31}{c} = \frac{1}{180}$$

$$c = \frac{\$.31 \times 180}{1}$$

$$= \$55.80$$

Answer: **(C)** $55.80

13. The amount earned is proportional to the number of days worked. If a is the unknown amount:

$$\frac{\$352}{a} = \frac{16}{117}$$

$$a = \frac{\$352 \times 117}{16}$$

$$a = \$2574$$

Answer: **(B)** $2575

14. If n is the unknown length:

$$\frac{\frac{1}{8}}{3\frac{3}{4}} = \frac{12}{n}$$

$$n = \frac{12 \times 3\frac{3}{4}}{\frac{1}{8}}$$

$$= \frac{\overset{3}{\cancel{12}} \times \frac{15}{4}\,\underset{1}{}}{\frac{1}{8}}$$

$$= \frac{45}{\frac{1}{8}}$$

$$= 45 \div \tfrac{1}{8}$$
$$= 45 \times \tfrac{8}{1}$$
$$= 360$$

Answer: **(D)** 360

15. The ratio of investment is:

$$9,000:7,000:6,000 \quad \text{or} \quad 9:7:6$$

$$9 + 7 + 6 = 22$$
$$\$825 \div 22 = \$37.50 \text{ each share of profit}$$
$$7 \times \$37.50 = \$262.50 \text{ B's share of profit}$$

$$\begin{array}{r} \$262.50 \\ -\ 230.00 \\ \hline \$\ 32.50 \end{array} \text{ amount B has left}$$

Answer: **(B)** $32.50

WORK AND TANK PROBLEMS

Work Problems

1. a. In work problems, there are three items involved: the number of people working, the time, and the amount of work done.

    b. The number of people working is directly proportional to the amount of work done; that is, the more people on the job, the more the work that will be done, and vice versa.

    c. The number of people working is inversely proportional to the time; that is, the more people on the job, the less time it will take to finish it, and vice versa.

    d. The time expended on a job is directly proportional to the amount of work done; that is, the more time expended on a job, the more work that is done, and vice versa.

Work at Equal Rates

2. a. When given the time required by a number of people working at equal rates to complete a job, multiply the number of people by their time to find the time required by one person to do the complete job.

    Example: If it takes 4 people working at equal rates 30 days to finish a job, then one person will take 30 × 4 or 120 days.

    b. When given the time required by one person to complete a job, to find the time required by a number of people working at equal rates to complete the same job, divide the time by the number of people.

    Example: If 1 person can do a job in 20 days, it will take 4 people working at equal rates 20 ÷ 4 or 5 days to finish the job.

3. To solve problems involving people who work at equal rates:

    a. Multiply the number of people by their

time to find the time required by 1 person.

    b. Divide this time by the number of people required.

Illustration: Four workers can do a job in 48 days. How long will it take 3 workers to finish the same job?

SOLUTION: One worker can do the job in 48 × 4 or 192 days.
3 workers can do the job in 192 ÷ 3 = 64 days.

Answer: It would take 3 workers 64 days.

4. In some work problems, the rates, though unequal, can be equalized by comparison. To solve such problems:

    a. Determine from the facts given how many equal rates there are.

    b. Multiply the number of equal rates by the time given.

    c. Divide this by the number of equal rates.

Illustration: Three workers can do a job in 12 days. Two of the workers work twice as fast as the third. How long would it take one of the faster workers to do the job himself?

SOLUTION: There are two fast workers and one slow worker. Therefore, there are actually five slow workers working at equal rates.

1 slow worker will take 12 × 5 or 60 days.
1 fast worker = 2 slow workers; therefore, he will take 60 ÷ 2 or 30 days to complete the job.

Answer: It will take 1 fast worker 30 days to complete the job.

5. Unit time is expressed in terms of 1 minute, 1 hour, 1 day, etc.

6. The rate at which a person works is the amount of work he can do in **unit time.**

7. If given the time it will take one person to do a job, then the reciprocal of the time is the part done in unit time.

   Example: If a worker can do a job in 6 days, then he can do $\frac{1}{6}$ of the work in 1 day.

8. The reciprocal of the work done in unit time is the time it will take to do the complete job.

   Example: If a worker can do $\frac{3}{7}$ of the work in 1 day, then he can do the whole job in $\frac{7}{3}$ or $2\frac{1}{3}$ days.

9. If given the various times at which each of a number of people can complete a job, to find the time it will take to do the job if all work together:

   a. Invert the time of each to find how much each can do in unit time.

   b. Add these reciprocals to find what part all working together can do in unit time.

   c. Invert this sum to find the time it will take all of them together to do the whole job.

   Illustration: If it takes A 3 days to dig a certain ditch, whereas B can dig it in 6 days, and C in 12, how long would it take all three to do the job?

   SOLUTION: A can do it in 3 days; therefore, he can do $\frac{1}{3}$ in one day. B can do it in 6 days; therefore, he can do $\frac{1}{6}$ in one day. C can do it in 12 days; therefore, he can do $\frac{1}{12}$ in one day.

   $$\frac{1}{3} + \frac{1}{6} + \frac{1}{12} = \frac{7}{12}$$

   A, B, and C can do $\frac{7}{12}$ of the work in one day; therefore, it will take them $\frac{12}{7}$ or $1\frac{5}{7}$ days to complete the job.

   Answer: A, B, and C, working together, can complete the job in $1\frac{5}{7}$ days.

10. If given the total time it requires a number of people working together to complete a job, and the times of all but one are known, to find the missing time:

    a. Invert the given times to find how much each can do in unit time.

    b. Add the reciprocals to find how much is done in unit time by those whose rates are known.

    c. Subtract this sum from the reciprocal of the total time to find the missing rate.

    d. Invert this rate to find the unknown time.

    Illustration: A, B, and C can do a job in 2 days. B can do it in 5 days, and C can do it in 4 days. How long would it take A to do it himself?

    SOLUTION: B can do it in 5 days; therefore, he can do $\frac{1}{5}$ in one day. C can do it in 4 days; therefore, he can do $\frac{1}{4}$ in one day. The part that can be done by B and C together in 1 day is:

    $$\frac{1}{5} + \frac{1}{4} = \frac{9}{20}$$

    The total time is 2 days; therefore, all can do $\frac{1}{2}$ in one day.

    $$\frac{1}{2} - \frac{9}{20} = \frac{1}{20}$$

    A can do $\frac{1}{20}$ in 1 day; therefore, he can do the whole job in 20 days.

    Answer: It would take A 20 days to complete the job himself.

11. In some work problems, certain values are given for the three factors—number of workers, the amount of work done, and the time. It is then usually required to find the changes that occur when one or two of the factors are given different values.

    One of the best methods of solving such problems is by directly making the necessary cancellations, divisions and multiplications.

    In this problem it is easily seen that more workers will be required since more houses are to be built in a shorter time.

    Illustration: If 60 workers can build 4 houses in 12 months, how many workers would be required to build 6 houses in 4 months?

    SOLUTION: To build 6 houses instead of 4 in the same amount of time, we would need $\frac{6}{4}$ of the number of workers.

    $$\frac{6}{4} \times 60 = 90$$

    Since we now have 4 months where previously we needed 12, we must triple the number of workers.

$$90 \times 3 = 270$$

Answer: 270 workers will be needed to build 6 houses in 4 months.

12. In general, a work problem in which the workers work at different rates can be fitted into the following formula for combining their work:

$$\frac{\text{work done by worker A}}{\text{time taken by worker A}}$$
$$+ \frac{\text{work done by worker B}}{\text{time taken by worker B}}$$
$$= \frac{\text{Total work done}}{\text{Total time taken}}$$

The problem will, directly or indirectly, give you five of the above six items. Plug in the known quantities and calculate the unknown one.

Note: Be sure your units of work and time are consistent throughout the formula.

Illustration: A can do the job in 4 hours. B can do it in 5. How long do they take together?

SOLUTION: $\dfrac{1 \text{ job}}{4 \text{ hrs.}} + \dfrac{1 \text{ job}}{5 \text{ hrs.}} = \dfrac{1 \text{ job}}{x \text{ hrs.}}$

$$\frac{1}{4} + \frac{1}{5} = \frac{1}{x}$$
$$\frac{5}{20} + \frac{4}{20} = \frac{1}{x}$$
$$\frac{9}{20} = \frac{1}{x}$$
$$\frac{20}{9} = \frac{x}{1}$$
$$2\frac{2}{9} = x$$

Answer: A and B together take $2\frac{2}{9}$ hours to do the job.

Tank Problems

13. The solution of tank problems is similar to that of work problems. Completely filling (or emptying) a tank may be thought of as completing a job.

14. a. If given the time it takes a pipe to fill or empty a tank, the reciprocal of the time will represent that part of the tank that is filled or emptied in unit time.

Example: If it takes a pipe 4 minutes to fill a tank, then $\frac{1}{4}$ of the tank is filled in one minute.

b. The amount that a pipe can fill or empty in unit time is its **rate.**

15. If given the part of a tank that a pipe or a combination of pipes can fill or empty in unit time, invert the part to find the total time required to fill or empty the whole tank.

Example: If a pipe can fill $\frac{2}{5}$ of a tank in 1 minute, then it will take $\frac{5}{2}$ or $2\frac{1}{2}$ minutes to fill the entire tank.

16. To solve tank problems in which only one action (filling or emptying) is going on:

a. Invert the time of each pipe to find how much each can do in unit time.

b. Add the reciprocals to find how much all can do in unit time.

c. Invert this sum to find the total time.

Illustration: Pipe A can fill a tank in 3 minutes whereas B can fill it in 4 minutes. How long would it take both pipes, working together, to fill it?

SOLUTION: Pipe A can fill it in 3 minutes; therefore, it can fill $\frac{1}{3}$ of the tank in one minute. Pipe B can fill it in 4 minutes; therefore, it can fill $\frac{1}{4}$ of the tank in one minute.

$$\frac{1}{3} + \frac{1}{4} = \frac{7}{12}$$

Pipe A and Pipe B can fill $\frac{7}{12}$ of the tank in one minute; therefore, they can fill the tank in $\frac{12}{7}$ or $1\frac{5}{7}$ minutes.

Answer: Pipes A and B, working together, can fill the tank in $1\frac{5}{7}$ minutes.

17. In problems in which both filling and emptying actions are occurring:

a. Determine which process has the faster rate.

b. The difference between the filling rate and the emptying rate is the part of the tank that is actually being filled or emptied in unit time. The fraction representing the slower action is subtracted from the fraction representing the faster process.

c. The reciprocal of this difference is the time it will take to fill or empty the tank.

Illustration: A certain tank can be filled by Pipe A in 12 minutes. Pipe B can empty the tank in 18 minutes. If both pipes are open, how long will it take to fill or empty the tank?

SOLUTION: Pipe A fills $\frac{1}{12}$ of the tank in 1 minute.

Pipe B empties $\frac{1}{18}$ of the tank in 1 minute.

$$\frac{1}{12} = \frac{3}{36}$$
$$\frac{1}{18} = \frac{2}{36}$$

Since $\frac{1}{12}$ is greater than $\frac{1}{18}$, the tank will ultimately be filled. In 1 minute, $\frac{3}{36} - \frac{2}{36} = \frac{1}{36}$ of the tank is actually filled. Therefore, the tank will be completely filled in 36 minutes.

Answer: It will take 36 minutes to fill the tank if both pipes are open.

Work and Tank Practice Problems

1. If 314 clerks filed 6594 papers in 10 minutes, what is the number filed per minute by the average clerk?
   (A) .2
   (B) 1.05
   (C) 2.1
   (D) 2.5
   (E) 21

2. Four men working together can dig a ditch in 42 days. They begin, but one man works only half-days. How long will it take to complete the job?
   (A) 38 days
   (B) 42 days
   (C) 43 days
   (D) 44 days
   (E) 48 days

3. A clerk is requested to file 800 cards. If he can file cards at the rate of 80 cards an hour,

the number of cards remaining to be filed after 7 hours of work is
   (A) 140
   (B) 240
   (C) 260
   (D) 560
   (E) 800

4. If it takes 4 days for 3 machines to do a certain job, it will take two machines
   (A) 6 days
   (B) $5\frac{1}{2}$ days
   (C) 5 days
   (D) $4\frac{1}{2}$ days
   (E) 2 days

5. A stenographer has been assigned to place entries on 500 forms. She places entries on 25 forms by the end of half an hour, when she is joined by another stenographer. The second stenographer places entries at the rate of 45 an hour. Assuming that both stenographers continue to work at their respective rates of speed, the total number of hours required to carry out the entire assignment is
   (A) 5
   (B) $5\frac{1}{2}$
   (C) $6\frac{1}{2}$
   (D) 7
   (E) $7\frac{1}{14}$

6. If in 5 days a clerk can copy 125 pages, 36 lines each, 11 words to the line, how many pages of 30 lines each and 12 words to the line can he copy in 6 days?
   (A) 145
   (B) 155
   (C) 160
   (D) 165
   (E) 175

7. A and B do a job together in two hours. Working alone A does the job in 5 hours. How long will it take B to do the job alone?
   (A) 2 hrs
   (B) $2\frac{1}{4}$ hrs
   (C) $2\frac{1}{2}$ hrs
   (D) 3 hrs
   (E) $3\frac{1}{3}$ hrs

8. A stenographer transcribes her notes at the rate of one line typed in ten seconds. At this

rate, how long (in minutes and seconds) will it take her to transcribe notes, which will require seven pages of typing, 25 lines to the page?

(A) 29 min 10 sec
(B) 20 min 30 sec
(C) 17 min 50 sec
(D) 15 min
(E) 9 min 30 sec

9. A group of five clerks have been assigned to insert 24,000 letters into envelopes. The clerks perform this work at the following rates of speed: Clerk A, 1100 letters an hour; Clerk B, 1450 letters an hour; Clerk C, 1200 letters an hour; Clerk D, 1300 letters an hour; Clerk E, 1250 letters an hour. At the end of two hours of work, Clerks C and D are assigned to another task. From the time that Clerks C and D were taken off the assignment, the number of hours required for the remaining clerks to complete this assignment is

(A) less than 2 hr
(B) more than 2 hr, but less than 4 hr
(C) more than 4 hr, but less than 6 hr
(D) more than 6 hr
(E) none of the above

10. If a certain job can be performed by 18 workers in 26 days, the number of workers needed to perform the job in 12 days is

(A) 24
(B) 30
(C) 39
(D) 45
(E) 52

11. A steam shovel excavates 2 cubic yards every 40 seconds. At this rate, the amount excavated in 45 minutes is

(A) 90 cu yd
(B) 135 cu yd
(C) 270 cu yd
(D) 1200 cu yd
(E) 3600 cu yd

12. If a plant making bricks turns out 1250 bricks in 5 days, the number of bricks that can be made in 20 days is

(A) 5000
(B) 6250

(C) 12,500
(D) 25,000
(E) none of the above

13. A tank is $\frac{3}{4}$ full. Fillpipe A can fill the tank in 12 minutes. Drainpipe B can empty it in 8 minutes. If both pipes are open, how long will it take to empty the tank?

(A) 8 min
(B) 12 min
(C) 16 min
(D) 18 min
(E) 24 min

14. A tank that holds 400 gallons of water can be filled by one pipe in 15 minutes and emptied by another in 40 minutes. How long would it take to fill the tank if both pipes are functioning?

(A) 20 min
(B) 21 min
(C) 23 min
(D) 24 min
(E) 28 min

15. An oil burner in a housing development burns 76 gallons of fuel oil per hour. At 9 A.M. on a very cold day the superintendent asks the housing manager to put in an emergency order for more fuel oil. At that time, he reports that he has on hand 266 gallons. At noon, he again comes to the manager, notifying him that no oil has been delivered. The maximum amount of time that he can continue to furnish heat without receiving more oil is

(A) $\frac{1}{2}$ hr
(B) 1 hr
(C) $1\frac{1}{2}$ hr
(D) 2 hr
(E) none of the above

Work and Tank Problems—Correct Answers

1.	**(C)**	6.	**(D)**	11.	**(B)**
2.	**(E)**	7.	**(E)**	12.	**(A)**
3.	**(B)**	8.	**(A)**	13.	**(D)**
4.	**(A)**	9.	**(B)**	14.	**(D)**
5.	**(B)**	10.	**(C)**	15.	**(A)**

Work and Tank Problem Solutions

1. 6594 papers ÷ 314 clerks = 21 papers per clerk in 10 minutes

    21 papers ÷ 10 minutes = 2.1 papers per minute filed by average clerk

    Answer: **(C)** 2.1

2. It would take 1 man 42 × 4 = 168 days to complete the job, working alone.

    If $3\frac{1}{2}$ men are working (one man works halfdays, the other 3 work full days), the job would take 168 ÷ $3\frac{1}{2}$ = 48 days.

    Answer: **(E)** 48 days

3. In 7 hours the clerk files 7 × 80 = 560 cards. Since 800 cards must be filed, there are 800 − 560 = 240 remaining.

    Answer: **(B)** 240

4. It would take 1 machine 3 × 4 = 12 days to do the job. Two machines could do the job in 12 ÷ 2 = 6 days.

    Answer: **(A)** 6 days

5. At the end of the first half-hour, there are 500 − 25 = 475 forms remaining. If the first stenographer completed 25 forms in half an hour, her rate is 25 × 2 = 50 forms per hour. The combined rate of the two stenographers is 50 + 45 = 95 forms per hour. The remaining forms can be completed in 475 ÷ 95 = 5 hours. Adding the first half-hour, the entire job requires $5\frac{1}{2}$.

    Answer: **(B)** $5\frac{1}{2}$

6. 36 lines × 11 words = 396 words on each page

    125 pages × 396 words = 49,500 words in 5 days

    49,500 ÷ 5 = 9900 words in 1 day

    12 words × 30 lines = 360 words on each page

    9900 ÷ 360 = $27\frac{1}{2}$ pages in 1 day

    $27\frac{1}{2}$ × 6 = 165 pages in 6 days.

    Answer: **(D)** 165

7. If A can do the job alone in 5 hours, A can do $\frac{1}{5}$ of the job in 1 hour. Working together, A and B can do the job in 2 hours, therefore in 1 hour they do $\frac{1}{2}$ the job.

    In 1 hour, B alone does

    $$\frac{1}{2} - \frac{1}{5} = \frac{5}{10} - \frac{2}{10}$$
    $$= \frac{3}{10} \text{ of the job.}$$

    It would take B $\frac{10}{3}$ hours = $3\frac{1}{3}$ hours to do the whole job alone.

    Answer: **(E)** $3\frac{1}{3}$ hr

8. She must type 7 × 25 = 175 lines. At the rate of 1 line per 10 seconds, it will take 175 × 10 = 1750 seconds.

    $$1750 \text{ seconds} \div 60 = 29\frac{1}{6} \text{ minutes}$$
    $$= 29 \text{ min } 10 \text{ sec}$$

    Answer: **(A)** 29 min 10 sec

9.

Clerk	Number of letters per hr
A	1100
B	1450
C	1200
D	1300
E	+ 1250
Total =	6300

    All 5 clerks working together process a total of 6300 letters per hour. After 2 hours, they have processed 6300 × 2 = 12,600. Of the original 24,000 letters there are

    $$
    \begin{array}{r}
    24,000 \\
    - 12,600 \\
    \hline
    11,400 \text{ letters remaining}
    \end{array}
    $$

    Clerks A, B, and E working together process a total of 3800 letters per hour. It will take them

    $$11,400 \div 3800 = 3 \text{ hours}$$

    to process the remaining letters.

    Answer: **(B)** more than 2 hr, but less than 4 hr

10. The job could be performed by 1 worker in 18 × 26 days = 468 days. To perform the job in 12 days would require 468 ÷ 12 = 39 workers.

    Answer: **(C)** 39

11. The shovel excavates 1 cubic yard in 20 seconds.

    There are $45 \times 60 = 2700$ seconds in 45 minutes.

    In 2700 seconds the shovel can excavate $2700 \div 20 = 135$ cubic yards.

    Answer: **(B)** 135 cu yd

12. In 20 days the plant can produce four times as many bricks as in 5 days.

    $$1250 \times 4 = 5000 \text{ bricks}$$

    Answer: **(A)** 5000

13. Pipe A can fill the tank in 12 min or fill $\frac{1}{12}$ of the tank in 1 min. Pipe B can empty the tank in 8 min or empty $\frac{1}{8}$ of the tank in 1 min. In 1 minute, $\frac{1}{8} - \frac{1}{12}$ of the tank is emptied (since $\frac{1}{8}$ is greater than $\frac{1}{12}$).

    $$\begin{array}{r} \frac{1}{8} \quad \frac{3}{24} \\ -\frac{1}{12} = -\frac{2}{24} \\ \hline \frac{1}{24} \end{array}$$ of the tank is emptied per minute

    It would take 24 min to empty whole tank, but it is only $\frac{3}{4}$ full:

    $$\frac{3}{4} \times \overset{6}{\cancel{24}} = 18 \text{ minutes}$$

    Answer: **(D)** 18 min

14. The first pipe can fill $\frac{1}{15}$ of the tank in 1 minute. The second pipe can empty $\frac{1}{40}$ of the tank in 1 minute. With both pipes open, $\frac{1}{15} - \frac{1}{40}$ of the tank will be filled per minute.

    $$\begin{array}{r} \frac{1}{15} \quad \frac{8}{120} \\ -\frac{1}{40} = -\frac{3}{120} \\ \hline \frac{5}{120} = \frac{1}{24} \end{array}$$

    In 1 minute, $\frac{1}{24}$ of the tank is filled; therefore, it will take 24 mintues for the entire tank to be filled.

    Answer: **(D)** 24 min

15. If 76 gallons are used per hour, it will take $266 \div 76 = 3\frac{1}{2}$ hours to use 266 gallons.

    From 9 a.m. to noon is 3 hours; therefore, there is only fuel for $\frac{1}{2}$ hour more.

    Answer: **(A)** $\frac{1}{2}$ hr

DISTANCE PROBLEMS

1. In distance problems, there are usually three quantities involved: the distance (in miles), the rate (in miles per hour—mph), and the time (in hours).

   a. To find the distance, multiply the rate by the time: distance = rate × time.

   Example: A man traveling 40 miles per hour for 3 hours travels 40×3 or 120 miles.

   b. The rate is the distance traveled in unit time. To find the rate, divide the distance by the time.

   Example: If a car travels 100 miles in 4 hours, the rate is $100 \div 4$ or 25 miles per hour.

   c. To find the time, divide the distance by the rate.

   Example: If a car travels 150 miles at the rate of 30 miles an hour, the time is $150 \div 30$ or 5 hours.

Combined Rates

2. a. When two people or objects are traveling towards each other, the rate at which they are approaching each other is the sum of their respective rates.

   b. When two people or objects are traveling in directly opposite directions, the rate at which they are separating is the sum of their respective rates.

3. To solve problems involving combined rates:

   a. Determine which of the three factors is to be found.

   b. Combine the rates and find the unknown factor.

   Illustration: A and B are walking towards each other over a road 120 miles long. A walks at a rate of 6 miles per hour, and B walks at a rate of 4 miles per hour. How soon will they meet?

SOLUTION: The factor to be found is the time.

Time = distance ÷ rate
Distance = 120 miles
Rate = 6 + 4 = 10 miles per hour
Time = 120 ÷ 10 = 12 hours

Answer: They will meet in 12 hours.

Illustration: Joe and Sam are walking in opposite directions. Joe walks at the rate of 5 miles per hour, and Sam walks at the rate of 7 miles per hour. How far apart will they be at the end of 3 hours?

SOLUTION: The factor to be found is distance.

Distance = time × rate
Time = 3 hours
Rate = 5 + 7 = 12 miles per hour
Distance = 12 × 3 = 36 miles

Answer: They will be 36 miles apart at the end of 3 hours.

4. To find the time it takes a faster person or object to catch up with a slower person or object:

a. Determine how far ahead the slower person or object is.

b. Subtract the slower rate from the faster rate to find the distance the faster person or object gains per unit time.

c. Divide the slower person or object's lead by the difference in rates (b).

Illustration: Two automobiles are traveling along the same road. The first one, which travels at the rate of 30 miles per hour, starts out 6 hours ahead of the second one, which travels at the rate of 50 miles per hour. How long will it take the second one to catch up with the first one?

SOLUTION: The first automobile starts out 6 hours ahead of the second. Its rate is 30 miles per hour. Therefore, it has traveled 6 × 30 or 180 miles by the time the second one starts. The second automobile travels at the rate of 50 miles per hour. Therefore, its gain is 50 − 30 or 20 miles per hour. The second auto has to cover 180 miles. There-

fore, it will take 180 ÷ 20 or 9 hours to catch up with the first automobile.

Answer: It will take the faster auto 9 hours to catch up with the slower one.

Average of Two Rates

5. In some problems, two or more rates must be averaged. When the times are the same for two or more different rates, add the rates and divide by the number of rates.

Example: If a man travels for 2 hours at 30 miles per hour, at 40 miles per hour for the next 2 hours, and at 50 miles per hour for the next 2 hours, then his average rate for the 6 hours is (30 + 40 + 50) ÷ 3 = 40 miles per hour.

6. When the times are not the same, but the distances are the same:

a. Assume the distance to be a convenient length.

b. Find the time at the first rate.

c. Find the time at the second rate.

d. Find the time at the third rate, if any.

e. Add up all the distances and divide by the total time to find the average rate.

Illustration: A boy travels a certain distance at the rate of 20 miles per hour and returns at the rate of 30 miles per hour. What is his average rate for both trips?

SOLUTION: The distance is the same for both trips. Assume that it is 60 miles. The time for the first trip is 60 ÷ 20 = 3 hours. The time for the second trip is 60 ÷ 30 = 2 hours. The total distance is 120 miles. The total time is 5 hours. Average rate is 120 ÷ 5 = 24 miles per hour.

Answer: The average rate is 24 miles per hour.

7. When the times are not the same and the distances are not the same:

a. Find the time for the first distance.

b. Find the time for the second distance.

c. Find the time for the third distance, if any.

d. Add up all the distances and divide by the total time to find the average rate.

Illustration: A man travels 100 miles at 20 miles per hour, 60 miles at 30 miles per hour, and 80 miles at 10 miles per hour. What is his average rate for the three trips?

SOLUTION: The time for the first trip is $100 \div 20 = 5$ hours. The time for the second trip is $60 \div 30 = 2$ hours. The time for the third trip is $80 \div 10 = 8$ hours. The total distance is 240 miles. The total time is 15 hours. Average rate is $240 \div 15 = 16$.

Answer: The average rate for the three trips is 16 miles an hour.

Gasoline Problems

8. Problems involving miles per gallon (mpg) of gasoline are solved in the same way as those involving miles per hour. The word gallon simply replaces the word hour.

9. Miles per gallon = distance in miles ÷ no. of gallons

   Example: If a car can travel 100 miles using 4 gallons of gasoline, then its gasoline consumption is $100 \div 4$, or 25 mpg.

Practice Problems Involving Distance

1. A ten-car train took 6 minutes to travel between two stations that are 3 miles apart. The average speed of the train was
   (A) 20 mph
   (B) 25 mph
   (C) 30 mph
   (D) 35 mph
   (E) 40 mph

2. A police car is ordered to report to the scene of a crime 5 miles away. If the car travels at an average rate of 40 miles per hour, the time it will take to reach its destination is
   (A) 3 min

(B) 7.5 min
(C) 10 min
(D) 13.5 min
(E) 15 min

3. If the average speed of a train between two stations is 30 miles per hour and the two stations are $\frac{1}{2}$ mile apart, the time it takes the train to travel from one station to the other is
   (A) 1 min
   (B) 2 min
   (C) 3 min
   (D) 4 min
   (E) 5 min

4. A car completes a 10-mile trip in 20 minutes. If it does one-half the distance at a speed of 20 miles per hour, its speed for the remainder of the distance must be
   (A) 25 mph
   (B) $33\frac{1}{3}$ mph
   (C) 40 mph
   (D) 50 mph
   (E) 60 mph

5. An express train leaves one station at 9:02 and arrives at the next station at 9:08. If the distance traveled is $2\frac{1}{2}$ miles, the average speed of the train (mph) is
   (A) 15 mph
   (B) 20 mph
   (C) 25 mph
   (D) 40 mph
   (E) 50 mph

6. A motorist averaged 60 miles per hour in going a distance of 240 miles. He made the return trip over the same distance in 6 hours. What was his average speed for the entire trip?
   (A) 40 mph
   (B) 48 mph
   (C) 50 mph
   (D) 60 mph
   (E) 64 mph

7. A city has been testing various types of gasoline for economy and efficiency. It has been found that a police radio patrol car can travel 18 miles on a gallon of Brand A

gasoline, costing $1.30 a gallon, and 15 miles on a gallon of Brand B gasoline, costing $1.25 a gallon. For a distance of 900 miles, Brand B will cost

(A) $10 more than Brand A
(B) $10 less than Brand A
(C) $100 more than Brand A
(D) $100 less than Brand A
(E) the same as Brand A

8. A suspect arrested in New Jersey is being turned over by New Jersey authorities to two New York City police officers for a crime committed in New York City. The New York officers receive their prisoner at a point 16 miles from their precinct station house, and travel directly toward their destination at an average speed of 40 miles per hour except for a delay of 10 minutes at one point because of a traffic tie-up. The time it should take the officers to reach their destination is, most nearly,

(A) 16 min
(B) 18 min
(C) 24 min
(D) 30 min
(E) 34 min

9. The Mayflower sailed from Plymouth, England, to Plymouth Rock, a distance of approximately 2800 miles, in 63 days. The average speed was closest to which one of the following?

(A) $\frac{1}{2}$ mph
(B) 1 mph
(C) 2 mph
(D) 3 mph
(E) 4 mph

10. If a vehicle is to complete a 20-mile trip at an average rate of 30 miles per hour, it must complete the trip in

(A) 20 min
(B) 30 min
(C) 40 min
(D) 50 min
(E) 60 min

11. A car began a trip with 12 gallons of gasoline in the tank and ended with $7\frac{1}{2}$ gallons. The car traveled 17.3 miles for each gallon of gasoline. During the trip gasoline was

bought for $10.00, at a cost of $1.25 per gallon. The total number of miles traveled during this trip was most nearly

(A) 79
(B) 196
(C) 216
(D) 229
(E) 236

12. A man travels a total of 4.2 miles each day to and from work. The traveling consumes 72 minutes each day. How many hours would he save in 129 working days if he moved to another residence so that he would travel only 1.7 miles each day, assuming he travels at the same rate?

(A) 98.3
(B) 97.0
(C) 95.6
(D) 93.2
(E) 90.3

13. A man can travel a certain distance at the rate of 25 miles per hour by automobile. He walks back the same distance on foot at the rate of 10 miles per hour. What is his average rate for both trips?

(A) $14\frac{2}{7}$ mph
(B) $15\frac{1}{3}$ mph
(C) $17\frac{1}{2}$ mph
(D) $28\frac{4}{7}$ mph
(E) 35 mph

14. Two trains running on the same track travel at the rates of 25 and 30 miles per hour. If the first train starts out an hour earlier, how long will it take the second train to catch up with it?

(A) 2 hr
(B) 3 hr
(C) 4 hr
(D) 5 hr
(E) 6 hr

15. Two ships are 1550 miles apart sailing towards each other. One sails at the rate of 85 miles per day and the other at the rate of 65 miles per day. How far apart will they be at the end of 9 days?

(A) 180 mi
(B) 200 mi
(C) 220 mi

(D) 785 mi
(E) 1350 mi

Distance Problems—Correct Answers

1. **(C)**	6. **(B)**	11. **(C)**
2. **(B)**	7. **(A)**	12. **(E)**
3. **(A)**	8. **(E)**	13. **(A)**
4. **(E)**	9. **(C)**	14. **(D)**
5. **(C)**	10. **(C)**	15. **(B)**

Problem Solutions—Distance

1.
$$6 \text{ min} = \tfrac{6}{60} \text{ hr} = .1 \text{ hr}$$
$$\text{Speed (rate)} = \text{distance} \div \text{time}$$
$$\text{Speed} = 3 \div .1 = 30 \text{ mph}$$

Answer: **(C)** 30 mph

2.
$$\text{Time} = \text{distance} \div \text{rate}$$
$$\text{Time} = 5 \div 40 = .125 \text{ hr}$$
$$.125 \text{ hr} = .125 \times 60 \text{ min}$$
$$= 7.5 \text{ min}$$

Answer: **(B)** 7.5 min

3.
$$\text{Time} = \text{distance} \div \text{rate}$$
$$\text{Time} = \tfrac{1}{2} \text{ mi} \div 30 \text{ mph}$$
$$= \tfrac{1}{60} \text{ hr}$$
$$\tfrac{1}{60} \text{ hr} = 1 \text{ min}$$

Answer: **(A)** 1 min

4. First part of trip = $\tfrac{1}{2}$ of 10 miles = 5 miles
$$\text{Time for first part} = 5 \div 20$$
$$= \tfrac{1}{4} \text{ hour}$$
$$= 15 \text{ minutes}$$

Second part of trip was 5 miles, completed in 20 − 15 minutes, or 5 minutes.

$$5 \text{ minutes} = \tfrac{1}{12} \text{ hour}$$
$$\text{Rate} = 5 \text{ mi} \div \tfrac{1}{12} \text{ hr}$$
$$= 60 \text{ mph}$$

Answer: **(E)** 60 mph

5. Time is 6 minutes, or .1 hour
$$\text{Speed} = \text{distance} \div \text{time}$$
$$= 2\tfrac{1}{2} \div .1$$
$$= 2.5 \div .1$$
$$= 25 \text{ mph}$$

Answer: **(C)** 25 mph

6.
$$\text{Time for first 240 mi} = 240 \div 60$$
$$= 4 \text{ hours}$$
$$\text{Time for return trip} = 6 \text{ hours}$$
$$\text{Total time for round trip} = 10 \text{ hours}$$
$$\text{Total distance for round trip} = 480 \text{ mi}$$
$$\text{Average rate} = 480 \text{ mi} \div 10 \text{ hr}$$
$$= 48 \text{ mph}$$

Answer: **(B)** 48 mph

7.
$$\text{Brand A requires } 900 \div 18 = 50 \text{ gal}$$
$$50 \text{ gal} \times \$1.30 \text{ per gal} = \$65$$

$$\text{Brand B requires } 900 \div 15 = 60 \text{ gal}$$
$$60 \text{ gal} \times \$1.25 \text{ per gal} = \$75$$

Answer: **(A)** Brand B will cost $10 more than Brand A

8.
$$\text{Time} = \text{distance} \div \text{rate}$$
$$\text{Time} = 16 \text{ mi} \div 40 \text{ mph}$$
$$= \tfrac{4}{10} \text{ hrs}$$
$$= \tfrac{4}{10} \times 60 \text{ minutes}$$
$$= 24 \text{ minutes}$$
$$24 + 10 = 34 \text{ minutes}$$

Answer: **(E)** 34 min

9.
$$63 \text{ days} = 63 \times 24 \text{ hours}$$
$$= 1512 \text{ hours}$$
$$\text{Speed} = 2800 \text{ mi} \div 1512 \text{ hr}$$
$$= 1.85 \text{ mph}$$

Answer: **(C)** 2 mph

10.
$$\text{Time} = 20 \text{ mi} \div 30 \text{ mph}$$
$$= \tfrac{2}{3} \text{ hr}$$
$$\tfrac{2}{3} \text{ hr} = \tfrac{2}{3} \times 60 \text{ min} = 40 \text{ min}$$

Answer: **(C)** 40 min

11. The car used

$$12 - 7\tfrac{1}{2} = 4\tfrac{1}{2} \text{ gal, plus}$$
$$\$10.00 \div \$1.25 = 8 \text{ gal,}$$

for a total of $12\tfrac{1}{2}$ gal, or 12.5 gal.

$$12.5 \text{ gal} \times 17.3 \text{ mpg} = 216.25 \text{ mi}$$

Answer: **(C)** 216

12.
$$72 \text{ min} = \tfrac{72}{60} \text{ hr} = 1.2 \text{ hr}$$
$$\text{Rate} = 4.2 \text{ mi} \div 1.2 \text{ hr} = 3.5 \text{ mph}$$

At this rate it would take 1.7 mi ÷ 3.5 mph

= .5 hours (approx.) to travel 1.7 miles. The daily savings in time is 1.2 hr − .5 hr = .7 hr.

.7 hr × 129 days = 90.3 hr

Answer: **(E)** 90.3

13. Assume a convenient distance, say, 50 mi.

Time by automobile = 50 mi ÷ 25 mph
= 2 hr
Time walking = 50 mi ÷ 10 mph
= 5 hr
Total time = 7 hours
Total distance = 100 mi
Average rate = 100 mi ÷ 7 hr
= $14\frac{2}{7}$ mph

Answer: **(A)** $14\frac{2}{7}$ mph

14. 30 mi − 25 mi = 5 mi gain per 1 hr

During first hour, the first train travels 25 miles.

25 mi ÷ 5 mph = 5 hr

Answer: **(D)** 5 hr

15. 85 mi × 9 da = 765 mi
65 mi × 9 da = 585 mi
1350

1550 mi − 1350 = 200 miles apart at end of 9 days.

Answer: **(B)** 200 mi

INTEREST

1. **Interest (I)** is the price paid for the use of money. There are three items considered in interest:

   a. The **principal (p),** which is the amount of money-bearing interest.

   b. The **interest rate (r),** expressed in percent on an annual basis.

   c. The **time (t)** during which the principal is used, expressed in terms of a year.

2. The basic formulas used in interest problems are:

   a. $I = prt$

   b. $p = \dfrac{I}{rt}$

   c. $r = \dfrac{I}{pt}$

   d. $t = \dfrac{I}{pr}$

3. a. For most interest problems, the year is considered to have 360 days. Months are considered to have 30 days, unless a particular month is specified.

   b. To use the interest formulas, time must be expressed as part of a year.

   Examples: 5 months = $\frac{5}{12}$ year

   36 days = $\frac{36}{360}$ year, or $\frac{1}{10}$ year

   1 year 3 months = $\frac{15}{12}$ year

   c. In reference to time, the prefix semi- means every half. The prefix bi- means every two.

   Examples: Semiannually means every half-year (every 6 months).
   Biannually means every 2 years.
   Semimonthly means every half-month (every 15 days, unless the month is specified).
   Biweekly means every 2 weeks (every 14 days).

4. There are two types of interest problems:

   a. **Simple interest,** in which the interest is calculated only once over a given period of time.

   b. **Compound interest,** in which interest is recalculated at given time periods based on previously earned interest.

Simple Interest

5. To find the interest when the principal, rate, and time are given:

   a. Change the rate of interest to a fraction.

   b. Express the time as a fractional part of a year.

   c. Multiply all three items.

Illustration: Find the interest on $400 at $11\frac{1}{4}\%$ for 3 months and 16 days.

SOLUTION: $11\frac{1}{4}\% = \frac{45}{4}\% = \frac{45}{400}$

3 months and 16 days = 106 days
(30 days per month)
106 days = $\frac{106}{360}$ of a year = $\frac{53}{180}$ year
(360 days per year)

$$\overset{1}{\underset{1}{400}} \times \frac{45}{\underset{1}{400}} \times \frac{53}{\underset{4}{180}} = \frac{53}{4}$$

$$= 13.25$$

Answer: Interest = $13.25

6. To find the principal if the interest, interest rate, and time are given:

   a. Change the interest rate to a fraction.

   b. Express the time as a fractional part of a year.

   c. Multiply the rate by the time.

   d. Divide the interest by this product.

Illustration: What amount of money invested at 6% would receive interest of $18 over $1\frac{1}{2}$ years?

SOLUTION: $6\% = \frac{6}{100}$

$1\frac{1}{2}$ years = $\frac{3}{2}$ years

$$\frac{6}{100} \times \frac{\overset{3}{\cancel{3}}}{\underset{1}{2}} = \frac{9}{100}$$

$$\$18 \div \frac{9}{100} = \$\overset{2}{\cancel{18}} \times \frac{100}{\underset{1}{9}}$$

$$= \$200$$

Answer: Principal = $200

7. To find the rate if the principal, time, and interest are given:

   a. Change the time to a fractional part of a year.

   b. Multiply the principal by the time.

   c. Divide the interest by this product.

   d. Convert to a percent.

Illustration: At what interest rate should $300 be invested for 40 days to accrue $2 in interest?

SOLUTION: 40 days = $\frac{40}{360}$ of a year

$$\overset{5}{\underset{6}{300}} \times \frac{\overset{20}{\cancel{40}}}{\cancel{360}} = \frac{100}{3}$$

$$\$2 \div \frac{100}{3} = \overset{1}{\cancel{2}} \times \frac{3}{\underset{50}{\cancel{100}}}$$

$$= \frac{3}{50}$$

$$\frac{3}{50} = 6\%$$

Answer: Interest rate = 6%

8. To find the time (in years) if the principal, interest, and interest rate are given:

   a. Change the interest rate to a fraction (or decimal).

   b. Multiply the principal by the rate.

   c. Divide the interest by this product.

Illustration: Find the length of time for which $240 must be invested at 5% to accrue $16 in interest.

SOLUTION: $5\% = .05$

$$240 \times .05 = 12$$
$$16 \div 12 = 1\frac{1}{3}$$

Answer: Time = $1\frac{1}{3}$ years

Compound Interest

9. Interest may be computed on a compound basis; that is, the interest at the end of a certain period (half-year, full year, or whatever time stipulated) is added to the principal for the next period. The interest is then computed on the new increased principal, and for the next period the interest is again computed on the new increased principal. Since the principal constantly increases, compound interest yields more than simple interest.

10. To find the compound interest when given the principal, the rate, and time period:

    a. Calculate the interest as for simple interest problems, using the period of compounding for the time.

    b. Add the interest to the principal.

    c. Calculate the interest on the new principal over the period of compounding.

d. Add this interest to form a new principal.

e. Continue the same procedure until all periods required have been accounted for.

f. Subtract the original principal from the final principal to find the compound interest.

Illustration: Find the amount that $200 will become if compounded semiannually at 8% for $1\frac{1}{2}$ years.

SOLUTION: Since it is to be compounded semiannually for $1\frac{1}{2}$ years, the interest will have to be computed 3 times:

Interest for the first period: .08 × $\frac{1}{2}$ × $200 = $8
First new principal: $200 + $8 = $208

Interest for the second period: .08 × $\frac{1}{2}$ × $208 = $8.32
Second new principal: $208 + $8.32 = $216.32

Interest for the third period: .08 × $\frac{1}{2}$ × $216.32 = $8.6528
Final principal: $216.32 + $8.6528 = $224.9728

Answer: $224.97 to the nearest cent

Bank Discounts

11. A **promissory note** is a commitment to pay a certain amount of money on a given date, called the **date of maturity.**

12. When a promissory note is cashed by a bank in advance of its date of maturity, the bank deducts a discount from the principal and pays the rest to the depositor.

13. To find the bank discount:

a. Find the time between the date the note is deposited and its date of maturity, and express this time as a fractional part of a year.

b. Change the rate to a fraction.

c. Multiply the principal by the time and the rate to find the bank discount.

d. If required, subtract the bank discount from the original principal to find the amount the bank will pay the depositor.

Illustration: A $400 note drawn up on August 12, 1980, for 90 days is deposited at the bank on September 17, 1980. The bank

charges a $6\frac{1}{2}$% discount on notes. How much will the depositor receive?

SOLUTION: From August 12, 1980, to September 17, 1980, is 36 days. This means that the note has 54 days to run.

$$54 \text{ days} = \tfrac{54}{360} \text{ of a year}$$
$$6\tfrac{1}{2}\% = \tfrac{13}{2}\% = \tfrac{13}{200}$$
$$\$400 \times \tfrac{13}{200} \times \tfrac{54}{360} = \tfrac{39}{10}$$
$$= \$3.90$$
$$\$400 - \$3.90 = \$396.10$$

Answer: The depositor will receive $396.10.

Practice Problems Involving Interest

1. What is the simple interest on $460 for 2 years at $8\frac{1}{2}$%? _____

2. For borrowing $300 for one month, a man was charged $6.00. The rate of interest was _____.

3. At a simple interest rate of 5% a year, the principal that will give $12.50 interest in 6 months is _____.

4. Find the interest on $480 on $10\frac{1}{2}$% for 2 months and 15 days. _____

5. The interest on $300 at 6% for 10 days is _____.

6. The scholarship board of a certain college loaned a student $200 at an annual rate of 6% from September 30 until December 15. To repay the loan and accumulated interest the student must give the college _____.

7. If $300 is invested at simple interest so as to yield a return of $18 in 9 months, the amount of money that must be invested at the same rate of interest so as to yield a return of $120 in 6 months is _____.

8. When the principal is $600, the difference in one year between simple interest at 12% per annum and interest compounded semiannually at 12% per annum is _____.

9. What is the compound interest on $600, compounded quarterly, at 6% for 9 months?
   _____.

10. A 90-day note for $1200 is signed on May 12. Seventy-five days later the note is deposited at a bank that charges 8% discount on notes. The bank discount is _____.

Problem Solutions—Interest

1. Principal = $460
    Rate = $8\frac{1}{2}\% = .085$
    Time = 2 years
    Interest = $460 × .085 × 2
    = $78.20

    Answer: $78.20

2. Principal = $300
    Interest = $6
    Time = $\frac{1}{12}$ year
    $300 × $\frac{1}{12}$ = $25
    $6 ÷ $25 = .24 = 24%

    Answer: 24%

3. Rate = 5% = .05
    Interest = $12.50
    Time = $\frac{1}{2}$ year
    .05 × $\frac{1}{2}$ = .025
    $12.50 ÷ .025 = $500.00

    Answer: $500

4. Time:
    2 months 15 days = 75 days or $\frac{75}{360}$ of a year
    Rate:
    $10\frac{1}{2}\% = \frac{21}{2}\% = \frac{21}{200}$
    Interest:
    $480 × \frac{21}{200} × \frac{75}{360} = \frac{21}{2} = 10.50$

    Answer: $10.50

5. Principal = $300
    Rate = .06 = $\frac{6}{100}$
    Time = $\frac{10}{360} = \frac{1}{36}$
    Interest = $300 × $\frac{6}{100}$ × $\frac{1}{36}$
    = $\frac{3}{6}$ = $.50

    Answer: $.50

6. Principal = $200
    Rate = .06 = $\frac{6}{100}$

    Time from Sept. 30 until Dec. 15 is 76 days. (31 days in October, 30 days in November, 15 days in December)
    76 days = $\frac{76}{360}$ year
    Interest = $200 × $\frac{6}{100}$ × $\frac{76}{360}$
    = $\frac{152}{60}$ = $2.53
    $200 + $2.53 = $202.53

    Answer: closest to $202.50

7. Principal = $300
    Interest = $18
    Time = $\frac{9}{12}$ years = $\frac{3}{4}$ year
    $300 × $\frac{3}{4}$ = $225
    $18 ÷ $225 = .08

    Rate is 8%.

    To yield $120 at 8% in 6 months,
    Interest = $120
    Rate = .08
    Time = $\frac{1}{2}$ year
    .08 × $\frac{1}{2}$ = .04
    $120 ÷ .04 = $3000 must be invested

    Answer: $3000

8. Simple interest:
    Principal = $600
    Rate = .12
    Time = 1
    Interest = $600 × .12 × 1
    = $72.00

    Compound interest:
    Principal = $600
    Period of compounding = $\frac{1}{2}$ year
    Rate = .12

    For the first period,
    Interest = $600 × .12 × $\frac{1}{2}$
    = $36
    New principal = $600 + $36
    = $636

    For the second period,
    Interest = $636 × .12 × $\frac{1}{2}$
    = $38.16
    New principal = $636 + $38.16
    = $674.16

Total interest = $74.16

Difference = $74.16 − 72.00

= $2.16

Answer: $2.16

9. Principal = $600

Rate = 6% = $\frac{6}{100}$

Time (period of
compounding) = $\frac{3}{12}$ year = $\frac{1}{4}$ year

In 9 months, the interest will be computed 3 times.

For first quarter,

Interest = $600 × $\frac{6}{100}$ × $\frac{1}{4}$

= $9

New principal at end of first quarter:
$600 + $9 = $609

For second quarter,

Interest = $609 × $\frac{6}{100}$ × $\frac{1}{4}$

= $\$\frac{3654}{400}$ = $9.135,

or $9.14

New principal at end of second quarter:
$609 + $9.14 = $618.14

For third quarter,

Interest = $618.14 × $\frac{6}{100}$ × $\frac{1}{4}$

= $\$\frac{3708.84}{400}$

= $9.27

Total interest for the 3 quarters:
$9 + $9.14 + $9.27 = $27.41

Answer: $27.41

10. Principal = $1200

Time = 90 days − 75 days

= 15 days

15 days = $\frac{15}{360}$ year

Rate = 8% = $\frac{8}{100}$

Bank discount = $\$\overset{12}{\cancel{1200}} × \underset{1}{\overset{1}{\frac{8}{\cancel{100}}}} × \underset{45}{\frac{15}{\cancel{360}}}$

= $\$\frac{180}{45}$ = $4

Answer: $4.00

TAXATION

1. a. Taxation problems are a form of percentage or fraction problems since the tax rate is often expressed as a percentage (parts per hundred) or as another sort of fraction such as tax per $100,000, etc.

   b. Taxation problems may also be a form of table or chart problem when the rate of taxation is not a single rate, but changes in accordance with something else, such as total to be taxed, time, etc.

2. In taxation, there are usually three items involved: the amount taxable, henceforth called the base, the tax rate, and the tax itself.

3. To find the tax when given the base and the tax rate in percent:

   a. Change the tax rate to a decimal.

   b. Multiply the base by the tax rate.

   Illustration: How much would be realized on $4000 if taxed 15%?

   SOLUTION: 15% = .15

   $4000 × .15 = $600

   Answer: Tax = $600

4. To find the tax rate in percent form when given the base and the tax:

   a. Divide the tax by the base.

   b. Convert to a percent.

   Illustration: Find the tax rate at which $5600 would yield $784.

   SOLUTION: $784 ÷ $5600 = .14

   .14 = 14%

   Answer: Tax rate = 14%

5. To find the base when given the tax rate and the tax:

   a. Change the tax rate to a decimal.

   b. Divide the tax by the tax rate.

   Illustration: What amount of money taxed 3% would yield $75?

   SOLUTION: 3% = .03

   $75 ÷ .03 = $2500

   Answer: Base = $2500

6. When the tax rate is fixed and expressed in terms of money, take into consideration the denomination upon which it is based; that is, whether it is based on every $100, or $1000, etc.

7. To find the tax when given the base and the tax rate in terms of money:

   a. Divide the base by the denomination upon which the tax is based.

   b. Multiply this quotient by the tax rate.

   Illustration: If the tax rate is $3.60 per $1000, find the tax on $470,500.

   SOLUTION:

   $$\$470,500 \div \$1000 = 470.5$$
   $$470.5 \times \$3.60 = \$1,693.80$$

   Answer: $1,693.80

8. To find the tax rate based on a certain denomination when given the base and the tax derived:

   a. Divide the base by the denomination indicated.

   b. Divide the tax by this quotient.

   Illustration: Find the tax rate per $100 that would be required to raise $350,000 on $2,000,000 of taxable property.

   SOLUTION: $\$2,000,000 \div \$100 = 20,000$
   $\$350,000 \div 20,000 = \$17.50$

   Answer: Tax rate = $17.50 per $100

9. Since a surtax is an additional tax besides the regular tax, to find the total tax:

   a. Change the regular tax rate to a decimal.

   b. Multiply the base by the regular tax rate.

   c. Change the surtax rate to a decimal.

   d. Multiply the base by the surtax rate.

   e. Add both taxes.

   Illustration: Assuming that the tax rate is $2\frac{1}{2}\%$ on liquors costing up to $3.00, and 3% on those costing from $3.00 to $6.00, and $3\frac{1}{2}\%$ on those from $6.00 to $10.00, what would be the tax on a bottle costing $8.00 if there is a surtax of 5% on all liquors above $5.00?

SOLUTION: An $8.00 bottle falls within the category of $6.00 to $10.00. The tax rate on such a bottle is

$$3\frac{1}{2}\% = .035$$
$$\$8.00 \times .035 = \$.28$$
$$\text{surtax rate} = 5\% = .05$$
$$\$8.00 \times .05 = \$.40$$
$$\$.28 + \$.40 = \$.68$$

Answer: Total tax = $.68

Practice Problems Involving Taxation

1. Mr. Jones' income for a year is $15,000. He pays $2250 for income taxes. The percent of his income that he pays for income taxes is _____.

2. If the tax rate is $3\frac{1}{2}\%$ and the amount to be raised is $64.40, what is the base? _____

3. What is the tax rate per $1000 if a base of $338,500 would yield $616.07? _____

4. A man buys an electric light bulb for 54¢, which includes a 20% tax. What is the cost of the bulb without tax? _____

5. What tax rate on a base of $3650 would raise $164.25? _____

6. A piece of property is assessed at $22,850 and the tax rate is $4.80 per thousand. What is the amount of tax that must be paid on the property? _____

7. $30,000 worth of land is assessed at 120% of its value. If the tax rate is $5.12 per $1000 assessed valuation, the amount of tax to be paid is _____.

8. Of the following real estate tax rates, which is the largest?
   $31.25 per $1000
   $3.45 per $100
   32¢ per $10
   3¢ per $1

9. A certain community needs $185,090.62 to cover its expenses. If its tax rate is $1.43 per $100 of assessed valuation, what must be the assessed value of its property? _____

10. A man's taxable income is $14,280. The state tax instructions tell him to pay 2% on the first $3000 of his taxable income, 3% on each of the second and third $3000, and 4% on the remainder. What is the total amount of income tax that he must pay? _____

Problem Solutions—Taxation

1. Tax = $2250
    Base = $15,000
    Tax rate = Tax ÷ Base
    Tax rate = $2250 ÷ $15,000 = .15
    Tax rate = .15 = 15%

    Answer: 15

2. Tax rate = $3\frac{1}{2}$% = .035
    Tax = $64.40
    Base = Tax ÷ Tax rate
    Base = $64.40 ÷ .035
        = $1840

    Answer: $1840

3. Base = $338,500
    Tax = $616.07
    Denomination = $1000
    $338,500 ÷ $1000 = 338.50
    $616.07 ÷ 338.50 = $1.82 per $1000

    Answer: $1.82

4. 54¢ is 120% of the base (cost without tax)
    Base = 54 ÷ 120%
        = 54 ÷ 1.20
        = 45

    Answer: 45¢

5. Base = $3650
    Tax = $164.25
    Tax rate = Tax ÷ Base
        = $164.25 ÷ $3650
        = .045
        = $4\frac{1}{2}$%

    Answer: $4\frac{1}{2}$%

6. Base = $22,850
    Denomination = $1000
    Tax rate = $4.80 per thousand
    $\frac{$22,850}{$1000}$ = 22.85
    22.85 × $4.80 = $109.68

    Answer: $109.68

7. Base = Assessed val. = 120% of $30,000
            = 1.20 × $30,000
            = $36,000

    Denomination = $1000
    Tax rate = $5.12 per thousand
    $\frac{$36,000}{$1000}$ = 36
    36 × $5.12 = $184.32

    Answer: $184.32

8. Express each tax rate as a decimal:

    $31.25 per $1000 = $\frac{31.25}{1000}$ = .03125

    $3.45 per $100 = $\frac{3.45}{100}$ = .0345

    32¢ per $10 = $\frac{.32}{10}$ = .0320

    3¢ per $1 = $\frac{.03}{1}$ = .0300

    The largest decimal is .0345

    Answer: $3.45 per $100

9. Tax rate = $1.43 per $100
        = $\frac{1.43}{100}$ = .0143
        = 1.43%
    Tax = $185,090.62
    Base = Tax ÷ rate
        = 185,090.62 ÷ .0143
        = $12,943,400

    Answer: $12,943,400

10. First $3000:   .02 × $3000 = $ 60.00
    Second $3000:   .03 × $3000 = $ 90.00
    Third $3000:   .03 × $3000 = $ 90.00
    Remainder
    ($14,280 − $9000): .04 × $5280 = $211.20
                        Total tax = $451.20

    Answer: $451.20

PROFIT AND LOSS

1. The following terms may be encountered in profit and loss problems:

   a. The **cost price** of an article is the price paid by a person who wishes to sell it again.

   b. There may be an **allowance** or **trade discount** reducing the cost price.

   c. The **list price** or **marked price** is the price at which the article is listed or marked to be sold.

   d. There may be a **discount** or **series of discounts** (usually expressed as a percent) on the list price.

   e. The **selling price** or **sales price** is the price at which the article is finally sold.

   f. If the selling price is greater than the cost price, there has been a **profit.**

   g. If the selling price is lower than the cost price, there has been a **loss.**

   h. If the article is sold at the same price as the cost, there has been no loss or profit.

   i. A percentage profit or loss may be based either on the cost price or on the selling price.

   j. Profit or loss may be stated in terms of dollars and cents, or in terms of percent.

   k. **Overhead** expenses include such items as rent, salaries, etc., and may be added to cost price or to the profit to increase the selling price.

2. The basic formulas used in profit and loss problems are:

   > Selling price = cost price + profit
   > Selling price = cost price − loss

   Example: If the cost of an article is $2.50, and the profit is $1.50, then the selling price is $2.50 + $1.50 = $4.00.

   Example: If the cost of an article is $3.00, and the loss is $1.20, then the selling price is $3.00 − $1.20 = $1.80.

3. a. To find the profit in terms of money, subtract the cost price from the selling price, or selling price − cost price = profit.

   Example: If an article costing $3.00 is sold for $5.00, the profit is $5.00 − $3.00 = $2.00.

   b. To find the loss in terms of money, subtract the selling price from the cost price, or: cost price − selling price = loss.

   Example: If an article costing $2.00 is sold for $1.50, the loss is $2.00 − $1.50 = $.50.

4. To find the selling price if the profit or loss is expressed in percent based on cost price:

   a. Multiply the cost price by the percent of profit or loss to find the profit or loss in terms of money.

   b. Add this product to the cost price if a profit is involved, or subtract for a loss.

   Illustration: Find the selling price of an article costing $3.00 that was sold at a profit of 15% of the cost price.

   SOLUTION: 15% of $3.00 = .15 × $3.00
   = $.45 profit
   $3.00 + $.45 = $3.45

   Answer: Selling price = $3.45

   Illustration: If an article costing $2.00 is sold at a loss of 5% of the cost price, find the selling price.

   SOLUTION: 5% of $2.00 = .05 × $2.00
   = $.10 loss
   $2.00 − $.10 = $1.90

   Answer: Selling price = $1.90

5. To find the cost price when given the selling price and the percent of profit or loss based on the selling price:

   a. Multiply the selling price by the percent of profit or loss to find the profit or loss in terms of money.

   b. Subtract this product from the selling price if a profit, or add the product to the selling price if a loss.

Illustration: If an article sells for $12.00 and there has been a profit of 10% of the selling price, what is the cost price?

SOLUTION:

$$10\% \text{ of } \$12,00 = .10 \times \$12.00$$
$$= \$1.20 \text{ profit}$$
$$\$12.00 - \$1.20 = \$10.80$$

Answer: Cost price = $10.80

Illustration: What is the cost price of an article selling for $2.00 on which there has been a loss of 6% of the selling price?

SOLUTION:
$$6\% \text{ of } \$2.00 = .06 \times \$2.00$$
$$= \$.12 \text{ loss}$$
$$\$2.00 + \$.12 = \$2.12$$

Answer: Cost price = $2.12

6. To find the percent of profit or percent of loss based on cost price:

a. Find the profit or loss in terms of money.

b. Divide the profit or loss by the cost price.

c. Convert to a percent.

Illustration: Find the percent of profit based on cost price of an article costing $2.50 and selling for $3.00.

SOLUTION: $3.00 - $2.50 = $.50 profit

$$2.50 \overline{)\ .50} = 250 \overline{)\ 50.00}^{.20}$$
$$.20 = 20\%$$

Answer: Profit = 20%

Illustration: Find the percent of loss based on cost price of an article costing $5.00 and selling for $4.80.

SOLUTION: $5.00 - $4.80 = $.20 loss

$$5.00 \overline{)\ .20} = 500 \overline{)\ 20.00}^{.04}$$
$$.04 = 4\%$$

Answer: Loss = 4%

7. To find the percent of profit or percent of loss on selling price:

a. Find the profit or loss in terms of money.

b. Divide the profit or loss by the selling price.

c. Convert to a percent.

Illustration: Find the percent of profit based on the selling price of an article costing $2.50 and selling for $3.00.

SOLUTION:

$$\$3.00 - \$2.50 = \$.50 \text{ profit}$$
$$3.00 \overline{)\ .50} = 300 \overline{)\ 50.00} = .16\tfrac{2}{3}$$
$$= 16\tfrac{2}{3}\%$$

Answer: Profit = $16\tfrac{2}{3}\%$

Illustration: Find the percent of loss based on the selling price of an article costing $5.00 and selling for $4.80.

SOLUTION:

$$\$5.00 - \$4.80 = \$.20 \text{ loss}$$
$$4.80 \overline{)\ .20} = 480 \overline{)\ 20.00} = .04\tfrac{1}{6}$$
$$= 4\tfrac{1}{6}\%$$

Answer: Loss = $4\tfrac{1}{6}\%$

8. To find the cost price when given the selling price and the percent of profit based on the cost price:

a. Establish a relation between the selling price and the cost price.

b. Solve to find the cost price.

Illustration: An article is sold for $2.50, which is a 25% profit of the cost price. What is the cost price?

SOLUTION: Since the selling price represents the whole cost price plus 25% of the cost price,

$$2.50 = 125\% \text{ of the cost price}$$
$$2.50 = 1.25 \text{ of the cost price}$$
$$\text{Cost price} = 2.50 \div 1.25$$
$$= 2.00$$

Answer: Cost price = $2.00

9. To find the selling price when given the profit based on the selling price:

a. Establish a relation between the selling price and the cost price.

b. Solve to find the selling price.

Illustration: A merchant buys an article for $27.00 and sells it at a profit of 10% of the selling price. What is the selling price?

SOLUTION: $27.00 + profit = selling price

Since the profit is 10% of the selling price, the cost price must be 90% of the selling price.

$$27.00 = 90\% \text{ of the selling price}$$
$$= .90 \text{ of the selling price}$$
$$\text{Selling price} = 27.00 \div .90$$
$$= 30.00$$

Answer: Selling price = $30.00

Trade Discounts

10. A **trade discount,** usually expressed in percent, indicates the part that is to be deducted from the list price.

11. To find the selling price when given the list price and the trade discount:

   a. Multiply the list price by the percent of discount to find the discount in terms of money.

   b. Subtract the discount from the list price.

Illustration: The list price of an article is $20.00. There is a discount of 5%. What is the selling price?

SOLUTION: $20.00 × 5%
$$= 20.00 \times .05 = \$1.00 \text{ discount}$$
$$\$20.00 - \$1.00 = \$19.00$$

Answer: Selling price = $19.00

An alternate method of solving the above problem is to consider the list price to be 100%. Then, if the discount is 5%, the selling price is 100% − 5% = 95% of the list price. The selling price is

$$95\% \text{ of } \$20.00 = .95 \times \$20.00$$
$$= \$19.00$$

Series of Discounts

12. There may be more than one discount to be deducted from the list price. These are called a **discount series.**

13. To find the selling price when given the list price and a discount series:

   a. Multiply the list price by the first percent of discount.

   b. Subtract this product from the list price.

   c. Multiply the difference by the second discount.

   d. Subtract this product from the difference.

   e. Continue the same procedure if there are more discounts.

Illustration: Find the selling price of an article listed at $10.00 on which there are discounts of 20% and 10%.

SOLUTION:

$$\$10.00 \times 20\% = 10.00 \times .20 = \$2.00$$
$$\$10.00 - \$2.00 = \$8.00$$
$$\$8.00 \times 10\% = 8.00 \times .10 = \$.80$$
$$\$8.00 - \$.80 = \$7.20$$

Answer: Selling price = $7.20

14. Instead of deducting each discount individually, it is often more practical to find the single equivalent discount first and then deduct. It does not matter in which order the discounts are taken.

15. The single equivalent discount may be found by assuming a list price of 100%. Leave all discounts in percent form.

   a. Subtract the first discount from 100%, giving the net cost factor (NCF) had there been only one discount.

   b. Multiply the NCF by the second discount. Subtract the product from the NCF, giving a second NCF that reflects both discounts.

   c. If there is a third discount, multiply the second NCF by it and subtract the product from the second NCF, giving a third NCF that reflects all three discounts.

   d. If there are more discounts, repeat the process.

   e. Subtract the final NCF from 100% to find the single equivalent discount.

Illustration: Find the single equivalent discount of 20%, 25%, and 10%.

SOLUTION:

$$
\begin{array}{ll}
& 100\% \\
- & 20\% \text{ first discount} \\
\hline
& 80\% \text{ first NCF} \\
-25\% \text{ of } 80\% = & 20\% \\
\hline
& 60\% \text{ second NCF} \\
-10\% \text{ of } 60\% = & 6\% \\
\hline
& 54\% \text{ third NCF}
\end{array}
$$

100% − 54% = 46% single equivalent
discount

Answer: 46%

Illustration: An article lists at $750.00. With discounts of 20%, 25%, and 10%, what is the selling price of this article?

SOLUTION: As shown above, the single equivalent discount of 20%, 25%, and 10% is 46%.

$$
\begin{aligned}
46\% \text{ of } \$750 &= .46 \times \$750 \\
&= \$345 \\
\$750 - \$345 &= \$405
\end{aligned}
$$

Answer: Selling price = $405

Practice Problems Involving Profit and Loss

1. Dresses sold at $65.00 each. The dresses cost $50.00 each. The percentage of increase of the selling price over the cost is _____.

2. A dealer bought a ladder for $27.00. What must it be sold for if he wishes to make a profit of 40% on the selling price? _____

3. A typewriter was listed at $120.00 and was bought for $96.00. What was the rate of discount? _____

4. A dealer sells an article at a loss of 50% of the cost. Based on the selling price, the loss is _____.

5. What would be the marked price of an article if the cost was $12.60 and the gain was 10% of the cost price? _____

6. A stationer buys note pads at $.75 per dozen and sells them at 25 cents apiece. The profit based on the cost is _____.

7. An article costing $18 is to be sold at a profit of 10% of the selling price. The selling price will be _____.

8. A calculating machine company offered to sell a city agency 4 calculating machines at a discount of 15% from the list price, and to allow the agency $85 for each of two old machines being traded in. The list price of the new machines is $625 per machine. If the city agency accepts this offer, the amount of money it will have to provide for the purchase of these 4 machines is _____.

9. Pencils are purchased at $9 per gross and sold at 6 for 75 cents. The rate of profit based on the selling price is _____.

10. The single equivalent discount of 20% and 10% is _____.

Problem Solutions—Profit and Loss

1.
$$
\begin{aligned}
\text{Selling price} - \text{cost} &= \$65 - \$50 \\
&= \$15 \\
\frac{\$15}{\$50} &= .30 = 30\%
\end{aligned}
$$

Answer: 30%

2. Cost price = 60% of selling price, since the profit is 40% of the selling price, and the whole selling price is 100%.

$$
\begin{aligned}
\$27 &= 60\% \text{ of selling price} \\
\text{Selling price} &= \$27 \div 60\% \\
&= \$27 \div .6 \\
&= \$45
\end{aligned}
$$

Answer: $45

3. The discount was $120 − $96 = $24

$$
\begin{aligned}
\text{Rate of discount} &= \frac{\$24}{\$120} = .20 \\
&= 20\%
\end{aligned}
$$

Answer: 20%

4. Loss = cost − selling price.

Considering the cost to be 100% of itself, if the loss is 50% of the cost, the selling price is also 50% of the cost. (50% = 100% − 50%)

Since the loss and the selling price are therefore the same, the loss is 100% of the selling price.

Answer: 100%

5.
$$\text{Gain (profit)} = 10\% \text{ of } \$12.60$$
$$= .10 \times \$12.60$$
$$= \$1.26$$

$$\text{Selling price} = \text{cost} + \text{profit}$$
$$= \$12.60 + \$1.26$$
$$= \$13.86$$

Answer: $13.86

6. Each dozen note pads cost $.75 and are sold for
$$12 \times \$.25 = \$3.00$$
The profit is $\$3.00 − \$.75 = \$2.25$

$$\text{Profit based on cost} = \frac{\$2.25}{\$.75}$$
$$= 3$$
$$= 300\%$$

Answer: 300%

7.
If profit = 10% of selling price,
then cost = 90% of selling price
$$\$18 = 90\% \text{ of selling price}$$
$$\text{Selling price} = \$18 \div 90\%$$
$$= \$18 \div .90$$
$$= \$20$$

Answer: $20.00

8. Discount for each new machine:
$$15\% \text{ of } \$625 = .15 \times \$625$$
$$= \$93.75$$

Each new machine will cost
$$\$625 − \$93.75 = \$531.25$$

Four new machines will cost
$$\$531.25 \times 4 = \$2125$$

But there is an allowance of $85 each for 2 old machines:
$$\$85 \times 2 = 170$$

Final cost to city:
$$\$2125 − \$170 = \$1955$$

Answer: $1955

9.
$$1 \text{ gross} = 144 \text{ units}$$
$$\text{Selling price for 6 pencils} = \$.75$$
$$\text{Selling price for 1 pencil} = \frac{\$.75}{6}$$
$$\text{Selling price for 1 gross of pencils} = \frac{\$.75}{\overset{1}{6}} \times \overset{24}{\cancel{144}}$$
$$= \$18.00$$
$$\text{Cost for 1 gross of pencils} = \$9.00$$
$$\text{Profit for 1 gross of pencils} = \$18.00 − \$9.00$$
$$= \$9.00$$
$$\frac{\text{profit}}{\text{selling price}} = \frac{\$9.00}{\$18.00}$$
$$= .5 = 50\%$$

Answer: 50%

10.
$$\begin{array}{r} 100\% \\ - \quad 20\% \\ \hline 80\% \end{array}$$
$$-10\% \text{ of } 80\% = \begin{array}{r} 80\% \\ - \quad 8\% \\ \hline 72\% \end{array}$$

100% − 72% = 28% single equivalent discount

Answer: 28%

TABLES

1. **Tables** are used to organize information in easily understandable form. The key to understanding tables is to read the title and the margins, or stubs as they are sometimes called. These items, plus the footnotes to the table, if any, will tell you what the numbers in the table mean. The numbers themselves have no meaning without the writing. For example, consider the following arrangement of numbers:

300	500	800
400	600	1000
700	1100	1800

You may think that the bottom row and the right-hand column represent totals since things seem to add up that way. It is possible that this is correct, but unless there is written information to tell you this, you do not know it to be true.

2. You should be particularly alert to the units that are used in a table, which may be

different from the units asked for in the problem. For example, a table may give you information in tons and the problem might ask for pounds.

3. Other than the fact that the information is presented in a table, there is nothing about a table problem that is different from any of the other sorts of problems which have been discussed.

4. As in other arithmetic computational problems, it is usually a good idea to estimate the numbers that you have to use from a table rather than using them in their printed form. Generally the first and second digits are all that is needed.

GRAPHS

1. **Graphs** illustrate comparisons and trends in statistical information. The most commonly used graphs are **bar graphs, line graphs, circle graphs,** and **pictographs.** The fundamental idea about graphs is that they all use some distance or area to represent value. The distance may be length, width, etc., and the value may be dollars, percents, etc. The graphs are always labelled to show what part of the graph means what value. So read the labels, margins, and notes of each graph carefully.

Bar Graphs

2. **Bar graphs** are used to compare various quantities. Each bar may represent a single quantity or may be divided to represent several quantities.

3. Bar graphs may have horizontal or vertical bars.

Illustration (next column):

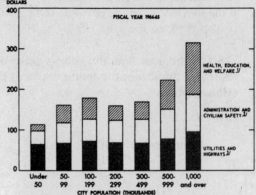

Municipal Expenditures, Per Capita

1/PUBLIC WELFARE, EDUCATION, HOSPITALS, HEALTH, LIBRARIES, AND HOUSING AND URBAN RENEWAL.
2/POLICE AND FIRE PROTECTION, FINANCIAL ADMINISTRATION, GENERAL CONTROL, GENERAL PUBLIC BUILDINGS, INTEREST ON GENERAL DEBT, AND OTHER.
3/HIGHWAYS, SEWERAGE, SANITATION, PARKS AND RECREATION, AND UTILITIES.
SOURCE: DEPARTMENT OF COMMERCE.

Question 1: What was the approximate municipal expenditure per capita in cities having populations of 200,000 to 299,000?

Answer: The middle bar of the seven shown represents cities having populations from 200,000 to 299,000. This bar reaches about halfway between 100 and 200. Therefore, the per capita expenditure was approximately $150.

Question 2: Which cities spent the most per capita on health, education, and welfare?

Answer: The bar for cities having populations of 1,000,000 and over has a larger striped section than the other bars. Therefore, those cities spent the most.

Question 3: Of the three categories of expenditures, which was least dependent on city size?

Answer: The expenditures for utilities and highways, the darkest part of each bar, varied least as city size increased.

Line Graphs

4. **Line graphs** are used to show trends, often over a period of time.

5. A line graph may include more than one line, with each line representing a different item.

    Illustration:

    The graph below indicates, at 5 year-intervals, the number of citations issued for various offenses from the year 1960 to the year 1980.

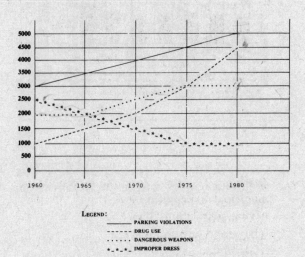

Question 4: Over the 20-year period, which offense shows an average rate of increase of more than 150 citations per year?

Answer: Drug-use citations increased from 1000 in 1960 to 4500 in 1980. The average increase over the 20-year period is $\frac{3500}{20} = 175$.

Question 5: Over the 20-year period, which offense shows a constant rate of increase or decrease?

Answer: A straight line indicates a constant rate of increase or decrease. Of the four lines, the one representing parking violations is the only straight one.

Question 6: Which offense shows a total increase or decrease of 50% for the full 20-year period?

Answer: Dangerous weapons citations increased from 2000 in 1960 to 3000 in 1980, which is an increase of 50%.

Circle Graphs

6. **Circle graphs** are used to show the relationship of various parts of a quantity to each other and to the whole quantity.

7. Percents are often used in circle graphs. The 360 degrees of the circle represents 100%.

8. Each part of the circle graph is called a **sector.**

    Illustration:

    The following circle graph shows how the federal budget of $300.4 billion was spent.

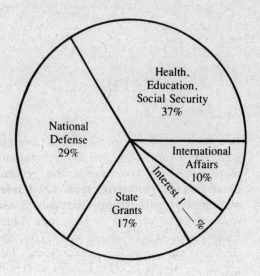

Question 7: What is the value of I?

Answer: There must be a total of 100% in a circle graph. The sum of the other sectors is:

$$17\% + 29\% + 37\% + 10\% = 93\%$$

Therefore, I = 100% − 93% = 7%.

Question 8: How much money was actually spent on national defense?

Answer: 29% × $300.4 billion
= $87.116 billion
= $87,116,000,000

Question 9: How much more money was spent on state grants than on interest?

Answer: 17% − 7% = 10%
10% × $300.4 billion
= $30.04 billion
= $30,040,000,000

Pictographs

9. **Pictographs** allow comparisons of quantities by using symbols. Each symbol represents a given number of a particular item.

Illustration:

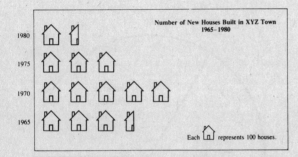

Question 10: How many more new houses were built in 1970 than in 1975?

Answer: There are two more symbols for 1970 than for 1975. Each symbol represents 100 houses. Therefore, 200 more houses were built in 1970.

Question 11: How many new houses were built in 1965?

Answer: There are 3½ symbols shown for 1965; 3½ × 100 = 350 houses.

Question 12: In which year were half as many houses built as in 1975?

Answer: In 1975, 3 × 100 = 300 houses were built. Half of 300, or 150, houses were built in 1980.

Practice Problems Involving Graphs

Questions 1–4 refer to the graph in the next column:

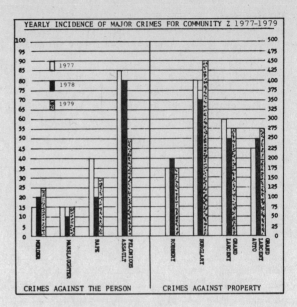

1. In 1979, the incidence of which of the following crimes was greater than in the previous two years?
   (A) murder
   (B) grand larceny
   (C) rape
   (D) robbery
   (E) manslaughter

2. If the incidence of burglary in 1980 had increased over 1979 by the same number as it had increased in 1979 over 1978, then the average for this crime for the four-year period from 1977 through 1980 would be most nearly
   (A) 100
   (B) 400
   (C) 425
   (D) 440
   (E) 550

3. The above graph indicates that the *percentage* increase in grand larceny auto from 1978 to 1979 was:
   (A) 5%
   (B) 10%
   (C) 15%
   (D) 20%
   (E) 25%

4. Which of the following cannot be determined because there is not enough information in the above graph to do so?
   (A) For the three-year period, what percentage of all "Crimes Against the Person" involved murders committed in 1978?
   (B) For the three-year period, what percentage of all "Major Crimes" was committed in the first six months of 1978?
   (C) Which major crimes followed a pattern of continuing yearly increases for the three-year period?
   (D) For 1979, what was the ratio of robbery, burglary, and grand larceny crimes?
   (E) What was the major crime with the greatest annual incidence for the period 1977–1979?

Questions 5–7 refer to the following graph:

In the graph below, the lines labeled "A" and "B" represent the cumulative progress in the work of two file clerks, each of whom was given 500 consecutively numbered applications to file in the proper cabinets over a five-day work week.

5. The day during which the largest number of applications was filed by both clerks was
   (A) Monday
   (B) Tuesday
   (C) Wednesday
   (D) Thursday
   (E) Friday

6. At the end of the second day, the percentage of applications still to be filed was
   (A) 25%
   (B) 30%
   (C) 50%
   (D) 66%
   (E) 75%

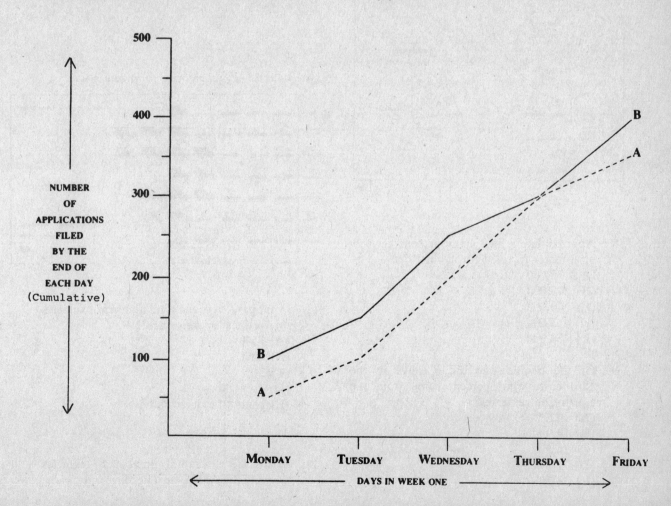

7. Assuming that the production pattern is the same the following week as the week shown in the chart, the day on which Clerk B will file application number 475 will be
   (A) Monday
   (B) Tuesday
   (C) Wednesday
   (D) Thursday
   (E) Friday

Questions 8–11 refer to the following graph:

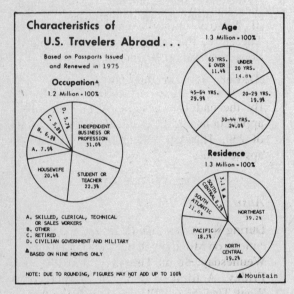

8. Approximately how many persons aged 29 or younger traveled abroad in 1975?
   (A) 175,000
   (B) 245,000
   (C) 350,000
   (D) 415,000
   (E) 450,000

9. Of the people who did *not* live in the Northeast, what percent came from the North Central states?
   (A) 19.2%
   (B) 19.9%
   (C) 26.5%
   (D) 31.6%
   (E) 38.7%

10. The fraction of travelers from the four smallest occupation groups is most nearly equal to the fraction of travelers
    (A) under age 20, and 65 and over, combined
    (B) from the North Central and Mountain states
    (C) between 45 and 64 years of age
    (D) from the Housewife and Other categories
    (E) Northeast and Pacific states

11. If the South Central, Mountain, and Pacific sections were considered as a single classification, how many degrees would its sector include?
    (A) 30°
    (B) 67°
    (C) 108°
    (D) 120°
    (E) 180°

Questions 12–15 refer to the following graph:

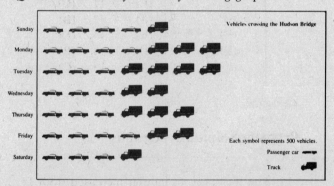

12. What percent of the total number of vehicles on Wednesday were cars?
    (A) 85%
    (B) 60%
    (C) 30%
    (D) 10%
    (E) cannot be determined

13. What was the total number of vehicles crossing the bridge on Tuesday?

(A) 7
(B) 700
(C) 1500
(D) 2000
(E) 3500

14. How many more trucks crossed on Monday than on Saturday?
    (A) 200
    (B) 1000
    (C) 1500
    (D) 2000
    (E) 3500

15. If trucks paid a toll of $1.00 and cars paid a toll of $.50, how much money was collected in tolls on Friday?
    (A) $400
    (B) $750
    (C) $2000
    (D) $2500
    (E) $3000

Graphs—Correct Answers

1.	(A)	6.	(E)	11.	(C)
2.	(D)	7.	(A)	12.	(B)
3.	(B)	8.	(E)	13.	(E)
4.	(B)	9.	(D)	14.	(B)
5.	(C)	10.	(A)	15.	(C)

Problem Solutions—Graphs

1. The incidence of murder increased from 15 in 1977 to 20 in 1978 to 25 in 1979.

   Answer: **(A)** murder

2. The incidence of burglary in 1977 was 400; in 1978 it was 350; and in 1979 it was 450. The increase from 1978 to 1979 was 100. An increase of 100 from 1979 gives 550 in 1980. The average of 400, 350, 450, and 550 is

   $$\frac{400 + 350 + 450 + 550}{4} = \frac{1750}{4}$$
   $$= 437.5$$

   Answer: **(D)** 440

3. The incidence of grand larceny auto went from 250 in 1978 to 275 in 1979, an increase of 25.
   The percent increase is

   $$\frac{25}{250} = .10 = 10\%$$

   Answer: **(B)** 10%

4. This graph gives information by year, not month. It is impossible to determine from the graph the percentage of crimes committed during the first six months of any year.

   Answer: **(B)**

5. For both A and B, the greatest increase in the cumulative totals occurred from the end of Tuesday until the end of Wednesday. Therefore, the largest number of applications was filed on Wednesday.

   Answer: **(C)** Wednesday

6. By the end of Tuesday, A had filed 100 applications and B had filed 150, for a total of 250. This left 750 of the original 1000 applications.

   $$\frac{750}{1000} = .75 = 75\%$$

   Answer: **(E)** 75%

7. **During Week One, Clerk B files 100 applications on Monday, 50 on Tuesday, 100 on Wednesday, 50 on Thursday, and 100 on Friday. A total of 400. On Monday of Week Two, he will file numbers 401 to 500.**

   Answer: **(A)** Monday

8. 20–29 yrs.:   19.9%
   Under 20 yrs.:   +14.8%
   _____
   34.7%

   34.7% × 1.3 million = .4511 million
   = 451,100

   Answer: **(E)** 450,000

9. 100% − 39.2% = 60.8% did not live in Northeast.

   19.2% lived in North Central

   $$\frac{19.2}{60.8} = .316 \text{ approximately}$$

   Answer: **(D)** 31.6%

10. Four smallest groups of occupation:

$$7.9 + 6.9 + 5.8 + 5.7 = 26.3$$

Age groups under 20 and over 65:

$$14.8 + 11.4 = 26.2$$

Answer: **(A)**

11. South Central: 8.2%
Mountain: 3.1%
Pacific: <u>18.7%</u>
               30.0%

$$30\% \times 360° = 108°$$

Answer: **(C)** 108°

12. There are 5 vehicle symbols, of which 3 are cars.

$$\tfrac{3}{5} = 60\%$$

Answer: **(B)** 60%

13. On Tuesday, there were $3 \times 500 = 1500$ cars and $4 \times 500 = 2000$ trucks. The total number of vehicles was 3500.

Answer: **(E)** 3500

14. The graph shows 2 more truck symbols on Monday than on Saturday. Each symbol represents 500 trucks, so there were $2 \times 500 = 1000$ more trucks on Monday.

Answer: **(B)** 1000

15. On Friday there were

$$4 \times 500 = 2000 \text{ cars}$$
$$2 \times 500 = 1000$$

Car tolls: 2000 × $ .50 = $1000
Truck tolls: 1000 × $1.00 = <u>+ $1000</u>
Total tolls: $2000

Answer: **(C)** $2000

POWERS AND ROOTS

1. The numbers that are multiplied to give a product are called the **factors** of the product.

Example: In $2 \times 3 = 6$, 2 and 3 are factors.

2. If the factors are the same, an **exponent** may be used to indicate the number of times the factor appears.

Example: In $3 \times 3 = 3^2$, the number 3 appears as a factor twice, as is indicated by the exponent 2.

3. When a product is written in exponential form, the number the exponent refers to is called the **base.** The product itself is called the **power.**

Example: In 2^5, the number 2 is the base and 5 is the exponent.
$2^5 = 2 \times 2 \times 2 \times 2 \times 2 = 32$, so 32 is the power.

4. a. If the exponent used is 2, we say that the base has been **squared,** or raised to the second power.

Example: 6^2 is read "six squared" or "six to the second power."

b. If the exponent used is 3, we say that the base has been **cubed,** or raised to the third power.

Example: 5^3 is read "five cubed" or "five to the third power."

c. If the exponent is 4, we say that the base has been raised to the fourth power. If the exponent is 5, we say the base has been raised to the fifth power, etc.

Example: 2^8 is read "two to the eighth power."

5. A number that is the product of a whole number squared is called a **perfect square.**

Example: 25 is a perfect square because $25 = 5^2$.

6. a. If a number has exactly two equal factors, each factor is called the **square root** of the number.

Example: $9 = 3 \times 3$; therefore, 3 is the square root of 9.

b. The symbol $\sqrt{}$ is used to indicate square root.

Example: $\sqrt{9} = 3$ means that the square root of 9 is 3, or $3 \times 3 = 9$.

c. In principle, all numbers have a square root. Although many square roots cannot be calculated exactly, they can be found to whatever degree of accuracy is needed (see item 8). Thus the square root of 10, $\sqrt{10}$, is *by definition* the number that equals 10 when it is squared—$\sqrt{10} \times \sqrt{10} = 10$.

d. If a number has exactly three equal factors, each factor is called a **cube root.** The symbol $\sqrt[3]{}$ is used to indicate a cube root.

Example: $8 = 2 \times 2 \times 2$; thus $2 = \sqrt[3]{8}$

e. In general, the nth root is indicated as $\sqrt[n]{}$

7. The square root of the most common perfect squares may be found by using the following table, or by trial and error; that is, by finding the number that, when squared, yields the given perfect square.

Number	Perfect Square	Number	Perfect Square
1	1	10	100
2	4	11	121
3	9	12	144
4	16	13	169
5	25	14	196
6	36	15	225
7	49	20	400
8	64	25	625
9	81	30	900

Example: To find $\sqrt{81}$, note that 81 is the perfect square of 9, or $9^2 = 81$. Therefore, $\sqrt{81} = 9$.

8. On the GMAT you will only rarely have to find the square root of a number that is not a perfect square. The two most common square roots with which you will have to deal with are $\sqrt{2}$, which equals approximately 1.4, and $\sqrt{3}$, which equals approximately 1.7. Most times you will not have to convert these square roots to their equivalents since the answer choices will be in terms of the square roots, e.g., (A) $4\sqrt{3}$, etc.

The following method is the way to compute square roots of numbers that are not perfect squares. It is very effective, but it is long and you are unlikely to actually need it on the GMAT.

a. Locate the decimal point.

b. Mark off the digits in groups of two in both directions beginning at the decimal point.

c. Mark the decimal point for the answer just above the decimal point of the number whose square root is to be taken.

d. Find the largest perfect square contained in the left-hand group of two.

e. Place its square root in the answer. Subtract the perfect square from the first digit or pair of digits.

f. Bring down the next pair.

g. Double the partial answer.

h. Add a trial digit to the right of the doubled partial answer. Multiply this new number by the trial digit. Place the correct new digit in the answer.

i. Subtract the product.

j. Repeat steps f–i as often as necessary.

You will notice that you get one digit in the answer for every group of two you marked off in the original number.

Illustration: Find the square root of 138,384.

SOLUTION:

$$\begin{array}{r} 3 \\ \sqrt{13'83'84.} \\ 3^2 = 9 \\ \hline 4\ 83 \end{array}$$

$$\begin{array}{r} 3\ 7\ 2. \\ \sqrt{13'83'84.} \\ 3^2 = 9 \\ \hline 4\ 83 \\ 7 \times 67 = 4\ 69 \\ \hline 14\ 84 \\ 2 \times 742 = 14\ 84 \end{array}$$

The number must first be marked off in groups of two figures each, beginning at the decimal point, which, in the case of a whole number, is at the right. The number of figures in the root will be the same as the number of groups so obtained.

The largest square less than 13 is 9. $\sqrt{9} = 3$

Place its square root in the answer. Subtract the perfect square from the first digit or pair of digits. Bring down the next pair. To form our trial divisor, annex 0 to this root "3" (making 30) and multiply by 2.

$483 \div 60 = 80$. Multiplying the trial divisor 68 by 8, we obtain 544, which is too large. We then try multiplying 67 by 7. This is correct. Add the trial digit to the right of the doubled partial answer. Place the new digit in the answer. Subtract the product. Bring down the final group. Annex 0 to the new root 37 and multiply by 2 for the trial divisor:

$$2 \times 370 = 740$$
$$1484 \div 740 = 2$$

Place the 2 in the answer.

Answer: The square root of 138,384 is 372.

Illustration: Find the square root of 3 to the nearest hundredth.

$$
\begin{array}{r}
1.\ 7\ 3\ 2 \\
\sqrt{3.00'00'00}
\end{array}
$$

SOLUTION:

$$
\begin{array}{rr}
1^2 = & 1 \\
20 & 2\ 00 \\
7 \times 27 = & 1\ 89 \\ \hline
340 & 11\ 00 \\
3 \times 343 = & 10\ 29 \\ \hline
3460 & 71\ 00 \\
2 \times 3462 = & 69\ 24 \\ \hline
\end{array}
$$

Answer: The square root of 3 is 1.73 to the nearest hundredth.

9. When more complex items are raised to powers, the same basic rules apply.

   a. To find the power of some multiplied item, find the power of each multiplicand and multiply those powers together.

Example: $(4x)^2 = (4x)(4x) = (4)(4)(x)(x) = (4)^2(x)^2 = 16x^2$

Example: $(2xy)^4 = (2)^4(x)^4(y)^4 = 16x^4y^4$

   b. To find the power of some divided item or fraction, find the power of each part of the fraction and then divide in the manner of the original fraction.

Example: $\left(\dfrac{2}{x}\right)^2 = \left(\dfrac{2}{x}\right)\left(\dfrac{2}{x}\right) = \left(\dfrac{4}{x^2}\right)$

   c. To find the result when two powers of the same base are multiplied together, *add* the exponents. You add the exponents because you are adding to the length of the string of the same base all being multiplied together.

Example: $(x^2)(x^3) = (x)(x) \cdot (x)(x)(x) = xxxxx = x^{(2+3)} = x^5$

Example: $2^a \cdot 2^b = 2^{(a+b)}$

   d. To find the result when a power is raised to an exponent, *multiply* the exponents. You multiply the exponents together because you are multiplying the length of the string of the same base all being multiplied together.

Example: $(x^2)^3 = (x^2)(x^2)(x^2) = xxxxxx = x^{(2 \cdot 3)} = x^6$

   e. When a power is divided by another power of the same base, the result is found by subtracting the exponent in the denominator (bottom) from the exponent in the numerator (top).

Example: $\dfrac{x^3}{x^2} = \dfrac{xxx}{xx} = x^{(3-2)} = x^1 = x$

   Note: Any base to the first power, x^1, equals the base.

Example: $\dfrac{x^9}{x^6} = x^{(9-6)} = x^3$

Example: $\dfrac{x^2}{x^2} = \dfrac{xx}{xx} = x^{(2-2)} = x^0 = 1$

   Note: Any base to the "zero-th" power, x^0, equals 1.

Example: $\dfrac{x^3}{x^4} = \dfrac{xxx}{xxxx} = \dfrac{1}{x} = x^{(3-4)} = x^{-1}$

f. A **negative exponent** is a reciprocal, as discussed in the earlier section on fractions.

Example: $z^{-3} = \left(\dfrac{z}{1}\right)^{-3} = \left(\dfrac{1}{z}\right)^{+3} = \dfrac{1^3}{z^3} = \dfrac{1}{z^3}$

Example: $(3p)^{-2} = \dfrac{1}{(3p)^{+2}} = \dfrac{1}{9p^2}$

Example: $(r^{-3})^{-6} = \dfrac{1}{(r^{-3})^{+6}} = \dfrac{1}{\left(\dfrac{1}{r^3}\right)^6} = \dfrac{1}{\dfrac{1}{r^{18}}}$

$$= (1)\left(\dfrac{r^{18}}{1}\right) = r^{18}$$
$$\text{or } (r^{-3}) = r^{(-3)(-6)} = r^{+18}$$

10. Some problems require that different powers be grouped together. Depending on the relationships, they can be grouped by doing the processes explained in #9 in the reverse direction.

Example: $9x^2 = 3^2 \cdot x^2 = (3x)^2$

Example: $\dfrac{81}{y^2} = \dfrac{9^2}{y^2} = \left(\dfrac{9}{y}\right)^2$

Example: $m^{12} = (m^5)(m^7)$ or $(m^{10})(m^2)$ etc.

Example: $z^{24} = (z^6)^4$ or $(z^8)^3$ etc.

11. The conditions under which radicals can be added or subtracted are much the same as the conditions for letters in an algebraic expression. The radicals act as a label, or unit, and must therefore be exactly the same. In adding or subtracting, we add or subtract the coefficients, or rational parts and carry the radical along as a label, which does not change.

Example: $\sqrt{2} + \sqrt{3}$ cannot be added
$\sqrt{2} + \sqrt[3]{2}$ cannot be added
$4\sqrt{2} + 5\sqrt{2} = 9\sqrt{2}$

Often, when radicals to be added or subtracted are not the same, simplification of one or more radicals will make them the same. To simplify a radical, we remove any perfect square factors from underneath the radical sign.

Example: $\sqrt{12} = \sqrt{4}\sqrt{3} = 2\sqrt{3}$
$\sqrt{27} = \sqrt{9}\sqrt{3} = 3\sqrt{3}$

If we wish to add $\sqrt{12} + \sqrt{27}$, we must first

simplify each one. Adding the simplified radicals gives a sum of $5\sqrt{3}$.

Example: $\sqrt{125} + \sqrt{20} - \sqrt{500}$

SOLUTION:

$$\sqrt{25}\,\sqrt{5} + \sqrt{4}\,\sqrt{5} - \sqrt{100}\,\sqrt{5}$$
$$5\sqrt{5} + 2\sqrt{5} - 10\sqrt{5}$$
$$-3\sqrt{5}$$

Answer: $-3\sqrt{5}$

12. In multiplication and division we again treat the radicals as we would letters in an algebraic expression. They are factors and must be treated as such.

Example: $(\sqrt{2})(\sqrt{3}) = \sqrt{(2)(3)} = \sqrt{6}$

Example: $4\sqrt{2} \cdot 5\sqrt{3} = 20 \cdot \sqrt{6}$

Example: $(3\sqrt{2})^2 = 3\sqrt{2} \cdot 3\sqrt{2} = 9 \cdot 2 = 18$

Example: $\dfrac{\sqrt{8}}{\sqrt{2}} = \sqrt{4} = 2$

Example: $\dfrac{10\sqrt{20}}{\sqrt{4}} = 10\sqrt{5}$

Example: $\sqrt{2}(\sqrt{8} + \sqrt{18}) = \sqrt{16} + \sqrt{36}$
$= 4 + 6 = 10$

13. In simplifying radicals that contain several terms under the radical sign, we must combine terms before taking the square root.

Example: $\sqrt{16 + 9} = \sqrt{25} = 5$

Note: It is not true that $\sqrt{16 + 9} = \sqrt{16} + \sqrt{9}$, which would be $4 + 3$, or 7.

Example: $\sqrt{\dfrac{x^2}{16} - \dfrac{x^2}{25}} = \sqrt{\dfrac{25x^2 - 16x^2}{400}}$

$$= \sqrt{\dfrac{9x^2}{400}} = \dfrac{3x}{20}$$

Practice Problems Involving Roots

1. Combine $4\sqrt{27} - 2\sqrt{48} + \sqrt{147}$
   (A) $27\sqrt{3}$
   (B) $-3\sqrt{3}$
   (C) $9\sqrt{3}$

(D) $10\sqrt{3}$

(E) $11\sqrt{3}$

2. Combine $\sqrt{80} + \sqrt{45} - \sqrt{20}$

(A) $9\sqrt{5}$

(B) $5\sqrt{5}$

(C) $-\sqrt{5}$

(D) $3\sqrt{5}$

(E) $-2\sqrt{5}$

3. Combine $6\sqrt{5} + 3\sqrt{2} - 4\sqrt{5} + \sqrt{2}$

(A) 8

(B) $2\sqrt{5} + 3\sqrt{2}$

(C) $2\sqrt{5} + 4\sqrt{2}$

(D) $5\sqrt{7}$

(E) 5

4. Combine $\frac{1}{2}\sqrt{180} + \frac{1}{3}\sqrt{45} - \frac{2}{5}\sqrt{20}$

(A) $3\sqrt{10} + \sqrt{15} + 2\sqrt{2}$

(B) $\frac{16}{5}\sqrt{5}$

(C) $\sqrt{97}$

(D) $\frac{24}{5}\sqrt{5}$

(E) none of these

5. Combine $5\sqrt{mn} - 3\sqrt{mn} - 2\sqrt{mn}$

(A) 0

(B) 1

(C) $\sqrt{mn}$

(D) mn

(E) $-\sqrt{mn}$

6. Multiply and simplify: $2\sqrt{18} \cdot 6\sqrt{2}$

(A) 72

(B) 48

(C) $12\sqrt{6}$

(D) $8\sqrt{6}$

(E) 36

7. Find $(3\sqrt{3})^3$

(A) $27\sqrt{3}$

(B) $81\sqrt{3}$

(C) 81

(D) $9\sqrt{3}$

(E) 243

8. Multiply and simplify: $\frac{1}{2}\sqrt{2}\,(\sqrt{6} + \frac{1}{2}\sqrt{2})$

(A) $\sqrt{3} + \frac{1}{2}$

(B) $\frac{1}{2}\sqrt{3}$

(C) $\sqrt{6} + 1$

(D) $\sqrt{6} + \frac{1}{2}$

(E) $\sqrt{6} + 2$

9. Divide and simplify: $\dfrac{\sqrt{32b^3}}{\sqrt{8b}}$

(A) $2\sqrt{b}$

(B) $\sqrt{2b}$

(C) $2b$

(D) $\sqrt{2b^2}$

(E) $b\sqrt{2b}$

10. Divide and simplify: $\dfrac{15\sqrt{96}}{5\sqrt{2}}$

(A) $7\sqrt{3}$

(B) $7\sqrt{12}$

(C) $11\sqrt{3}$

(D) $12\sqrt{3}$

(E) $40\sqrt{3}$

11. Simplify $\sqrt{\dfrac{x^2}{9} + \dfrac{x^2}{16}}$

(A) $\dfrac{25x^2}{144}$

(B) $\dfrac{5x}{12}$

(C) $\dfrac{5x^2}{12}$

(D) $\dfrac{x}{7}$

(E) $\dfrac{7x}{12}$

12. Simplify $\sqrt{36y^2 + 64x^2}$

(A) $6y + 8x$

(B) $10xy$

(C) $6y^2 + 8x^2$

(D) $10x^2y^2$

(E) cannot be simplified

13. Simplify $\sqrt{\dfrac{x^2}{64} - \dfrac{x^2}{100}}$

(A) $\dfrac{x}{40}$

(B) $-\dfrac{x}{2}$

(C) $\dfrac{x}{2}$

(D) $\dfrac{3x}{40}$

(E) $\dfrac{3x}{80}$

14. Simplify $\sqrt{\dfrac{y^2}{2} - \dfrac{y^2}{18}}$

(A) $\dfrac{2y}{3}$

(B) $\dfrac{y\sqrt{5}}{3}$

(C) $\dfrac{10y}{3}$

(D) $\dfrac{y\sqrt{3}}{6}$

(E) cannot be simplified

15. $\sqrt{a^2 + b^2}$ is equal to
    (A) $a + b$
    (B) $a - b$
    (C) $\sqrt{a^2} + \sqrt{b^2}$
    (D) $(a + b)(a - b)$
    (E) none of these

16. Which of the following square roots can be found exactly?
    (A) $\sqrt{.4}$
    (B) $\sqrt{.9}$
    (C) $\sqrt{.09}$
    (D) $\sqrt{.02}$
    (E) $\sqrt{.025}$

Root Problems—Correct Answers

1.	**(E)**	9.	**(C)**
2.	**(B)**	10.	**(D)**
3.	**(C)**	11.	**(B)**
4.	**(B)**	12.	**(E)**
5.	**(A)**	13.	**(D)**
6.	**(A)**	14.	**(A)**
7.	**(B)**	15.	**(E)**
8.	**(A)**	16.	**(C)**

Problem Solutions—Roots

1. $4\sqrt{27} = 4\sqrt{9}\sqrt{3} = 12\sqrt{3}$
   $2\sqrt{48} = 2\sqrt{16}\sqrt{3} = 8\sqrt{3}$
   $\sqrt{147} = \sqrt{49}\sqrt{3} = 7\sqrt{3}$
   $12\sqrt{3} - 8\sqrt{3} + 7\sqrt{3} = 11\sqrt{3}$

   Answer: **(E)** $11\sqrt{3}$

2. $\sqrt{80} = \sqrt{16}\sqrt{5} = 4\sqrt{5}$
   $\sqrt{45} = \sqrt{9}\sqrt{5} = 3\sqrt{5}$
   $\sqrt{20} = \sqrt{4}\sqrt{5} = 2\sqrt{5}$
   $4\sqrt{5} + 3\sqrt{5} - 2\sqrt{5} = 5\sqrt{5}$

   Answer: **(B)** $5\sqrt{5}$

3. Only terms with the same radical may be combined.

   $6\sqrt{5} - 4\sqrt{5} = 2\sqrt{5}$
   $3\sqrt{2} + \sqrt{2} = 4\sqrt{2}$

   Therefore we have $2\sqrt{5} + 4\sqrt{2}$

   Answer: **(C)** $2\sqrt{5} + 4\sqrt{2}$

4. $\frac{1}{2}\sqrt{180} = \frac{1}{2}\sqrt{36}\sqrt{5} = 3\sqrt{5}$
   $\frac{1}{3}\sqrt{45} = \frac{1}{3}\sqrt{9}\sqrt{5} = \sqrt{5}$
   $\frac{2}{5}\sqrt{20} = \frac{2}{5}\sqrt{4}\sqrt{5} = \frac{4}{5}\sqrt{5}$
   $3\sqrt{5} + \sqrt{5} - \frac{4}{5}\sqrt{5} = 4\sqrt{5} - \frac{4}{5}\sqrt{5} = 3\frac{1}{5}\sqrt{5} = \frac{16}{5}\sqrt{5}$

   Answer: **(B)** $\frac{16}{5}\sqrt{5}$

5. $5\sqrt{mn} - 5\sqrt{mn} = 0$

   Answer: **(A)** 0

6. $2\sqrt{18} \cdot 6\sqrt{2} = 12\sqrt{36} = 12 \cdot 6 = 72$

   Answer: **(A)** 72

7. $3\sqrt{3} \cdot 3\sqrt{3} \cdot 3\sqrt{3} = 27(3\sqrt{3}) = 81\sqrt{3}$

   Answer: **(B)** $81\sqrt{3}$

8. Using the distributive law, we have

   $\frac{1}{2}\sqrt{12} + \frac{1}{4} \cdot 2 = \frac{1}{2}\sqrt{4}\sqrt{3} + \frac{1}{2} = \sqrt{3} + \frac{1}{2}$

   Answer: **(A)** $\sqrt{3} + \frac{1}{2}$

9. Dividing the numbers in the radical sign, we have $\sqrt{4b^2} = 2b$

   Answer: **(C)** $2b$

10. $3\sqrt{48} = 3\sqrt{16}\sqrt{3} = 12\sqrt{3}$

    Answer: **(D)** $12\sqrt{3}$

11. $\sqrt{\dfrac{16x^2 + 9x^2}{144}} = \sqrt{\dfrac{25x^2}{144}} = \dfrac{5x}{12}$

    Answer: **(B)** $\dfrac{5x}{12}$

12. The terms cannot be combined and it is not possible to take the square root of separated terms.

    Answer: **(E)** cannot be done

13. $\sqrt{\dfrac{100x^2 - 64x^2}{6400}} = \sqrt{\dfrac{36x^2}{6400}} = \dfrac{6x}{80} = \dfrac{3x}{40}$

    Answer: **(D)** $\dfrac{3x}{40}$

14. $\sqrt{\dfrac{18y^2 - 2y^2}{36}} = \sqrt{\dfrac{16y^2}{36}} = \dfrac{4y}{6} = \dfrac{2y}{3}$

    Answer: **(A)** $\dfrac{2y}{3}$

15. It is not possible to find the square root of separate terms.

    Answer: **(E)** none of these

16. In order to take the square root of a decimal, it must have an even number of decimal places so that its square root will have exactly half as many. In addition to this, the digits must form a perfect square ($\sqrt{.09} = .3$).

    Answer: **(C)** $\sqrt{.09}$

ALGEBRAIC FRACTIONS

1. In reducing algebraic fractions, we must divide the numerator and denominator by the same factor, just as we do in arithmetic. We can never cancel terms, as this would be adding or subtracting the same number from the numerator and denominator, which changes the value of the fraction. When we reduce $\dfrac{6}{8}$ to $\dfrac{3}{4}$, we are really saying that $\dfrac{6}{8} = \dfrac{2 \cdot 3}{2 \cdot 4}$ and then dividing numerator and denominator by 2. We do not say $\dfrac{6}{8} = \dfrac{3+3}{3+5}$ and then say $\dfrac{6}{8} = \dfrac{3}{5}$. This is faulty reasoning in algebra as well. If we have $\dfrac{6t}{8t}$, we can divide numerator and denominator by 2t, giving $\dfrac{3}{4}$ as an answer. However, if we have $\dfrac{6 + t}{8 + t}$, we can do no more, as there is no factor that divides into the *entire* numerator as well as the *entire* denominator. Cancelling terms is one of the most frequent student errors. Don't get caught! Be careful!

Example: Reduce $\dfrac{3x^2 + 6x}{4x^3 + 8x^2}$ to its lowest terms.

SOLUTION: Factoring the numerator and denominator, we have $\dfrac{3x(x + 2)}{4x^2(x + 2)}$. The factors common to both numerator and denominator are x and (x + 2). Dividing these out, we arrive at $\dfrac{3}{4x}$.

Answer: $\dfrac{3}{4x}$

2. In adding or subtracting fractions, we must work with a common denominator and the same shortcuts we used in arithmetic.

Example: Find the sum of $\dfrac{1}{a}$ and $\dfrac{1}{b}$.

SOLUTION: Remember to add the two cross products and put the sum over the denominator product.

Answer: $\dfrac{b + a}{ab}$

Example: Add: $\dfrac{2n}{3} + \dfrac{3n}{2}$

SOLUTION: $\dfrac{4n + 9n}{6} = \dfrac{13n}{6}$

Answer: $\dfrac{13n}{6}$

3. In multiplying or dividing fractions, we may cancel a factor common to any numerator and any denominator. Always remember to invert the fraction following the division sign. Where exponents are involved, they are added in multiplication and subtracted in division.

Example: Find the product of $\dfrac{a^3}{b^2}$ and $\dfrac{b^3}{a^2}$.

SOLUTION: We divide a^2 into the first numerator and second denominator, giving $\dfrac{a}{b^2} \cdot \dfrac{b^2}{1}$. Then we divide b^2 into the first denominator and second numerator, giving $\dfrac{a}{1} \cdot \dfrac{b}{1}$. Finally, we multiply the resulting fractions, giving an answer of ab.

Answer: ab

Example: Divide $\dfrac{6x^2y}{5}$ by $2x^3$.

SOLUTION: $\dfrac{6x^2y}{5} \cdot \dfrac{1}{2x^3}$. Divide the first numerator and second denominator by $2x^2$, giving $\dfrac{3y}{5} \cdot \dfrac{1}{x}$. Multiplying the resulting fractions, we get $\dfrac{3y}{5x}$.

Answer: $\dfrac{3y}{5x}$

4. Complex algebraic fractions are simplified by the same methods used in arithmetic. Multiply *each term* of the complex fraction by the lowest quantity that will eliminate the fraction within the fraction.

Example: $\dfrac{\dfrac{1}{a} + \dfrac{1}{b}}{ab}$

SOLUTION: We must multiply *each term* by ab, giving $\dfrac{b + a}{a^2b^2}$ Since no reduction beyond this is possible, $\dfrac{b + a}{a^2b^2}$ is our final answer. Remember *never* to cancel terms unless they apply to the entire numerator or the entire denominator.

Answer: $\dfrac{b + a}{a^2b^2}$

Practice Problems Involving Algebraic Fractions

1. Find the sum of $\dfrac{n}{6} + \dfrac{2n}{5}$.
   (A) $\dfrac{13n}{30}$
   (B) $17n$
   (C) $\dfrac{3n}{30}$
   (D) $\dfrac{17n}{30}$
   (E) $\dfrac{3n}{11}$

2. Combine into a single fraction: $1 - \dfrac{x}{y}$
   (A) $\dfrac{1-x}{y}$
   (B) $\dfrac{y - x}{y}$
   (C) $\dfrac{x - y}{y}$
   (D) $\dfrac{1 - x}{1 - y}$

(E) $\dfrac{y - x}{xy}$

3. Divide $\dfrac{x - y}{x + y}$ by $\dfrac{y - x}{y + x}$.
   (A) 1
   (B) -1
   (C) $\dfrac{(x-y)^2}{(x+y)^2}$
   (D) $-\dfrac{(x-y)^2}{(x+y)^2}$
   (E) 0

4. Simplify: $\dfrac{1 + \dfrac{1}{x}}{\dfrac{y}{x}}$
   (A) $\dfrac{x + 1}{y}$
   (B) $\dfrac{x + 1}{x}$
   (C) $\dfrac{x + 1}{xy}$
   (D) $\dfrac{x^2 + 1}{xy}$
   (E) $\dfrac{y + 1}{y}$

5. Find an expression equivalent to $\left(\dfrac{2x^2}{y}\right)^3$.
   (A) $\dfrac{8x^5}{3y}$
   (B) $\dfrac{6x^6}{y^3}$
   (C) $\dfrac{6x^5}{y^3}$
   (D) $\dfrac{8x^5}{y^3}$
   (E) $\dfrac{8x^6}{y^3}$

6. Simplify: $\dfrac{\dfrac{1}{x} + \dfrac{1}{y}}{3}$
   (A) $\dfrac{3x + 3y}{xy}$
   (B) $\dfrac{3xy}{x + y}$
   (C) $\dfrac{xy}{3}$
   (D) $\dfrac{y + x}{3xy}$
   (E) $\dfrac{x + y}{3}$

7. $\frac{1}{a} + \frac{1}{b} = 7$ and $\frac{1}{a} - \frac{1}{b} = 3$.

Find $\frac{1}{a^2} - \frac{1}{b^2}$.

(A) 10
(B) 7
(C) 3
(D) 21
(E) 4

Algebraic Fractions—Correct Answers

1.	**(D)**	5.	**(E)**
2.	**(B)**	6.	**(D)**
3.	**(B)**	7.	**(D)**
4.	**(A)**		

Solutions—Algebraic Fractions

1. $\frac{n}{6} + \frac{2n}{5} = \frac{5n + 12n}{30} = \frac{17n}{30}$

Answer: **(D)** $\frac{17n}{30}$

2. $\frac{1}{1} - \frac{x}{y} = \frac{y - x}{y}$

Answer: **(B)** $\frac{y - x}{y}$

3. $\frac{x - y}{x + y} \cdot \frac{y + x}{y - x}$

Since addition is commutative, we may cancel x + y with y + x, as they are the same quantity. However, subtraction is not commutative, so we may not cancel x − y with y − x, as they are *not* the same quantity. We can change the form of y − x by factoring out a − 1. Thus, y − x = (−1)(x − y). In this form, we can cancel x − y, leaving an answer of $\frac{1}{-1}$, or −1.

Answer: **(B)** −1

4. Multiply every term in the fraction by x, giving $\frac{x + 1}{y}$.

Answer: **(A)** $\frac{x + 1}{y}$

5. $\frac{2x^2}{y} \cdot \frac{2x^2}{y} \cdot \frac{2x^2}{y} = \frac{8x^6}{y^3}$

Answer: **(E)** $\frac{8x^6}{y^3}$

6. Multiply every term of the fraction by xy, giving $\frac{y + x}{3xy}$.

Answer: **(D)** $\frac{y + x}{3xy}$

7. $\frac{1}{a^2} - \frac{1}{b^2}$ is equivalent to $\left(\frac{1}{a} + \frac{1}{b}\right)\left(\frac{1}{a} - \frac{1}{b}\right)$. We therefore multiply 7 by 3 for an answer of 21.

Answer: **(D)** 21

PROBLEM-SOLVING IN ALGEBRA

1. In solving verbal problems, the most important technique is to read accurately. Be sure you understand clearly what you are asked to find. Then try to evaluate the problem in common-sense terms; use this to eliminate answer choices.

   Example: If two people are working together, their combined speed is greater than either one, but not more than twice as fast as the fastest one.

   Example: The total number of the correct answers cannot be greater than the total number of answers. Thus if x questions are asked and you are to determine from other information how many correct answers there were, they cannot come to 2x.

2. The next step, when common sense alone is not enough, is to translate the problem into algebra. Keep it as simple as possible.

   Example: 24 = what % of 12?

   Translation: 24 = x% · 12
   or 24 = x$\frac{1}{100}$ · 12
   or 24 = $\frac{x}{100} \cdot \frac{12}{1}$

   Divide both sides by 12.

   $2 = \frac{x}{100}$

   Multiply both sides by 100.

   200 = x IN PERCENT

3. Be alert for the "hidden equation." This is some necessary information so obvious in the stated situation that the question assumes that you know it.

   Example: Boys plus girls = total class

   Example: Imported wine plus domestic wine = all wine.

   Example: The wall and floor, or the shadow and the building, make a right angle (thus permitting use of the Pythagorean Theorem).

4. Always remember that a variable (letter) can have any value whatsoever within the terms of the problem. Keep the possibility of fractional and negative values constantly in mind.

5. **Manipulating Equations.** You can perform any mathematical function you think helpful to one side of the equation, *provided* you do precisely the same thing to the other side of the equation. You can also substitute one side of an equality for the other in another equation.

6. **Manipulating Inequalities.** You can add to or subtract from both sides of an inequality without changing the direction of the inequality.

   Example:
   $$8 > 5$$
   $$8 + 10 > 5 + 10$$
   $$18 > 15$$

   Example:
   $$3x > y + z$$
   $$3x + 5 > y + z + 5$$

   You can also multiply or divide both sides of the inequality by any POSITIVE number without changing the direction of the inequality.

   Example:
   $$12 > 4$$
   $$3(12) > 3(4)$$
   $$36 > 12$$

   Example:
   $$x > y$$
   $$3x > 3y$$

   If you multiply or divide an inequality by a NEGATIVE number, you REVERSE the direction of the inequality.

   Example:
   $$4 > 3$$
   $$(-2)(4) < (-2)(3)$$
   $$-8 < -6$$

   Example:
   $$x^2y > z^2x$$
   $$-3(x^2y) < -3(z^2x)$$

7. **Solving Equations.** The first step is to determine what quantity or letter you wish to isolate. Solving an equation for x means getting x on one side of the equals sign and everything else on the other.

   Example: $5x + 3 = y$
   Subtract 3.
   $$5x = y - 3$$
   Divide by 5.
   $$x = \frac{y - 3}{5}$$

   Aside from factoring, discussed later in this review, unwrapping an equation is a matter of performing three steps. These rules are stated in terms of *x*, but apply equally to all variables or variable expressions.

   Put all x on one side of the equation, if not already there. This can be done by adding, subtracting, dividing or multiplying. Sometimes other quantities come along.

   Example: $4x + 2 = 29 + bxy$
   Subtract bxy.
   $$4x + 2 - bxy = 29$$
   (continued below)

   Unpeel x by considering the structure of the whole side x is on as a single expression and perform the opposite operation. Addition and subtraction are opposites; multiplication and division are opposites; raising to powers and taking roots are opposites.

   Example: $14k + 8 = 22$
   Left is addition, so subtract 8.
   $$14k = 14$$
   Divide by 14.
   $$k = 1$$

   Continue step b until only terms with x in them are left.

   Example: (from above)

   $$4x + 2 - bxy = 29$$
   Subtract 2.
   $$4x - bxy = 29 - 2 = 27$$

   If only one x term is left, unravel to just x.

Example: 8x = 24
              Divide by 8.
              x = 3

Example: 4x² = 36
           Divide by 4.
           x² = 9
           Take square root. Note ±.
           x = ±3

If more than one term with x in it is left, try to factor. While, in principle, many things are not factorable, on the GMAT most polynomials will be factorable. (Factoring and polynomial multiplication are discussed in the next section of the math review.)

8. If there are two variables in an equation, it may be helpful to put all expressions containing one variable on one side and all the others on the other.

9. Expressing x in terms of y means having an equation with x alone on one side and some expression of y on the other, such as x = 4y² + 3y + 4.

10. We will review some of the frequently encountered types of algebra problems, although not every problem you may get will fall into one of these categories. However, thoroughly familiarizing yourself with the types of problems that follow will help you to translate and solve all kinds of verbal problems.

A. Coin Problems

In solving coin problems, it is best to change the value of all monies involved to cents before writing an equation. Thus, the number of nickels must be multiplied by 5 to give their value in cents; dimes must be multiplied by 10; quarters by 25; half-dollars by 50; and dollars by 100.

Example: Richard has $3.50 consisting of nickels and dimes. If he has 5 more dimes than nickels, how many dimes does he have?

SOLUTION:

Let x = the number of nickels
x + 5 = the number of dimes
5x = the value of the nickels in cents
10x + 50 = the value of the dimes in cents
350 = the value of the money he has in cents
5x + 10x + 50 = 350
15x = 300
x = 20

Answer: He has 20 nickels and 25 dimes.

In a problem such as this, you can be sure that 20 would be among the multiple-choice answers. You must be sure to read carefully what you are asked to find and then continue until you have found the quantity sought.

B. Consecutive Integer Problems

Consecutive integers are one apart and can be represented by x, x+1, x+2, etc. Consecutive even or odd integers are two apart and can be represented by x, x+2, x+4, etc.

Illustration: Three consecutive odd integers have a sum of 33. Find the average of these integers.

Solution: Represent the integers as x, x+2 and x+4. Write an equation indicating the sum is 33.

$$3x + 6 = 33$$
$$3x = 27$$
$$x = 9$$

The integers are 9, 11, and 13. In the case of evenly spaced numbers such as these, the average is the middle number, 11. Since the sum of the three numbers was given originally, all we really had to do was to divide this sum by 3 to find the average, without ever knowing what the numbers were.

Answer: 11

C. Age Problems

Problems of this type usually involve a comparison of ages at the present time, several years from now, or several years ago. A person's age x years from now is found by adding x to his present age. A person's age x years ago is found by subtracting x from his present age.

Illustration: Michelle was 12 years old y years ago. Represent her age b years from now.

SOLUTION: Her present age is 12 + y. In b years. her age will be 12 + y + b.

Answer: 12 + y + b

D. Interest Problems

The annual amount of interest paid on an investment is found by multiplying the amount of principal invested by the rate (percent) of interest paid.

Principal · Rate = Interest income

Illustration: Mr. Strauss invests $4,000, part at 6% and part at 7%. His income from these investments in one year is $250. Find the amount invested at 7%.

SOLUTION: Represent each investment.
Let x = the amount invested at 7%. Always try to let x represent what you are looking for.
4000 − x = the amount invested at 6%
.07x = the income from the 7% investment
.06(4000 − x) = the income from the 6% investment
.07x + .06(4000 − x) = 250
7x + 6(4000 − x) = 25000
7x + 24000 − 6x = 25000
x = 1000

Answer: He invested $1,000 at 7%.

E. Mixture

There are two kinds of mixture problems with which you could be familiar. These problems are rare, so this is best regarded as an extra-credit section and not given top priority. The first is sometimes referred to as dry mixture, in which we mix dry ingredients of different values, such as nuts or coffee.

Also solved by the same method are problems such as those dealing with tickets at different prices. In solving this type of problem, it is best to organize the data in a chart of three rows and three columns, labeled as illustrated in the following problem.

Illustration: A dealer wishes to mix 20 pounds of nuts selling for 45 cents per pound with some more expensive nuts selling for 60 cents per pound, to make a mixture that will sell for 50 cents per pound. How many pounds of the more expensive nuts should he use?

SOLUTION:

	No. of lbs.	Price/lb.	= Total Value
Original	20	.45	.45(20)
Added	x	.60	.60(x)
Mixture	20 + x	.50	.50(20+x)

The value of the original nuts plus the value of the added nuts must equal the value of the mixture. Almost all mixture problems require an equation that comes from adding the final column.

.45(20) + .60(x) = .50(20 + x)
Multiply by 100 to remove decimals.
45(20) + 60(x) = 50(20 + x)
900 + 60x = 1000 + 50x
10x = 100
x = 10

Answer: He should use 10 lbs. of 60-cent nuts.

In solving the second type, or chemical. mixture problem, we are dealing with percents rather than prices, and amounts instead of value.

Illustration: How much water must be added to 20 gallons of solution that is 30% alcohol to dilute it to a solution that is only 25% alcohol?

SOLUTION:

	No. of gals.	% alcohol	= Amt. alcohol
Original	20	.30	.30(20)
Added	x	0	0
New	20 + x	.25	.25(20+x)

Note that the percent of alcohol in water is 0. Had we added pure alcohol to strengthen the solution, the percent would have been 100. The equation again comes from the last column. The amount of alcohol added (none in this case) plus the amount we had to start with must equal the amount of alcohol in the new solution.

$$.30(20) = .25(20 + x)$$
$$30(20) = 25(20 + x)$$
$$600 = 500 + 25x$$
$$100 = 25x$$
$$x = 4$$

Answer: 4 gallons.

F. Motion Problems

The fundamental relationship in all motion problems is that Rate · Time = Distance. The problems at the level of this examination usually derive their equation from a relationship concerning distance. Most problems fall into one of three types.

Motion in opposite directions. When two objects start at the same time and move in opposite directions, or when two objects start at points at a given distance apart and move toward each other until they meet, then twice the distance the second travels will equal the total distance covered.

In either of the above cases, $d_1 + d_2 =$ Total distance.

Motion in the same direction. This type of problem is sometimes called the "catch-up" problem. Two objects leave the same place at different times and different rates, but one "catches up" to the other. In such a case, the two distances must be equal.

Round trip. In this type of problem, the rate going is usually different from the rate

returning. The times are also different. But if we go somewhere and then return to the starting point, the distances must be the same.

To solve any motion problem, it is helpful to organize the data in a box with columns for rate, time, and distance. A separate line should be used for each moving object. Remember that if the rate is given in *miles per hour*, the time must be in *hours* and the distance in *miles*.

Illustration: Two cars leave a restaurant at 1 P.M., with one car traveling east at 60 miles per hour and the other west at 40 miles per hour along a straight highway. At what time will they be 350 miles apart?

SOLUTION:

	Rate	× Time	= Distance
Eastbound	60	x	60x
Westbound	40	x	40x

Notice that the time is unknown, since we must discover the number of hours traveled. However, since the cars start at the same time and stop when they are 350 miles apart, their times are the same.

$$60x + 40x = 350$$
$$100x = 350$$
$$x = 3\frac{1}{2}$$

Answer: In $3\frac{1}{2}$ hours, it will be 4:30 P.M.

Illustration: Gloria leaves home for school, riding her bicycle at a rate of 12 MPH. Twenty minutes after she leaves, her mother sees Gloria's English paper on her bed and leaves to bring it to her. If her mother drives at 36 MPH, how far must she drive before she reaches Gloria?

SOLUTION:

	Rate	× Time	= Distance
Gloria	12	x	12x
Mother	36	$x - \frac{1}{3}$	$36(x - \frac{1}{3})$

Notice that 20 minutes has been changed to $\frac{1}{3}$ of an hour. In this problem the times are not equal, but the distances are.

$$12x = 36(x - \frac{1}{3})$$
$$12x = 36x - 12$$
$$12 = 24x$$
$$x = \frac{1}{2}$$

Answer: If Gloria rode for $\frac{1}{2}$ hour at 12 m.p.h., the distance covered was 6 miles.

Illustration: Judy leaves home at 11 A.M. and rides to Mary's house to return her bicycle. She travels at 12 miles per hour and arrives at 11:30 A.M. She turns right around and walks home. How fast does she walk if she returns home at 1 P.M.?

SOLUTION:

	Rate	× Time	= Distance
Going	12	$\frac{1}{2}$	6
Return	x	$1\frac{1}{2}$	$\frac{3}{2}x$

The distances are equal.

$$6 = \frac{3}{2}x$$
$$12 = 3x$$
$$x = 4$$

Answer: She walked at 4 m.p.h.

G. Work Problems

In most work problems, a complete job is broken into several parts, each representing a fractional part of the entire job. For each fractional part, which represents the portion completed by one man, one machine, one pipe, etc., the numerator should represent the time actually spent working, while the denominator should represent the total time needed to do the entire job alone. The sum of all the individual fractions should be 1.

Illustration: John can wax his car in 3 hours. Jim can do the same job in 5 hours. How long will it take them if they work together?

SOLUTION: If multiple-choice answers are given, you should realize that the correct answer must be smaller than the quickest worker, for no matter how slow a helper may be, he does part of the job and therefore it will be completed in less time.

	John	Jim
$\dfrac{\text{Time spent}}{\text{Total time needed to do job alone}}$	$\dfrac{x}{3}$ +	$\dfrac{x}{5}$ = 1

Multiply by 15 to eliminate fractions.

$$5x + 3x = 15$$
$$8x = 15$$
$$x = 1\frac{7}{8} \text{ hours}$$

11. In general, you need as many equations as you have unknowns in order to get a unique numerical solution.

12. The two methods for coping with two or more equations are called **substitution** and **simultaneous.** They overlap. You have used both many times.

Substitution. Whenever one unknown equals something, you can substitute that something for it.

Example: (1) $2x + 3y = 14$ }
  (2) $x = 2y$ } given

Substitute 2y for x in first equation.

$$2(2y) + 3y = 14$$
$$4y + 3y = 14$$

Add up y's; divide by 7.

$$7y = 14$$
$$y = 2$$

Substitute for y in second equation.
$$x = 2(2)$$
$$x = 4$$

Simultaneous. Sometimes adding or subtracting whole equations is shorter.

Example: (1) $5x + 3y = 13$
  (2) $2x + 3y = 7$

Subtract (2) from (1).
$$5x + 3y = 13$$
$$- [2x + 3y = 7]$$
$$[5x - 2x] + [3y - 3y] = [13 - 7]$$
$$3x = 6$$

Divide by 3.
$$x = 2$$
$$y = 1 \qquad \text{by substitution}$$

Practice Problems—Algebra

1. Sue and Nancy wish to buy a gift for a friend. They combine their money and find they have $4.00, consisting of quarters, dimes, and nickels. If they have 35 coins and the number of quarters is half the number of nickels, how many quarters do they have?
(A) 5
(B) 10
(C) 20
(D) 3
(E) 6

2. Three times the first of three consecutive odd integers is 3 more than twice the third. Find the third integer.
(A) 9
(B) 11
(C) 13
(D) 15
(E) 7

3. Robert is 15 years older than his brother Stan. However, y years ago Robert was twice as old as Stan. If Stan is now b years old and $b > y$, find the value of $b - y$.
(A) 13
(B) 14
(C) 15
(D) 16
(E) 17

4. How many ounces of pure acid must be added to 20 ounces of a solution that is 5% acid to strengthen it to a solution that is 24% acid?
(A) $2\frac{1}{2}$
(B) 5
(C) 6
(D) $7\frac{1}{2}$
(E) 10

5. A dealer mixes a lbs. of nuts worth b cents per pound with c lbs. of nuts worth d cents per pound. At what price should he sell a pound of the mixture if he wishes to make a profit of 10 cents per pound?

(A) $\dfrac{ab + cd}{a + c} + 10$

(B) $\dfrac{ab + cd}{a + c} + .10$

(C) $\dfrac{b + d}{a + c} + 10$

(D) $\dfrac{b + d}{a + c} + .10$

(E) $\dfrac{b + d + 10}{a + c}$

6. Barbara invests $2,400 in the Security National Bank at 5%. How much additional money must she invest at 8% so that the total annual income will be equal to 6% of her entire investment?
(A) $2,400
(B) $3,600
(C) $1,000
(D) $3,000
(E) $1,200

7. Frank left Austin to drive to Boxville at 6:15 P.M. and arrived at 11:45 P.M. If he averaged 30 miles per hour and stopped one hour for dinner, how far is Boxville from Austin?
(A) 120
(B) 135
(C) 180
(D) 165
(E) 150

8. A plane traveling 600 miles per hour is 30 miles from Kennedy Airport at 4:58 P.M. At what time will it arrive at the airport?
(A) 5:00 P.M.
(B) 5:01 P.M.
(C) 5:02 P.M.
(D) 5:20 P.M.
(E) 5:03 P.M.

9. Mr. Bridges can wash his car in 15 minutes, while his son Dave takes twice as long to do the same job. If they work together, how many minutes will the job take them?
(A) 5
(B) $7\frac{1}{2}$
(C) 10
(D) $22\frac{1}{2}$
(E) 30

10. The value of a fraction is $\frac{2}{5}$. If the numerator is decreased by 2 and the denominator increased by 1, the resulting fraction is equivalent to $\frac{1}{4}$. Find the numerator of the original fraction.
    (A) 3
    (B) 4
    (C) 6
    (D) 10
    (E) 15

Algebra Problem-Solving— Correct Answers

1.	**(B)**	6.	**(E)**
2.	**(D)**	7.	**(B)**
3.	**(C)**	8.	**(B)**
4.	**(B)**	9.	**(C)**
5.	**(A)**	10.	**(C)**

Problem Solutions—Algebra Problem-Solving

1.   Let x = number of quarters
     2x = number of nickels
     35 − 3x = number of dimes
     Write all money values in cents.
     25(x) + 5(2x) + 10(35 − 3x) = 400
     25x + 10x + 350 − 30x = 400
     5x = 50
     x = 10

   Answer: **(B)** 10

2. Let x = first integer
   x + 2 = second integer
   x + 4 = third integer
   3(x) = 3 + 2(x + 4)
   3x = 3 + 2x + 8
   x = + 11
   The third integer is 15.

   Answer: **(D)** 15

3. b = Stan's age now
   b + 15 = Robert's age now
   b − y = Stan's age y years ago
   b + 15 − y = Robert's age y years ago
   b + 15 − y = 2(b − y)
   b + 15 − y = 2b − 2y
   15 = b − y

   Answer: **(C)** 15

4.

	No. of oz.	% acid	Amt. acid
Original	20	.05	1
Added	x	1.00	x
Mixture	20 + x	.24	.24(20 + x)

   1 + x = .24(20 + x) Multiply by 100 to eliminate decimal.
   100 + 100x = 480 + 24x
   76x = 380
   x = 5

   Answer: **(B)** 5

5. The a lbs. of nuts are worth a total of ab cents. The c lbs. of nuts are worth a total of cd cents. The value of the mixture is ab + cd cents. Since there are a + c pounds, each pound is worth $\frac{ab + cd}{a + c}$ cents.

   Since the dealer wants to add 10 cents to each pound for profit, and the value of each pound is in cents, we add 10 to the value of each pound.

   Answer: **(A)** $\frac{ab + cd}{a + c} + 10$

6. If Barbara invests x additional dollars at 8%, her total investment will amount to 2400 + x dollars.
   .05(2400) + .08(x) = .06(2400 + x)
   5(2400) + 8(x) = 6(2400 + x)
   12,000 + 8x = 14400 + 6x
   2x = 2400
   x = 1200

   Answer: **(E)** $1,200

7. Total time elapsed is $5\frac{1}{2}$ hours. However, one hour was used for dinner. Therefore, Frank drove at 30 m.p.h. for $4\frac{1}{2}$ hours, covering 135 miles.

   Answer: **(B)** 135

8. Time $= \dfrac{\text{Distance}}{\text{Rate}} = \dfrac{30}{600} = \dfrac{1}{20}$ hour, or 3 minutes.

   Answer: **(B)** 5:01 P.M.

9. Dave takes 30 minutes to wash the car alone.

   $\dfrac{x}{15} + \dfrac{x}{30} = 1$

   $2x + x = 30$

   $3x = 30$

   $x = 10$

   Answer: **(C)** 10

10. Let $2x =$ original numerator

    $5x =$ original denominator

    $\dfrac{2x - 2}{5x + 1} = \dfrac{1}{4}$ Cross multiply

    $8x - 8 = 5x + 1$

    $3x = 9$

    $x = 3$

    Original numerator is 2(3), or 6.

    Answer: **(C)** 6

POLYNOMIAL MULTIPLICATION AND FACTORING

1. A polynomial is any expression with two or more terms, such as $2x + y$ or $3z + 9m^2$.

2. A single term multiplied by another expression must multiply *every* term in the second expression.

   Example: $4(x + y + 2z) = 4x + 4y + 8z$

3. The same holds true for division.

   Example: $\dfrac{(a + b + 3c)}{3} = \dfrac{a}{3} + \dfrac{b}{3} + \dfrac{3c}{3}$

   $= \dfrac{a}{3} + \dfrac{b}{3} + c$

4. The FOIL method should be used when multiplying two binomials together.

Example: $(x + y)(x + y)$

First $(x + y)(x + y) = x^2$

Outer $(x + y)(x + y) = xy$

Inner $(x + y)(x + y) = xy$

Last $(x + y)(x + y) = y^2$

$(x + y)(x + y) = x^2 + 2xy + y2$

5. You should know these three equivalencies by heart for the GMAT.

   $(x + y)^2 = (x + y)(x + y) = x^2 + 2xy + y^2$

   $(x - y)^2 = (x - y)(x - y) = x^2 - 2xy + y^2$

   $(x + y)(x - y) = x^2 - y^2$

   Work all three out with the FOIL method. The x or y could stand for a letter, a number, or an expression.

   Example: $(m + 3)^2 = m^2 + 2 \cdot 3 \cdot m + 3^2$

   $= m^2 + 6m + 9$

   Example: $(2k - p)^2 = (2k)^2 - 2 \cdot 2k \cdot p + p^2$

   $= 4k^2 - 4kp + p^2$

6. You will not need much factoring on the exam. Most of what you do need was covered in the preceding points—if you just reverse the process of multiplication.

   Example: $3x + 6xy = 3x(1 + 2y)$

   Example: $2xyz + 4xy = 2xy(z + 2)$

7. One special situation (called a quadratic equation) occurs when an algebraic multiplication equals zero. Since zero can only be achieved in multiplication by multiplying by zero itself, one of the factors must be zero.

   Example: $(x + 1)(x + 2) = 0$
   Therefore, either $x + 1 = 0$, $x = -1$
   or $x + 2 = 0$, $x = -2$.

   In such a situation you simply have to live with two possible answers. This uncertainty may be important in Quantitative Comparison questions.

8. You may also need to factor to achieve a quadratic format.

Example: $x^2 + 2x + 1 = 0$
$(x + 1)(x + 1) = 0$

Thus, x + 1 = 0
x = −1 since both factors are the same.

GEOMETRY

Symbols

The most common symbols used in GMAT geometry problems are listed below. The concepts behind the symbols will be explained in this section.

Angles
∠ or ∡   angle (∠ C = angle C or ∡ C = angle C)
  ∟   right angle (90°)

Lines
  ⊥   perpendicular, at right angles to
  ∥   parallel (line B ∥ line C)
  $\overline{BD}$ line or line segment BD

Circles
  ⊙   circle
  $\overset{\frown}{AC}$ arc AC

Angles

1. a. An **angle** is the figure formed by two lines meeting at a point.

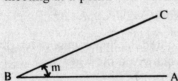

   b. The point B is the **vertex** of the angle and the lines BA and BC are the **sides** of the angle.

2. There are three common ways of naming an angle:

   a. By a small letter or figure written within the angle, as ∡m.

   b. By a capital letter at its vertex, as ∡ʙ.

   c. By three capital letters, the middle letter being the vertex letter, as ∠ABC.

3. a. When two straight lines intersect (cut each other), four angles are formed. If these four angles are equal, each angle is a **right angle** and contains 90°. The symbol ∟ is used to indicate a right angle.

Example:

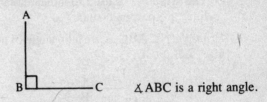

∡ABC is a right angle.

   b. An angle less than a right angle is an **acute angle.**

   c. If the two sides of an angle extend in opposite directions forming a straight line, the angle is a **straight angle** and contains 180°.

   d. An angle greater than a right angle (90°) and less than a straight angle (180°) is an **obtuse angle.**

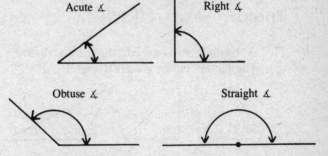

4. a. Two angles are **complementary** if their sum is 90°.

   b. To find the complement of an angle, subtract the given number of degrees from 90°.

Example: The complement of 60° is 90° − 60° = 30°.

5. a. Two angles are **supplementary** if their sum is 180°.

b. To find the supplement of an angle, subtract the given number of degrees from 180°.

Example: The supplement of 60° is 180° − 60° = 120°.

Lines

6. a. Two lines are **perpendicular** to each other if they meet to form a right angle. The symbol ⊥ is used to indicate that the lines are perpendicular.

Example: ∠ABC is a right angle. Therefore, AB ⊥ BC.

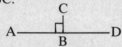

b. Lines that do not meet no matter how far they are extended are called **parallel lines.** Parallel lines are always the same perpendicular distance from each other. The symbol ∥ is used to indicate that two lines are parallel.

Example: AB ∥ CD

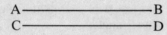

Triangles

7. A **triangle** is a closed, three-sided figure. The figures below are all triangles.

8. a. The sum of the three angles of a triangle is 180°.

b. To find an angle of a triangle when you are given the other two angles, add the given angles and subtract their sum from 180°.

Illustration: Two angles of a triangle are 60° and 40°. Find the third angle.

SOLUTION: 60° + 40° = 100°
                180° − 100° = 80°

Answer: The third angle is 80°.

9. a. A triangle that has two equal sides is called an **isosceles triangle.**

b. In an isosceles triangle, the angles opposite the equal sides are also equal.

10. a. A triangle that has all three sides equal is called an **equilateral triangle.**

b. Each angle of an equilateral triangle is 60°.

11. a. A triangle that has a right angle is called a **right triangle.**

b. In a right triangle, the two acute angles are complementary.

c. In a right triangle, the side opposite the right angle is called the **hypotenuse** and is the longest side. The other two sides are called **legs.**

Example: AC is the hypotenuse.
AB and BC are the legs.

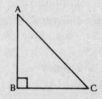

12. The **Pythagorean Theorem** states that in a right triangle the square of the hypotenuse equals the sum of the squares of the legs. In the triangle above, this would be expressed as $\overline{AB}^2 + \overline{BC}^2 = \overline{AC}^2$. The simplest whole number example is $3^2 + 4^2 = 5^2$.

13. a. To find the hypotenuse of a right triangle when given the legs:

   a. Square each leg.

   b. Add the squares.

   c. Extract the square root of this sum.

Illustration: In a right triangle the legs are 6 inches and 8 inches. Find the hypotenuse.

SOLUTION: $6^2 = 36$ $8^2 = 64$
                      $36 + 64 = 100$
                      $\sqrt{100} = 10$

Answer: The hypotenuse is 10 inches.

b. To find a leg when given the other leg and the hypotenuse of a right triangle:

   a. Square the hypotenuse and the given leg.

   b. Subtract the square of the leg from the square of the hypotenuse.

   c. Extract the square root of this difference.

Illustration: One leg of a right triangle is 12 feet and the hypotenuse is 20 feet. Find the other leg.

SOLUTION: $12^2 = 144$ $20^2 = 400$
                    $400 - 144 = 256$
                    $\sqrt{256} = 16$

Answer: The other leg is 16 feet.

14. Within a given triangle, the largest side is opposite the largest angle; the smallest side is opposite the smallest angle; and equal sides are opposite equal angles.

Quadrilaterals

15. a. A **quadrilateral** is a closed, four-sided figure in two dimensions. Common quadrilaterals are the **parallelogram, rectangle,** and **square.**

   b. The sum of the four angles of a quadrilateral is 360°.

16. a. A **parallelogram** is a quadrilateral in which both pairs of opposite sides are parallel.

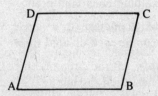

   b. Opposite sides of a parallelogram are also equal.

   c. Opposite angles of a parallelogram are equal.

17. A **rectangle** has all of the properties of a parallelogram. In addition, all four of its angles are right angles.

18. A **square** is a rectangle having the additional property that all four of its sides are equal.

Circles

19. A **circle** is a closed plane curve, all points of which are equidistant from a point within called the **center.**

20. a. A **complete circle** contains 360°.

   b. A **semicircle** contains 180°.

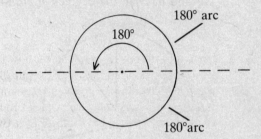

21. a. A **chord** is a line segment connecting any two points on the circle.

   b. A **radius** of a circle is a line segment connecting the center with any point on the circle.

   c. A **diameter** is a chord passing through the center of the circle.

   d. A **secant** is a chord extended in either one or both directions.

   e. A **tangent** is a line touching a circle at one and only one point.

   f. The **circumference** is the curved line bounding the circle.

   g. An **arc** of a circle is any part of the circumference.

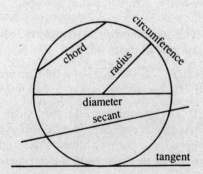

Note: The terms secant and chord are rarely used on the test.

22. a. A **central angle,** as ∠AOB in the figure below, is an angle whose vertex is the center of the circle and whose sides are radii. A central angle is equal to, or has the same number of degrees as, its intercepted arc.

    b. An **inscribed angle,** as ∠MNP, is an angle whose vertex is on the circle and whose sides are chords. An inscribed angle has half the number of degrees as its intercepted arc. ∠MNP intercepts arc MP and has half the degrees of arc MP.

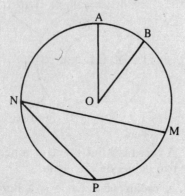

Perimeter

23. The **perimeter** of a two-dimensional figure is the distance around the figure.

    Example: The perimeter of the figure above is $9 + 8 + 4 + 3 + 5 = 29$.

24. a. The perimeter of a triangle is found by adding all of its sides.

    Example: If the sides of a triangle are 4, 5, and 7, its perimeter is $4 + 5 + 7 = 16$.

    b. If the perimeter and two sides of a triangle are given, the third side is found by adding the two given sides and subtracting this sum from the perimeter.

Illustration: Two sides of a triangle are 12 and 15, and the perimeter is 37. Find the other side:

SOLUTION: $12 + 15 = 27$
$37 - 27 = 10$

Answer: The third side is 10.

25. The perimeter of a rectangle equals twice the sum of the length and the width. The formula is $P = 2(l + w)$.

    Example: The perimeter of a rectangle whose length is 7 feet and width is 3 feet equals $2 \times 10 = 20$ feet.

26. The perimeter of a square equals one side multiplied by 4. The formula is $P = 4s$.

    Example: The perimeter of a square, one side of which is 5 feet, is 4×5 feet $= 20$ feet.

27. a. The circumference of a circle is equal to the product of the diameter multiplied by π. The formula is $C = \pi d$.

    b. The number π (pi) is approximately equal to $\frac{22}{7}$, or 3.14 (3.1416 for greater accuracy). A problem will usually state which value to use; otherwise, express the answer in terms of "pi," π.

Example: The circumference of a circle whose diameter is 4 inches $= 4\pi$ inches; or, if it is stated that $\pi = \frac{22}{7}$, the circumference is $4 \times \frac{22}{7} = \frac{88}{7} = 12\frac{4}{7}$ inches.

    c. Since the diameter is twice the radius, the circumference equals twice the radius multiplied by π. The formula is $C = 2\pi r$.

Example: If the radius of a circle is 3 inches, then the circumference $= 6\pi$ inches.

    d. The diameter of a circle equals the circumference divided by π.

Example: If the circumference of a circle is 11 inches, then, assuming

$$\pi = \frac{22}{7},$$
$$\text{diameter} = 11 \div \frac{22}{7} \text{ inches}$$
$$= \overset{1}{\cancel{11}} \times \frac{7}{\cancel{22}} \text{ incheses}$$
$$= \frac{7}{2} \text{ inches, or } 3\frac{1}{2} \text{ inches}$$

Area

28. a. In a figure of two dimensions, the total space within the figure is called the **area.**

    b. Area is expressed in square denominations, such as square inches, square centimeters, and square miles.

    c. In computing area, all dimensions must be expressed in the same denomination.

29. The area of a square is equal to the square of the length of any side. The formula is A = s^2.

    Example: The area of a square, one side of which is 6 inches, is 6 × 6 = 36 square inches.

30. a. The area of a rectangle equals the product of the length multiplied by the width. The length is any side; the width is the side next to the length. The formula is A = l × w.

    Example: If the length of a rectangle is 6 feet and its width 4 feet, then the area is 6 × 4 = 24 square feet.

    b. If given the area of a rectangle and one dimension, divide the area by the given dimension to find the other dimension.

    Example: If the area of a rectangle is 48 square feet and one dimension is 4 feet, then the other dimension is 48 ÷ 4 = 12 feet.

31. a. The altitude, or height, of a parallelogram is a line drawn from a vertex perpendicular to the opposite side, or base.

    Example: DE is the height.
    AB is the base.

    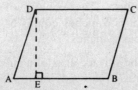

    b. The area of a parallelogram is equal to the product of its base and its height: A = b × h.

Example: If the base of a parallelogram is 10 centimeters and its height is 5 centimeters, its area is 5 × 10 = 50 square centimeters.

c. If given one of these dimensions and the area, divide the area by the given dimension to find the base or the height of a parallelogram.

Example: If the area of a parallelogram is 40 square inches and its height is 8 inches, its base is 40 ÷ 8 = 5 inches.

32. a. The altitude, or height, of a triangle is a line drawn from a vertex perpendicular to the opposite side, called the base. Each triangle has three sets of altitudes and bases.

    b. The area of a triangle is equal to one-half the product of the base and the height: A = ½b × h.

    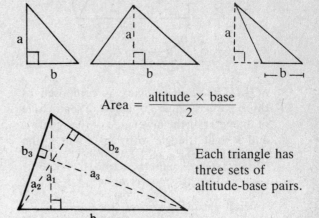

    $$\text{Area} = \frac{\text{altitude} \times \text{base}}{2}$$

    Each triangle has three sets of altitude-base pairs.

    Example: The area of a triangle having a height of 5 inches and a base of 4 inches is ½ × 5 × 4 = ½ × 20 = 10 square inches.

    c. In a right triangle, one leg may be considered the height and the other leg the base. Therefore, the area of a right triangle is equal to one-half the product of the legs.

    Example: The legs of a right triangle are 3 and 4. Its area is ½ × 3 × 4 = 6 square units.

33. a. The area of a circle is equal to the radius squared, multiplied by π: A = πr^2.

    Example: If the radius of a circle is 6 inches, then the area = 36π square inches.

b. To find the radius of a circle given the area, divide the area by π and find the square root of the quotient.

Example: To find the radius of a circle of area 100π:

$$\frac{100\pi}{\pi} = 100$$
$$\sqrt{100} = 10 = radius.$$

34. Some figures are composed of several geometric shapes. To find the area of such a figure it is necessary to find the area of each of its parts.

Illustration: Find the area of the figure below:

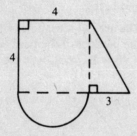

SOLUTION: The figure is composed of three parts: a square of side 4, a semi-circle of diameter 4 (the lower side of the square), and a right triangle with legs 3 and 4 (the right side of the square).

Area of square = 4^2 = 16
Area of triangle = $\frac{1}{2} \times 3 \times 4$ = 6
Area of semicircle is $\frac{1}{2}$ area of circle = $\frac{1}{2}\pi r^2$
Radius = $\frac{1}{2} \times 4$ = 2
Area = $\frac{1}{2}\pi r^2$
= $\frac{1}{2} \times \pi \times 2^2$
= 2π

Answer: Total area = $16 + 6 + 2\pi = 22 + 2\pi$.

Three-Dimensional Figures

35. a. In a three-dimensional figure, the total space contained within the figure is called the **volume;** it is expressed in **cubic denominations.**

b. The total outside surface is called the **surface area;** it is expressed in **square denominations.**

c. In computing volume and surface area, all dimensions must be expressed in the same denomination.

36. a. A **rectangular solid** is a figure of three dimensions having six rectangular faces meeting each other at right angles. The three dimensions are length, width and height.

The figure below is a rectangular solid; "l" is the length, "w" is the width, and "h" is the height.

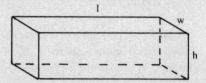

b. The volume of a rectangular solid is the product of the length, width, and height; $V = l \times w \times h$.

Example: The volume of a rectangular solid whose length is 6 feet, width 3 feet, and height 4 feet is $6 \times 3 \times 4 = 72$ cubic feet.

37. a. A **cube** is a rectangular solid whose edges are equal. The figure below is a cube; the length, width, and height are all equal to "e."

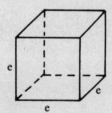

b. The volume of a cube is equal to the edge cubed: $V = e^3$.

Example: The volume of a cube whose height is 6 inches equals $6^3 = 6 \times 6 \times 6 = 216$ cubic inches.

c. The surface area of a cube is equal to the area of any side multiplied by 6.

Example: The surface area of a cube whose length is 5 inches = $5^2 \times 6 = 25 \times 6 = 150$ square inches.

38. The volume of a **circular cylinder** is equal to the product of π, the radius squared, and the height.

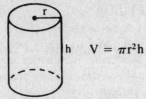

$$V = \pi r^2 h$$

Example: A circular cylinder has a radius of 7 inches and a height of $\frac{1}{2}$ inch. Using $\pi = \frac{22}{7}$, its volume is

$$\frac{22}{7} \times 7 \times 7 \times \frac{1}{2} = 77 \text{ cubic inches}$$

39. The volume of a **sphere** is equal to $\frac{4}{3}$ the product of π and the radius cubed.

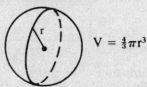

$$V = \frac{4}{3}\pi r^3$$

Example: If the radius of a sphere is 3 cm, its volume in terms of π is

$$\frac{4}{3} \times \pi \times 3 \text{ cm} \times 3 \text{ cm} \times 3 \text{ cm} = 36\pi \text{ cm}^3$$

Practice Problems Involving Geometry

1. If the perimeter of a rectangle is 68 yards and the width is 48 feet, the length is
   (A) 10 yd
   (B) 18 yd
   (C) 20 ft
   (D) 46 ft
   (E) 56 ft

2. The total length of fencing needed to enclose a rectangular area 46 feet by 34 feet is
   (A) 26 yd 1 ft
   (B) $26\frac{2}{3}$ yd
   (C) 48 yds
   (D) 52 yd 2 ft
   (E) $53\frac{1}{3}$ yd

3. An umbrella 50″ long can lie on the bottom of a trunk whose length and width are, respectively,
   (A) 26″, 30″

(B) 39″, 36″
(C) 31″, 31″
(D) 40″, 21″
(E) 40″, 30″

4. A road runs 1200 ft from A to B, and then makes a right angle going to C, a distance of 500 ft. A new road is being built directly from A to C. How much shorter will the new road be?
   (A) 400 ft
   (B) 609 ft
   (C) 850 ft
   (D) 1000 ft
   (E) 1300 ft

5. A certain triangle has sides that are, respectively, 6 inches, 8 inches, and 10 inches long. A rectangle equal in area to that of the triangle has a width of 3 inches. The perimeter of the rectangle, expressed in inches, is
   (A) 11
   (B) 16
   (C) 22
   (D) 24
   (E) 30

6. A ladder 65 feet long is leaning against the wall. Its lower end is 25 feet away from the wall. How much further away will it be if the upper end is moved down 8 feet?
   (A) 60 ft
   (B) 52 ft
   (C) 14 ft
   (D) 10 ft
   (E) 8 ft

7. A rectangular bin 4 feet long, 3 feet wide, and 2 feet high is solidly packed with bricks whose dimensions are 8 inchs, 4 inches, and 2 inches. The number of bricks in the bin is
   (A) 54
   (B) 320
   (C) 648
   (D) 848
   (E) none of these

8. If the cost of digging a trench is $2.12 a cubic yard, what would be the cost of digging a trench 2 yards by 5 yards by 4 yards?
   (A) $21.20
   (B) $40.00

(C) $64.00
(D) $84.80
(E) $104.80

9. A piece of wire is shaped to enclose a square, whose area is 121 square inches. It is then reshaped to enclose a rectangle whose length is 13 inches. The area of the rectangle, in square inches, is
   (A) 64
   (B) 96
   (C) 117
   (D) 144
   (E) 234

10. The area of a 2-foot-wide walk around a garden that is 30 feet long and 20 feet wide is
    (A) 104 sq ft
    (B) 216 sq ft
    (C) 680 sq ft
    (D) 704 sq ft
    (E) 1416 sq ft

11. The area of a circle is 49π. Find its circumference, in terms of π.
    (A) 14π
    (B) 28π
    (C) 49π
    (D) 98π
    (E) 147π

12. In two hours, the minute hand of a clock rotates through an angle of
    (A) 90°
    (B) 180°
    (C) 360°
    (D) 720°
    (E) 1080°

13. A box is 12 inches in width, 16 inches in length, and 6 inches in height. How many square inches of paper would be required to cover it on all sides?
    (A) 192
    (B) 360
    (C) 720
    (D) 900
    (E) 1440

14. If the volume of a cube is 64 cubic inches, the sum of its edges is
    (A) 48 in

(B) 32 in
(C) 24 in
(D) 16 in
(E) 12 in

Geometry Problems—Correct Answers

1.	**(B)**	6.	**(C)**	11.	**(A)**
2.	**(E)**	7.	**(C)**	12.	**(D)**
3.	**(E)**	8.	**(D)**	13.	**(C)**
4.	**(A)**	9.	**(C)**	14.	**(A)**
5.	**(C)**	10.	**(B)**		

Problem Solutions—Geometry

1.

   Perimeter = 68 yards
   Each width = 48 feet = 16 yards
   Both widths = 16 yd + 16 yd = 32 yd
   Perimeter = sum of all sides
   Remaining two sides must total 68 − 32 = 36 yards.
   Since the remaining two sides are equal, they are each 36 ÷ 2 = 18 yards.

   Answer: **(B)** 18 yd

2. Perimeter = 2(46 + 34) feet
   $\qquad\qquad$ = 2 × 80 feet
   $\qquad\qquad$ = 160 feet
   160 feet = 160 ÷ 3 yards = $53\frac{1}{3}$ yards

   Answer: **(E)** $53\frac{1}{3}$ yd

3. The umbrella would be the hypotenuse of a right triangle whose legs are the dimensions of the trunk.

   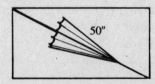

   The Pythagorean Theorem states that in a right triangle, the square of the hypotenuse equals the sum of the squares of the legs. Therefore, the sum of the dimensions of the trunk squared must at least equal the length of the umbrella squared, which is 50^2 or 2500.

The only set of dimensions filling this condition is **(E)**:

$$40^2 + 30^2 = 1600 + 900$$
$$= 2500$$

Answer: **(E)** 40″, 30″

4. The new road is the hypotenuse of a right triangle, whose legs are the old road.

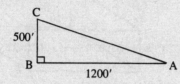

$$AC^2 = AB^2 + BC^2$$
$$AC = \sqrt{500^2 + 1200^2}$$
$$= \sqrt{250,000 + 1,440,000}$$
$$= \sqrt{1,690,000}$$
$$= 1300 \text{ feet}$$
$$\text{Old road} = 1200 + 500 \text{ feet}$$
$$= 1700 \text{ feet}$$
$$\text{New road} = 1300 \text{ feet}$$
$$\text{Difference} = 400 \text{ feet}$$

Answer: **(A)** 400 ft

5. Since $6^2 + 8^2 = 10^2$ $(36 + 64 = 100)$, the triangle is a right triangle. The area of the triangle is $\frac{1}{2} \times 6 \times 8 = 24$ square inches. Therefore, the area of the rectangle is 24 square inches.

If the width of the rectangle is 3 inches, the length is $24 \div 3 = 8$ inches. Then the perimeter of the rectangle is $2(3 + 8) = 2 \times 11 = 22$ inches.

Answer: **(C)** 22

6. The ladder forms a right triangle with the wall and the ground.

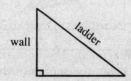

First, find the height that the ladder reaches when the lower end of the ladder is 25 feet from the wall:

$$65^2 = 4225$$
$$25^2 = 625$$
$$65^2 - 25^2 = 3600$$
$$\sqrt{3600} = 60$$

The ladder reaches 60 feet up the wall when its lower end is 25 feet from the wall.

If the upper end is moved down 8 feet, the ladder will reach a height of $60 - 8 = 52$ feet.

The new triangle formed has a hypotenuse of 65 feet and one leg of 52 feet. Find the other leg:

$$65^2 = 4225$$
$$52^2 = 2704$$
$$65^2 - 52^2 = 1521$$
$$\sqrt{1521} = 39$$

The lower end of the ladder is now 39 feet from the wall. This is $39 - 25 = 14$ feet further than it was before.

Answer: **(C)** 14 ft

7. Convert the dimensions of the bin to inches:

$$4 \text{ feet} = 48 \text{ inches}$$
$$3 \text{ feet} = 36 \text{ inches}$$
$$2 \text{ feet} = 24 \text{ inches}$$
$$\text{Volume of bin} = 48 \times 36 \times 24 \text{ cubic inches}$$
$$= 41,472 \text{ cubic inches}$$
$$\text{Volume of each brick} = 8 \times 4 \times 2 \text{ cubic inches}$$
$$= 64 \text{ cubic inches}$$
$$41,472 \div 64 = 648 \text{ bricks}$$

Answer: **(C)** 648

8. The trench contains

$$2 \text{ yd} \times 5 \text{ yd} \times 4 \text{ yd} = 40 \text{ cubic yards}$$
$$40 \times \$2.12 = \$84.80$$

Answer: **(D)** \$84.80

9. Find the dimensions of the square: If the area of the square is 121 square inches, each side is $\sqrt{121} = 11$ inches, and the perimeter is $4 \times 11 = 44$ inches.

Next, find the dimensions of the rectangle: The perimeter of the rectangle is the same as the perimeter of the square, since the same length of wire is used to enclose either figure. Therefore, the perimeter of the rectangle is 44 inches. If the two lengths are each 13 inches, their total is 26 inches, and 44 − 26 inches, or 18 inches, remain for the two widths. Each width is equal to 18 ÷ 2 = 9 inches.

The area of a rectangle with length 13 in and width 9 in is 13 × 9 = 117 sq in.

Answer: **(C)** 117

10.

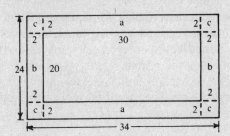

The walk consists of:

a. 2 rectangles of length 30 feet and width 2 feet.

Area of each rectangle = 2 × 30 = 60 sq ft
Area of both rectangles: = 120 sq ft

b. 2 rectangles of length 20 feet and width 2 feet.

Area of each = 2 × 20 = 40 sq ft
Area of both = 80 sq ft

c. 4 squares, each having sides measuring 2 feet.

Area of each square = 2^2 = 4 sq ft
Area of 4 squares = 16 sq ft

Total area of walk = 120 + 80 + 16
= 216 sq ft

Alternate solution:

Area of walk = Area of large rectangle
− area of small rectangle
= 34 × 24 − 30 × 20
= 816 − 600
= 216 sq ft

Answer: **(B)** 216 sq ft

11. If the area of a circle is 49π, its radius is $\sqrt{49}$

= 7. Then, the circumference is equal to 2 × 7 × π = 14π.

Answer: **(A)** 14π

12. In one hour, the minute hand rotates through 360°. In two hours, it rotates through 2 × 360° = 720°.

Answer: **(D)** 720°

13. Find the area of each surface:

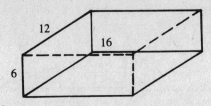

Area of top =	12 × 16 =	192 sq in
Area of bottom =	12 × 16 =	192 sq in
Area of front =	6 × 16 =	96 sq in
Area of back =	6 × 16 =	96 sq in
Area of right side =	6 × 12 =	72 sq in
Area of left side =	6 × 12 =	+ 72 sq in
Total surface area =		720 sq in

Answer: **(C)** 720

14. For a cube, $V = e^3$. If the volume is 64 cubic inches, each edge is $\sqrt[3]{64}$ = 4 inches.

A cube has 12 edges. If each edge is 4 inches, the sum of the edges is 4 × 12 = 48 inches.

Answer: **(A)** 48 in

COORDINATE GEOMETRY

Perhaps the easiest way to understand the coordinate axis system is as an analog to the points of the compass. If we take a plot of land, we can divide it into quadrants:

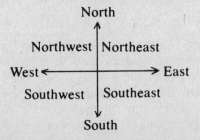

Now, if we add measuring units along each of the directional axes, we can actually describe any location on this piece of land by two numbers. For example, point P is located at 4 units East and 5 units North. Point Q is located at 4 units West and 5 units North. Point R is located at 5 units West and 2 units South. And Point T is located at 3 units East and 4 units South.

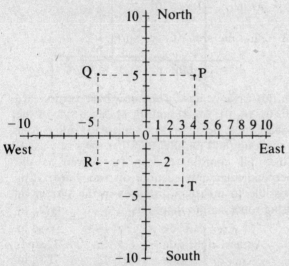

The coordinate system used in coordinate geometry differs from our map of a plot of land in two respects. First, it uses x and y axes divided into negative and positive regions.

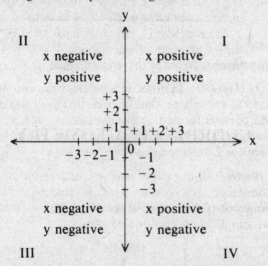

It is easy to see that Quadrant I corresponds to our Northeast quarter, and in it the measurements on both the x and y axes are positive. Quadrant II corresponds to our Northwest quarter, and in it the measurements on the x axis are negative and the measurements on the y axis are positive. Quadrant III corresponds to the Southwest quarter, and in it both the x axis measurements and the y axis measurements are negative. Finally, Quadrant IV corresponds to our Southeast quarter, and there the x values are positive while the y values are negative.

Second, mathematicians adopt a convention called **ordered pairs** to eliminate the necessity of specifying each time whether one is referring to the x axis or the y axis. An ordered pair of coordinates has the general form (a, b). The first element always refers to the x value (distance left or right of the *origin*, or intersection, of the axes) while the second element gives the y value (distance up or down from the origin).

To make this a bit more concrete, let us *plot* some examples of ordered pairs, that is, find their locations in the system: Let us start with the point (3, 2). We begin by moving to the positive 3 value on the x axis. Then from there we move up two units on the y axis.

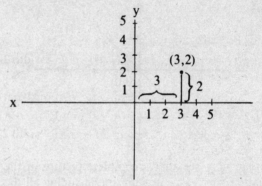

An alternative way of speaking about this is to say that the point (3, 2) is located at the intersection of a line drawn through the x value 3 parallel to the y axis and a line drawn through the y value 2 parallel to the x axis:

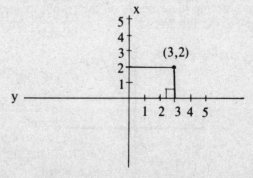

Both methods locate the same point. Let us now use the ordered pairs (−3, 2), (−2, −3) and (3, −2):

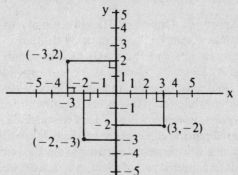

One important use of the coordinate axis system is that it can be used to draw a picture of an equation. For example, we know that the equation $x = y$ has an infinite number of solutions:

x	1	2	3	5	0	−3	−5	etc.
y	1	2	3	5	0	−3	−5	

We can plot these pairs of x and y on the axis system:

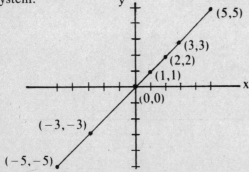

We can now see that a complete picture of the equation $x = y$ is a straight line including all the real numbers such that x is equal to y.

Similarly, we might graph the equation $2x = y$

x	−4	−2	−1	0	1	2	4
y	−8	−4	−2	0	2	4	8

After entering these points on the graph, we can complete the picture:

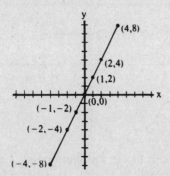

It too is a straight line, but it rises at a more rapid rate than does $x = y$.

A final use one might have for the coordinate system on the GMAT is in graphing geometric figures:

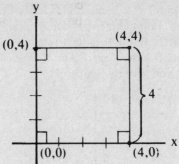

In this case we have a square whose vertices are (0, 0), (4, 0), (4, 4) and (0, 4). Each side of the square must be equal to 4 since each side is four units long (and parallel to either the x or y axis). Since all coordinates can be viewed as the perpendicular intersection of two lines, it is possible to measure distances in the system by using some simple theorems.

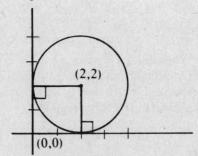

Illustration: What is the area of circle 0?

SOLUTION: In order to solve this problem, we need to know the radius of circle 0. The center of the circle is located at the intersection of $x = 2$ and $y = 2$, or the point (2, 2). So we know the radius is 2 units long and the area is 4π.

Answer: 4π

Illustration: What is the length of PQ?

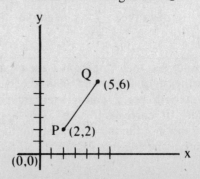

SOLUTION: We can find the length of PQ by constructing a triangle:

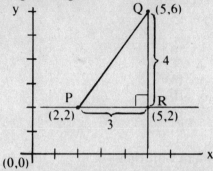

Now, we see that QR runs from (5,6) to (5,2) and so it must be 4 units long. We see that PR runs from (2,2) to (5, 2) so it is 3 units long. We then use the Pythagorean Theorem to determine that PQ, which is the hypotenuse of our triangle, is 5 units long.

Answer: 5 units

It is actually possible to generalize on this example. Let us take any two points on the graph (for simplicity's sake we will confine the discussion to the First Quadrant, but the method is generally applicable, that is, will work in all quadrants and even with lines covering two or more quadrants) P and Q. Now let us assign the value (x_1, y_1) to P and (x_2, y_2) to Q.

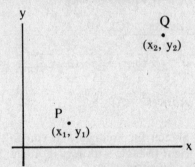

Then, following our method above, we construct a triangle so that we can use the Pythagorean Theorem:

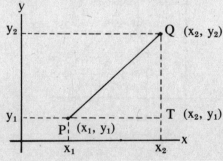

Point T now has the coordinates (x_2, y_1). Side PT will be $x_2 - x_1$ units long (the y coordinate does not change, so the length is only the distance moved on the x axis), and QT will be $y_2 - y_1$ (again, the distance is purely vertical, moving up from y_1 to y_2, with no change in the x value). Using the Pythagorean Theorem:

$$PQ^2 = PT^2 + QT^2$$
$$PQ^2 = (x_2 - x_1)^2 + (y_2 - y_1)^2$$
$$PQ = \sqrt{(x_2 - x_1)^2 + (y_2 - y_1)^2}$$

And we have just derived what is called the **Distance Formula.** We can find the length of any straight line segment drawn in a coordinate axis system (that is, the distance between two points in the system) using this formula.

Illustration: What is the distance between P and Q?

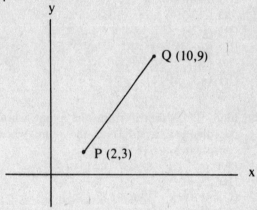

SOLUTION: Point P has the coordinates (2,3) and Q the coordinates (10,9). Using the formula:

$$PQ^2 = \sqrt{(10 - 2)^2 + (9 - 3)^2}$$
$$PQ = \sqrt{8^2 + 6^2}$$
$$PQ = \sqrt{64 + 36}$$
$$PQ = \sqrt{100}$$
$$PQ = 10$$

Answer: 10

For those students who find the Distance Formula a bit too technical, be reassured that the Pythagorean Theorem (which is more familiar) will work just as well on the GMAT. In fact, as a general rule, any time one is asked to calculate a distance which does not move parallel to one of the axes, the proper attack is to use the Pythagorean Theorem.

Practice Problems Involving Coordinate Geometry

1. AB is the diameter of a circle whose center is O. If the coordinates of A are (2,6) and the coordinates of B are (6,2), find the coordinates of O.
(A) (4,4)
(B) (4,−4)
(C) (2,−2)
(D) (0,0)
(E) (2,2)

2. AB is the diameter of a circle whose center is O. If the coordinates of O are (2,1) and the coordinates of B are (4,6) find the coordinates of A.
(A) $(3,3\frac{1}{2})$
(B) $(1,2\frac{1}{2})$
(C) (0,−4)
(D) $(2\frac{1}{2},1)$
(E) $(-1,-2\frac{1}{2})$

3. Find the distance from the point whose coordinates are (4,3) to the point whose coordinates are (8,6).
(A) 5
(B) 25
(C) $\sqrt{7}$
(D) $\sqrt{67}$
(E) 15

4. The vertices of a triangle are (2,1), (2,5), and (5,1). The area of the triangle is
(A) 12
(B) 10
(C) 8
(D) 6
(E) 5

5. The area of a circle whose center is at (0,0) is 16π. The circle passes through each of the following points *except*
(A) (4,4)
(B) (0,4)
(C) (4,0)
(D) (−4,0)
(E) (0,−4)

Coordinate Geometry Problems— Correct Answers

1. **(A)**
2. **(C)**
3. **(A)**
4. **(D)**
5. **(A)**

Problem Solutions— Coordinate Geometry

1. Find the midpoint of AB by averaging the x coordinates and averaging the y coordinates.
$$\left(\frac{6+2}{2}, \frac{2+6}{2}\right) = (4, 4)$$

Answer: **(A)** (4,4)

2. O is the midpoint of AB.

$\dfrac{x+4}{2} = 2 \qquad x + 4 = 4 \qquad x = 0$

$\dfrac{y+6}{2} = 1 \qquad y + 6 = 2 \qquad y = -4$

A is the point (0,−4)

Answer: **(C)** (0,−4)

3. $d = \sqrt{(8-4)^2 + (6-3)^2} = \sqrt{4^2 + 3^2} = \sqrt{16+9} = \sqrt{25} = 5$

Answer: **(A)** 5

4. Sketch the triangle and you will see it is a right triangle with legs of 4 and 3.

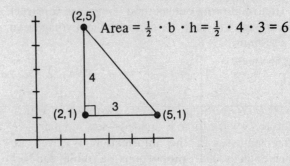

Area = $\frac{1}{2} \cdot b \cdot h = \frac{1}{2} \cdot 4 \cdot 3 = 6$

Answer: **(D)** 6

5. Area of a circle $= \pi r^2$

$\pi r^2 = 16\pi \qquad r = 4$

Points B, C, D, and E are all 4 units from the origin. Point A is not.

Answer: **(A)** (4, 4)

SETS

In the past few years a new type of problem—called set problems—has been introduced in the Discrete Quantitative Math sections of the GMAT. These problems give you information about the relationships between different groupings and combinations of persons or objects and ask for the number or percentage in one of the combinations or groupings. The information given in the problem is often in the form of totals for two or more groupings and the approach is to break the situation into separate groupings. This means that your diagram or analysis must always be in terms of the smallest groupings. If the members of a class of students are referred to by sex and by major, then the smallest groupings are males with a certain major, females with that major, etc.

Set problems can also be classified in terms of what is being counted. Usually it is the number of persons or objects that is being discussed, as shown in the following two examples. The third example shows a problem in which the number of memberships, entries, etc., is being counted.

Example: In the ABC Coat Company 85% of the employees are non-managerial and three-quarters are women. If two-thirds of the managers are men, what proportion of the men are non-managers?

(A) 10%
(B) 15%
(C) $33\frac{1}{3}\%$
(D) 60%
(E) 75%

SOLUTION: Since there are two ways in which the total work force is divided—sex and managerial status—and the information is given in percentages and proportions, a table can be constructed and filled in, in percentages of the total work force.

	Men	Women	Total
Manager			**15**
Non-Manager			85
Total	**25**	75	100

The numbers in bold type can be calculated by subtraction from 100%. Then we can use the information that two-thirds of the managers are men, which is 10% of the total ($\frac{2}{3} \times 15\% = 10\%$). From this, the entire table can be constructed by subtraction from the known totals:

	Men	Women	Total
Manager	10	5	15
Non-Manager	15	70	85
Total	25	75	100

Answer: $\frac{15}{25} = 60\%$ of the men are non-managers, choice (D).

Such a problem could be solved by making a system of equations, but it is much quicker and simpler to do it with a chart.

Another type of problem which is also classified as a set problem is one in which there are two categories and a group of people or objects that are in one or the other of the categories or in both. The key to approaching such a problem is to consider there to be three categories: the first alone, the second alone, and both together.

Example: Thirty-five members of the Sigma fraternity are taking German or French classes. If 25 fraternity members are taking German and eighteen members are taking French, how many are taking both French and German?

(A) 6
(B) 8
(C) 10
(D) 12
(E) 14

SOLUTION: Labeling our three types of fraternity members as F for those taking only French, G for those taking only German, and FG for those taking both classes, we can establish the following equations: F + FG = 18, G + FG = 25, and F + FG + G = 35.

By comparing these three equations we can see that: F must be 10 (difference between second and third equations), G must be 17 (difference between first and third equations), and FG must be 8 (by plugging the values of F and G into the third equation).

Answer: **(B)** 8

This same solution can be achieved by using a diagram, such as two overlapping circles, to indicate the relationships.

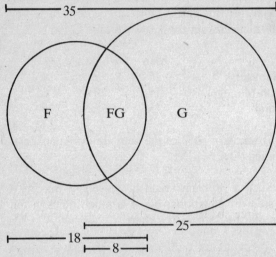

When a problem gives information about the number of memberships, etc., there will be multiple memberships. The solution can be most easily found by counting the number of memberships, etc.

Example: Of 30 adults, 12 belong to club A, 15 belong to club B and 19 belong to club C. If 7 belong to all three clubs and exactly 6 belong to two clubs, how many belong to none of the clubs?
(A) 0
(B) 2
(C) 4
(D) 6
(E) 8

SOLUTION: Adding up the number of memberships in the three clubs gives a total of 12 + 15 + 19 = 46 memberships to be accounted for by the 30 adults. The seven adults with triple memberships account for 21 memberships among them and the six with two memberships account for another 12. Thus 33 memberships are accounted for and only adults with one or no memberships remain. The 46 − 33 = 13 remaining memberships must be 13 people with one membership apiece. Thus

```
 7 adults × 3 memberships = 21 memberships
 6 adults × 2 memberships = 12 memberships
13 adults × 1 membership  = 13 memberships
 4 adults × 0 memberships =  0 memberships
```
───
30 adults   46 memberships

Answer: **(C)** 4

Practice Problems Involving Sets

1. Nineteen diners at Joe's Pizzeria are eating only pizza and 26 diners are eating only calzone. If a total of 55 different people are eating either calzone or pizza or both, how many diners are eating both calzone and pizza?
   (A) 10
   (B) 12
   (C) 14
   (D) 16
   (E) 18

2. Twenty percent of the animals at the Westside Dog and Cat Shelter are male cats. If there are twice as many male dogs as male cats and three times as many dogs as cats at the shelter, what percentage of the cats in the shelter are female?
   (A) 5%
   (B) 15%
   (C) 20%
   (D) 30%
   (E) 50%

3. A troop of 20 scouts earned a total of 14 merit badges in first aid, 13 merit badges in woodcraft, and 12 merit badges in knot tying. If 10 scouts had earned three merit badges and 5 scouts had earned only one merit badge each, what percentage of the troop had earned no merit badges?
   (A) 0%
   (B) 5%
   (C) 10%
   (D) 15%
   (E) 25%

Set Problems—Correct Answers

1. (A)   2. (C)   3. (D)

Problem Solutions—Sets

1. There are three categories: calzone only, pizza only, and both. Pizza only plus calzone only comes to 19 + 26 = 45, so 55 − 45 = 10 are eating both. The problem states that the 55 total of diners does not include any other possibility.

   Answer: **(A)**

2. Setting up the table with only the male cats:

	Dogs	Cats	Total
Male		20	
Female			
Total			100

   Then, noting the fact that the number of male dogs is twice that of male cats (2 × 20 = 40), and that dogs plus cats must come to 100%, there must be 75% dogs in order for there to be three times as many dogs as cats. (You would know that dogs and cats are the total population both from the title of the shelter and from the fact that those are the only animals mentioned.)
   This yields the following table:

	Dogs	Cats	Total
Male	40	20	
Female			
Total	75	25	100

Filling in the remaining boxes by addition and subtraction:

	Dogs	Cats	Total
Male	40	20	60
Female	35	5	40
Total	75	25	100

Thus there are 5% female cats and 25% total cats out of the total animal population, and one-fifth or 20% of the cats are females.

Answer: **(C)**

3. The total number of merit badges earned is 14 + 13 + 12 = 39. The ten scouts with three badges each account for 30 of the badges and the five with one badge each account for another five. This leaves only 4 badges to be earned by those with exactly two badges each, which is two scouts with two badges each. Thus 3 scouts had no badges and $\frac{3}{20}$ = 15% of the scouts had no badges.

   10 scouts × 3 badges = 30 badges
   2 scouts × 2 badges = 4 badges
   5 scouts × 1 badge = 5 badges
   3 scouts × 0 badges = 0 badges
   _____
   20 scouts   39 badges

   Answer: **(D)**

Part Four

Full-Length Practice Examinations

ANSWER SHEET—PRACTICE EXAMINATION 1

SECTION I

1 Ⓐ Ⓑ Ⓒ Ⓓ Ⓔ	6 Ⓐ Ⓑ Ⓒ Ⓓ Ⓔ	11 Ⓐ Ⓑ Ⓒ Ⓓ Ⓔ	16 Ⓐ Ⓑ Ⓒ Ⓓ Ⓔ	21 Ⓐ Ⓑ Ⓒ Ⓓ Ⓔ
2 Ⓐ Ⓑ Ⓒ Ⓓ Ⓔ	7 Ⓐ Ⓑ Ⓒ Ⓓ Ⓔ	12 Ⓐ Ⓑ Ⓒ Ⓓ Ⓔ	17 Ⓐ Ⓑ Ⓒ Ⓓ Ⓔ	22 Ⓐ Ⓑ Ⓒ Ⓓ Ⓔ
3 Ⓐ Ⓑ Ⓒ Ⓓ Ⓔ	8 Ⓐ Ⓑ Ⓒ Ⓓ Ⓔ	13 Ⓐ Ⓑ Ⓒ Ⓓ Ⓔ	18 Ⓐ Ⓑ Ⓒ Ⓓ Ⓔ	23 Ⓐ Ⓑ Ⓒ Ⓓ Ⓔ
4 Ⓐ Ⓑ Ⓒ Ⓓ Ⓔ	9 Ⓐ Ⓑ Ⓒ Ⓓ Ⓔ	14 Ⓐ Ⓑ Ⓒ Ⓓ Ⓔ	19 Ⓐ Ⓑ Ⓒ Ⓓ Ⓔ	24 Ⓐ Ⓑ Ⓒ Ⓓ Ⓔ
5 Ⓐ Ⓑ Ⓒ Ⓓ Ⓔ	10 Ⓐ Ⓑ Ⓒ Ⓓ Ⓔ	15 Ⓐ Ⓑ Ⓒ Ⓓ Ⓔ	20 Ⓐ Ⓑ Ⓒ Ⓓ Ⓔ	25 Ⓐ Ⓑ Ⓒ Ⓓ Ⓔ

SECTION II

1 Ⓐ Ⓑ Ⓒ Ⓓ Ⓔ	5 Ⓐ Ⓑ Ⓒ Ⓓ Ⓔ	9 Ⓐ Ⓑ Ⓒ Ⓓ Ⓔ	13 Ⓐ Ⓑ Ⓒ Ⓓ Ⓔ	17 Ⓐ Ⓑ Ⓒ Ⓓ Ⓔ
2 Ⓐ Ⓑ Ⓒ Ⓓ Ⓔ	6 Ⓐ Ⓑ Ⓒ Ⓓ Ⓔ	10 Ⓐ Ⓑ Ⓒ Ⓓ Ⓔ	14 Ⓐ Ⓑ Ⓒ Ⓓ Ⓔ	18 Ⓐ Ⓑ Ⓒ Ⓓ Ⓔ
3 Ⓐ Ⓑ Ⓒ Ⓓ Ⓔ	7 Ⓐ Ⓑ Ⓒ Ⓓ Ⓔ	11 Ⓐ Ⓑ Ⓒ Ⓓ Ⓔ	15 Ⓐ Ⓑ Ⓒ Ⓓ Ⓔ	19 Ⓐ Ⓑ Ⓒ Ⓓ Ⓔ
4 Ⓐ Ⓑ Ⓒ Ⓓ Ⓔ	8 Ⓐ Ⓑ Ⓒ Ⓓ Ⓔ	12 Ⓐ Ⓑ Ⓒ Ⓓ Ⓔ	16 Ⓐ Ⓑ Ⓒ Ⓓ Ⓔ	20 Ⓐ Ⓑ Ⓒ Ⓓ Ⓔ

SECTION III

1 Ⓐ Ⓑ Ⓒ Ⓓ Ⓔ	6 Ⓐ Ⓑ Ⓒ Ⓓ Ⓔ	11 Ⓐ Ⓑ Ⓒ Ⓓ Ⓔ	16 Ⓐ Ⓑ Ⓒ Ⓓ Ⓔ	21 Ⓐ Ⓑ Ⓒ Ⓓ Ⓔ
2 Ⓐ Ⓑ Ⓒ Ⓓ Ⓔ	7 Ⓐ Ⓑ Ⓒ Ⓓ Ⓔ	12 Ⓐ Ⓑ Ⓒ Ⓓ Ⓔ	17 Ⓐ Ⓑ Ⓒ Ⓓ Ⓔ	22 Ⓐ Ⓑ Ⓒ Ⓓ Ⓔ
3 Ⓐ Ⓑ Ⓒ Ⓓ Ⓔ	8 Ⓐ Ⓑ Ⓒ Ⓓ Ⓔ	13 Ⓐ Ⓑ Ⓒ Ⓓ Ⓔ	18 Ⓐ Ⓑ Ⓒ Ⓓ Ⓔ	23 Ⓐ Ⓑ Ⓒ Ⓓ Ⓔ
4 Ⓐ Ⓑ Ⓒ Ⓓ Ⓔ	9 Ⓐ Ⓑ Ⓒ Ⓓ Ⓔ	14 Ⓐ Ⓑ Ⓒ Ⓓ Ⓔ	19 Ⓐ Ⓑ Ⓒ Ⓓ Ⓔ	24 Ⓐ Ⓑ Ⓒ Ⓓ Ⓔ
5 Ⓐ Ⓑ Ⓒ Ⓓ Ⓔ	10 Ⓐ Ⓑ Ⓒ Ⓓ Ⓔ	15 Ⓐ Ⓑ Ⓒ Ⓓ Ⓔ	20 Ⓐ Ⓑ Ⓒ Ⓓ Ⓔ	25 Ⓐ Ⓑ Ⓒ Ⓓ Ⓔ

SECTION IV

1 Ⓐ Ⓑ Ⓒ Ⓓ Ⓔ	6 Ⓐ Ⓑ Ⓒ Ⓓ Ⓔ	11 Ⓐ Ⓑ Ⓒ Ⓓ Ⓔ	16 Ⓐ Ⓑ Ⓒ Ⓓ Ⓔ	21 Ⓐ Ⓑ Ⓒ Ⓓ Ⓔ
2 Ⓐ Ⓑ Ⓒ Ⓓ Ⓔ	7 Ⓐ Ⓑ Ⓒ Ⓓ Ⓔ	12 Ⓐ Ⓑ Ⓒ Ⓓ Ⓔ	17 Ⓐ Ⓑ Ⓒ Ⓓ Ⓔ	22 Ⓐ Ⓑ Ⓒ Ⓓ Ⓔ
3 Ⓐ Ⓑ Ⓒ Ⓓ Ⓔ	8 Ⓐ Ⓑ Ⓒ Ⓓ Ⓔ	13 Ⓐ Ⓑ Ⓒ Ⓓ Ⓔ	18 Ⓐ Ⓑ Ⓒ Ⓓ Ⓔ	23 Ⓐ Ⓑ Ⓒ Ⓓ Ⓔ
4 Ⓐ Ⓑ Ⓒ Ⓓ Ⓔ	9 Ⓐ Ⓑ Ⓒ Ⓓ Ⓔ	14 Ⓐ Ⓑ Ⓒ Ⓓ Ⓔ	19 Ⓐ Ⓑ Ⓒ Ⓓ Ⓔ	24 Ⓐ Ⓑ Ⓒ Ⓓ Ⓔ
5 Ⓐ Ⓑ Ⓒ Ⓓ Ⓔ	10 Ⓐ Ⓑ Ⓒ Ⓓ Ⓔ	15 Ⓐ Ⓑ Ⓒ Ⓓ Ⓔ	20 Ⓐ Ⓑ Ⓒ Ⓓ Ⓔ	25 Ⓐ Ⓑ Ⓒ Ⓓ Ⓔ

SECTION V

1 Ⓐ Ⓑ Ⓒ Ⓓ Ⓔ	6 Ⓐ Ⓑ Ⓒ Ⓓ Ⓔ	11 Ⓐ Ⓑ Ⓒ Ⓓ Ⓔ	16 Ⓐ Ⓑ Ⓒ Ⓓ Ⓔ	21 Ⓐ Ⓑ Ⓒ Ⓓ Ⓔ
2 Ⓐ Ⓑ Ⓒ Ⓓ Ⓔ	7 Ⓐ Ⓑ Ⓒ Ⓓ Ⓔ	12 Ⓐ Ⓑ Ⓒ Ⓓ Ⓔ	17 Ⓐ Ⓑ Ⓒ Ⓓ Ⓔ	22 Ⓐ Ⓑ Ⓒ Ⓓ Ⓔ
3 Ⓐ Ⓑ Ⓒ Ⓓ Ⓔ	8 Ⓐ Ⓑ Ⓒ Ⓓ Ⓔ	13 Ⓐ Ⓑ Ⓒ Ⓓ Ⓔ	18 Ⓐ Ⓑ Ⓒ Ⓓ Ⓔ	23 Ⓐ Ⓑ Ⓒ Ⓓ Ⓔ
4 Ⓐ Ⓑ Ⓒ Ⓓ Ⓔ	9 Ⓐ Ⓑ Ⓒ Ⓓ Ⓔ	14 Ⓐ Ⓑ Ⓒ Ⓓ Ⓔ	19 Ⓐ Ⓑ Ⓒ Ⓓ Ⓔ	24 Ⓐ Ⓑ Ⓒ Ⓓ Ⓔ
5 Ⓐ Ⓑ Ⓒ Ⓓ Ⓔ	10 Ⓐ Ⓑ Ⓒ Ⓓ Ⓔ	15 Ⓐ Ⓑ Ⓒ Ⓓ Ⓔ	20 Ⓐ Ⓑ Ⓒ Ⓓ Ⓔ	25 Ⓐ Ⓑ Ⓒ Ⓓ Ⓔ

SECTION VI

1 Ⓐ Ⓑ Ⓒ Ⓓ Ⓔ	6 Ⓐ Ⓑ Ⓒ Ⓓ Ⓔ	11 Ⓐ Ⓑ Ⓒ Ⓓ Ⓔ	16 Ⓐ Ⓑ Ⓒ Ⓓ Ⓔ	21 Ⓐ Ⓑ Ⓒ Ⓓ Ⓔ
2 Ⓐ Ⓑ Ⓒ Ⓓ Ⓔ	7 Ⓐ Ⓑ Ⓒ Ⓓ Ⓔ	12 Ⓐ Ⓑ Ⓒ Ⓓ Ⓔ	17 Ⓐ Ⓑ Ⓒ Ⓓ Ⓔ	22 Ⓐ Ⓑ Ⓒ Ⓓ Ⓔ
3 Ⓐ Ⓑ Ⓒ Ⓓ Ⓔ	8 Ⓐ Ⓑ Ⓒ Ⓓ Ⓔ	13 Ⓐ Ⓑ Ⓒ Ⓓ Ⓔ	18 Ⓐ Ⓑ Ⓒ Ⓓ Ⓔ	23 Ⓐ Ⓑ Ⓒ Ⓓ Ⓔ
4 Ⓐ Ⓑ Ⓒ Ⓓ Ⓔ	9 Ⓐ Ⓑ Ⓒ Ⓓ Ⓔ	14 Ⓐ Ⓑ Ⓒ Ⓓ Ⓔ	19 Ⓐ Ⓑ Ⓒ Ⓓ Ⓔ	24 Ⓐ Ⓑ Ⓒ Ⓓ Ⓔ
5 Ⓐ Ⓑ Ⓒ Ⓓ Ⓔ	10 Ⓐ Ⓑ Ⓒ Ⓓ Ⓔ	15 Ⓐ Ⓑ Ⓒ Ⓓ Ⓔ	20 Ⓐ Ⓑ Ⓒ Ⓓ Ⓔ	25 Ⓐ Ⓑ Ⓒ Ⓓ Ⓔ

SECTION VII

1 Ⓐ Ⓑ Ⓒ Ⓓ Ⓔ	5 Ⓐ Ⓑ Ⓒ Ⓓ Ⓔ	9 Ⓐ Ⓑ Ⓒ Ⓓ Ⓔ	13 Ⓐ Ⓑ Ⓒ Ⓓ Ⓔ	17 Ⓐ Ⓑ Ⓒ Ⓓ Ⓔ
2 Ⓐ Ⓑ Ⓒ Ⓓ Ⓔ	6 Ⓐ Ⓑ Ⓒ Ⓓ Ⓔ	10 Ⓐ Ⓑ Ⓒ Ⓓ Ⓔ	14 Ⓐ Ⓑ Ⓒ Ⓓ Ⓔ	18 Ⓐ Ⓑ Ⓒ Ⓓ Ⓔ
3 Ⓐ Ⓑ Ⓒ Ⓓ Ⓔ	7 Ⓐ Ⓑ Ⓒ Ⓓ Ⓔ	11 Ⓐ Ⓑ Ⓒ Ⓓ Ⓔ	15 Ⓐ Ⓑ Ⓒ Ⓓ Ⓔ	19 Ⓐ Ⓑ Ⓒ Ⓓ Ⓔ
4 Ⓐ Ⓑ Ⓒ Ⓓ Ⓔ	8 Ⓐ Ⓑ Ⓒ Ⓓ Ⓔ	12 Ⓐ Ⓑ Ⓒ Ⓓ Ⓔ	16 Ⓐ Ⓑ Ⓒ Ⓓ Ⓔ	20 Ⓐ Ⓑ Ⓒ Ⓓ Ⓔ

PRACTICE EXAMINATION 1

SECTION I

Time—30 Minutes
25 Questions

Directions: Below each of the following passages, you will find questions or incomplete statements about the passage. Each statement or question is followed by five lettered words or expressions. Select the word or expression that most satisfactorily completes each statement, or answers each question in accordance with the meaning of the passage. After you have chosen the best answer, blacken the corresponding space on the answer sheet.

War has escaped the battlefield and now can, with modern guidance systems on missiles, touch virtually every square yard of the earth's surface. It no longer involves only the military profession, but engulfs also
5 entire civilian populations. Nuclear weapons have made major war unthinkable. We are forced, however, to think about the unthinkable because a thermonuclear war could come by accident or miscalculation. We must accept the paradox of maintaining a capacity
10 to fight such a war so that we will never have to do so.

War has also lost most of its utility in achieving the traditional goals of conflict. Control of territory carries with it the obligation to provide subject
15 peoples certain administrative, health, education, and other social services; such obligations far outweigh the benefits of control. If the ruled population is ethnically or racially different from the rulers, tensions and chronic unrest often exist which further reduce the
20 benefits and increase the costs of domination. Large populations no longer necessarily enhance state power and, in the absence of high levels of economic development, can impose severe burdens on food supply, jobs, and the broad range of services expected of mod-
25 ern governments. The noneconomic security reasons for the control of territory have been progressively undermined by the advances of modern technology. The benefits of forcing another nation to surrender its wealth are vastly outweighed by the benefits of per-
30 suading that nation to produce and exchange goods and services. In brief, imperialism no longer pays.

Making war has been one of the most persistent of human activities in the 80 centuries since men and women settled in cities and became thereby "civi-
35 lized," but the modernization of the past 80 years has fundamentally changed the role and function of war. In pre-modernized societies, successful warfare

brought significant material rewards, the most obvious of which were the stored wealth of the defeated.
40 Equally important was human labor——control over people as slaves or levies for the victor's army——and the productive capacity of agricultural lands and mines. Successful warfare also produced psychic benefits. The removal or destruction of a threat brought a
45 sense of security, and power gained over others created pride and national self-esteem.

Warfare was also the most complex, broad-scale and demanding activity of pre-modernized people. The challenges of leading men into battle, organizing,
50 moving and supporting armies, attracted the talents of the most vigorous, enterprising, intelligent and imaginative men in the society. "Warrior" and "statesman" were usually synonymous, and the military was one of the few professions in which an able, ambitious
55 boy of humble origin could rise to the top. In the broader cultural context, war was accepted in the pre-modernized society as a part of the human condition, a mechanism of change, and an unavoidable, even noble, aspect of life. The excitement and drama of war
60 made it a vital part of literature and legends.

1. The primary purpose of the passage is to
   (A) theorize about the role of the warrior-statesman in pre-modernized society
   (B) explain the effects of war on both modernized and pre-modernized societies
   (C) contrast the value of war in a modernized society with its value in pre-modernized society
   (D) discuss the political and economic circumstances which lead to war in pre-modernized societies
   (E) examine the influence of the development of nuclear weapons on the possibility of war

2. According to the passage, leaders of pre-modernized society considered war to be
   (A) a valid tool of national policy
   (B) an immoral act of aggression
   (C) economically wasteful and socially unfeasible
   (D) restricted in scope to military participants
   (E) necessary to spur development of unoccupied lands

197

3. The author most likely places the word "civilized" in quotation marks (lines 34–35) in order to
   (A) show dissatisfaction at not having found a better word
   (B) acknowledge that the word was borrowed from another source
   (C) express irony that war should be a part of civilization
   (D) impress upon the reader the tragedy of war
   (E) raise a question about the value of war in modernized society

4. The author mentions all of the following as possible reasons for going to war in a pre-modernized society EXCEPT
   (A) possibility of material gain
   (B) promoting deserving young men to higher positions
   (C) potential for increasing the security of the nation
   (D) desire to capture productive farming lands
   (E) need for workers to fill certain jobs

5. The author is primarily concerned with discussing how
   (A) political decisions are reached
   (B) economic and social conditions have changed
   (C) technology for making war has improved
   (D) armed conflict has changed
   (E) war lost its value as a policy tool

6. Which of the following best describes the tone of the passage?
   (A) outraged and indignant
   (B) scientific and detached
   (C) humorous and wry
   (D) fearful and alarmed
   (E) concerned and optimistic

7. With which of the following statements about a successfully completed program of nuclear disarmament would the author most likely agree?
   (A) Without nuclear weapons, war in modernized society would have the same value it had in pre-modernized society.
   (B) In the absence of the danger of nuclear war, national leaders could use powerful conventional weapons to make great gains from war.
   (C) Eliminating nuclear weapons is likely to increase the danger of an all-out, world-wide military engagement.

(D) Even without the danger of a nuclear disaster, the costs of winning a war have made armed conflict on a large scale virtually obsolete.
(E) War is caused by aggressive instincts, so if nuclear weapons were no longer available, national leaders would use conventional weapons to reach the same end.

8. According to the author, maintaining a nuclear weapons capacity is paradoxical because
   (A) the cost of creating such weapons and training people to use them is prohibitive
   (B) the intention of policy makers is that such weapons never be used
   (C) the human and economic cost of a nuclear war would be incalculable
   (D) a nuclear war could only occur as a result of an error in judgment
   (E) an uncontrolled arms race endangers everyone on the earth

Until Josquin des Prez, 1440–1521, Western music was liturgical, designed as an accompaniment to worship. Like the intricately carved gargoyles perched atop medieval cathedrals beyond sight of any human,
5 music was composed to please God before anybody else; its dominant theme was reverence. Emotion was there, but it was the grief of Mary standing at the foot of the Cross, the joy of the faithful hailing Christ's resurrection. Even the secular music of the Middle
10 Ages was tied to predetermined patterns that sometimes seemed to stand in the way of individual expression.
  While keeping one foot firmly planted in the divine world, Josquin stepped with the other into the human.
15 He scored magnificent masses, but also newly expressive motets such as the lament of David over his son Absalom or the "Deploration d'Ockeghem," a dirge on the death of Ockeghem, the greatest master before Josquin, a motet written all in black notes, and one of
20 the most profoundly moving scores of the Renaissance. Josquin was the first composer to set psalms to music. But alongside *Benedicite omnia opera Domini Domino* ("Bless the Lord, all ye works of the Lord") he put *El Grillo* ("The cricket is a good singer who
25 manages long poems") and *Allegez moy* ("Solace me, sweet pleasant brunette"). Josquin was praised by Martin Luther, for his music blends respect for tradition with a rebel's willingness to risk the horizon. What Galileo was to science, Josquin was to music.
30 While preserving their allegiance to God, both asserted a new importance for man.
  Why then should Josquin languish in relative obscurity? The answer has to do with the separation of

concept from performance in music. In fine art, con-
35 cept and performance are one; both the art lover and
the art historian have thousands of years of paintings,
drawings and sculptures to study and enjoy. Similarly
with literature: Poetry, fiction, drama, and criticism
survive on the printed page or in manuscript for judg-
40 ment and admiration by succeeding generations. But
musical notation on a page is not art, no matter how
lofty or excellent the composer's conception; it is,
crudely put, a set of directions for producing art.
Being highly symbolic, musical notation requires
45 training before it can even be read, let alone performed. Moreover, because the musical conventions
of other days are not ours, translation of a Renaissance
score into modern notation brings difficulties of its
own. For example, the Renaissance notation of Jos-
50 quin's day did not designate the tempo at which the
music should be played or sung. It did not indicate all
flats or sharps; these were sounded in accordance with
musicianly rules, which were capable of transforming
major to minor, minor to major, diatonic to chromatic
55 sound, and thus affect melody, harmony, and musical
expression. A Renaissance composition might include
several parts—but it did not indicate which were to
be sung, which to be played, nor even whether instruments were to be used at all.
60   Thus, Renaissance notation permits of several in-
terpretations and an imaginative musician may give an
interpretation that is a revelation. But no matter how
imaginative, few modern musicians can offer any
interpretation of Renaissance music. The public for it
65 is small, limiting the number of musicians who can
afford to learn, rehearse, and perform it. Most of
those who attempt it at all are students organized in
collegia musica whose memberships have a distress-
ing habit of changing every semester, thus preventing
70 directors from maintaining the year-in, year-out con-
tinuity required to achieve excellence of performance.
Finally, the instruments used in Renaissance times—
drummhorns, recorders, rauschpfeifen, shawms,
sackbuts, organettos—must be specially procured.

9. The primary purpose of the passage is to
   (A) introduce the reader to Josquin and account
   for his relative obscurity
   (B) describe the main features of medieval music and show how Josquin changed them
   (C) place Josquin's music in an historical context and show its influence on later composers
   (D) enumerate the features of Josquin's music
   and supply critical commentary
   (E) praise the music of Josquin and interest the
   reader in further study of medieval music

10. The passage contains information which would
help answer all of the following questions EX-
CEPT
   (A) What are the titles of some of Josquin's secular compositions?
   (B) What are the names of some Renaissance
   musical instruments?
   (C) Who was the greatest composer before Josquin?
   (D) Where might it be possible to hear Renaissance music performed?
   (E) What are the names of some of Josquin's
   most famous students?

11. It can be inferred from the passage that modern
musical notation has which of the following characteristics?
   I. The tempo at which a composition is to be
   played is indicated in the notation.
   II. Whether a note is sharp or a flat is indicated
   in the notation.
   III. The notation indicates which parts of the
   music are to be played by which instruments.

   (A) I only
   (B) II only
   (C) I and III only
   (D) II and III only
   (E) I, II, and III

12. The author would most likely agree with which of
the following statements?
   (A) Music is a more perfect art form than paint-
   ing or sculpture.
   (B) Music can be said to exist only when it is
   being performed.
   (C) Josquin was the greatest composer of the
   Middle Ages.
   (D) Renaissance music is superior to music pro-
   duced in modern times.
   (E) Most people dislike Josquin because they do
   not understand his music.

13. The passage leads most logically to a proposal
to
   (A) establish more *collegia musica*
   (B) study Josquin's compositional techniques in
   greater detail
   (C) include Renaissance music in college studies
   (D) provide funds for musicians to study and
   play Josquin
   (E) translate Josquin's music into modern notation

14. The author cites all of the following as reasons for Josquin's relative obscurity EXCEPT
    (A) the difficulty one encounters in attempting to read his musical notation
    (B) the inability of modern musicians to play instruments of the Renaissance
    (C) the difficulty of procuring unusual instruments needed to play the music
    (D) the lack of public interest in Renaissance music
    (E) problems in finding funding for the study of Renaissance music

15. The author's attitude toward Galileo (line 29) can best be described as
    (A) admiring
    (B) critical
    (C) accepting
    (D) analytical
    (E) noncommittal

16. In the first paragraph the author employs
    (A) an analogy
    (B) a counter example
    (C) a generalization
    (D) a contradiction
    (E) an emotional appeal

17. The author apparently regards Josquin des Prez as
    (A) a composer whose works are insignificant
    (B) a rustic musician untrained in musical theory
    (C) primarily a composer of secular music
    (D) a poet and a scholar who was also interested in music
    (E) a composer of considerable merit

There is extraordinary exposure in the United States to the risks of injury and death from motor vehicle accidents. More than 80 percent of all households own passenger cars or light trucks and each of these is driven an average of more than 11,000 miles each year. Almost one-half of fatally injured drivers have a blood alcohol concentration (BAC) of 0.1 percent or higher. For the average adult, over five ounces of 80 proof spirits would have to be consumed over a short period of time to attain these levels. A third of drivers who have been drinking, but fewer than 4 percent of all drivers, demonstrate these levels. Although less than 1 percent of drivers with BAC's of 0.1 percent or more are involved in fatal crashes, the probability of their involvement is 27 times higher than for those without alcohol in their blood.

There are a number of different approaches to reducing injuries in which intoxication plays a role. Based on the observation that excessive consumption correlates with the total alcohol consumption of a country's population, it has been suggested that higher taxes on alcohol would reduce both. While the heaviest drinkers would be taxed the most, anyone who drinks at all would be penalized by this approach.

To make drinking and driving a criminal offense is an approach directed only at intoxicated drivers. In some states, the law empowers police to request breath tests of drivers cited for any traffic offense and elevated BAC can be the basis for arrest. The National Highway Traffic Safety Administration estimates, however, that even with increased arrests, there are about 700 violations for every arrest. At this level there is little evidence that laws serve as deterrents to drinking while intoxicated. In Britain, motor vehicle fatalities fell 25 percent immediately following implementation of the Road Safety Act in 1967. As Britishers increasingly recognized that they could drink and not be stopped, the effectiveness declined, although in the ensuing three years the fatality rate seldom reached that observed in the seven years prior to the Act.

Whether penalties for driving with a high BAC or excessive taxation on consumption of alcoholic beverages will deter the excessive drinker responsible for most fatalities is unclear. In part, the answer depends on the extent to which those with high BAC's involved in crashes are capable of controlling their intake in response to economic or penal threat. Therapeutic programs which range from individual and group counseling and psychotherapy to chemotherapy constitute another approach, but they have not diminished the proportion of accidents in which alcohol was a factor. In the few controlled trials that have been reported there is little evidence that rehabilitation programs for those repeatedly arrested for drunken behavior have reduced either the recidivism or crash rates. Thus far, there is no firm evidence that Alcohol Safety Action Project-supported programs, in which rehabilitation measures are requested by the court, have decreased recidivism or crash involvement for clients exposed to them, although knowledge and attitudes have improved. One thing is clear, however; unless we deal with automobile and highway safety and reduce accidents in which alcoholic intoxication plays a role, many will continue to die.

18. The author is primarily concerned with
    (A) interpreting the results of surveys on traffic fatalities
    (B) reviewing the effectiveness of attempts to curb drunk driving

(C) suggesting reasons for the prevalence of drunk driving in the United States

(D) analyzing the causes of the large number of annual traffic fatalities

(E) making an international comparison of experience with drunk driving

19. It can be inferred that the 1967 Road Safety Act in Britain
(A) changed an existing law to lower the BAC level which defined driving while intoxicated

(B) made it illegal to drive while intoxicated

(C) increased the number of drunk driving arrests

(D) placed a tax on the sale of alcoholic drinks

(E) required drivers convicted under the law to undergo rehabilitation therapy

20. The author implies that a BAC of 0.1 percent
(A) is unreasonably high as a definition of intoxication for purposes of driving

(B) penalizes the moderate drinker while allowing the heavy drinker to consume without limit

(C) will operate as an effective deterrent to over 90 percent of the people who might drink and drive

(D) is well below the BAC of most drivers who are involved in fatal collisions

(E) proves that a driver has consumed five ounces of 80 proof spirits over a short time

21. With which of the following statements about making driving while intoxicated a criminal offense versus increasing taxes on alcohol consumption would the author most likely agree?
(A) Making driving while intoxicated a criminal offense is preferable to increased taxes on alcohol because the former is aimed only at those who abuse alcohol by driving while intoxicated.

(B) Increased taxation on alcohol consumption is likely to be more effective in reducing traffic fatalities because taxation covers all consumers and not just those who drive.

(C) Increased taxation on alcohol will constitute less of an interference with personal liberty because of the necessity of blood alcohol tests to determine BAC's in drivers suspected of intoxication.

(D) Since neither increased taxation nor enforcement of criminal laws against drunk drivers is likely to have any significant impact, neither measure is warranted.

(E) Because arrests of intoxicated drivers have proved to be expensive and administratively cumbersome, increased taxation on alcohol is the most promising means of reducing traffic fatalities.

22. The author cites the British example in order to
(A) show that the problem of drunk driving is worse in Britain than in the U.S.

(B) prove that stricter enforcement of laws against intoxicated drivers would reduce traffic deaths

(C) prove that a slight increase in the number of arrests of intoxicated drivers will not deter drunk driving

(D) suggest that taxation of alcohol consumption may be more effective than criminal laws

(E) demonstrate the need to lower BAC levels in states that have laws against drunk driving

23. Which of the following, if true, most weakens the author's statement that the effectiveness of proposals to stop the intoxicated driver depends, in part, on the extent to which the high-BAC driver can control his intake?
(A) Even if the heavy drinker cannot control his intake, criminal laws against driving while intoxicated can deter him from driving while intoxicated.

(B) Rehabilitation programs aimed at drivers convicted of driving while intoxicated have not significantly reduced traffic fatalities.

(C) Many traffic fatalities are caused by factors unrelated to the excessive consumption of alcohol of the driver.

(D) Even though severe penalties may not deter the intoxicated driver, these laws will punish him for the harm he causes if he drives while intoxicated.

(E) Some sort of therapy may be effective in helping the problem drinker to control his intake of alcohol, thereby keeping him off the road.

24. The author's closing remarks can best be described as
(A) ironic

(B) indifferent

(C) admonitory

(D) indecisive

(E) indignant

25. In the first paragraph, the author implies that
    (A) two-thirds of drivers have not been drinking
    (B) two-thirds of the drivers who have been drinking have BAC's of less than 0.1 percent

(C) half of all fatally injured drivers have not been drinking
(D) fewer than 4 percent of all drivers involved in accidents have been drinking
(E) one out of every 27 fatal crashes involves a driver with a BAC in excess of 0.1 percent

STOP

END OF SECTION. IF YOU HAVE ANY TIME LEFT, GO OVER YOUR WORK IN THIS SECTION ONLY. DO NOT WORK IN ANY OTHER SECTION OF THE TEST.

SECTION II

Time—30 Minutes
20 Questions

Directions: For each of the following questions, select the best of the answer choices and blacken the corresponding space on your answer sheet.
Numbers: All numbers used are real numbers.
Figures: The diagrams and figures that accompany these questions are for the purpose of providing information useful in answering the questions. Unless it is stated that a specific figure is not drawn to scale, the diagrams and figures are drawn as accurately as possible. All figures are in a plane unless otherwise indicated.

1. If w, x, y, and z are real numbers, each of the following equals $w(x + y + z)$ EXCEPT
   - (A) $wx + wy + wz$
   - (B) $(x + y + z)w$
   - (C) $wx + w(y + z)$
   - (D) $3w + x + y + z$
   - (E) $w(x + y) + wz$

2. A carpenter needs four boards, each 2 feet 10 inches long. If wood is sold only by the foot, what is the minimum length, in feet, of wood he must buy?
   - (A) 9
   - (B) 10
   - (C) 11
   - (D) 12
   - (E) 13

3. If $x = +4$, then $(x - 7)(x + 2) =$
   - (A) -66
   - (B) -18
   - (C) 0
   - (D) 3
   - (E) 17

4. If $2x + y = 7$ and $x - y = 2$, then $x + y =$
   - (A) 6
   - (B) 4
   - (C) $\frac{3}{2}$
   - (D) 0
   - (E) -5

5. A girl rode her bicycle from home to school, a distance of 15 miles, at an average speed of 15 miles per hour. She returned home from school by walking at an average speed of 5

miles per hour. What was her average speed for the round trip if she took the same route in both directions?
   - (A) 7.5 miles per hour
   - (B) 10 miles per hour
   - (C) 12.5 miles per hour
   - (D) 13 miles per hour
   - (E) 25 miles per hour

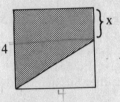

6. In the square above with side 4, the ratio
   $$\frac{\text{area of shaded region}}{\text{area of unshaded region}} =$$
   - (A) $\frac{2 + x}{4}$
   - (B) $\frac{4 - x}{8}$
   - (C) 2
   - (D) $\frac{4 + x}{4 - x}$
   - (E) $2x$

7. Ned is two years older than Mike, who is twice as old as Linda. If the ages of the three total 27 years, how old is Mike?
   - (A) 5 years
   - (B) 8 years
   - (C) 9 years
   - (D) 10 years
   - (E) 12 years

8. A taxicab charges $1.00 for the first one-fifth mile of a trip and 20¢ for each following one-fifth mile or part thereof. If a trip is $2\frac{1}{2}$ miles long, what will be the fare?
   - (A) $2.60
   - (B) $3.10
   - (C) $3.20
   - (D) $3.40
   - (E) $3.60

9. What is the side of a square if its area is $36x^2$?
   (A) 9
   (B) 9x
   (C) $6x^2$
   (D) 6
   (E) 6x

10. If Susan has $5 more than Tom, and if Tom has $2 more than Ed, which of the following exchanges will ensure that each of the three has an equal amount of money?
    (A) Susan must give Ed $3 and Tom $1.
    (B) Tom must give Susan $4 and Susan must give Ed $5.
    (C) Ed must give Susan $1 and Susan must give Tom $1.
    (D) Susan must give Ed $4 and Tom must give Ed $5.
    (E) Either Susan or Ed must give Tom $7.

11. A perfect number is one which is equal to the sum of all its positive factors that are less than the number itself. Which of the following is a perfect number?
    (A) 1
    (B) 4
    (C) 6
    (D) 8
    (E) 10

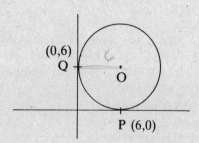

12. In the figure above, the coordinates of points P and Q are (6,0) and (0,6), respectively, What is the area of the circle O?
    (A) 36π
    (B) 12π
    (C) 9π
    (D) 6π
    (E) 3π

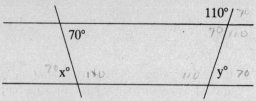

13. In the figure above, x + y =
    (A) 50
    (B) 140
    (C) 180
    (D) 220
    (E) 240

14. A cylinder has a radius of 2 ft and a height of 5 ft. If it is already 40% filled with a liquid, how many more cubic feet of liquid must be added to completely fill it?
    (A) 6π
    (B) 8π
    (C) 10π
    (D) 12π
    (E) 16π

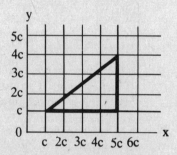

15. If the area of the above triangle is 54, then c =
    (A) 3
    (B) 6
    (C) 10
    (D) 12
    (E) Cannot be determined from the information given.

16. A carpenter is building a frame for a large wall painting. The painting is in the shape of a rectangle. If the sides of the rectangle are in the ratio of 3:2 and the shorter side has a length of 15 inches, how much framing material does the carpenter need to frame the painting?
    (A) 12 inches
    (B) $22\frac{1}{2}$ inches
    (C) $37\frac{1}{2}$ inches

(D) 50 inches

(E) 75 inches

17. In 1972, country X had a population of P and M cases of meningitis, for a per capita rate of meningitis of $\frac{M}{P}$. If, over the next ten years, the number of cases of meningitis decreased by 50% and the population of country X increased by 50%, what is the percentage change in the per capita rate of meningitis over the ten-year period?

(A) $33\frac{1}{3}$% increase

(B) no change

(C) $33\frac{1}{3}$% decrease

(D) 50% decrease

(E) $66\frac{2}{3}$% decrease

18. In the Excel Manufacturing Company, 46 percent of the employees are men. If 60 percent of the employees are unionized and 70 percent of these are men, what percent of the non-unionized workers are women?

(A) 90%

(B) 87.5%

(C) 66.7%

(D) 50%

(E) 36%

19. A slot machine in a Las Vegas casino has an average profit of $600 for each 8-hour shift for the five days Sunday through Thursday, inclusive. If the average per-shift profit on Friday and Saturday is 25% greater than on the other days of the week and the slot machine is in operation every hour of every day, what is the total weekly profit that the casino makes from the slot machine?

(A) $4,500

(B) $9,000

(C) $13,500

(D) $15,500

(E) $27,000

20. An apartment dweller pays $125 per quarter for theft insurance. The policy will cover the loss of cash and valuables during the course of a year in excess of $350 by reimbursing him 75% of the value of the loss above $350. During the course of a certain year, the apartment dweller suffers the theft of $1250 in cash—but no other losses—by theft. What is the difference between the combined amount he pays in theft insurance and his unreimbursed losses for that year, and the amount that he would have lost if he had not had any insurance?

(A) $125

(B) $175

(C) $225

(D) $350

(E) $675

STOP

END OF SECTION. IF YOU HAVE ANY TIME LEFT, GO OVER YOUR WORK IN THIS SECTION ONLY. DO NOT WORK IN ANY OTHER SECTION OF THE TEST.

SECTION III

Time—30 Minutes
25 Questions

Directions: Each question below is followed by two numbered facts. You are to determine whether the data given in the statements is sufficient for answering the question. Use the data given, plus your knowledge of math and everyday facts, to choose between the five possible answers.

(A) if statement 1 alone is sufficient to answer the question, but statement 2 alone is not sufficient

(B) if statement 2 alone is sufficient to answer the question, but statement 1 alone is not sufficient

(C) if both statements together are needed to answer the question, but neither statement alone is sufficient

(D) if either statement by itself is sufficient to answer the question

(E) if not enough facts are given to answer the question

1. What is the value of x?
   (1) $x^2 + x = 2$
   (2) $x^2 + 2x - 3 = 0$

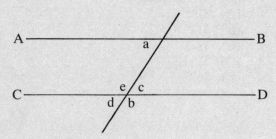

2. Is AB parallel to CD?
   (1) Angle a + angle b = 180°
   (2) Angle a + angle c + angle d + angle e = 360°

3. A, B, and C are three consecutive even integers (not necessarily in order). Which has the greatest value?
   (1) A + B = C
   (2) C is a positive number.

4. How many hours does it take Bill to do a certain job?
   (1) Working together, Bill and Jim can complete it in eight hours.
   (2) Jim can do the job in twelve hours.

5. If x and y are non-negative, is (x + y) greater than xy?
   (1) x = y
   (2) x + y is greater than $x^2 + y^2$

6. How heavy is one brick?
   (1) Two bricks weigh as much as three 6-lb. weights.
   (2) Three bricks weigh as much as one brick plus 18 lbs.

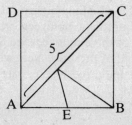

7. In the diagram, find the length of AB.
   (1) ABCD is a rectangle.
   (2) AC − AE = AB + BE

8. A man has eight 3-lb weights, ten 5-lb weights, and seven 10-lb weights. He places eight of these weights on a scale. How many 5-lb weights are used?
   (1) The scale registers 47 lbs.
   (2) The number of 10-lb weights used is one less than the number of 3-lb weights used.

9. What is the value of p?
   (1) p=4q
   (2) q=4p

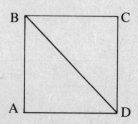

10. Is ABCD a square?
    (1) AB is parallel to CD.
    (2) BCD is an equilateral triangle.

11. A marathon runner running along a prescribed route passes through neighborhoods J, K, L and M, not necessarily in that order. How long does he take to run from J to M?
    (1) The runner averages 8 miles per hour on the route from J to M.
    (2) M is 4 miles from K and 12 miles from L, but J is 15 miles from K.

12. Mary has qualified to become a police officer. Has Albert qualified to become a police officer?
    (1) If Albert qualifies to become a police officer, then Mary will qualify to become a police officer.
    (2) If Albert does not qualify to become a police officer, then Mary will not qualify to become a police officer.

13. A package of 40 cookies is divided among three children, W, X and Y. How many cookies did X get?
    (1) W got one-fifth as many cookies as Y.
    (2) W got 16 fewer cookies than Y.

14. Is $\frac{x}{5}$ an integer?
    (1) $\frac{x}{12,345}$ is an integer.
    (2) $\frac{x}{336}$ is an integer.

15. What is the volume of cube X?
    (1) The diagonal of one of the faces of X is $\sqrt{6}$.
    (2) The diagonal of the cube from the upper rear left corner to the lower front right corner is 3.

16. What is the value of $p^8 - q^8$?
    (1) $p^7 + q^7 = 127$
    (2) $p - q = 0$

17. Is x a negative number?
    (1) $4x + 24 > 0$
    (2) $4x - 24 < 0$

18. In 1980 the Maximo Corporation spent $12,000 on employee pension payments. How much did the corporation spend on employee pension payments in 1981?
    (1) In 1981 the number of employees on the Maximo Corporation pension plan decreased by 15% compared to 1980.

    (2) In 1981 the average cost of employee pension payments per employee increased by 30% over the cost of such payments in 1980.

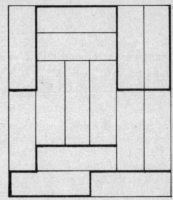

19. In the figure above, a rectangle is divided into smaller rectangles of the same shape and size. What is the area of the large rectangle?
    (1) The length of the darkened path at the top of the diagram is 45.
    (2) The length of the darkened path at the bottom of the diagram is 39.

20. Does $(x + y)^2 + (x - y)^2$ equal 130?
    (1) $x^2 + y^2 = 65$
    (2) $x = 7$ and $y = 7$.

21. What is the 999th term of the series S?
    (1) The first 4 four terms of S are $(1 + 1)^2$, $(2 + 1)^2$, $(3 + 1)^2$, and $(4 + 1)^2$.
    (2) For every x, the xth term of S is $(x + 1)^2$.

22. If x and y are integers, is x less than y?
    (1) The cube of x is less than the cube of y.
    (2) The square of x is less than the square of y.

23. When one piece of fruit is taken at random from a fruit bowl, what is the chance that it is an apple?
    (1) There are twice as many apples as oranges in the fruit bowl.
    (2) A third of the fruit in the fruit bowl are oranges.

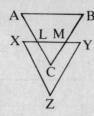

24. Triangles ABC and XYZ are equilateral triangles. Are lines AB and XY parallel?
    (1)   ∠ BAL = ∠ CLM

(2)   Triangle CLM is an equilateral triangle.

25. How many chocolate bars 2 inches wide and 4 inches long can be packed into carton Q?
    (1)   The inside dimensions of carton Q are 8 inches by 8 inches by 12 inches.
    (2)   The width of carton Q is equal to the height and $\frac{3}{4}$ of the length.

STOP

END OF SECTION. IF YOU HAVE ANY TIME LEFT, GO OVER YOUR WORK IN THIS SECTION ONLY. DO NOT WORK IN ANY OTHER SECTION OF THE TEST.

SECTION IV

Time—30 Minutes
25 Questions

Directions: In this section, the questions ask you to analyze and evaluate the reasoning in short paragraphs or passages. For some questions, all of the answer choices may conceivably be answers to the question asked. You should select the *best* answer to the question, that is, an answer which does not require you to make assumptions which violate commonsense standards by being implausible, redundant, irrelevant, or inconsistent. After choosing the best answer, blacken the corresponding space on the answer sheet.

Questions 1 and 2

On his trip to the People's Republic of China, a young U.S. diplomat of very subordinate rank embarrassed himself by asking a Chinese official how it was that Orientals managed to be so inscrutable. The Chinese official smiled and then gently responded that he preferred to think of the inscrutability of his race in terms of a want of perspicacity in Occidentals.

1. Which of the following best describes the point of the comment made by the Chinese official?
   (A) It is not merely the Chinese, but all Oriental people who are inscrutable.
   (B) Most Americans fail to understand Chinese culture.
   (C) What one fails to perceive may be attributable to carelessness in observation rather than obscurity inherent in the object.
   (D) Since the resumption of diplomatic relations between the United States and Communist China, many older Chinese civil servants have grown to distrust the Americans.
   (E) If the West and the East are ever to truly understand one another, there will have to be considerable cultural exchange between the two.

2. Which of the following best characterizes the attitude and response of the Chinese official?
   (A) angry
   (B) fearful
   (C) emotional
   (D) indifferent
   (E) compassionate

3. People waste a surprising amount of money on gadgets and doodads that they hardly ever use. For example, my brother spent $25 on an electric ice-cream maker two years ago, but he has used it on only three occasions. Yet, he insists that regardless of the number of times he actually uses the ice-cream maker, the investment was a good one because ——————.

   Which of the following best completes the thought of the paragraph?
   (A) The price of ice cream will go up in the future.
   (B) He has purchased the ice-cream maker for the convenience of having it available if and when he needs it.
   (C) In a society that is oriented toward consumer goods, one should take every opportunity to acquire things.
   (D) Today $25 is not worth what it was two years ago on account of the inflation rate.
   (E) By using it so infrequently he has conserved a considerable amount of electrical energy.

4. A poet was once asked to interpret a particularly obscure passage in one of his poems. He responded, "When I wrote that verse, only God and I knew the meaning of that passage. Now, only God knows."

   What is the point of the poet's response?
   (A) God is infinitely wiser than man.
   (B) Most men are unable to understand poetry.
   (C) Poets rarely know the source of their own creative inspiration.
   (D) A great poem is inspired by the muse.
   (E) He has forgotten what he had originally meant by the verse.

5. A recent survey by the economics department of an Ivy League university revealed that increases in the salaries of preachers are accompanied by increases in the nationwide average of rum consumption. From 1965 to 1970 preachers' salaries increased on the average of 15% and rum sales grew by 14.5%. From 1970 to 1975 average preachers' salaries rose by 17% and rum sales by

17.5%. From 1975 to 1980 rum sales expanded by only 8% and average preachers' salaries also grew by only 8%.

Which of the following is the most likely explanation for the findings cited in the paragraph?
(A) When preachers have more disposable income, they tend to allocate that extra money to alcohol.
(B) When preachers are paid more, they preach longer; and longer sermons tend to drive people to drink.
(C) Since there were more preachers in the country, there were also more people; and a larger population will consume greater quantities of liquor.
(D) The general standard of living increased from 1965 to 1980, which accounts for both the increase in rum consumption and preachers' average salaries.
(E) A consortium of rum importers carefully limited the increases in imports of rum during the test period cited.

6. Since all four-door automobiles I have repaired have eight-cylinder engines, all four-door automobiles must have eight-cylinder engines.
The author argues on the basis of
(A) special training
(B) generalization
(C) syllogism
(D) ambiguity
(E) deduction

7. Two women, one living in Los Angeles, the other living in New York City, carried on a lengthy correspondence by mail. The subject of the exchange was a dispute over certain personality traits of Winston Churchill. After some two dozen letters, the Los Angeles resident received the following note from her New York City correspondent: "It seems you were right all along. Yesterday I met someone who actually knew Sir Winston, and he confirmed your opinion."

The two women could have been arguing on the basis of all of the following EXCEPT
(A) published biographical information
(B) old news film footage
(C) direct personal acquaintance
(D) assumption
(E) third party reports

8. The protection of the right of property by the Constitution is tenuous at best. It is true that the Fifth Amendment states that the government may not take private property for public use without compensation, but it is the government that defines private property.

Which of the following is most likely the point the author is leading up to?
(A) Individual rights that are protected by the Supreme Court are secure against government encroachment.
(B) Private property is neither more nor less than that which the government says is private property.
(C) The government has no authority to deprive an individual of his liberty.
(D) No government that acts arbitrarily can be justified.
(E) The keystone of American democracy is the Constitution.

9. *Daily Post* newspaper reporter Roger Nightengale let it be known that Andrea Johnson, the key figure in his award-winning series of articles on prostitution and drug abuse, was a composite of many persons and not a single, real person, and so he was the subject of much criticism by fellow journalists for having failed to disclose that information when the articles were first published. But these were the same critics who voted Nightengale a prize for his magazine serial *General*, which was a much dramatized and fictionalized account of a Korean War military leader whose character was obviously patterned closely after that of Douglas MacArthur.

In which of the following ways might the critics mentioned in the paragraph argue that they were NOT inconsistent in their treatment of Nightengale's works?

I. Fictionalization is an accepted journalistic technique for reporting on sensitive subject matter such as prostitution.
II. Critic disapproval is one of the most important ways members of the writing community have for ensuring that reporting is accurate and to the point.
III. There is a critical difference between dramatizing events in a piece of fiction and presenting distortions of the truth as actual fact.

(A) I only
(B) I and II only
(C) II and III only
(D) III only
(E) I, II, and III

10. Why pay outrageously high prices for imported sparkling water when there is now an inexpensive water carbonated and bottled here in the United States at its source—Cold Springs, Vermont. Neither you nor your guests will taste the difference, but if you would be embarrassed if it were learned that you were serving a domestic sparkling water, then serve Cold Springs Water— but serve it in a leaded crystal decanter.

The advertisement rests on which of the following assumptions?

  I. It is difficult if not impossible to distinguish Cold Springs Water from imported competitors on the basis of taste.

  II. Most sparkling waters are not bottled at the source.

  III. Some people may purchase an imported sparkling water over a domestic one as a status symbol.

(A) I only
(B) II only
(C) III only
(D) I and II only
(E) I and III only

11. Choose the best completion of the following paragraph.

Parochial education serves the dual functions of education and religious instruction, and church leaders are justifiably concerned to impart important religious values regarding relationships between the sexes. Thus, when the administrators of a parochial school system segregate boys and girls in separate institutions, they believe they are helping to keep the children pure by removing them from a source of temptation. If the administrators realized, however, that children would be more likely to develop the very attitudes they seek to engender in the company of the opposite sex, they would ——————.

(A) put an end to all parochial education
(B) no longer insist upon separate schools for boys and girls
(C) abolish all racial discrimination in the religious schools
(D) stop teaching foolish religious tripe, and concentrate instead on secular educational programs
(E) reinforce their policies of isolating the sexes in separate programs

12. Professor Branch, who is chairman of the sociology department, claims she saw a flying saucer the other night. But since she is a sociologist instead of a physicist, she cannot possibly be acquainted with the most recent writings of our finest scientists that tend to discount such sightings, so we can conclude her report is unreliable.

Which of the following would be the most appropriate criticism of the author's analysis?

(A) He makes an irrelevant attack on Professor Branch's credentials.
(B) He himself may not be a physicist, and therefore may not be familiar with the writings he cites.
(C) Even the U.S. Air Force cannot explain all of the sightings of UFOs which are reported to them each year.
(D) A sociologist is sufficiently well educated that he can probably read and understand scientific literature in a field other than his own.
(E) It is impossible to get complete agreement on matters such as the possibility of life on other planets.

13. INQUISTOR: Are you in league with the devil?

VICTIM: Yes.

INQUISITOR: Then you must be lying, for those in league with the "Evil One" never tell the truth. So you are not in league with the devil.

The inquisitor's behavior can be described as paradoxical because he

(A) charged the victim with being in a league with the devil but later recanted
(B) relies on the victim's answer to reject the victim's response
(C) acts in accordance with religious law but accuses the victim of violating that law
(D) questions the victim about his ties with the devil but does not himself believe there is a devil
(E) asked the question in the first place, but then refused to accept the answer that the victim gave

14. "Whom did you pass on the road?" the King went on, holding his hand out to the messenger for some hay.

"Nobody," said the messenger.

"Quite right," said the King. "This young lady saw him, too. So, of course, Nobody walks slower than you."

The King's response shows that he believes
(A) the messenger is a very good messenger
(B) "Nobody" is a person who might be seen
(C) the young lady's eyesight is better than the messenger's
(D) the messenger is not telling him the truth
(E) there was no person actually seen by the messenger on the road

15. MARY: All of the graduates from Midland High School go to State College.
    ANN: I don't know. Some of the students at State College come from North Hills High School.

Ann's response shows that she has interpreted Mary's remark to mean that
(A) most of the students from North Hills High School attend State College
(B) none of the students at State College are from Midland High School
(C) only students from Midland High School attend State College
(D) Midland High School is a better school than North Hills High School
(E) some Midland High School graduates do not attend college

16. Total contributions by individuals to political parties were up 25 percent in this most recent presidential election over those of four years earlier. Hence, it is obvious that people are no longer as apathetic as they were, but are taking a greater interest in politics.

Which of the following, if true, would considerably weaken the preceding argument?
(A) The average contribution per individual actually declined during the same four-year period.
(B) Per capita income of the population increased by 15 percent during the four years in question.
(C) Public leaders continue to warn citizens against the dangers of political apathy.
(D) Contributions made by large corporations to political parties declined during the four-year period.
(E) Fewer people voted in the most recent presidential election than in the one four years earlier.

17. The harmful effects of marijuana and other drugs have been considerably overstated. Although parents and teachers have expressed much con-

cern over the dangers which widespread usage of marijuana and other drugs pose for high school and junior high school students, a national survey of 5,000 students of ages 13 to 17 showed that fewer than 15% of those students thought such drug use was likely to be harmful.

Which of the following is the strongest criticism of the author's reasoning?
(A) The opinions of students in the age group surveyed are likely to vary with age.
(B) Alcohol use among students of ages 13 to 17 is on the rise, and is now considered by many to present greater dangers than marijuana usage.
(C) Marijuana and other drugs may be harmful to users even though the users are not themselves aware of the danger.
(D) A distinction must be drawn between victimless crimes and crimes in which an innocent person is likely to be involved.
(E) The fact that a student does not think a drug is harmful does not necessarily mean he will use it.

18. AL: If an alien species ever visited Earth, it would surely be because they were looking for other intelligent species with whom they could communicate. Since we have not been contacted by aliens, we may conclude that none have ever visited this planet.
    AMY: Or, perhaps, they did not think human beings intelligent.

How is Amy's response related to Al's argument?
(A) She misses Al's point entirely.
(B) She attacks Al personally rather than his reasoning.
(C) She points out that Al made an unwarranted assumption.
(D) She ignores the detailed internal development of Al's logic.
(E) She introduces a false analogy.

19. I maintain that the best way to solve our company's present financial crisis is to bring out a new line of goods. I challenge anyone who disagrees with this proposed course of action to show that it will not work.

A flaw in the preceding argument is that it
(A) employs group classifications without regard to individuals
(B) introduces an analogy which is weak

(C) attempts to shift the burden of proof to those who would object to the plan

(D) fails to provide statistical evidence to show that the plan will actually succeed

(E) relies upon a discredited economic theory

20. If quarks are the smallest subatomic particles in the universe, then gluons are needed to hold quarks together. Since gluons are needed to hold quarks together, it follows that quarks are the smallest subatomic particles in the universe.

The logic of the above argument is most nearly paralleled by which of the following?

(A) If this library has a good French literature collection, it will contain a copy of *Les Conquerants* by Malraux. The collection does contain a copy of *Les Conquerants;* therefore, the library has a good French literature collection.

(B) If there is a man-in-the-moon, the moon must be made of green cheese for him to eat. There is a man-in-the-moon, so the moon is made of green cheese.

(C) Either helium or hydrogen is the lightest element of the periodic table. Helium is not the lightest element of the periodic table, so hydrogen must be the lightest element of the periodic table.

(D) If Susan is taller than Bob, and if Bob is taller than Elaine, then if Susan is taller than Bob, Susan is also taller than Elaine.

(E) Whenever it rains, the streets get wet. The streets are not wet. Therefore, it has not rained.

21. In the earliest stages of the common law, a party could have his case heard by a judge only upon the payment of a fee to the court, and then only if his case fit within one of the forms for which there existed a writ. At first the number of such formalized cases of action was very small, but judges invented new forms which brought more cases and greater revenues.

Which of the following conclusions is most strongly suggested by the paragraph above?

(A) Early judges often decided cases in an arbitrary and haphazard manner.

(B) In most early cases, the plaintiff rather than the defendant prevailed.

(C) The judiciary at first had greater power than either the legislature or the executive.

(D) One of the motivating forces for the early expansion in judicial power was economic considerations.

(E) The first common law decisions were inconsistent with one another and did not form a coherent body of law.

22. If Martin introduces an amendment to Evans' bill, then Johnson and Lloyd will both vote the same way. If Evans speaks against Lloyd's position, Johnson will defend anyone voting with him. Martin will introduce an amendment to Evans' bill only if Evans speaks against Johnson's position.

If the above statements are true, each of the following can be true EXCEPT

(A) if Evans speaks against Johnson's position, Lloyd will not vote with Johnson.

(B) if Martin introduces an amendment to Evans' bill, then Evans has spoken against Johnson's position.

(C) if Evans speaks against Johnson's position, Martin will not introduce an amendment to Evans' bill.

(D) if Martin introduces an amendment to Evans' bill, then either Johnson will not vote with Lloyd or Evans did not speak against Johnson's position.

(E) if either Evans did not speak against Lloyd's position or Martin did not introduce an amendment to Evans' bill, then either Johnson did not defend Lloyd or Martin spoke against Johnson's position.

23. Once at a conference on the philosophy of language, a professor delivered a lengthy and tiresome address the central thesis of which was that "yes" and related slang words such as "yeah" can only be used to show agreement with a proposition. At the end of the paper, a listener in the back of the auditorium stood up and shouted in a sarcastic voice, "Oh, yeah?" This constituted a complete refutation of the paper.

The listener argued against the paper by

(A) offering a counter example

(B) pointing out an inconsistency

(C) presenting an analogy

(D) attacking the speaker's character

(E) citing additional evidence

Questions 24–25

The blanks in the following passage indicate deletions from the text. Select the completion that is most appropriate to the context.

Contemporary legal positivism depends upon the methodological assumption that a theory of law may be conceptual without, at the same time, being normative. In point of fact this assumption is a composite principle. It makes the fairly obvious claim that a conceptual theory, which strives to be descriptive rather than normative, says what the law is——not what it ought to be. A conceptual theory must be supplemented by a normative theory, and the arguments in favor of a particular content for law are couched in terms of the results which are expected to flow from proposed legal acts. It is never a part of an argument for what the law ought to be, in the positivist's view, that to be a law it must have a certain content. While the normative argument refers ultimately to agreed-upon ends, it does not assert that these ends——(24)——. Rather, that they are accepted and acted upon is merely a contingent matter. The second part of the methodological premise is more subtle: A conceptual theory such as legal positivism does not claim that the particular description it offers is uniquely correct. Proponents of legal positivism regard their study of law as analogous to the physicists' study of the universe: They have one theory of legal institutions, ——(25)——.

24. (A) must be pursued as a matter of logical necessity
    (B) are not the best ends for any modern legal system
    (C) would not be adopted by courts in a democratic society
    (D) could be undermined by dissident elements in the community
    (E) are shared by everyone

25. (A) and that is the only possible correct theory of law
    (B) and someday, with sufficient work, that theory will be able to generate societal goals for us to pursue
    (C) but that theory may, someday, be displaced by a better one
    (D) although no theory of the physical universe is as reliable as the positivistic theory of law
    (E) which is, however, strongly supported by the findings of modern science

STOP

END OF SECTION. IF YOU HAVE ANY TIME LEFT, GO OVER YOUR WORK IN THIS SECTION ONLY. DO NOT WORK IN ANY OTHER SECTION OF THE TEST.

SECTION V

Time—30 Minutes
20 Questions

Directions: For each of the following questions, select the best of the answer choices and blacken the corresponding space on your answer sheet.
Numbers: All numbers used are real numbers.
Figures: The diagrams and figures that accompany these questions are for the purpose of providing information useful in answering the questions. Unless it is stated that a specific figure is not drawn to scale, the diagrams and figures are drawn as accurately as possible. All figures are in a plane unless otherwise indicated.

1. If $x + 6 = 3$, then $x + 3 =$
   (A) -9
   (B) -3
   (C) 0
   (D) 3
   (E) 9

2. A person is standing on a staircase. He walks down 4 steps, up 3 steps, down 6 steps, up 2 steps, up 9 steps, and down 2 steps. Where is he standing in relation to the step on which he started?
   (A) 2 steps above
   (B) 1 step above
   (C) the same place
   (D) 1 step below
   (E) 4 steps above

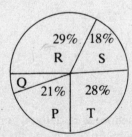

3. What portion of the circle graph above belongs to sector Q?
   (A) 4%
   (B) 5%
   (C) 6%
   (D) 75%
   (E) 96%

4. A professor begins his class at 1:21 P.M. and ends it at 3:36 P.M. the same afternoon. How many minutes long was the class?
   (A) 457
   (B) 215
   (C) 150
   (D) 135
   (E) 75

5. A sales representative will receive a 15% commission on a sale of $2800. If she has already received an advance of $150 on that commission, how much more is she due on the commission?
   (A) $120
   (B) $270
   (C) $320
   (D) $420
   (E) $570

6. If a circle has an area of $9\pi x^2$ units, what is its radius?
   (A) 3
   (B) $3x$
   (C) $3\pi x$
   (D) $9x$
   (E) $81x^4$

7. Hans is taller than Gertrude, but he is shorter than Wilhem. If Hans, Gertrude, and Wilhelm are heights x, y, and z, respectively, which of the following accurately expresses the relationships of their heights?
   (A) $x > y > z$
   (B) $x < y < z$
   (C) $y > x > z$
   (D) $z < x < y$
   (E) $z > x > y$

8. For which of the following figures can the area of the figure be determined if the perimeter is known?

   I. a square
   II. a trapezoid

III. an equilateral triangle

IV. a parallelogram

(A) I only

(B) II only

(C) III only

(D) I and III only

(E) I, II, III, and IV

9. A child withdraws from his piggy bank 10% of the original sum in the bank. If he must add 90¢ to bring the amount in the bank back up to the original sum, what was the original sum in the bank?

(A) $1.00

(B) $1.90

(C) $8.10

(D) $9.00

(E) $9.90

10. If cylinder P has a height twice that of cylinder Q and a radius half that of cylinder Q, what is the ratio between the volume of cylinder P and the volume of cylinder Q?

(A) 1:8

(B) 1:4

(C) 1:2

(D) 1

(E) 2:1

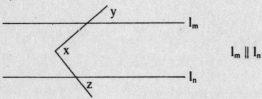

11. In the figure above, which of the following is true?

(A) $y + z = x$

(B) $y = 90°$

(C) $x + y + z = 180$

(D) $y = x + z$

(E) $z = x + y$

12. If the width of a rectangle is increased by 25% while the length remains constant, the resulting area is what percent of the original area?

(A) 25%

(B) 75%

(C) 125%

(D) 225%

(E) Cannot be determined from the information given.

13. The average of four consecutive odd positive integers is always

(A) an odd number

(B) divisible by 4

(C) a prime number

(D) a multiple of 3

(E) an even number

14. A snapshot measures $2\frac{1}{2}$ inches by $1\frac{7}{8}$ inches. It is to be enlarged so that the longer dimension will be 4 inches. The length of the enlarged shorter dimension will be

(A) $2\frac{1}{2}$ inches

(B) 3 inches

(C) $3\frac{3}{8}$ inches

(D) $2\frac{5}{8}$ inches

(E) none of these

15. From a piece of tin in the shape of a square 6 inches on a side, the largest possible circle is cut out. Of the following, the ratio of the area of the circle to the area of the original square is closest in value to

(A) $\frac{3}{4}$

(B) $\frac{2}{3}$

(C) $\frac{3}{5}$

(D) $\frac{1}{2}$

(E) $\frac{1}{4}$

16. In the Peterson Company, the ratio of upper-management to middle-management personnel is 4:3. If 75% of upper management has experience on the production line, what is the greatest proportion of the total of upper- and middle-management personnel who could have experience on the production line?

(A) $\frac{5}{7}$

(B) $\frac{3}{4}$

(C) $\frac{6}{7}$

(D) $\frac{7}{6}$

(E) $\frac{7}{4}$

17. The function # is defined for any positive whole number N as being the product $\#N = (N - 1)(N - 2)(N - 3)$. What is the sum of #1, #2, #3, and #4?

(A) −10

(B) 6

(C) 12

(D) 60

(E) 256

18. A basketball club meets on a certain night with 12 members in attendance. The club members form two 6-member teams to play against each other. If five players on each team must be on the basketball court for a game to be played, how many different groups of players could be playing during the course of the game?

(A) 6
(B) 18
(C) 24
(D) 36
(E) 144

19. Two crystal spheres of diameter $\frac{x}{2}$ are being packed in a cubic box with a side of x. If the crystal spheres are in the box and the rest of the box is completely filled with packing powder, approximately what proportion of the box is filled with packing powder? (The volume of a sphere of radius r is $\frac{4}{3}\pi r^3$.)

(A) $1\frac{1}{16}$
(B) $\frac{1}{8}$
(C) $\frac{1}{2}$
(D) $\frac{3}{4}$
(E) $\frac{7}{8}$

20. All of the coffee mixtures sold in a certain store contain either Colombian, Jamaican, or Brazilian coffee or some combination of these. Of all the mixtures, 33 contain Colombian coffee, 43 contain Jamaican coffee, and 42 contain Brazilian coffee. Of these, 16 contain at least Colombian and Jamaican coffees, 18 contain at least Jamaican and Brazilian coffees, 8 contain at least Brazilian and Colombian coffees, and 5 contain all three. How many different coffee mixtures are sold in the store?

(A) 71
(B) 81
(C) 109
(D) 118
(E) 165

STOP

END OF SECTION. IF YOU HAVE ANY TIME LEFT, GO OVER YOUR WORK IN THIS SECTION ONLY. DO NOT WORK IN ANY OTHER SECTION OF THE TEST.

SECTION VI

Time—30 Minutes
25 Questions

Directions: In each problem below, either part or all of the sentence is underlined. The sentence is followed by five ways of writing the underlined part. Answer choice (A) repeats the original; the other answer choices vary. If you think that the original phrasing is the best, choose (A). If you think one of the other answer choices is the best, select that choice.

This section tests the ability to recognize correct and effective expression. Follow the requirements of Standard Written English: grammar, choice of words, and sentence construction. Choose the answer which results in the clearest, most exact sentence, but do not change the meaning of the original sentence.

1. During the summer of 1981, when it looked like parts of New York and New Jersey were going to run short of water, many businesses and homes were affected by the stringent restrictions on the use of water.
   (A) it looked like parts of New York and New Jersey were going to run
   (B) it looked as if parts of New York and New Jersey would have run
   (C) it appeared that parts of New York and New Jersey would run
   (D) appearances were that parts of New York and New Jersey would run
   (E) it was the appearance that parts of New York and New Jersey would be running

2. The books of W.E.B. DuBois before World War I constituted as fundamental a challenge to the accepted ideas of race relations that, two generations later, will be true of the writings of the radical writers of the 1960's.
   (A) that, two generations later, will be true of
   (B) that, two generations later, would be true of
   (C) as, two generations later, would be true of
   (D) as, two generations later, would
   (E) just in the way that, two generations later, did

3. For the reason that gasoline was relatively cheap and twenty-five cents per gallon in the 1960's, the average American came to view unfettered, inexpensive driving as a right rather than a lucky privilege.
   (A) For the reason that gasoline was relatively cheap and
   (B) Because gasoline was relatively cheap and
   (C) Due to the fact that gasoline was a relatively inexpensive
   (D) In that gasoline was a relatively inexpensive
   (E) Because gasoline was a relatively cheap

4. The political masters of the health care system have not listened to professional health planners because it has not been profitable for them to do that thing.
   (A) has not been profitable for them to do that thing.
   (B) has not been profitable for them to do so.
   (C) has been unprofitable for them to do that thing.
   (D) has been unprofitable for them to do so.
   (E) doing so had not been profitable for them.

5. Because of the efforts of Amory Lovins and other advocates of the "soft" path of solar energy, the economics of nuclear power are being more closely examined now than ever before.
   (A) being more closely examined now than ever before.
   (B) being attacked more vigorously than ever before.
   (C) open to closer examination than they ever were before.
   (D) more closely examined than before.
   (E) more examined than they ever were before now.

6. Most bacterial populations grown in controlled conditions will quickly expand to the limit of the food supply, <u>produce toxic waste products that inhibit further growth, and reached an equilibrium state within a relatively short time.</u>

   (A) produce toxic waste products that inhibit further growth, and reached an equilibrium state within a relatively short time.

   (B) will have produced toxic waste products that inhibit further growth and also will reach an equilibrium state within a relatively short time.

   (C) will then produce a toxic waste product that inhibits further growth and thus reached an equilibrium state in a very short time.

   (D) produce toxic waste products that inhibit further growth and reach equilibrium.

   (E) produce toxic waste products that inhibit further growth, and reach an equilibrium state in a fairly prompt way.

7. A little-known danger of potent hallucinogens such as lysergic acid diethylamide-25 is that not only is the user immediately disoriented, <u>but also he will experience significant ego suppression for a period of three weeks as well.</u>

   (A) but also he will experience significant ego suppression for a period of three weeks as well.

   (B) but also he will experience significant ego suppression for a period of three weeks.

   (C) but also there will be a three-week period of ego suppression as well.

   (D) but the ego is suppressed for a period of three weeks as well.

   (E) but the user's ego is suppressed for a period of three weeks in addition.

8. Many people mistakenly believe that the body's nutritional requirements remain the same <u>irregardless of the quantity and form of other nutrients ingested, physical activity and emotional state.</u>

   (A) irregardless of the quantity and form of other nutrients ingested, physical activity and emotional state.

   (B) irregardless of the other nutrients, physical activity and emotional state.

   (C) regardless of the quantity of nutrients or physical exercise or emotional excitation.

   (D) regardless of the quantity or form of nutrients or physical exercise and emotional statement.

   (E) regardless of the quantity or form of other nutrients ingested, physical activity or emotional state.

9. Measuring the brainwaves of human beings while they are engaged in different types of thought <u>hopefully will enable</u> neuropsychologists to better understand the relationship between the structures of the brain and thinking.

   (A) hopefully will enable

   (B) hopefully might enable

   (C) will, it is hoped, enable

   (D) would hopefully enable

   (E) will, it is to be hoped by all, enable

10. <u>It appears from a study of the detailed grammar of the Hopi Indians that their system</u> of assigning tenses is very different from that of English or other European languages.

    (A) It appears from a study of the detailed grammar of the Hopi Indians that their system

    (B) It seems that study of the Hopi Indians indicates that their system

    (C) A detailed study of the grammar of the Hopi Indian language indicates that its system

    (D) Detailed study of Hopi Indians reveals that their system

    (E) The Hopi Indians have a system

11. While everyone continues to hope for their survival, it is unlikely that the astronauts <u>could have made it back to the shelter before the power plant exploded.</u>

    (A) could have made it back to the shelter before the power plant exploded.

    (B) were making it back to the shelter before the power plant exploded.

    (C) were able to make it back to the shelter before the power plant explodes.

(D) have been able to make it back to the shelter before the power plant will explode.

(E) could have made it to the shelter before the power plant explosion would have destroyed them.

12. By the time peace and happiness will have come to the planet, many lives will be wasted.
(A) will have come to the planet, many lives will be wasted.
(B) come to the planet, many lives will have been wasted.
(C) will have come to the planet, many lives will have been wasted.
(D) shall have come to the planet, many lives shall be wasted.
(E) would have come to the planet, many lives would have been wasted.

13. It could be argued that the most significant virtue of a popular democracy is not the right to participate in the selection of leaders, but rather that it affirms our importance in the scheme of things.
(A) but rather that it affirms
(B) but rather its affirmation of
(C) but rather it's affirmation in terms of
(D) but instead of that, its affirming that
(E) affirming rather

14. Long popular among the connoisseurs of Indian music, Ravi Shankar first impressed Western listeners with his phenomenal technical virtuosity, but they soon came to appreciate his music as an artful expression of an older culture's musical insights.
(A) but they soon came to appreciate his music as an artful
(B) but it soon occurred that they appreciated his artful music as an
(C) but soon this was surpassed by an appreciation of it as an artful
(D) which was soon surpassed by an even deeper appreciation of it as an artful
(E) soon surpassed by an artful appreciation of an

15. Primarily accomplished through the use of the electron microscope, researchers have

recently vastly increased their knowledge of the process of cell division.
(A) Primarily accomplished through the use of the electron microscope,
(B) Through the competent use of advanced electron microscopy,
(C) Primarily through the use of electron microscopy,
(D) In a large sense through the use of the electron microscope,
(E) In the main, particularly through the use of electron microscopes,

16. Though garlic is often associated with Italian cuisine, it is actually the use of oregano which most distinguishes the Italians from the French.
(A) which most distinguishes the Italians from the French.
(B) which primarily distinguishes Italians from Frenchmen.
(C) which generally serves to distinguish an Italian sauce from a French one.
(D) which is the major distinction between the two great cuisines.
(E) which most distinguishes Italian cookery from French.

17. While controversy rages over whether the sign language taught to some great apes is truly human-like speech, there is no similar dispute that our powers of communication are greater by far than that of any other animal.
(A) are greater by far than that of any other animal.
(B) are far greater than that of any other animal.
(C) are greater by far than any other animal.
(D) are far greater than those of any other animal.
(E) have been far greater than those of other animals.

18. Despite the money that has been invested by industry in the attempt to persuade Americans that highly processed foods are the best foods, the populace stubbornly clings to the belief that such foods are neither particularly healthy or tasty.

(A) are neither particularly healthy or tasty.

(B) are neither particularly healthful nor tasty.

(C) are not particularly healthy or tasty.

(D) are not particularly healthful or tasteful.

(E) are not very healthy nor tasty.

19. While it is certainly true that almost all literate citizens could be taught to improve their ability to read and reason, it must first be demonstrated that such an undertaking would increase the general welfare.

(A) While it is certainly true that almost all literate citizens could be taught to improve their ability to read and reason, it must first be demonstrated that such an undertaking would increase the general welfare.

(B) While it is certainly true that almost all literate citizens could improve their reading and reasoning skills, such a vast undertaking requires a clear demonstration of benefit before being undertaken.

(C) Before undertaking to improve the reading and reasoning of almost all citizens, it is necessary to show that the project will work.

(D) Before the project of improving almost all citizens' reading and reasoning skills is undertaken, that the outcome will be increased happiness must be demonstrated.

(E) Prior to the improvement of citizens' reading and reasoning skills, it must be shown that they will be happier with the improved skills than they are now.

20. The closing of small, inexpensive hospitals while large expensive hospitals remain open seems a luxury that we can no longer afford in order to maintain them.

(A) seems a luxury that we can no longer afford in order to maintain them.

(B) seems to emphasize luxury over economy, which we can no longer afford.

(C) seems to be a waste of valuable resources.

(D) seems a luxury we can no longer afford.

(E) seems too luxurious to be any longer affordable.

21. The ancient question of the exact difference between plants and animals, which was so complicated with the discovery of microscopic members of both groups, was somewhat sidestepped with the establishment of a third phylum, the Protista, reserved just for them.

(A) reserved just for them.

(B) consisting only of them.

(C) inhabited only by them.

(D) which includes all microscopic life.

(E) which would have included all microscopic plants and animals.

22. The Lake Manyara Park in Tanzania affords the visitor with unequalled opportunities to photograph lions playing in trees without the aid of telephoto lenses.

(A) The Lake Manyara Park in Tanzania affords the visitor with unequalled opportunities to photograph lions playing in trees without the aid of telephoto lenses.

(B) The Lake Manyara Park in Tanzania permits the visitor unequalled opportunities to photograph lions playing in trees without the aid of telephoto lenses.

(C) The Lake Manyara Park in Tanzania gives the visitor the unequalled opportunity to photograph lions playing in trees without telephoto lenses.

(D) The visitor to the Lake Manyara Park in Tanzania has the unequalled opportunity to photograph lions playing in trees without the aid of telephoto lenses.

(E) Even without the aid of telephoto lenses, the visitor to Tanzania's Lake Manyara Park has an unequalled opportunity to photograph lions playing in trees.

23. One school of thought maintains that a person's susceptibility to hypnosis is able to

be measured by their performance on the "eye roll" test.

(A) is able to be measured by their
(B) can be measured by their
(C) can be measured by his
(D) is measurable by their
(E) is possibly measurable by his

24. Many observers of the demonstration were appalled at the violence with which it was broken up, grieved by the large number of injuries to both demonstrators and militia, and promising that this sort of horror would never be repeated.

(A) grieved by the large number of injuries to both demonstrators and militia, and promising that this sort of horror would never be repeated.
(B) aggrieved by the large number of injuries to both demonstrators and militia, and promised that this sort of horror would never be repeated.
(C) grieved by the large number of injuries to both demonstrators and militia and determined that this sort of horror would never be repeated.
(D) saddened by the large number of injuries to both sides and promised that this horror would never be repeated.

(E) grieving about the large number of injuries to both demonstrators and militia and promising that this sort of horror would never be repeated.

25. In order to survive, prisoners may have to adapt to the harsh conditions of jail, but to do so may be to lose much that is human and admirable in their original personalities.

(A) In order to survive, prisoners may have to adapt to the harsh conditions of jail, but to do so may be to lose much that is human and admirable in their original personalities.
(B) To survive, prisoners may have to jettison much that is human and admirable in the original personality.
(C) In order to survive, prisoners must adapt to the harsh conditions of jail, thus losing much that is human and admirable of their original personalities.
(D) Survival in jail may require the prisoner to discard much that was human and admirable from their original personality.
(E) Survival in a harsh prison environment often requires the discarding of much that is human and admirable in the prisoner's original personalities.

STOP

END OF SECTION. IF YOU HAVE ANY TIME LEFT, GO
OVER YOUR WORK IN THIS SECTION ONLY. DO NOT
WORK IN ANY OTHER SECTION OF THE TEST.

SECTION VII

Time—30 Minutes
20 Questions

Directions: For each of the following questions, select the best of the answer choices and blacken the corresponding space on your answer sheet.

Numbers: All numbers used are real numbers.

Figures: The diagrams and figures that accompany these questions are for the purpose of providing information useful in answering the questions. Unless it is stated that a specific figure is not drawn to scale, the diagrams and figures are drawn as accurately as possible. All figures are in a plane unless otherwise indicated.

1. What is 40% of $\frac{10}{7}$?
   (A) $\frac{2}{7}$
   (B) $\frac{4}{7}$
   (C) $\frac{10}{28}$
   (D) $\frac{1}{28}$
   (E) $\frac{28}{10}$

2. A prime number is one with 2 divisors and which is divisble only by itself and 1. Which of the following are prime numbers?

   I.   17
   II. 27
   III. 51
   IV. 59

   (A) I only
   (B) I and II only
   (C) I, III, and IV only
   (D) I and IV only
   (E) III and IV only

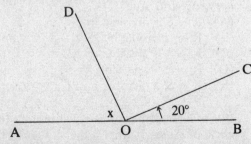

3. As shown in the above diagram, AB is a straight line and angle BOC = 20°. If the number of degrees in angle DOC is 6 more than the number of degrees in angle x, find the number of degrees in angle x.
   (A) 77
   (B) 75
   (C) 78
   (D) $22\frac{6}{7}$
   (E) 87

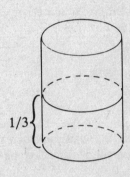

4. As shown in the figure, a cylindrical oil tank is $\frac{1}{3}$ full. If 3 more gallons are added, the tank will be half full. What is the capacity, in gallons, of the tank?
   (A) 15
   (B) 16
   (C) 17
   (D) 18
   (E) 19

5. A boy receives grades of 91, 88, 86, and 78 in four of his major subjects. What must he receive in his fifth major subject in order to average 85?
   (A) 86
   (B) 85
   (C) 84
   (D) 83
   (E) 82

6. If a steel bar is 0.39 feet long, its length in *inches* is
   (A) less than 4
   (B) between 4 and $4\frac{1}{2}$
   (C) between $4\frac{1}{2}$ and 5
   (D) between 5 and 6
   (E) more than 6

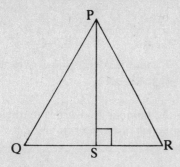

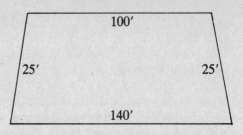

7. In the figure, PS is perpendicular to QR. If PQ = PR = 26 and PS = 24, then QR =
   (A) 14
   (B) 16
   (C) 18
   (D) 20
   (E) 22

8. If x = 0, for what value of y is the following equation valid? $5x^3 + 7x^2 - (4y + 13)x - 7y + 15 = 0$
   (A) $-2\frac{1}{7}$
   (B) 0
   (C) $+2\frac{1}{7}$
   (D) $\frac{15}{11}$
   (E) $3\frac{1}{7}$

9. A man buys some shirts and some ties. The shirts cost $7 each and the ties cost $3 each. If the man spends exactly $81 and buys the maximum number of shirts possible under these conditions, what is the ratio of shirts to ties?
   (A) 5:3
   (B) 4:3
   (C) 5:2
   (D) 4:1
   (E) 3:2

10. If a man walks $\frac{2}{5}$ mile in 5 minutes, what is his average rate of walking in miles per hour?
    (A) 4
    (B) $4\frac{1}{2}$
    (C) $4\frac{4}{5}$
    (D) $5\frac{1}{5}$
    (E) $5\frac{3}{4}$

11. One end of a dam has the shape of a trapezoid with the dimensions indicated. What is the dam's area in square feet?
    (A) 1000
    (B) 1200
    (C) 1500
    (D) 1800
    (E) Cannot be determined from the information given.

12. If $1 + \frac{1}{t} = \frac{t+1}{t}$, what does t equal?
    (A) +2 only
    (B) +2 or −2 only
    (C) +2 or −1 only
    (D) −2 or +1 only
    (E) t is any number except 0

13. Point A is 3 inches from line b as shown in the diagram. In the plane that contains point A and line b, what is the total number of points which are 6 inches from A and also 1 inch from b?
    (A) 0
    (B) 1
    (C) 2
    (D) 3
    (E) 4

14. If R and S are different integers, both divisible by 5, then which of the following is *not necessarily* true?
    (A) R − S is divisible by 5
    (B) RS is divisible by 25
    (C) R + S is divisible by 5
    (D) $R^2 + S^2$ is divisible by 5
    (E) R + S is divisible by 10

15. If a triangle of base 7 is equal in area to a circle of radius 7, what is the altitude of the triangle?
    (A) 8π
    (B) 10π

(C) 12π

(D) 14π

(E) Cannot be determined from the information given.

16. If the following numbers are arranged in order from the smallest to the largest, what will be their correct order?

I. $\dfrac{9}{13}$

II. $\dfrac{13}{9}$

III. 70%

IV. $\dfrac{1}{.70}$

(A) II, I, III, IV

(B) III, II, I, IV

(C) III, IV, I, II

(D) II, IV, III, I

(E) I, III, IV, II

17. The coordinates of the vertices of quadrilateral PQRS are P(0, 0), Q(9, 0), R(10, 3) and S(1, 3), respectively. The area of PQRS is

(A) $9\sqrt{10}$

(B) $\frac{9}{2}\sqrt{10}$

(C) $\frac{27}{2}$

(D) 27

(E) not determinable from the information given

18. In circle O shown, AB is a diameter. If secant AP = 8 and tangent CP = 4, find the number of units in the diameter of the circle.

(A) 6

(B) $6\frac{1}{2}$

(C) 8

(D) $3\sqrt{2}$

(E) Cannot be determined from the information given.

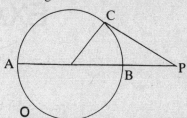

19. A certain type of siding for a house costs $10.50 per square yard. What does it cost for the siding for a wall 4 yards wide and 60 feet long?

(A) $800

(B) $840

(C) $2520

(D) $3240

(E) $5040

20. A circle whose radius is 7 has its center at the origin. Which of the following points are outside the circle?

I. (4, 4)

II. (5, 5)

III. (4, 5)

IV. (4, 6)

(A) I and II only

(B) II and III only

(C) II, III, and IV only

(D) II and IV only

(E) III and IV only

STOP

END OF SECTION. IF YOU HAVE ANY TIME LEFT, GO
OVER YOUR WORK IN THIS SECTION ONLY. DO NOT
WORK IN ANY OTHER SECTION OF THE TEST.

ANSWER KEY — PRACTICE EXAMINATION 1

SECTION I

1. C	6. B	11. E	16. A	21. A
2. A	7. D	12. B	17. E	22. C
3. C	8. B	13. D	18. B	23. A
4. B	9. A	14. B	19. B	24. C
5. E	10. E	15. A	20. A	25. B

SECTION II

1. D	5. A	9. E	13. B	17. E
2. D	6. D	10. A	14. D	18. A
3. B	7. D	11. C	15. A	19. C
4. B	8. D	12. A	16. E	20. B

SECTION III

1. C	6. D	11. E	16. B	21. B
2. A	7. B	12. B	17. E	22. A
3. C	8. A	13. C	18. C	23. C
4. C	9. C	14. A	19. D	24. D
5. B	10. B	15. D	20. D	25. E

SECTION IV

1. C	6. B	11. B	16. E	21. D
2. E	7. C	12. A	17. C	22. D
3. B	8. B	13. B	18. C	23. A
4. E	9. D	14. B	19. C	24. A
5. D	10. E	15. C	20. A	25. C

SECTION V

1.	C	5.	B	9.	D	13.	E	17.	B
2.	A	6.	B	10.	C	14.	B	18.	D
3.	A	7.	E	11.	A	15.	A	19.	E
4.	D	8.	D	12.	C	16.	C	20.	B

SECTION VI

1.	C	6.	D	11.	A	16.	E	21.	D
2.	D	7.	B	12.	B	17.	D	22.	E
3.	E	8.	E	13.	B	18.	B	23.	C
4.	B	9.	C	14.	A	19.	A	24.	C
5.	A	10.	C	15.	C	20.	D	25.	A

SECTION VII

1.	B	5.	E	9.	E	13.	E	17.	D
2.	D	6.	C	10.	C	14.	E	18.	A
3.	A	7.	D	11.	D	15.	D	19.	B
4.	D	8.	C	12.	E	16.	E	20.	D

EXPLANATORY ANSWERS

Section I

1. **(C)** This is a main idea question, and the task is to find a choice which expresses the main thesis of the passage without being too narrow and without being overly broad and going beyond the scope of the argument. (A) is too narrow, since this is but a minor feature of the discussion. (E) can be eliminated on the same grounds, since the possibility of nuclear destruction is but one important difference between war in a modernized society and war in a pre-modernized society. (B) is an attractive choice, but it is not the main thesis of the passage. The author does indeed discuss some of the effects of war on both modernized and pre-modernized societies, but this discussion is subordinate to a larger goal: to show that because of changing circumstance (effects are different), the value of war has changed. (D) is incorrect because it misses this main point, and it is incorrect for the further reason that the author discusses more than just pre-modernized societies.

2. **(A)** The second paragraph describes the attitude of pre-modernized society toward war: accepted, even noble, necessary. Coupled with the goals of war in pre-modernized societies, described in the first paragraph, we can infer that leaders of pre-modernized society regarded war as a valid policy tool. On this ground we select (A), eliminating (B) and (C). As for (D), although this can be inferred to have been a feature of war in pre-modernized society, (D) is not responsive to the question: What did the leaders think of war, that is, what was their attitude? (E) can be eliminated on the same ground and on the further ground that "necessity" for war was not that described in (E).

3. **(C)** The author is discussing war, a seemingly uncivilized activity. Yet, the author argues that war, at least in pre-modernized times, was the necessary result of certain economic and social forces. His use of the term "civilized" is ironic. Under other circumstances, the explanations offered by (A) and (B) might be plausible, but there is nothing in this text to support either of those. (D), too, might under other circumstances be a reason for placing the word in quotation marks, but it does not appear that this author is attempting to affect the reader's emotions; the passage is too detached and scientific for that. Finally, (E) does articulate one of the author's objectives, but this is not the reason for putting the one word in quotations. The explanation for that is something more specific than an overall idea of the passage.

4. **(B)** This is an explicit idea question, and (A), (C), (D), and (E) are all mentioned at various points in the passage as reasons for going to war. (B), too, is mentioned, but it is mentioned as a feature of the military establishment in pre-modernized society—not as a reason for going to war.

5. **(E)** This is another main idea question, and (B), (C), and (D) can be eliminated as too narrow. It is true the author mentions that economic and social conditions, technology, and armed conflict have all changed, but this is not the ultimate point to be proved. The author's main point is that *because* of such changes, the value of war has changed. (A) is only tangentially related to the text. Though we may learn a bit about how decisions are made, in part, this is not the main burden of the argument.

6. **(B)** We have already mentioned that the tone of the passage is neutral—scientific and detached. As for the remaining choices, (A) and (D) can be eliminated as overstatements. To be sure, the author seems to deplore the destruction which might result from a nuclear war, but that concern does not rise to the status of outrage, indignation, fear, or alarm. (E) is a closer call. While it is true

that the author expresses concern about the ability of modernized society to survive war, and while there is arguably a hint of optimism or hope, it cannot be said that these are the *defining* features of the passage. A better description of the prevailing tone is offered by (B). As for (C), the one ironic reference ("civilized") does not make the entire passage humorous.

7. **(D)** This is an application question, and we must take the information from the passage and apply it to a new situation. The author offers two reasons for the conclusion that war is no longer a viable policy tool: (1) the danger of world-wide destruction and (2) the costs after victory outweigh the benefits to be won. We can conclude that even in the absence of nuclear weapons, war will still lack its traditional value, as argued by the author in the fourth paragraph. Thus, we can eliminate (A) and (B) on the grounds that they are contradicted by the author's thinking. (E) can be eliminated for the same reason and because no such "instincts" are discussed in the text. A close look at (C) shows that it is not in agreement with the author's view, since the author believes that though nuclear weapons deter nuclear war, war is obsolete for other reasons as well.

8. **(B)** This is an explicit idea question, and the reference you need is the first paragraph. There the author specifically states that maintaining a nuclear capability is paradoxical because it is hoped that the capability will never be used.

9. **(A)** This is a main idea question. The passage actually makes two points: Who is Josquin, and why have we never heard of him? (A) correctly mentions both of these. (B) is incorrect for the main focus is not to describe medieval music at all. Rather, the author focuses on Josquin, a man of the Renaissance. (C) is incorrect because the author is more concerned to introduce the reader to Josquin than to place Josquin into a context. And in any event, though the author mentions some ways in which Josquin broke with his predecessors, this is not a discussion of his "influence on later composers." (D) is incorrect, for the enumeration of features of Josquin's music is incidental to the task of introducing the reader to Josquin. Moreover, the author does not offer critical commentary. The mere fact that he praises Josquin's music does not constitute critical analysis. Finally, (E) is incorrect because it fails to refer to the second major aspect of the passage: Why is Josquin not better known?

10. **(E)** This is an explicit idea question. (A) is answered in paragraph two ("Solace me, ..."). (B) is answered in the final paragraph (sackbut). (C) is answered in the second paragraph (Ockeghem). An answer to (D) is suggested in the final paragraph. (E) must be the correct answer, since the author never makes reference to any students.

11. **(E)** This is an inference question. In the third paragraph the author lists certain difficulties in reading a Renaissance score: no tempo specified, missing flats and sharps, and no instrument/voice indication. Since these are regarded as deficiencies of Renaissance scoring, we may infer that modern music notation contains all of these.

12. **(B)** This is an application question. The support for (B) is found in paragraph 3, where the author discusses the distinction between concept and performance. The author states that music does not exist as printed notes. The notation is just a set of instructions for producing music. So the author would agree with (B). As for (A), it is conceivable that the author might endorse this statement—though it is also possible that the author would reject it. It is clear, however, that as between the statement in (B) and that in (A) we can be sure that the author would endorse (B). So (B), rather than (A), must be correct. (C) is incorrect because Josquin belongs to the Renaissance, not the Middle Ages. (D) fails for the same reason that (A) fails. Finally, there is no support for the statement in (E).

13. **(D)** Here, too, we have an application question. There is some merit to each of the choices, but we are looking for the one answer that is most closely connected with the text. Since the author discusses the lack of funding as one important reason for Josquin's obscurity, an obscurity the author deplores, the argument might be used to support a proposal for funds to promote Josquin's music. That is (D). (A) is less clearly supported by the text. To the extent that it is read as a device to promote Josquin's music, it would be less effective than (D) since the author states that *collegia musica* have a high turnover of students. Establishing yet another one would not do as much to bring Josquin's music to more people as (D). As for (B) and (E), these do not tie in with the idea of publicizing Josquin's music. Finally, (C) has some plausibility, but (D) has a connection with the passage which (C) lacks.

14. **(B)** This is an explicit idea question. (C), (D), and (E) are mentioned in the final paragraph. (A) is mentioned in the third paragraph. (B) is never mentioned. The author states that musicians who read modern notation have difficulty reading Renaissance notation——not that these musicians lack talent.

15. **(A)** This is a tone question. The author compares Josquin to Galileo in order to praise Josquin. This must mean that the author has a very high opinion of Galileo. So (D) and (E) can be eliminated because they are merely neutral. (B) can be eliminated because of its negative connotations. And (C) can be eliminated as being lukewarm, when the author is clearly enthusiastic about Josquin and therefore Galileo as well.

16. **(A)** In the first paragraph the author likens music before Josquin des Prez to certain architectural features of medieval cathedrals. The best description of this rhetorical move is an analogy.

17. **(E)** This is obviously another author's attitude question. There are several clues in the passage to help you. For example, the author refers to the composer's "magnificent masses" and to a "profoundly moving" score. This indicates that the author believes the composer's works have considerable merit (even though they may not be well known).

18. **(B)** This is a main idea question. The author begins by stating that a large number of auto traffic fatalities can be attributed to drivers who are intoxicated. He then reviews two approaches to controlling this problem, taxation and drunk driving laws. Neither is very successful. The author finally notes that therapy may be useful, though the extent of its value has not yet been proved. (B) fairly well describes this development. (A) can be eliminated since any conclusions drawn by the author from studies on drunk driving are used for the larger objective described in (B). (C) is incorrect since, aside from suggesting possible ways to reduce the extent of the problem, the author never treats the causes of drunk driving. (D) is incorrect for the same reason. Finally, (E) is incorrect, because the comparison between the U.S. and Britain is only a small part of the passage.

19. **(B)** This is an inference question. In the third paragraph, the author discusses the effect of drunk driving laws. He states that after the implementation of the Road Safety Act in Britain, motor vehicle fatalities fell considerably. On this basis, we infer that the RSA was a law aimed at drunk driving. We can eliminate (D) and (E) on this ground. (C) can be eliminated as not warranted on the basis of this information. It is not clear whether the number of arrests increased. Equally consistent with the passage is the conclusion that the number of arrests dropped because people were no longer driving while intoxicated. (C) is incorrect for a further reason, the justification for (B). (B) and (A) are fairly close since both describe the RSA as a law aimed at drunk driving. But the last sentence of the third paragraph calls for (B) over (A). As people learned that they would not get caught for drunk driving, the law became less effective. This suggests that the RSA made drunk driving illegal, not that it lowered the BAC required for conviction. This makes sense of the sentence ". . . they could drink and not be stopped." If (A) were correct, this sentence would have to read, ". . . they could drink the same amount and not be convicted."

20. **(A)** This is an inference question. In the first paragraph, the author states that for a person to attain a BAC of 0.1 percent, he would need to drink over five ounces of 80 proof spirits over a *short period of time*. The author is trying to impress on us that that is a considerable quantity of alcohol for most people to drink. (A) explains why the author makes this comment. (B) is incorrect and confuses the first paragraph with the second paragraph. (C) is incorrect since the point of the example is that the BAC is so high most people will not exceed it. This is not to say, however, that people will not drink and drive because of laws establishing maximum BAC levels. Rather, they can continue to drink and drive because the law allows them a considerable margin in the level of BAC. (D) is a misreading of that first paragraph. Of all the very drunk drivers (BAC in excess of 0.1), only 1 percent are involved in accidents. But this does not say that most drivers involved in fatal collisions have BAC levels in excess of 0.1 percent, and that is what (D) says. As for (E), the author never states that the only way to attain a BAC of 0.1 percent is to drink five ounces of 80 proof spirits in a short time——there may be other ways of becoming intoxicated.

21. **(A)** This is an application question. In the second paragraph, the author states that increased taxation on alcohol would tax the heaviest drinkers

most, but he notes that this would also penalize the moderate and light drinker. In other words, the remedy is not sufficiently focused on the problem. Then, in the third paragraph, the author notes that drunk driving laws are aimed at the specific problem drivers. We can infer from this discussion that the author would likely advocate drunk driving laws over taxation for the reasons just given. This reasoning is presented in answer (A). (B) is incorrect for the reasons just given and for the further reason that the passage never suggests that taxation is likely to be more effective in solving the problem. The author never really evaluates the effectiveness of taxation in reducing drunk driving. (C) is incorrect for the reason given in support of (A) and for the further reason that the author never raises the issue of personal liberty in conjunction with the BAC test. (D) can be eliminated because the author does not discount the effectiveness of anti-drunk driving measures entirely. Even the British example gives some support to the conclusion that such laws have an effect. (E) is incorrect for the author never mentions the expense or administrative feasibility of BAC tests.

22. **(C)** This is a question about the logical structure of the passage. In paragraph 3, the author notes that stricter enforcement of laws against drunk driving may result in a few more arrests; but a few more arrests is not likely to have much impact on the problem because the number of arrests is small compared to those who do not get caught. As a consequence, people will continue to drink and drive. The author supports this with the British experience. Once people realize that the chances of being caught are relatively small, they will drink and drive. This is the conclusion of answer (C). (A) is incorrect since the passage does not support the conclusion that the problem is any worse or any better in one country or the other. (B) is incorrect since this is the conclusion the author is arguing against. (D) is wrong because the author is not discussing the effectiveness of taxation in paragraph 3. (E) is a statement the author would likely accept, but that is not the reason for introducing the British example. So answer (E) is true but non-responsive.

23. **(A)** This is an application question which asks us to examine the logical structure of the argument. In the fourth paragraph, the author argues that the effectiveness of deterrents to drunk driving will depend upon the ability of the drinker to control his consumption. But drunk driving has two as-

pects: drunk and driving. The author assumes that drunk driving is a function of drinking only. Otherwise, he would not suggest that control on consumption is *necessary* as opposed to *helpful*. (A) attacks this assumption by pointing out that it is possible to drink to excess without driving. It is possible that stiff penalties could be effective deterrents to drunk driving if not to drinking to excess. (B) is incorrect because the author himself makes this point, so this choice does not weaken the argument. (C) is incorrect since the author is concerned only with the problem of fatalities caused by drunk driving. It is hardly an attack on his argument to contend that he has not solved all of the world's ills. Then (D) can be eliminated since the author is concerned to eliminate fatalities caused by drunk driving. He takes no position on whether the drunk driver ought to be punished, only that he ought to be deterred from driving while intoxicated. (E) is not a strong attack on the argument since the author does leave open the question of the value of therapy in combating drunk driving.

24. **(C)** This is a tone question which focuses on the final sentence of the paragraph. There the author states again that the problem is a serious one and that we must find a solution. Since he admonishes us to look for a solution, (C) is an excellent description. (A) can be eliminated since there is no irony in the passage. (B) can be eliminated since the author is concerned to find a solution. (E), however, overstates the case. Concern is not indignation. Finally, (D) may seem plausible. The author does leave us with a project. But to acknowledge that a problem exists and that a clear solution has not yet been found is not to be indecisive. The author is decisive in his assessment of the problem.

25. **(B)** This is an implied idea question. In the first paragraph, the author states that a third of drivers who have been drinking reach the 0.1 percent BAC level. So we can conclude that two-thirds of drivers who have been drinking do not reach that level. (A) represents a misreading of this point. (C) also is a misreading of the selection. The author does state that half of all fatally injured drivers have a BAC in excess of 0.1 percent, and that means that half do not. But that just means that the other half either were not drinking at all or had BAC's of less than 0.1 percent. Finally, (D) and (E) also represent misreadings of that paragraph.

Section II

1. **(D)** By multiplying out the given expression, we learn $w(x + y + z) = wx + wy + wz$, which shows that (A) is an equivalent expression. Second, given that it does not matter in multiplication in which order the elements are listed (i.e., $2 \times 3 = 3 \times 2 = 6$), we can see that (B) is also an equivalent expression. From $wx + wy + wz$, we can factor the w's out of the first two terms: $w(x + y) + wz$, which shows that (E) is an equivalent expression. Finally, we could also factor the w's from the last two terms: $wx + w(y + z)$, which shows that (C) is an equivalent expression. (D) is not, however, equivalent: $w + w + w + x + y + z$. The 3 would make you suspicious of (D).

2. **(D)** The problem requires you to find the amount of wood that is needed and then find the number of whole feet that will give you the wood that is needed. In this particular problem there is no question about trying to fit different lengths together, as there might be if, for instance, the wood were only available in 5-foot sections. To find the total wood needed, you must multiply 2 feet, 10 inches by four. Two feet times 4 is 8 feet. Ten inches times 4 is 40 inches, which is between 3 feet (36 inches) and 4 feet (48 inches). There is no way to get 40 inches of wood out of 3 feet. You should round up, so that there is enough wood and the answer is thus 8 feet plus 4 feet = 12 feet.

3. **(B)** The most direct solution to this problem is to substitute the value $+4$ for x: $(+4-7)(+4+2) = (-3)(6) = -18$. Substitute before multiplying to keep it simple.

4. **(B)** Here we need to solve the simultaneous equations. Though there are different methods, one way to find the values of x and y is first to redefine y in terms of x. Since $x - y = 2$, $x = 2 + y$. We can now use $2 + y$ as the equivalent of x and substitute $2 + y$ for x in the other equation:

$$2(2 + y) + y = 7$$
$$4 + 2y + y = 7$$
$$3y = 3$$
$$y = 1$$

Once we have a value of y, we substitute that value into either of the equations. Since the second is a bit simpler, we may prefer to use it:

$x - 1 = 2$, so $x = 3$. Now we can determine that $x + y$ is $3 + 1$, or 4.

Another approach would be to add the two equations together so that the y terms will cancel themselves out:

$$2x + y = 7$$
$$+ \underline{(x - y = 2)}$$
$$3x \qquad = 9, \text{ thus } x = 3.$$

Find y by substituting 3 for x in either equation.

5. **(A)** Average speed requires total distance divided by total time. Therefore it is incorrect to average the two speeds together, for, after all, the girl moved at the slower rate for three times as long as she moved at the faster rate, so they cannot be weighted equally. The correct way to solve the problem is to reason that the girl covered the 15 miles by bicycle in 1 hour. She covered the 15 miles by walking in 3 hours. Therefore, she traveled a total of 30 miles in a total of 4 hours. 30 miles/4 hours = 7.5 miles per hour.

6. **(D)** While we know by inspection that the shaded area is larger—the diagonal of a rectangle divides the rectangle in half—the answer choices tell us more is needed, though (C) is eliminated. We begin by noting that the area which is left unshaded is a triangle with a 90° angle. This means that we have an altitude and a base at our disposal. Then we note that the shaded area is the area of the square minus the area of the triangle. So we are in a position to compute the area of the square, the triangle, and the shaded part of the figure. In the first place, the base of the triangle—which is the unshaded area of the figure—is equal to the side of the square, 4. The altitude of that triangle is four units long less the unknown distance x, or $4 - x$. So the area of the triangle, $\frac{1}{2}ab$, is $\frac{1}{2}(4 - x)(4)$. The area of the square is 4×4, or 16, so the shaded area is 16 minus the triangle, which we have just determined is $\frac{1}{2}(4 - x)(4)$. Let us first pursue the area of the triangle:

$$\tfrac{1}{2}(4 - x)(4) = (4 - x)(2) = 8 - 2x$$

Substituting in the shaded portion:

$$16 - (8 - 2x) = 8 + 2x$$

Now we complete the ratio. $8 + 2x$ goes on the top, since that is the shaded area, and $8 - 2x$ goes on the bottom, since that is the unshaded area:

$\dfrac{8 + 2x}{8 - 2x}$. And we reduce by 2 to yield $\dfrac{4 + x}{4 - x}$.

7. **(D)** Since Linda is the youngest and the other ages are derived from hers, let us assign the value x for Linda's age. In that case Mike will be 2x years old, since he is twice as old as Linda. Finally, Ned will be 2x + 2 since he is two years older than Mike. Our three ages are: Linda, x; Mike, 2x; and Ned, 2x + 2. We know that these three ages total 27. Hence, x + 2x + 2x + 2 = 27. And now we solve for x:

$$5x + 2 = 27$$
$$5x = 25$$
$$x = 5$$

So Linda is 5 years old. Then, if Linda is 5, Mike must be 10 years old.

If Mike is used as a basis, $M = y$, $L = \frac{y}{2}$, $N = y + 2$. Thus, $y + \frac{y}{2} + (y + 2) = 27$; $2\frac{1}{2}y = 25$, $y = 10$.

8. **(D)** Since our rates are by fifths of a mile, let us begin the solution by figuring out how many fifths of a mile (or parts thereof) there are in this trip. In $2\frac{2}{5}$ miles there are 12 fifths. Then we add another fifth for the additional bit of distance between $2\frac{2}{5}$ and $2\frac{1}{2}$ miles. So the whole trip can be broken down into 13 segments of one-fifth (or part of one-fifth) of a mile. For the first, the charge is $1.00. That leaves 12 more segments, the charge for each of which is 20¢, giving a total charge for those 12 segments of $2.40. Now, the total charge for the trip is $1.00 for the first one-fifth of a mile and $2.40 for the remaining segments, or $3.40.

9. **(E)** We know that the formula for the area of a square is $s^2 = \text{area}$. So $s^2 = 36x^2$, and, taking the square root of both sides, we learn $s = 6x$. (Note: there is no question here of a negative solution, since geometrical distances are always positive.)

10. **(A)** Since we do not know how much money Ed has, we must assign that amount the value of x. We now establish that Tom has x + $2 since he has $2 more than Ed; and we know that Susan has (x + $2) + $5, which is x + $7, since she has $5 more than Tom. We want to divide this money equally. The natural thing to do, then, is to add up all the money and divide it by 3. The total held by all three individuals is: x + (x + 2) + (x + 2 + 5) = 3x + 9. Dividing that by 3, we want everyone to have x + 3. Ed has x, so he needs to receive 3. Tom has x + 2, so he needs to receive 1. Susan has x + 7, so she needs to rid herself of 4. Susan gets rid of this 4 by giving 1 to Tom and 3 to Ed, giving us answer choice (A).

Some shortcutting is possible by considering that Susan has the most money, and then Tom and then Ed. Therefore, any answer which has Ed give up money cannot result in equal shares, eliminating (C) and (E). Furthermore, since Susan has the most, she must give up the most. In (D) Tom gives more than Susan, so this is eliminated. In (B), Susan gives out more than Tom, but she also receives from Tom, so her net giving out is only $1, compared to Tom's $4, so this is also wrong, which leaves (A).

11. **(C)** Do not let the term perfect number throw you. Accept the definition of any such oddball term and apply it to the problem. Since the factors of 6 less than 6 itself are 1, 2, and 3, 6 is the perfect number (1 + 2 + 3 = 6). 1 is not a perfect number since there are no factors of 1 less than itself. 4 is not a perfect number since the factors of 4 less than 4 are 1 and 2 and 1 + 2 ≠ 4. Nor is 8 a perfect number since the factors of 8 which are less than 8 itself are 1, 2, and 4, and those total 7, not 8. Finally, 10 is not a perfect number since the key factors here are 1, 2, and 5, which total 8, not 10.

12. **(A)** By connecting Q and O or P and O, it can be seen that the radius of circle O is 6 units. (Remember, when a circle is named after a point, that point is the center of the circle.) The formula for the area of a circle is πr^2, so the area of circle O is: $\pi(6)^2 = 36\pi$.

13. **(B)** We are given information about angles in the top of the figure and asked about angles in the bottom. The task, then, is to connect these items. We do not know that the horizontal lines are parallel, nor can we prove it. We do, however, have a quadrilateral figure and several straight lines to work with. Considering the figure with a, b, and c as the three angles of the quadrilateral other than the 70°, we see:

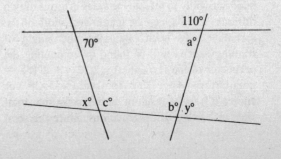

Angle A is on a straight line with 110° and thus equals 70°. We are looking only for x + y, so we need not have each individually. Working our way down through the quadrilateral, we see that the total degrees in the quadrilateral, as for all such figures, is 360°. Thus, b + c + 70° + 70° = 360° and b + c = 220°. Now, at last, we are on the right line. Again using the fact that a straight line totals 180°, we see:

$$
\begin{aligned}
x + c &= 180 \\
y + b &= 180 \\
\hline
x + y + b + c &= 360
\end{aligned}
$$

Since we know b + c = 220, we can solve by substituting to get x + y + 220 = 360; thus x + y = 140.

14. **(D)** We begin by computing the capacity of the cylinder, which is πr^2 times height. Since the radius is 2 and the height is 5, the capacity of this cylinder is $\pi(2)^2 \times 5 = 20\pi$ cu. ft. It is already 40% full, which means that 60% of the capacity is left. 60% of 20π cu. ft. = 12π cu. ft., and this is the answer we seek.

15. **(A)** We are seeking c, but the given information is about the area of the triangle, while c is a distance. However, the formula for the area of triangles connects distance to area, so we should compute the area in terms of c. We know that we have a right angle in the lower right-hand corner of the figure. So this gives us an altitude and a base. The altitude is 3c units long and the base is 4c units long. So, the area is $\frac{1}{2}ab$ or $\frac{1}{2}(3c)(4c) = \frac{1}{2}(12c^2) = 6c^2$. And this is equal to 54. $6c^2 = 54$; so $c^2 = 9$ and c = 3.

16. **(E)** Since the shorter side of the rectangle is 15 inches, the statement that the sides of the rectangle have the ratio of 3:2 means that the long side is found by the equation $\frac{3}{2} = \frac{x}{15}$, which becomes 45 = 2x by cross-multiplication, leading to the result that the long side of the rectangle is $22\frac{1}{2}$ inches long. Since a rectangle has two pairs of sides (the two lengths and the two widths), it is necessary only to refer to the sides in terms of two different sizes. Once the length and width of the rectangle have been calculated, the length of framing needed will be found by computing the perimeter of the rectangle by $2(22\frac{1}{2}) + 2(15) =$ perimeter = 45 + 30 = 75 inches. Answer choice (C) is the result of adding only one set of sides. Choice (D) is reached through the error of

considering the side of 15 to be the longer side.

17. **(E)** Since the number of cases is the numerator of the fraction that represents the per capita rate of meningitis and the population is the denominator, both a decrease in the number of cases and an increase in the population will tend to lower the rate. Since we have both, and both changes are substantial, we may expect a substantial decrease in the rate. Thus (A) and (B) may be eliminated on logical grounds. The new rate is found by computing $\frac{50\% \, M}{150\% \, P} = \frac{1M}{3P}$, which is $\frac{1}{3}$ of the original rate of $\frac{M}{P}$. If the new rate is one-third of the old rate, then the percentage change is a decrease of $1 - \frac{1}{3} = \frac{2}{3}$, or $66\frac{2}{3}\%$.

18. **(A)** Since we have a set of non-overlapping groupings, we can construct a table showing the sex and union status of the workers. Putting in the original information and the fact that 70% of 60% is 42%, we get:

	Men	Women	Total
Unionized	42%		60%
Non-unionized			
Total	46%		100%

Filling in the table by subtraction and addition:

	Men	Women	Total
Unionized	42%	18%	60%
Non-unionized	4%	36%	40%
Total	46%	54%	100%

Thus the percentage of the non-unionized workers that are women can be determined by the computation $\frac{36\%}{40\%} = \frac{36}{40} = \frac{9}{10} = 90\%$.

19. **(C)** The total profit is the sum of the profit for the five-day period and the profit for the two-day period Friday and Saturday. You must also remember that there are 24 hours in a day, and thus the profit per 8-hour shift must be multiplied by 3 in order to get the daily profit. For the five-day period, the profit is $600 (per shift) × 3 (shifts per day) × 5 (days) = $9000. The profit per shift for the other days is 25% greater and is thus $600 + $\frac{1}{4}$($600) = $600 + $150 = $750. The total profit for the two-day period is calculated as $750 (per shift) × 3 (shifts per day) × 2 (days) =

$4500. The total profit for the week is $9000 + $4500 = $13,500.

20. **(B)** When a question is as convoluted as this one, the issue must assuredly be the unraveling of just what is being asked for. Thinking backwards is a good approach. We are asked for the difference between two numbers: (cost of insurance + unreimbursed losses) − (loss if no insurance) = answer. The cost of the insurance is $125 per quarter, which means that the annual cost is 4 × $125 = $500. That is the first number in our equation. The unreimbursed losses consist of two items. First, there is the deductible, that is, the amount of loss that must be sustained before any reimbursement is made. Here, the first $350 of loss is not reimbursed, so that is one part of the unreimbursed loss. In addition, even when reimbursement is made, it is only made for 75%, or $\frac{3}{4}$ of the value of the loss above $350. The total loss was $1250, $900 above the $350 deductible. Three-quarters of $900 is $675, but that is the portion of the $900 that *is* reimbursed; so $\frac{1}{4}$ × $900 = $225 is the portion that is *not* reimbursed. Thus the total non-reimbursed amount is $350 + 225 = $575, which is the second figure we needed for our computation. The third figure is the total amount of the loss, since without insurance it would all have been a loss; this is $1250. We thus can compute ($500 + $575) − $1250 = −$175. But the negative sign is irrelevant because the difference is all that is asked, not whether one is greater than the other.

Section III

1. **(C)** From equation (1), x may be either 1 or −2. From equation (2), x may be 1 or −3. Thus, if both are true, x = 1.

2. **(A)** Angle b = angle e, a + e = 180°, which means AB is parallel to CD. Equation (2) shows us only that a = b, which makes the two lines parallel only where a = b = 90°.

3. **(C)** There are three possible combinations fulfilling (1): −2 + (−4) = (−6); −2 + 2 = 0; and 2 + 4 = 6. Of these, only the last satisfies property (2).

4. **(C)** Jim does $1\frac{1}{2}$ of the job in 1 hour. Together, Jim and Bill do $\frac{1}{8}$ of the job in 1 hour. Bill alone,

therefore, does $\frac{1}{8} - \frac{1}{12}$ of the job in 1 hour = $\frac{1}{24}$. Accordingly, it will take Bill 24 hours to do the entire job by himself.

5. **(B)** (1) does not work by itself since x = y = 0 and x = y = 1 give different answers. (2) means that either x or y are both fractions between 0 and 1, since that is the only way squaring can reduce the result. Adding a fraction (x + y) increases the result, but multiplying by a fraction (xy) decreases it. Thus x + y > xy under (2). Checking for zero gives a compatible result.

6. **(D)** Since there is only one unknown, the weight of a brick, you only need a single equation to give you sufficient information. Each of the propositions (1) and (2) give an equation, so each is sufficient. You should not bother to calculate the actual weight of the brick, though it is 9 pounds.

7. **(B)** It is tempting to leap to an answer saying that both propositions are needed, but although (1) is clearly not sufficient by itself because it leaves open the issue of the relative proportions of the sides of the rectangle, (2) must be evaluated separately. As it happens, (2) is sufficient. Taking equation (2) and adding AE to both sides, we have: AC = AB + BE + AE. Since BE + AE = AB, AC = 2AB, so AB = $2\frac{1}{2}$.

8. **(A)** For the last digit of the total weight to be a 7, there must be either four 3's or nine 3's, or more. Nine or more are impossible, so there must be four 3's. This leaves four weights chosen from the 5's and 10's to make up 35 lbs. The only possible way to do this is by using three 10's and one 5.

9. **(C)** On one level, this is an easy problem. There are two unknowns in the situation, p and q. There are two different equations without any squares or exponents, so there is enough information using both equations. If you try to actually solve the problem, which is not really necessary, you may have some difficulty since it appears insoluble at first. Since we are interested in p, substitute from equation (2) into (1), getting p = 4(4p); p = 16p, which seems impossible. However, there is one value of p that will work, and that is zero. Thus p is determined by the two equations.

10. **(B)** This is one of the rare problems in which you are asked a "yes/no" question, and the answer is

"no." (1) is nice, but not enough by itself. (2) makes it impossible for ABCD to be a square since the diagonal of a square is not equal to its sides. Some suspicion that this might be a "no" question is raised by the fact that equilateral triangles have nothing to do with squares.

11. **(E)** In order to know how long a moving object takes, you need to know the distance traveled and the rate of speed: Neither is given in the original information. The rate is given in (1), but that is not enough by itself; nor is (2). The question then comes down to whether (2) actually gives the distance between J and M. Note that the order of the neighborhoods along the marathon route is not necessarily in alphabetic order. (2) is not sufficient because the order of the neighborhoods could be either with K between J and M, or with J between K and M. Thus the distance is not specified and the answer is (E).

12. **(B)** Both of the given propositions establish a definite relationship between the officerships of Albert and Mary. Since the original information gives us the actual officership status of Mary (she is qualified), the temptation is to say that both propositions are sufficient. (1), however is not sufficient by itself. It leaves open the question of what happens if Albert does not qualify, because Mary may still qualify even if Albert doesn't. (2) is sufficient because it tells us that if Albert did not qualify, then it is certain that Mary did not qualify. Since Mary did qualify, we must know that Albert must also have qualified.

13. **(C)** There are three unknowns—the number of cookies received by W, X, and Y. We have one equation in the original information—that the sum of the three is 40—and we get one more equation in each of the propositions, making three equations for three unknowns, which is enough. You do not need to actually solve the equations.

14. **(A)** The issue is whether 5 is an integral factor of x. According to (1), x can be divided by 12,345 and yield an integer. Since 12,345 ends in 5, it has a factor of five, and thus x must have a factor of five in order to have 12,345 divide evenly into it. (2) is not enough because 336 does not have a factor of five in it, so that we cannot say for certain that x/5 is an integer; although it is still possible [suppose x = (12345)(336)].

15. **(D)** A cube is a highly structured figure. All the edges must, by definition, be equal to each other and all the opposite faces parallel, and all the other symmetries of a cube maintained no matter what size the cube may be. Therefore, in principle, if you know any well-defined line in the cube—any edge or any diagonal of a side, or the diagonal of the whole cube—you can compute the lengths of any other line, the area of the sides, or the volume of the cube. Thus, in principle, both statement (1) and statement (2) are sufficient to permit the computation of the volume of the cube. On the actual test, you would leave it there, answer (D), and go on to the next problem. For instructional purposes only, we include a brief description of the way in which each statement could be used.

Statement (1): Each face of a cube is a square. Since the diagonal of a square forms a 45-45-90 right triangle with two of the sides, the length of the diagonal can be computed as $\sqrt{2}$ times the length of a side using the Pythagorean Theorem, or from your knowledge of right triangles. Once an edge of the cube is known, the volume of the cube can be computed as the third power (or cube) of the edge.

Statement (2): The diagonal of the cube forms a right triangle with the diagonal of a face and one of the edges, as shown below. By the same process described in the explanation of statement (1), the length of a diagonal is $\sqrt{2}$ times the length of an edge. Thus the Pythagorean Theorem equation for the triangle which includes the diagonal of the whole cube is $d^2 = (\sqrt{2}s)^2(s)^2$, and thus the diagonal = $\sqrt{3}$ times the length of the side. Therefore, knowing the length of the diagonal permits calculation of the length of an edge and of the volume of the cube.

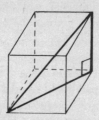

16. **(B)** Since the p and q terms are to the eighth power, simply having two equations for two unknowns is not sufficient. Usually, it is a good idea to try and factor polynomials if they are not easy to deal with in their original form. In this case, we can factor $p^8 - q^8$ into the difference between squares since the square of something to

the fourth power is the same base to the eighth power. Thus:

$p^8 - q^8 = (p^4 - q^4)(p^4 + q^4)$. This in turn factors to
$$(p^2 - q^2)(p^2 + q^2)(p^4 + q^4),$$
which factors to
$$(p - q)(p + q)(p^2 + q^2)(p^4 + q^4)$$

This gives us something that we can use since $(p - q)$ is stated in proposition (2) and is equal to zero. If $p - q$ is equal to zero, then anything multiplied by zero is equal to zero and the whole thing is equal to zero.

A shorter method would be to note that (2) transforms into $p = q$, which means that $p^8 = q^8$, which means that $p^8 - q^8 = 0$. The factoring approach might be needed if the propositions referred to $p^2 + q^2 = 0$ or to some other intermediate factor.

17. **(E)** Manipulating (1) to get x alone, we get:

$4x + 24 > 0$
$4x \qquad > -24$ (subtract $+24$ from both sides)
$x \qquad > -6$ (divide both sides by $+4$)

Manipulating (2), we get:

$4x - 24 < 0$
$4x \qquad < +24$ (add $+24$ to both sides)
$x \qquad < +6$ (divide both sides by $+4$)

Each statement allows for the possibility that x may be either positive or negative, and the question cannot be answered.

18. **(C)** In order to know the dollar amount that the corporation spent on pension payments, it is necessary to know the number of employees and the average payment per employee. The alternative of adding up all the individual payments is impractical on the test and, in any case, the propositions point you toward the idea of averages. The given information is the amount in 1980. Since we need the amount in 1981, this could be gotten either by a direct comparison, or linkage, between the two years or by using 1980 information to reconstruct 1981.

(1) and (2) address part of the needed information and thus are not enough by themselves. They do not link the 1980 total to the 1981 total. If 1980 is viewed as the product of two numbers: 1980 total payments = (1980 no. of employees)(1980 average payment). Then we can link 1980 to 1981 by making the adjustments called

for in (1) and (2): 1981 total payments = (85%)(1980 no. of employees) (130%)(1980 average payment).

Rearrange the items: 1981 total payments = (85%)(130%) (1980 no. of employees) (1980 average payment); but the last two are equal to the 1980 total payments, or $12,000. Thus 1981 total payments = (85%) (130%) ($12,000) = $13,260.

You should not calculate this answer. It is worked out only to show you that you have enough information with the two propositions.

19. **(D)** In order to find the area of the large rectangle, you need to find its length and width. The only measures of those dimensions that the problem gives you are the small rectangles. Since the only information that is given is that all of the small rectangles are the same shape and size, the first place to look for additional understanding is to the ways that the small rectangles build up into the large rectangle. In addition, the fact that both of the statements concern paths made up of pieces of small rectangles should also focus your attention on the small rectangles. Since the small rectangles are rectangles, their length and width are the key dimensions. Since all of the small rectangles are the same shape and size, the fact that three widths equal one length gives you the proportions of the small rectangles. This is shown in the following details from the diagram:

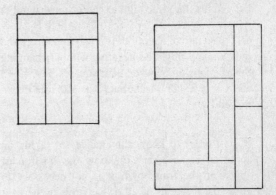

Once you know that three widths of a small rectangle is equal to one length, the information given in the propositions becomes very useful. The upper path referred to in proposition (1) is composed of four lengths and three widths, which is equal to 15 widths (or 5 lengths). Since the proposition gives the value of this path as 45, you can calculate that one width is equal to 45 divided by 15 or 3. Knowing the value of a width of the small rectangle allows you to calculate the value of the length of the small rectangle and thus its area and the area of the large rectangle. You could also directly calculate the length and width of the large rectangle 21 (7 small rectangle widths) and 18 (6 small rectangle widths), respectively. Similarly, the lower path is equivalent to 13 small rectangle widths and knowing its length as 39 permits the area of the large rectangle to be calculated.

20. **(D)** As usual with polynomials, when they are not helpful in one form, change them to the other form. Here they are in factors, but the expanded form will be most useful.

$$(x^2 + y^2) + (x^2 - y^2) = x^2 + 2xy + y^2 + x^2 - 2xy + y^2 = 2x^2 + 2y^2 = 2(x^2 + y^2)$$

(2) is certainly sufficient by itself; the only issue is whether (1) is also sufficient. As the simplification of the equation shows, (1) is sufficient because it gives the value needed to compute $2(x^2 + y^2)$.

21. **(B)** (2) is sufficient because it gives a rule for calculating any term of the series. (1) looks good, but does not actually tell us that the series continues in the same manner beyond the terms listed; thus it is not sufficient.

22. **(A)** (1) is sufficient because the cube of a number retains the same sign as the original number or base, e.g., $(-2)^3 = -8; (+2)^3 = +8$. However, the square of a number is always positive, and thus x and y might be negative without changing the relationship between their squares. If $x = -2$ and $y = +3$, (2) is true; but (2) is also true if $x = +2$ and $y = -3$.

23. **(C)** In order to know the chances of taking an apple, it is necessary to know the fraction of apples in the fruit bowl. It is not necessary to know the fractions of all of the fruits in the fruit bowl. (1) only tells the relationship between oranges and apples, but there may be other fruits. (2) only tells the fraction of oranges. Together they permit the calculation that one-sixth of the fruits in the fruit bowl are apples.

24. **(D)** In order to prove that two lines are parallel, you will usually need to either know that there are equal corresponding angles, or that the two lines are opposite sides of a rectangle or square. Since

there are no rectangles or squares in this diagram, you should concentrate on the corresponding angles approach. Statement (1) gives the information that two angles are equal. If these are corresponding angles, that will immediately be enough to show that the two lines AB and XY are parallel. Extending some of the lines to make the intersections clearer we see that the angles cited are, in fact, corresponding angles of the intersection of line CA with the two lines we are interested in:

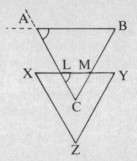

Statement (2) tells you that the smaller, interior triangle is an equilateral triangle. This connects to the facts given in the original question that the larger triangles are also equilateral triangles. Since you are interested in finding out whether the corresponding angles are equal, you should consider what you know about angles of equilateral triangles. Of course, the angles of equilateral triangles are all equal to 60 degrees. Thus, $\angle BAL = 60°$ and $\angle CLM = 60°$, which are the same corresponding angles discussed for statement (1). Angles ABM and CML would also be equal to 60 degrees and form a pair of corresponding angles.

25. **(E)** To know the number of chocolate bars that can be packed into the carton, you need to know at least the three dimensions of the chocolate bars and the three dimensions of the carton. Only two dimensions of the chocolate bar are given in the initial information and the third dimension is never supplied, hence (E). The two propositions do give the three dimensions of the carton, but that is not enough.

Section IV

1. **(C)** The point of the Chinese official's comment is that the Chinese may appear to some Westerners to be "inscrutable" because those Westerners simply do not pay very careful attention to what is directly before them. Thus, (C) is the best

answer. (A) is misleading. The Chinese official refers to Occidentals in general, but he never mentions Orientals in general. Even so, (A) misses the main point of the anecdote. (B) is better than (A) since it is at least generally related to the point of the Chinese official, but the precise point is not that Americans (rather than Occidentals) fail to understand Chinese culture, but rather that they suffer from a more specific myopia: They find they are not able to penetrate the motivations of the Chinese. In any event, the point of the passage is not just that there is such a failure, but that such failure is attributable to the lack of insight of Westerners——not any real inscrutability of the Chinese. (E) mentions the problem of understanding, but the difficulty described in the passage is one way only. Nowhere is it suggested that the Chinese have difficulty in understanding Westerners. Finally, (D) would be correct only if the passage had contained some key word to qualify the official's response, such as *hesitatingly* or *cautiously*.

2. **(E)** Once it is seen that the passage is humorous, this question is fairly easy. The official "smiles" and he "gently" responds. Further, the scenario is set by the first sentence: a *junior* official *embarrassed* himself. This shows the situation is uncomfortable for the American, but it is not a serious international incident. And the Chinese official's response is kind——not angry (A), not fearful (B), not indifferent (D). (C) requires an assumption of malice on the part of the Chinese official. By comparison, "compassion" better fits the description of the official's action—— smiling and gentle.

3. **(B)** Here the problem is to make sense out of the brother's claim that a device he rarely used and may never use again is still a good investment. It is not land, a work of art, or some similar thing, so it does not appear as though it will appreciate in value. The advantage, then, of owning must come from merely being able to possess it. Thus, answer (B), which cites the convenience of having the item to use if and when he should decide to do so, is best. (A) can be disregarded because the brother regards the investment as a good one *even if* he never again uses the device. To save money on ice cream, he would have to use it. (C) is highly suggestive——is the brother saying that it is a good idea to have things around in case one needs them? If so, then (C) sounds a bit like (B). But (C) is not nearly so direct as (B), and it

requires some work to make it into (B). (D) is wrong because saving money by having purchased earlier would be worthwhile only if the item is actually needed. After all, a great deal you made by buying a ton of hay is not a great deal just because the price of hay is going up——you need an elephant (or a horse, or a plan to resell, or something) to make it worthwhile. Just buying hay because it's a "bargain" is no bargain at all. (E) is fairly silly. It is like saying: "The bad news is you are to be executed tomorrow morning; the good news is you would have had liver for lunch." Or perhaps closer to this example would be: "The bad news is that someone stole your car; the good news is that the price of gasoline went up by 25¢ a gallon this morning." The point is that you will avoid some trivial injury or cost at the expense of something more serious.

4. **(E)** Again, the passage is somewhat lighthearted. The poet is saying that the poem is obscure: When he wrote it only he and the Almighty could understand it, and now (it is so difficult) even he has forgotten the point of the verse. (A) is somewhat attractive because the passage does state that God knows what man does not. Of course, once one understands the point of the passage, (A) can be discarded. Even so, there is something about (A) that lets you know it is wrong——"infinitely." One might infer from the poet's comments that man is not as wise as God, but it is not possible to conclude, on the basis of the one example, that God is infinitely wiser than man. (B) is also attractive, for the poet is saying that it is difficult to understand this particular poem. But (B) is wrong because he is not saying that men cannot understand poetry in general. (C) and (D) are distractions. They play on the term "God" in the paragraph. The poet cites God as the one who understands the verse——not the one who inspired it.

5. **(D)** You must always be careful of naked correlations. Sufficient research would probably turn up some sort of correlation between the length of skirts and the number of potatoes produced by Idaho, but such a correlation is obviously worthless. Here, too, the two numbers are completely unrelated to one another at any concrete cause-and-effect level. What joins them is the very general movement of the economy. The standard of living increases; so, too, does the average salary of a preacher, the number of vacations taken by factory workers, the consumption of beef, the

number of color televisions, and the consumption of rum. (D) correctly points out that these two are probably connected only this way. (A) is incorrect for it is inconceivable that preachers, a small portion of the population, could account for so large an increase in rum consumption. (B) is wildly implausible. (C), however, is more likely. It strives for that level of generality of correlation achieved by (D). The difficulty with (C) is that it focuses upon *total* preachers, not the *average* preacher; and the passage correlated not *total* income for preachers with rum consumption, but *average* income for preachers with consumption of rum. (E) might be arguable if only one period had been used, but the paragraph cites three different times during which this correlation took place.

6. **(B)** This is a relatively easy question. The argument is similar to "All observed instances of S are P; therefore, all S must be P." (All swans I have seen are white; therefore, all swans must be white.) There is little to suggest the author is a mechanic or a factory worker in an automobile plant; therefore, (A) is incorrect—and would be so even if the author were an expert because he does not argue using that expertise. A syllogism is a formal logical structure such as: "All S are M; all M are P; therefore, all S are P," and the argument about automobiles does not fit this structure—so (C) is wrong. By the same token, (E) is wrong since the author generalizes—he does not deduce, as by logic, anything. Finally, (D) is incorrect because the argument is not ambiguous, and one could hardly argue on the basis of ambiguity anyway.

7. **(C)** The key phrase here—and the problem is really just a question of careful reading—is "who actually knew." This reveals that neither of the two knew the person whom they were discussing. There are many ways, however, of debating about the character of people with whom one is not directly acquainted. We often argue about the character of Napoleon or even fictional characters such as David Copperfield. When we do, we are arguing on the basis of indirect information. Perhaps we have read a biography of Napoleon (A), or maybe we have seen a news film of Churchill (B). We may have heard from a friend, or a friend of a friend, that so and so does such and such (E). Finally, sometimes we just make more or less educated guesses, (D). At any event, the two people described in the paragraph

could have done all of these things. What they could not have done—since they finally resolved the problem by finding someone who actually knew Churchill—was to have argued on the basis of their own personal knowledge.

8. **(B)** Here we have a question which asks us to draw a conclusion from a set of premises. The author points out that the Constitution provides that the government may not take private property. The irony, according to the author, is that government itself defines what it will classify as private property. We might draw an analogy to a sharing practice among children: You divide the cake and I will choose which piece I want. The idea behind this wisdom is that this ensures fairness to both parties. The author would say that the Constitution is set up so that the government not only divides (defines property), it chooses (takes what and when it wants). (A) is contradicted by this analysis. (C) is wide of the mark since the author is discussing property rather than liberty. While the two notions are closely connected in the Constitution, this connection is beyond the scope of this argument. (D) is also beyond the scope of the argument. It makes a broad and unqualified claim that is not supported by the text. (E) is really vacuous and, to the extent that we try to give it content, it must fail for the same reason as (A).

9. **(D)** The insight required to solve this problem is that the apparent contradiction can be resolved by observing that the two cases are essentially different. The one is supposed to be a factual story; the other is a fictional account. Only III properly expresses this distinction, and II is simply irrelevant. While it may be true that disapproval is one way of trying to keep members of the profession honest, that has nothing to do with the seeming contradiction in the behavior of the critics. Finally, I contradicts the explicit wording of the passage, which stated that the critics rejected the fictionalization.

10. **(E)** The main point of the advertisement is that you should not hesitate to buy Cold Springs Water even though it is not imported. According to the ad, you will not be able to taste the difference. Thus, I is an assumption of the ad: "Neither you nor your guests will taste the difference," and it is explicitly mentioned. We know it is an assumption because if there were a taste difference, the appeal of the ad would be serious-

ly undermined. III is an assumption, too—but it is hidden or suppressed. Implicit in the ad is a rebuttal to the objection: "Yes, but it is not imported." Whether it is imported or not can have only to do with status since the ad also states (assumes) that the tastes of Cold Springs and imported waters are indistinguishable. II is not an assumption. Although it is mentioned that Cold Springs is bottled at the source, the ad does not depend on where other imported or domestic waters are bottled. They could be bottled 50 miles away from the source, and that would not affect the appeal of the ad.

11. **(B)** Careful reading of the paragraph shows that the author's attitude toward parochial education is that he believes the insistence on instruction in religious values is *justifiable;* he disagrees, however, on the question of how best to inculcate those values. He believes that the proper attitude toward relations between the sexes could best be learned by children in the company of the other sex. Thus, (E) is diametrically opposite to the policy the author would recommend. (A) and (D) must be wrong because the passage clearly indicates that the author supports parochial schools and the religious instruction they provide. (C) is a distraction. It plays on the association of segregation and racial discrimination. Racial segregation is not the only form of segregation. The word *segregation* means generally to separate or to keep separate.

12. **(A)** In this story, the identity of the person who reports the incident is irrelevant. So long as it is not someone with a special infirmity (very poor eyesight, for example) or poor credibility (an inveterate liar), the person is quite capable of reporting what he saw—or what he thought he saw. The most serious weakness of the analysis presented is that it attacks Professor Branch's credentials. To be sure, one might want to question the accuracy of the report: At what time did it occur? What were the lighting conditions? Had the observer been drinking or smoking? But these can be asked independently of attacking the qualifications of the source. Thus, (D) must be wrong, for special credentials are just not needed in this case, so the wrong way to defend Professor Branch is to defend those. By the same token, it makes no sense to defend Branch by launching a counter-*ad hominem* attack on her attacker, so (B) is incorrect. (C) and (E) may or may not be true, but they are surely irrelevant to the question

of whether this particular sighting is to be trusted.

13. **(B)** The inquisitor's behavior is paradoxical—that is, internally inconsistent or contradictory. The victim tells him that he is in league with the devil, so the inquisitor refuses to believe him because those in league with the devil never tell the truth. In other words, the inquisitor refuses to believe the victim because he accepts the testimony of the victim. Thus, (B) is correct. (A) is incorrect because the inquisitor does not *withdraw* anything he has said; in fact, he lets everything he has said stand, and that is how he manages to contradict himself. (E) is a bit more plausible, but it is incomplete. In a certain sense, the inquisitor does not accept the answer, but the real point of the passage is that his basis for *not* accepting the answer is that he *does* accept the answer: He believes the victim when he says he is in league with the devil. (C) and (D) find no support in the paragraph. Nothing suggests that the inquisitor is violating any religious law, and nothing indicates that the inquisitor does not himself believe in the devil.

14. **(B)** The key here is that the word "nobody" is used in a cleverly ambiguous way and, as many of you probably know, the "young lady" in the story is Lewis Carroll's Alice. This is fairly representative of his word play. (E) must be incorrect since it misses completely the little play on words: "I saw Nobody," encouraging a response such as "Oh, is he a handsome man?" (D) is beside the point, for the King is not interested in the messenger's veracity. He may be interested in his reliability (A); but, if anything, we should conclude the King finds the messenger unreliable since "nobody walks slower" than the messenger. (C) is wrong because the question is not a matter of eyesight. The King does not say, "If you had better eyes, you might have seen Nobody."

15. **(C)** Ann's response would be appropriate only if Mary had said, "All of the students at State College come from Midland High." That is why (C) is correct. (D) is wrong, because they are talking about the background of the students, not the reputations of the schools. (E) is wrong, for the question is from where the students at State College come. (B) is superficially relevant to the exchange, but it, too, is incorrect. Ann would not reply to this statement, had Mary made it, in the

way she did reply. Rather, she would have said, "No, there are some Midland students at State College." Finally, Ann would have correctly said (A) only if Mary had said, "None of the students from North Hills attend State College," or "Most of the students from North Hills do not attend State College." But Ann makes neither of these responses, so we know that (A) cannot have been what she thought she heard Mary say.

16. **(E)** If you wanted to determine how politically active people are, what kind of test would you devise? You might do a survey to test political awareness; you might do a survey to find out how many hours people devote to political campaigning each week or how many hours they spend writing letters, etc.; or you might get a rough estimate by studying the voting statistics. The paragraph takes contributions as a measure of political activity. (E) is correct for two reasons. One, the paragraph says nothing about individual activity. It says total contributions were up, not average or per person contributions. Second, (E) cites voting patterns which seem as good as or better an indicator of political activity than giving money. This second reason explains why (A) is wrong. (A) may weaken the argument, but a stronger attack would use voting patterns. (D) confuses individual and corporate contributions, so even if campaign giving were a strong indicator of activity, (D) would still be irrelevant. (B) does not even explain why contributions *in toto* rose during the four years, nor does it tell us anything about the pattern of giving by individual persons. Finally, (C) seems the worst of all the answers, for it hardly constitutes an attack on the author's reasoning. It seems likely that even in the face of increased political activity, public leaders would continue to warn against the dangers of political apathy.

17. **(C)** If you want to determine whether or not drug use is harmful to high school students, you surely would not conduct a survey of the students themselves. This is why (C) is correct. That a student does not *think* a drug is harmful does not mean that it *is not* actually harmful. (E) misses the point of the argument. The author is not attempting to prove that drug use is not widespread; he is trying to show it is not dangerous. (D) is part of an argument often used in debates over legalization of drugs by proponents of legalization. Here, however, it is out of place. The question is whether the drugs are harmless, that is, whether they are,

in fact, victimless. (D) belongs to some other part of the debate. (A) sounds like the start of an argument. One might suggest that students change their minds as they get older, and eventually many acknowledge the danger of such drugs. But (A) does not get that far; and, even if it did, (C) would be stronger for it gives us the final statement up to which that argument would only be leading. Finally, (B) is irrelevant. The question here is the harm of drugs, and that issue can be resolved independent of whether other things are harmful, e.g., alcohol or drag-racing.

18. **(C)** Amy points out that Al assumes that any extraterrestrial visitors to Earth, seeking intelligent life, would regard human beings here on Earth as intelligent, and therefore contact us. Amy hints that we might not be intelligent enough to interest them in contacting us. This is why (C) is the best answer. (A) is wrong. Amy does not miss Al's point: She understands it very well and criticizes it. (B) is wrong since Amy is not suggesting that Al is any less intelligent than any other human being, just that the aliens might regard us all as below the level of intelligence which they are seeking. (D) is more nearly correct than any other choice save (C). The difficulties with it are threefold: One, there really is not all that much internal development of Al's argument, so (D) does not seem on target; two, in a way she does examine what internal structure there is—she notes there is a suppressed assumption which is unsound; finally, even assuming that what (D) says is correct, it really does not describe the point of Amy's remark nearly so well as (C) does. Finally, (E) is incorrect because Amy does not offer an analogy of any sort.

19. **(C)** The problem with this argument is that it contains no argument at all. Nothing is more frustrating than trying to discuss an issue with someone who will not even make an attempt to prove his case, whose only constructive argument is: "Well, that is my position; if I am wrong, you prove I am wrong." This is an illegitimate attempt to shift the burden of proof. The person who advances the argument naturally has the burden of giving some argument for it. (C) points out this problem. (A) is incorrect because the author uses no group classifications. (B) is incorrect because the author does not introduce any analogy. (D) is a weak version of (C). It is true that the author does not provide statistical evidence to prove his claim, but then again he provides no

kind of argument at all to prove his claim. So if (D) is a legitimate objection to the paragraph (and it is), then (C) must be an even stronger objection. So any argument for answer (D)'s being the correct choice ultimately supports (C) even more strongly. The statement contained in (E) may or may not be correct, but the information in the passage is not sufficient to allow us to isolate the theory upon which the speaker is operating. Therefore, we cannot conclude that it is or is not discredited.

20. **(A)** Let us assign letters to represent the complete clauses of the sentence from which the argument is built. "If quarks . . . universe" will be represented by the letter P, the rest of the sentence by Q. The structure of the argument is therefore: "If P then Q. Q. Therefore, P." The argument is obviously not logically valid. If it were, it would work for any substitutions of clauses for the letters, but we can easily think up a case in which the argument will not work: "If this truck is a fire engine, it will be painted red. This truck is painted red; therefore, it is a fire engine." Obviously, many trucks which are not fire engines could also be painted red. The argument's invalidity is not the critical point. Your task was to find the answer choice that paralleled it—and since the argument first presented was incorrect, you should have looked for the argument in the answer choices which makes the same mistake: (A). It has the form: "If P then Q. Q. Therefore, P" (B) has the form: "If P, then Q. P. Therefore, Q," which is both different from our original form and valid to boot. (C) has the form: "P or Q. Not P. Therefore, Q." (D) has the form: "If P, then Q. If Q, then R. Therefore, if P, then R." Finally, (E) has the form: "If P then Q. Not Q. Therefore, not P."

21. **(D)** The author explains that the expansion of judicial power by increasing the number of causes of action had the effect of filling the judicial coffers. A natural conclusion to be drawn from this information is that the desire for economic gain fueled the expansion. (A) is not supported by the text since the judges may have made good decisions—even though they were paid to make them. (E) is incorrect for the same reason. (C) is not supported by the text since no mention is made of the other two bodies (even assuming they existed at the time the author is describing). (B) is also incorrect because there is nothing in the text to support such a conclusion.

22. **(D)** As we did in question 20, let us use letters to represent the form of the argument. The first sentence is our old friend: "If P, then Q." Now we must be careful not to use the same letter to stand for a different statement. No part of the second sentence is also a part of the first one, so we must use a new set of letters: "If R, then S." Do not be confused by the internal structure of the sentences. Though the second clause of the first sentence speaks about Johnson and Lloyd voting the same way, the second clause of the second sentence speaks about Johnson's defending someone. So the two statements are different ideas and require different letters. The first clause of the third sentence is the same idea as the first clause of the first sentence, so we use letter P again, but the second clause is different, T. The third sentence uses the phrase "only if," "P only if T," which can also be written: "If P, then T." Our three sentences are translated as:

1. If P, then Q.
2. If R, then S.
3. If P, then T.

Now we can find which of the answers cannot be true.
(A) "If R, then not Q." That is a possibility. While it cannot be deduced from our three assumptions, nothing in the three assumptions precludes it. So (A) could be true.
(B) "If P, then T." This is true, a restatement of the final assumption.
(C) "If T, then not-P." This is possibly true. Sentence 3 tells us, "If P then T," which is the same thing as "if not-T, then not-P"; but it does not dictate consequences when the antecedent clause (the if-clause) is T.
(D) "If P, then either not-Q or not-T." This must be false, since sentences 1 and 3 together tell us that from P must follow both Q and T.
(E) "If not-T or not-P, then either not-S or U." We have to add a new letter: U. In any event, this is possible for the reasons mentioned in (C).

23. **(A)** The listener's comment constitutes a counter-example. He shows by his sarcasm that "yeah" can be used to show disagreement. Obviously, the listener does not point out an inconsistency within the speaker's address (even though the listener's remark is inconsistent with the speaker's position). There is no analogy developed by the listener, whose remark is very brief, so (C) is incorrect. The argument is directed

against the speaker's contention, not his character, so (D) is incorrect. Finally, though the listener's comment is high evidence that the speaker is wrong, the comment itself does not cite evidence, so (E) is incorrect.

24. **(A)** The ends of law, according to legal positivism, are to be agreed upon—"accepted as a contingent matter." They are values which the community adopts; they are not handed down by God, nor are they dictated by logic. (B) actually reverses the point. The legal positivist probably would say he does not claim these ends are the best for all modern legal systems. He does not want to commit himself to anything beyond a mere factual description of things as they are. The normative theory ultimately reduces to a question of practical politics—whatever succeeds. (C) can be rejected because the question raised by the normative theory is what values the law ought to generally embody, not just what values the courts ought to promote. (D) is incorrect because while it is perhaps true, it does not address itself to the *status* of the normative values: Are they universally held and dictated by logic? Are they given by God? etc. (E) is similar to (D) in that it may be true simply as a matter of fact, but, again, (E) does not address itself to the status of the values. It is true that the values are those the community chooses, but that such status is *selected* rather than dictated is not undermined because there is not complete agreement on the values. Whatever values are selected will be chosen by more or less unanimous agreement.

25. **(C)** The analogy to physical theory is highly suggestive. The physicist advances a theory which represents an improvement on existing theories, but he is aware that tomorrow another theory may be proposed which is more correct than his. So the legal positivist advances a descriptive theory, that is, a description of existing legal institutions, but new information or advances in theory may displace that theory. (A) is directly contrary to the legal positivist's position that no one theory is uniquely correct. (B) ignores the radical and complete divorce of description and normative recommendation upon which the legal positivist insists. (D) just confuses the point of the analogy to physics. The author introduces the analogy to explain how the legal positivist views his theory—in the same way the physicist views his—not to compare the reliability of physics with

jurisprudence. (E) makes a mistake similar to that committed by (D).

Section V

1. **(C)** Since $x + 6 = 3$, $x = -3$. Then, substituting -3 for x in the second expression, $x + 3$ is $-3 + 3 = 0$.

2. **(A)** Probably the easiest way to solve this problem is just to count the steps on your fingers, but the same process can be expressed mathematically. Let those steps he walks down be assigned negative values, and those steps he walks up be positive. We then have: $-4 + 3 - 6 + 2 + 9 - 2 = +2$. So the person comes to rest two steps above where he started.

3. **(A)** In a circle graph such as this, the sectors must total 100%. The sectors P, R, S, and T account for 21%, 29%, 18%, and 28%, respectively, for a total of 96%. So Q must be 4%.

4. **(D)** This is a problem which is most easily solved directly. From 1:21 to 2:21 is 60 minutes. From 2:21 to 3:21 is 60 minutes. So far we have a total of 120 minutes. Then, from 3:21 to 3:36 is 15 minutes, for a total of 135 minutes.

5. **(B)** First, we must compute the total commission that will be owed: 15% of $3200 = $420. Then we must take into account the fact that the sales representative has already received $150 of that sum. So she is now owed: $420 - $150 = $270.

6. **(B)** The area of a circle is pi times radius squared, or $A = \pi r^2$. Here the area is $9\pi x^2$. So we write: $9\pi x^2 = \pi r^2$. Notice that the π terms cancel out, leaving: $9x^2 = r^2$. Taking the square root of both sides of the equation: $\sqrt{9x^2} = \sqrt{r^2}$, so $r = 3x$.

7. **(E)** Since this problem deals with the heights of the individuals, a quite natural starting point would be to draw a diagram:

Hans is taller than Gertrude:
H
G

Hans is shorter than Wilhelm:
W (z)
H (x)
G (y)

Given the picture, it is easily determined that W is taller than H, who is taller than G; so z is greater than x is greater than y, or z > x > y.

8. **(D)** First, we can show that the area of the square and the area of the equilateral triangle are determinable from their respective perimeters. The square is more easily handled. Since the perimeter of the square is 4 times the length of one side, given the perimeter of the square it is possible to determine the side of the square. Then, once the side of the square is known, the area can be computed as side times side. The equilateral triangle is a bit trickier:

$$P = 3x \qquad A = \frac{1}{2}\left(\frac{\sqrt{3x}}{2}\right)\left(\frac{x}{2}\right)$$

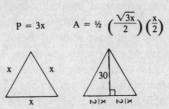

Given the perimeter, it is possible to determine the length of each leg of the triangle (leg = P/3, since each leg is equal). Now, since we know that an equilateral triangle has angles of 60°, and that a perpendicular in this triangle drawn to the opposite base bisects the angle, we can set up a 90° − 30° = 60° triangle. It will be possible to compute the length of each leg of such a triangle, given the length of the hypotenuse. Therefore, we can determine the altitude, and we know the base; so, given the perimeter, we can compute the area. Then, the easiest way to demonstrate that it is not possible to compute the area of a trapezoid or of a parallelogram on the basis of perimeter alone is to draw some pictures:

PARALLELOGRAM:

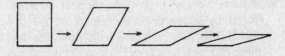

TRAPEZOID:

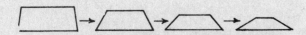

To prove this algebraically would require too much detailed work, but the student should be able to see intuitively that the area of the figures from left to right decreases, and that when the angles eventually become sharp enough, the area will be nearly zero.

9. **(D)** In simple English, the 90¢ the child must replace to bring the amount back up to its original amount is 10% of the original amount. Expressed in notation, that is:

$$90¢ = .10 \text{ of } x$$
$$\$9.00 = x$$

10. **(C)** Let us begin by assigning letters to the height and radius of each cylinder. Since most people find it easier to deal with whole numbers instead of fractions, let us say that cylinder Q has a radius of 2r, so that cylinder P can have a radius of r. Then, we assign cylinder Q a height of h so that P can have a height of 2h. Now, the formula for the volume of a cylinder is $\pi r^2 \times h$. So P and Q have volumes:

$$\text{Volume } P = \pi(r)^2 \times 2h$$
$$P = \pi 2r^2 h$$

$$\text{Volume } Q = \pi(2r)^2 \times h$$
$$Q = \pi 4r^2 h$$

Thus, the ratio of P:Q is $\dfrac{\pi 2r^2 h}{\pi 4r^2 h} = \frac{2}{4} = \frac{1}{2}$.

Another way of solving the problem is to use the knowledge that the area of a circle goes up with the square of the radius. This means that if P and Q had equal heights, the volume of Q would be *four* times that of P, since the radius of Q is *twice* that of P. On the other hand, if their radii were equal, P would have a volume of only twice that of Q—the height of P is twice that of Q and the volume increases directly with height. Therefore, the ratio must be two to four, or 1:2.

11. **(A)** We begin by extending the lines to give this picture:

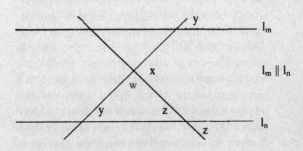

x + w = 180°, and we know that y + z + w = 180°. So, x + w = y + z + w, and x = y + z.

12. **(C)** Let us begin by drawing the rectangle:

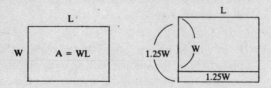

The original area is WL. The width of the new rectangle is W + .25%W, or 1.25W. So the new area is 1.25WL. It then follows that the new area is

$$\frac{1.25WL}{WL}, \text{ or } 125\% \text{ of the old area.}$$

13. **(E)** Let us take any four consecutive odd positive integers, a,b,c, and d. Between b and c there will be an even integer; let us call that x. The average of the four odd integers will be the even integer between b and c. Therefore the average will always be an even number.

14. **(B)** The proportion to be solved is 2½:4 = 1⅞:x, where x is the length of the shorter dimension of the enlargement. Solving, we get x = 3.

15. **(A)** The area of the circle is π times the square of the radius, or 9π. The area of the square is 36. Thus, the ratio is $\frac{9\pi}{36}$, or $\frac{\pi}{4}$. Approximating π as slightly more than 3, the answer is slightly more than ¾.

16. **(C)** First of all, (D) and (E) are impossible on logical grounds since they are greater than 1, and the proportion of something that has a characteristic cannot be greater than 1. That would be like saying, "Five out of three doctors recommend. . . ." We need the total of upper and middle management with production line experience. The ratio 4:3 tells us that the total number of middle- and upper-management personnel in the company can be divided into 7 equal parts, with 4 of them in upper management and 3 in middle management. Of the 4 parts in upper management, 75%, or $\frac{3}{4}$, have experience on the production line. Three-quarters of 4 parts amounts to 3 parts ($\frac{3}{7}$ of the total). You are not told how many of the middle-management personnel have production line experience, but the key word "greatest" tells you that you should consider *all* of the middle-management personnel as having production line experience. This means that there are 3 parts from the upper-management personnel who have production line experience and that

there are 3 more parts from the middle-management personnel that are assumed to have production line experience, for a total of 6 parts out of 7, or $\frac{6}{7}$.

17. **(B)** This sort of problem can seem much more difficult than it actually is. The first step is to understand the instructions for doing the "#" game. For the number N = 1, #1 = (1 − 1)(1 − 2)(1 − 3). The key thing to notice is that the first term in this series of terms being multiplied together (1 − 1) is zero. When you multiply by zero, the result is zero no matter what the other numbers are. Not only should this immediately make you realize that you do not need to compute #1, but it should also alert you to the same sort of possibility in at least some of the other # functions with which you are working. In fact, #2 and #3 also come to zero because they also contain terms which equal zeros (2 − 2 and 3 − 3). Thus, only #4 needs to be evaluated (#4 = (4 − 1)(4 − 2)(4 − 3) = 3 × 2 × 1 = 6).

18. **(D)** The question asks us to determine how many different quintets can be made from each 6-man team, and then how many combinations can there be between the two teams. Taking each team by itself, finding how many quintets can be formed from a given six players is the same as determining how many different single players can be on the sidelines. That is, the same decision that sends a given five players into the game also selects a single player to stay out of the game. Taking the six players one at a time gives six different possibilities; thus there are six different quintets that can be formed out of six players. If there are six different possibilities for each team, the combined possibilities are 6 × 6 = 36.

19. **(E)** The volume of the powder will be determined by subtracting the volume of the two spheres from the volume of the box. The first thing that you must notice is that the quantity $\frac{x}{2}$, which is given to you to show the size of the spheres, is the *diameter*. Thus $\frac{x}{4}$ is the radius of the spheres. Before calculating the answer, it is probably a good idea to try to visualize the situation.

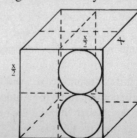

There would be room for 8 spheres in the box if they were placed so that they touched each other. Thus we know that if we divided the box into 8 smaller cubes of side $\frac{x}{2}$, two of them would have spheres in them and the other six would only have packing powder. Having six cubes with only packing powder in them would mean that $\frac{3}{4}$ of the box is completely filled with packing powder, in addition to the powder that is in the two cubes containing the spheres. Thus (E) is the only possible answer.

By calculation, the volume of one sphere is $V = (\frac{4}{3})\pi(\frac{x}{4})^3 = \frac{4\pi x^3}{(3)(64)} = \frac{\pi x^3}{48}$. The volume of a cube of side x is x^3, so the volume of the powder will be $x^3 - 2(\frac{\pi x^3}{48}) = x^3(1 - \frac{\pi}{24})$. If we estimate that π is approximately equal to 3, then we can say that the fraction $\frac{\pi}{24}$ is approximately equal to $\frac{1}{8}$ and the powder makes up approximately $\frac{7}{8}$ of the total volume of the box. You will not often, if ever, need to know the actual value of π; and if you do need to know, it will be sufficient to know that it is slightly more than 3.

20. **(B)** As with all set problems, the key is to break the situation down into non-overlapping groups. There are three basic coffees (B,J, and C) and these three categories can combine in 7 possible ways: B only, C only, J only, B + J only, B + C only, J + C only, and B + J + C. Therefore, your work must start with the information that is given to you in the form of a single category. The only single non-overlapping category that is given is the B + J + C group, of which there are 5 mixtures. The key words at least, when used to describe the information given about combinations of two coffees, tell you that these numbers describe the number of coffee mixtures containing the two coffees only plus the number of coffee mixtures containing all three coffees. Thus the given information that 16 mixtures contain at least Colombian and Jamaican coffees leads to the conclusion that $16 - 5 = 11$ mixtures contain Colombian and Jamaican coffees only; $18 - 5 = 13$ mixtures contain Jamaican and Brazilian coffees only; and $8 - 5 = 3$ mixtures contain Brazilian and Colombian coffees only.

Perhaps the clearest way of seeing how to do the remaining subtractions is to draw three overlapping circles, which show all possible combinations. The final breakdown looks like this:

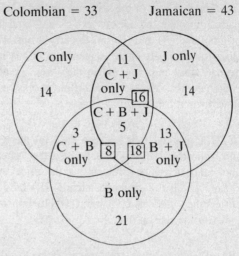

Colombian = 33   Jamaican = 43

Brazilian = 42

Once the four middle groupings are tied down, then the number of mixtures with only Colombian coffee can be determined by subtraction $33 - 3 - 5 - 11 = 14$; Jamaican only is $43 - 11 - 5 - 13 = 14$; and Brazilian only is $42 - 3 - 5 - 13 = 21$. Adding the seven categories together gives a total of 81.

Another method of approaching this problem is to consider the total number of inclusions of a coffee into a mixture. There are $43 + 42 + 33 = 118$ total inclusions. Fifteen of these are from the five mixtures that include all three coffees. The given information states that there are $16 + 18 + 8 = 42$ multiple mentions (at least 2 coffees). Since the multiple mentions can only be two or three coffees, we can see that 15 of the 42 multiple mentions are from the three-coffee blends (counted three times, as shown in the diagram), which leaves 27 double mentions. The number of single mentions can be determined by subtraction: $118 - 3(5) - 2(27) = 49$. The total number of mixtures is thus $49 + 5 + 27 = 81$. This method is a little more abstract and the first method is therefore preferable for most students.

Section VI

1. **(C)** A future possibility of this sort is not expressed by "like." "Looked like" should not be used to mean "appeared." (B) errs in saying "would have" since it is a simple future idea not requiring that construction. (C) correctly uses "appeared" and "would" without the "have." (D) is not so much wrong as an unnecessary change in the sentence structure. (E) similarly is unnecessary and too wordy.

2. **(D)** The first part of the sentence sets up a comparison through the use of "as . . . as," and the original and (B) and (E) fail to carry it out. The "be true of" part of the sentence in (C) is not needed since it is implied in the "as . . . as" construction by the fact that DuBois' work was a fundamental challenge.

3. **(E)** The original fails because the "for the reason" construction is poor, and also the "cheap and" fails to make it clear that the price was cheap, which the sentence intends. (B) fails to correct the "and" and (C) and (D) fail to improve the "for the reason that."

4. **(B)** (A) fails because "that thing" refers to a diffuse idea in the sentence better expressed by (B), (C) and (D) allege that it was *un*profitable, while only a lack of profit was stated. (E) has an unneeded change of tense.

5. **(A)** The original is correct. (B) introduces the new idea of attack, which is not in the original. (C) and (D) lose the idea of "now." (E) trades the idea of the closeness of the examination for one of quantity, which changes the meaning.

6. **(D)** The three verbs in parallel are: "will expand," "(will) produce" and "(will) reached." This shows the original error. Also, the adverb "quickly" will carry forward to all three verbs. (B) fails for introducing a "have" for "produced." (C) fails to correct the "reached" and adds a gratuitous "then." (E)'s addition of "fairly prompt way" is an error, for level of usage. (D) corrects the "reached" and drops the unneeded time of equilibrium, and the redundant "state."

7. **(B)** "Not only" requires "but also"; hence (D) and (E) fail. "Not only" already includes the idea of an additional item, so the "as well" of the original and (C) are wrong.

8. **(E)** "Irregardless" is not an English word, eliminating the original and (B). (C) and (D) carelessly drop the term "ingested," which changes the meaning. (E) also correctly uses "or" as a connector since the intended meaning of the sentence is to refer to these ideas severally and not as a single group.

9. **(C)** "Hopefully" is not acceptable in standard written English. The correct phrase is "it is hoped" as in (C). (E)'s phrase denies the fact of the hope expressed by the original sentence.

10. **(C)** There is a lack of coordination between the underlined part's reference to the system of the Hopis and the other part's reference to the system of certain languages. (C) corrects that error. In addition, it seems more likely that it is a detailed study that is at issue than a detailed grammar studied at some unknown depth.

11. **(A)** The original is correct. (B) changes the meaning to a discussion of what they were doing rather than one of their possible success. (C) and (D) change the time of the explosion for no good reason. (E) erroneously has both a "would" and a "could." One of these is sufficient to give the idea of uncertainty.

12. **(B)** The future perfect should be used to refer to an event between the present and some future reference point. In the original it refers to the future reference point, thus (A) is wrong. In (C) and (D) it is used for both the future reference point (time peace . . . comes) and the intermediate point (lives . . . wasted). This is wrong. The use of "shall" is without meaning here. (E) uses "would have," which introduces an uncertainty not present in the original. (B) does everything correctly.

13. **(B)** Parallelism is the issue here. The parallel creating elements are "not . . . but rather" and the parts after those two must be similar in construction. After the "not" we have a noun, and that is what we should have after "but rather" as well. (E) drops the "but," and (C) and (D) add unneeded words.

14. **(A)** The original is correct. (C), (D), and (E) add the idea of "surpassing," which is not in the original and merely speaks of first and second. (B) is not wrong, but is wordy without cause.

15. **(C)** The element of the sentence following the introductory descriptor or modifier must apply to the first noun after the comma. The researchers were not "primarily accomplished" through the use of electron microscopes, so (A) is out. Though (B)'s idea of competence is not unacceptable, (B) drops the idea of the primacy of the electron microscope in the work, which is wrong. (D) and (E) use locutions that are either meaningless or wordy. (C) keeps everything in order.

16. **(E)** The first part of the sentence speaks of the cuisine, so we do not want to shift suddenly to the peoples themselves as the original does. (B) fails for the same reason. (C) limits itself to sauces, which is unfounded. (D) fails to mention the French cuisine, which is in error. Thus (E) is correct, because then the word "cookery" can be carried forward in the reader's mind to yield French cookery being compared to Italian cookery.

17. **(D)** The original errs in its use of "that," which is singular, while "powers," for which it stands, is plural. This eliminates (A) and (B). (C) fails because it is comparing our powers of communication with other animals, rather than with the powers of communication of the other animals. (E) is inferior to (D) because it changes the tense to "have been" without cause. (D)'s change to "far greater," while not strictly necessary, does leave the meaning intact and even improves the sentence.

18. **(B)** "Healthy" refers to the state of health of some organism. "Healthful" is the proper way to describe something that promotes health. "Tasty" refers to the quality of having a good taste when eaten. "Tasteful" refers to being in accord with good aesthetic taste, or having such taste. In addition, the original erred in having "neither . . . or," when "neither . . . nor" is required. Only (B) conveys the intended meaning of the original.

19. **(A)** The original, while not a wonderful sentence, is not wrong. (B) omits the standard of judging benefit (general welfare). (C) leaves aside all consideration of benefit and focuses only on the feasibility of the project. (D) is perhaps second best, though a little convoluted. However, it omits the certainty that the project could be accomplished. (E) incorrectly refers to the happiness of the individuals, while the original referred to the general welfare, which might not be the same thing at all.

20. **(D)** The first part of the sentence, after "in," is surplus. (D) correctly dispenses with that part and preserves the rest.

21. **(D)** The "them" is unclear, eliminating (A), (B), and (C). (D)'s use of the present tense is acceptable since the classification presumably still does what it was set up to do. (E)'s use of the

"would" construction is not acceptable since there is no doubt about what is included.

22. **(E)** The original sentence has the lions playing with lenses while in the trees. This is clearly unacceptable. Only (E) corrects the situation to make it clear that the visitor is the one concerned with telephoto lenses, not the lions.

23. **(C)** We are concerned with the capacity for something to be done, which is expressed best by "can," eliminating (A), (D), and (E). Also, the original refers to "a person," which is singular even with the apostrophe and "s" of the possessive case appended. Thus "his" is needed rather than "their," making (C) preferable to (B).

24. **(C)** The original sentence sets up a parallel structure of "were appalled," "(were) grieved," and "(were) promised." (B)'s use of "aggrieved" is wrong since they were not injured. "Saddened," used in (D), is essentially the same meaning as "grieved," though somewhat weaker. (D) and (E) fail to correct the error with "promise," which leaves (C).

25. **(A)** The original sentence is correct. (B) fails primarily because of its reference to "the" personality rather than "his." The use of "jettison" is not so major a problem. (C) introduces the idea of "must," which is quite different from the "may" of the original and not required by the meaning of the sentence. (D) speaks of "the prisoner" (singular) and "their" (plural) "personality" (singular). (E) fails for similar reasons, since it refers to "prisoner's" (singular) "personalities" (plural), implying multiple personalities for the prisoner, which the original certainly does not support.

Section VII

1. **(B)** $40\% = \frac{2}{5}$
   $\frac{2}{5} \times \frac{10}{7} = \frac{4}{7}$

2. **(D)** 27 and 51 are each divisible by 3. 17 and 59 are prime numbers. Hence, I and IV only.

3. **(A)** Angle DOC = 6 + x
   Angle AOC = (6 + x) + x = 180 − 20
   $$6 + 2x = 160$$
   $$2x = 154$$
   $$x = 77$$

4. **(D)** Let C = the capacity in gallons. Then $\frac{1}{3}$C + 3 = $\frac{1}{2}$C. Multiplying through by 6, we obtain 2C + 18 = 3C, or C = 18.

5. **(E)**
$$\frac{91 + 88 + 86 + 78 + x}{5} = 85$$
$$343 + x = 425$$
$$x = 82$$

6. **(C)** $12 \times .39 = 4.68$ inches; that is, between $4\frac{1}{2}$ and 5.

7. **(D)**

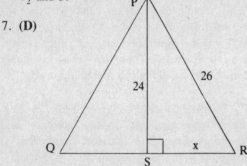

In the figure above, PS ⊥ QR. Then, in right triangle PSR:

$$x^2 + 24^2 = 26^2$$
$$x^2 = 26^2 - 24^2$$
$$= (26 + 24)(26 - 24)$$
$$x^2 = 50\cdot2 = 100$$
$$x = 10$$

Thus, QR = 20.

8. **(C)** All terms involving x are 0. Hence, the equation reduces to:

$$0 - 7y + 15 = 0$$
$$\text{or } 7y = 15$$
$$y = 2\frac{1}{7}$$

9. **(E)** Let s = number of shirts and t = number of ties, where s and t are integers:

$$\text{Then } 7s + 3t = 81$$
$$7s = 81 - 3t$$
$$s = \frac{81 - 3t}{7}$$

Since s is an integer, t must have an integral value such that 81 − 3t is divisible by 7. Trial shows that t = 6 is the smallest such number, making $s = \frac{81 - 18}{7} = \frac{63}{7} = 9$. Hence, s:t = 9:6 = 3:2.

10. **(C)** Rate = $\dfrac{\text{distance}}{\text{time}} = \dfrac{\frac{2}{5}\text{ mile}}{\frac{5}{60}\text{ hour}} = \dfrac{\frac{2}{5}}{\frac{1}{12}}$
rate $= \frac{2}{5}\cdot\frac{12}{1} = \frac{24}{5} = 4\frac{4}{5}$ miles per hour.

11. **(D)** Draw the altitudes indicated. A rectangle and two right triangles are produced. From the figure, the base of each triangle is 20 feet. By the Pythagorean Theorem, the altitude is 15 feet. Hence, the area:

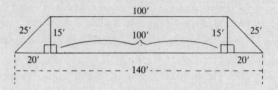

$$K = \frac{1}{2} \cdot 15(100 + 140)$$
$$= \frac{1}{2} \cdot 15 \cdot 240$$
$$= 15 \cdot 120$$
$$= 1800 \text{ square feet}$$

12. **(E)** If $1 + \dfrac{1}{t} = \dfrac{t + 1}{t}$, then the right-hand fraction can also be reduced to $1 + \dfrac{1}{t}$, and we have an identity, which is true for all values of t except 0.

13. **(E)** All points 6 inches from A are on a circle of radius 6 with center at A. All points 1 inch from b are on 2 straight lines parallel to b and 1 inch from it on each side. These two parallel lines intersect the circle in 4 points.

14. **(E)** Let R = 5P and S = 5Q where P and Q are integers. Then R − S = 5P − 5Q = 5(P − Q) is divisible by 5. RS = 5P · 5Q = 25PG is divisible by 25. R + S = 5P + 5Q = 5(P + Q) is divisible by 5. $R^2 + S^2 = 25P^2 + 25Q^2 = 25(P^2 + Q^2)$ is divisible by 5. R + S = 5P + 5Q = 5(P + Q), which is not necessarily divisible by 10.

15. **(D)** $\frac{1}{2} \cdot 7 \cdot h = \pi \cdot 7^2$. Dividing both sides by 7, we get ½h = 7π, or h = 14π.

16. **(E)**

$\begin{array}{r} .69 \\ 13\overline{)9.00} \\ 78 \\ \hline 120 \\ 117 \\ \hline \end{array}$	$\begin{array}{r} 1.44 \\ 9\overline{)13.00} \\ 9 \\ \hline 40 \\ 36 \\ \hline 40 \\ 36 \end{array}$	$70\% = .7$ $\dfrac{1}{.70} = \dfrac{1}{\frac{7}{10}}$ $\begin{array}{r} 1.42 \\ 7\overline{)10.00} \\ 7 \\ \hline 30 \\ 28 \\ \hline 20 \end{array}$

Correct order is $\frac{9}{13}$, 70%, $\frac{1}{.70}$, $\frac{13}{9}$ ——or I, III, IV, II.

17. **(D)**

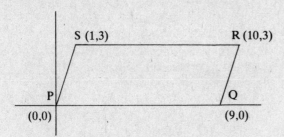

Since PQ and RS are parallel and equal, the figure is a parallelogram of base = 9 and height = 3. Hence, area = 9 · 3 = 27.

18. **(A)**

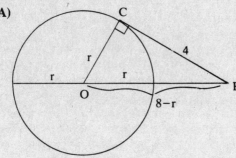

From the figure, in right △PCO:

$$PO^2 = r^2 + 4^2$$
$$(8 - r)^2 = r^2 + 16$$
$$64 - 16r + r^2 = r^2 + 16$$
$$48 = 16r$$
$$r = 3$$

Hence, diameter = 6.

19. **(B)** Area of wall = $4 \cdot \frac{60}{3} = 4 \cdot 20 = 80$ sq. yd. Cost = $80 \times \$10.50 = \$840.00$.

20. **(D)** Using the distance formula, derived from the Pythagorean Theorem, that the distance from (a,b) to (c,d) is $\sqrt{(a - c)^2 + (b - d)^2}$:

Distance of (4,4) from origin =
$\sqrt{16 + 16} = \sqrt{32} < 7$

Distance of (5,5) from origin =
$\sqrt{25 + 25} = \sqrt{50} > 7$

Distance of (4,5) from origin =
$\sqrt{16 + 25} = \sqrt{41} < 7$

Distance of (4,6) from origin =
$\sqrt{16 + 36} = \sqrt{52} > 7$

Hence, only II and IV are outside the circle.

ANSWER SHEET—PRACTICE EXAMINATION 2

SECTION I

1 Ⓐ Ⓑ Ⓒ Ⓓ Ⓔ   6 Ⓐ Ⓑ Ⓒ Ⓓ Ⓔ   11 Ⓐ Ⓑ Ⓒ Ⓓ Ⓔ   16 Ⓐ Ⓑ Ⓒ Ⓓ Ⓔ   21 Ⓐ Ⓑ Ⓒ Ⓓ Ⓔ

2 Ⓐ Ⓑ Ⓒ Ⓓ Ⓔ   7 Ⓐ Ⓑ Ⓒ Ⓓ Ⓔ   12 Ⓐ Ⓑ Ⓒ Ⓓ Ⓔ   17 Ⓐ Ⓑ Ⓒ Ⓓ Ⓔ   22 Ⓐ Ⓑ Ⓒ Ⓓ Ⓔ

3 Ⓐ Ⓑ Ⓒ Ⓓ Ⓔ   8 Ⓐ Ⓑ Ⓒ Ⓓ Ⓔ   13 Ⓐ Ⓑ Ⓒ Ⓓ Ⓔ   18 Ⓐ Ⓑ Ⓒ Ⓓ Ⓔ   23 Ⓐ Ⓑ Ⓒ Ⓓ Ⓔ

4 Ⓐ Ⓑ Ⓒ Ⓓ Ⓔ   9 Ⓐ Ⓑ Ⓒ Ⓓ Ⓔ   14 Ⓐ Ⓑ Ⓒ Ⓓ Ⓔ   19 Ⓐ Ⓑ Ⓒ Ⓓ Ⓔ   24 Ⓐ Ⓑ Ⓒ Ⓓ Ⓔ

5 Ⓐ Ⓑ Ⓒ Ⓓ Ⓔ   10 Ⓐ Ⓑ Ⓒ Ⓓ Ⓔ   15 Ⓐ Ⓑ Ⓒ Ⓓ Ⓔ   20 Ⓐ Ⓑ Ⓒ Ⓓ Ⓔ   25 Ⓐ Ⓑ Ⓒ Ⓓ Ⓔ

SECTION II

1 Ⓐ Ⓑ Ⓒ Ⓓ Ⓔ   5 Ⓐ Ⓑ Ⓒ Ⓓ Ⓔ   9 Ⓐ Ⓑ Ⓒ Ⓓ Ⓔ   13 Ⓐ Ⓑ Ⓒ Ⓓ Ⓔ   17 Ⓐ Ⓑ Ⓒ Ⓓ Ⓔ

2 Ⓐ Ⓑ Ⓒ Ⓓ Ⓔ   6 Ⓐ Ⓑ Ⓒ Ⓓ Ⓔ   10 Ⓐ Ⓑ Ⓒ Ⓓ Ⓔ   14 Ⓐ Ⓑ Ⓒ Ⓓ Ⓔ   18 Ⓐ Ⓑ Ⓒ Ⓓ Ⓔ

3 Ⓐ Ⓑ Ⓒ Ⓓ Ⓔ   7 Ⓐ Ⓑ Ⓒ Ⓓ Ⓔ   11 Ⓐ Ⓑ Ⓒ Ⓓ Ⓔ   15 Ⓐ Ⓑ Ⓒ Ⓓ Ⓔ   19 Ⓐ Ⓑ Ⓒ Ⓓ Ⓔ

4 Ⓐ Ⓑ Ⓒ Ⓓ Ⓔ   8 Ⓐ Ⓑ Ⓒ Ⓓ Ⓔ   12 Ⓐ Ⓑ Ⓒ Ⓓ Ⓔ   16 Ⓐ Ⓑ Ⓒ Ⓓ Ⓔ   20 Ⓐ Ⓑ Ⓒ Ⓓ Ⓔ

SECTION III

1 Ⓐ Ⓑ Ⓒ Ⓓ Ⓔ   6 Ⓐ Ⓑ Ⓒ Ⓓ Ⓔ   11 Ⓐ Ⓑ Ⓒ Ⓓ Ⓔ   16 Ⓐ Ⓑ Ⓒ Ⓓ Ⓔ   21 Ⓐ Ⓑ Ⓒ Ⓓ Ⓔ

2 Ⓐ Ⓑ Ⓒ Ⓓ Ⓔ   7 Ⓐ Ⓑ Ⓒ Ⓓ Ⓔ   12 Ⓐ Ⓑ Ⓒ Ⓓ Ⓔ   17 Ⓐ Ⓑ Ⓒ Ⓓ Ⓔ   22 Ⓐ Ⓑ Ⓒ Ⓓ Ⓔ

3 Ⓐ Ⓑ Ⓒ Ⓓ Ⓔ   8 Ⓐ Ⓑ Ⓒ Ⓓ Ⓔ   13 Ⓐ Ⓑ Ⓒ Ⓓ Ⓔ   18 Ⓐ Ⓑ Ⓒ Ⓓ Ⓔ   23 Ⓐ Ⓑ Ⓒ Ⓓ Ⓔ

4 Ⓐ Ⓑ Ⓒ Ⓓ Ⓔ   9 Ⓐ Ⓑ Ⓒ Ⓓ Ⓔ   14 Ⓐ Ⓑ Ⓒ Ⓓ Ⓔ   19 Ⓐ Ⓑ Ⓒ Ⓓ Ⓔ   24 Ⓐ Ⓑ Ⓒ Ⓓ Ⓔ

5 Ⓐ Ⓑ Ⓒ Ⓓ Ⓔ   10 Ⓐ Ⓑ Ⓒ Ⓓ Ⓔ   15 Ⓐ Ⓑ Ⓒ Ⓓ Ⓔ   20 Ⓐ Ⓑ Ⓒ Ⓓ Ⓔ   25 Ⓐ Ⓑ Ⓒ Ⓓ Ⓔ

SECTION IV

1 Ⓐ Ⓑ Ⓒ Ⓓ Ⓔ   6 Ⓐ Ⓑ Ⓒ Ⓓ Ⓔ   11 Ⓐ Ⓑ Ⓒ Ⓓ Ⓔ   16 Ⓐ Ⓑ Ⓒ Ⓓ Ⓔ   21 Ⓐ Ⓑ Ⓒ Ⓓ Ⓔ

2 Ⓐ Ⓑ Ⓒ Ⓓ Ⓔ   7 Ⓐ Ⓑ Ⓒ Ⓓ Ⓔ   12 Ⓐ Ⓑ Ⓒ Ⓓ Ⓔ   17 Ⓐ Ⓑ Ⓒ Ⓓ Ⓔ   22 Ⓐ Ⓑ Ⓒ Ⓓ Ⓔ

3 Ⓐ Ⓑ Ⓒ Ⓓ Ⓔ   8 Ⓐ Ⓑ Ⓒ Ⓓ Ⓔ   13 Ⓐ Ⓑ Ⓒ Ⓓ Ⓔ   18 Ⓐ Ⓑ Ⓒ Ⓓ Ⓔ   23 Ⓐ Ⓑ Ⓒ Ⓓ Ⓔ

4 Ⓐ Ⓑ Ⓒ Ⓓ Ⓔ   9 Ⓐ Ⓑ Ⓒ Ⓓ Ⓔ   14 Ⓐ Ⓑ Ⓒ Ⓓ Ⓔ   19 Ⓐ Ⓑ Ⓒ Ⓓ Ⓔ   24 Ⓐ Ⓑ Ⓒ Ⓓ Ⓔ

5 Ⓐ Ⓑ Ⓒ Ⓓ Ⓔ   10 Ⓐ Ⓑ Ⓒ Ⓓ Ⓔ   15 Ⓐ Ⓑ Ⓒ Ⓓ Ⓔ   20 Ⓐ Ⓑ Ⓒ Ⓓ Ⓔ   25 Ⓐ Ⓑ Ⓒ Ⓓ Ⓔ

SECTION V

1 Ⓐ Ⓑ Ⓒ Ⓓ Ⓔ   5 Ⓐ Ⓑ Ⓒ Ⓓ Ⓔ   9 Ⓐ Ⓑ Ⓒ Ⓓ Ⓔ   13 Ⓐ Ⓑ Ⓒ Ⓓ Ⓔ   17 Ⓐ Ⓑ Ⓒ Ⓓ Ⓔ

2 Ⓐ Ⓑ Ⓒ Ⓓ Ⓔ   6 Ⓐ Ⓑ Ⓒ Ⓓ Ⓔ   10 Ⓐ Ⓑ Ⓒ Ⓓ Ⓔ   14 Ⓐ Ⓑ Ⓒ Ⓓ Ⓔ   18 Ⓐ Ⓑ Ⓒ Ⓓ Ⓔ

3 Ⓐ Ⓑ Ⓒ Ⓓ Ⓔ   7 Ⓐ Ⓑ Ⓒ Ⓓ Ⓔ   11 Ⓐ Ⓑ Ⓒ Ⓓ Ⓔ   15 Ⓐ Ⓑ Ⓒ Ⓓ Ⓔ   19 Ⓐ Ⓑ Ⓒ Ⓓ Ⓔ

4 Ⓐ Ⓑ Ⓒ Ⓓ Ⓔ   8 Ⓐ Ⓑ Ⓒ Ⓓ Ⓔ   12 Ⓐ Ⓑ Ⓒ Ⓓ Ⓔ   16 Ⓐ Ⓑ Ⓒ Ⓓ Ⓔ   20 Ⓐ Ⓑ Ⓒ Ⓓ Ⓔ

SECTION VI

1 Ⓐ Ⓑ Ⓒ Ⓓ Ⓔ   5 Ⓐ Ⓑ Ⓒ Ⓓ Ⓔ   9 Ⓐ Ⓑ Ⓒ Ⓓ Ⓔ   13 Ⓐ Ⓑ Ⓒ Ⓓ Ⓔ   17 Ⓐ Ⓑ Ⓒ Ⓓ Ⓔ

2 Ⓐ Ⓑ Ⓒ Ⓓ Ⓔ   6 Ⓐ Ⓑ Ⓒ Ⓓ Ⓔ   10 Ⓐ Ⓑ Ⓒ Ⓓ Ⓔ   14 Ⓐ Ⓑ Ⓒ Ⓓ Ⓔ   18 Ⓐ Ⓑ Ⓒ Ⓓ Ⓔ

3 Ⓐ Ⓑ Ⓒ Ⓓ Ⓔ   7 Ⓐ Ⓑ Ⓒ Ⓓ Ⓔ   11 Ⓐ Ⓑ Ⓒ Ⓓ Ⓔ   15 Ⓐ Ⓑ Ⓒ Ⓓ Ⓔ   19 Ⓐ Ⓑ Ⓒ Ⓓ Ⓔ

4 Ⓐ Ⓑ Ⓒ Ⓓ Ⓔ   8 Ⓐ Ⓑ Ⓒ Ⓓ Ⓔ   12 Ⓐ Ⓑ Ⓒ Ⓓ Ⓔ   16 Ⓐ Ⓑ Ⓒ Ⓓ Ⓔ   20 Ⓐ Ⓑ Ⓒ Ⓓ Ⓔ

SECTION VII

1 Ⓐ Ⓑ Ⓒ Ⓓ Ⓔ   6 Ⓐ Ⓑ Ⓒ Ⓓ Ⓔ   11 Ⓐ Ⓑ Ⓒ Ⓓ Ⓔ   16 Ⓐ Ⓑ Ⓒ Ⓓ Ⓔ   21 Ⓐ Ⓑ Ⓒ Ⓓ Ⓔ

2 Ⓐ Ⓑ Ⓒ Ⓓ Ⓔ   7 Ⓐ Ⓑ Ⓒ Ⓓ Ⓔ   12 Ⓐ Ⓑ Ⓒ Ⓓ Ⓔ   17 Ⓐ Ⓑ Ⓒ Ⓓ Ⓔ   22 Ⓐ Ⓑ Ⓒ Ⓓ Ⓔ

3 Ⓐ Ⓑ Ⓒ Ⓓ Ⓔ   8 Ⓐ Ⓑ Ⓒ Ⓓ Ⓔ   13 Ⓐ Ⓑ Ⓒ Ⓓ Ⓔ   18 Ⓐ Ⓑ Ⓒ Ⓓ Ⓔ   23 Ⓐ Ⓑ Ⓒ Ⓓ Ⓔ

4 Ⓐ Ⓑ Ⓒ Ⓓ Ⓔ   9 Ⓐ Ⓑ Ⓒ Ⓓ Ⓔ   14 Ⓐ Ⓑ Ⓒ Ⓓ Ⓔ   19 Ⓐ Ⓑ Ⓒ Ⓓ Ⓔ   24 Ⓐ Ⓑ Ⓒ Ⓓ Ⓔ

5 Ⓐ Ⓑ Ⓒ Ⓓ Ⓔ   10 Ⓐ Ⓑ Ⓒ Ⓓ Ⓔ   15 Ⓐ Ⓑ Ⓒ Ⓓ Ⓔ   20 Ⓐ Ⓑ Ⓒ Ⓓ Ⓔ   25 Ⓐ Ⓑ Ⓒ Ⓓ Ⓔ

PRACTICE EXAMINATION 2

SECTION I

Time—30 Minutes
25 Questions

Directions: In this section, the questions ask you to analyze and evaluate the reasoning in short paragraphs or passages. For some questions, all of the answer choices may conceivably be answers to the question asked. You should select the *best* answer to the question, that is, an answer which does not require you to make assumptions which violate commonsense standards by being implausible, redundant, irrelevant or inconsistent. After choosing the best answer, blacken the corresponding space on the answer sheet.

1. Which of the following activities would depend upon an assumption which is inconsistent with the judgment that you cannot argue with taste?
   (A) a special exhibition at a museum
   (B) a beauty contest
   (C) a system of garbage collection and disposal
   (D) a cookbook filled with old New England recipes
   (E) a movie festival

2. If George graduated from the University after 1974, he was required to take Introductory World History.

   The statement above can be logically deduced from which of the following?
   (A) Before 1974, Introductory World History was not a required course at the University.
   (B) Every student who took Introductory World History at the University graduated after 1974.
   (C) No student who graduated from the University before 1974 took Introductory World History.
   (D) All students graduating from the University after 1974 were required to take Introductory World History.
   (E) Before 1974, no student was permitted to graduate from the University without having taken Introductory World History.

3. Largemouth bass are usually found living in shallow waters near the lake banks wherever minnows are found. There are no largemouth bass living on this side of the lake.

Which of the following would logically complete an argument with the preceding premises given?

   I. Therefore, there are no minnows on this side of the lake.
   II. Therefore, there are probably no minnows on this side of the lake.
   III. Therefore, there will never be any minnows on this side of the lake.

   (A) I only
   (B) II only
   (C) III only
   (D) I and III only
   (E) II and III only

4. TOMMY: That telephone always rings when I am in the shower and can't hear it.

   JUANITA: But you must be able to hear it; otherwise you couldn't know that it was ringing.

   Juanita's response shows that she presupposes that
   (A) the telephone does not ring when Tommy is in the shower
   (B) Tommy's callers never telephone except when he is in the shower
   (C) Tommy's callers sometimes hang up thinking he is not at home
   (D) Tommy cannot tell that the telephone has rung unless he actually heard it
   (E) the telephone does not always function properly

5. ADVERTISEMENT: You cannot buy a more potent pain-reliever than RELIEF without a prescription.

   Which of the following statements is inconsistent with the claim made by the advertisement?

   I. RELIEF is not the least expensive non-prescription pain-reliever one can buy.
   II. Another non-prescription pain-reliever, TOBINE, is just as powerful as RELIEF.

III. Some prescription pain-relievers are not as powerful as RELIEF.

(A) I only
(B) II only
(C) I and II only
(D) I, II, and III
(E) None of the statements is inconsistent with the advertisement.

Questions 6 and 7

A behavioral psychologist interested in animal behavior noticed that dogs who are never physically disciplined (e.g., with a blow from a rolled-up newspaper) never bark at strangers. He concluded that the best way to keep a dog from barking at strange visitors is to not punish the dog physically.

6. The psychologist's conclusion is based on which of the following assumptions?

   I. The dogs he studied never barked.
   II. Dogs should not be physically punished.
   III. There were no instances of an unpunished dog barking at a stranger which he had failed to observe.

   (A) I only
   (B) II only
   (C) III only
   (D) II and III only
   (E) I, II and III

7. Suppose the psychologist decides to pursue his project further, and he studies 25 dogs which are known to bark at strangers. Which of the following possible findings would undermine his original conclusion?

   I. Some of the owners of the dogs studied did not physically punish the dog when it barked at a stranger.
   II. Some of the dogs studied were never physically punished.
   III. The owners of some of the dogs studied believe that a dog which barks at strangers is a good watchdog.

   (A) I only
   (B) II only
   (C) I and II only
   (D) II and III only
   (E) I, II, and III

8. Everything a child does is the consequence of

some experience he has had before. Therefore, a child psychologist must study the personal history of his patient.

The author's conclusion logically depends upon the premise that

(A) everything that a child is doing he has already done before
(B) every effect is causally generated by some previous effect
(C) the study of a child's personal history is the best way of learning about that child's parents
(D) a child will learn progressively more about the world because experience is cumulative
(E) it is possible to ensure that a child will grow up to be a mature, responsible adult

9. It is sometimes argued that we are reaching the limits of the earth's capacity to supply our energy needs with fossil fuels. In the past ten years, however, as a result of technological progress making it possible to extract resources from even marginal wells and mines, yields from oil and coal fields have increased tremendously. There is no reason to believe that there is a limit to the earth's capacity to supply our energy needs.

Which of the following statements most directly contradicts the conclusion drawn above?

(A) Even if we exhaust our supplies of fossil fuel, the earth can still be mined for uranium for nuclear fuel.
(B) The technology needed to extract fossil fuels from marginal sources is very expensive.
(C) Even given the improvements in technology, oil and coal are not renewable resources; so we will eventually exhaust our supplies of them.
(D) Most of the land under which marginal oil and coal supplies lie is more suitable to cultivation or pasturing than to production of fossil fuels.
(E) The fuels that are yielded by marginal sources tend to be high in sulphur and other undesirable elements which aggravate the air pollution problem.

Questions 10–12 refer to the following arguments.

(A) The Bible must be accepted as the revealed word of God, for it is stated several times in the Bible that it is the one, true word of God.

And since the Bible is the true word of God, we must accept what it says as true.

(B) It must be possible to do something about the deteriorating condition of the nation's interstate highway system. But the repairs will cost money. Therefore, it is foolish to reduce federal appropriations for highway repair.

(C) The Learner Commission's Report on Pornography concluded that there is a definite link between pornography and sex crimes. But no one should accept that conclusion because the Learner Commission was funded by the Citizens' Committee Against Obscenity, which obviously wanted the report to condemn pornography.

(D) People should give up drinking coffee. Of ten people who died last year at City Hospital from cancer of the pancreas, eight of them drank three or more cups of coffee a day.

(E) Guns are not themselves the cause of crime. Even without firearms crimes would be committed. Criminals would use knives or other weapons.

10. Which of the above arguments contains circular reasoning?

11. Which of the above arguments contains a generalization which is based on a sample?

12. Which of above arguments addresses itself to the source of the claim rather than to the merits of the claim itself?

13. Some sociologists believe that religious sects such as the California-based Waiters, who believe the end of the world is imminent and seek to purify their souls by, among other things, abstaining completely from sexual relations, are a product of growing disaffection with modern, industrialized and urbanized living. As evidence, they cite the fact that there are no other active organizations of the same type which are more than 50 or 60 years old. The evidence, however, fails to support the conclusion for _____.

Which of the following is the most logical completion of the passage?

(A) the restrictions on sexual relations are such that the only source of new members is outside recruitment, so such sects tend to die out after a generation or two.

(B) it is simply not possible to gauge the intensity of religious fervor by the length of time

the religious sect remains viable.

(C) the Waiters group may actually survive beyond the second generation of its existence.

(D) there are other religious sects that emphasize group sexual activity which currently have several hundred members.

(E) the Waiters are a California-based organization and have no members in the Northeast, which is even more heavily urban and industrialized than California.

14. Any truthful auto mechanic will tell you that your standard 5,000-mile checkup can detect only one-fifth of the problems which are likely to go wrong with your car. Therefore, such a checkup is virtually worthless and a waste of time and money.

Which of the following statements, if true, would weaken the above conclusion?

I. Those problems which the 5,000-mile checkup will turn up are the ten leading causes of major engine failure.

II. For a new car, a 5,000-mile checkup is required to protect the owner's warranty.

III. During a 5,000-mile checkup the mechanic also performs routine maintenance which is necessary to the proper functioning of the car.

(A) I only
(B) II only
(C) I and II only
(D) II and III only
(E) I, II, and III

Questions 15 and 16

In recent years, unions have begun to include in their demands at the collective bargaining table requests for contract provisions which give labor an active voice in determining the goals of a corporation. Although it cannot be denied that labor leaders are highly skilled administrators, it must be recognized that their primary loyalty is and must remain to their membership, not to the corporation. Thus, labor participation in corporate management decisions makes about as much sense as _____.

15. Which of the following represents the best continuation of the passage?
(A) allowing inmates to make decisions about prison security
(B) a senior field officer asking the advice of a

junior officer on a question of tactics
- (C) a university's asking the opinion of the student body on the scheduling of courses
- (D) Chicago's mayor inviting the state legislators for a ride on the city's subway system
- (E) the members of a church congregation discussing theology with the minister

16. The author's reasoning leads to the further conclusion that
- (A) the authority of corporate managers would be symbolically undermined if labor leaders were allowed to participate in corporate planning
- (B) workers have virtually no idea of how to run a large corporation
- (C) workers would not derive any benefit from hearing the goals of corporate management explained to them at semiannual meetings
- (D) the efficiency of workers would be lowered if they were to divide their time between production line duties and management responsibilities
- (E) allowing labor a voice in corporate decisions would involve labor representatives in a conflict of interest

17. DRUGGIST: Seventy percent of the people questioned stated that they would use Myrdal for relief of occasional headache pain. Only 30 percent of those questioned indicated that they would take Blufferin for such pain.

CUSTOMER: Oh, then over twice as many people preferred Myrdal to Blufferin.

DRUGGIST: No, 25 percent of those questioned stated they never took any medication.

In what manner may the seeming inconsistency in the druggist's statements be explained?
- (A) The 30 percent who indicated they would take Blufferin are contained within the 70 percent of those who indicated they would take Myrdal.
- (B) The questioner asked more than 100 people.
- (C) The questioner did not accurately record the answers of at least 25 percent of those questioned.
- (D) The sampling population was too small to yield results that were statistically significant.

- (E) Some of those questioned indicated that they would take both brands of pain relievers.

18. I. No student who commutes from home to a university dates a student who resides at a university.
   II. Every student who lives at home commutes to his university, and no commuter student ever dates a resident student.

Which of the following best describes the relationship between the two preceding sentences?
- (A) If II is true, I must also be true.
- (B) If II is true, I must be false.
- (C) If II is true, I may be either true or false.
- (D) If I is true, II is unlikely to be false.
- (E) If II is false, I must also be false.

19. All books from the Buckner collection are kept in the Reserve Room.
   All books kept in the Reserve Room are priceless.
   No book by Hemingway is kept in the Reserve Room.
   Every book kept in the Reserve Room is listed in the card catalogue.

If all of the statements above are true, which of the following must also be true?
- (A) All priceless books are kept in the Reserve Room.
- (B) Every book from the Buckner collection which is listed in the card catalogue is not valuable.
- (C) No book by Hemingway is priceless.
- (D) The Buckner collection contains no books by Hemingway.
- (E) Every book listed in the card catalogue is kept in the Reserve Room.

20. The new car to buy this year is the Goblin. We had 100 randomly selected motorists drive the Goblin and the other two leading subcompact cars. Seventy-five drivers ranked the Goblin first in handling. Sixty-nine rated the Goblin first in styling. From the responses of these 100 drivers, we can show you that they ranked Goblin first overall in our composite category of style, performance, comfort, and drivability.

The persuasive appeal of the advertisement's claim is most weakened by its use of the undefined word
- (A) randomly
- (B) handling
- (C) first

(D) responses
(E) composite

21. Recently the newspaper published the obituary notice of a novelist and poet that had been written by the deceased in anticipation of the event. The last line of the verse advised the reader that the author had expired a day earlier and gave as the cause of death "a deprivation of time."

The explanation of the cause of the author's death is
(A) circular
(B) speculative
(C) self-serving
(D) medically sound
(E) self-authenticating

22. Since Ronnie's range is so narrow, he will never be an outstanding vocalist.
The statement above is based on which of the following assumptions?

   I. A person's range is an important indicator of his probable success or failure as a professional musician.
   II. Vocalizing requires a range of at least two and one-half octaves.
   III. Physical characteristics can affect how well one sings.

(A) I only
(B) II only
(C) I and II
(D) III only
(E) I, II, and III

23. During the 1970's the number of clandestine CIA agents posted to foreign countries increased 25 percent and the number of CIA employees not assigned to field work increased by 21 percent. In the same period, the number of FBI agents assigned to case investigation rose by 18 percent, but the number of non-case-working agents rose by only 3 percent.

The statistics best support which of the following claims?
(A) More agents are needed to administer the CIA than are needed for the FBI.
(B) The CIA needs more people to accomplish its mission than does the FBI.

(C) The proportion of field agents tends to increase more rapidly than the number of non-field agents in both the CIA and the FBI.
(D) The rate of change in the number of supervisory agents in an intelligence-gathering agency or a law-enforcement agency is proportional to the percentage change in the results produced by the agency.
(E) At the end of the 1960's, the CIA was more efficiently administered than the FBI.

The following material contains blanks that represent deleted material. For Questions 24 and 25, select the most appropriate completion of the passage.

When we reflect on the structure of moral decisions, we come across cases in which we seem to be subject to mutually exclusive moral demands. But the conflict is just that, a seeming one. We must be careful to distinguish two levels of moral thinking: The *prima facie* and the critical. A *prima facie* moral principle is analogous to a workaday tool, say a(n)__(24)__. It is versatile, that is, useful in many situations, and at your fingertips, to wit, no special skill is needed to use it. Unfortunately, the value of a *prima facie* principle derives from its non-specific language, which means that in some situations it will turn out to be an oversimplification. For example, two fairly straightforward moral rules such as "keep all promises" and "assist others in dire need," which work well enough in most cases, seem to clash in the following scenario: "I have promised a friend I will run a very important errand on his behalf (and he is relying on me); but while en route I happen across a person in need of emergency medical assistance, which I can provide, but only at the cost of leaving my original purpose unaccomplished." The appearance of conflict arises from the choice of tools used in analyzing the situation——the two *prima facie* rules do not cut finely enough. What is wanted, therefore, is a more refined analysis which will be applicable to the specific situation. At this, the second level of moral thinking, critical moral thinking employs a finer system of categories so that the end result is__(25)__.

24. (A) surgical scalpel
    (B) kitchen knife
    (C) electrical generator
    (D) tuning fork
    (E) library book

25. (A) not two conflicting moral judgments, but a single consistent moral judgment

(B) an advance for the human species over the savagery of our forebears

(C) the improvement of medical care for the population in general

(D) moral principles of higher levels of abstraction which are applicable to larger numbers of cases

(E) that value judgments will no longer depend on the particulars of any given situation

STOP

END OF SECTION. IF YOU HAVE ANY TIME LEFT, GO OVER YOUR WORK IN THIS SECTION ONLY. DO NOT WORK IN ANY OTHER SECTION OF THE TEST.

SECTION II

Time—30 Minutes
20 Questions

Directions: For each of the following questions, select the best of the answer choices and blacken the corresponding space on your answer sheet.
Numbers: All numbers used are real numbers.
Figures: The diagrams and figures that accompany these questions are for the purpose of providing information useful in answering the question. Unless it is stated that a specific figure is not drawn to scale, the diagrams and figures are drawn as accurately as possible. All figures are in a plane unless otherwise indicated.

1. From the time 6:15 P.M. to the time 7:45 P.M. of the same day, the minute hand of a standard clock describes an arc of
   (A) 30°
   (B) 90°
   (C) 180°
   (D) 540°
   (E) 910°

2. Which of the following fractions is the LEAST?
   (A) $\frac{7}{8}$
   (B) $\frac{7}{12}$
   (C) $\frac{8}{9}$
   (D) $\frac{1}{2}$
   (E) $\frac{6}{17}$

3. The length of each side of a square is $\frac{3x}{4} + 1$.

   What is the perimeter of the square?
   (A) $x + 1$
   (B) $3x + 1$
   (C) $3x + 4$
   (D) $\frac{9}{16}x^2 + \frac{3}{2}x + 1$
   (E) It cannot be determined from the information given.

4. A truck departed from Newton at 11:53 A.M. and arrived in Far City, 240 miles away, at 4:41 P.M. on the same day. What was the approximate average speed of the truck on this trip?
   (A) $\frac{5640}{5}$ MPH
   (B) $\frac{16}{1200}$ MPH
   (C) 50 MPH
   (D) $\frac{240}{288}$ MPH
   (E) $\frac{1494}{240}$ MPH

5. If m, n, o and p are real numbers, each of the following expressions equals m(nop) EXCEPT
   (A) (op)(mn)
   (B) ponm
   (C) p(onm)
   (D) (mp)(no)
   (E) (mn)(mo)(mp)

ABCD is a square

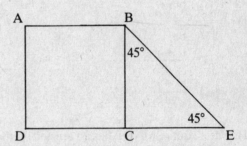

6. If the area of the triangle BCE is 8, what is the area of the square ABCD?
   (A) 16
   (B) 82
   (C) 8
   (D) 4
   (E) 22

7. The diagonal of the floor of a rectangular closet is $7\frac{1}{2}$ feet. The shorter side of the closet is $4\frac{1}{2}$ feet. What is the area of the closet in square feet?
   (A) 37
   (B) 27
   (C) $\frac{54}{4}$
   (D) $\frac{21}{4}$
   (E) 5

8. If the ratio of women to men in a meeting is 4 to 1, what percent of the persons in the meeting are men?
   (A) 20%
   (B) 25%

(C) $33\frac{1}{3}\%$
(D) 80%
(E) 100%

9. Which of the following fractions expressed in the form $\frac{P}{Q}$ is most nearly approximated by the decimal .PQ, where P is the tenths' digit and Q is the hundredths' digit?
(A) $\frac{1}{8}$
(B) $\frac{2}{9}$
(C) $\frac{3}{4}$
(D) $\frac{4}{5}$
(E) $\frac{8}{9}$

10. If b books can be purchased for d dollars, how many books can be purchased for m dollars?
(A) $\frac{bm}{d}$
(B) bdm
(C) $\frac{d}{bm}$
(D) $\frac{b + m}{d}$
(E) $\frac{b - m}{d}$

11. If a square MNOP has an area of 16, then its perimeter is
(A) 4
(B) 8
(C) 16
(D) 32
(E) 64

12. John has more money than Mary but less than Bill. If the amounts held by John, Mary and Bill are x, y, and z, respectively, which of the following is true?
(A) $z < x < y$
(B) $x < z < y$
(C) $y < x < z$
(D) $y < z < x$
(E) $x < y < z$

13. If $x = 3$ and $(x - y)^2 = 4$, then y could be
(A) −5
(B) −1
(C) 0
(D) 5
(E) 9

14. 10% of 360 is how much more than 5% of 360?
(A) 5
(B) 9
(C) 18
(D) 36
(E) 48

15. If $x^2 + 3x + 10 = 1 + x^2$, then $x^2 =$
(A) 0
(B) 1
(C) 4
(D) 7
(E) 9

16. Which of the following must be true?

  I. Any of two lines which are parallel to a third line are also parallel to each other.
  II. Any two planes which are parallel to a third plane are parallel to each other.
  III. Any two lines which are parallel to the same plane are parallel to each other.

(A) I only
(B) II only
(C) I and II only
(D) II and III only
(E) I, II, and III

17. An item costs 90% of its original price. If 90¢ is added to the discount price, the cost of the item will be equal to its original price. What is the original price of the item?
(A) $.09
(B) $.90
(C) $9.00
(D) $9.90
(E) $9.99

18. In the figure below, the coordinates of the vertices A and B are (2,0) and (0,2), respectively. What is the area of the square ABCD?
(A) 2
(B) 4
(C) $4\sqrt{2}$
(D) 8
(E) $8\sqrt{2}$

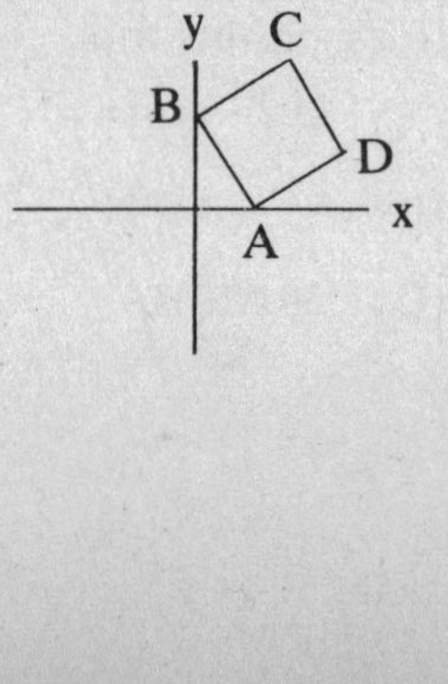

19. If $mx + ny = 12my$, and $my \neq 0$, then $\dfrac{x}{y} + \dfrac{n}{m} =$

    (A) 12
    (B) 12 mn
    (C) 12 m + 12y
    (D) 0
    (E) mx + ny

20. In circle 0 shown to the right, MN > NO. All of the following must be true EXCEPT

    (A) MN < 2 MO
    (B) x > y
    (C) z = y
    (D) x = y + z
    (E) x > 60°

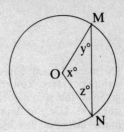

STOP

END OF SECTION. IF YOU HAVE ANY TIME LEFT, GO
OVER YOUR WORK IN THIS SECTION ONLY. DO NOT
WORK IN ANY OTHER SECTION OF THE TEST.

SECTION III

Time—30 Minutes
25 Questions

Directions: Each question below is followed by two numbered facts. You are to determine whether the data given in the statements is sufficient for answering the question. Use the data given, plus your knowledge of math and everyday facts, to choose between the five possible answers.

(A) if statement 1 alone is sufficient to answer the question, but statement 2 alone is not sufficient
(B) if statement 2 alone is sufficient to answer the question, but statement 1 alone is not sufficient
(C) if both statements together are needed to answer the question, but neither statement alone is sufficient
(D) if either statement by itself is sufficient to answer the question
(E) if not enough facts are given to answer the question

1. If the area of a rectangle is 20, what is its perimeter?
   (1) The length of the rectangle is 5.
   (2) The width of the rectangle is 1 unit less than its length.

2. Is the average of ten integers greater than 10?
   (1) Half of the integers are greater than 10.
   (2) Half of the integers are less than 10.

3. Is A > B?
   (1) AX > BX
   (2) X < 0

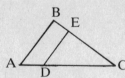

4. Is AB parallel to DE?
   (1) DC = EC
   (2) ∠EDC = ∠BAC

5. What is the length of the diagonal of a certain rectangle?
   (1) The area of the rectangle is 16.
   (2) The perimeter of the rectangle is 16.

6. If Tim weighs X, where X is a whole number, what is Tim's weight?
   (1) If Tim gains 6 pounds, he will weigh less than 186 pounds.
   (2) If Tim gains 8 pounds, he will weigh more than 186 pounds.

7. Is the integer T divisible by 15?
   (1) The sum of the digits of T equals 15.
   (2) The units digit of T is a 3.

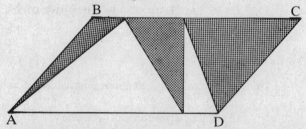

8. What is the area of the shaded region above?
   (1) ABCD is a parallelogram.
   (2) The area of ABCD is 46.

9. What is the length of the diagonal of a cube?
   (1) The sides of the cube have length 1.
   (2) The diagonals of the faces of the cube have length $\sqrt{2}$.

10. How long did a round trip take?
    (1) The outward journey took 1 hour longer than the return journey.
    (2) The return journey was 75 miles.

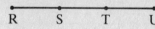

11. Points R, S, T and U are on line RU as shown. Which is larger, TU or ST?
    (1) RU is 15 units long.
    (2) Points S and T trisect line segment RU.

12. John, Peter and Paul together have ten marbles. If each has at least one marble, how many marbles does each boy have?
    (1) John has 5 more than Paul.
    (2) Peter has half as many as John.

13. Is A + B > B?
    (1) B > 0
    (2) A < 0

14. Is x positive?
    (1) $x^2 - 1 = 0$
    (2) $x^3 + 1 = 0$

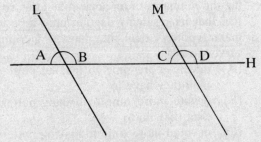

15. L, M and H are straight lines with L ∥ M. Is ∠B equal to 90°?
    (1) ∠A = 55°
    (2) ∠D > 90°

16. A rectangle is 40 inches long. What is its area?
    (1) Its perimeter is 140 inches.
    (2) The length of the diagonal is 50 inches.

17. What are the values of A and B?
    (1) 2A − 3B = 17
    (2) 6B − 4A = −34

18. There are 150 bushels to unload from a truck. Joe and Tom, working together take $\frac{1}{2}$ hour to unload the truck. How long should it take Tom working by himself to unload the truck?
    (1) Joe unloads twice as many bushels as Tom.
    (2) Joe would take 45 minutes by himself to unload it.

19. Is A > B?
    (1) A is positive.
    (2) $(A + B)^2$ is positive.

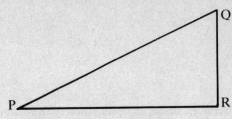

20. Is triangle PQR a right triangle?
    (1) ∠P < ∠Q
    (2) ∠P + ∠Q = ∠R

21. Is K greater than L?
    (1) K is greater than 2L.
    (2) The difference K − L is positive.

22. A piece of wood 7 feet long is cut into three pieces. What is the length of each of the pieces?
    (1) The length of the longest piece is equal to the sum of the lengths of the other two pieces.
    (2) The length of the shortest piece is 6 inches.

23. Is A greater than B?
    (1) A + B > 2A
    (2) $A^2 > B^2$

24. N is an integer. Is N divisible by 12?
    (1) N is divisible by 6.
    (2) N is divisible by 2.

25. Is X a whole number?
    (1) 2X is even.
    (2) 3X is odd.

STOP

END OF SECTION. IF YOU HAVE ANY TIME LEFT, GO
OVER YOUR WORK IN THIS SECTION ONLY. DO NOT
WORK IN ANY OTHER SECTION OF THE TEST.

SECTION IV

Time—30 Minutes
25 Questions

Directions: In each problem below, either part or all of the sentence is underlined. The sentence is followed by five ways of writing the underlined part. Answer choice (A) repeats the original; the other answer choices vary. If you think that the original phrasing is the best, choose (A). If you think one of the other answer choices is the best, select that choice.

This section tests the ability to recognize correct and effective expression. Follow the requirements of Standard Written English: grammar, choice of words, and sentence construction. Choose the answer which results in the clearest, most exact sentence, but do not change the meaning of the original sentence.

1. If they would have found the receipt by mid-April, they would have paid less tax.
   - (A) If they would have found the receipt by mid-April, they would have paid less tax.
   - (B) If they would have found the receipt by mid-April, they had paid less tax.
   - (C) If they had found the receipt by mid-April, they would have paid fewer tax.
   - (D) If they had found the receipt by mid-April, they would have paid less tax.
   - (E) If they find the receipt by mid-April, they will pay less tax.

2. The libraries with the Corinthian columns that contain almost a million volumes opened last evening.
   - (A) The libraries with the Corinthian columns that contain almost a million volumes
   - (B) The libraries with the Corinthian columns that contained almost a million volumes
   - (C) The libraries with the Corinthian columns that contains almost a million volumes
   - (D) The libraries with the Corinthian columns and which contain almost a million volumes
   - (E) The libraries which contain almost a million volumes with the Corinthian columns

3. The Russian scientists who have been studying the remnants of an ancient Siberian city feel that its residents devote more time to making pottery than they have to learning survival skills.
   - (A) devote more time to making pottery than they have to
   - (B) devote more time to making pottery than they do to
   - (C) devoted more time to making pottery than they did to
   - (D) devote more time to the making of their pottery than to
   - (E) devoted more time to making pottery than they do to

4. The leader of the Neanderthal tribe rarely hunted for food, and because of it was never acknowledged as a great hunter.
   - (A) The leader of the Neanderthal tribe rarely hunted for food, and because of it
   - (B) Because the leader of the Neanderthal tribe rarely hunted for food, he
   - (C) In that he rarely hunted for food, the leader of the Neanderthal tribe was
   - (D) Rarely hunting for food was the reason that the leader of the Neanderthal tribe
   - (E) Hunts were rare, and because of this the leader of the Neanderthal tribe

5. The physicians explained that had the patient known the warning signs of cancer, he would have come in earlier for a check-up.
   - (A) had the patient known the warning signs of cancer, he would have come in earlier
   - (B) if the patient had known the warning signs of cancer, he would have come in earlier
   - (C) if the patient knew the warning signs of cancer, he would have come in earlier

(D) had the patient known the warning signs of cancer, he would come in earlier

(E) if the patient would have known the warning signs of cancer, he would have come in earlier

6. The general's hopes for success in battle were dashed <u>as a result of the willingness of the native population to cooperate with the enemy.</u>

(A) as a result of the willingness of the native population to cooperate with the enemy.

(B) because the native population was willing to cooperate with the enemy.

(C) insofar as the native population was willing to cooperate with the enemy.

(D) because the native population would have a willingness to cooperate with enemy.

(E) by the native population's apparent willingness to cooperate with the enemy.

7. <u>The marines who landed on the beaches of Iwo Jima effected the rescue of several prisoners of war whose assault took the enemy by surprise.</u>

(A) The marines who landed on the beaches at Iwo Jima effected the rescue of several prisoners of war whose assault took the enemy by surprise.

(B) The marines effected the rescue of several prisoners of war who had landed on the beaches at Iwo Jima and whose assult had taken the enemy by surprise.

(C) The marines who landed on the beaches at Iwo Jima effected the rescue of several prisoners of war whose assault had taken the enemy by surprise.

(D) The marines who landed on the beaches at Iwo Jima affected the rescue of several prisoners of war whose assault had taken the enemy by surprise.

(E) The marines who landed on the beaches at Iwo Jima, and whose assault took the enemy by surprise, effected the rescue of several prisoners of war.

8. <u>Unafraid of neither lightning nor thunder</u> during a storm, Mr. Jones enjoyed walking in the park during heavy downpours.

(A) Unafraid of neither lightning nor thunder

(B) Afraid of both lightning and thunder

(C) Unafraid of neither lightning or thunder

(D) Unafraid of either lightning or thunder

(E) Afraid of either lightning or thunder

9. <u>Should we be told that our recommendations pertinent to the kind of use made of our vehicles have been accepted, we will</u> gladly cooperate with the ultimate plan.

(A) Should we be told that our recommendations pertinent to the kind of use made of our vehicles have been accepted, we will

(B) If we are told that recommendations about use of our vehicles has been accepted, we will

(C) Should we be told that our recommendations for the use of our vehicles have been accepted, we will

(D) Our being told of the acceptance of our recommendations pertinent to use made of our vehicles should cause us to

(E) Our being told of all recommendations about the use of our vehicles being accepted will cause us to

10. <u>Authors of the seventeenth century used alliteration to both refine their writing and increase</u> a listener's pleasure.

(A) Authors of the seventeenth century used alliteration to both refine their writing and increase

(B) Authors of the seventeenth century utilized alliteration both to refine their writing and to increase

(C) Seventeenth-century authors utilized alliteration both to refine their writing and to increase

(D) Seventeenth-century authors used alliteration both to refine their writing and to increase

(E) Seventeenth-century authors used alliteration to refine their writing, and also to increase

11. Married women raising young children do not respond to social stresses as poorly as unmarried women do.
    (A) as poorly as unmarried women do.
    (B) as much as unmarried women do
    (C) as poorly as unmarried women.
    (D) as much as unmarried women have.
    (E) as well as unmarried women.

12. Your incessant meddling in my affairs, your obnoxious ridiculing of my suggestions and sudden departure prevented our conference from yielding significant results.
    (A) and sudden departure prevented
    (B) and your suddenness of departure prevented
    (C) and your sudden departing prevented
    (D) and your sudden departing caused the prevention of
    (E) plus your sudden departure prevented

13. Breeding and education establishes the rules of behavior for any person, as does occupation and income.
    (A) establishes the rules of behavior for any person, as does
    (B) establish the rules of behavior for any person, as does
    (C) establish the rules of behavior for any person, and so does
    (D) establish the rules of behavior for any person, as do
    (E) establishes the rules of behavior for any person, and so does

14. If science can find a cure for cancer, if the nuclear arms race can be stopped, and if people can work together to resolve mutual differences are the topics around which the seminar has been planned.
    (A) If science can find a cure for cancer, if the nuclear arms race can be stopped, and if people can work together to resolve mutual differences are
    (B) Whether science can find a cure for cancer, whether the nuclear arms race can be stopped, and whether people can work together to resolve mutual differences are
    (C) If science can find a cure for cancer, if the nuclear arms race can be stopped, and if people can work together to resolve mutual differences is

    (D) Whether science can find a cure for cancer, whether the nuclear arms race can be stopped, and whether people can work together toward the resolution of mutual differences
    (E) That science can find a cure for cancer, that the nuclear arms race can be stopped, and that people can work together to resolve mutual differences is

15. In the Renaissance, painters were so impressed with Da Vinci that they ignored their own training and designated as a masterpiece anything he painted.
    (A) were so impressed with Da Vinci that they ignored
    (B) were impressed with Da Vinci to such an extent that they were to ignore
    (C) were so impressed with Da Vinci as to ignore
    (D) were so impressed with Da Vinci that they had to ignore
    (E) were as impressed with Da Vinci as to ignore

16. Most members of the trade union rejected the mayor's demand that they return to work.
    (A) that they return to work.
    (B) that the members return to work.
    (C) for them to return to work.
    (D) that they would return to work.
    (E) that they ought to return to work.

17. The players were often punished by the referee's lack of alertness who penalized all those who were involved in fighting, regardless of who had instigated it.
    (A) The players were often punished by the referee's lack of alertness who penalized
    (B) The referee's lack of alertness often caused him to penalize
    (C) The players were punished by the lack of alertness of the referee who penalized often
    (D) Lacking alertness, the referee's choice was to penalize often
    (E) His lack of alertness to brutality often caused the referee to penalize

18. The New York City Police Department was not only responsible for the maintenance of order in the metropolitan area but also for rebuilding the bonds among the various ethnic groups.
    (A) not only responsible for the maintenance of order in the metropolitan area but also for rebuilding the bonds
    (B) responsible not only for maintaining order in the metropolitan area but also for rebuilding the bonds
    (C) responsible not only for the maintenance of order in the metropolitan area and also for rebuilding
    (D) responsible not only for the maintenance of order in the metropolitan area and also for the rebuilding of bonds
    (E) not only responsible for maintaining order in the metropolitan area but also for rebuilding the bonds

19. In comparison with the literature created by the ancient Greeks, today's Greeks have written nothing worth describing.
    (A) In comparison with the literature created by the ancient Greeks, today's Greeks have written nothing worth describing.
    (B) In comparison with the literature created by the ancient Greeks, the literature of today's Greeks are containing nothing worth describing.
    (C) Compared to that of the ancient Greeks, today's Greeks have written nothing worth describing.
    (D) Compared to that of the ancient Greeks, the literature of today's Greeks is not worth describing.
    (E) Compared to the ancient Greek's literature, today's Greeks have written nothing worth describing.

20. Steve, along with his oldest brothers, are going to make a large real estate investment.
    (A) Steve, along with his oldest brothers, are
    (B) Steve, along with his oldest brothers, is
    (C) Steve, in addition to his oldest brothers, are

    (D) Steve, as well as his oldest brothers, are
    (E) Steve and his oldest brothers is

21. During the war, when it looked as if the German army was going to cross into France, English mercenaries joined the French to resist the assault.
    (A) it looked as if the German army was going to cross
    (B) it looked like the German army was going to cross
    (C) it looked like the German army would have crossed
    (D) appearances were that the German army would be crossing
    (E) it appeared that the German army would cross

22. In stating the argument that President Reagan does not care about the plight of the poor, a prominent Democrat inferred that Republicans have never been concerned about them.
    (A) a prominent Democrat inferred that Republicans have never been concerned about them.
    (B) a prominent Democrat inferred that Republicans have never been concerned about the poor.
    (C) a prominent Democrat implied that Republicans have never been concerned about them.
    (D) a prominent Democrat inferred that Republicans have never been concerned about it.
    (E) a prominent Democrat implied that Republicans have never been concerned about it.

23. Although both are rich and famous, Bill and his twin brother differ considerably in temperament; the ambition and sincerity of both are also different.
    (A) Although both are rich and famous, Bill and his twin brother differ considerably in temperament; the ambition and sincerity of both are also different.
    (B) Although both are rich and famous, Bill and his twin brother differ in temperament, ambition, and in how sincere they are.

(C) Although both are rich and famous, the temperament of Bill differs from that of his twin brother; the ambition and sincerity of both are also different.

(D) Although both are rich and famous, Bill and his twin brother differ in temperament, ambition, and sincerity.

(E) Although both rich and famous, the temperament, ambition and sincerity of Bill are different from those of his twin brother.

24. To insist on an oath of allegiance to the government is violating a worker's basic constitutional rights.

(A) To insist on an oath of allegiance to the government is violating a

(B) To insist on an oath of allegiance to the government is to violate a

(C) Insisting on an oath of allegiance to the government is to violate a

(D) Insisting on an oath of allegiance to the government amounts to a violation of a

(E) To insist on an oath to demonstrate loyalty to the government is violating a

25. Excessive exposure to microwave radiation in rats not only damages hearing but also decreases visual acuity as well, thereby reducing the survival potential of the affected organisms.

(A) but also decreases visual acuity as well, thereby reducing

(B) but also decreases visual acuity, thereby reducing

(C) but also decreases visual acuity as well, which reduces

(D) but decreases visual acuity, thereby reducing

(E) but decreases visual acuity, which reduces

STOP

END OF SECTION. IF YOU HAVE ANY TIME LEFT, GO
OVER YOUR WORK IN THIS SECTION ONLY. DO NOT
WORK IN ANY OTHER SECTION OF THE TEST.

Section V

Time: 30 Minutes
20 Questions

Directions: For each of the following questions, select the best of the answer choices and blacken the corresponding space on your answer sheet.
Numbers: All numbers used are real numbers.
Figures: The diagrams and figures that accompany these questions are for the purpose of providing information useful in answering the questions. Unless it is stated that a specific figure is not drawn to scale, the diagrams and figures are drawn as accurately as possible. All figures are in a plane unless otherwise indicated.

1. If $x = 3$ and $y = 2$, then $2x + 3y =$
    (A) 5
    (B) 10
    (C) 12
    (D) 14
    (E) 15

2. If the profit on an item is $4 and the sum of the cost and the profit is $20, what is cost of the item.
    (A) $24
    (B) $20
    (C) $16
    (D) $12
    (E) Cannot be determined from the information given.

3. In 1950, the number of students enrolled at a college was 500. In 1970, the number of students enrolled at the college was $2\frac{1}{2}$ times as great as that in 1950. What was the number of students enrolled at the college in 1970?
    (A) 1250
    (B) 1000
    (C) 1750
    (D) 500
    (E) 250

4. If n is an integer between 0 and 100, then any of the following could be $3n + 3$ EXCEPT
    (A) 300
    (B) 297
    (C) 208
    (D) 63
    (E) 6

5. A figure that can be folded over along a straight line so that the result is two equal halves which are then lying on top of one another with no overlap is said to have a line of symmetry. Which of the following figures has only one line of symmetry?
    (A) square
    (B) circle
    (C) equilateral triangle
    (D) isosceles triangle
    (E) rectangle

6. A laborer is paid $8 per hour for an 8-hour day and $1\frac{1}{2}$ times that rate for each hour in excess of 8 hours in a single day. If the laborer received $80 for a single day's work, how long did he work on that day?
    (A) 6 hr. 40 min.
    (B) 9 hr. 20 min.
    (C) 9 hr. 30 min.
    (D) 9 hr. 40 min.
    (E) 10 hr.

7. The vertex of the square MNOP is located at the center of circle O. If arc NP is 4π units long, then the perimeter of the square MNOP is

    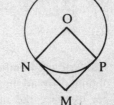

    (A) 32
    (B) 32π
    (C) 64
    (D) 64π
    (E) cannot be determined from the information given

8. How many minutes will it take to completely fill a water tank with a capacity of 3750 cubic feet if the water is being pumped into the tank at the rate of 800 cubic feet per minute and is being drained out of the tank at the rate of 300 cubic feet per minute?
    (A) 3 min. 36 sec.
    (B) 6 minutes
    (C) 7 min. 30 sec.
    (D) 8 minutes
    (E) 1875 minutes

9. Paul is standing 180 yards due north of point P. Franny is standing 240 yards due west of point P. What is the shortest distance between Franny and Paul?
(A) 60 yards
(B) 300 yards
(C) 420 yards
(D) 900 yards
(E) 9000 yards

10. If a rectangle has an area of $81x^2$ and a length of $27x$, then what is its width?
(A) $3x$
(B) $9x$
(C) $3x^2$
(D) $9x^2$
(E) $2128x^3$

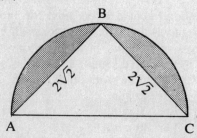

11. Triangle ABC is inscribed in a semicircle. What is the area of the shaded region above?
(A) $2\pi - 2$
(B) $2\pi - 4$
(C) $4\pi - 4$
(D) $8\pi - 4$
(E) $8\pi - 8$

12. The * of any number is defined as the result obtained by adding the square of the number to twice the number. What number is the * of 12?
(A) 12
(B) 168
(C) 1728
(D) 1752
(E) 2024

13. A motorist travels 120 miles to his destination at an average speed of 60 miles per hour and returns to his starting point at an average speed of 40 miles per hour. His average speed for the entire trip is
(A) 53 miles per hour
(B) 50 miles per hour
(C) 48 miles per hour
(D) 45 miles per hour
(E) 52 miles per hour

14. In the figure, AB = BC and angles BAD and BCD are right angles. Which one of the following conclusions may be drawn?

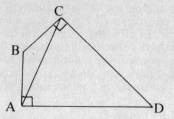

(A) angle BCA = angle CAD
(B) angle B is greater than angle D
(C) AC = CD
(D) AD = CD
(E) BC is shorter than CD

15. A merchant sells a radio for $80, thereby making a profit of 25% of the cost. What is the ratio of cost to selling price?
(A) $\frac{4}{5}$
(B) $\frac{3}{4}$
(C) $\frac{5}{6}$
(D) $\frac{2}{3}$
(E) $\frac{3}{5}$

16. How many degrees are between the hands of a clock at 3:40?
(A) 150°
(B) 140°
(C) 130°
(D) 125°
(E) 120°

17. Two fences in a field meet at an angle of 120°. A cow is tethered at their intersection with a 15-foot rope, as shown in the figure. Over how many square feet may the cow graze?
(A) 50π
(B) 75π
(C) 80π
(D) 85π
(E) 90π

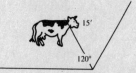

18. If $\frac{17}{10}y = 0.51$, then y =
   (A) 3
   (B) 1.3
   (C) 1.2
   (D) .3
   (E) .03

19. A junior class of 50 girls and 70 boys sponsored a dance. If 40% of the girls and 50% of the boys attended the dance, approximately what percent attended?
   (A) 40
   (B) 42
   (C) 44
   (D) 46
   (E) 48

20. In the same amount of time a new production assembly robot can assemble 8 times as many transmissions as an old assembly line. If the new robot can assemble x transmissions per hour, how many transmissions can the new robot and the old assembly line produce together in five days of round-the-clock production?
   (A) $\frac{45x}{8}$
   (B) 15x
   (C) $\frac{135x}{8}$
   (D) 135x
   (E) 1080x

STOP

END OF SECTION. IF YOU HAVE ANY TIME LEFT GO OVER YOUR WORK IN THIS SECTION ONLY. DO NOT WORK IN ANY OTHER SECTION OF THE TEST.

SECTION VI

Time—30 Minutes
20 Questions

Directions: For each of the following questions, select the best of the answer choices and blacken the corresponding space on your answer sheet.
Numbers: All numbers used are real numbers.
Figures: The diagrams and figures that accompany these questions are for the purpose of providing information useful in answering the questions. Unless it is stated that a specific figure is not drawn to scale, the diagrams and figures are drawn as accurately as possible. All figures are in a plane unless otherwise indicated.

1. Into how many line segments, each 2 inches long, can a line segment one and one-half yards long be divided?
   (A) 9
   (B) 18
   (C) 27
   (D) 36
   (E) 48

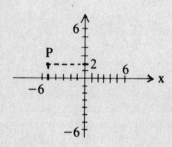

2. In the figure above, the coordinates of point P are
   (A) (−5, −2)
   (B) (−5, 2)
   (C) (−2, 5)
   (D) (2, −5)
   (E) (5, 2)

3. If circle O has a radius of 4, and if P and Q are points on circle O, then the maximum length of arc which could separate P and Q is
   (A) 8π
   (B) 4π
   (C) 4
   (D) 2π
   (E) 2

4. All of the following are prime numbers EXCEPT
   (A) 13
   (B) 17
   (C) 41
   (D) 79
   (E) 91

5. A girl at point X walks 1 mile east, then 2 miles north, then 1 mile east, then 1 mile north, then 1 mile east, then 1 mile north to arrive at point Y. From point Y, what is the shortest distance to point X?
   (A) 7 miles
   (B) 6 miles
   (C) 5 miles
   (D) 2.5 miles
   (E) 1 mile

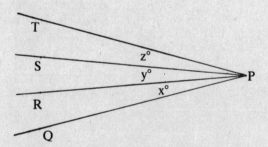

6. In the figure above, the measure of ∠QPS is equal to the measure of ∠TPR. Which of the following must be true?
   (A) x = y
   (B) y = z
   (C) x = z
   (D) x = y = z
   (E) none of the above

7. Newtown is due north of Oscarville. Highway L runs 31° south of east from Newtown and Highway M runs 44° north of east from Oscarville. If L and M are straight, what is the measure of the acute angle they form at their intersection?
   (A) 105°
   (B) 89°
   (C) 75°

(D) 59°
(E) 46°

DISTRIBUTION	NUMBER IN POPULATION
Having X Having Y	25
Having X Lacking Y	10
Lacking X Having Y	25
Lacking X Lacking Y	40

8. If a sum of money is divided equally among n children, each child will receive $60. If another child is added to the group, then when the sum is divided equally among all the children, each child will receive a $50 share. What is the sum of money?
(A) $3000
(B) $300
(C) $110
(D) $10
(E) Cannot be determined from the information given.

9. If an item which ordinarily costs $90 is discounted by 25%, what is the new selling price?
(A) $22.50
(B) $25.00
(C) $45.00
(D) $67.50
(E) $112.50

10. In the rectangle above, what is the ratio of $\dfrac{\text{area of shaded region}}{\text{area of unshaded region}}$?
(A) $\frac{1}{4}$
(B) $\frac{1}{2}$
(C) 1
(D) $\frac{2}{1}$
(E) Cannot be determined from the information given.

11. Earl can stuff advertising circulars into envelopes at the rate of 45 envelopes per minute and Ellen requires a minute and a half to stuff the same number of envelopes. Working together, how long will it take Earl and Ellen to stuff 300 envelopes?
(A) 15 minutes
(B) 4 minutes
(C) 3 minutes 30 seconds
(D) 3 minutes 20 seconds
(E) 2 minutes

12. The table above gives the distribution of two genetic characteristics, X and Y, in a population of 100 subjects. What is the ratio of $\dfrac{\text{number of subjects having X}}{\text{number of subjects having Y}}$?
(A) $\frac{7}{5}$
(B) 1
(C) $\frac{5}{7}$
(D) $\frac{7}{10}$
(E) $\frac{1}{4}$

13. If the ratio of the number of passenger vehicles to all other vehicles passing a checkpoint on a highway is 4 to 1, what percent of the vehicles passing the checkpoint are passenger vehicles?
(A) 20%
(B) 25%
(C) 75%
(D) 80%
(E) 400%

14. If the price of an item is increased by 10% and then decreased by 10%, the net effect on the price of the item is
(A) an increase of 99%
(B) an increase of 1%
(C) no change
(D) a decrease of 1%
(E) a decrease of 11%

15. Lines l_m and l_n lie in the plane x and intersect one another on the perpendicular at point P. Which of the following statements must be true?

   I. A line which lies in plane x and intersects line l_m on the perpendicular at a point other than P does not intersect l_n.

   II. Line segment MN, which does not intersect l_m, does not intersect l_n.

   III. If line l_o lies in plane y and intersects l_m and point P, plane y is perpendicular to plane x.

   (A) I only
   (B) II only
   (C) I and II only
   (D) I and III only
   (E) I, II, and III

16. A student conducts an experiment in biology lab and discovers that the ratio of the number of insects in a given population having characteristic X to the number of insects in the population not having characteristic X is 5:3, and that $\frac{3}{8}$ of the insects having characteristic X are male insects. What proportion of the total insect population are male insects having the characteristic X?

   (A) 1
   (B) $\frac{5}{8}$
   (C) $\frac{6}{13}$
   (D) $\frac{15}{64}$
   (E) $\frac{1}{5}$

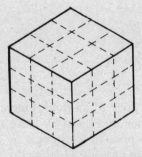

17. The figure above represents a wooden block 3 inches on an edge, all of whose faces are painted black. If the block is cut up along the dotted lines, 27 blocks result, each 1 cubic inch in volume. Of these, how many will have no painted faces?

   (A) 1
   (B) 3
   (C) 4
   (D) 5
   (E) 7

18. The fountain in the above illustration is located exactly at the center of the circular path. How many cubic feet of gravel are required to cover the circular garden path six inches deep with gravel?

   (A) 5400 π cu. ft.
   (B) 4500 π cu. ft.
   (C) 1250 π cu. ft.
   (D) 450 π cu. ft.
   (E) 5 π cu. ft.

19. A business firm reduces the number of hours its employees work from 40 hours per week to 36 hours per week while continuing to pay the same amount of money. If an employee earned x dollars per hour before the reduction in hours, how much does he earn per hour under the new system?

   (A) $\dfrac{1}{10}$

   (B) $\dfrac{x}{9}$

   (C) $\dfrac{9x}{10}$

   (D) $\dfrac{10x}{9}$

   (E) 9x

20. A painter has painted one-third of a rectangular wall which is ten feet high. When she has painted another 75 square feet of wall she will be three-quarters finished with the job. What is the length (the horizontal dimension) of the wall?

   (A) 18 feet
   (B) 12 feet
   (C) 10 feet
   (D) 9 feet
   (E) 6 feet

STOP

END OF SECTION. IF YOU HAVE ANY TIME LEFT, GO
OVER YOUR WORK IN THIS SECTION ONLY. DO NOT
WORK IN ANY OTHER SECTION OF THE TEST.

SECTION VII

Time—30 Minutes
25 Questions

Directions: Below each of the following passages, you will find questions or incomplete statements about the passage. Each statement or question is followed by lettered words or expressions. Select the word or expression that most satisfactorily completes each statement or answers each question in accordance with the meaning of the passage. After you have chosen the best answer, blacken the corresponding space on the answer sheet.

Under existing law, a new drug may be labeled, promoted, and advertised only for those conditions in which safety and effectiveness have been demonstrated and of which the Food and Drug
5 Administration (FDA) has approved, or so-called "approved uses." Other uses have come to be called "unapproved uses" and cannot be legally promoted. In a real sense, the term "unapproved" is a misnomer because it includes
10 in one phrase two categories of marketed drugs that are very different: drugs which are potentially harmful and will never be approved, and already approved drugs that have "unapproved" uses. It is common for new research and new
15 insights to demonstrate valid new uses for drugs already on the market. Also, there are numerous examples of medical progress resulting from the serendipitous observations and therapeutic innovations of physicians, both important methods of
20 discovery in the field of therapeutics. Before such advances can result in new indications for inclusion in drug labeling, however, the available data must meet the legal standard of substantial evidence derived from adequate and well-con-
25 trolled clinical trials. Such evidence may require time to develop, and, without initiative on the part of the drug firm, it may not occur at all for certain uses. However, because medical literature on new uses exists and these uses are medically
30 beneficial, physicians often use these drugs for such purposes prior to FDA review or changes in labeling. This is referred to as "unlabeled uses" of drugs.

A different problem arises when a particular
35 use for a drug has been examined scientifically and has been found to be ineffective or unsafe,

and yet physicians who either are uninformed or who refuse to accept the available scientific evidence continue to use the drug in this way.
40 Such use may have been reviewed by the FDA and rejected, or, in some cases, the use may actually be warned against in the labeling. This subset of uses may be properly termed "disapproved uses."

45 Government policy should minimize the extent of unlabeled uses. If such uses are valid—and many are—it is important that scientifically sound evidence supporting them be generated and that the regulatory system accommodate them into
50 drug labeling. Continuing rapid advances in medical care and the complexity of drug usage, however, makes it impossible for the government to keep drug labeling up to date for every conceivable situation. Thus, when a particular use
55 of this type appears, it is also important, and in the interest of good medical care, that no stigma be attached to "unapproved usage" by practitioners while the formal evidence is assembled between the time of discovery and the time the
60 new use is included in the labeling. In the case of "disapproved uses," however, it is proper policy to warn against these in the package insert. Whether use of a drug for these purposes by the uninformed or intransigent physician constitutes a
65 violation of the current Federal Food, Drug and Cosmetic Act is a matter of debate that involves a number of technical and legal issues. Regardless of that, the inclusion of disapproved uses in the form of contraindications, warnings and other
70 precautionary statements in package inserts is an important practical deterrent to improper use. Except for clearly disapproved uses, however, it is in the best interests of patient care that physicians not be constrained by regulatory stat-
75 utes from exercising their best judgment in prescribing a drug for both its approved uses and any unlabeled uses it may have.

1. The author is primarily concerned with
   (A) refuting a theory
   (B) drawing a distinction

(C) discrediting an opponent

(D) describing a new development

(E) condemning an error

2. According to the passage, an unlabeled use of a drug is any use which

(A) has been reviewed by the FDA and specifically rejected

(B) is medically beneficial despite the fact that such use is prohibited by law

(C) has medical value but has not yet been approved by FDA for inclusion as a labeled use

(D) is authorized by the label as approved by the FDA on the basis of scientific studies

(E) is made in experiments designed to determine whether a drug is medically beneficial

3. It can be inferred from the passage that the intransigent physician (line 64)

(A) continues to prescribe a drug even though he knows it is not in the best interests of the patient

(B) refuses to use a drug for an unlabeled purpose out of fear that he may be stigmatized by its use

(C) persists in using a drug for disapproved uses because he rejects the evidence of its ineffectiveness or dangers

(D) experiments with new uses for tested drugs in an attempt to find medically beneficial uses for the drugs

(E) should be prosecuted for violating the Federal Food, Drug, and Cosmetic Act in using drugs for disapproved uses

4. All of the following are mentioned in the passage as reasons for allowing unlabeled uses of drugs EXCEPT

(A) the increased cost to the patient of buying an FDA-approved drug

(B) the medical benefits which can accrue to the patient through unlabeled use

(C) the time lag between initial discovery of a medical use and FDA approval of that use

(D) the possibility that a medically beneficial use may never be clinically documented

(E) the availability of publications to inform physicians of the existence of such uses

5. With which of the following statements about the distinction between approved and unlabeled uses would the author most likely agree?

(A) Public policy statements have not adequately distinguished between uses already approved by the FDA and medically beneficial uses which have not yet been approved.

(B) The distinction between approved and unlabeled uses has been obscured because government regulatory agencies approve only those uses which have been clinically tested.

(C) Practicing physicians are in a better position than the FDA to distinguish between approved and unlabeled uses because they are involved in patient treatment on a regular basis.

(D) The distinction between approved and unlabeled uses should be discarded so that the patient can receive the full benefits of any drug use.

(E) The practice of unlabeled uses of drugs exists because of the time lag between discovery of a beneficial use and the production of data needed for FDA approval.

6. The author regards the practice of using drugs for medically valid purposes before FDA approval as

(A) a necessary compromise

(B) a dangerous policy

(C) an illegal activity

(D) an unqualified success

(E) a short-term phenomenon

7. Which of the following statements best summarizes the point of the passage?

(A) Patients have been exposed to needless medical risk because the FDA has not adequately regulated unlabeled uses as well as disapproved uses.

(B) Physicians who engage in the practice of unlabeled use make valuable contributions to medical science and should be protected from legal repercussions of such activity.

(C) Pharmaceutical firms develop and test new drugs which initially have little or no medical value but later are found to have value in unlabeled uses.

(D) Doctors prescribe drugs for disapproved purposes primarily because they fail to read manufacturers' labels or because they disagree with the clinical data about the value of drugs.

(E) The government should distinguish between unlabeled use and disapproved use of a drug, allowing the practice of unlabeled use and condemning disapproved uses.

8. Which of the following pairs of terms would the author regard as most nearly opposite?
    (A) approved use and unapproved use
    (B) approved use and disapproved use
    (C) approved use and labeled use
    (D) disapproved use and unapproved use
    (E) labeled use and legal use

The existence of both racial and sexual discrimination in employment is well documented, and policy makers and responsible employers are particularly sensitive to the plight of the black
5 female employee on the theory that she is doubly the victim of discrimination. That there exist differences in income between whites and blacks is clear, but it is not so clear that these differences are solely the result of racial discrimination in
10 employment. The two groups differ in productivity, so basic economics dictates that their incomes will differ.

To obtain a true measure of the effect of racial discrimination in employment it is necessary to
15 adjust the gross black/white income ratio for these productivity factors. White women in urban areas have a higher educational level than black women and can be expected to receive larger incomes. Moreover, state distribution of resi-
20 dence is important because blacks are overrepresented in the South where wage rates are typically lower than elsewhere and where racial differentials in income are greater. Also, blacks are overrepresented in large cities; incomes of blacks
25 would be greater if blacks were distributed among cities of different sizes in the same manner as whites.

After standardization for these productivity factors, the income of black urban women is estimated to be between 108 and 125 percent of 30 the income of white women. This indicates that productivity factors more than account for the actual white/black income differential for women. Despite their greater education, white women's *actual* median income is only 2 to 5 percent higher 35 than that of black women in the North. Unlike the situation of men, the evidence indicates that the money income of black urban women was as great as, or greater than, that of whites of similar productivity in the North, and probably in the 40 United States as a whole. For men, however, the adjusted black/white income ratio is approximately 80 percent.

At least two possible hypotheses may explain why the adjustment for productivity more than 45 accounts for the observed income differential for women, whereas the income differential persists for men. First, there may be more discrimination against black men than against black women. The different occupational structures for men and 50 women give some indication why this could be the case, and institutionalized considerations—for example, the effect of unionization in cutting competition—may also contribute. Second, the data are consistent with the hypothesis that the 55 intensity of discrimination against women differs little between whites and blacks. Therefore, racial discrimination adds little to the effects of existing sex discrimination.

These findings suggest that a black woman does 60 not necessarily suffer relatively more discrimination in the labor market than does a white woman. Rather, for women, the effects of sexual discrimination are so pervasive that the effects of racial discrimination are negligible. Of course, 65 this is not to say that the more generalized racial discrimination of which black women, like black men, are victims does not disadvantage black women in their search for work. After all, one important productivity factor is level of educa- 70 tion, and the difference between white and black women on this scale is largely the result of racial discrimination.

9. The primary purpose of the passage is to
    (A) explain the reasons for the existence of income differentials between men and women

(B) show that racial discrimination against black women in employment is less important than sexual discrimination

(C) explore the ways in which productivity factors such as level of education influence the earning power of black workers

(D) sketch a history of racial and sexual discrimination against black and female workers in the labor market

(E) offer some suggestions as to how public officials and private employers can act to solve the problem of discrimination against black women

10. According to the passage, the gross black/ white income ratio is not an accurate measure of discrimination in employment because the gross ratio

(A) fails to include large numbers of black workers who live in the large cities and in the South

(B) must be adjusted to reflect the longer number of hours and greater number of days worked by black employees

(C) represents a subjective interpretation by the statistician of the importance of factors such as educational achievement

(D) is not designed to take account of the effects of the long history of racial discrimination

(E) includes income differences attributable to real economic factors and not to discrimination

11. Which of the following best describes the relationship between the income level of black women and that of black men?

(A) In general, black men earn less money than do black women.

(B) On the average, black women in the South earn less money than do black men in large northern cities.

(C) Productivity factors have a greater dollar value in the case of black women.

(D) Black men have a higher income level than black women because black men have a higher level of education.

(E) The difference between income levels for black and white women is less than that for black and white men.

12. Which of the following best describes the logical relationship between the two hypotheses presented in lines 44–59?

(A) The two hypotheses may both be true since each phenomenon could contribute to the observed differential.

(B) The two hypothess are contradictory, and if one is proved to be correct, the other is proved incorrect.

(C) The two hypotheses are dependent on each other, and empirical disconfirmation of the one is disconfirmation of the other.

(D) The two hypotheses are logically connected, so that proof of the first entails the truth of the second.

(E) The two hypotheses are logically connected, so that it is impossible to prove either one to be true without also proving the other to be true.

13. Which of the following best describes the tone of the passage?

(A) confident and overbearing

(B) ill-tempered and brash

(C) Objective and critical

(D) tentative and inconclusive

(E) hopeful and optimistic

14. If the second hypothesis mentioned by the author (lines 54–59) is correct, a general lessening of the discrimination against women should lead to

(A) a higher white/black income ratio for women

(B) a lower white/black income ratio for women

(C) a lower female/male income ratio

(D) an increase in the productivity of women

(E) an increase in the level of education of women

15. The author's attitude toward racial and sexual discrimination in employment can best be described as one of

(A) apology

(B) concern

(C) indifference

(D) indignation

(E) anxiety

16. The author mentions which of the following as factors which ought to be taken into consideration in determining the actual median income of a group?

    I. the level of education of group members

   II. wage levels in geographical regions where group members are employed

  III. the average number of years of group members in work force

(A) I only
(B) II only
(C) I and II only
(D) I and III only
(E) I, II, and III

Helplessness and passivity are central themes in describing human depression. Laboratory experiments with animals have uncovered a phenomenon designated "learned helplessness." Dogs
5 given inescapable shock initially show intense emotionality, but later become passive in the same situation. When the situation is changed from inescapable to escapable shock, the dogs fail to escape even though escape is possible. Neuro-
10 chemical changes resulting from learned helplessness produce an avoidance–escape deficit in laboratory animals.

Is the avoidance deficit caused by prior exposure to inescapable shock learned helplessness or
15 is it simply stress-induced noradrenergic deficiency leading to a deficit in motor activation? Avoidance-escape deficit can be produced in rats by stress alone, i.e., by a brief swim in cold water. But a deficit produced by exposure to extremely
20 traumatic events must be produced by a very different mechanism than the deficit produced by exposure to the less traumatic uncontrollable aversive events in the learned-helplessness experiments. A nonaversive parallel to the learned
25 helplessness induced by uncontrollable shock, e.g., induced by uncontrollable food delivery, produces similar results. Moreover, studies have shown the importance of prior experience in learned helplessness. Dogs can be "immunized"
30 against learned helplessness by prior experience with controllable shock. Rats also show a "mastery effect" after extended experience with escapable shock. They work far longer trying to escape

from inescapable shock than do rats lacking this prior mastery experience. Conversely, weanling 35 rats given inescapable shock fail to escape shock as adults. These adult rats are also poor to nonaversive discrimination learning.

Certain similarities have been noted between conditions produced in animals by the learned- 40 helplessness procedure and by the experimental neurosis paradigm. In the latter, animals are first trained on a discrimination task and are then tested with discriminative stimuli of increasing similarity. Eventually, as the discrimination be- 45 comes very difficult, animals fail to respond and begin displaying abnormal behaviors: first agitation, then lethargy.

It has been suggested that both learned helplessness and experimental neurosis involve inhibi- 50 tion of motivation centers and pathways by limbic forebrain inhibitory centers, especially in the septal area. The main function of this inhibition is compensatory, providing relief from anxiety or distress. In rats subjected to the learned-helpless- 55 ness and experimental-neurosis paradigms, stimulation of the septum produces behavioral arrest, lack of behavioral initiation and lethargy, while rats with septal lesions do not show learned helplessness. 60

How analogous the model of learned helplessness and the paradigm of stress-induced neurosis are to human depression is not entirely clear. Inescapable noise or unsolvable problems have been shown to result in conditions in humans 65 similar to those induced in laboratory animals, but an adequate model of human depression must also be able to account for the cognitive complexity of human depression.

17. The primary purpose of the passage is to
 (A) propose a cure for depression in human beings
 (B) discuss research possibly relevant to depression in human beings
 (C) criticize the result of experiments which induce depression in laboratory animals
 (D) raise some questions about the propriety of using laboratory animals for research
 (E) suggest some ways in which depression in animals differs from depression in humans

18. The author raises the question at the beginning of the second paragraph in order to
    - (A) prove that learned helplessness is caused by neurochemical changes
    - (B) demonstrate that learned helplessness is also caused by nonaversive discrimination learning
    - (C) suggest that further research is needed to determine the exact causes of learned helplessness
    - (D) refute a possible objection based on an alternative explanation of the cause of learned helplessness
    - (E) express doubts about the structure of the experiments which created learned helplessness in dogs

19. It can be inferred from the passage that rats with septal lesions (lines 59–60) do not show learned helplessness because
    - (A) such rats were immunized against learned helplessness by prior training
    - (B) the lesions blocked communication between the limbic forebrain inhibitory centers and motivation centers
    - (C) the lesions prevented the rats from understanding the inescapability of the helplessness situation
    - (D) a lack of stimulation of the septal area does not necessarily result in excited behavior
    - (E) lethargy and other behavior associated with learned helplessness can be induced by the neurosis paradigm

20. It can be inferred that the most important difference between experiments inducing learned helplessness by inescapable shock and the nonaversive parallel mentioned at line 24 is that the nonaversive parallel
    - (A) did not use pain as a stimuli to be avoided
    - (B) failed to induce learned helplessness in subject animals
    - (C) reduced the extent of learned helplessness
    - (D) caused a more traumatic reaction in the animals
    - (E) used only rats rather than dogs as subjects

21. The author cites the "mastery effect" primarily in order to
    - (A) prove the avoidance deficit caused by

exposure to inescapable shock is not caused by shock per se but by the inescapability
    - (B) cast doubts on the validity of models of animal depression when applied to depression in human beings
    - (C) explain the neurochemical changes in the brain which cause learned helplessness
    - (D) suggest that the experimental-neurosis paradigm and the learned-helplessness procedure produce similar behavior in animals
    - (E) argue that learned helplessness is simply a stress-induced noradrenergic deficiency

22. Which of the following would be the most logical continuation of the passage?
    - (A) an explanation of the connection between the septum and the motivation centers of the brains of rats
    - (B) an examination of techniques used to cure animals of learned helplessness
    - (C) a review of experiments designed to created stress-induced noradrenergic deficiencies in humans
    - (D) a proposal for an experiment to produce learned helplessness and experimental neurosis in humans
    - (E) an elaboration of the differences between human depression and similar animal behavior

23. In developing her argument, the author relies on conclusions based on all of the following EXCEPT
    - (A) studies of humans exposed to inescapable noise
    - (B) experiments exposing animals to inescapable shock
    - (C) experiments exposing animals to escapable shock
    - (D) reports on neurochemical changes in experimental subjects
    - (E) programs to cure human beings of learned helplessness

24. The author regards any conclusions about human depression based upon studies of laboratory animals as
    - (A) unwarranted

(B) confirmed
(C) tentative
(D) disproved
(E) disingenuous

25. An avoidance-escape deficit (line 17) refers to the
    (A) failure of a laboratory animal to swim when immersed in cold water
    (B) failure of a subject to take normal actions to avoid or escape an undesirable situation
    (C) improved ability of animals to make decisions after proper training
    (D) reduced ability of a subject to discriminate among very similar simuli
    (E) stress artificially induced in a laboratory animal by subjecting it to trauma

STOP

END OF SECTION. IF YOU HAVE ANY TIME LEFT, GO OVER YOUR WORK IN THIS SECTION ONLY. DO NOT WORK IN ANY OTHER SECTION OF THE TEST.

ANSWER KEY—PRACTICE EXAMINATION 2

SECTION I

1.	B	8.	B	15.	A	22.	D
2.	D	9.	C	16.	E	23.	C
3.	B	10.	A	17.	E	24.	B
4.	D	11.	D	18.	A	25.	A
5.	E	12.	C	19.	D		
6.	C	13.	A	20.	E		
7.	B	14.	E	21.	A		

SECTION II

1.	D	6.	A	11.	C	16.	C
2.	E	7.	B	12.	C	17.	C
3.	C	8.	A	13.	D	18.	D
4.	C	9.	E	14.	C	19.	A
5.	E	10.	A	15.	E	20.	D

SECTION III

1.	D	8.	C	15.	D	22.	C
2.	E	9.	D	16.	D	23.	A
3.	C	10.	E	17.	E	24.	E
4.	B	11.	B	18.	D	25.	A
5.	C	12.	C	19.	E		
6.	C	13.	B	20.	B		
7.	B	14.	B	21.	B		

SECTION IV

1.	D	8.	D	15.	C	22.	E
2.	D	9.	C	16.	A	23.	D
3.	C	10.	D	17.	B	24.	B
4.	B	11.	A	18.	B	25.	B
5.	A	12.	C	19.	D		
6.	B	13.	D	20.	B		
7.	E	14.	B	21.	E		

SECTION V

1.	C	6.	B	11.	B	16.	C
2.	C	7.	A	12.	B	17.	B
3.	A	8.	C	13.	C	18.	D
4.	C	9.	B	14.	D	19.	D
5.	D	10.	A	15.	A	20.	D

SECTION VI

1.	C	6.	C	11.	B	16.	D
2.	B	7.	C	12.	D	17.	A
3.	B	8.	B	13.	D	18.	D
4.	E	9.	D	14.	D	19.	D
5.	C	10.	C	15.	A	20.	A

SECTION VII

1.	B	8.	B	15.	B	22.	E
2.	C	9.	B	16.	C	23.	E
3.	C	10.	E	17.	B	24.	C
4.	A	11.	E	18.	D	25.	B
5.	E	12.	A	19.	B		
6.	A	13.	C	20.	A		
7.	E	14.	A	21.	A		

EXPLANATORY ANSWERS

Section I

1. **(B)** The proposition that you cannot argue with taste says that taste is relative. Since we are looking for an answer choice inconsistent with that proposition, we seek an answer choice that argues that taste, or aesthetic value, is absolute, or at least not relative—that there are standards of taste. (B) is precisely that.

   (C) and (D) are just distractions, playing on the notion of taste in the physical sense and the further idea of the distasteful; but these superficial connections are not strong enough.

   (A), (B), and (E) are all activities in which there is some element of aesthetic judgment or appreciation. In (A), the holding of an exhibition, while implying some selection principle and thus some idea of a standard of taste, does not truly purport to judge aesthetics in the way that (B), precisely a beauty *contest*, does. The exhibition may be of historical or biographical interest, for example. (E) also stresses more of the exhibition aspect than the judging aspect. You should not infer that all movie festivals are contests, since the word "festival" does not require this interpretation and, in fact, there are festivals at which the judging aspect is minimal or non-existent. The Cannes Film Festival, while perhaps the best known, is not the only type of movie festival there is. The questions are not tests of your knowledge of the movie industry.

2. **(D)** Note the question stem very carefully: We are to find the answer choice *from which* we can deduce the sample argument. You must pay very careful attention to the question stem in every problem. (D) works very nicely as it gives us the argument structure: All post-1974 students are required. . . . George is a post-1974 student. Therefore, George is required. . . ." Actually, the middle premise is phrased in the conditional (with an "if"), but our explanation is close enough, even if it is a bit oversimplified. (A) will not suffice, for while it describes the situation before 1974, it just does not address itself to the post-1974 situation. And George is a post-1974 student. (B) also fails. From the fact that all of those who took the course graduated after 1974, we cannot conclude that George was one of them (any more than we can conclude from the proposition that all airline flight attendants lived after 1900 and that Richard Nixon, who lived after 1900, was one of them). (C) fails for the same reason that (A) fails. (E) is a bit tricky because of the double negative. It makes the sentence awkward. The easiest way to handle such a sentence is to treat the double negative as an affirmative. The negative cancels the negative, just as in arithmetic a negative number times a negative number yields a positive number. So (E) actually says that before 1974 the course was not required. That is equivalent to (A) and must be wrong for the same reason.

3. **(B)** II is the only one of the three which is completely supported by the argument. III is easily dismissed. That there are no minnows on this side of the lake now surely does not mean that there will never be any, any more than the fact that there are no children in the park now means that there never will be any children in the park. I is very close to II and differs only in the qualification introduced by the word "probably," but that is an important qualification. The author states specifically that bass are *usually* found wherever there are minnows. So where there are no bass, he *expects* to find no minnows. But, of course, he cannot be certain. Perhaps there are other reasons for the absence of bass: The water is too cold or too shallow or too muddy for bass, though not for minnows. So I overstates the case. The author apparently allows that you may find minnows without bass—but not usually.

4. **(D)** Juanita wonders how Tommy knows the phone has rung if he couldn't hear it because of the shower. She overlooks the possibility that he learned the phone had rung without actually hear-

ing it himself. Perhaps someone else lives with him who heard it; perhaps Tommy has an answering machine and later learned that the phone rang while he was in the shower; maybe the caller calls back and tells Tommy he called earlier and Tommy says "Oh, I must have been in the shower and didn't hear it." Juanita overlooks these possibilities. (A) is incorrect because Juanita apparently assumes the phone does ring and that Tommy can hear it ringing. (C) and (E) may or may not be true, but they do not address themselves to Juanita's statement. (B) could only underlie Juanita's objection to Tommy's remarks if hearing calls were the only possible way in which Tommy could learn of the call. But as we show, there are other possibilities.

5. **(E)** I is not inconsistent with the advertisement since the ad is touting the strength of the pain-reliever, not its price. III, too, can easily be seen not to be inconsistent. The ad speaks of non-prescription pain-relievers, but III brings up the irrelevant matter of prescription pain-relievers. II is not inconsistent because RELIEF does not claim to be the one strong*est* pain-reliever, only that no other non-prescription pain-reliever is stronger. So none of the statements contradicts the ad.

6. **(C)** III is an assumption of the psychologist. He observed the dogs for a certain period of time, and found that each time a stranger approached they kept silent. From those observed instances he concluded that the dogs never barked at strangers. Obviously his theory would be disproved (or at least it would have to be seriously qualified) if, when he was not watching, the dogs barked their heads off at strangers. I is not assumed, however. The psychologist was concerned only with the dogs' reactions to strangers. As far as we know, he may have seen the dogs barking during a frolic in the park, or while they were being bathed, or at full moon. II is not an assumption the author makes. The author makes a factual claim: Dogs treated in this way do not bark at strangers. We have no basis for concluding that the author does or does not think that dogs ought or ought not to bark at strangers. In fact, it seems as likely that the author thinks a great way to train watchdogs is to hit them with rolled-up newspapers.

7. **(B)** II would undermine the psychologist's thesis that "only a beaten dog barks." It cites instances

in which the dog was not beaten and still barked at strangers. This would force the psychologist to reconsider his conclusion about the connection between beating and barking. I is not like II. It does not state the dogs were never beaten; it states only that the dogs were not beaten when they barked at strangers. It is conceivable that they were beaten at other times. If they were, then even though they might bark at strangers (and not be beaten at that moment), they would not be counter-examples to the psychologist's theory. III is not an assumption of the psychologist, as we saw in the preceding question, so denying it does not affect the strength of his argument. The psychologist is concerned with the factual connection between beating a dog and its barking; information about the owners' feelings can hardly be relevant to the factual issue.

8. **(B)** Here the author must assume that every effect which is part of the child's experience has been generated by a cause which was also a part of the child's experience, but that is possible only on the assumption that the cause, which is an effect itself, is the result of some previous cause. In other words, every effect flows from some earlier effect. Now, admittedly, that seems to lead to a pretty absurd conclusion: Therefore, there could be no beginning of experience for the child—it must stretch back infinitely. But the question stem does not ask us to critique the argument, only to analyze it and uncover its premises. (A) is wrong because the author does not say all experiences are alike, only that the one today has its roots in the one yesterday. For example, sometimes the presence of moisture in the atmosphere causes rain, sometimes snow. (C) oversimplifies matters in two respects. One, while the author may agree that a child's experiences may tell us *something* about the parents (assuming the child is in intimate contact with them), we surely would not want to conclude that is the *best* way to learn about the parents. Two, the parents are not the only source of experience the child has, so the later effects would be the result of non-parental causes as well. (D) is incorrect because the author need not assume that experience is cumulative. In some cases, the cause-and-effect sequence may only reiterate itself so that experience is circular rather than cumulative. Finally, (E) is another example of going too far—of extending a simple factual statement beyond the scope the author originally gave it. Here the author says that experience causes experience, but he never suggests

that we are in a position to use this principle practically, to manipulate the input to mold the child.

9. **(C)** The author's claim is that we have unbounded resources, and he tries to prove this by showing that we are getting better and better at extracting those resources from the ground. But that is like saying, "I have found a way to get the last little bit of toothpaste out of the tube; therefore, the tube will never run out." (C) calls our attention to this oversight. (A) does not contradict the author's claim. In fact, it seems to support it. He might suggest, "Even if we run out of fossil fuels, we still have uranium for nuclear power." Now, this is not to suggest that he would. The point is only to show that (A) supports rather than undermines the author's contention. (B) is an attack on the author's general stance, but it does not really *contradict* the particular conclusion he draws. The author says, "We have enough." (B) says, "It is expensive." Both could very well be true, so they cannot contradict one another. (D) is similar to (B). Yes, you may be correct, the technology is expensive, or in this case wasteful, but it will still get us the fuel we need. Finally, (E) is incorrect for pretty much these same reasons. Yes, the energy will have unwanted side effects, but the author claimed only that we could get the energy. The difficulty with (B), (D), and (E) is that though they attack the author's general *position,* though they undermine his general suggestion, they do not *contradict* his *conclusion.*

Questions 10–12

10. **(A)** 11. **(D)** 12. **(C)** Argument (A) is circular. It is like saying, "I never tell a lie; and you must believe that because, as I have just told you, I never tell a lie." So (A) is the answer to question 10. (E) might seem circular: Guns do not cause crimes, people do. But it is not. The author's point is that these crimes would be committed anyway, and he explains how they would be committed. (C) is an *ad hominem* attack. It rejects the conclusion of the argument not because the argument is illogical but because it comes from a particular source. Remember, not all *ad hominem* are illegitimate. It is perfectly all right to inquire into possible biases of the source, and that is just what occurs here. So (C) is the answer to question 12. (D) is a fairly weak argument. It takes a handful of observed instances and generalizes to a strong conclusion. But even

though it may be weak, it does fit the description "generalization," so (D) is the answer to question 11. (B) is just left over and fits none of the descriptions.

13. **(A)** The author places himself in opposition to the sociologists whom he cites. He claims an alternative interpretation of the evidence. In other words, the most logical continuation of the passage will be the one which explains why such sects are not a recent phenomenon even though there are no old ones around. (A) does this neatly. Since the members abstain from sexual relations, they will not reproduce members and the sect will tend to die out. This explains why there are none more than 50 or 60 years old. (C), if anything, supports the position of the sociologists, for it implicitly gives up trying to explain the evidence differently and also undercuts the explanation the author might have given. (B) is irrelevant because intensity of religious fervor is irrelevant to the length of the sect's existence; it cannot possibly help the author explain away the evidence of the sociologists. (D) is irrelevant for another reason. The author needs to explain why the sects are all relatively young without having recourse to the thesis of the sociologists that they are a recent phenomenon. That there are other organizations which encourage sexual relations of whatever kind cannot help the author explain a phenomenon such as the Waiters. Finally, (E) is a distraction, picking up as it does on a minor detail. The author needs to explain the short-livedness of groups of which the Waiters is only an example.

14. **(E)** The conclusion of the speaker is that the checkup has *no* value, so anything which suggests the checkup does have value will undermine the conclusion. I shows a possible advantage of having the checkup. It says, in effect, while the checkup is not foolproof and will not catch everything, it does catch some fairly important things. II also gives us a possible reason for visiting our mechanic for a 5,000-mile checkup. Even if it won't keep our car in running order, it is necessary if we want to take advantage of our warranty. Finally, III also gives us a good reason to have a checkup: The mechanic will make some routine adjustments. All three of these propositions, then, mention possible advantages of having a checkup. So all three weaken the author's conclusion that the checkup is *worthless* and a waste of money and time.

15. **(A)** Here we are looking for the most perfect analogy. Keep in mind, first, that the author opposes the move, and second, all of the features of the union-management situation in particular that they are adversaries. (A) captures both elements. The relationship between prison administrators and inmates is adversarial, and the suggestion that inmates make decisions on security is outrageous enough that it captures also the first element. (B) fails on both counts. First, the two are not on opposites of the fence; second, the senior officer is *asking* for advice——not deferring to the opinion of his junior officer. (C) is very similar. First, the administration of the university and the student body are not necessarily adversaries; at least, although they may disagree on the best means for advancing the goals of the university, there is often agreement about those goals. Second, the administration is, as with (B), *asking* advice, not abdicating responsibility for the decision. In (D) we lack both elements; the mayor need not be an adversary of the state legislators (he may be seeking their assistance), nor is he giving them his authority to make decisions. Finally, (E) lacks both elements as well; the minister is a leader, not an adversary, who is discussing questions, not delegating authority.

16. **(E)** The author's reason for rejecting the notion of labor participation in management decisions is that the labor leaders first have a responsibility to the people they represent and that the responsibility would color their thinking about the needs of the corporation. His thinking is reflected in the adage: No man can serve two masters. (B) is incorrect for the author is referring to the labor *leaders,* not the rank-and-file; and he specifically mentions that the leaders are skilled administrators. (D) is incorrect because it, too, fails to respect the distinction between union leader and union member. (A) is a distraction. The notion that the authority would be "symbolically undermined" is edifying but finds no support in the paragraph. In any event, it entirely misses the main point of the paragraph as we have explained it. (C) also fails to observe the distinction between leader and worker, not to mention also that it is only remotely connected with the discussion.

17. **(E)** The question stem advises us that the inconsistency is only "seeming." (E) explains it away. Of the total population, 70 percent take X and 30 percent take Y, yet only 75 percent of the population take anything at all. This means that some people took both X and Y. (A) is close, but it gets no cigar. While we can infer that there must be some overlap, we cannot conclude that the 30 percent is totally contained within the 70 percent. It is possible that only 25 percent of the population take both. In that case, we would have 5 percent who take Y only, 45 percent who take X only, and 25 percent who take both X and Y. This still leaves 25 percent of the population who take neither. (B) seems totally unrelated to the logic of the argument. As for (C) and (D), while these are possible weaknesses in any statistical argument, there is nothing to indicate that they operate here specifically.

18. **(A)** If II is true, then both independent clauses of II must be true. This is because a sentence which has the form "P and Q" (Eddie is tall and John is short) can be true only if both subparts are true. If either is false (Eddie is not tall or John is not short) or if both are false, then the entire sentence makes a false claim. If the second clause of II is true, then I must also be true, for I is actually equivalent to the second clause in II. That is, if "P and Q" is true then Q must itself be true. On this basis, (B) and (C) can be seen to be incorrect. (D) is wrong, for we can actually define the interrelationship of I and II as a matter of logic: We do not have to have recourse to a probabilistic statement; i.e., it is *unlikely.* (E) is incorrect since a statement of the form "P and Q" might be false and Q could still be true——if P is false, "P and Q" is false even though Q is true.

19. **(D)** Again, let us resort to the use of capital letters to make it easier to talk about the propositions. Incidentally, you may or may not find this technique useful under test conditions. Some people do, but others do not. We use it here because it makes explanation easier. Let us render the four premises as:

(1) All B are R. (All Buckner are Reserve)
(2) All R are P. (All Reserve are Priceless)
(3) No H is R. (No Hemingway is Reserve)
(4) All R are C. (All Reserve are Catalogue)

From this we can deduce: (5) All B are P. (using 1 and 2)
and: (6) No H is B. (using 1 and 3)

Since "no B is H" is equivalent to "no H is B" (there is no overlap between the two categories), (D) must be our correct answer. From (2), we would not want to conclude "all P are R," any more than we would go from "all station wagons are cars" to "all cars are station wagons"; so (A) is not a proper inference and cannot be our answer. As for (B), we can show that "all B are C" (using 1 and 4) and also "all B are P" (5), so we would be wrong in concluding that "no B are not P." As for (C), while we know that "no H is R," we would not want to conclude that "no H is P." After all, books by Hemingway may be priceless, but the Buckner collection and the Reserve Room may just not contain any. Finally, (E) is not deducible from our four propositions. We cannot deduce "all C is R" from "all R is C."

20. **(E)** Now, it must be admitted that a liar can abuse just about any word in the English language, and so it is true that each of the five answer choices is *conceivably* correct. But it is important to keep in mind that you are looking for the BEST answer, which will be the one word which, more than all the others, is likely to be abused. As for (A), while there may be different ways of doing a random selection, we should be able to decide whether a sample was, in fact, selected fairly. Although the ad may be lying about the selection of participants in the study, we should be able to determine whether they are lying. In other words, though they may not have selected the sample randomly, they cannot escape by saying, "Oh, by *random* we meant anyone who liked the Goblin." The same is true of (C), *first*. That is a fairly clear term. You add up the answers you got, and one will be at the top of the list. The same is true of (D), a "response" is an answer. Now, (B) is open to manipulation. By asking our question correctly, that is, by finagling a bit with what we mean by "handling," we can influence the answers we get. For example, compare: "Did you find the Goblin handled well?" "Did you find the Goblin had a nice steering wheel?" "Did you find the wheel was easy to turn?" We could keep it up until we found a question that worked out to give a set of "responses" from "randomly" selected drivers who would rank the Goblin "first." Now, if the one category itself is susceptible to manipulation, imagine how much easier it will be to manipulate a "composite" category. We have only to take those individual categories in which the Goblin scored well, construct from them a "composite" category, and announce the Goblin "first" in the overall category. There is also the question of how the composite was constructed, weighted, added, averaged, etc.

21. **(A)** The explanation given is no explanation at all. It is like a mechanic saying to a motorist, "Your car did not get over this steep hill because it did not have enough grade climbing power." While the author may have speculated about when and how his death would occur, it cannot be said that his explanation was speculative. So (A) is correct, not (B). Of course, since the explanation is merely circular, it cannot be considered medically sound, any more than our hypothetical mechanic's answer is sound as a matter of automotive engineering, so (D) must be wrong. As for (C), while the author's *announcement* may be self-serving, designed to aggrandize his reputation, the *explanation* he gives in the announcement is not. Finally, the explanation is not self-authenticating, that is, it does not provide that standard by which its own validity is to be measured. So (E) can be overruled.

22. **(D)** It is important not to attribute more to an author than he actually says or implies. Here the author states only that Ronnie's range is narrow so he will not be an *outstanding vocalist*. *Vocalizing* is only one kind of music career, so I, which speaks of professional *musicians*, takes us far beyond the claim the author actually makes. II also goes beyond what the author says. He never specifies what range an outstanding vocalist needs, much less what range is required to vocalize without being outstanding. Finally, III is an assumption since the author moves from a physical characteristic to a conclusion regarding ability.

23. **(C)** You should remember that there is a very important distinction between "numbers" and "percentages." For example, an increase from one murder per year to two murders per year can be described as a "whopping big 100% increase." The argument speaks only of percentages, so we would not want to conclude anything about the numbers underlying those percentages. Therefore, both (A) and (B) are incorrect. They speak of "more agents," and "more people," and those are numbers rather than percentages. Furthermore, if we would not want to draw a conclusion about numbers from data given in percentage terms, we surely would not want to base on percentages a conclusion about efficiency or work accomplished. Thus, (D) and (E) are incorrect. What makes (C) the best answer of the five

is the possibility of making percentage comparisons *within* each agency. Within both agencies, the number of field agents increased by a greater *percentage or proportion* than the non-field agents.

24. **(B)** This is essentially an analogy question. Argument from analogy is an important form of argument, and the GMAT has many different ways of determining whether or not a student can use that argumentative technique. In this question, we are looking for the tool which is most analogous to a rule-of-thumb moral principle. Our task is made easier by the string of adjectives that follows the blank. We need a tool which is useful in many situations, which rules out a tuning fork (D) and an electrical generator (C), both of which have highly specialized functions. Moreover, we need a tool which requires no special training, so we can eliminate answer (A). Finally, although a library book requires no special training, it has only one use—to be read. Though the knowledge it contains may be generally useful, the book itself, *qua* book, has only one use.

25. **(A)** The point of the passage is that a moral decision sometimes seems difficult because we are using moral principles which are too general. They work most of the time, but sometimes they are too abstract, and as a result, two or more of them give contradictory results. (D) and (E) are wrong, then, for they confuse the value of abstract and particular principles. When a conflict arises, we need principles which are more specific, not more abstract, (D) and particularly (E). (C) is a distraction; the medical character of the example was purely fortuitous and irrelevant to the author's point about moral reasoning. (B) is edifying but hardly a logical completion of the paragraph. The author is not trying to explain advances in moral reasoning; he is explaining two different levels of moral reasoning available to us now.

Section II

1. **(D)** The minute hand will make one complete circle of the dial by 7:15. Then it will complete another half circle by 7:45. Since there are 360° in a circle, the arc travelled by the minute hand will be one full 360° plus half of another full 360°, yielding 360° + 180° = 540°.

2. **(E)** One way of solving this problem would be to convert each of the fractions to a decimal or find a common denominator so that a direct comparison can be made. This is too time-consuming. Instead, anytime the GMAT asks a question similar to this one, the student can be confident that there is very likely some shortcut available. Here the shortcut is to recognize that every answer choice, except for (E), is either equal to or greater than $\frac{1}{2}$. $\frac{7}{8}$ and $\frac{8}{9}$ are clearly much larger than $\frac{1}{2}$. $\frac{7}{12}$ must be greater than $\frac{1}{2}$ since $\frac{6}{12}$ is equal to $\frac{1}{2}$. But $\frac{6}{17}$ is less than $\frac{1}{2}$—$\frac{6}{12}$ would be $\frac{1}{2}$. So (E) is the smallest of the fractions. Even if the shortcut had eliminated only two or three answers, it would have been worthwhile.

3. **(C)** Even though it is not absolutely necessary to draw a figure to solve this problem, anyone finding the solution elusive will likely profit from a "return to basics":

$$\frac{3x}{4} + 1 \qquad \boxed{} \qquad \frac{3x}{4} + 1 \qquad P = 4\left(\frac{3x}{4} + 1\right)$$

Quickly sketching the figure may help you avoid the mistake of multiplying the side of the square by another side, giving the area, answer (D), not the perimeter. The perimeter will be 4s, not s²: $4\left(\frac{3x}{4} + 1\right) = \frac{12x}{4} + 4 = 3x + 4$.

4. **(C)** Average speed is nothing more than miles traveled over the time taken: $\text{rate speed} = \frac{\text{distance}}{\text{time}}$. The elapsed time here is 4 hours and 48 minutes. 48 minutes is $\frac{4}{5}$ hours. Our formula then will be: $\frac{240 \text{ miles}}{4\frac{4}{5}}$. We attack the problem by converting the denominator to a fraction: $4\frac{4}{5} = \frac{24}{5}$, and then we invert and multiply:

$$\frac{240 \text{ miles}}{4\frac{4}{5}} = \frac{240}{\frac{24}{5}} = \frac{5 \times 240}{24} = \text{miles/hr.}$$

Notice that setting up the problem in this way avoids a lot of needless arithmetic. This is characteristic of the GMAT. Most problems do not require a lengthy calculation. Usually the numbers used in constructing the questions are selected in a way that will allow for cancelling, factoring, or other shortcut devices. On the test, fractions are usually easier to work with than decimals.

5. **(E)** Multiplication is both associative and commutative. By associative, we mean that the grouping of the elements is not important—for example, $(5 \times 6) \times 7 = 5 \times (6 \times 7)$. By commutative we mean that the order of the elements is unimportant—for example, $5 \times 6 = 6 \times 5$. So (A), (B), (C), and (D) are all alternative forms for m(nop), but (E) is not: $(mn)(mo)(mp) = m^3nop$.

6. **(A)** There is an easy and a more complicated way to handle this question. The more complex method is to begin with the formula for the area of a triangle: Area = $\frac{1}{2}$(altitude)(base). Since angle CBE is equal to angle E, BC must be equal to CE, and it is possible to reduce the altitude to the base (or vice versa). So Area = $\frac{1}{2}$(side)². The area is 8, so $8 = \frac{1}{2}s^2$, and s = 4. Of course, s is also the side of the square, so the area of the square ABCD is s² or 16.

Now, an easier method of solving the problem is to recognize that BC and CE are equal to sides of the square ABCD, so the area of BCE is simply half that of the square. So the square must be double the triangle, or 16. A 45–45–90 right triangle is half of a square, and its hypotenuse is the diagonal of the square.

7. **(B)** Although some students will be able to solve this problem without the use of a diagram, for most drawing the floor plan of the closet is the logical starting point:

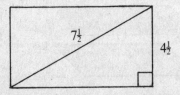

Now it becomes clear that the Pythagorean Theorem is the key to solving this problem. Once the dimensions are converted to fractions, the problem is simplified further: the triangle is a 3–4–5 right triangle ($\frac{9}{2}$, $\frac{12}{2}$, $\frac{15}{2}$). The two legs of the right triangle are simultaneously the width and length of the rectangle. So the area of the closet is: $\frac{9}{2} \times 6 = \frac{54}{2} = 27$.

8. **(A)** There are four times as many women as there are men, so if there are x men in the meet-

ing, there are 4x women. This means that there is a total of 5x persons in the meeting (x + 4x). Since the men are x men out of a total of 5x, the men constitute one-fifth, or 20%. Choices (D) and (E) can be avoided by noting that there are more women than men in the room and men thus come to less than 50%.

9. **(E)** This is an unusual problem, one which requires careful reading rather than some clever mathematical insight. The question asks us to compare the fractions in the form $\frac{P}{Q}$ with the decimal .PQ. For example, we convert the fraction $\frac{1}{8}$ into the decimal .18 for purposes of comparison and ask how closely the second approximates the first. Since $\frac{1}{8}$ is .125, we see that the fit is not a very precise one. Similarly, with $\frac{2}{9}$, the corresponding decimal we are to compare is .29, but the actual decimal equivalent of $\frac{2}{9}$ is .22$\frac{2}{9}$. The equivalent for $\frac{3}{4}$ is .34, not even close to the actual decimal equivalent of .75. Similarly, for $\frac{4}{5}$, the artificially derived .45 is not very close to the actual decimal equivalent of .80; but for $\frac{8}{9}$ we use the decimal .89, and this is fairly close—the closest of all the fractions listed—to the actual decimal equivalent of $\frac{8}{9}$, which is .888.

If you have difficulties in finding the decimals for fractions, try to relate the fractions to percentages, which are in hundredths, or to other, more common decimal-fraction equivalencies. For example, one-third is probably known to you as approximately .33 or 33%. A ninth is one-third of a third; hence a ninth is approximately 33%/3 = 11% or .11. Eight-ninths is thus 8(11%) = 88%.

10. **(A)** If a problem seems a bit too abstract to handle using algebraic notation, a sometimes useful technique is to try to find a similar, more familiar situation. For example, virtually everyone could answer the following question: Books cost $5 each; how many books can be bought for $100? The calculation goes: $\frac{1 \text{ book}}{\$5} \times \$100 = 20$ books. So, too, here the number of books which can be purchased per d dollars must be multiplied by the number of dollars to be spent, m: $\frac{b}{d} \times m$, or $\frac{bm}{d}$. Pursuing this line of attack, it might be worthwhile to point out that substitution of real numbers in problems like this is often an effective way of solving the problem. Since the variables and the formulas are general—that is, they do

not depend upon any given number of books or dollars—the correct answer choice must work for all possible values. Suppose we assume, therefore, 2(b) books can be purchased for $5(d), and that the amount to be spent is $50(m). Most people can fall back onto common sense to calculate the number of books that can be purchased with $50: 20 books. But of the five formulas offered as answer choices, only (A) gives the number 20 when the values are substituted: For

$b = 2$, $d = 5$ and $m = 50$, (A) $= \dfrac{(2)(50)}{5} = 20$,

(B) $= (2)(5)(50) = 500$, (C) $= \dfrac{5}{(2)(50)} = \dfrac{1}{20}$,

(D) $= \dfrac{2 + 50}{5} = \dfrac{52}{5}$, (E) $= \dfrac{2 - 50}{5} = \dfrac{-48}{5}$.

Substitution will take longer than a direct algebraic approach, but it is much better than simply guessing if you have the time and can't get the algebra to work right.

11. **(C)** The formula for the area of a square is *side times side*. Since the square has an area of 16, we know $s \times s = 16$, $s^2 = 16$, so side = 4. Then we compute the perimeter of the square as the sum of the lengths of its four sides: $4 + 4 + 4 + 4 = 16$.

12. **(C)** Since John has more money than Mary, we note that x is greater than y. Then, John has less money than Bill has, so x is less than z. This gives us $x > y$ or $y < x$ and $x < z$. Thus (C), $y < x < z$.

13. **(D)** One way to attack this question is to multiply the expression $(x - y)^2$ and then substitute the value 3 for x. $(x - y)^2 = 4$, so $x^2 - 2xy + y^2 = 4$. Then, if $x = 3$, we have $(3)^2 - 2(3)y + y^2 = 4$, or $9 - 6y + y^2 = 4$. Now we rewrite that in standard form (grouping like terms and arranging terms in descending order of exponents): $y^2 - 6y + 5 = 0$. At this juncture, the mathematicians will factor the expression on the left: $(y - 5)(y - 1) = 0$. Thus, the two roots of the equation are 5 and 1. So, 5 is a possible value.

Of course, a non-mathematical attack is also possible. We know that one of the five answers must be correct. So, we can simply try each one until we find one that will fit in the equation. For this we begin by putting 3 in for x: $(3 - y)^2 = 4$. We then test (A): $(3 - -5)^2 = (8)^2 = 64$ and $64 \neq 4$, so we know that -5 is not a possible value for y. On the other hand, if we try (D): (3 -

$5)^2 = (-2)^2 = 4$, and 4 does equal 4. We have taken a shortcut here by not working each of the answer choices.

14. **(C)** There are several ways of running the calculation for this problem. One way is to reason: 10% of 360 is 36. Since 5% is one half of 10%, 5% of 360 is one half of 36, or 18. Since 10% of 360 is 36, and since 5% of 360 is 18, the difference between the two is $36 - 18 = 18$.

15. **(E)** Again, perhaps the most natural starting point for a solution is working on the expression, rearranging by grouping like terms. $x^2 + 3x + 10 = 1 + x^2$. By transposing (subtracting from both sides) the x^2 term, we see that the x^2 is eliminated:

$$3x + 10 = 1, \text{ so } 3x = -9, \text{ and } x = -3$$

Although the x^2 term was eliminated from our initial expression, we know the value of x. It is now a simple matter to substitute -3 for x in the expression x^2, and we learn $x^2 = 9$.

16. **(C)** Proposition I is true. It is the geometry theorem that two lines parallel to a third must be parallel to each other.

$$
\begin{array}{ll}
\underline{\hspace{2cm}} l_1 & l_1 \parallel l_2 \\
\underline{\hspace{2cm}} l_2 & l_3 \parallel l_2 \\
\underline{\hspace{2cm}} l_3 & \therefore l_1 \parallel l_3
\end{array}
$$

Proposition II is also necessarily true. Just as with lines, if two planes are parallel to a third plane, they must likewise be parallel to each other.

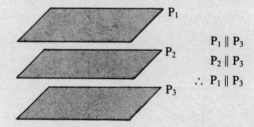

$P_1 \parallel P_3$
$P_2 \parallel P_3$
$\therefore \; P_1 \parallel P_3$

Proposition III, however, is not necessarily true. Two lines might be drawn in a plane parallel to another plane and yet intersect one another:

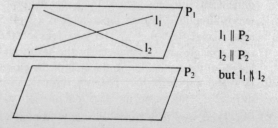

$l_1 \parallel P_2$
$l_2 \parallel P_2$
but $l_1 \nparallel l_2$

17. **(C)** We all know the simple formula that price minus discount equals discounted price—that much is just common-sense arithmetic. What we sometimes overlook, however, is the fact that the discounted price can be expressed either in monetary terms, e.g., $5.00 or 37¢, or in percentage terms, e.g., 50% of the original price. In this case, the discount is given as a percentage of the original price. So we have original price − 90¢ = 90% of original price; or, using x for the original price: $x − \$.90 = .9x$. This is an equation with only one variable, so we proceed to solve for x: $.1x = \$.90$, so $x = \$9.00$.

18. **(D)** We begin by computing the length of the side of the square ABCD. Since the x and y axes meet on the perpendicular, we have a right triangle formed by the origin (the point of intersection of x and y) and points A and B. Since point A has the coordinates (2,0), we know that OA is two units long—the x coordinate is 2. Similarly, point B is two units removed from 0, so OB is also two units long. Thus, the two legs of our right triangle are 2 and 2. Using the Pythagorean Theorem:

$$2^2 + 2^2 = s^2, \text{ so } s = \sqrt{8} = 2\sqrt{2}$$

Now that we have the length of the side, we compute the area of ABCD by side × side: $(2\sqrt{2})(2\sqrt{2}) = 8$.

19. **(A)** This problem is particularly elusive since there is no really clear starting point. One way of getting a handle on it is to manipulate the expression $\frac{x}{y} + \frac{n}{m}$. If we add the two terms together using the common denominator of my, we have $\frac{mx + ny}{my}$. We can see that this bears a striking similarity to the first equation given in the problem: $mx + ny = 12my$. If we manipulate that equation by dividing both sides by my, we have $\frac{mx + ny}{my} = 12$. But since $\frac{x}{y} + \frac{n}{m}$ is equivalent to $\frac{mx + ny}{my}$, we are entitled to conclude that $\frac{x}{y} + \frac{n}{m}$ is also equal to 12.

20. **(D)** This problem, too, is fairly difficult. The difficulty stems from the fact that its solution requires several different formulas. For example,

we can conclude that (A) is necessarily true. MN is not a diameter. We know this since a diameter passes through the center of the circle. So whatever the length of MN, it is less than that of the diameter (the diameter is the longest chord which can be drawn in a circle). Since 2MO would be equal to a diameter (twice the radius is the diameter), and since MN is less than a diameter, we can conclude that MN is less than 2MO. We also know that z = y. Since MO and NO are both radii of circle O, they must be equal. So we know that in triangle MNO, MO = NO; and since angles opposite equal sides are equal, we conclude that z = y. (B) requires still another line of reasoning. Since MN is greater than NO, the angle opposite MN, which is x, must be greater than the angle opposite NO, which is y. So x is greater than y. Finally, (E) requires yet another line of reasoning. If MN were equal to NO, it would also be equal to MO, since MO and NO are both radii. In that case, we would have an equilateral triangle and all angles would be 60°. Since MN is greater than MO and NO, the angle opposite MN, which is x, must be greater than 60°. So (D) must be the correct answer. A moment's reflection will show that it is not necessarily true that x = y + z. This would be true only in the event that MNO is a right triangle, but there is no information given in the problem from which we are entitled to conclude that x° = 90°.

Section III

1. **(D)** The area of a rectangle equals its length times its width, and the perimeter of a rectangle is the sum of its sides, or twice the sum of its length and its width. From (1) you can find the width of the rectangle:

$$5W = 20$$
$$W = 4.$$

You can then find the perimeter of the rectangle:

$$2(L + W) = P$$
$$2(5 + 4) = P = 18$$

From (2) you can also determine the length and width of the rectangle by setting up an equation with one unknown $x(x − 1) = 20$, where x equals the length and $(x − 1)$ equals the width. Then, solving for x:

$$x^2 − x − 20 = 0$$
$$(x − 5)(x + 4) = 0$$

$x = 5$ or $x = -4$. Since a negative length is impossible, the length, x, is 5, and the width, $x - 1$, is 4. Thus the perimeter is $2(5 + 4) = 18$. To answer the question, it is not necessary to solve the equations and actually find the perimeter using (1) and (2) separately. It is sufficient (the name of the section is Data *Sufficiency*) to know that the length and width *can* be found by each of the two statements separately.

2. **(E)** From (1) or (2) separately, you know that the average can be either greater than 10 or less than 10; just think of groups of numbers that yield averages both less than 10 and greater than 10. For example, five 11's and five 1's yield an average of 6, but five 9's and five 15's yield an average of 12. Using (1) and (2) together will not produce an answer to the question either; the same two groups above can be used to answer the question either "yes" or "no."

3. **(C)** If $AX > BX$, $A > B$ if X is positive, but $A < B$ is X is negative because multiplying or dividing both sides of an inequality by the same negative number changes the direction of the inequality, but multiplying or dividing by a positive number does not change the direction. (2) by itself tells you nothing about A or B. (1) and (2) together, however, tell you that $A < B$. Thus the answer to the question is "no."

4. **(B)** In order for AB to be parallel to DE, you must be told either that $\angle BAC = \angle EDC$ or that $\angle ABC = \angle DEC$. Since (1) tells you only that $DC = EC$, and nothing about the relationship among the above angles, you do not know whether AB is parallel to DE. (2) tells you that AB is parallel to DE because $\angle EDC$ and $\angle BAC$ are equal corresponding angles.

5. **(C)** If the area of the rectangle is 16, the length and width are variable, e.g., 4 and 4, 8 and 2, 16 and 1, and thus the length of the diagonal is variable. If the perimeter is 16, the length and width are also variable, e.g., 1 and 7, 2 and 6, 3 and 5, and thus the length of the diagonal is also variable. If (1) and (2) are both used, then the length must be 4 and the width must be 4, so that the diagonal, according to the Pythagorean Theorem, is $4\sqrt{2}$. Using (1) and (2) together gives two equations with two unknowns, an area equation and a perimeter equation, enabling you to determine the length and width of the rectangle and, therefore, the length of the diagonal by means of the Pythagorean Theorem.

6. **(C)** (1) tells you that $X + 6 < 186$ and $X < 180$ (subtracting 6 from both sides), which is not sufficient to answer the question. (2) tells you that $X + 8 > 186$ and $X > 178$ (subtracting 8 from both sides), which is not sufficient to answer the question. Both (1) and (2) together tell you that $178 < X < 180$ (X is greater than 178 *and* less than 180), which implies that X is 179 (since X must be a whole number).

7. **(B)** If (1) is true, then T may or may not be divisible by 15; for example, T could be 555, which is divisible by 15 (divisible means that the result of dividing is an integer with no remainder, or an integer rather than an integer plus a proper fraction), or T could be 348, which is not divisible by 15. (2) tells you that T is definitely not divisible by 15, because in order for an integer to be divisible by 15 it must also be divisible by 5 (since 5 is a factor of 15). An integer divisible by 5 must end in 5 or 0. Since in (2) the units digit is 3 (not 5 or 0), the integer is not divisible by 5 and hence not by 15. Thus, given (2) only, the answer to the question is "no."

8. **(C)** (1) gives you no idea of the size of the parallelogram and is therefore insufficient to answer the question. (2) by itself also is insufficient to answer the question because you don't know what shape the quadrilateral is. (1) and (2) together are sufficient to answer the question (the answer is 23) because the two unshaded triangles together have half of the area of the parallelogram: the area of the entire parallelogram is its base times its height. The area of the unshaded triangle on the left is *half* of its base times its height (which is the same as the height of the parallelogram), and the area of the unshaded triangle on the right is *half* of its base times its height (which is also the same as the height of the parallelogram). Since the bases of the two unshaded triangles together add up to the base of the parallelogram, the areas of the two triangles must be half of the area of the parallelogram, and the shaded region must be the other half.

9. **(D)** (1) by itself fixes the size of the cube completely and is therefore sufficient to answer the question (the answer is $\sqrt{3}$). Likewise, (2) by itself fixes the size of the cube completely, because from the length of the diagonals of the faces you can deduce that the sides are of length 1, and it is therefore sufficient to answer the question.

10. **(E)** (1) tells you nothing about the time the return journey took. Using (1) by itself, you can conclude only that the round trip took more than one hour. (2) by itself tells you nothing about how long the return journey or the round trip took. (1) and (2) together likewise tell you nothing about the length of time that any portion of the trip took.

11. **(B)** If (1) is true, you cannot answer the question without knowing the relative positions of points S and T. (Remember that geometric figures in the Data Sufficiency section are not necessarily drawn to scale, i.e., the lengths or sizes may not be what they appear to be.) If (2) is true, then the lengths of TU, ST, and RS are equal to each other, and therefore the answer to the question is "neither."

12. **(C)** If John has 5 more than Paul, there are two possible combinations: Paul could have 1 and John 6, or Paul could have 2 and John 7. Note that 3 and 8 are impossible since the total number of marbles is only 10. So (1) is not sufficient to answer the question. If Peter has half as many as John, there are three possible combinations: Peter could have 1 and John 2, Peter could have 2 and John 4, or Peter could have 3 and John 6. Again, (2) is not sufficient by itself. If both conditions are known, the only possibility is that Paul has 1, John has 6 and Peter has 3.

13. **(B)** (1) tells you nothing about the value of A. If A is positive, the answer to the question is "yes"; if A is not positive, the answer to the question is "no." Therefore, (1) by itself is insufficient to answer the question. In (2), since $A < 0$, $A + B < B$ (adding B to both sides of $A < 0$), so the answer to the question is "no."

14. **(B)** (1) tells you that x equals 1 or -1, so (1) is insufficient to answer the question. (2) tells you that x equals -1, so (2) by itself is sufficient to answer the question.

15. **(D)** In (1), if $\angle A = 55°$, then $\angle B = 180° - 55° = 125°$. Therefore, (1) is sufficient to answer the question. In (2), if $\angle D > 90°$, then $\angle B$ is also greater than 90° because $\angle B$ and $\angle D$ are corresponding angles with respect to parallel lines l and m and are therefore equal. So the answer to the question is "no" and (2) is sufficient.

16. **(D)** The area of a rectangle equals its length times its width. The length is given as 40. The perimeter (twice the sum of the length and the width) is given in (1), so the width can be found as follows:

$$2(L + W) = 140$$
$$2(40 + W) = 140$$
$$40 + W = 70$$
$$W = 30$$

Now you know the length and the width which are sufficient to find the area. In (2) you are given the length of the diagonal. By using the Pythagorean Theorem you can find the width as follows:

$$40^2 + W^2 = 50^2$$
$$W = 30$$

Now the area can also be found.

17. **(E)** If you divide both sides of the second equation by -2, the result is the equation in (1). Therefore, equation (2) is equivalent to equation (1). There are many solutions to equation (1)— and equation (2). For example, $A = 0$ and $B = \frac{-17}{3}$, and $A = 1$ and $B = -5$.

18. **(D)** In general, the relationship among the lengths of time that it takes for two persons or machines to perform a task is illustrated by the equation $\frac{1}{x} + \frac{1}{y} = \frac{1}{z}$, where x equals the number of units of time that it takes one person or machine to complete the task, y equals the number of units that it takes the other person or machine, and z equals the number of units that it takes both, working together, to complete the task (1) tells you that the equation is $\frac{1}{x} + \frac{1}{2x} = \frac{1}{30}$, where x equals the number of minutes that it takes Joe to unload the bushels, y equals 2x equals the number of minutes that it takes Tom, and z equals 30 minutes, the time it takes Tom and Joe working together to unload the bushels. Since the equation can be solved for x, (1) is sufficient. Likewise, (2) is sufficient because it also yields one equation with one unknown, which may be solved for the unknown: $\frac{1}{45} + \frac{1}{x} = \frac{1}{30}$.

19. **(E)** (1) gives no information about B, so (1) is insufficient to answer the question. (2) tells you nothing about the relative values of A and B, but only that the square of $(A + B)$ is positive, so (2) is also insufficient.

20. **(B)** If $\angle P < \angle Q$, it is possible for any one of the three angles to be a right angle, which would make the triangle a right triangle, or it is possible for none of the three angles to be a right angle, so (1) by itself is insufficient to answer the question. (2) tells you that $\angle R$ is a right angle ($\angle R = 90°$), since the sum of the three angles is 180°: $\angle P + \angle Q + \angle R = 180°$; $\angle P + \angle Q = \angle R$; $\angle R + \angle R = 180°$ (by substituting $\angle R$ for $\angle P + \angle Q$ in $\angle P + \angle Q + \angle R = 180°$); $2\angle R = 180°$; therefore $\angle R = 90°$ (by dividing both sides of the equation by 2). Thus (2) is sufficient to answer the question.

21. **(B)** In (1), if $K > 2L$, K could equal 3 and L could equal 0 ($K > L$); or K could equal -4 and L could equal -3 ($K < L$). In (2), if $K - L$ is positive, then $K - L > 0$ and $K > L$ (adding L to both sides in $K - L > 0$), so (2) is sufficient to answer the question.

22. **(C)** In this problem there are three unknown quantities. In order to determine them, you need three equations. From the given conditions you can write $x + y + z = 7$, where x, y, and z represent the lengths of each of the three pieces. From (1) you can write $x = y + z$. These two equations are not sufficient to answer the question. From (2) you can write $y = 6$ or $z = 6$. Now, with both (1) and (2), there is sufficient information to arrive at an answer (3 equations and 3 unknowns). You need not solve the equations, but the longest piece is three feet six inches long, the shortest piece is six inches long, and the other piece is three feet long.

23. **(A)** Subtracting A from both sides in (1), $B > A$ or $A < B$. So the answer to the question is "no." From statement (2) you could get different results as follows: if $A^2 > B^2$, then A could equal 3 and B could equal 2 ($A > B$). Alternatively, A could equal -5 and B could equal 2 ($A < B$).

24. **(E)** In (1) N could be divisible by 6 and not by 12, e.g., $N = 18$. Alternatively, N could be divisible by 6 and by 12, e.g., $N = 24$. So (1) is not sufficient to answer the question. In (2) the same argument could be presented. A number divisible by 2 may or may not be divisible by 12. The two statements together are still not sufficient because any number divisible by 6 is automatically divisible by 2. So (2) gives no new information.

25. **(A)** An even number is always twice some whole number. So (1) yields the answer "yes." In (2) X could be, for example, $\frac{1}{3}$ (not a whole number) or 3 (a whole number). So (2) is not sufficient to answer the question.

Section IV

1. **(D)** (A) is incorrect because the "if" clause, expressing past condition contrary to fact, requires the past-perfect subjunctive ("had found"). (B) is wrong because the "possible conclusion" clause requires the perfect form of a modal auxiliary ("would have paid"). (C) fails because "fewer" refers to items that can be counted; tax, as a collective quantity, requires "less." (E) changes the meaning.

2. **(D)** (D) is not elegant but at least it is unambiguous and correct. Poor phrasing in (A) and (E) results in ambiguities: Do the columns contain volumes? Do the volumes have columns? (B) changes the tense and hence the overall meaning. (C) errs in agreement of subject and verb: the plural noun "libraries" must take the plural verb "contain."

3. **(C)** When seen from the context of the present, activities of ancient peoples should be described in the past (or past perfect) tenses. (A), (B), (D), and (E) put one or both of the ancient activities in the present or present perfect tenses. (D) also errs in adding three superfluous words. Only (C) is completely correct.

4. **(B)** (A), (C), and (D) require 14 words each to say what (B) says, more gracefully, in 12. (E) changes the meaning.

5. **(A)** (C) and (E) are incorrect because the clause expressing past condition contrary to fact requires past-perfect subjunctive ("had known"). (D) is incorrect because the clause stating a possible conclusion requires the perfect form of a modal auxiliary ("would have come"). (A) and (B) both use the correct verb forms in both clauses but (B) adds "if"; this word is superfluous and alters the word order required by Standard Written English.

6. **(B)** (A) requires 15 words, and (C) 12, to say what B says in 11. (D) and (E) change the meaning.

7. **(E)** (A), (B), (C), and (D) are obviously confused: men whose landing and assault surprised the enemy could not have been prisoners at the time. (D) also confuses "affected" with "effected."

8. **(D)** Context indicates Jones is not afraid of bad weather; all that is required is a single negative. (A) uses a double negative ("Un-" and "neither . . . nor"). (C) incorrectly mixes the "either . . . or" and "neither . . . nor" constructions. (B) and (E) change the meaning.

9. **(C)** (A) requires 22 words to say what (C) says in 18. (B), (D), and (E) all change the meaning of the original; B also uses the singular verb "has" with the plural noun "recommendations."

10. **(D)** (A) is wordier than need be, fails to repeat "to" in the parallel structure ("to refine . . . to increase"), and misplaces the modifier "both." (B) and (C) needlessly substitute "utilized" for the short, simple "used." (E) uses a loose "also" instead of the tight "both" construction and incorrectly adds a comma.

11. **(A)** (B), (D), and (E) change the meaning. (C) omits the "do" needed to focus the contrast with married women who "do not."

12. **(C)** In its first two phrases, the original sentence establishes a pattern of parallelism ("Your . . . meddling, your . . . ridiculing"). (A), (B), and (E) fail to continue the pattern. Both (C) and (D) do continue it ("your . . . departing"), but (D) adds three unnecessary words, leaving (C) as the best version.

13. **(D)** (A), (B), (C), and (E) each contain one or two errors in agreement of subject and verb. Plural subject "breeding and education" requires plural verb "establish," just as plural subject "occupation and income" requires "do."

14. **(B)** (A) and (C) are wrong because when a noun clause is used to pose this kind of indirect question, the conjunction required is "whether," not "if." (D) fails to link its "whether" clauses to the predicate with a verb. (C) and (E) err in using "is" instead of "are"; (E) also changes the meaning.

15. **(C)** (A) and (D) express simple result ("so impressed . . . that"), but (C) adds the sense of *to such an extent* ("so impressed . . . as to.") That this sense is the one intended is shown in the original by the second result "designate," which is in the infinitive form; the two results together then should be "so impressed . . . as to ignore . . . and designate. . . ." (B) takes more wordage than (C) to stress "to such an extent that," and "were to ignore" changes the time sense. (E) is not idiomatic.

16. **(A)** (A) is correct because the way to specify a "demand" that someone do something is in a "that" clause using the present subjunctive (*do*, "return"). (C) weakens the effect by confusing "demand that" with "demand for." (D) and (E) make incorrect use of the auxiliary verbs "would" and "ought." With "ought" (E) even changes the meaning. (B) needlessly repeats "the members" instead of using the pronoun "they."

17. **(B)** The original confuses two sources of punishment, the "referee's lack" and the referee himself, resulting in awkward use of "who" and needless use of both "punished" and "penalized." (C) better manages to link "referee" and "who," but it still requires both "punished" and "penalized." (D) and (E) change the meaning, (D) by implying that the referee is conscious of his "lack," (E) by adding "brutality."

18. **(B)** (A) and (E) suffer from faulty parallelism. When two or more phrases/clauses branch off from the same word, that word should come first and they should be in parallel structure ("responsible not only for . . . but also for . . ."). (C) and (D) have the right word order but a wrong word—the idiom is "not only . . . but also," and (C) changes the meaning. Furthermore, (A), (C), and (D) are wordy, using "the maintenance of order" when "maintaining order" will do.

19. **(D)** (A), (C), and (E) are marred by faulty parallelism: ancient Greek literature is compared with today's Greek people. (C) even leaves "literature" to be inferred, and (E) compares the ancient *Greek* with modern *Greeks*. (B) does achieve parallelism, but errs in using the plural (and here unidiomatic) verb "are containing" with the singular noun "literature." Only (D) lines up the ideas correctly.

20. **(B)** In (A), (C), and (D), the phrases about the "oldest brothers" are parenthetical; they are not part of the subject. Steve, the true subject, is sin-

gular, requiring not "are" but "is," as in (B). In (E), "his oldest brothers" is linked with "Steve" by "and," thus creating a plural subject requiring not "is" but "are."

21. **(E)** In Standard Written English, "looked like" and "looked as if" are not synonyms for "appeared that," eliminating (A), (B), and (C). "Would have" (C) changes the meaning. "Appearances were that" and "would be crossing" make (D) wordier than the succinct, and correct, (E).

22. **(E)** (A), (B), and (D) incorrectly use "inferred" to mean "implied." (A) and (C) use the pronoun "them" instead of "it" (the antecedent is "plight").

23. **(D)** (A) and (C) each use two statements that can be condensed into one. (B) and (E) do condense them, but they fail in other ways: (B) uses faulty parallelism—a series of like items is awkwardly expressed in unlike forms, two nouns and a "how" clause—while (E) uses a dangling modifier—"rich and famous" here describes the traits instead of the men. (C) makes an error similar to (E). (D) achieves clarity and brevity by lining up like items in a series of like grammatical forms, and by placing modifiers next to the words they modify.

24. **(B)** (B) is correct because in likening two things, it puts the second into the same grammatical form as the first ("To insist . . . is to violate"). The others are incorrect because they put the second item in a different grammatical form: (A) and (E) use "violating" instead of "to violate"; (C) uses "to violate" instead of "violating"; and (D) has "violation" instead of "violating." (D) and (E) are also wordier than need be.

25. **(B)** (A) and (C) are redundant: "as well" means "also." The "which reduces" phrase in (C) and (E) may change the meaning, suggesting that only the damaged vision figures in the reduced survival potential. (D) and (E) need "also" after "but" to carry out the pattern of "not only . . . but also."

Section V

1. **(C)** This problem simply requires finding the value of the expression $2x + 3y$, when $x = 3$ and $y = 2$: $2(3) + 3(2) = 12$.

2. **(C)** You do not need a course in business arithmetic to solve this problem, only the common-sense notion that profit is equal to gross revenue less cost. Expressed algebraically, we have $P = GR - C$; then, transposing the C term, we have $C + P = GR$, which is read: cost plus profit (or mark-up) is equal to gross revenue (or selling price). In this case, $P = \$4$, $GR = \$20$: $C + 4 = 20$, so $C = 16$.

3. **(A)** The information given says that the 1970 student population is $2\frac{1}{2}$ times as great as the 1950 student population. So: '70SP = '50SP $\times$ $2\frac{1}{2}$, or '70SP = $500 \times 2\frac{1}{2} = 500 \times \frac{5}{2} = 1250$.

4. **(C)** We must test each of the answer choices. The question asks for the one choice in which the answer is not equal to $3n + 3$. In (A), for example, does $300 = 3n + 3$? A quick manipulation will show that there is an integer, n, which solves the equation: $297 = 3n$, so $n = 99$. For (C), however, no integral n exists: $3n + 3 = 208$, $3n = 205$, $n = 68\frac{1}{3}$. So (C) is the answer we want. Another approach is to test each of the answer choices for being divisible by 3 since $3n + 3$ is divisible by 3 when n is an integer. If the sum of all the single digits in a number add up to a number divisible by 3, the number is itself divisible by 3; if not, not (208, for example: $2 + 0 + 8 = 10$, is not divisible by 3). Being divisible by 3 does not mean an answer fits the conditions, but not being divisible by 3 means that it doesn't.

5. **(D)** The easiest approach to this problem is to draw the figures.

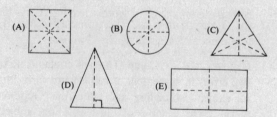

The dotted lines show possible lines of symmetry—that is, these are lines along which a paper cutout of the figure could be folded and the result will be that the two halves exactly match one another. (D) must be our answer, since it is the only figure with but one line of symmetry.

6. **(B)** This problem can, of course, be solved using an equation. We know that the laborer worked 8 hours @ $8 per hour, but what we need to know is how much overtime he worked. We let x be the number of overtime hours: (8 hrs. × $8/hr.) + (x

hrs. × \$12/hr.) = \$80. The \$12/hr. is the laborer's overtime rate——that is, \$8 × $1\frac{1}{2}$ = \$12. Now it is a fairly simple matter to manipulate the equation:

$$64 + 12x = 80$$
$$12x = 16$$
$$x = \frac{16}{12}$$
$$x = 1\frac{1}{3}$$

Since $\frac{1}{3}$ of an hour is 20 minutes, the laborer worked 1 hour and 20 minutes of overtime, which, when added to the standard 8 hours, gives a total work day of 9 hours and 20 minutes.

Now, common sense reasoning might have gone like this: Well, I know he made \$64 in a regular day. If he made \$80 on a given day, \$16 must have been overtime pay. His overtime rate is time-and-a-half, that is, $1\frac{1}{2}$ times \$8/hr., or \$12/hr. In the first hour of overtime he made \$12, that leaves \$4 more. Since \$4 is one-third of \$12, he has to work another one-third of an hour to make that, which is twenty minutes. So he works 8 hours at standard rates of \$64, one full hour of overtime for another \$12, and another $\frac{1}{3}$ of an overtime hour for \$4. So \$80 represents 9 hours and 20 minutes of work.

7. **(A)** Since MNOP is a square, we know that angle O must be a right angle, that is, 90°. From that we can conclude that arc NP is one-fourth of the entire circle. If arc NP is 4π units long, then the circumference of the circle must be 4 times that long, or 16π units. We are now in a position to find the length of the radius of circle O, and once we have the radius, we will also know the length of the sides of square MNOP, since MN and OP are both radii. The formula for the circumference of a circle is $C = 2\pi r$, so:

$$2\pi r = 16\pi$$
$$2r = 16$$
$$r = 8$$

So the side of the square MNOP must be 8, and its perimeter must be $s + s + s + s$ or $4(8) = 32$.

8. **(C)** The most direct way of solving this problem is first to compute the rate at which the water is filling the tank. Water is flowing into the tank at 800 cu. ft. per minute, but it is also draining out at the rate of 300 cu. ft. per minute. The net gain each minute, then, is 500 cu. ft. We then divide 3750 cu. ft. by 500 cu. ft./min., which equals 7.5 minutes. We convert the .5 minute to 30 seconds, so our answer is 7 min. 30 sec.

9. **(B)** A quick sketch of the information provided in the problem shows that we need to employ the Pythagorean Theorem:

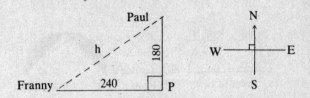

The shortest distance from Paul to Franny is the hypotenuse of this right triangle:

$$180^2 + 240^2 = h^2$$

It is extremely unlikely that the GMAT would present a problem requiring such a lengthy calculation. So there must be a shortcut available. The key is to recognize that 180 and 240 are multiples of 60——3 × 60 and 4 × 60, respectively. This must be a 3,4,5 right triangle, so our hypotenuse must be 5 × 60 = 300.

10. **(A)** This problem requires a very simple insight: Area of rectangle = width × length. What makes it difficult is that many students——while they are able to compute the area of any rectangle in which the dimensions are given——"freak out" when dimensions are expressed in terms of a variable rather than real numbers. Those who keep a cool head will say, "Oh, the area is the width times the length. The area here is $81x^2$, the length is 27x, therefore:

$$(W)(L) = \text{Area}$$
$$(W)(27x) = (81x^2)$$
Divide both sides by x:
$$(W)(27) = 81x$$
$$W = 3x$$

11. **(B)** To solve this problem, you must recognize that angle ABC is a right angle. This is because the triangle is *inscribed* in a semicircle (the vertex of the triangle is situated on the circumference of the circle), and an inscribed angle intercepts twice the arc. For example:

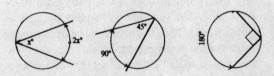

Once it is recognized that ABC is a right triangle, the shaded area can be computed by taking the area of the triangle from the area of the semicircle, or expressed in pictures:

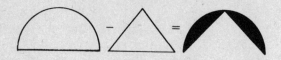

Line AC is the hypotenuse of ABC, so its length is:

$$AC^2 = (2\sqrt{2})^2 + (2\sqrt{2})^2$$
$$AC^2 = 8 + 8$$
$$AC = 4$$

AC is also the diameter of the circle, so the radius of the entire circle is 2 (radius is one-half diameter). We are now in a position to compute the area of the semicircle. Since the area of the entire circle would be πr^2, the area of the semicircle is

$$\frac{\pi r^2}{2} = \frac{\pi(2)^2}{2} = 2\pi.$$

Then we compute the area of the triangle. The area of a triangle is $\frac{1}{2}$ ab, and in any right triangle either of the two sides will serve as the altitude, the other serving as the base. For example:

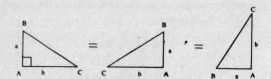

In this case, we have area = $\frac{1}{2}(2\sqrt{2})(2\sqrt{2}) =$ 4. Referring to our pictorial representation of the problem:

$$\bigcirc - \triangle = 2\pi - 4.$$

12. **(B)** This problem does not actually need to be calculated. The symbol * is standing for a set of instructions. These instructions start with the square of the number and then add twice the number, which could be symbolized by * of x = x^2 + 2x. Since 12 squared is 144, the answer must be something in that general neighborhood, and the only answer that is close is (B) 168. The calculation would be $12^2 + 2 \cdot 12 = 144 + 24 = 168$.

13. **(C)** In the first trip, the motorist travels 120 miles at 60 m.p.h., which takes 2 hours. On the way back, he travels the same distance at 40 m.p.h., which takes 3 hours. His average rate is the total distance (240 miles) divided by the total time (5 hours), which yields 48 m.p.h.

14. **(D)** If angles BAD and BCD are right angles, they are equal. Angle BAC equals angle BCA, since they are base angles of an isosceles triangle. Subtracting equals from equals, angle DAC equals angle DCA. Therefore, ACD is an isosceles triangle, and AD = CD.

15. **(A)** Let x = the cost.

$$\text{Then } x + \tfrac{1}{4}x = 80$$
$$4x + x = 320$$
$$5x = 320$$
$$= \$64 \text{ (cost)}$$
$$\frac{\text{Cost}}{\text{S.P.}} = \frac{64}{80}$$
$$= \frac{4}{5}$$

16. **(C)**

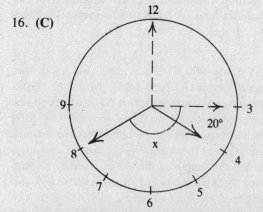

At 3:00, large hand is at 12 and small hand is at 3. During the next 40 minutes, large hand moves to 8 and small hand moves $\frac{40}{60} = \frac{2}{3}$ of the distance between 3 and 4; $\frac{2}{3} \times 30° = 20°$. Since there is 30° between two numbers on a clock $\angle x = 5(30°) - 20° = 150° - 20° = 130°$.

17. **(B)** Area of sector = $\frac{120}{360} \cdot \pi \cdot 15^2$
$$= \frac{1}{3} \cdot \pi \cdot 15 \cdot 15$$
$$= 75\pi$$

18. **(D)** $\frac{17}{10}y - 0.51$
Multiplying both sides by 10, we get 17y = 5.1, or y = .3.

19. **(D)** $40\% = \frac{2}{5} \times 50 = 20$ girls attended
$50\% = \frac{1}{2} \times 70 = 35$ boys attended

$$\frac{55}{50+70} = \frac{55}{120} = \frac{11}{24}$$

$$\begin{array}{r} .458 \\ 24\overline{)11.000} \\ 96 \\ \overline{140} \\ 120 \\ \overline{200} \\ 192 \end{array} = 45.8\%$$

Approx. 46%

20. **(D)** In order to find out the total production for the five days of round-the-clock production, you first need to know the rate of production for some time period and the number of that time period in the five days. To find the rate of production, we need to add the rate of production of the new machine ($\frac{x}{\text{hour}}$) to the rate of production of the old machine, which is $\frac{1}{8}$ as much ($\frac{x}{8}$ per hour). Adding these two together you get a total production rate of $x + \frac{x}{8} = (\frac{9}{8})x$ per hour. This must be multiplied by the number of hours in five days (5)(24) to give the total production: $\frac{(9)(x)(5)(24)}{8} = 135x$ transmissions.

Section VI

1. **(C)** First we must convert one and one-half yards into inches. There are 36 inches in a yard, so one and one-half yards must contain 36 + 18 or 54 inches. Now, to determine how many two-inch segments there are in 54 inches, we just divide 54 by 2, which equals 27. So there must be 27 two-inch segments in a segment which is one and one-half yards long.

2. **(B)** It is important to remember that the positive x values are to the right of the origin (the intersection between the x and y axes), and that the negative values on the x axis are to the left of the origin. Also, the positive y values are above the origin, while the negative y values are below the x axis.

```
            y
  (−,+)  |  (+,+)
         |
    II   |   I
  _____|_____ x
         |
   III   |   IV
  (−,−)  |  (+,−)
```

When reading an ordered pair such as (x,y) (called ordered because the first place is always

the x-coordinate and the second place is always the y-coordinate), we know the first element is the movement on the horizontal or x axis (from left to right), while the second element of the pair gives us the vertical distance. In this case, we are five units to the left of the origin, so that gives us an (x) value of negative 5. We are 2 units above the horizontal axis, so that gives us the second value (y) of +2. Thus our ordered pair is (−5, 2), answer (B).

3. **(B)** The formula for computing the circumference of a circle is $2\pi r$. In this case our radius is 4, so the circumference of the circle is 8π. Now, P and Q will be as far apart as they can possibly be when they are directly opposite one another:

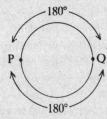

Or a half circle away from each other. So the maximum distance by which P and Q could be separated—measured by the circumference of the circle and not as the crow flies—is one-half the circumference, or 4π.

4. **(E)** Remember that a prime number is an integer which has only itself and 1 as integral factors. Thus, 13, 17, 41, and 79 are all prime numbers because their only factors are 13 and 1, 17 and 1, 41 and 1, and 79 and 1, respectively. 91, however, is not a prime number since it can be factored by 7 and 13 as well as by 1 and 91.

5. **(C)** The natural starting point here would be to draw the picture:

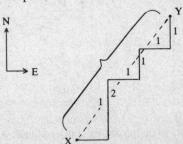

Since directions are perpendicular, we can perform the needed calculation with the Pythagorean Theorem. To simplify things, we can show that the picture above is equivalent to this:

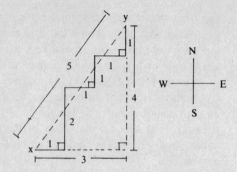

Now we can solve for the distance between X and Y with one use of the Pythagorean Theorem. Since the two legs of the right triangle are 3 and 4, we know that the hypotenuse must be 5. (Remember that 3, 4, and 5, or any multiples thereof, such as 6, 8, and 10, always make a right triangle.)

6. **(C)** Let us begin by substituting x, y, and z for ∠QPS and ∠TPR. Since ∠QPS and ∠TPR are equal, we know x + y = z + y, and since y = y, we know that x = z. As for (A) and (B), we do not know whether y is equal to x and z; it could be larger or smaller or equal:

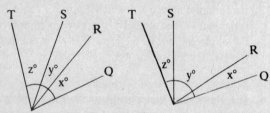

We can also eliminate (D), since we have no information that would lead us to conclude that all three are of equal measure.

7. **(C)** By this juncture the drill should be well known. We must begin by drawing a picture:

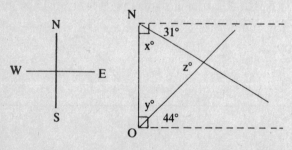

Now, since the angles at N and O are 90°, we can compute the magnitude of x and y. x = 90° − 31° = 59°, and y = 90° − 44° = 46°. Then, since x, y, and z are the interior angles of a triangle, we know x + y + z = 180°. Substituting for x and y, we have 59° + 46° + z = 180°, and we solve for

z: z = 75°. Since z is the angle of intersection between the two highways, our answer must be (C).

8. **(B)** Let us use x to represent the sum of money. Then we know that when x is divided equally by n, the result is $60; or, expressed in formal notation: $\frac{x}{n} = 60$. We then know that when x is divided by n + 1 (that is the original number plus another child), the result is $50, or $\frac{x}{n+1} = 50$. Now, let us manipulate these equations so that we isolate n:

$$\frac{x}{n} = 60 \qquad \frac{x}{n+1} = 50$$

$$\frac{x}{60} = n \qquad \frac{x}{50} = n + 1$$

$$\frac{x}{60} = n \qquad \frac{x}{50} - 1 = n$$

Since n = n, we know that x/60 = x/50 − 1, and we have an equation with only one variable: x/60 − x/50 = −1, so:

$$\frac{5x - 6x}{300} = -1$$

AND: $-x = -300$

SO: $x = 300$

The sum of money is $300 and our answer is (B). (Note that you could also solve for n; in this case n = 5.)

9. **(D)** While it is possible to set up a formula for this problem, Original Price − Discount = Discounted Price, a little common sense is a better attack. The discount is 25% of the original price, and 25% of $90 is $22.50. If the item originally cost $90, and we are getting a discount of $22.50, the new price will be $67.50.

10. **(C)** Let us begin our solution by dropping a perpendicular from the upper vertex of the triangle:

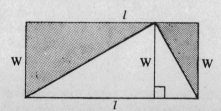

This divides the rectangle into two other rectangles, each with a diagonal running across it:

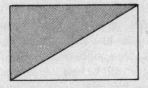

It should be intuitively clear that the diagonal of a rectangle divides the rectangle in half since all sides and angles are equal. Therefore, the left shaded area is equal to the left unshaded area and the right shaded area is equal to the right unshaded area, which means the total shaded area is equal to the total unshaded area. Thus, the triangle has half the area of the rectangle. This is actually the proof of the formula you use to find the area of a triangle—A = (height)(base)$\frac{1}{2}$. Remember this situation since it could easily come up in one problem or another.

11. **(B)** Since Earl and Ellen will be working together, we add their work rates:

$$\frac{\text{Number of tasks}}{\text{Time}} + \frac{\text{Number of tasks}}{\text{Time}}$$
$$= \frac{\text{Number of tasks together}}{\text{Time}}$$

In this case:

$$\frac{45 \text{ envelopes}}{60 \text{ seconds}} + \frac{45 \text{ envelopes}}{90 \text{ seconds}} = \frac{300 \text{ envelopes}}{x \text{ seconds}}$$

Or: $\frac{45}{60} + \frac{45}{90} = \frac{300}{x}$

To make the arithmetic simpler, we reduce fractions:

$\frac{3}{4} + \frac{1}{2} = \frac{300}{x}$.

Then we add: $\frac{10}{8} = \frac{300}{x}$.

And solve for x: $x = 300(\frac{8}{10}) = 240$ seconds.

Since 240 seconds is equal to 4 minutes, our answer is (B). If you are not comfortable with fractions, you could have kept to minutes.

Another way to approach this problem would be to try to get the rate of each worker in envelopes per minute. Earl is already known to work at 45 envelopes per minute. Ellen takes $1\frac{1}{2}$ minutes for the same work. Thus, 45 envelopes are done in three half-minutes. 45 divides by 3 nicely, as we often find on the GMAT, so Ellen does 15 envelopes in $\frac{1}{2}$ minute or 30 envelopes per minute, 45 per minute + 30 per minute = 75 per minute, which means $\frac{300}{75} = 4$ minutes.

12. **(D)** First, let us count the number of subjects having characteristic X. The first two categories are those subjects having X (25 which also have Y, 10 which do not have Y but do have X), which is a total of 35. Then those subjects having Y are entered in the first and third categories (25 also have X, 25 have Y but lack X), for a total of 50: Our ratio is $\frac{35}{50}$, which, when reduced by a factor of 5, is equal to $\frac{7}{10}$.

13. **(D)** This problem is a bit tricky, but not really difficult. When dealing with a ratio, say 4 to 1, it is important to remember that the number of parts is the sum of these two numbers. So we might say we have five parts—four parts are passenger vehicles, one part is all other vehicles— and that is how we get a ratio of 4 to 1. But this means that 4 parts out of the total of 5 parts are passenger vehicles, and 4 out of 5 is $\frac{4}{5}$, or 80%. Answer (E) makes the mistake of forgetting that although there are four times as many passenger cars as all other vehicles, the passenger vehicles constitute only $\frac{4}{5}$ of the total number.

14. **(D)** Let us logically approach this problem before even trying to calculate it. Although we have a 10% increase and then a 10% decrease, we must always ask ourselves "10% of what?" The increase was 10% of the original price, but the decrease was 10% of the higher price and consequently the decrease is bigger than the increase and the result at the end is less than the starting price, which eliminates answer choices (A), (B), and (C). Similarly, on logical grounds, it is hard to see how a 10% decrease from a 10% higher price could be equal to an 11% decrease from the starting price; that seems too much, which leaves (D) as the answer.

If we wish to compute the answer, let us start by saying that the original price of the item is x. A 10% increase in that price will be one-tenth of x, or .1x. When we add the increase to the original price, we find our increased price is 1.1x. We must then take away 10% of that. Ten percent of 1.1x is .11x, and subtracting .11x from 1.1x, we get .99x. We started with x; we ended with .99x, so we lost .01x, which is 1%.

15. **(A)** Proposition I is necessarily true. Since lines l_m and l_n are perpendicular to one another, a line that intersects l_m on the perpendicular must be parallel to line l_n.

Proposition II is not necessarily true. Line segment MN may fail to intersect l_m simply because it is too short—that is, if extended, for all we know MN will intersect l_n.

Proposition III is not necessarily true. Line l_o may intersect l_m at point P without plane y being perpendicular to plane x.

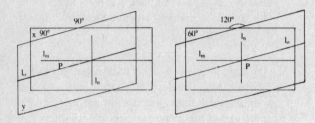

16. **(D)** Since the ratio of insects with X to those without X is 5:3, we know that $\frac{5}{8}$ of the population has X. (There are 8 equal units—5 + 3— 5 of which are insects with X.) Then, of those $\frac{5}{8}$, $\frac{3}{8}$ are male. So we take $\frac{3}{8}$ of the $\frac{5}{8}(\frac{3}{8} \times \frac{5}{8})$, and that tells us that $\frac{15}{64}$ of the total population are male insects with X.

17. **(A)** This is an interesting problem in that no formula is going to solve it. Instead, it requires the use of some good old common sense. Perhaps the solution is more easily visualized if we explode the cube.

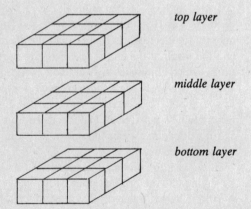

top layer

middle layer

bottom layer

All of the small cubes on the top and the bottom layers will have at least one side painted. In the middle layer, the outer eight smaller cubes encircle the center cube, which is protected on top by the top layer, on the bottom by the bottom layer, and on the remaining four sides by the outside of the sandwich layer.

18. **(D)** The proper way to "visualize" this problem is to imagine that the gravel-covered walk will be a very squat-shaped cylinder with a donut hole removed (the circular region inside the walk). Expressed more abstractly, we need to compute

the volume of a cylinder with a radius of 50 feet ($\frac{1}{2}$ of 100 = 50) and a height of 6 inches, or $\frac{1}{2}$ foot. Then we compute the volume of a cylinder with a radius of 40 feet ($\frac{1}{2}$ of 80 = 40) and a height of 6 inches, or $\frac{1}{2}$ foot. Then we subtract the second from the first and what is left is the volume we seek. Now, since both cylinders have the same height, it will be easier to compute the areas of the bases first and subtract before multiplying by $\frac{1}{2}$ foot.

Area of larger circle: Area = $\pi r^2 = \pi(50)^2 =$ 2500 π.

Area of smaller circle: Area = $\pi r^2 = \pi(40)^2 =$ 1600π.

By subtracting 1600π from 2500π, we determine that the area of the garden path is 900π square feet. To determine the volume of gravel we need, we then multiply the figure by $\frac{1}{2}$ foot (the depth of the gravel), and arrive at our answer 450π cu. ft.

19. **(D)** Let d stand for the hourly rate under the new system. Since the employee is to make the same amount per week under both systems, it must be the case that:

$$\frac{\$x}{\text{hr.} \times 40 \text{ hrs.}} = \frac{\$d}{\text{hr.} \times 36 \text{ hrs.}}$$

Now we must solve for d:

$$40x = 36d, \quad d = \frac{10x}{9}$$

The problem can also be solved in an intuitive way. Since the employee is working less time yet making the same weekly total, he must be earning slightly more per hour under the new system than under the old. Answer (A) is just the naked fraction $\frac{1}{10}$, without making reference to monetary units. Answer (B) implies that the employee is making $\frac{1}{9}$ as much per hour under the new system as under the old—that would be a decrease in the hourly rate. Similarly, (C) says that the employee is making only 90% of his old hourly rate and that, too, is a decrease. Finally, (E) says that the employee is making 9 *times* the hourly rate he made under the old system, a figure which is obviously out of line. The only reasonable choice is (D). The moral is: Even if you cannot set up the math in a technically correct way, use a little common sense.

20. **(A)** This problem must be solved in two stages. First, we need to calculate the total area of the

wall. The information given in the problem states that $\frac{1}{3}$ of the job plus another 75 square feet equals $\frac{3}{4}$ of the job. In algebraic notation, this is:

$$\frac{1}{3} x + 75 = \frac{3}{4} x$$
$$75 = \frac{3}{4} x - \frac{1}{3} x$$
$$75 = \frac{5}{12} x$$
$$x = 180$$

So the entire wall is 180 square feet—that is, $W \times L = 180$. We know that the height of the wall is 10 feet; so $10 \times L = 180$, and $L = 18$.

Section VII

1. **(B)** This is a main idea question. In the very first paragraph the author presents the distinction between unlabeled and prohibited uses and then proceeds to develop the important implications of the distinction. (B) correctly describes this form of argument. (A) must be incorrect since no theory is cited for refutation. (C) is incorrect since no opponent is mentioned. (D) can be eliminated since there is no evidence that the practice of unlabeled uses is a recent development. (E) can be eliminated for either of two reasons. First, if one interprets "error" here to mean the practice of forbidden uses, then that is not the main point of the argument. Or if one interprets "error" to mean the confusing of unlabeled with prohibited uses, then (E) is eliminated because "condemn" is inappropriate. The author may wish to correct a misconception, but that is not the wording of (E). Moreover, the method he uses to accomplish that end is by drawing a distinction. Thus, (B) stands as correct.

2. **(C)** This is an explicit idea question. The reference we need is to be found in the first paragraph. There the author explains that he uses the term "unlabeled use" to refer to any medically valuable use of any already approved drug that has not yet been specifically recognized by the FDA. (A) is incorrect because this is a prohibited use, as that term is used in the text. (B) is incorrect because an unlabeled use is one that was not considered when the drug was originally labeled; it is one discovered later, not one proposed, tested and rejected. (D) is incorrect because this use the author would term a labeled use. Finally, (E) is

incorrect since this refers to research designed to determine whether a drug has labeled uses because it meets the legal standard of substantial evidence of such uses.

3. **(C)** This is an inference question that requires that we collate information from two parts of the passage. In paragraph two the author refers to physicians who persist in prohibited use for one of two reasons: ignorance or refusal to accept evidence. Then, in the third paragraph, the author refers to physicians who use drugs in violation of labeling instructions as either uninformed or intransigent. The parallelism here tells us that the intransigent physician is the one who rejects the evidence that the drug is ineffective. This is neatly captured by (C). (A) is incorrect since the intransigent physician prescribes the drug in violation of the labeling provision because he believes that the drug is effective. (B) is incorrect, for this would be a physician who is anything but intransigent. As for (D), an intransigent physician might take such actions, but his is not the defining characteristic of an intransigent physician. Finally, (E) can be eliminated since the author specifically expresses reservations as to whether such behavior is illegal.

4. **(A)** Here we have an explicit detail question, with a thought reverser. Four of the five choices will be incorrect because they are mentioned in the passage. The remaining choice will be correct because it is the one *not* explicitly mentioned. (B) can be eliminated since the medical benefits of an unlabeled usage are specifically mentioned in both the first and final paragraphs. (C) is incorrect since the time lag that might delay application of a new usage is mentioned in the first paragraph as a reason for permitting that usage, even though that usage has not been formally approved. (D), too, must be incorrect since the possibility that a manufacturer might not incur the expenses to secure formal approval of a new usage is explicitly mentioned in the first paragraph. Finally, (E) can be eliminated since the first paragraph also points out that literature is available to ensure that doctors are familiar with the limitations of the unlabeled use. (A) must be the correct answer, for nowhere in the passage is the cost to the consumer mentioned as a reason for allowing unlabeled usage.

5. **(E)** This is an application, and we must find the statement that is most likely to be acceptable to

the author. (E) would likely be embraced by the author since he explains in the first paragraph that unlabeled uses are created by the time lag between the discovery of the use and the accumulation of data needed to prove that use effective. (A) is an attractive answer, but it fails upon careful reading. The distinction referred to there is that between approved and unlabeled uses. The distinction which the author attempts to draw is between two types of unapproved uses: unlabeled and prohibited. This is the distinction which has been blurred, says the author, not the distinction between approved and unlabeled. (B) is incorrect for the same reason. The blurred distinction is between unlabeled and prohibited uses (both types of unapproved uses), not between approved and unlabeled uses. (C) is incorrect since the distinction between unlabeled and approved uses is a matter of practice, not categorization. The unlabeled use exists because a physician *uses* the drug in a beneficial but not yet approved way, not because the physician or government decides that the use is unlabeled versus approved. (D) is incorrect since the author calls for caution in unlabeled use in the final paragraph.

6. **(A)** This is a tone question. What is the author's attitude toward unlabeled usage? In the passage, the author notes benefits to be derived from unlabeled usages, but the author also points out some dangers in such usage. Unlabeled usage, then, on the author's view, can best be described as a compromise necessitated by economic and perhaps social (governmental) factors. Thus, (A) is correct. (B) is incorrect for it states the case too strongly. To be sure, the author recognizes the dangers of unlabeled usages, but he also recognizes the benefits of such usages. (D) is incorrect for overstating the case in the other direction. The author mentions not only advantages but disadvantages to the policy. (C) can be eliminated for it does not describe the author's attitude. Unlabeled uses are arguably (but only arguably, see final paragraph) illegal, but that is not the defining characteristic of the author's attitude toward the *policy* of tolerating the unlabeled usages. Finally, (E) is incorrect for two reasons. One, it, like (C), is not responsive to the question, that is, (E) is not descriptive of the author's attitude. Two, if anything, the passage supports the conclusion that the practice of unlabeled usage is not short-term but inherent in the licensing process.

7. **(E)** This is a main idea question, and the main idea of this passage, already discussed at some

length, is neatly summarized by (E). Answer (B) is surely the second best answer, but (B) must fail by comparison with (E) because it is too narrow. To be sure, one point the author makes is that the physician who prescribes unlabeled uses should not be subject to legal liability. But that is only part of the argument. That recommendation depends on the distinction between the two types of unapproved uses. (E) makes reference to this additional point. Notice also that in a way (B) is included in (E), so (E) is broad enough to describe the overall point of the author. (A) is incorrect since the author is cautioning against overzealous enforcement of laws against unlabeled uses. (C) is incorrect because it is never mentioned in the passage. Finally, (D) is incorrect because this is at best a minor part of the argument.

8. **(B)** In the first paragraph, the authors states that approved uses are ordinarily contrasted with unapproved uses, but this, the author states, is a misunderstanding because it fails to distinguish between forbidden uses (called "disapproved uses" in paragraph two) and unlabeled uses (not authorized but not harmful). So the nearest opposite of "approved" would be the stricter term "disapproved." (A) is incorrect because those terms represent the common misunderstanding about the distinction just discussed. (C) is incorrect because those terms are synonymous. (D) is incorrect since the author regards "disapproved" as a subset of "unapproved." Finally, (E) is incorrect since those two terms would be nearly synonymous.

9. **(B)** This is a main idea question. The author begins by acknowledging that there exists an actual differential between the earnings of whites and blacks, but then the author moves quickly to block the automatic presupposition that this is attributable to discrimination *in employment*. The author then examines the effect of various productivity variables on the differentials between black and white men and between black and white women, with particular emphasis on the latter. The conclusion of the argument is that there is little difference in the adjusted earnings of black and white women, and the reason for this is the overpowering influence of sexual discrimination. (B) captures this analysis. (A) is incorrect since the author's primary focus is the black woman. He studies black female workers by comparing them with white female workers. The differentials between men and women generally

are only incidentally related to this analysis. (C) fails because this is a subordinate level of argumentation. To be sure, the author does introduce productivity factors to adjust actual earnings, but that is so he can better evaluate the effects of discrimination. (D) is incorrect since no history is offered aside from casual references to the distribution of workers. Finally, (E) is incorrect since the author makes no such recommendations.

10. **(E)** This is an explicit idea question, the answer to which is found in paragraphs one and two. There the author states that the actual ratio is not an accurate measure of discrimination *in employment* because it fails to take account of productivity factors. (A) is incorrect because of the word ''include''—the gross ratio fails to *adjust* for distribution. (B) is not mentioned and so cannot be an answer to a question which begins with the phrase ''According to the passage . . .'' (C), too, is never mentioned in the passage, and so it fails for the same reason, as does (D).

11. **(E)** This is an explicit detail question and our needed reference is the third paragraph, which gives us comparisons, or ratios, of the earnings of black men to the earnings of white men and of the earnings of black women to the earnings of white women. Notice that the comparisons are relative. We never get actual dollar amounts, nor do we get comparisons between women and men. (E) recognizes that the only conclusion that can be drawn on this basis is that the differential between black and white women is less than the differential between black and white men. The first is a difference of only 2 to 5 percent (before adjustment for productivity factors), while the second is about 20 percent (before adjustment). (A), (C), and (D) can be eliminated on the ground that no such male/female comparison is possible. (B) can be eliminated since no such information is supplied.

12. **(A)** This is a logical structure question. The author states that there are two explanations to be considered: (1) black men are found in jobs characterized by greater racial discrimination, and (2) sexual discrimination in the case of women renders insignificant the racial discrimination against black women. But each of these could be true since both could contribute to the phenomenon being studied. There is only an empirical, not a logical, connection between the two, that is, the extent to which each does have explanatory pow-

er as a matter of fact. On this ground we can eliminate every other answer choice.

13. **(C)** This is a tone question, and the best description of the treatment of the subject matter is provided by (C). (A) can be eliminated for the treatment, while confident, is not offensive. (B) can be eliminated for that reason as well. (D) is incorrect since there is nothing tentative or inconclusive about the treatment. To acknowledge that one is unable to determine which of two competing theories is preferable is not to be inconclusive or tentative. Finally, though some readers may find in the author's discussion reason for hope or optimism, we cannot say that the author himself shows us these attitudes.

14. **(A)** This is an application question. What would happen if sexual discrimination against women were no longer a factor? On the assumption that the second hypothesis is correct, racial discrimination against women is not a significant factor because it is overpowered by sexual discrimination. The author acknowledges the existence of the racial discrimination, so elimination of the sexual discrimination should result in the manifestation of increased racial discrimination against black women (on the assumption that the second theory is correct). The result should be a greater disparity between white and black female workers, with white female workers enjoying the higher end of the ratio. This is articulated by (A). (B) is contradicted by this analysis and must be incorrect. (C) is irrelevant since male earning levels are not being explained. Finally, there is nothing to suggest that (D) or (E) would occur.

15. **(B)** This is a tone question. Notice that this question asks not about the tone of the presentation but about the author's attitude toward a particular subject. We must take our cue from the first paragraph, where the author refers to the efforts of ''responsible employers.'' This indicates that the author is sympathetic to the situation of workers who are victims of discrimination. (B) is the best way of describing this attitude. (E) is much too strong, for concern is not anxiety. Further, (C) is much too weak, for the reference to responsible employers indicates the author is not indifferent. (D), like (E), overstates the case. Finally, (A) is incorrect since the author offers no apology.

16. **(C)** This is strictly an explicit idea question. Both statements I and II are mentioned in the sec-

ond paragraph. Statement III, while plausible enough, is nowhere mentioned in the passage, so the correct answer choice must be I and II only.

17. **(B)** This is obviously a main idea question. The main purpose of the passage is to review the findings of some research on animal behavior and suggest that this may have implications for the study of depression in humans. (B) neatly restates this. (A) can be overruled since the author proposes no such cure; indeed, he concludes by noting that there are complex issues remaining to be solved. (C) is incorrect since the author does not criticize any experiments. It is important to recognize that in the second paragraph the author is not being critical of any study in which rats were immersed in cold water; it is just that he anticipates a possible interpretation of those results and moves to block it. So, to the extent that the author criticizes anything at that juncture, he criticizes a possible interpretation of the experiment, not the experiment or results. In any event, that can in no way be interpreted as the main theme of the passage. (D) is wide of the mark. Though one might object to the use of animals for experimentation, that is not a burden the author has elected to carry. Finally, (E) is incorrect because the author mentions this only in closing, almost as a qualification on the main theme of the passage.

18. **(D)** This is a logical detail question. As we have just noted, the author introduces the question in the second paragraph to anticipate a possible objection: Perhaps the animal's inability to act was caused by the trauma of the shock rather than the fact that it could not escape the shock. The author then lists some experiments the conclusions of which he believes refute this alternative explanation. (A) is incorrect since the question represents an interruption of the flow of argument, not a continuation of the first paragraph. (B) is incorrect and might be just a confusion of answer and question. (C) can be eliminated since that is not the reason for raising the question, though it may be the overall theme of the passage. Here we cannot answer a question about a specific logical detail by referring to the main point of the text. Finally, (E) is incorrect since the author does not criticize the experiments; he defends them.

19. **(B)** This is an inference question. We are referred by the question stem to lines 9–60. There we find that stimulation of the septal region

inhibits behavior "while rats with septal lesions do not show learned helplessness." We infer that the septum somehow sends "messages" which tell the action centers not to act. If ordinary rats learn helplessness and rats with septal lesions do not, this suggests that the communication between the two areas of the brain has been interrupted. This idea is captured by (B). (A) is incorrect and confuses the indicated reference with the discussion of "immunized" dogs at line 29. (C) seems to offer an explanation, but the text never suggests that rats have "understanding." (D) is incorrect since it does not offer an explanation: Why don't rats with septal lesions learn helplessness? Finally, (E) is irrelevant to the question asked.

20. **(A)** This is an inferred idea question. The author contrasts the inescapable shock experiment with a "nonaversive parallel" in order to demonstrate that inescapability rather than trauma caused inaction in the animals. So the critical difference must be the trauma—it is present in the shock experiments and not in the nonaversive parallels. This is further supported by the example of a nonaversive parallel, the uncontrollable delivery of food. So the relevant difference is articulated by (A). (B) is incorrect since the author specifically states that the nonaversive parallels did succeed in inducing learned helplessness. (C) is incorrect for the same reason. (D) is incorrect since the value of the nonaversive parallel to the logical structure of the argument is that it was not traumatic at all. Finally, (E) is incorrect because even if one experiment used rats and the other dogs, that is not the defining difference between the shock experiments and the nonaversive-parallel experiments.

21. **(A)** This is a logical detail question, and it is related to the matters discussed above. The author raises the question in paragraph two in order to anticipate a possible objection; namely, that the shock, not the unavoidability, caused inaction. The author then offers a refutation of this position by arguing that we get the same results using similar experiments with nonaversive stimuli. Moreover, if trauma of shock caused the inaction, then we would expect to find learned helplessness induced in rats by the shock, regardless of prior experience with shock. The "mastery effect," however, contradicts this expectation. This is essentially the explanation provided in (A). (B) is incorrect since the author does not

mention this until the end of the passage. (C) can be eliminated since the "mastery effect" reference is not included to support the conclusion that neurochemical changes cause the learned helplessness. (D) is incorrect, for though the author makes such an assertion, the "mastery effect" data is not adduced to support that particular assertion. Finally, (E) is the point against which the author is arguing when he mentions the "mastery effect" experiments.

22. **(E)** This is a further application question. The author closes with a disclaimer that the human cognitive makeup is more complex than that of laboratory animals and that for this reason the findings regarding learned helplessness and induced neurosis may or may not be applicable to humans. He does not, however, explain what the differences are between the experimental subjects and humans. A logical continuation would be to supply the reader with this elaboration. By comparison, the other answer choices are less likely. (B) is unlikely since the author begins and ends with references to human depression, and that is evidently the motivation for writing the article. (C) is not supported by the text since it is nowhere indicated that any such experiments have been undertaken. (D) fails for a similar reason. We cannot conclude that the author would want to test humans by similar experimentation. Finally, (A) is perhaps the second best answer. Its value is that it suggests the mechanism should be studied further. But the most important question is not how the mechanism works in rats but whether that mechanism also works in humans.

23. **(E)** This is an explicit idea question. (A) is mentioned in the final paragraph. (B) is mentioned on several occasions. (C) is mentioned in the second paragraph. (D) is mentioned in the first paragraph. Nowhere, however, does the author mention programs to cure humans of learned helplessness.

24. **(C)** The justification for this choice is found in the concluding paragraph. There the author implies that there is some basis for drawing conclusions about human behavior based on laboratory studies of animals, thus eliminating (A), (D) and (E). But the author cautions that further research is required, and we eliminate (B). The best description of this cautious tone is given by (C).

25. **(B)** This is an explicit idea question. The avoidance-escape deficit must be a deficiency of something: It is the deficiency of action which would normally be expected. (A) is incorrect since this is a way of inducing an avoidance-escape deficit by stress. (E) is incorrect for a similar reason. The term refers not to the stress but to the behavior induced by the stress. (C) must be a confusion with the "mastery effect," and (D) must be a confusion with the reference to the neurosis paradigm.

ANSWER SHEET—PRACTICE EXAMINATION 3

SECTION I

1 Ⓐ Ⓑ Ⓒ Ⓓ Ⓔ   6 Ⓐ Ⓑ Ⓒ Ⓓ Ⓔ   11 Ⓐ Ⓑ Ⓒ Ⓓ Ⓔ   16 Ⓐ Ⓑ Ⓒ Ⓓ Ⓔ   21 Ⓐ Ⓑ Ⓒ Ⓓ Ⓔ

2 Ⓐ Ⓑ Ⓒ Ⓓ Ⓔ   7 Ⓐ Ⓑ Ⓒ Ⓓ Ⓔ   12 Ⓐ Ⓑ Ⓒ Ⓓ Ⓔ   17 Ⓐ Ⓑ Ⓒ Ⓓ Ⓔ   22 Ⓐ Ⓑ Ⓒ Ⓓ Ⓔ

3 Ⓐ Ⓑ Ⓒ Ⓓ Ⓔ   8 Ⓐ Ⓑ Ⓒ Ⓓ Ⓔ   13 Ⓐ Ⓑ Ⓒ Ⓓ Ⓔ   18 Ⓐ Ⓑ Ⓒ Ⓓ Ⓔ   23 Ⓐ Ⓑ Ⓒ Ⓓ Ⓔ

4 Ⓐ Ⓑ Ⓒ Ⓓ Ⓔ   9 Ⓐ Ⓑ Ⓒ Ⓓ Ⓔ   14 Ⓐ Ⓑ Ⓒ Ⓓ Ⓔ   19 Ⓐ Ⓑ Ⓒ Ⓓ Ⓔ   24 Ⓐ Ⓑ Ⓒ Ⓓ Ⓔ

5 Ⓐ Ⓑ Ⓒ Ⓓ Ⓔ   10 Ⓐ Ⓑ Ⓒ Ⓓ Ⓔ   15 Ⓐ Ⓑ Ⓒ Ⓓ Ⓔ   20 Ⓐ Ⓑ Ⓒ Ⓓ Ⓔ   25 Ⓐ Ⓑ Ⓒ Ⓓ Ⓔ

SECTION II

1 Ⓐ Ⓑ Ⓒ Ⓓ Ⓔ   5 Ⓐ Ⓑ Ⓒ Ⓓ Ⓔ   9 Ⓐ Ⓑ Ⓒ Ⓓ Ⓔ   13 Ⓐ Ⓑ Ⓒ Ⓓ Ⓔ   17 Ⓐ Ⓑ Ⓒ Ⓓ Ⓔ

2 Ⓐ Ⓑ Ⓒ Ⓓ Ⓔ   6 Ⓐ Ⓑ Ⓒ Ⓓ Ⓔ   10 Ⓐ Ⓑ Ⓒ Ⓓ Ⓔ   14 Ⓐ Ⓑ Ⓒ Ⓓ Ⓔ   18 Ⓐ Ⓑ Ⓒ Ⓓ Ⓔ

3 Ⓐ Ⓑ Ⓒ Ⓓ Ⓔ   7 Ⓐ Ⓑ Ⓒ Ⓓ Ⓔ   11 Ⓐ Ⓑ Ⓒ Ⓓ Ⓔ   15 Ⓐ Ⓑ Ⓒ Ⓓ Ⓔ   19 Ⓐ Ⓑ Ⓒ Ⓓ Ⓔ

4 Ⓐ Ⓑ Ⓒ Ⓓ Ⓔ   8 Ⓐ Ⓑ Ⓒ Ⓓ Ⓔ   12 Ⓐ Ⓑ Ⓒ Ⓓ Ⓔ   16 Ⓐ Ⓑ Ⓒ Ⓓ Ⓔ   20 Ⓐ Ⓑ Ⓒ Ⓓ Ⓔ

SECTION III

1 Ⓐ Ⓑ Ⓒ Ⓓ Ⓔ   6 Ⓐ Ⓑ Ⓒ Ⓓ Ⓔ   11 Ⓐ Ⓑ Ⓒ Ⓓ Ⓔ   16 Ⓐ Ⓑ Ⓒ Ⓓ Ⓔ   21 Ⓐ Ⓑ Ⓒ Ⓓ Ⓔ

2 Ⓐ Ⓑ Ⓒ Ⓓ Ⓔ   7 Ⓐ Ⓑ Ⓒ Ⓓ Ⓔ   12 Ⓐ Ⓑ Ⓒ Ⓓ Ⓔ   17 Ⓐ Ⓑ Ⓒ Ⓓ Ⓔ   22 Ⓐ Ⓑ Ⓒ Ⓓ Ⓔ

3 Ⓐ Ⓑ Ⓒ Ⓓ Ⓔ   8 Ⓐ Ⓑ Ⓒ Ⓓ Ⓔ   13 Ⓐ Ⓑ Ⓒ Ⓓ Ⓔ   18 Ⓐ Ⓑ Ⓒ Ⓓ Ⓔ   23 Ⓐ Ⓑ Ⓒ Ⓓ Ⓔ

4 Ⓐ Ⓑ Ⓒ Ⓓ Ⓔ   9 Ⓐ Ⓑ Ⓒ Ⓓ Ⓔ   14 Ⓐ Ⓑ Ⓒ Ⓓ Ⓔ   19 Ⓐ Ⓑ Ⓒ Ⓓ Ⓔ   24 Ⓐ Ⓑ Ⓒ Ⓓ Ⓔ

5 Ⓐ Ⓑ Ⓒ Ⓓ Ⓔ   10 Ⓐ Ⓑ Ⓒ Ⓓ Ⓔ   15 Ⓐ Ⓑ Ⓒ Ⓓ Ⓔ   20 Ⓐ Ⓑ Ⓒ Ⓓ Ⓔ   25 Ⓐ Ⓑ Ⓒ Ⓓ Ⓔ

SECTION IV

1 Ⓐ Ⓑ Ⓒ Ⓓ Ⓔ   6 Ⓐ Ⓑ Ⓒ Ⓓ Ⓔ   11 Ⓐ Ⓑ Ⓒ Ⓓ Ⓔ   16 Ⓐ Ⓑ Ⓒ Ⓓ Ⓔ   21 Ⓐ Ⓑ Ⓒ Ⓓ Ⓔ

2 Ⓐ Ⓑ Ⓒ Ⓓ Ⓔ   7 Ⓐ Ⓑ Ⓒ Ⓓ Ⓔ   12 Ⓐ Ⓑ Ⓒ Ⓓ Ⓔ   17 Ⓐ Ⓑ Ⓒ Ⓓ Ⓔ   22 Ⓐ Ⓑ Ⓒ Ⓓ Ⓔ

3 Ⓐ Ⓑ Ⓒ Ⓓ Ⓔ   8 Ⓐ Ⓑ Ⓒ Ⓓ Ⓔ   13 Ⓐ Ⓑ Ⓒ Ⓓ Ⓔ   18 Ⓐ Ⓑ Ⓒ Ⓓ Ⓔ   23 Ⓐ Ⓑ Ⓒ Ⓓ Ⓔ

4 Ⓐ Ⓑ Ⓒ Ⓓ Ⓔ   9 Ⓐ Ⓑ Ⓒ Ⓓ Ⓔ   14 Ⓐ Ⓑ Ⓒ Ⓓ Ⓔ   19 Ⓐ Ⓑ Ⓒ Ⓓ Ⓔ   24 Ⓐ Ⓑ Ⓒ Ⓓ Ⓔ

5 Ⓐ Ⓑ Ⓒ Ⓓ Ⓔ   10 Ⓐ Ⓑ Ⓒ Ⓓ Ⓔ   15 Ⓐ Ⓑ Ⓒ Ⓓ Ⓔ   20 Ⓐ Ⓑ Ⓒ Ⓓ Ⓔ   25 Ⓐ Ⓑ Ⓒ Ⓓ Ⓔ

SECTION V

1 Ⓐ Ⓑ Ⓒ Ⓓ Ⓔ	6 Ⓐ Ⓑ Ⓒ Ⓓ Ⓔ	11 Ⓐ Ⓑ Ⓒ Ⓓ Ⓔ	16 Ⓐ Ⓑ Ⓒ Ⓓ Ⓔ	21 Ⓐ Ⓑ Ⓒ Ⓓ Ⓔ
2 Ⓐ Ⓑ Ⓒ Ⓓ Ⓔ	7 Ⓐ Ⓑ Ⓒ Ⓓ Ⓔ	12 Ⓐ Ⓑ Ⓒ Ⓓ Ⓔ	17 Ⓐ Ⓑ Ⓒ Ⓓ Ⓔ	22 Ⓐ Ⓑ Ⓒ Ⓓ Ⓔ
3 Ⓐ Ⓑ Ⓒ Ⓓ Ⓔ	8 Ⓐ Ⓑ Ⓒ Ⓓ Ⓔ	13 Ⓐ Ⓑ Ⓒ Ⓓ Ⓔ	18 Ⓐ Ⓑ Ⓒ Ⓓ Ⓔ	23 Ⓐ Ⓑ Ⓒ Ⓓ Ⓔ
4 Ⓐ Ⓑ Ⓒ Ⓓ Ⓔ	9 Ⓐ Ⓑ Ⓒ Ⓓ Ⓔ	14 Ⓐ Ⓑ Ⓒ Ⓓ Ⓔ	19 Ⓐ Ⓑ Ⓒ Ⓓ Ⓔ	24 Ⓐ Ⓑ Ⓒ Ⓓ Ⓔ
5 Ⓐ Ⓑ Ⓒ Ⓓ Ⓔ	10 Ⓐ Ⓑ Ⓒ Ⓓ Ⓔ	15 Ⓐ Ⓑ Ⓒ Ⓓ Ⓔ	20 Ⓐ Ⓑ Ⓒ Ⓓ Ⓔ	25 Ⓐ Ⓑ Ⓒ Ⓓ Ⓔ

SECTION VI

1 Ⓐ Ⓑ Ⓒ Ⓓ Ⓔ	5 Ⓐ Ⓑ Ⓒ Ⓓ Ⓔ	9 Ⓐ Ⓑ Ⓒ Ⓓ Ⓔ	13 Ⓐ Ⓑ Ⓒ Ⓓ Ⓔ	17 Ⓐ Ⓑ Ⓒ Ⓓ Ⓔ
2 Ⓐ Ⓑ Ⓒ Ⓓ Ⓔ	6 Ⓐ Ⓑ Ⓒ Ⓓ Ⓔ	10 Ⓐ Ⓑ Ⓒ Ⓓ Ⓔ	14 Ⓐ Ⓑ Ⓒ Ⓓ Ⓔ	18 Ⓐ Ⓑ Ⓒ Ⓓ Ⓔ
3 Ⓐ Ⓑ Ⓒ Ⓓ Ⓔ	7 Ⓐ Ⓑ Ⓒ Ⓓ Ⓔ	11 Ⓐ Ⓑ Ⓒ Ⓓ Ⓔ	15 Ⓐ Ⓑ Ⓒ Ⓓ Ⓔ	19 Ⓐ Ⓑ Ⓒ Ⓓ Ⓔ
4 Ⓐ Ⓑ Ⓒ Ⓓ Ⓔ	8 Ⓐ Ⓑ Ⓒ Ⓓ Ⓔ	12 Ⓐ Ⓑ Ⓒ Ⓓ Ⓔ	16 Ⓐ Ⓑ Ⓒ Ⓓ Ⓔ	20 Ⓐ Ⓑ Ⓒ Ⓓ Ⓔ

SECTION VII

1 Ⓐ Ⓑ Ⓒ Ⓓ Ⓔ	6 Ⓐ Ⓑ Ⓒ Ⓓ Ⓔ	11 Ⓐ Ⓑ Ⓒ Ⓓ Ⓔ	16 Ⓐ Ⓑ Ⓒ Ⓓ Ⓔ	21 Ⓐ Ⓑ Ⓒ Ⓓ Ⓔ
2 Ⓐ Ⓑ Ⓒ Ⓓ Ⓔ	7 Ⓐ Ⓑ Ⓒ Ⓓ Ⓔ	12 Ⓐ Ⓑ Ⓒ Ⓓ Ⓔ	17 Ⓐ Ⓑ Ⓒ Ⓓ Ⓔ	22 Ⓐ Ⓑ Ⓒ Ⓓ Ⓔ
3 Ⓐ Ⓑ Ⓒ Ⓓ Ⓔ	8 Ⓐ Ⓑ Ⓒ Ⓓ Ⓔ	13 Ⓐ Ⓑ Ⓒ Ⓓ Ⓔ	18 Ⓐ Ⓑ Ⓒ Ⓓ Ⓔ	23 Ⓐ Ⓑ Ⓒ Ⓓ Ⓔ
4 Ⓐ Ⓑ Ⓒ Ⓓ Ⓔ	9 Ⓐ Ⓑ Ⓒ Ⓓ Ⓔ	14 Ⓐ Ⓑ Ⓒ Ⓓ Ⓔ	19 Ⓐ Ⓑ Ⓒ Ⓓ Ⓔ	24 Ⓐ Ⓑ Ⓒ Ⓓ Ⓔ
5 Ⓐ Ⓑ Ⓒ Ⓓ Ⓔ	10 Ⓐ Ⓑ Ⓒ Ⓓ Ⓔ	15 Ⓐ Ⓑ Ⓒ Ⓓ Ⓔ	20 Ⓐ Ⓑ Ⓒ Ⓓ Ⓔ	25 Ⓐ Ⓑ Ⓒ Ⓓ Ⓔ

SECTION VIII

1 Ⓐ Ⓑ Ⓒ Ⓓ Ⓔ	8 Ⓐ Ⓑ Ⓒ Ⓓ Ⓔ	15 Ⓐ Ⓑ Ⓒ Ⓓ Ⓔ	22 Ⓐ Ⓑ Ⓒ Ⓓ Ⓔ	29 Ⓐ Ⓑ Ⓒ Ⓓ Ⓔ
2 Ⓐ Ⓑ Ⓒ Ⓓ Ⓔ	9 Ⓐ Ⓑ Ⓒ Ⓓ Ⓔ	16 Ⓐ Ⓑ Ⓒ Ⓓ Ⓔ	23 Ⓐ Ⓑ Ⓒ Ⓓ Ⓔ	30 Ⓐ Ⓑ Ⓒ Ⓓ Ⓔ
3 Ⓐ Ⓑ Ⓒ Ⓓ Ⓔ	10 Ⓐ Ⓑ Ⓒ Ⓓ Ⓔ	17 Ⓐ Ⓑ Ⓒ Ⓓ Ⓔ	24 Ⓐ Ⓑ Ⓒ Ⓓ Ⓔ	31 Ⓐ Ⓑ Ⓒ Ⓓ Ⓔ
4 Ⓐ Ⓑ Ⓒ Ⓓ Ⓔ	11 Ⓐ Ⓑ Ⓒ Ⓓ Ⓔ	18 Ⓐ Ⓑ Ⓒ Ⓓ Ⓔ	25 Ⓐ Ⓑ Ⓒ Ⓓ Ⓔ	32 Ⓐ Ⓑ Ⓒ Ⓓ Ⓔ
5 Ⓐ Ⓑ Ⓒ Ⓓ Ⓔ	12 Ⓐ Ⓑ Ⓒ Ⓓ Ⓔ	19 Ⓐ Ⓑ Ⓒ Ⓓ Ⓔ	26 Ⓐ Ⓑ Ⓒ Ⓓ Ⓔ	33 Ⓐ Ⓑ Ⓒ Ⓓ Ⓔ
6 Ⓐ Ⓑ Ⓒ Ⓓ Ⓔ	13 Ⓐ Ⓑ Ⓒ Ⓓ Ⓔ	20 Ⓐ Ⓑ Ⓒ Ⓓ Ⓔ	27 Ⓐ Ⓑ Ⓒ Ⓓ Ⓔ	34 Ⓐ Ⓑ Ⓒ Ⓓ Ⓔ
7 Ⓐ Ⓑ Ⓒ Ⓓ Ⓔ	14 Ⓐ Ⓑ Ⓒ Ⓓ Ⓔ	21 Ⓐ Ⓑ Ⓒ Ⓓ Ⓔ	28 Ⓐ Ⓑ Ⓒ Ⓓ Ⓔ	35 Ⓐ Ⓑ Ⓒ Ⓓ Ⓔ

PRACTICE EXAMINATION 3

SECTION I

Time—30 Minutes
25 Questions

Directions: Below each of the following passages, you will find questions or incomplete statements about the passage. Each statement or question is followed by five lettered words or expressions. Select the word or expression that most satisfactorily completes each statement or answers each question in accordance with the meaning of the passage. After you have chosen the best answer, blacken the corresponding space on the answer sheet.

Although it is now possible to bring most high blood pressure under control, the causes of essential hypertension remain elusive. Understanding how hypertension begins is at least partly
5 a problem of understanding when in life it begins, and this may be very early—perhaps within the first few months of life. Since the beginning of the century, physicians have been aware that hypertension may run in families, but before the 1970's,
10 studies of the familial aggregation of blood pressure treated only populations 15 years of age or older. Few studies were attempted in younger persons because of a prevailing notion that blood pressures in this age group were difficult to
15 measure and unreliable and because essential hypertension was widely regarded as a disease of adults.

In 1971, a study of 700 children, ages 2 to 14, used a special blood pressure recorder which
20 minimizes observer error and allows for standardization of blood pressure readings. Before then, it had been well established that the blood pressure of adults aggregates familially, that is, the similarities between the blood pressure of an individ-
25 ual and his siblings are generally too great to be explained by chance. The 1971 study showed that familial clustering was measurable in children as well, suggesting that factors responsible for essential hypertension are acquired in childhood.
30 Additional epidemiological studies demonstrated

a clear tendency for the children to retain the same blood pressure patterns, relative to their peers, four years later. Thus, a child with blood pressure higher or lower than the norm would tend to remain higher or lower with increasing 35 age.

Meanwhile, other investigators uncovered a complex of physiologic roles—including blood pressure—for a vasoactive system called the kallikrein-kinin system. Kallikreins are enzymes 40 in the kidney and blood plasma which act on precursors called kininogens to produce vasoactive peptides called kinins. Several different kinins are produced, at least three of which are powerful blood vessel dilators. Apparently, the 45 kallikrein-kinin system normally tends to offset the elevations in arterial pressure that result from the secretion of salt-conserving hormones such as aldosterone on the one hand and from activation of the sympathetic nervous system (which tends 50 to constrict blood vessels) on the other hand.

It is also known that urinary kallikrein excretion is abnormally low in subjects with essential hypertension. Levels of urinary kallikrein in children are inversely related to the diastolic 55 blood pressures of both children and their mothers. Children with the lowest kallikrein levels are found in the families with the highest blood pressures. In addition, black children tend to show somewhat lower urinary kallikrein levels 60 than white children, and blacks are more likely to have high blood pressure. There is a great deal to be learned about the biochemistry and physiologic roles of the kallikrein-kinin system. But there is the possibility that essential hypertension 65 will prove to have biochemical precursors.

1. The author is primarily concerned with
   (A) questioning the assumption behind

certain experiments involving children under the age of 15

(B) describing the new scientific findings about high blood pressure and suggesting some implications

(C) describing two different methods for studying the causes of high blood pressure

(D) revealing a discrepancy between the findings of epidemiological studies and laboratory studies on essential hypertension

(E) arguing that high blood pressure may be influenced by familial factors

2. Which of the following are factors mentioned by the author which discouraged studies of essential hypertension in children?

   I. the belief that children generally did not suffer from essential hypertension
   II. the belief that it was difficult or impossible to measure accurately blood pressures in children
   III. the belief that blood pressure in adults aggregates familially

   (A) I only
   (B) II only
   (C) III only
   (D) I and II only
   (E) I, II, and III

3. The argument in the passage leads most naturally to which of the following conclusions?

   (A) A low output of urinary kallikrein is a likely cause of high blood pressure in children.
   (B) The kallikrein-kinin system plays an important role in the regulation of blood pressure.
   (C) Essential hypertension may have biochemical precursors which may be useful predictors in children.
   (D) The failure of the body to produce sufficient amounts of kinins is the cause of essential hypertension.
   (E) It is now possible to predict high blood pressure by using familial aggregations and urinary kallikrein measurement.

4. The author refers to the somewhat lower urinary kallikrein levels in black children (lines 59–62) in order to

   (A) support the thesis that kallikrein levels are inversely related to blood pressure
   (B) highlight the special health problems involved in treating populations with high concentrations of black children
   (C) offer a causal explanation for the difference in urinary kallikrein levels between black and white children
   (D) suggest that further study needs to be done on the problem of high blood pressure among black adults
   (E) prove that hypertension can be treated if those persons likely to have high blood pressure can be found

5. The author suggests that the kallikrein-kinin system may affect blood pressure in which of the following ways?

   I. by directly opposing the tendency of the sympathetic nervous system to constrict blood vessels
   II. by producing kinins, which tend to dilate blood vessels
   III. by suppressing the production of hormones such as aldosterone

   (A) I only
   (B) II only
   (C) I and III only
   (D) II and III only
   (E) I, II, and III

6. The evidence that a child with blood pressure higher or lower than the norm would tend to remain so with increasing age (lines 30–33) is introduced by the author in order to

   (A) suggest that essential hypertension may have biochemical causes
   (B) show that high blood pressure can be detected in children under the age of 15
   (C) provide evidence that factors affecting blood pressure are already present in children
   (D) propose that increased screening of children for high blood pressure should be undertaken

(E) refute arguments that blood pressure in children cannot be measured reliably

7. The author presents his argument primarily by
(A) contrasting two methods of doing scientific research
(B) providing experimental evidence against a conclusion
(C) presenting new scientific findings for a conclusion
(D) analyzing a new theory and showing its defects
(E) criticizing scientific research on blood pressure done before 1971

8. According to the passage, kallikreins may act to reduce blood pressure by
(A) dilating blood vessels
(B) increasing enzymes in the kidneys and blood plasma
(C) secreting salt-conserving hormones
(D) activating the sympathetic nervous system
(E) increasing urinary kallikrein excretion

9. The author regards further research on the relationship between the kallikrein-kinin system and blood pressure as
(A) misdirected
(B) hazardous
(C) difficult
(D) unneeded
(E) warranted

Many critics of the current welfare system argue that existing welfare regulations foster family instability. They maintain that those regulations, which exclude most poor husband-and-
5 wife families from Aid to Families with Dependent Children assistance grants, contribute to the problem of family dissolution. Thus, they conclude that expanding the set of families eligible for family assistance plans or guaranteed income
10 measures would result in a marked strengthening of the low-income family structure.

If all poor families could receive welfare, would the incidence of instability change markedly? The answer to this question depends on the relative
15 importance of three categories of potential wel-

fare recipients. The first is the "cheater"—the husband who is reported to have abandoned his family, but in fact disappears only when the social caseworker is in the neighborhood. The second
20 consists of a loving husband and devoted father who, sensing his own inadequacy as a provider, leaves so that his wife and children may enjoy the relative benefit provided by public assistance. There is very little evidence that these categories
25 are significant.

The third category is the unhappily married couple who remain together out of a sense of economic responsibiity for their children, because of the high costs of separation, or because of the
30 consumption benefits of marriage. This group is numerous. The formation, maintenance and dissolution of the family is in large part a function of the relative balance between the benefits and costs of marriage as seen by the individual
35 members of the marriage. The major benefit generated by the creation of a family is the expansion of the set of consumption possibilities. The benefits from such a partnership depend largely on the relative dissimilarity of the re-
40 sources or basic endowments each partner brings to the marriage. Persons with similar productive capacities have less economic "cement" holding their marriage together. Since the family performs certain functions society regards as vital, a
45 complex network of social and legal buttresses has evolved to reinforce marriage. Much of the variation in marital stability across income classes can be explained by the variation in costs of dissolution imposed by society, e.g., division of
50 property, alimony, child support, and the social stigma attached to divorce.

Marital stability is related to the costs of achieving an acceptance agreement on family consumption and production and to the prevailing
55 social price of instability in the marriage partners' social-economic group. Expected AFDC income exerts pressures on family instability by reducing the cost of dissolution. To the extent that welfare is a form of government-subsidized alimony
60 payments, it reduces the institutional costs of separation and guarantees a minimal standard of living for wife and children. So welfare opportunities are a significant determinant of family instability in poor neighborhoods, but this is not the
65 result of AFDC regulations that exclude most intact families from coverage. Rather, welfare-related instability occurs because public assistance

lowers both the benefits of marriage and the costs of its disruption by providing a system of govern-
70 ment-subsidized alimony payments.

10. The author is primarily concerned to
   (A) interpret the results of a survey
   (B) discuss the role of the father in low-income families
   (C) analyze the causes of a phenomenon
   (D) recommend reforms in the welfare system
   (E) change public attitude toward welfare recipients

11. Which of the following would provide the most logical continuation of the final paragraph?
   (A) Paradoxically, any liberalization of AFDC eligibility restrictions is likely to intensify, rather than mitigate, pressures on family stability.
   (B) Actually, concern for the individual recipients should not be allowed to override considerations of sound fiscal policy.
   (C) In reality, there is virtually no evidence that AFDC payments have any relationship at all to problems of family instability in low-income marriages.
   (D) In the final analysis, it appears that government welfare payments, to the extent that the cost of marriage is lowered, encourages the formation of low-income families.
   (E) Ultimately, the problem of low-income family instability can be eliminated by reducing welfare benefits to the point where the cost of dissolution equals the cost of staying married.

12. All of the following are mentioned by the author as factors tending to perpetuate a marriage EXCEPT
   (A) the stigma attached to divorce
   (B) the social class of the partners
   (C) the cost of alimony and child support
   (D) the loss of property upon divorce
   (E) the greater consumption possibilities of married people

13. Which of the following best summarizes the main idea of the passage?
   (A) Welfare restrictions limiting the eligibility of families for benefits do not contribute to low-income family instability.
   (B) Contrary to popular opinion, the most significant category of welfare recipients is not the "cheating" father.
   (C) The incidence of family dissolution among low-income families is directly related to the inability of families with fathers to get welfare benefits.
   (D) Very little of the divorce rate among low-income families can be attributed to fathers' deserting their families so that they can qualify for welfare.
   (E) Government welfare payments are at present excessively high and must be reduced in order to slow the growing divorce rate among low-income families.

14. The tone of the passage can best be described as
   (A) confident and optimistic
   (B) scientific and detached
   (C) discouraged and alarmed
   (D) polite and sensitive
   (E) calloused and indifferent

15. With which of the following statements about marriage would the author most likely agree?
   (A) Marriage is an institution that is largely shaped by powerful but impersonal economic and social forces.
   (B) Marriage has a greater value to persons in higher income brackets than to person in lower income brackets.
   (C) Society has no legitimate interest in encouraging people to remain married to one another.
   (D) Marriage as an institution is no longer economically viable and will gradually give way to other forms of social organization.
   (E) The rising divorce rate across all income brackets indicates that people are more self-centered and less concerned about others than before.

16. The passage would most likely be found in a
    (A) pamphlet on civil rights
    (B) basic economics text
    (C) book on the history of welfare
    (D) religious tract on the importance of marriage
    (E) scholarly journal devoted to public policy questions

17. The author mentions the category of the "cheater" (line 16) in order to
    (A) demonstrate that some persons are not eligible for Aid to Families with Dependent Children assistance grants
    (B) correct a possible misconception about the effect of welfare on family stability
    (C) cite an example of the type of family which is likely to disintegrate as a result of welfare payments
    (D) introduce a counterexample to the thesis that welfare encourages family dissolution
    (E) compare the attitudes of honest but poor working persons with dishonest welfare cheaters

Reverse discrimination, minority recruitment, racial quotas, and, more generally, affirmative action are phrases that carry powerful emotional charges. But why should affirmative action, of all
5 government policies, be so controversial? In a sense, affirmative action is like other government programs, e.g., defense, conservation and public schools. Affirmative action programs are designed to achieve legitimate government objec-
10 tives such as improved economic efficiency, reduced social tension and general betterment of the public welfare. While it cannot be denied that there is no guarantee that affirmative action will achieve these results, neither can it be denied that
15 there are plausible, even powerful, sociological and economic arguments pointing to its likely success.

Government programs, however, entail a cost; i.e., the expenditure of social or economic
20 resources. Setting aside cases in which the specific user is charged a fee for service (toll roads and tuition at state institutions), the burdens and benefits of publicly funded or mandated programs are widely shared. When an
25 individual benefits personally from a government program, it is only because she or he is one member of a larger beneficiary class, e.g., a farmer; and most government revenue is obtained through a scheme of general taxation to which all are subject. 30

Affirmative action programs are exceptions to this general rule, though not, as it might at first seem, because the beneficiaries of the programs are specific individuals. It is still the case that those who ultimately benefit from affirmative 35 action do so only by virtue of their status as a member of a larger group, a particular minority. Rather the difference is the location of the burden. In affirmative action, the burden of "funding" the program is not shared universally, 40 and that is inherent in the nature of the case, as can be seen clearly in the case of affirmative action in employment. Often job promotions are allocated along a single dimension—seniority. When an employer promotes a less senior worker 45 from a minority group, the person disadvantaged by the move is easily identified: the worker with greatest seniority on a combined minority-nonminority list passed over for promotion.

Now we are confronted with two competing 50 moral sentiments. On the one hand, there is the idea that those who have been unfairly disadvantaged by past discriminatory practices are entitled to some kind of assistance. On the other, there is the feeling that no person ought to be deprived of 55 what is rightfully his, even for the worthwhile service of his fellow humans. In this respect, disability due to past racial discrimination, at least in so far as there is no connection to the passed-over worker, is like a natural evil. When a 60 villainous man willfully and without provocation strikes and injures another, there is not only the feeling that the injured person ought to be compensated but there is also consensus that the appropriate party to bear the cost is the one who 65 inflicted the injury. Yet, if the same innocent man stumbled and injured himself, it would be surprising to hear someone argue that the villainous man ought to be taxed for the injury simply because he might have tripped the victim had he been given 70 the opportunity. There may very well be agreement that the victim should be aided in his recovery with money and personal assistance, and many will give willingly, but there is also agreement that no one individual ought to be singled 75 out and forced to do what must ultimately be considered an act of charity.

18. The passage is primarily concerned with
   (A) comparing affirmative action programs to other government programs
   (B) arguing that affirmative action programs are morally justified
   (C) analyzing the basis for moral judgments about affirmative action programs
   (D) introducing the reader to the importance of affirmative action as a social issue
   (E) describing the benefits which can be obtained through affirmative action programs

19. The author mentions toll roads and tuition at state institutions (lines 21–22) in order to
   (A) anticipate a possible objection based on counterexamples
   (B) avoid a contradiction between moral sentiments
   (C) provide illustrations of common government programs
   (D) voice doubts about the social and economic value of affirmative action
   (E) offer examples of government programs that are too costly

20. With which of the following statements would the author most likely agree?
   (A) Affirmative action programs should be discontinued because they place an unfair burden on nonminority persons who bear the cost of the programs.
   (B) Affirmative action programs may be able to achieve legitimate social and economic goals such as improved efficiency.
   (C) Affirmative action programs are justified because they are the only way of correcting injustices created by past discrimination.
   (D) Affirmative action programs must be redesigned so that society as a whole, rather than particular individuals, bears the cost of the programs.
   (E) Affirmative action programs should be abandoned because they serve no useful social function and place unfair burdens on particular individuals.

21. The author most likely places the word "funding" in quotation marks (line 41) in order to remind the reader that
   (A) affirmative action programs are costly in terms of government revenues
   (B) particular individuals may bear a disproportionate share of the burden of affirmative action
   (C) the cost of most government programs is shared by society at large
   (D) the beneficiaries of affirmative action are members of larger groups
   (E) the cost of affirmative action is not only a monetary expenditure

22. The "villainous man" introduced at line 60 functions primarily as a(n)
   (A) illustration
   (B) counterexample
   (C) authority
   (D) analogy
   (E) disclaimer

23. According to the passage, affirmative action programs are different from most other government programs in which of the following ways?

   I. the goals the programs are designed to achieve
   II. the ways in which costs of the programs are distributed
   III. the ways in which benefits of the programs are allocated

   (A) I only
   (B) II only
   (C) III only
   (D) II and III only
   (E) I, II, and III

24. It can be inferred that the author believes the reader will regard affirmative action programs as
   (A) posing a moral dilemma
   (B) based on unsound premises
   (C) containing self-contradictions
   (D) creating needless suffering
   (E) offering a panacea

25. The primary purpose of the passage is to
   (A) reconcile two conflicting points of view

(B)   describe and refute a point of view
(C)   provide a historical context for a
      problem

(D)   suggest a new method for studying
      social problems
(E)   analyze the structure of an intuition

STOP

END OF SECTION. IF YOU HAVE ANY TIME LEFT, GO
OVER YOUR WORK IN THIS SECTION ONLY. DO NOT
WORK IN ANY OTHER SECTION OF THE TEST.

SECTION II

Time—30 Minutes
20 Questions

Directions: For each of the following questions, select the best of the answer choices and blacken the corresponding space on your answer sheet.
Numbers: All numbers used are real numbers.
Figures: The diagrams and figures that accompany these questions are for the purpose of providing information useful in answering the questions. Unless it is stated that a specific figure is not drawn to scale, the diagrams and figures are drawn as accurately as possible. All figures are in a plane unless otherwise indicated.

1. A certain machine processes 8 quarts of milk every 6 seconds. How many gallons of milk can the machine process in 3 minutes?
    (A) 18
    (B) 20
    (C) 60
    (D) 75
    (E) 120

2. During a half-price sale, Ms. Baker bought a toothbrush for the usual price and a second toothbrush for one-half the usual price. If she paid $1.80 for the 2 toothbrushes, what was the usual price of a toothbrush?
    (A) $ .60
    (B) $ .50
    (C) $. 90
    (D) $1.20
    (E) $2.40

3. If a sales representative earned a total of $18,000 in commissions in one year, what was the amount she earned in March if the total commissions she earned in that month was half her monthly average for the year?
    (A) $3,000
    (B) $1,500
    (C) $900
    (D) $750
    (E) $500

4. For which of the following lengths of a side of a square would the perimeter be divisible by both 4 and 7?
    (A) 3

    (B) 4
    (C) 5
    (D) 6
    (E) 7

5. On a certain day, a news vendor began the day with P papers. Between opening and noon, he sold 40 percent of the papers, and between noon and closing, he sold 60 percent of the papers which remained. What percent of the original P papers did he sell?
    (A) 0%
    (B) 20%
    (C) 24%
    (D) 76%
    (E) 100%

6. The value of a certain office machine depreciates in such a way that its value at the end of each year is $\frac{4}{5}$ of its value at the beginning of the same year. If the initial value of the machine is $5,000, what is its value at the end of 3 years?
    (A) $4,750.25
    (B) $4,000.00
    (C) $2,560.00
    (D) $2,000.00
    (E) $640.00

7. In a certain year, corporation X produced 40 percent of the total world production of a certain drug. If corporation X produced 18 kilograms of the drug, how many kilograms were produced by producers other than corporation X?
    (A) 22
    (B) 27
    (C) 36
    (D) 40
    (E) 45

8. A certain metropolitan area consists of six counties. The poorest county in terms of income has an average income of $12,500 per x persons. The richest county in terms of

income has an average income of $16,250 per x persons. Which of the following could NOT be the average income per x persons for the entire six-county metropolitan area as a whole?

(A) $12,750
(B) $13,250
(C) $14,250
(D) $16,115
(E) $16,775

9. If x < 0, which of the following is NOT necessarily true?

(A) $\frac{1}{x^2} > 0$
(B) $x^2 > x^3$
(C) $x^5 < x^4$
(D) $x^2 + x^3 > 0$
(E) $x^3 < 0$

10. In a certain year, the income of an individual from her investments amounted to 45 percent of her total income. If municipal bonds accounted for $\frac{2}{3}$ of her investment income, then the ratio of income derived from municipal bonds to total *noninvestment* income was

(A) $\frac{2}{3}$
(B) $\frac{6}{11}$
(C) $\frac{3}{10}$
(D) $\frac{3}{11}$
(E) $\frac{3}{20}$

11. For a certain concert, 560 tickets were sold for a total of $2,150. If an orchestra seat sold for twice the balcony seat price of $2.50, how many of the tickets sold were balcony seat tickets?

(A) 235
(B) 260
(C) 300
(D) 325
(E) 358

12. A certain liquid fertilizer contains 10 percent mineral X by volume. If a farmer wishes to treat a crop with $\frac{3}{4}$ of a liter of mineral X per acre, how many acres can he treat with 300 liters of the liquid fertilizer?

(A) 40
(B) 24
(C) 18
(D) 16
(E) 12

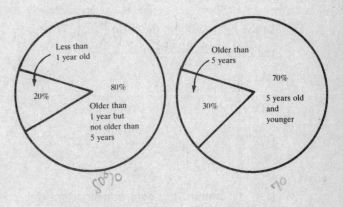

13. The diagrams above show the percent of all children of the ages specified at a day-care center. What percent of all children are one year old or older, but not older than five years?

(A) 10%
(B) 24%
(C) 50%
(D) 55%
(E) 56%

14. At the beginning of a class, a classroom has 3 empty chairs and all students are seated. No student leaves the classroom, and additional students equal to 20 percent of the number of students already seated enter the class late and fill the empty chairs. What is the total number of chairs in the classroom?

(A) 18
(B) 15
(C) 10
(D) 6
(E) 3

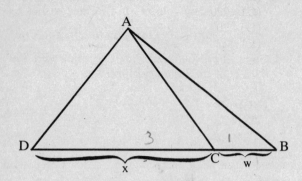

15. In the figure above, the ratio $\frac{w}{x}$ is $\frac{1}{3}$. What is the ratio $\frac{area\ \Delta\ ABC}{area\ \Delta\ ACD}$?

(A) $\frac{1}{6}$

(B) $\frac{1}{3}$

(C) $\frac{3}{1}$

(D) $\frac{6}{1}$

(E) It cannot be determined from the information given.

16. In a certain shipment, x out of every y items were found to be defective. If 10 defective items were found in the shipment, what was the total number of items in the shipment?

(A) $\frac{10y}{x}$

(B) $\frac{10x}{y}$

(C) $10y$

(D) $\frac{10y}{y - x}$

(E) $\frac{10x}{x - y}$

17. Four cylindrical cans each with a radius of 2 inches are placed on their bases inside an open square pasteboard box. If the four sides of the box bulge slightly, which of the following could be the internal perimeter of the base of the box, expressed in inches?

(A) 20

(B) 16

(C) 30

(D) 32

(E) 64

18. In a certain office each day, the number of cases to be handled is divided evenly among p workers. If $\frac{1}{8}$ of the workers are absent and the cases they would have handled are divided evenly among the workers present, the increase in the share of each of these workers would be what fraction of his or her original share of cases?

(A) $\frac{1}{8}$

(B) $\frac{1}{7}$

(C) $\frac{7}{8}$

(D) $\frac{8}{7}$

(E) $\frac{1}{7p}$

19. Machine M can produce x units in $\frac{3}{4}$ of the time it takes machine N to produce x units. Machine N can produce x units in $\frac{2}{3}$ the time it takes machine O to produce x units. If all three machines are working simultaneously, what fraction of the total output is produced by machine N?

(A) $\frac{1}{2}$

(B) $\frac{1}{3}$

(C) $\frac{4}{13}$

(D) $\frac{8}{29}$

(E) $\frac{6}{33}$

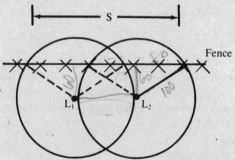

20. In the figure above, two security lights, L_1 and L_2, are located 100 feet apart. Each illuminates an area of radius 100 feet, and

both are located 60 feet from a chain-link
fence. What is the total length s of fence, in
feet, illuminated by the two lights?

(A) 260

(B) 240

(C) 220

(D) 200

(E) 180

STOP

END OF SECTION. IF YOU HAVE ANY TIME LEFT, GO
OVER YOUR WORK IN THIS SECTION ONLY. DO NOT
WORK IN ANY OTHER SECTION OF THE TEST.

SECTION III

Time—30 Minutes
25 Questions

Directions: Each question below is followed by two numbered facts. You are to determine whether the data given in the statements is sufficient for answering the question. Use the data given, plus your knowledge of math and everyday facts, to choose between the five possible answers.

(A) if statement 1 alone is sufficient to answer the question, but statement 2 alone is not sufficient
(B) if statement 2 alone is sufficient to answer the question, but statement 1 alone is not sufficient
(C) if both statements together are needed to answer the question, but neither statement alone is sufficient
(D) if either statement by itself is sufficient to answer the question
(E) if not enough facts are given to answer the question

1. 149 people were aboard Flight 222 when it arrived at Los Angeles from New York City with Chicago as the only intermediate stop. How many people first boarded the flight in Chicago?
   (1) 170 people were aboard the flight when it left New York City.
   (2) 23 people from the flight deplaned in Chicago and did not reboard.

2. The total number of active members in a college fraternity is $12\frac{1}{2}$ percent higher this year than last year. How many active members does the fraternity have this year?
   (1) Last year, 23 members of the fraternity graduated.
   (2) Last year, there were 56 active members in the fraternity.

3. Is p a positive number?
   (1) 5p is a positive number
   (2) −p is a negative number

4. An author is paid how much in royalties by a publisher in a certain year?
   (1) The publisher pays her a guaranteed minimum of $10,000 per year plus royalty.

   (2) The author receives a yearly royalty of $6\frac{1}{2}$ percent on the gross sales of her book in excess of $100,000.

5. Is 15 the average (arithmetic mean) of x, y, and 15?
   (1) x + y = 30
   (2) x − y = 4

6. Mary, Paul and Susan all played in a summer softball league, and each hit at least one home run during the season. Which of the three players hit the most home runs?
   (1) Paul hit $\frac{4}{5}$ as many home runs as Mary.
   (2) Mary hit $\frac{5}{4}$ as many home runs as Susan.

7. What is the perimeter of a rectangle if the ratio of its width to its length is 3 to 4?
   (1) The width of the rectangle is 6.
   (2) The area of the rectangle is 48.

8. Amy's graduate seminar in history meets once each week, on Thursday afternoons. If it met every Thursday in the month of May, how many times did the seminar meet that month?
   (1) There were five Wednesdays in the month.
   (2) The seventeenth of May was a Friday.

9. Was Mark's average running speed for the first hour of his 26-mile marathon 11 miles per hour?
   (1) He ran the entire 26 miles in 2.5 hours.
   (2) He ran the last 15 miles in 1.5 hours.

10. If p > 0, what percent is p of q?
    (1) q = 2p
    (2) p + q = 36

11. A certain packing crate contains between 50 and 60 books. How many books are there in the packing crate?

(1) If the books are counted out by threes, there will be one book left over.

(2) If the books are counted out by sixes, there will be one book left over.

12. If x, y and z are the lengths of three sides of a triangle, is z > 8?
    (1) x + y = 8
    (2) x = 6

13. At 9 A.M., a hiker was due south of point P. What direction was point P from her position at noon?
    (1) From 9 A.M. until 11 A.M., she walked due east at 2 miles per hour; and from 11 A.M. until noon, she walked due north at 3 miles per hour.
    (2) At noon, she is exactly 4.5 miles from point P.

14. If N and P denote the nonzero digits of a four-digit number NNPP, is NNPP divisible by 4?
    (1) NPP is divisible by 8.
    (2) NPP is divisible by 4.

15. A supermarket sells both a leading brand of laundry powder and its own brand of laundry powder. On all sizes of the leading brand it makes a profit of 15 percent of cost per box. On all sizes of its own brand it makes a profit of 10 percent of cost per box. For a certain month, from the sales of which of the two brands does the supermarket realize the greater profit?
    (1) Ounce for ounce, the supermarket pays a higher wholesale price for the leading brand than it does for its own brand.
    (2) Ounce for ounce, the supermarket sells 25 percent more of its own brand than of the leading brand.

16. If x and y are positive integers, is x > y?
    (1) $x^2 < y$
    (2) $\sqrt{x} < y$

17. If the number of square units in the area of a circle is A and the number of linear units in the circumference is C, what is the radius of the circle?

(1) $\dfrac{A}{C} = \dfrac{3}{2}$

(2) A > C + 3

18. If all of the 30 students living in a dormitory are taking physics or math or both, how many of the students are taking both physics and math?
    (1) Of the 30 students, 10 are taking only physics.
    (2) Of the 30 students, 20 are taking math and 16 are taking physics.

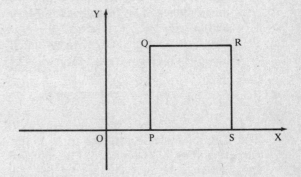

19. In the figure above, P and S are points on the x-axis. What is the area of square PQRS?
    (1) The coordinates of point P are (2, 0).
    (2) The coordinates of point R are (6, 4).

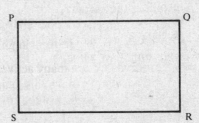

20. Is quadrilateral PQRS a square?
    (1) PR = SQ
    (2) All of the interior angles are equal.

21. If S is a sequence of numbers the first term of which is 1 and each succeeding term of which is x more than the preceding term, what is the value of x?
    (1) The sum of the third and fourth terms of S is 22.

(2) The sum of the second and ninth terms of S is 39.

22. Two children, Bob and Mary, have piggy banks into which they deposit money earned from doing odd jobs. In a certain year, both Bob and Mary each deposited $5 on the first of every month into their respective piggy banks. If these were the only deposits made into the piggy banks during the year, on December 31 does Bob have more money in his piggy bank than Mary has in her piggy bank? (Assume no withdrawals.)

(1) On March 15 Bob had three times as much money in his piggy bank as Mary had in hers.

(2) On June 15 Bob had twice as much money in his piggy bank as Mary had in hers.

23. The Central Hotel contracted to have the carpeting in its lobby replaced. The contract specified that the only charges for the job would be a charge for purchasing the carpet and a charge for installing it. What percent of the total amount paid for purchasing and installing the carpet was the installation charge?

(1) The installation charge was $240 less than the total cost of purchasing and installing the carpet.

(2) Without the installation charge, the total cost of the carpet would have been only $\frac{3}{4}$ as much.

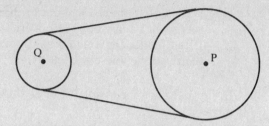

24. Two pulleys are connected by a belt as shown in the drawing above. If pulley Q makes 300 revolutions per minute, how many revolutions per minute does pulley P make?

(1) The length of the belt is 12π.

(2) The ratio of the radius of pulley P to the radius of pulley Q is 2 to 1.

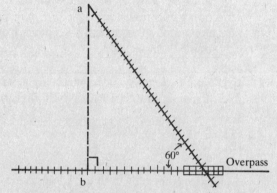

25. In the diagram above, trains P and Q start from stations a and b, respectively, and at the same time. Do they arrive at the overpass at the same time?

(1) The speed of train P is exactly twice that of train Q.

(2) Train Q is traveling at 30 miles per hour.

STOP

END OF SECTION. IF YOU HAVE ANY TIME LEFT, GO OVER YOUR WORK IN THIS SECTION ONLY. DO NOT WORK IN ANY OTHER SECTION OF THE TEST.

SECTION IV

Time—30 Minutes
25 Questions

Directions: In this section, the questions ask you to analyze and evaluate the reasoning in short paragraphs or passages. For some questions, all of the answer choices may conceivably be answers to the question asked. You should select the *best* answer to the question, that is, an answer which does not require you to make assumptions which violate commonsense standards by being implausible, redundant, irrelevant or inconsistent. After choosing the best answer, blacken the corresponding space on the answer sheet.

1. Children in the first three grades who attend private schools spend time each day working with a computerized reading program. Public schools have very few such programs. Tests prove, however, that public-school children are much weaker in reading skills when compared to their private-school counterparts. We conclude, therefore, that public-school children can be good readers only if they participate in a computerized reading program.

    The author's initial statements logically support his conclusion only if which of the following is also true?
    (A) All children can learn to be good readers if they are taught by a computerized reading program.
    (B) All children can learn to read at the same rate if they participate in a computerized reading program.
    (C) Better reading skills produce better students.
    (D) Computerized reading programs are the critical factor in the better reading skills of private-school students.
    (E) Public-school children can be taught better math skills.

2. Is your company going to continue to discriminate against women in its hiring and promotion policies?

    The above question might be considered unfair for which of the following reasons?

    I. Its construction seeks a "yes" or "no" answer where both might be inappropriate.
    II. It is internally inconsistent.

III. It contains a hidden presupposition which the responder might wish to contest.

    (A) I only
    (B) II only
    (C) I and II only
    (D) I and III only
    (E) I, II, and III

Questions 3 and 4

Ms. Evangeline Rose argued that money and time invested in acquiring a professional degree are totally wasted. As evidence supporting her argument, she offered the case of a man who, at considerable expense of money and time, completed his law degree and then married and lived as a house-husband, taking care of their children and working part time at a day care center so his wife could pursue her career.

3. Ms. Rose makes the unsupported assumption that
    (A) an education in the law is useful only in pursuing law-related activities
    (B) what was not acceptable 25 years ago may very well be acceptable today
    (C) wealth is more important than learning
    (D) professional success is a function of the quality of one's education
    (E) only the study of law can be considered professional study

4. The logical reasoning of Ms. Rose's argument is closely parallelled by which of the following?
    (A) A juvenile delinquent who insists that his behavior should be attributable to the fact that his parents did not love him.
    (B) A senator who votes large sums of money for military equipment, but who votes against programs designed to help the poor.
    (C) A conscientious objector who bases his draft resistance on the premise that there can be no moral wars.
    (D) When a policeman is found guilty of murdering his wife, an opponent of police brutality who says, "That's what these people mean by law and order."

(E) A high school senior who decides that rather than go to college he will enroll in a vocational training program to learn to be an electrician.

5. A cryptographer has intercepted an enemy message that is in code. He knows that the code is a simple substitution of numbers for letters. Which of the following would be the least helpful in breaking the code?
   (A) knowing the frequency with which the vowels of the language are used
   (B) knowing the frequency with which two vowels appear together in the language
   (C) knowing the frequency with which odd numbers appear relative to even numbers in the message
   (D) knowing the conjugation of the verb *to be* in the language on which the code is based
   (E) knowing every word in the language that begins with the letter *R*

6. One way of reducing commuting time for those who work in the cities is to increase the speed at which traffic moves in the heart of the city. This can be accomplished by raising the tolls on the tunnels and bridges connecting the city with other communities. This will discourage auto traffic into the city and will encourage people to use public transportation instead.

   Which of the following, if true, would LEAST weaken the argument above?
   (A) Nearly all of the traffic in the center of the city is commercial traffic which will continue despite toll increases.
   (B) Some people now driving alone into the city would choose to car-pool with each other rather than use public transportation.
   (C) Any temporary improvement in traffic flow would be lost because the improvement itself would attract more cars.
   (D) The numbers of commuters who would be deterred by the toll increases would be insignificant.
   (E) The public transportation system is not able to handle any significant increase in the number of commuters using the system.

7. An independent medical research team recently did a survey at a mountain retreat founded to help heavy smokers quit or cut down on their cigarette smoking. Eighty percent of those persons smoking three packs a day or more were able to cut

down to one pack a day after they began to take End-Smoke with its patented desire suppressant. Try End-Smoke to help you cut down significantly on your smoking.

Which of the following could be offered as valid criticism of the above advertisement?

I. Heavy smokers may be physically as well as psychologically addicted to tobacco.
II. A medicine that is effective for very heavy smokers may not be effective for the population of smokers generally.
III. A survey conducted at a mountain retreat to aid smokers may yield different results than one would expect under other circumstances.

(A) I only
(B) II only
(C) III only
(D) II and III only
(E) I, II, and III

8. JOCKEY: Horses are the most noble of all animals. They are both loyal and brave. I knew of a farm horse which died of a broken heart shortly after its owner died.

VETERINARIAN: You're wrong. Dogs can be just as loyal and brave. I had a dog who would wait every day on the front steps for me to come home, and if I did not arrive until midnight, he would still be there.

All of the following are true of the claims of the jockey and the veterinarian EXCEPT:
(A) both claims assume that loyalty and bravery are characteristics which are desirable in animals.
(B) both claims assume that the two most loyal animals are the horse and the dog.
(C) both claims assume that human qualities can be attributed to animals.
(D) both claims are supported by only a single example of animal behavior.
(E) neither claim is supported by evidence other than the opinions and observations of the speakers.

9. Rousseau assumed that human beings in the state of nature are characterized by a feeling of sympathy toward their fellow humans and other living creatures. In order to explain the existence of social ills, such as the exploitation of man by man, Rousseau maintained that our natural feelings are crushed under the weight of unsympathetic social institutions.

Rousseau's argument described above would be most strengthened if it could be explained how

(A) creatures naturally characterized by feelings of sympathy for all living creatures could create unsympathetic social institutions

(B) we can restructure our social institutions so that they will foster our natural sympathies for one another

(C) modern reformers might lead the way to a life which is not inconsistent with the ideals of the state of nature

(D) non-exploitative conduct could arise in conditions of the state of nature

(E) a return to the state of nature from modern society might be accomplished

10. Every element on the periodic chart is radioactive, though the most stable elements have half-lives which are thousands and thousands of years long. When an atom decays, it splits into two or more smaller atoms. Even considering the fusion taking place inside of stars, there is only a negligible tendency for smaller atoms to transmute into larger ones. Thus, the ratio of lighter to heavier atoms in the universe is increasing at a measurable rate.

Which of the following sentences provides the most logical continuation of this paragraph?

(A) Without radioactive decay of atoms, there could be no solar combustion and no life as we know it.

(B) Therefore, it is imperative that scientists begin developing ways to reverse the trend and restore the proper balance between the lighter and the heavier elements.

(C) Consequently, it is possible to use a shifting ratio of light to heavy atoms to calculate the age of the universe.

(D) Therefore, there are now more light elements in the universe than heavy ones.

(E) As a result, the fusion taking place inside stars has to produce enough atoms of the heavy elements to offset the radioactive decay of large atoms elsewhere in the universe.

Questions 11 and 12

SPEAKER: The great majority of people in the United States have access to the best medical care available anywhere in the world.

OBJECTOR: There are thousands of poor in this country who cannot afford to pay to see a doctor.

11. Which of the following is true of the objector's comment?

(A) It uses emotionally charged words.

(B) It constitutes a hasty generalization on few examples.

(C) It is not necessarily inconsistent with the speaker's remarks.

(D) It cites statistical evidence which tends to confirm the speaker's points.

(E) It overlooks the distinction the speaker draws between a cause and its effect.

12. A possible objection to the speaker's comments would be to point to the existence of

(A) a country which has more medical assistants than the United States

(B) a nation where medical care is provided free of charge by the government

(C) a country in which the people are given better medical care than Americans

(D) government hearings in the United States on the problems poor people have getting medical care

(E) a country which has a higher hospital bed per person ratio than the United States

13. We must do something about the rising cost of our state prisons. It now costs an average of $132 per day to maintain a prisoner in a double-occupancy cell in a state prison. Yet, in the most expensive cities in the world, one can find rooms in the finest hotels which rent for less than $125 per night.

The argument above might be criticized in all of the following ways EXCEPT:

(A) it introduces an inappropriate analogy

(B) it relies on an unwarranted appeal to authority

(C) it fails to take account of costs which prisons have but hotels do not have

(D) it misuses numerical data

(E) it draws a faulty comparison

Questions 14–16

The blanks in the following paragraph indicate deletions from the text. For questions 14 and 15, select the completion that is most appropriate.

I often hear smokers insisting that they have a *right* to smoke whenever and wherever they choose, as though there are no conceivable circumstances in which the law might not legitimately prohibit smoking. This contention is obviously indefensible. Implicit in the development of the concept of a right is the notion that one person's freedom of action is circumscribed by the——(14)——. It requires nothing more than common sense to realize that there are situations in which smoking presents a clear and present danger: in a crowded theater, around flammable materials, during take-off in an airplane. No one would seriously deny that the potential harm of smoking in such circumstances more than outweighs the satisfaction a smoker would derive from smoking. Yet, this balancing is not unique to situations of potential catastrophe. It applies equally as well to situations where the potential injury is small, though in most cases, as for example a person's table manners, the injury of the offended person is so slight we automatically strike the balance in favor of the person acting. But once it is recognized that a balance of freedoms must be struck, it follows that a smoker has a *right* to smoke only when and where——(15)——.

14. (A) Constitution of our nation
    (B) laws passed by Congress and interpreted by the Supreme Court
    (C) interest of any other person to not be injured or inconvenienced by that action
    (D) rights of other persons not to smoke
    (E) rights of non-smoking persons not to have to be subjected to the noxious fumes of tobacco smoking

15. (A) the government chooses to allow him to smoke
    (B) he finally decides to light up
    (C) his interest in smoking outweighs the interests of other persons in his not smoking
    (D) he can ensure that no other persons will be even slightly inconvenienced by his smoking
    (E) there are signs which explicitly state that smoking is allowed in that area

16. The author's strategy in questioning the claim that smokers have a right to smoke is to

(A) cite facts which are not generally known
(B) clarify and fully define a key concept
(C) entertain arguments on a hypothetical case
(D) uncover a logical inconsistency
(E) probe the reliability of an empirical generalization

17. Some judges are members of the bar. No member of the bar is a convicted felon. Therefore, some judges are not convicted felons.

Which of the following is logically most similar to the argument developed above?
(A) Anyone who jogs in the heat will be sick. I do not jog in the heat, and will therefore likely never be sick.
(B) People who want to avoid jury duty will not register to vote. A person may not vote until he is 18. Therefore, persons under 18 are not called for jury duty.
(C) All businesses file a tax return, but many businesses do not make enough money to pay taxes. Therefore, some businesses do not make a profit.
(D) All men are excluded from the women's dormitory, but some men are polite. Therefore, some polite men are not allowed in the women's dormitory.
(E) The Grand Canyon is large. The Grand Canyon is in Arizona. Therefore, Arizona is large.

Questions 18 and 19

A study published by the Department of Education shows that children in the central cities lag far behind students in the suburbs and the rural areas in reading skills. The report blames this differential on the overcrowding in the classrooms of city schools. I maintain, however, that the real reason that city children are poorer readers than non-city children is that they do not get enough fresh air and sunshine.

18. Which of the following best describes the form of the above argument?
    (A) It attacks the credibility of the Department of Education.
    (B) It indicts the methodology of the study of the Department of Education.
    (C) It attempts to show that central city students read as well as non-city students.
    (D) It offers an alternative explanation for the differential.
    (E) It argues from analogy.

19. Which of the following would LEAST strengthen the author's point in the preceding argument?
    (A) medical research which shows a correlation between air pollution and learning disabilities
    (B) a report by educational experts demonstrating there is no relationship between the number of students in a classroom and a student's ability to read
    (C) a notice released by the Department of Education retracting that part of their report which mentions overcrowding as the reason for the differential
    (D) the results of a federal program which indicates that city students show significant improvement in reading skills when they spend the summer in the country
    (E) a proposal by the federal government to fund emergency programs to hire more teachers for central city schools in an attempt to reduce overcrowding in the classrooms

20. Some judges have allowed hospitals to disconnect life-support equipment of patients who have no prospects for recovery. But I say that is murder. Either we put a stop to this practice now, or we will soon have programs of euthanasia for the old and infirm as well as others who might be considered a burden. Rather than disconnecting life-support equipment, we should let nature take its course.

    Which of the following are valid objections to the above argument?

    I. It is internally inconsistent.
    II. It employs emotionally charged terms.
    III. It presents a false dilemma.

    (A) I only
    (B) II only
    (C) III only
    (D) II and III only
    (E) I, II, and III

21. If Paul comes to the party, Quentin leaves the party. If Quentin leaves the party, either Robert or Steve asks Alice to dance. If Alice is asked to dance by either Robert or Steve and Quentin leaves the party, Alice accepts. If Alice is asked to dance by either Robert or Steve and Quentin does not leave the party, Alice does not accept.

    If Quentin does not leave the party, which of the following statements can be logically deduced from the information given?

    (A) Robert asks Alice to dance.
    (B) Steve asks Alice to dance.
    (C) Alice refuses to dance with either Robert or Steve.
    (D) Paul does not come to the party.
    (E) Alice leaves the party.

22. All students have submitted applications for admission. Some of the applications for admission have not been acted upon. Therefore, some more students will be accepted.

    The logic of which of the following is most similar to that of the argument above?
    (A) Some of the barrels have not yet been loaded on the truck, but all of the apples have been put into barrels. So, some more apples will be loaded onto the truck.
    (B) All students who received passing marks were women. X received a passing mark. Therefore, X is a woman.
    (C) Some chemicals will react with glass bottles, but not with plastic bottles. Therefore, those chemicals should be kept in plastic bottles and not glass ones.
    (D) All advertising must be approved by the Council before it is aired. This television spot for a new cola has not yet been approved by the Council. Therefore, it is not to be aired until the Council makes its decision.
    (E) There are six blue marbles and three red marbles in this jar. Therefore, if I blindly pick out seven marbles, there should be two red marbles left to pick.

23. New Evergreen Gum has twice as much flavor for your money as Spring Mint Gum, and we can prove it. You see, a stick of Evergreen Gum is twice as large as a stick of Spring Mint Gum, and the more gum, the more flavor.

    Which of the following, if true, would undermine the persuasive appeal of the above advertisement?

    I. A package of Spring Mint Gum contains twice as many sticks as a package of Evergreen Gum at the same price.
    II. Spring Mint Gum has more concentrated flavor than Evergreen Gum.
    III. Although a stick of Evergreen Gum is twice as large in volume as a stick of Spring Mint Gum, it weighs only 50% as much.

    (A) I only
    (B) II only

(C) I and II only

(D) II and III only

(E) I, II, and III

24. Judging from the tenor of the following statements and the apparent authoritativeness of their sources, which is the most reasonable and trustworthy?

(A) FILM CRITIC: Beethoven is really very much overrated as a composer. His music is not really that good; it's just very well known.

(B) SPOKESMAN FOR A MANUFACTURER: The jury's verdict against us for $2 million is ridiculous, and we are sure that the Appeals Court will agree with us.

(C) SENIOR CABINET OFFICER: Our administration plans to cut inefficiency, and we have already begun to discuss plans which we calculate will save the federal government nearly $50 billion a year in waste.

(D) FRENCH WINE EXPERT: The best buy in wines in America today is the California chablis which is comparable to the French chablis and is available at half the cost.

(E) UNION LEADER: We plan to stay out on strike until management meets each and every one of the demands we have submitted.

25. PUBLIC ANNOUNCEMENT: When you enroll with Future Careers Business Institute (FCBI), you will have access to our placement counseling service. Last year, 92% of our graduates who asked us to help them find jobs found them. So go FCBI for your future!

Which of the following would be appropriate questions to ask in order to determine the value of the preceding claim?

I. How many of your graduates asked FCBI for assistance?

II. How many people graduated from FCBI last year?

III. Did those people who asked for jobs find ones in the areas for which they were trained?

IV. Was FCBI responsible for finding the jobs or did graduates find them independently?

(A) I and II only

(B) I, II, and III only

(C) I, II, and IV only

(D) III and IV only

(E) I, II, III, and IV

STOP

END OF SECTION. IF YOU HAVE ANY TIME LEFT, GO OVER YOUR WORK IN THIS SECTION ONLY. DO NOT WORK IN ANY OTHER SECTION OF THE TEST.

SECTION V

Time—30 Minutes
25 Questions

Directions: In each problem below, either part or all of the sentence is underlined. The sentence is followed by five ways of writing the underlined part. Answer choice (A) repeats the original; the other answer choices vary. If you think that the original phrasing is the best, choose (A). If you think one of the other answer choices is the best, select that choice.

This section tests the ability to recognize correct and effective expression. Follow the requirements of Standard Written English: grammar, choice of words, and sentence construction. Choose the answer which results in the clearest, most exact sentence, but do not change the meaning of the original sentence.

1. It has been said that to be afraid of the dark is being afraid of all those things we cannot comprehend and, therefore, instinctively fear.
   - (A) said that to be afraid of the dark is being afraid
   - (B) said, that to be afraid of the dark, is being afraid
   - (C) said being afraid of the dark is to be afraid
   - (D) said that to be afraid of the dark is to be afraid
   - (E) said that to be being afraid of the dark is to be being afraid

2. Hurtling through space, Anna saw a shooting star and was transfixed by the rare beauty of this sight.
   - (A) Hurtling through space, Anna saw a shooting star and was transfixed by the rare beauty of this sight.
   - (B) Anna saw a shooting star and was transfixed by the rare beauty of this sight hurtling through space.
   - (C) Anna saw a shooting star hurtling through space and was transfixed by the rare beauty of this sight.
   - (D) Anna saw, hurtling through space, a shooting star and was transfixed by the rare beauty of this sight.
   - (E) Transfixed by the rare beauty of this sight, Anna saw a shooting star hurtling through space.

3. A study on the therapeutic value of pets as companions for the elderly has shown that cats are more superior than dogs as far as household companions are concerned.
   - (A) are more superior than dogs as far as household companions are concerned.
   - (B) are superior to dogs as household companions.
   - (C) are superior to dogs as far as household companions are concerned.
   - (D) are more superior to dogs as household companions.
   - (E) are superior household companions than dogs.

4. Tibetan rugs are so expensive because the weaver still pursues his art as they have for centuries, by hand-dyeing all their wool and then knotting each thread individually to achieve a unique pattern for every piece.
   - (A) the weaver still pursues his art as they have
   - (B) the weaver still pursues his art as he has
   - (C) weavers still pursue their art as they have
   - (D) weavers still pursue their art as was done
   - (E) the weaver still pursues his art as has been done

5. A number of prominent educators question whether the decreasing enrollment of students in colleges and universities is a reversible trend and fear that if the numbers do not go up, many institutions of higher learning will simply go out of business.
   - (A) whether the decreasing
   - (B) decreased
   - (C) that the decreasing
   - (D) if the decreasing
   - (E) the decreased

6. If I was President, I would call an immediate halt to the development of all nuclear weapons.

(A) If I was President, I would call an immediate halt

(B) If President, I would call an immediate halt

(C) If I was President, I would immediately call a halt

(D) As President, I would call an immediate halt

(E) If I were President, I would call an immediate halt

7. A survey of American business schools concludes that <u>female students are more concerned about job discrimination than male students.</u>

(A) female students are more concerned about job discrimination than male students.

(B) female students are more concerned about job discrimination than male students are.

(C) female students, as opposed to male students, are more concerned about job discrimination.

(D) female students are more concerned about job discrimination than male students are concerned.

(E) female students are more concerned about job discrimination than their male counterparts.

8. The revelation that Shakespeare wrote certain of his plays expressly for Queen Elizabeth I lends credence to the theory that the dark lady of the sonnets was <u>not Shakespeare's mistress nor any other woman the playwright had romanced</u> but, in fact, the Queen herself.

(A) not Shakespeare's mistress nor any other woman the playwright had romanced

(B) neither Shakespeare's mistress or any other woman the playwright had romanced

(C) neither Shakespeare's mistress nor any other woman the playwright had romanced

(D) not Shakespeare's mistress or any other woman the playwright had romanced

(E) not Shakespeare's mistress neither any other woman he had romanced

9. The recent drop in the prime interest rate probably results from the Federal Reserve Bank's tight money policy and <u>its effect on lending institutions rather than to the drop in the overall</u> rate of inflation.

(A) its effect on lending institutions rather than to the drop in the overall

(B) its affect on lending institutions, as opposed to the drop in the overall

(C) it's effect on lending institutions, rather than from the drop in the overall

(D) its effect on lending institutions rather than from the drop in the overall

(E) the effect on lending institutions, rather than to the drop in the overall

10. Before they will sit down and resume bargaining, the strikers demand that management halt legal proceedings, including current court actions aimed at incarcerating demonstrators, <u>and releases all strike leaders who have already been jailed.</u>

(A) and releases all strike leaders who have already been jailed.

(B) and releasing all strike leaders who have already been placed in jailed.

(C) and release all strike leaders who have already been jailed.

(D) in addition to releasing all presently jailed strike leaders.

(E) but release all strike leaders who have already been jailed.

11. Since they shared so much when they were growing up, Elizabeth and Sarah have cultivated a very special friendship and even now confide their most intimate thoughts only <u>to one another.</u>

(A) to one another.

(B) one with the other.

(C) one with another.

(D) each to the other.

(E) to each other.

12. Henrik Ibsen's plays posed as great a challenge to middle-class Scandinavians' expectations of the drama <u>that almost a century later Edward Albee will offer</u> to theatergoers in America.

(A) that almost a century later Edward Albee will offer

(B) that, almost a century later, Edward Albee would offer

(C) as, almost a century later, Edward Albee did offer

(D) just as, almost a century later, Edward Albee offered

(E) as, almost a century later, Edward Albee would offer

13. Although Bill Tilden was perhaps the greatest tennis player of all time, his real accomplishments were overshadowed for many years by rumors about his personal life.

(A) Although Bill Tilden was perhaps the greatest tennis player of all time, his real accomplishments were overshadowed for many years by rumors about his personal life.

(B) Perhaps the greatest tennis player of all time, Bill Tilden's real accomplishments were nevertheless overshadowed for many years by rumors about his personal life.

(C) Perhaps the greatest tennis player of all time, rumors about his personal life overshadowed Bill Tilden's real accomplishments for many years.

(D) For many years Bill Tilden's real accomplishments were overshadowed by rumors about his personal life, despite being perhaps the greatest tennis player of all time.

(E) Although Bill Tilden's real accomplishments were overshadowed for many years by rumors about his personal life, perhaps he was the greatest tennis player of all time.

14. The commission studying mass transportation suggested that the Metropolitan Transit Authority hold off purchasing new subway cars and spend money instead on preventive maintenance of all cars, on repairs of substandard cars, on crime prevention in all stations and better lighting for the busiest stations.

(A) on crime prevention in all stations and better lighting for the busiest stations.

(B) on crime prevention in all stations, and better lighting for the busiest stations.

(C) on crime prevention in all stations and

for better lighting in the busiest stations.

(D) on crime prevention in all stations, and on better lighting for the busiest stations.

(E) on the prevention of crime in all stations and for better lighting in the busiest stations.

15. Connoisseurs state unequivocally that the women in Paris are more beautiful than any other city.

(A) that the women in Paris are more beautiful than any other city.

(B) that the women in Paris are more beautiful than those in any other city.

(C) that Parisien women are more beautiful than in any other city.

(D) that, unlike any other city, Parisien women are more beautiful.

(E) that the women of Paris are more beautiful than the women in any other city.

16. The mayor's media advisor, together with his three top aides, are traveling with him on a tour of European capital cities.

(A) media advisor, together with his three top aides, are

(B) media advisor, also his three top aides, are

(C) media advisor, as well as his three top aides, is

(D) media advisor, along with his three top aides, are

(E) media advisor, all in the company of his three top aides, is

17. Lawyers and doctors alike both agree that something should be done about the rise in medical malpractice suits which are on the increase.

(A) alike both agree that something should be done about the rise in medical malpractice suits which are on the increase.

(B) alike agree that something should be done about the rise in medical malpractice suits.

(C) both agree that something should be done about the increasing rise in medical malpractice suits.

(D) agree that something should be done about the rise in medical malpractice suits, which are increasing.

(E) agree that something should be done about the rise in medical malpractice suits.

18. The obviously bitter actress stated that <u>had the director known what he was doing, the play would have run</u> for more than one night.

(A) had the director known what he was doing, the play would have run

(B) if the director would have known what he was doing, the play would have run

(C) if the director had known what he was doing, they would run

(D) had the director known what he was doing, they would run

(E) if the director knew what he was doing, they would have run

19. Dr. Smith's findings that emotions <u>affect blood pressure are different from those</u> published by his colleague, Dr. Loeb.

(A) affect blood pressure are different from those

(B) effect blood pressure are different from those

(C) effect blood pressure are different than those

(D) affect blood pressure are different than those

(E) affect blood pressure are different from that

20. <u>Entering professional tennis as a talented but shy and awkward teenager, for the past eight years Chris Evert was the dominant</u> force on the woman's circuit, a graceful and consistent player.

(A) Entering professional tennis as a talented but shy and awkward teenager, for the past eight years Chris Evert was

(B) A talented yet shy and awkward teenager when she entered professional tennis, for the last eight years Chris Evert has been

(C) Chris Evert entered professional tennis as a talented yet shy and awkward teenager, and was

(D) For the past eight years, having entered professional tennis as a talented yet shy and awkward teenager, Chris Evert has been

(E) Having entered professional tennis as a teenager who was talented yet shy and awkward, for the past eight years Chris Evert has been

21. The jurors agreed that of all the reasons the defense attorney gave for finding his client not guilty, <u>the last two of them were the most absurd.</u>

(A) the last two of them were the most absurd.

(B) the latter two were the most absurd.

(C) the last two of these were the most absurd.

(D) the last two of them were the absurdest.

(E) the last two were the most absurd.

22. The director of the Miss America pageant continues to maintain that the judges' ultimate choice is based less on the physical appearance of the contestant <u>as on</u> her intelligence, talent, and personality.

(A) as on

(B) and more on

(C) than on

(D) but more on

(E) than

23. The number of people jogging in New York City in the parks, in the playgrounds, and even in the streets, <u>is at least ten times what they were</u> a mere five years ago.

(A) is at least ten times what they were

(B) are at least ten times what they were

(C) is at least ten times what it was

(D) are at least ten times what it was

(E) is at least ten times what the numbers were

24. <u>Insofar as poultry is still a good bargain and under a dollar a pound,</u> the per-person consumption of chicken and turkey has increased in the last ten years, while that of the more expensive meats—beef, lamb, and pork—has declined.

(A) Insofar as poultry is still a good bargain and under a dollar a pound,

(B) Because poultry is still a good bargain and under a dollar a pound,

(C) For the reason that poultry is still a good bargain at under a dollar a pound,

(D) Because poultry is still a good bargain at under a dollar a pound,

(E) Insofar as poultry is still a good bargain, selling for under a dollar a pound,

25. Alicia de la Santina, <u>who danced with the famous Ballet de la France from 1942 to 1947, established</u> her own performance group, the renowned Ballet de Paris, in 1948.

(A) who danced with the famous Ballet de la France from 1942 to 1947, established

(B) who had danced with the famous Ballet de la France from 1942 to 1947, established

(C) who had been dancing with the famous Ballet de la France from 1942 to 1947, established

(D) who danced with the famous Ballet de la France from 1942 to 1947, had established

(E) dancing with the famous Ballet de la France from 1942 to 1947, established

STOP

END OF SECTION. IF YOU HAVE ANY TIME LEFT, GO OVER YOUR WORK IN THIS SECTION ONLY. DO NOT WORK IN ANY OTHER SECTION OF THE TEST.

SECTION VI

Time—30 Minutes
20 Questions

Directions: For each of the following questions, select the best of the answer choices and blacken the corresponding space on your answer sheet.
Numbers: All numbers used are real numbers.
Figures: The diagrams and figures that accompany these questions are for the purpose of providing information useful in answering the questions. Unless it is stated that a specific figure is not drawn to scale, the diagrams and figures are drawn as accurately as possible. All figures are in a plane unless otherwise indicated.

1. Mr. Johnson grosses $2000 per month from his mail-order business. If 40 percent of that amount goes for business expenses and 10 percent of the remainder is reinvested in the business, how much of the gross receipts is reinvested in the business?
   (A) $80
   (B) $100
   (C) $110
   (D) $120
   (E) $200

2. $8^4 \div 2^{10} =$
   (A) 4^{-6}
   (B) 4
   (C) 8
   (D) 16
   (E) 32

3. The number 50 is what percent of 2000?
   (A) 2.5%
   (B) 5%
   (C) 10%
   (D) 40%
   (E) 400%

4. $(4 + \sqrt{5})(4 - \sqrt{5})$ is equal to:
   (A) -1
   (B) 0
   (C) 11
   (D) 21
   (E) $11 + 8\sqrt{5}$

5. A rope 32 feet long was cut into two pieces, one piece 8 feet longer than the other. What is the ratio of the larger piece to the smaller piece?
   (A) $\frac{1}{16}$
   (B) $\frac{1}{8}$
   (C) $\frac{3}{5}$
   (D) $\frac{3}{2}$
   (E) $\frac{5}{3}$

6. If 3 people working together at the same rate can do a job in $5\frac{1}{3}$ days, what fraction of that job can two of these people do in one day?
   (A) $\frac{1}{16}$
   (B) $\frac{1}{8}$
   (C) $\frac{3}{16}$
   (D) $\frac{1}{2}$
   (E) $\frac{2}{3}$

7. If interest on a savings account is paid monthly at an annual rate of $6\frac{1}{4}$ percent and if the interest is not reinvested, then in how many years will the total amount of interest earned equal the amount of money saved in the account?
   (A) 36
   (B) 24
   (C) 18
   (D) 16
   (E) 12

8. A rectangular playground has a length that is twice as great as its width. If its length is halved while its width is quadrupled, what is the ratio of its original area to its new area?
   (A) $\frac{1}{8}$

(B) $\frac{1}{2}$

(C) 1

(D) 2

(E) 8

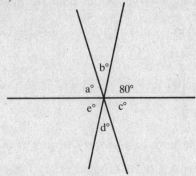

9. In the figure above, if a = 3d, b =
(A) 25
(B) 80
(C) 75
(D) 35
(E) 100

10. $(3508)^2 - (3510 \times 3508) =$
(A) 7020
(B) 0
(C) −2
(D) −3508
(E) −7016

11. A fruitseller bought 2000 quarts of berries at 80 cents per quart. If $\frac{1}{4}$ of the berries become too ripe for sale, what should be the selling price per quart of the remainder so that the gross profit will be 20 percent of the total cost?
(A) $0.25
(B) $0.80
(C) $1.00
(D) $1.10
(E) $1.28

12. Charlene spent $\frac{2}{5}$ of her income for January for rent, and $\frac{3}{4}$ of remainder on other expenses. If she put the remaining $180 in he savings account, how much was her income in January?
(A) $1000

(B) $1200
(C) $1400
(D) $1600
(E) $1800

13. George went to the drugstore and spent $25.00, including 30 cents tax on his taxable purchases. What was the cost of the tax-free items if the tax rate was 6 percent?
(A) $19.00
(B) $19.70
(C) $20.00
(D) $20.70
(E) $24.70

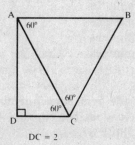

DC = 2

14. In the figure above, what is the area of triangle ABC?
(A) $8\sqrt{3}$
(B) $8\sqrt{2}$
(C) 8
(D) $4\sqrt{3}$
(E) $2\sqrt{3}$

15. If the numerator of a fraction is decreased 25 percent and the demoninator of that fraction is increased 25 percent, then the difference between the resulting and the original fractions represents what percentage decrease?
(A) 40%
(B) 45%
(C) 50%
(D) 60%
(E) 75%

16. A racetrack bounded by two concentric circles, one with a diameter of 160 yards and the other with a diameter of 140 yards, is to covered with asphalt. If the asphalt layer is to be 1 foot deep, how many cubic yards of asphalt will be needed?
(A) 75π
(B) 90π
(C) 500π

(D) 1500π

(E) 2000π

17. A new fast-growing strain of yeast cells reproduces by dividing every two minutes. Thus, one yeast cell becomes two yeast cells after two minutes, four after four minutes, eight after .eight minutes, and so on. If one newly divided cell is placed in a rectangular vat 6 inches by 8 inches by 12 inches, and after one hour the vat is full of yeast, how long did it take to fill half the vat?

(A) 15 minutes

(B) 24 minutes

(C) 30 minutes

(D) 48 minutes

(E) 58 minutes

18. If aPb = ab/(b−a) for all numbers a and b such that a does not equal b, what is the value of 5P(2P3)?

(A) 30

(B) 25

(C) 24

(D) 10

(E) 1

19. In going from city A to city B by car, Mr. Brown averaged 50 miles per hour. What must be his average speed in miles per hour on his return trip over the same route if he is to average 40 miles per hour for the entire trip?

(A) 30

(B) $33\frac{1}{3}$

(C) 36

(D) 40

(E) 42

20. A sale item in a grocery store was marked down to $\frac{5}{6}$ of its original price. Joe bought the item with a coupon that provided for a further 20 percent discount off the new price. By what percent would the amount paid by Joe have to be increased to equal the original price?

(A) 25%

(B) $33\frac{1}{3}\%$

(C) 50%

(D) $67\frac{2}{3}\%$

(E) 75%

STOP

END OF SECTION. IF YOU HAVE ANY TIME LEFT, GO
OVER YOUR WORK IN THIS SECTION ONLY. DO NOT
WORK IN ANY OTHER SECTION OF THE TEST.

SECTION VII

Time—30 Minutes
25 Questions

Directions: Each question below is followed by two numbered facts. You are to determine whether the data given in the statements is sufficient for answering the question. Use the data given, plus your knowledge of math and everyday facts, to choose between the five possible answers.

(A) if statement 1 alone is sufficient to answer the question, but statement 2 alone is not sufficient
(B) if statement 2 alone is sufficient to answer the question, but statement 1 alone is not sufficient
(C) if both statements together are needed to answer the question, but neither statement alone is sufficient
(D) if each statement by itself is sufficient to answer the question
(E) if not enough facts are given to answer the question

1. What is the area of triangle ABC?
   (1) AC = 5
   (2) $\angle ABC = 90$ degrees

2. Four women and three men work in an office. What is the average age of all seven office workers?
   (1) The average age of the four female workers is 27.
   (2) The average age of the three male workers is 33.

3. Is $a > 0$?
   (1) $-2a < 0$
   (2) $5a > 0$

4. If milk costs 59 cents per carton, what is the cost of the milk that George drinks per week?
   (1) A carton contains one quart of milk.
   (2) Every day George drinks a carton of milk.

5. An elevator in a large office building contains riders who range in weight from 95 to 205 pounds. How many riders are in the elevator?
   (1) The total weight of all the elevator riders is 1500 pounds.

   (2) The maximum capacity of the elevator is 1600 pounds.

6. Is the sum of two given numbers greater than 100?
   (1) Each of the numbers is greater than 60.
   (2) The product of the two numbers is greater than 2500.

7. What is the perimeter of quadrilateral ABCD?
   (1) Each of the angles of quadrilateral ABCD are right angles.
   (2) AB = 10

8. How many shovelfuls of sand are needed to fill the sandbox?
   (1) 600 pounds of sand will fill the sandbox.
   (2) 50 shovelfuls of sand will make the sandbox $\frac{1}{3}$ full.

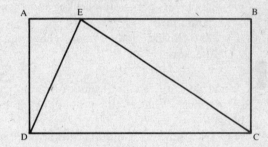

9. If ABCD above is a rectangle, what is the area of triangle CDE?
   (1) The area of triangle ADE is 4.
   (2) The area of triangle BCE is 8.

10. Mary sells vacuum cleaners and earns a commission on each vacuum cleaner sold. How much money must she collect from vacuum cleaner sales to earn $100 in commissions?
    (1) Vacuum cleaners sell for $50 each and Mary's commission is $10 per sale.
    (2) Mary earns a 20 percent commission on every vacuum she sells.

11. Students in five sections, F, G, H, J, and K, of an introductory accounting course were given a final exam. What is the average test score on all the students in the five sections?
    (1) The average of the final exam scores of students in sections F, G, and H was 72.
    (2) The average of the final exam scores of students in sections J and K was 78.

12. Is xy an integer?
    (1) $x^2 + y^2 = 25$ and $y = 4$
    (2) x^2y^4 is an integer

13. How long will it take a bricklayer to erect a wall if he works steadily and lays bricks at a constant rate?
    (1) He lays 100 bricks per hour.
    (2) After 4 hours, he has erected $\frac{2}{3}$ of the wall.

14. At the Chairman of the Boards Club only chess, checkers, and backgammon are played. If there are 100 players in the club and all players play at least two types of games, how many play both backgammon and chess?
    (1) 20 players play both checker and backgammon.
    (2) 30 players play both chess and checkers.

15. A marble is selected at random from a bag of marbles. What is the probability of its being a cat's eye?
    (1) One-quarter of the marbles in the bag are milkies.
    (2) There are twice as many cat's-eyes as milkies in the bag.

16. 120 students at college X are enrolled in English or French or both. How many students are enrolled in English?
    (1) 10 students are enrolled in English and French.
    (2) 50 students are enrolled only in French.

17. It will rain today. Will it rain tomorrow?
    (1) If it does not rain tomorrow, then it will not rain today.

    (2) If it rains tomorrow, then it will rain today.

18. If $p = r^2$, what is the value of $p + r$?
    (1) $p - r = 20$
    (2) $p = 16$

19. How many hours long is time period A?
    (1) Time period A started at 12 noon Monday and ended at 12 noon Wednesday.
    (2) Time period A is exactly two days long.

20. Driving 20 hours per day, a bus can travel from city A to city B in exactly three days if it takes route X. How many miles are there between city A and city B along route X?
    (1) The bus takes 10 percent longer for the trip if it takes route Y.
    (2) If the average speed of the bus using route X were 10 miles per hour slower, it would take exactly one extra day to make the trip.

21. If y is a positive integer, what is the remainder when y is divided by 6?
    (1) The remainder is 1 when $y - 1$ is divided by 6.
    (2) The remainder is 0 when 3y is divided by 6.

22. If c and d are positive intergers, is c even?
    (1) $c^2 - 1$ is odd.
    (2) $(c - 3)(d + 2)$ is odd.

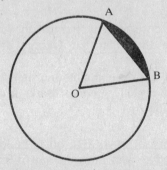

23. If circle O above has a diameter of 4, what is the area of the shaded region?
    (1) $\angle AOB = 60°$
    (2) $AO = AB$

24. What is the value of $(x + y)(x - z)$?
    (1) $y + z = 10$
    (2) $x + y = 5$

25. A company's profit was $600,000 in 1980. What was its profit in 1981?

(1) There was a 20 percent increase in income in 1981.
(2) There was a 25 percent increase in costs in 1981.

STOP

END OF SECTION. IF YOU HAVE ANY TIME LEFT, GO OVER YOUR WORK IN THIS SECTION ONLY. DO NOT WORK ON ANY OTHER SECTION OF THE TEST.

ANSWER KEY—PRACTICE EXAMINATION 3

SECTION I

1.	B	6.	C	11.	A	16.	E	21.	E
2.	D	7.	C	12.	B	17.	B	22.	D
3.	C	8.	A	13.	A	18.	C	23.	B
4.	A	9.	E	14.	B	19.	A	24.	A
5.	B	10.	C	15.	A	20.	B	25.	E

SECTION II

1.	C	6.	C	11.	B	16.	A
2.	D	7.	B	12.	A	17.	C
3.	D	8.	E	13.	E	18.	B
4.	E	9.	D	14.	A	19.	B
5.	D	10.	B	15.	B	20.	A

SECTION III

1.	C	6.	C	11.	B	16.	A	21.	D
2.	B	7.	D	12.	A	17.	A	22.	D
3.	D	8.	B	13.	E	18.	B	23.	B
4.	E	9.	C	14.	D	19.	B	24.	B
5.	A	10.	A	15.	E	20.	E	25.	A

SECTION IV

1.	D	8.	B	15.	C	22.	A
2.	D	9.	A	16.	B	23.	E
3.	A	10.	C	17.	D	24.	D
4.	D	11.	C	18.	D	25.	E
5.	C	12.	C	19.	E		
6.	B	13.	B	20.	E		
7.	D	14.	C	21.	D		

SECTION V

1.	D	6.	E	11.	E	16.	C	21.	E
2.	C	7.	B	12.	E	17.	E	22.	C
3.	B	8.	C	13.	A	18.	A	23.	C
4.	C	9.	D	14.	D	19.	A	24.	D
5.	A	10.	C	15.	B	20.	D	25.	B

SECTION VI

1.	D	6.	B	11.	E	16.	C
2.	B	7.	D	12.	B	17.	E
3.	A	8.	B	13.	B	18.	A
4.	C	9.	A	14.	D	19.	B
5.	E	10.	E	15.	A	20.	C

SECTION VII

1.	E	6.	A	11.	E	16.	C	21.	A
2.	C	7.	E	12.	A	17.	A	22.	D
3.	D	8.	B	13.	B	18.	C	23.	D
4.	B	9.	C	14.	E	19.	B	24.	C
5.	E	10.	D	15.	C	20.	B	25.	E

EXPLANATORY ANSWERS

Section I

1. **(B)** This is a main idea question. As correctly described by (B), the author explains the results of some studies and suggests some implications of new findings for detecting high blood pressure. (E) is incorrect since it is but a minor aspect of the passage. Although the author does note that there is such a correlation, he is not primarily concerned with proving the existence of such a relationship. (C) can be eliminated because the main point in not to describe the epidemiological and clinical studies from a methodological point of view. Rather, the author is concerned with the findings of these studies. (D) can be eliminated on similar ground, for the author indicates that both methods of study point to the existence of a familial connection. (A) can be eliminated since the author does not criticize, but rather relies on, these experiments.

2. **(D)** This is an explicit idea question. We find both statement I and statement II mentioned at the end of the first paragraph as factors discouraging studies of blood pressure in children. As for III, though this belief is mentioned in the passage, it is not mentioned as a factor discouraging research on children. If anything, this belief suggested that such research might be valuable, but the research was never undertaken for the reasons just mentioned.

3. **(C)** This is a question which asks us to make a further application of the arguments given in the passage, and the greatest danger may be the temptation to overstate the case. This is the difficulty with answer (E). The author qualifies his remarks in the closing sentences. It may be "possible," but it is

never asserted that it is now possible to do this. (D) also overstates the case. The author states that these chemical deficiencies are associated with high blood pressure, not that such deficiencies *cause* high blood pressure. And to the extent that one wants to argue that such deficiencies *contribute* to high blood pressure (based on paragraph three), that is not sufficient to support the causal statement expressed in (D). As for (A), the author notes that the low output of urinary kallikrein is associated with high blood pressure, that is, it may be another symptom of whatever physiological disorder causes high blood pressure, but that means it is an effect of the underlying cause and not the cause itself. Finally, (B) can be eliminated because it is not a further conclusion of the passage. To the extent that (B) reiterates what is stated already—and note that (B) states the kallikrein-kinin system is important in determining blood pressure, not that the system *causes* high blood pressure—it is not appropriate as a further statement based on arguments presented. (C) is, however, a natural extension of the argument. Remember, the author begins by noting that it is important to determine when high blood pressure begins, and he suggests that it may begin as early as infancy.

4. **(A)** This is a logical detail question. In essence, the questions stipulates that the author does introduce such evidence and then asks for what reason. In the final paragraph the author is discussing the connection between low urinary kallikrein excretion and high blood pressure. By noting that black children often show this and that blacks often have high blood pressure, he hopes to provide further evidence for the connection. As for (B), though this may be

an incidental effect of the reference, it cannot be said that this is the logical function of the argument in the overall development of the passage. (C) is incorrect since the author is not asserting a causal connection but only a correlation. (D) is incorrect for a reason similar to that which eliminates (B). Though this might be a further application for the point, it is not the reason the author incorporates the data into the argument of this passage. Finally, (E) is one of the main themes of the passage, but it does not explain why the author introduced the particular point at the particular juncture in the argument.

5. **(B)** This is an explicit detail question. In the third paragraph, the author discusses the operation of the kallikreinkinin system. There he mentions that it produces chemicals which operate to dilate blood vessels, so II is part of the correct answer. I and III, however, are not part of the correct answer. The author does not state that the kallikrein-kinin system interferes directly with either the sympathetic nervous system or the production of aldosterone—only that it *offsets* the effects of those actions.

6. **(C)** This is a logical detail question: Why does the author introduce this information. In the second paragraph the author is describing new research done on children, which suggest that the factors related to high blood pressure are already detectable in children. (A) is incorrect since the author has not yet begun to discuss the biochemical research; he is only discussing epidemiological surveys. (B) is incorrect since it is not a correct response to the question. The author does state that such research is actually possible, but he does not cite the results of the study in order to prove the study was possible. Rather, he cites the results to prove the further conclusion outlined in (C). (D) is incorrect because it is not a response to the question. To be sure, one might use the results of the study cited to support the recommendation articulated in (D), but that is not the author's motivation for introducing it in his argument. As for (E), this fails for the same reason that (B) fails.

7. **(C)** This is a logical structure question. The author develops his argument primarily by describing findings and supporting a conclusion. As for (A), though the author does mention two types of research, epidemiological studies and clinical studies, he does not contrast these. (B) is incorrect since his main purpose is to support a conclusion, and, whatever refutation is offered in the passage (e.g., against the position that blood pressure in children cannot be measured accurately), it is offered in the service of a greater point. (E) must fail for a similar reason. And (D) fails for this reason as well: The author is supporting a position, not refuting it.

8. **(A)** This is an explicit idea question. The answer is found in the third paragraph. There it is stated that kallikreins act on kininogens to produce kinins and that some kinins are dilators. It must be admitted that answer (A) does not describe the entire connection in such great detail, but (A) is the only plausible connection. (B) must be incorrect since kallikreins are enzymes in the kidneys and blood plasma. (C) is incorrect since this effect is counteracted by the kinins. (D) is incorrect for the same reason. Finally, (E) must be wrong since it is a symptom of the lack of kallikrein.

9. **(E)** This is a tone question. The warrant for (D) is found in the final paragraph. After discussing the recent findings on the kallikrein-kinin system, the author states that there is still "a great deal to be learned." From that we infer that the author regards such further research as important, or (E), warranted.

10. **(C)** This is a main idea question. The main point of the passage is that those who believe AFDC restrictions contribute to family dissolution are in error. It is not the restrictions on aid but the aid itself, according to the author, that contributes to the dissolution of low-income families. So the primary purpose of the passage is to analyze the causes of a phenomenon. (A) is incorrect, for any such results are mentioned only obliquely and are only incidental to the main

development. (B) describes something that is integral to the argument but is not the main point of the argument. As for (D), the author himself offers no such recommendation. While an argument for reform might use the argument in the passage for such recommendations, we cannot attribute any proposal for reform to the author. Finally, (E) describes what may be a result of the argument, but changing the attitude of the public, as opposed to engaging in scholarly debate, does not appear to be the objective of the text.

11. **(A)** As we noted above, the author argues that it is not the restrictions on aid that create pressures on low-income families; it is the aid itself. We can apply this reasoning to answer this question. The analysis in the text can be used to predict that an increase in the availability of aid would tend to increase pressures on the family unit. Thus, reducing restrictions, because it would result in an increase in aid availability, would actually tend to create more pressure for divorce. This would have the exact opposite effect predicted by those who call for welfare reforms such as eliminating restrictions. (A) is nice also because of the word "paradoxically" which opens the statement, for the result would be paradoxical from the standpoint of the reformer. (C) and (D) can be eliminated because they are contradicted by the analysis given in the passage. (B) is eliminated because the author never addresses questions of fiscal policy. Finally, (E) goes too far in two respects. First, it overstates the author's case. The author does not suggest that the only factor operating in the dissolution of low-income families is welfare; therefore, he would not likely suggest that the problem could be entirely controlled by manipulating benefit levels. Further, it is not clear that the author advocates any particular policy. The scholarly tone of the article suggests that the author may or may not believe public policy on welfare should take into account the problem of divorce.

12. **(B)** This is an explicit idea question. In discussing the costs of divorce in the third paragraph (costs meaning both economic and social costs), the author mentions (B), (C), and (D) as encouraging people to stay married. Earlier in that same paragraph, he mentions consumption possibilities as a factor tending to hold a marriage together. (B) is never mentioned in this respect. Although the author is primarily interested in low-income family stability, he never states that social or economic class is a factor in perpetuating a marriage. And to the extent that one mounts an argument to the effect that the pressures described in paragraph three (costs of divorce and greater consumption possibilities) would naturally tend to operate more powerfully for lower-income families, he is applying that reasoning to a new situation. So that argument, since it is new, cannot be a factor mentioned by the author in this passage and cannot, therefore, be an answer to the question asked.

13. **(A)** This is obviously a main idea question, and we have already analyzed the main point of the passage. It is nicely stated by (A). (B) is not the main idea but only an incidental feature of the argument. (C) is incorrect since this is in direct contradiction to the main point of the passage. (D) fails for the same reason that (B) fails. Finally, (E) is incorrect because there is no warrant in the passage to support the conclusion that the author himself would make such a recommendation. The author argues his point in a very scholarly and neutral fashion. Given that, we cannot attribute any attitude to him about the wisdom of welfare policy.

14. **(B)** As we have just noted, the scholarly treatment of the passage is best described as scientific and detached. As for (A), though the author may be confident in his presentation, there is no hint of optimism. (C) can be eliminated for a similar reason: There is no hint of alarm or discouragement. As for (D), to the extent that it can be argued that the author's treatment is scholarly, and therefore polite and sensitive, (B) is a better description of the overall tone. The defining elements of a scholarly treatment are those set forth in (B). Those elements suggested by (D) would be merely incidental to, and

parasitic upon, the main features of scientific neutrality and detachment. Finally, though the author's treatment is detached, it would be wrong to say that the author is calloused and indifferent—any more than we would want to say that the doctor who analyzes the causes of a disease in clinical terms is therefore calloused and indifferent.

15. **(A)** With an application question of this sort, we must be careful not to overstate the strength of the author's case. This is the reason (D) is incorrect. Though the author points out that there are economic pressures on families which tend to encourage divorce, it would go beyond that analysis to attribute to the author the statement in choice (D). (E), too, overstates the case. Though the author prefers to analyze family stability primarily in economic terms, the text will not support the judgment that people are getting more self-centered. If anything, a rising divorce rate would be analyzed by the author in broad social and economic terms, rather than in personal terms as suggested by (E). (B) is incorrect because it takes us too far beyond the analysis given in paragraph three. While it is conceivable that further analysis would generate the conclusion in (B), (A) is much closer to the actual text. This is not to say that (B) is necessarily a false statement. Rather, this is to accept the structure of the question: Would the author *most likely* agree. Finally, (C) attributes to the author a value judgment which has no support in the text.

16. **(E)** Here, too, is an application question. And, as we just pointed out, we are looking for the most likely source. It is not impossible that the passage was taken from a basic economics text or a book on the history of welfare. It could conceivably be one of several readings included in such books, but it seems more likely, given the scholarly tone and the particular subject, that (E) is the correct answer. It seems unlikely that this would have appeared in (A) or (D).

17. **(B)** This is a logical structure question. In the second paragraph the author states that the question of a connection between welfare and family instability cannot be properly analyzed unless a distinction is drawn between different types of recipients. He says that one seeming category is the cheater, and then he denies that this category is important. Why does he bother to do this? The reason must be that he wants to clear the deck, so to speak, for his own argument. That is, he wants to raise a possible argument (restrictions cause cheating) in order to dismiss it, so that he can concentrate on what he believes to be the real connection. (A) is incorrect, for though the author implicitly acknowledges that some people will not qualify for aid, this is not the reason for dividing recipients into three groups. (C) is incorrect for the same reason. (D) is incorrect because the author ultimately will support the thesis that welfare per se (though not restrictions) encourages family breakup. In any event, the argument is not introduced as a counterexample to the thesis that welfare encourages family dissolution. Rather, it is introduced to minimize the significance of an example that might be introduced to prove that thesis. Finally, (E) goes well beyond the scope of the passage.

18. **(C)** This is a main idea question. The author begins by posing the following question: Why are affirmative action programs so controversial? He then argues that affirmative action is unlike ordinary government programs in the way it allocates the burden of the program. Because of this, he concludes, we are torn between supporting the programs (because they have legitimate goals) and condemning the programs (because of the way the cost is allocated). (C) neatly describes this development. The author analyzes the structure of the moral dilemma. (A) is incorrect since the comparison is but a subpart of the overall development and is used in the service of the larger analysis. (B) is incorrect since the author reaches no such clear-cut decision. Rather, we are left with the question posed by the dilemma. (D) is incorrect since the author presupposes in his presentation that the reader already understands the importance of the issue. Finally, (E) is incorrect since

the advantages of the programs are mentioned only in passing.

19. **(A)** This is a logical structure question. In the second paragraph the author will describe the general structure of government programs in order to set up the contrast with affirmative action. The discussion begins with "Setting aside . . . ," indicating that the author recognizes such cases and does not wish to discuss them in detail. Tolls and tuition are exceptions to the general rule, so the author explicitly sets them aside in order to preempt a possible objection to his analysis based on claimed counterexamples. (B) is incorrect since the overall point of the passage is to discuss this dilemma, but the main point of the passage will not answer the question about the logical substructure of the argument. (C) is incorrect since tolls and tuition are not ordinary government programs. (D) is incorrect since the author never raises such doubts. Finally, (E) misses the point of the examples. The point is not that they are costly but that the cost is born by the specific user.

20. **(B)** This is an application question. In the first paragraph the author states that affirmative action is designed to achieve social and economic objectives. Although he qualifies his claim, he seems to believe that the arguments are in favor of affirmative action. So (B) is clearly supported by the text. (A) is not supported by the text since the author leaves us with a question; he does not resolve the issue. (C) can be eliminated on the same ground. The author neither embraces nor rejects affirmative action. (D) goes beyond the scope of the argument. While the author might wish this were possible, nothing in the passage indicates such restructuring is possible. Indeed, in paragraph three the author remarks that the "funding" problem seems to be inherent. Finally, (E) can be eliminated on the same ground as (A). Though the author recognizes the unfairness of affirmative action, he also believes that the programs are valuable.

21. **(E)** In paragraph two the author mentions that government programs entail both social and economic costs. Then, the cost of a specific example, the passed-over worker, is not a government expenditure in the sense that money is laid out to purchase something. So the author is using the term "funding" in a nonstandard way, and he wishes to call his readers' attention to this. (E) parallels this explanation. (A) is incorrect since it is inconsistent with the reasoning just provided. (B) is incorrect, for though the author may believe that individuals bear a disproportionate share of the burden, this is not a response to the question asked. (C) is incorrect for the same reason: It is a true but nonresponsive statement. Finally, (D) fails for the same reason. Though the author notes that affirmative action programs are similar to other government programs in this respect, this is not an explanation for the author's placing "funding" in quotation marks.

22. **(D)** This is a logical structure question. In the final paragraph, the author analyzes another similar situation. This technique is called "arguing from analogy." The strength of the argument depends on our seeing the similarity and accepting the conclusion of the one argument (the villainous man) as applicable to the other argument (affirmative action). (A) is perhaps the second-best response, but the author is not offering an illustration, e.g., an example of affirmative action. To be sure, the author is attempting to prove a point, but attempting to prove a conclusion is not equivalent to illustrating a contention. (B) is incorrect since the author adduces the situation to support his contention. (C) is incorrect, for the author cites no authority. Finally, (E) can be eliminated since the author uses the case of the villainous man to support, not to weaken, the case.

23. **(B)** This is an explicit idea question. In paragraph one the author mentions that affirmative action is like other government programs in that it is designed to achieve certain social and economic goals. So, statement I cites a similarity rather than a difference. Statement III can also be eliminated. In paragraph three the author states

that the relevant difference is not the method of allocating benefits. The salient difference is set forth in the same paragraph, and it is the difference described by statement II.

24. **(A)** This is an inference question. In the first paragraph the author asks why affirmative action is so controversial. In the final paragraph he reveals the answer: the moral dilemma. The wording of the passage, e.g., "we are confronted with . . . ," indicates that the author expects his reader will share this tension. So the passage is addressed to those who think affirmative action has value but also believe it is unfair to nonminority persons. As for (B), the author believes that affirmative action is based on sound premises and achieving a legitimate social goal, but that the world is built so that we encounter this conflict. As for (C), it is not the programs themselves that contain contradictions; rather, it is our value structure that creates the conflict. As for (D), the author believes the reader will regard the programs as creating suffering, but not that the suffering is needless. It may very well be the cost that must be paid. (E) is easily eliminated since the author expresses reservations about the programs.

25. **(E)** This is a main idea question, but one which asks about the main idea in the abstract. The discussion thus far makes clear the justification for (E). The author has a sense of this moral dilemma, which he believes will be shared by his readers, and he wants to explain why we experience this as conflict. As for (A), though the author develops a dilemma, he does not suggest that it is possible to slip between the horns of the dilemma. As for (B), he offers no refutation, so we will eliminate this as incorrect. As for (C), any historical references are purely incidental to the overall development of the thesis. And as for (D), though the analysis of affirmative action may suggest to the reader a method of analyzing other social problems, the focus of the passage is a particular problem, not methodology.

Section II

1. **(C)** This question can be analyzed in several ways, all of them acceptable, but it is obviously important to make the proper conversions: quarts to gallons and seconds to minutes. We recommend that once you have analyzed a question such as this, you make a marginal notation in your test booklet of the final form the answer must assume; gal/3 min. This will remind you to do the needed conversions.

Some students will analyze this as a rate problem:

$$\text{output} = \text{rate} \times \text{time}$$

The rate at which the machine processes milk is 8 qt/6 sec, which is equal to 2 gal/6 sec or 1 gal/3 sec. Then the running time is 3 minutes, or 180 seconds. Substituting into the rate formula:

$$\text{output} = 1 \text{ gal}/3 \text{ sec} \times 180 \text{ sec} = 60 \text{ gal}$$

Other students will prefer to use a proportion. Since output varies directly with running time (the longer the running time, the greater the output), we can set up a direct proportion. Let R stand for running time and O for output, and we will use subscripts 1 and 2 to designate the shorter (6 second) and longer (3 minute) running times, respectively. Using these notational devices, we can set up the direct proportion in any of four different ways:

$$\frac{O_1}{O_2} = \frac{R_1}{R_2} \quad \frac{O_2}{O_1} = \frac{R_2}{R_1} \quad \frac{R_1}{O_1} = \frac{R_2}{O_2} \quad \frac{O_1}{R_1} = \frac{O_2}{R_2}$$

Each of these formulas is a mathematical summary for a statement such as, "The output in case 1 *is to* the output in case 2 as the running time in case 1 *is to* the running time in case 2." That is, the ratio of the two outputs is the same as the ratio of the two running times. Taking the first formula (as a matter of arbitrary selection) and substituting numbers, we have

$$\frac{2 \text{ gal}}{x \text{ gal}} = \frac{6 \text{ sec}}{180 \text{ sec}}$$

Cross-multiplying:

$$360 = 6x$$
$$x = 60$$

2. **(D)** We begin by recognizing that Ms. Baker spent $1.80 and that this $1.80 represents, in a sense, two separate purchases at two different prices (one item at full price and a second item at half price). We do not know the usual price, so we use x to designate this unknown. Then we relate the second price to x. If x is the full price, then the sale price is one-half of that, or $\frac{1}{2}$x. When added, these two equal $1.80, so we have

$$x + \frac{1}{2}x = \$1.80$$

Solving for x,

$$\frac{3}{2}x = 1.80$$
$$x = 1.80(\frac{2}{3})$$
$$x = 1.20$$

It is also possible to answer this question by testing each of the answer choices. Since it is characteristic of the exam that choices are arranged in order of magnitude (least to greatest or vice versa), we test (C) first. If the regular price were $.90, then the sale price for the second item would be $\frac{1}{2}$($.90), or $.45, for a total price of $1.35. But the question stem tells us that Ms. Baker paid a total of $1.80, not $1.35. This tells us that (C) is not the correct answer, and it also tells us that the usual price is more than $.90 (otherwise, she would not have paid so much for both combined). So we test (D) next. If the usual price is $1.20, then the price for the second item is $.60, and the combined total is $1.80, which confirms that (D) is correct. Suppose the answer choices had been arranged differently, for example, (C) $ .50, (D) $ .90, (E) $1.20. We would have tested (C) and (D) and found them to be incorrect. That would have proved (by the process of elimination) that (E) was correct. There would have been no need then to test (E).

3. **(D)** We know the sales representative earned $18,000 over the 12-month period, which is an average of $\frac{\$18,000}{12}$ or $1,500 per month. If her commission for March was

exactly one-half that average, then it must have been $750.

4. **(E)** This is a problem in which it is essential to keep in mind that the array of answer choices dictates your attack on the question. After all, there is an infinite number of squares the perimeters of which are divisible by both 4 and 7, e.g., 28, 56, 112, etc.—in other words, any square the perimeter of which is divisible by 28 (4 × 7). The most efficient way of attacking this question is to test each choice. (A), (B), (C), and (D) have perimeters of 12, 16, 20, and 24, respectively, numbers that are not divisible by both 4 and 7. (E), however, has a perimeter of 28, divisible by both 4 and 7, and that is the correct choice.

5. **(D)** This problem is largely a matter of bookkeeping—that is, making sure you keep straight the difference between what was sold and what remained. We can attack the question by using P to designate the number of papers the vendor started with. He sold 40 percent of this, or .4P, which left .6P newspapers. In the afternoon, he sold 60 percent of this .6P, or .36P, which left .24P papers. So the vendor sold .76P out of a total of P papers, or 76 percent of all the papers. You can arrive at the same conclusion by arbitrarily picking a number to use instead of P. Since the problem does not specify the actual number of papers at the beginning of the day, the conditions are valid for any number—provided we do not wind up with fractions of papers. To avoid this problem, we pick a number large enough to avoid fractions of papers, yet not so large as to be cumbersome, say, 100 papers. If the vendor started with 100 papers and sold 40 percent in the morning, he had 60 papers for the afternoon. He sold 60 percent of those, or 36 papers, leaving 24 papers at the end of the day. This means he sold 76 out of 100 papers, or 76 percent of the papers he had at the beginning of the day.

6. **(C)** One way of attacking this question is to compute $\frac{1}{5}$ of the value of the machine at the

beginning of a year and subtract that from the total value of the machine at the beginning of the year. For example, the machine is valued at $5,000 in the first year, so it depreciates by $\frac{1}{5}$, or $1,000, leaving a value at the end of the year of $4,000. Then you would repeat this process two more times to get the value at the end of the third year. A simpler attack is to recognize that at the end of the year the machine has only $\frac{4}{5}$, or .8, of its value at the beginning of the year. So at the end of the first year, the machine has the value .8 × $5,000 = $4,000. At the end of the second year, it has the value .8 × $4,000 = $3,200. At the end of the third year, its value is .8 × $3,200 = $2,560.

7. **(B)** Again, there are several valid approaches to the problem. Some students will first want to determine the total amount of the drug produced. Using T to designate the total amount, we set the equation:

40 percent of T = 18. So,

$$.4T = 18$$
$$T = 45$$

Since 45 is the total amount produced, and since corporation X accounted for 18, the others produced 27.

Another way of attacking the question is to set up a proportion:

$$\frac{40\%}{18} = \frac{60\%}{x}$$

Notice that we use 60 percent since that is the proportion of the total produced by all other producers. To solve the proportion, you cross-multiply and solve for x.

Finally, if you were unable to solve the problem using a mathematical formula, you could always fall back on the technique of testing each choice. You would select (C) to test first. Assuming other producers produced 36 kilos of the drug, this would give total production of 36 plus 18, or 54 kilos. But $\frac{18}{54}$ is equal to $\frac{1}{3}$ which is only $33\frac{1}{3}$ percent, so other producers did not produce

as much as 36 kilos. Next you would test (B), and a quick calculation would prove (B) to be the correct choice.

8. **(E)** Although this question seems to be complicated, it is actually fairly easy. Since the smallest value is 12,500 and the largest is 16,250, the average must be somewhere between those two. (E) is outside of the range. So (E) could NOT be the average for the six counties.

9. **(D)** For this question, there really is no substitute for testing each answer choice. (D) is the correct answer, for it makes a statement which is NOT necessarily true. If x is -1, the value of $x^2 + x^3$ is exactly 0. Again, if x is -2, then the value of the statement is $(-2)^2 + (-2)^3$ which is -4. As for (A), since x^2 will always be positive, $\frac{1}{x^2}$ must be positive, and the statement is always true. Similar reasoning shows (B) to be necessarily true. x^2 will always be positive while x^3 will always be negative. (C) is proved true by the same reasoning. Any even-numbered power of a negative value will be positive, and any odd-numbered power will be negative. Finally, (E) makes a true statement since x^3 will always be negative.

10. **(B)** This question is largely a matter of careful reading. We are looking for the ratio "municipal bond income: noninvestment income." Municipal bonds accounted for $\frac{2}{3}$ of 45 percent of total income, or 30 percent of the total. Noninvestment income was 55 percent of the total. So the ratio we need is: $\frac{30\% \text{ of total}}{55\% \text{ of total}} = \frac{6}{11}$ You will notice that this ratio will be 6:11 regardless of the total amount of income. So we do not need to know the actual dollar value of income to solve the problem.

11. **(B)** One way of attacking this question is to use simultaneous equations. Let x be the number of balcony tickets sold and y the number of orchestra tickets sold. How many tickets were sold in total? The answer is 560,

the sum of the number of balcony and the number of orchestra tickets: x + y = 560. How much money was taken in? $2,150. Where did it come from? It came from x tickets at $2.50 and y tickets at $5.00: 2.50x + 5.00 y = 2,150. Now, both of the statements are true:

$$x + y = 560$$
$$2.5x + 5y = 2,150$$

And that it is why we call these statements simultaneous equations—both are true at the same time. Now, we use algebraic techniques to solve for x:

Isolating y: y = 560 − x
Substituting for y: 2.5x + 5(560 − x) = 2,150
Solving for x: 2.5x + 2800 − 5x = 2,150
                              −2.5x = −650
                                  x = 260

For the "mathophobes," this question can be attacked by testing answer choices. Begin with (C). Assume that 300 tickets were sold at $2.50 each. How many tickets were then sold at $5.00? 260. So what would be total revenues? (300 @ $2.50) + (260 @ $5.00) = $2,050. But that is not equal to $2,150; it is $100 short. So, did we assume too few or too many cheap tickets? Obviously, we assumed too many cheap tickets, so you would test the next smaller answer, (B). A quick calculation will show that (B) is the correct answer.

12. **(A)** The key to this question is keeping track of the interrelationships between the pieces of information. One way of attacking the problem is first to determine what volume of mineral X the farmer has in 300 liters of the fertilizer. Since the fertilizer is 10 percent mineral, X, 300 liters of the fertilizer will contain 30 liters of mineral X.

Then, we want to put $\frac{3}{4}$ of a liter on each acre. So we need to divide:

$$\frac{30 \text{ liters}}{\frac{3}{4} \text{ liter/acre}}$$

To divide, we invert and multiply:

$$30 \text{ liters} \times \frac{4 \text{ acres}}{3 \text{ liter}} = 40 \text{ acres}$$

Notice that just as we inverted the numerical fraction, so too we converted the units "fraction": liter per acre to acre per liter. Then, we had the unit "liter" in the numerator (30 liters) and the unit "liter" in the denominator ($\frac{\text{acres}}{\text{liter}}$), and just as numbers cancel, so do units cancel. This left only one type of unit in the problem, "acres," and that unit was in the numerator. In other words, our answer was 40 acres, and this little bookkeeping device confirms that we did the problem correctly. Notice that if you attempt to multiply 30 liters by $\frac{3}{4}$ liter per acre (rather than dividing), you will have two units of "liters" in the numerator and the unit "acres" in the denominator. Your answer would then read so many liters² per acre; and that is obviously not an answer to the question "How many acres. . .?"

13. **(E)** This question is primarily a matter of carefully reading the two pie graphs. The graph on the right breaks down the population into two groups: "older than 5 years" and "5 years or younger." The pie on the left also breaks down a population into two groups: "less than 1 year old" and "older than 1 year but not older than 5 years." Notice that the entire pie on the left is equal to that part of the pie on the right which is labeled "5 years old and younger" (both represent all children 5 years old or under). The pie on the right, however, gives us the entire population at the day care center because, logically speaking, a child is either 5 years old or younger *or* older than 5 years. So 70 percent of the entire population is 5 years old or younger, and that is the same as saying 70 percent of the population is not older than 5 years. Then, the pie on the left informs us that of that 70 percent, 80 percent are one year or older but still not older than 5 years. 80 percent of 70 percent is 56 percent, which means that 56 percent of the entire population at the day-care center is one year old or older but not older than five years.

14. **(A)** As with many problems on the test, there is more than one line of attack that can

be used. One way of approaching this question is to set up an algebraic statement. Let x designate the number of students already seated at the beginning of class; then the three additional late-comers are equal to 20 percent of that.

So: .20x = 3
And x = 15

The number of students originally seated was 15. But the question asks not about the number originally seated, but about the total number of chairs in the classroom. So we must add in the three late-comers, and 15 + 3 = 18.

15. **(B)** To find the area of a triangle, we will need an altitude:

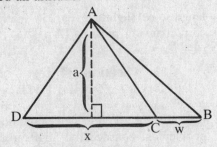

You will observe that our altitude is the altitude not only for △ ADC but also the altitude for △ ABC. Using a for altitude, we set up the ratio required:

$$\frac{\frac{1}{2}aw}{\frac{1}{2}ax} = \frac{w}{x} = \frac{1}{3}$$

Notice that the $\frac{1}{2}$ in the numerator and the $\frac{1}{2}$ in the denominator cancel, as does the a, leaving only the ratio w/x, which is stipulated in the problem to be 1:3.

16. **(A)** This question can be answered using a proportion.

$$\frac{x}{y} = \frac{10}{T}$$

This asserts that the ratio of 10 defective items to total (T) items shipped is x:y. Cross-multiplying, we have

$$Tx = 10\ y$$

and dividing by x,

$$T = \frac{10y}{x}$$

17. **(C)** A sketch of the bottom of the box may be helpful:

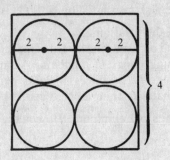

Since the radius of each can is 2, the diameter of each can is 4. If the cans fit exactly into the box, the box would have a side of 8 and a perimeter of 32. But we are told the box bulges slightly, so the inside perimeter must be slightly less than 32.

18. **(B)** We can solve the problem algebraically. Let n be the number of cases to be handled. If all workers are present, each person would handle $\frac{n}{p}$ cases. Since $\frac{1}{8}$ of the workers are absent, only $\frac{7}{8}p$ workers will have to handle all the cases. So each person will be assigned $\frac{n}{\frac{7}{8}p}$ which is $\frac{8}{7}(\frac{n}{p})$. So instead of handling just $\frac{n}{p}$ cases, each worker will handle an additional $\frac{1}{7}(\frac{n}{p})$ cases.

19. **(B)** To answer this question, we must find a way of relating all three rates to each other. Since M is given in terms of N, and N in terms of O, let us use N as our standard. If N operates at rate r, then at what rate does M operate? Since M can produce x units in $\frac{3}{4}$ the time it takes N to produce x units, M is operating at $\frac{4}{3}r$. Then, since N takes only $\frac{2}{3}$ the time to produce x units as machine O requires, O is operating at only $\frac{2}{3}r$. If all three machines are operating together, the total rate will be the sum of all three individual rates: $\frac{4}{3}r + r + \frac{2}{3} = 3r$.

The total rate of output for all three machines working together is 3r, of which r is being contributed by N. So N is producing $\frac{1}{3}$ of the total units.

You can reach the same conclusion by using concrete numbers. Assume that machine N produces 10 units per minute (or whatever time unit). Then, M produces 10 units per $\frac{3}{4}$ minute. How many units is that per minute?

$$\frac{10 \text{ units}}{3/4 \text{ min.}} = \frac{40}{3} \text{ units per minute}$$

Then, O will produce only $\frac{2}{3}$ of 10 units, or $\frac{20}{3}$ units, per minute. So our three machines operate at $\frac{40}{3}$, $\frac{30}{3}$, and $\frac{20}{3}$ units per minute, respectively. If all three machines are operating together, how many units will they produce totally in one minute? $\frac{90}{3}$, or 30 units per minute. And how many of those are produced by N? 10! So N produced $\frac{1}{3}$ of the total output.

20. **(A)** Here we have a geometry problem. Since this is a standardized test, you know there must be some key to the question, some insight that is required. Here it is useful to sketch some additional lines:

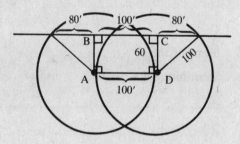

For convenience, we letter the points as shown. Now, ABCD is a rectangle. Since the two lights are 100 feet apart, BC is also 100. Then, we observe that AB and CD are sides of right triangles, the hypotenuses of which are radii and equal to 100. Since AB and CD are both 60, the one remaining side of each triangle is

$$x^2 + (60)^2 = (100)^2$$
$$x = 80$$

(You should have noticed the 3, 4, 5 relationship.) So the total length is 80 + 100 + 80 = 260.

There is actually an easier way to solve the problem. In this section (though not in the Data Sufficiency section), unless otherwise indicated ("Note: Figure not drawn to scale."), figures are drawn to scale. Why not measure the distance? Use the edge of your answer sheet as a straight edge. Measure the distance between the two lights, making light pencil marks to indicate the distance. That distance represents 100 feet on the map. Now measure the length of fence. You should find that it is slightly over $2\frac{1}{2}$ of those lengths, or slightly over 250 feet. So the correct answer must be (A).

Section III

1. **(C)** We are asked to determine how many people first boarded the flight in Chicago. (A) is not sufficient by itself. Though we know that 149 people were aboard the plane when it arrived in Los Angeles and (1) specifies the number on board when it left New York City, we cannot assume that those people on the plane when it arrived in Los Angeles were originally on board when the flight left New York City because the flight stopped in Chicago. Nor is (2) sufficient by itself, for we need to know how many passengers were on board when the flight left New York City. Both statements together, however, are sufficient. If we know how many people were on board when the flight left New York City, how many got off in Chicago, and how many arrived in Los Angeles, simple arithmetic will tell us how many first boarded in Chicago (though, of course, there is no reason to do the arithmetic).

2. **(B)** We are asked to determine the number of active members in the fraternity this year. Statement (1) is not sufficient since it does not tell us anything about the number of

active members last year or this year, only something about the number of active members lost upon graduation. (2), however, is sufficient. If we know the number last year, and the percentage increase in membership, a simple calculation will give us the number of active members this year: Number of Active Members Last Year $\times\ 112\frac{1}{2}$ percent = Number of Active Members This Year. Since we are concerned only about the number of active members and not about where they went or where they came from, (1) is not needed for this calculation.

3. **(D)** We are asked a very limited question: Is p positive, not what is the value of p? This question will give a yes or no answer. (1) is sufficient. Since 5 is positive and the product of 5 times p is positive, p must be positive. So the answer to the question is, "Yes, p is positive." That shows that (1) is sufficient to answer the question posed. Similarly, (2) is sufficient. Since $-p$ is equivalent to -1 times p and since the product of that multiplication is negative, p must be positive.

4. **(E)** (1) is not sufficient since this gives only the minimum, not the actual, royalties paid. (2) is insufficient since this gives the royalty schedule as a percentage of gross sales but does not tell us the actual sales. Then you will observe that neither statement supplies what is missing in the other statement. (2) does not give actual royalties paid, so it does not supply the information missing in (1). (1) does not give gross sales, so it does not supply the information missing in (2). So even if we take both statements together, we cannot answer the question posed: How much were the royalties?

5. **(A)** Here we are asked a yes or no question. Is 15 the average of x, y, and 15? What does this mean? This is asking whether $\frac{x + y + 15}{3} = 15$. A quick manipulation shows that this is asking whether $x + y = 30$. (1) answers that question in the affirmative, so statement (1), by itself, establishes that the answer to the question is yes. (2), however, is not sufficient to establish anything about the

sum of x and y (as opposed to the *difference* between x and y). To be sure, if we wanted to find exact values for x and y, both (1) and (2) would be needed, but that is not necessary for this particular question.

6. **(C)** We need only establish the identity of the player who hit the most home runs. It is not necessary to rank the other two players. (1) is not sufficient since it establishes only that Paul hit fewer home runs than Mary. (2) is not sufficient since it establishes only that Mary hit more home runs than Susan. Both together establish that Mary hit more home runs than either of the other two players. This establishes the identity of the number one home run hitter, so both statements taken together are sufficient to answer the question.

7. **(D)** Here we must establish the perimeter of the rectangle. Remember that knowing width and length will give us the perimeter. When coupled with the information provided in the question stem about the ratio between width and length, (1) is sufficient to answer the question about the perimeter. We could calculate the length (it is 8) and compute the perimeter (it is 28). That (2) is also sufficient is perhaps a little more difficult to see. (2) tells us that width times length equals 48; this is an equation with two unknowns. But since we know that $\frac{\text{width}}{\text{length}} = \frac{3}{4}$, we can express one of the two variables in terms of the other. For example, $w = \frac{3}{4}(l)$. Substituting this value for w in the equation for area, we have $\frac{3}{4}(l)\,(l) = 48$. Although the equation gives us two solutions ($l^2 = 64$, so $l = +8$ or -8), since we are dealing with distance, only one value, the positive value, is possible. So (2) also is sufficient by itself.

8. **(B)** This question is more a matter of common sense than mathematical reasoning ability. We are asked to determine how many times the seminar met in May, which essentially asks how many Thursdays there were in that May. Now, you are expected to

know that May has 31 days. (1), therefore, is not sufficient, for if the first was a Monday, there would have been only four Thursdays in the month, but if the first was a Wednesday, there would have been five Thursdays in that month. (2), however, is sufficient. Knowing on what day of the week the seventeenth fell enables us to construct a calendar for the entire month—by counting backward and forward on our fingers. Of course, there is no need to do that. Just knowing that we could do it is sufficient to determine that (2) is enough information to answer the question posed.

9. **(C)** We are asked a yes or no question: Was the speed 11 MPH for the first hour? (1) is not sufficient, for we cannot assume that Mark maintained a constant pace for the entire 2.5 hours. (2) is not sufficient, for it gives us Mark's running speed for the last 15 miles and for the last 1.5 hours. Both statements taken together, however, answer the question. From (1) we learn that the total running time was 2.5 hours. From (2) we learn that the last 15 miles were covered in 1.5 hours. This means that the first 11 miles were covered in the first hour. This is sufficient to answer the question posed. Incidentally, the answer to the question is yes, but that is a step we do not have to take within the Data Sufficiency format.

10. **(A)** Since the question stipulates that p is greater than 0, to determine what percent p is of q, we need only to know the ratio between p and q. (1) gives us this. It establishes that $p = \frac{1}{2}q$, which means 50 percent of q. (2), however, does not do the trick. Knowing the sum of two numbers, in and of itself, will not allow us to say anything about the ratio between those two numbers.

11. **(B)** Here the question is really asking whether we can pinpoint one integer between 50 and 60. (1) is not sufficient since it establishes that the number of books is 52, 55, or 58. (2), however, is sufficient. There is only one number between 50 and 60 which is one greater than a number divisible by 6. That number is 55 (54 divided by 6 = 9, then

adding 1 makes the number 55). So (2) alone is sufficient to establish the exact number of books in the crate, but (1) alone is not sufficient.

12. **(A)** To answer the question, is z > 8, you may want to sketch a triangle:

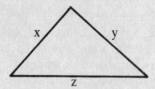

(1) is sufficient to establish that z is not greater than 8. If x + y = 8, then z cannot be greater than 8, for then x, y, and z could not be the lengths of three sides of a triangle. This is because the length of any one side of a triangle must always be less than the sum of the lengths of the remaining two sides. (2), however, is not sufficient to answer the question. Knowing that x = 6 leaves open the possibility that z is greater than, less than, or even equal to 8.

13. **(E)** To answer the question asked, we must be able to pinpoint the hiker's exact location at noon. Is that possible? (1) is surely not sufficient. It establishes only that the hiker is 4 miles to the east and 3 miles to the north of her original position at noon:

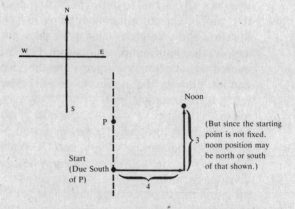

But since the starting point is not known, we cannot fix the position at noon. (2) alone is no better. By itself, it establishes only that the hiker is somewhere on a circle with radius of 4.5 miles and center P:

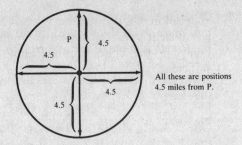

All these are positions 4.5 miles from P.

Nor are both together sufficient, for there are two points which satisfy both statements, one to the northeast of P and one to the southeast of P, as can be shown by superimposing one diagram on the other:

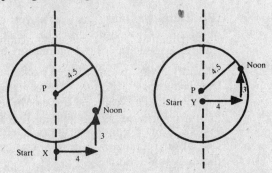

The circle with radius 4.5 miles represents the information provided by (2), while the arrows represent the information provided by (1). But the hiker's starting point is not specified by either location, so it could be X, as shown by the diagram on the left, or Y, as shown by the diagram on the right. Hence her position at noon is indeterminate.

14. **(D)** The question asks whether NNPP is divisible by 4. We can analyze the problem as follows. (1) is sufficient for the following reason: What is the difference between NPP and NNPP? Obviously, the extra N on the left of the number. But what does that mean? Since it is located in the fourth place to the left of the decimal point, it means "N × 1000." Therefore, NPP + (N × 1000) = NNPP. We are told in (1) that NPP is divisible by 8, so NNPP will be divisible by 8 provided that N × 1000 is also divisible by 8. Since 1000 is divisible by 8, N × 1000 will be divisible by 8, so NNPP must also be divisible by 8. And if a number is divisible by 8, it must be divisible by 4 as well. So (1) is sufficient. The same reasoning can be used

to show that (2) is sufficient. Since N × 1000 is divisible by 4 and since NPP is divisible by 4, NPP + (N × 1000) or NNPP, must also be divisible by 4.

15. **(E)** The question requires that we determine which brand accounted for the greater dollar profit. It should be fairly clear that (1) will not do the trick because it does not tell us how much of each was sold. (2) also is insufficient since it does not establish the wholesale price, and without that we cannot compute the dollar profit per item. The question is now whether both statements together answer the question. A moment's reflection will show the answer is no. (1), coupled with information provided in the stem, establishes that the monetary profit is higher on the name-brand items. But how much greater? If we sell enough of the generic brand, we will make more money on the generic brand. But how much is enough? That will depend on the difference in the per item profit. And that critical piece of information is missing.

16. **(A)** This question is a bit easier. Is x > y? (1) establishes that the answer to this question is no. Since x and y are both positive integers (as stipulated in the stem), x must be less than x^2, and if x^2 is less than y, then x must be less, not greater, than y. (2), however, is not sufficient. That the square root of x is less than y does not establish anything about x and y. For example, if x is 4 and y is 3, then the square root of x, which is 2, is less than y; and yet x is greater than y. On the other hand, if x is 4 and y is 5, then both x and the square root of x are less than y.

17. **(A)** We determine whether we have sufficient information to determine the radius of the circle. Using (1), we have

$$\frac{\pi r^2}{2\pi r} = \frac{3}{2}$$

We reduce the left-hand fraction by both π and by r. Cross-multiplying and solving for r, we learn r = 3. So (1) is sufficient. (2), however, does not contain enough information. It establishes only that the number of square units in the area is more than 3 greater than the number of linear units in the circumference. But an infinite number of radii will satisfy that statement.

18. **(B)** The question is how many students are taking both subjects. A student living in the dormitory must be taking only physics, only math, or both physics and math. These three possibilities can be represented by overlapping circles:

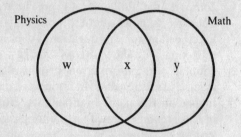

Region w is the area which represents students taking only Physics. Region y is the area representing students taking only math. Region x is the area for those taking both. We know that w + x + y = 30. (1) is insufficient, for when substituting 10 in the equation for w, we still have two variables: x + y = 20. So we cannot yet determine the value of x. (2), however, is sufficient. (2) tells us that w + x = 16 (w and x together represent students taking physics, and (2) also tells us that y + x = 20 (y and x are for those taking math). Now we can manipulate our three equations to find x:

$$
\begin{array}{r}
w + x = 16 \\
\underline{y + x = 20} \\
w + y + 2x = 36
\end{array}
$$

Taking the other equation:

$$
\begin{array}{r}
w + y + 2x = 36 \\
\underline{w + y + x = 30} \\
x = 6
\end{array}
$$

For those students who do not care to use the overlapping circles, the same conclusion can be reached by reasoning that 20 plus 16 gives a total of 36 courses being taken by only 30 students, so 6 students must be taking both courses.

19. **(B)** To answer this question, we need only find one side of the square, for all sides are equal and the area of the square is computed by the formula: side × side. (1) is not sufficient to establish any conclusion about the length of the sides of the figure. (1) proves only that P is located on the x-axis (which is stipulated in the stem also) and that P is two units to the right of the origin (O). (2), however, gives more information. Knowing that R has a y-coordinate of 4, tells us that the distance from R to S is four units. This gives us the one side of the square we need.

20. **(E)** Here we must answer a yes or no question. (1) is not sufficient because it establishes only that the diagonals are equal, and that is consistent with PQRS being a rectangle or a square. Even adding the information provided by (2), PQRS might still be a rectangle. Of course, it is possible that PQRS is a square (a square is a special case of the rectangle), but we cannot answer the question definitely.

21. **(D)** This question is actually easier than it might, at first glance, seem to be. We have a sequence in which each succeeding term is related to the preceding term in this way:

$$1;\ 1 + x;\ 1 + x + (x);\ 1 + 2x + (x) \ldots$$

Thus, if we are told the sum of any two terms in the sequence, we can construct an equation with x as the only variable, and then solve for x. For example, the third term is 1 + 2x (as shown), so the fourth term must be 1 + 3x. If (1 + 2x) + (1 + 3x) = 22, then x = 4. So (1) is sufficient. (2) must also be sufficient. Though the equation for (2) would be a bit more complex, we could still solve for x. Remember that once you recognize this you are finished.

22. **(D)** This question also is much easier than it at first appears to be. The question asks us to compare the amount of money Bob has at the end of the year with the amount Mary has at the end of the year. Now, the only deposits made during the year are those in the amount of $5 made on the first of each month. In other words, both Bob and Mary

deposit the same amount during the year. How then could there be any difference in the totals at the end of the year? The only difference between the two would have to be the result of some residual funds already in the bank at the start of the year. (1) establishes that after three deposits Bob had more money than Mary. (2) establishes a similar conclusion. But for Bob to have had more money than Mary at any time, it must be that Bob had more than Mary to begin with. Consequently, both statements establish that Bob will finish the year with more money than Mary (since each deposits 12 × $5). Now, it would be a more difficult task to calculate exactly how much each began and ended with. It could be done using simultaneous equations, but that is not relevant to the problem given the phrasing of the question.

23. **(B)** What question is asked? The question asks for the ratio of installation charge of total cost— expressed in percent terms. But if we can get the ratio between the two numbers, that will be sufficient. (1) does not supply the needed information. Knowing the difference between two numbers does not allow us to compute the ratio between them. (2), however, is sufficient. (2) establishes that the total minus installation would be only $\frac{3}{4}$ of the total. So the installation cost was only $\frac{1}{4}$, or 25 percent, of the total.

24. **(B)** The question is how many revolutions per minute pulley P makes. We know that pulley Q revolves at 300 RPM. What do we need to know to compute the RPMs of P? Only the relative sizes, that is, the ratio of their circumferences. Knowing the ratio of the radii of the circles will give us the needed information, so (2) is sufficient. (1) is not sufficient, since the pulleys may be closer together or farther apart, but the number of revolutions made by P in a minute depends only on how fast Q is turning and on the ratio of their radii.

25. **(A)** The question is whether the two trains arrive at the overpass at the same time. That is, do the two trains require the same length of time to move from their respective stations to the overpass? Clearly, (2) alone is not going to answer that question. (1), however, in and of itself, gives us the answer. Applying the special case of the Pythagorean Theorem to the diagram (30 : 60 : 90), we deduce that the distance from b to the overpass is exactly one-half of that from a to the overpass (a to the overpass is the hypotenuse and

b to the overpass is opposite a 30° angle). By (1), P travels twice as fast as Q, but since P has twice as far to travel as Q, the two trains will arrive at the overpass simultaneously.

Section IV

1. **(D)** The author's recommendation that public schools should have computerized reading programs depends upon the correctness of his explanation of the present deficiency in reading skills in the public schools. His contrast with private-school students shows that he thinks the deficiency can be attributed to the lack of such a program in the public schools. So, one of the author's assumptions, and that is what the question stem is asking about, is that the differential in reading skills is a result of the availability of a computerized program in the private-school system and the lack thereof in the public-school system. (E) is, of course, irrelevant to the question of *reading* skills. (C) tries to force the author to assume a greater burden than he has undertaken. He claims that the reading skills of public-school children could be improved by a computerized reading program. He is not concerned to argue the merits of having good reading skills. (A) and (B) are wrong for the same reason. The author's claim must be interpreted to mean "of children who are able to learn, all would benefit from a computerized reading program." When the author claims that "public-school children can be good readers," he is not implying that all children can learn to be good readers nor that all can learn to read equally well.

2. **(D)** The question contains a hidden assumption: that the person questioned agrees that his company has, in the past, discriminated. So I is applicable, since the speaker may wish to answer neither "yes" nor "no." He may wish to object to the question: "But I do not admit that our company has ever discriminated, so your question is unfair." III is just another way of describing the difficulty we have just outlined. II is not applicable to the question. Since a simple question never actually makes a statement, it would seem impossible for it to contradict itself. A contradiction occurs only between statements or assertions.

3. **(A)** There are two weaknesses in Ms. Rose's argument. One will be treated in the explanation

of the following question—she reaches a very general conclusion on the basis of one example. We are concerned for the moment with the second weakness. Even if Rose had been able to cite numerous examples like the case she mentions, her argument would be weak because it overlooks the possibility that an education may be valuable even if it is not used to make a living. Importantly, Rose may be correct in her criticism of the man she mentions—we need make no judgment about that—but the assumption is nonetheless *unsupported* in that she gives no arguments to support it. (B) plays on the superficial detail of the paragraph—the inversion of customary role models. But that is not relevant to the structure of the argument; the form could have been as easily shown using a woman with a law degree who decided to become a sailor, or a child who studied ballet but later decided to become a doctor. (D) also is totally beside the point. Rose never commits herself to so specific a conclusion. She simply says professional education is a waste; she never claims success is related to quality of education. (E) is wrong because Rose is making a general claim about professional education—the man with the law degree was used merely to illustrate her point. (C) is perhaps the second-best answer, but it is still not nearly as good as (A). The author's objection is that the man she mentions did not use his law degree in a law-related field. She never suggests that such a degree should be used to make money. She might not have objected to his behavior if he had used the degree to work in a public interest capacity.

4. **(D)** As we noted at the beginning of our discussion of question 3, there is another weakness in Rose's argument: She takes a single example and from it draws a very general conclusion. (D) exemplifies this weakness. Here, too, we have a person who rests his claim on a single example, and obviously this makes the claim very weak. (E) mentions education, but here education is a detail of the argument. The form of the argument—a foolish generalization—is not restricted to education. (A), (B), and (C) are all wrong because they do not reflect the form of the argument, a generalization on a single example.

5. **(C)** To break the code, the cryptographer needs information about the language which the code conceals. (A), (B), (D), and (E) all provide such information. (C), however, says nothing about the underlying language. The code could even use all even or all odd numbers for the symbol substitutions without affecting the information to be encoded.

6. **(B)** The question is one which tests the validity or strength of a causal inference. Often such arguments can be attacked by finding intervening causal linkages, that is, variables which might interfere with the predicted result. (A) cites such a variable. If the traffic problem is created by commercial traffic which will not be reduced by toll increases, then the proposed increases will not solve the problem. (C), too, is such a variable. It suggests that the proposal is essentially self-defeating. (D) undermines the claim by arguing that the deterrent effect of a price increase is simply not significant, so the proposal will have little, if any, effect. (E) attacks the argument on a different ground. The ultimate objective of the plan is to reduce commuting time. Even assuming a drop in auto traffic because some commuters use public transportation, no advantage is gained if the public transportation system cannot handle the increase in traffic. (B), however, does very little to the argument. In fact, it could be argued that (B) is one of the predicted results of the plan: a drop in the number of autos because commuters begin to car-pool.

7. **(D)** The ad is weak for two reasons. First, although it is addressed to smokers in general, the evidence it cites is restricted to heavy (three-packs-a-day) smokers. Second, the success achieved by the product was restricted to a highly specific and unusual location—the mountain retreat of a clinic with a population trying hard to quit smoking. Thus, II will undermine the appeal of the advertisement because it cites the first of the weaknesses. III also will tell against the ad since it mentions the second of these weaknesses. I, however, is irrelevant to the ad's appeal since the cause of a smoker's addiction plays no role in the claim of this ad to assist smokers in quitting or cutting down.

8. **(B)** Notice that there is much common ground between the jockey and the veterinarian. The question stem asks you to uncover the areas on which they are in agreement, by asking which of the answer choices in NOT a shared assumption. Note that the exception can be an area neither has as well as an area only one has. Examine the dialogue. Both apparently assume that human emotions can be attributed to animals since they talk

about them being loyal and brave (C), and both take those characteristics as being noble——that is, admirable (A). Neither speaker offers scientific evidence; each rests content with an anecdote (E) and (D). As for (B), though each speaker defends his choice for the first (*most* loyal), neither speaker takes a position on the second most loyal animal. For example, the jockey might believe that horses are the most loyal animals and that goldfish are the second most loyal animals.

9. **(A)** Although we do not want to argue theology, perhaps a point taken from that discipline will make this question more accessible: "If God is only good, from where does evil come?" Rousseau, at least as far as his argument is characterized here, faced a similar problem. If man is by his very nature sympathetic, what is the source of his non-sympathetic social institutions? (A) poses this critical question. The remaining choices each commit the same fundamental error. Rousseau *describes* a situation. The paragraph never suggests that he proposed a *solution*. Perhaps Rousseau considered the problem of modern society irremediable.

10. **(C)** The last sentence of the paragraph is very important. It tells us that the proportion of light atoms in the universe is increasing (because heavy ones decay into light ones, but the reverse process does not occur) and that this trend can be measured. By extrapolation back into time on the basis of present trends, scientists can find out when it all began. (B) and (E) are incorrect for the same reason. The author describes a physical phenomenon occurring on a grand scale. He never hints that it will be possible for man to reverse it (B). Further, (E) is in direct contradiction with information given in the paragraph: The ratio is not stable because the stars do not produce enough heavy atoms to offset the decay. (D) cannot be inferred from the passage. Although the *ratio* of light to heavy atoms is increasing, we should not conclude that the ratio is greater than 1:1. And, in any event, this would not be nearly so logical a conclusion to the passage as (C). Finally, (A) is a distraction. It picks up on a minor detail in the passage and inflates that into a conclusion. Moreover, the passage clearly states that the process which keeps the stars going is fusion, not decay.

11. **(C)** It is important to pay careful attention to the ways in which a speaker qualifies his claims. In this case, the speaker has said only that the *great*

majority of people can get medical care——he does not claim that *all* can. Thus, built into the claim is the implicit concession that some people may not have access to medical care. Thus, the objector's response fails to score against the speaker. The speaker could just respond, "Yes, I realize that and that is the reason why I qualified my remarks." (A) is incorrect for the only word in the objector's statement which is the least bit emotional is "poor," and it seems rather free from emotional overtones here. It would have been a different case had the objector claimed, "There are thousands of poor and starving people who have no place to live. . . ."(D) is wrong for two reasons. First, the evidence is really not statistical; it is only numerical. Second, and more important, the evidence, if anything, cuts against the speaker's claim——not that it does any damage given the speaker's qualifications on his claim; but it surely does not strengthen the speaker's claim. Finally, inasmuch as the speaker does not offer a cause-effect explanation, (E) must be wrong.

12. **(C)** There are really two parts to the speaker's claim. First, he maintains that the majority of Americans can get access to the medical care in this country; and, second, that the care they have access to is the best in the world. As for the second, good medical care is a function of many variables: number and location of facilities, availability of doctors, quality of education, etc. (A) and (E) may both be consistent with the speaker's claim. Even though we have fewer assistants (A) than some other country, we have more doctors, and that more than makes up for the fewer assistants. Or, perhaps, we have such good preventive medicine that people do not need to go into the hospital as frequently as the citizens of other nations, (E). (B) is wrong for a similar reason. Although it suggests there is a country in which people have greater access to the available care, it does not come to grips with the second element of the speaker's claim: that the care we get is the best. (C), however, does meet both because it cites the existence of a country in which people are *given* (that is the first element) *better* (the second element) care. (D) hardly tells against the speaker's claim since he has implicitly conceded that some people do not have access to the care.

13. **(B)** The chief failing of the argument is that it draws a false analogy. Since prisons are required to feed and maintain as well as house prisoners

(not to mention the necessity for security), the analogy to a hotel room is weak at best. (C) focuses on this specific shortcoming. Remember, in evaluating the strength of an argument from analogy it is important to look for dissimilarities which might make the analogy inappropriate. Thus, (A) and (E) are also good criticisms of the argument. They voice the general objection of which (C) is the specification. (D) is also a specific objection——the argument compares two numbers which are not at all similar. So the numerical comparison is a false one. (B) is not a way in which the argument can be criticized, for the author never cites any authority.

14. **(C)** Note the word *right* is italicized in the first sentence of the paragraph. The author is saying that this idea of a right can be only understood as the outcome of a balancing of demands. The smoker has an interest in smoking; the non-smoker has an interest in being free from smoke; so the question of which one actually has a *right* to have his *interest* protected depends upon which of those interests is considered to be more important. In some cases the balance is easily struck; in other cases it is difficult; but in all cases, the weighing, implicitly or explicitly, occurs. (C) captures the essence of this thought. In the case of smoking, the interests of both parties must be taken into account. (A) is a distraction. It is true the passage treats "rights," and it is also true that our Constitution protects our rights; but the connection suggested by (A) is a spurious one. It fails to address itself to the logic of the author's argument. The same objections can be leveled against (B). The wording of (D) makes it wrong. The passage is concerned with the demands of the nonsmoker *to be free from* the smoke of others, not with whether he himself chooses to smoke. (E) is premature. At this juncture the author is laying the foundation for his argument. He is speaking about rights in general. He reaches his conclusion with regard to smoking only at the end of the paragraph. (See discussion of the following question.) (E) is wrong also because it mentions the "rights" of non-smoking persons. The whole question the author is addressing is whether the non-smoking person has a *right* as opposed to an interest or a mere claim.

15. **(C)** Here is where the author makes his general discussion of the balancing of interests to determine rights specifically applicable to the question of smoking. A smoker will have a *right* to smoke

when and where his interests outweigh the interests of those who object, and (C) provides a pretty clear statement of this conclusion. (A) overstates the author's case. While it may be true that ultimately it will be some branch of the government which strikes the balance of interests, the phrase "chooses to allow" does not do justice to the author's concept of the balancing. The government is not simply choosing; it is weighing. Of course, since the balance may or may not be struck in favor of the smoker, (B) is incorrect. (E) confuses the problem of enforcement with the process of balancing. The passage leads to the conclusion that the balance must be struck. How that decision is later enforced is a practical matter the author is not concerned to discuss in this passage. Finally, (D), like (A), overstates the case. The smoker has an interest in being allowed to smoke, just as much as the non-smoker has an interest in being free from the smoke. A balance must be struck by giving proper weight to both. The author never suggests that the interest of the smokers can be completely overridden. Thus, for example, a smoker may have a more powerful interest in smoking than a non-smoker has in his being free from smoke, if the non-smoker can——with some small inconvenience——protect himself from the smoke.

16. **(B)** The whole passage is to clear up a misunderstanding about the concept of a *right*. The author explains that the term is misused since most people fail to realize that the right is not absolute, but is qualified by the interests and claims of other persons. While it is true that this is not generally known, (A) is incorrect because the author's *strategy* in argument is to clarify that term, not merely to bring up facts to support a contention that is already well defined. (C) also fails to describe his strategy. It is true that the author mentions hypothetical cases, but that is a detail, not his principal strategy. As for (D), though the author argues that smokers who claim an unqualified right to smoke are wrong, he does not argue that they have fallen into contradiction. Finally, although the author argues that the general claim of smokers is ill-founded, the general claim he attacks (smokers have a right to smoke) is not an induction based on *empirical* evidence. A person who makes such a claim is not generalizing on observed instances (All swans I have seen are white. . . .); he is making a conceptual claim.

17. **(D)** Let us use the technique of substituting cap-

ital letters for categories. The sample argument can be rendered:

Some J are B. (Some Judges are Bar members)

No B are F. (No Bar members are Felons)

Therefore, Some J are not F. (Some Judges are not Felons)

This is a perfectly valid (logical) argument. (D) shares its form and validity:

Some M are P. (Some Men are Polite)

No M are D. (No Men are Dorm-allowed)

Therefore, Some P are not D. (Some Polite Men are not Dorm-allowed)

(E) has the invalid argument form:

G is L.

G is A.

Therefore, A is L.

(B) and (C) are both set up using more than three categories; therefore, they cannot possibly have the structure of the sample argument which uses only three categories:

(B)——people, people who want to avoid jury duty, people who do not register to vote, persons under 18

(C)——business, entities filing tax returns, business making enough money to pay taxes, business making a profit.

Finally, (A) does not parallel the sample argument since it contains the qualification "likely."

18. **(D)** The author's argument is admittedly not a very persuasive one, but the question stem does not ask us to comment on its relative strength. Rather, we are asked to identify the form of argumentation. Here the author suggests an alternative explanation, albeit a somewhat outlandish one. Thus, (D) is correct, (E) is incorrect because the claim about fresh air and the country is introduced as a causal explanation, not an analogy to the city. (C) is wrong for the author accepts the differential described by the report; he just tries to explain the existence of the differential in another way. By the same token we can reject both (A) and (B) since the author takes the report's conclusion as his starting point. Although he attacks the explanation provided by the *report* published by the Department of Education, he does not attack the *credibility* of the *department* itself. Further, though he disagrees with the *conclusion* drawn by

the report, he does not attack the way in which the *study* itself was *conducted*. Rather, he disagrees with the interpretation of the data gathered.

19. **(E)** The question stem asks us to find the one item which will not strengthen the author's argument. That is (E). Remember, the author's argument is an attempt (to be sure, a weak one) to develop an alternative causal explanation. (A) would provide some evidence that the author's claim—which at first glance seems a bit farfetched—actually has some empirical foundation. While (B) does not add any strength to the author's own explanation of the phenomenon being studied, it does strengthen the author's overall position by undermining the explanation given in the report. (C) strengthens the author's position for the same reason that (B) does: It weakens the position he is attacking. (D) strengthens the argument in the same way that (A) does, by providing some empirical support for the otherwise seemingly far-fetched explanation.

20. **(E)** Perhaps the most obvious weakness in the argument is that it oversimplifies matters. It is like the domino theory arguments adduced to support the war in Vietnam: Either we fight Communism now or it will take us over. The author argues, in effect: Either we put a stop to this now, or there will be no stopping it. Like the proponents of the domino theory, he ignores the many intermediate positions one might take. III is one way of describing this shortcoming: The dilemma posed by the author is a false one because it overlooks positions between the two extremes. II is also a weakness of the argument: "Cold-blooded murder" is obviously a phrase calculated to excite negative feelings. Finally, the whole argument is also internally inconsistent. The conclusion is that we should allow nature to take its course. How? By prolonging life with artificial means.

21. **(D)** We can summarize the information, using capital letters to represent each statement:

If P, then Q.

If Q, then R or S.

If R or S, and if Q, then A.

If R or S and if not-Q, then not-A.

where P represents "Paul comes to the party," Q represents "Quentin leaves the party," R represents ''Robert asks Alice to dance,'' S represents ''Steve asks Alice to dance,'' (and conversely R represents ''Alice is asked by Robert to dance'' and S represents ''Alice is asked by Steve to dance''), and A represents Alice accepts. If we have not-Q, then we can deduce not-P from the first statement; thus, we have (D). (A), (B) and (C) are incorrect since there is no necessity that Robert or Steve ask Alice to dance. (E) is incorrect since this statement is different from our other statements and must be assigned a different letter, perhaps X. Notice that ''Alice will accept . . . '' tells us nothing about whether Alice leaves the party.

22. **(A)** The question stem has the form:

All S are AP. (All Students are APplicants)
Some AP are AC (Some APplicants are ACcepted)
Some *more* S are AC. (Some more Students are ACcepted)

Notice that (A) preserves very nicely the parallel in the conclusion because it uses the word ''more.'' Thus, the error made in the stem argument (that some *more* students will be *accepted*) is preserved in (A): *more* apples will be *loaded*. (B) has a valid argument form (All S are W; X is an S; therefore, X is a W), so it is not parallel to the sample argument. (C) is not similar for at least two reasons. First, its conclusion is a recommendation (''should''), not a factual claim. Second, (C) uses one premise, not two premises as the sample argument does. (D) would have been parallel to the sample argument only if the sample had the conclusion ''some more applications must be acted upon.'' Finally, (E) contains an argument which is fallacious, but the fallacy is not similar to that of the question stem.

23. **(E)** The advertisement employs the term ''more'' in an ambiguous manner. In the context, one might expect the phrase ''more flavor'' to mean ''more highly concentrated flavor,'' that is, ''more flavor per unit weight.'' What the ad actually says, however, is that the sticks of Evergreen are *larger*, so if they are larger, there must be more *total* flavor. All three propositions, if they are true (as we are asked to assume they are), are good attacks on the ad. First, in I, it is possible to beat the ad at its own game. If flavor is just a matter of chewing enough sticks, then Spring Mint is as good a deal because, flavor unit for flavor unit, it is no more expensive than Evergreen. Second, II would also undermine the ad by focusing on the ambiguity we have just discussed. Finally, III also uncovers another potential ambiguity. If the ad is comparing volume rather than weight, Spring Mint may be a better value. After all, who wants to buy a lot of air?

24. **(D)** Again, we remind ourselves that we are looking for the most reliable statement. Even the most reliable, however, will not necessarily be perfectly reliable. Here (D) is fairly trustworthy. We note that the speaker is an expert and so is qualified to speak about wines. In (A), the speaker is making a judgment about something on which he is not qualified to speak. Also, in (D) there is no hint of self-interest—if anything, the speaker is admitting against a possible self-interest that American chablis is a better buy than French chablis. By comparison, (B) and (C), which smack of a self-serving bias, are not so trustworthy. Finally, (E) sounds like a statement made for dramatic effect and so is not to be taken at face value.

25. **(E)** This advertisement is simply rife with ambiguity. The wording obviously seeks to create the impression that FCBI found jobs for its many graduates and generally does a lot of good for them. But first we should ask how many graduates FCBI had—one, two, three, a dozen, or a hundred. If it had only 12 or so, finding them jobs might have been easy; but if many people enroll at FCBI, they may not have the same success. Further, we might want to know how many people graduated compared with how many enrolled. Do people finish the program, or does FCBI just take their money and then force them out of the program? So II is certainly something we need to know in order to assess the validity of the claim. Now, how many of those who graduated came in looking for help in finding a job? Maybe most people had jobs waiting for them (only a few needed help), in which case the job placement assistance of FCBI is not so impressive. Or, perhaps the graduates were so disgusted they did not even seek assistance. So I is relevant. III is also important. Perhaps FCBI found them jobs sweeping streets—not in business. The ad does not say what jobs FCBI helped its people find. Finally, maybe the ad is truthful—FCBI graduates found jobs—but maybe they did it on their own. So IV also is a question worth asking.

Section V

1. **(D)** (D) is correct because in likening two things it expresses them in like grammatical forms: "to be afraid of . . . is to be afraid of" (infinitives). (A), (B), and (C) fail because they compare unlike forms: "to be afraid" (infinitive) with "being afraid" (gerund). (E) uses the same form for both parts, but is is an unnecessary combination of the two possibilities. (B) also uses commas incorrectly. Using the gerund form in both parts would also be correct.

2. **(C)** The problem is raised by placement of the modifier "hurtling through." Who or what is hurtling, Anna [(A), (D)], the sight (B), or the shooting star [(C), (E)]? Of the two clearest statements—(C) and (E)—(C) presents the facts in a better order.

3. **(B)** (A) errs in three ways: "superior" is already a comparative adjective and does not need the comparative form "more"; the idiom is "superior to," not "superior than"; and the "far as . . . concerned" phrase embodies an unneeded repetition. (C), (D) and (E) each make one of these errors; (E) also is awkward in its word order.

4. **(C)** A is incorrect because it switches from the singular ("weaver," "his") to the plural ("they"). Changing this segment to all singular, as in (B), would not tie in with "their wool" later in the sentence. So it is better to change all references to the plural, as in (C). (D) and (E) unpleasantly switch from the personal active to the impersonal passive.

5. **(A)** (C), (B) and (E) change the meaning; in (B) and (E) the result is gibberish. (D) would make sense but would not be Standard Written English: the required conjunction in such an indirect question is "whether."

6. **(E)** Since the writer talks of a condition contrary to fact (he is not President), he should use the subjunctive form "I were," as in (E). "I was," as in (A) and (C), would be acceptable in informal speech but not in Standard Written English. (B) is too elliptical. (C) and (D) slightly change the meaning: (C) makes the "halt" the President's very first action; (D) implies he has a realistic chance of being President.

7. **(B)** (A) and (E) err in being ambiguous: they could mean that females are more concerned about discrimination than about males. (D) goes further than it has to by repeating the full phrase "are concerned." All that is necessary is the key word "are," as in (B). (C) is not incorrect, but it is less graceful and too wordy.

8. **(C)** In Standard Written English, the negative correlative conjunctions "neither . . . nor" function together, as in (C). If one of them appears in a negating construction like (A), (B), or (E), the other should also appear, but in the appropriate order of "neither . . . nor." In (D), "or" is wrong because when it is used as a correlative conjunction, it appears only with "either," which would be contrary to the meaning here.

9. **(D)** (D) is correct because it extends the structure begun with "results from" by repeating the "from" at the crucial point. The others are incorrect. (A) used "to" where "from" is needed; (B) confuses "affect" with "effect" and fails to extend the "results from" structure; (C) makes two errors in punctuation—neither the apostrophe nor the comma is used correctly; (E) repeats (A)'s error with an unnecessary comma.

10. **(C)** (C) is correct because after a verb like "demand" the action called for must be expressed in the subjunctive mood, e.g., "that management halt . . . and release. . . ." (B) uses the correct verb form but the wrong conjunction: "but" violates the meaning. (A), (B) and (D) all violate the parallelism required. (D) also creates an awkward final phrase.

11. **(E)** In Standard Written English, "each other" is the reciprocal pronoun for two persons, "one another" for more than two. Hence (E) is the only correct answer. In informal speech, (A) would be acceptable.

12. **(E)** (A) errs in three ways: it uses "as . . . that" instead of "as . . . as," which is required in comparing things to an equal degree; it fails to put "almost a century later" in commas, required since the phrase is nonessential; and it uses "will offer" where, in the sequence of tenses after the past verb "posed," the past form of "will" ("would offer") is required. (B) and (C) each correct only two of the three errors; (D), only one; (E) is entirely correct.

13. **(A)** The original is best because it relates the circumstances in the most logical, most dramatic order, and without error. (B) and (C) leave their opening phrase dangling: (B) links "the greatest player" not to Tilden, but to his "accomplishments"; and (C), to the "rumors"! (C), (D) and (E) fail to arrange the facts as effectively as (A) does; (D) is especially awkward.

14. **(D)** (A) errs in parallelism and in punctuation. A series of times branches off from the idea "spend money . . . on." Effective parallelism requires repetition of "on" before each item; effective punctuation requires a comma after each item standing before "and." (B) supplies the comma but not the "on"; (C) and (E) supply "for" instead of "on" and no comma; (E) is wordier than need be.

15. **(B)** (A) creates ambiguity through faulty parallelism: are women being compared with women or with cities? (E) eliminates confusion by using strict parallel structure: "the women in Paris" is balanced by "the women in any other city." But (B) is better because it saves a word by using "those" instead of repeating "the women." (C) and (D) not only worsen the parallelism, they misspell "Parisian," ironically hitting on the French masculine form for the English adjective.

16. **(C)** The phrase about the "aides" simply supplies extra, parenthetical information. It is not part of the subject, which remains the singular "media advisor." (A), (B) and (D) therefore err in using the plural verb "are." (E) uses the correct singular "is" but reverses the facts—it's the "aides" who "are all in the company" of the "advisor."

17. **(E)** The original is repetitious: if "Lawyers and doctors . . . agree," then "alike" and "both" are superfluous; if there's a "rise in . . . suits," the clause "which are on the increase" is redundant. Only (E) avoids all these errors.

18. **(A)** (B) is wrong because the "if" clause, stating a past condition contrary to fact, requires a past-perfect subjunctive ("had known"). (C) and (D) are wrong because the "possible conclusion" clause requires the perfect form of a modal auxiliary ("would have run"). (E) uses the wrong tense of the subjunctive. (B), (C) and (E) all needlessly add the "if" already implicit in the "had . . . known" construction, which is required in Standard Written English.

19. **(A)** (B) and (C) confuse "effect" with "affect." (C) and (D) use "than" instead of "from": things differ "from" one another. (E) uses the singular "that" instead of the plural "those" to refer back to the plural antecedent "findings." Only (A) avoids all these traps.

20. **(D)** (A) is poor on two counts: (1) "the past eight years," or past action continuing into the present, requires the present perfect ("has been") rather than the past tense ("was"); and (2) the two parts of the sentence that should be close for comparative purposes—"shy and awkward" and "graceful and consistent"—are separated. (C) echoes (1) and corrects (2) at the expense of vital information. (B) and (E) echo (2).

21. **(E)** In (A), (C) and (D), "of them" or "of these" is superfluous. In (B), "the latter" is incorrect. Since there are more than two items to refer back to, the correct term is "the last." (If four items were specified, the writer could refer to "the latter two," as distinct from "the former two," but "of all the reasons" implies many more than four.)

22. **(C)** In Standard Written English, the pattern is "less . . . than" and of course the two parts thus introduced should be in parallel structure. (A)'s use of "as" is totally unacceptable. (B)'s use of "and more on" might be acceptable in informal speech. (D) is illiterate. (E) uses the correct adverb, "than," but omits the "on" that cinches the parallelism.

23. **(C)** The subject of the sentence is singular ("the number"). Therefore verbs related to the "the number" should be singular (is, was) and a pronoun referring back to "the number" should be singular (it). (A), (B) and (D) each violate one or both of these requirements. (E) only appears to correct the error by substituting "the numbers" for "they" but still makes an incorrect reference back to "the number."

24. **(D)** The original has two faults: "Insofar as" is used incorrectly—it means "to such an extent," not "because"—and "a good bargain" and "under a dollar a pound" are only loosely related by the conjunction "and." Only (D) corrects both faults. (E)'s solution for the second fault is

good, but the sentence requires 15 words compared to (D)'s 13.

25. **(B)** Context indicates that of two past actions, "danced" and "established," one occurred before the other. Therefore, the earlier action must be set in the past perfect tense ("had danced") as in (B). (C) is not incorrect, but there seems to be no reason for using the longer form, the past perfect progressive ("had been dancing"). (E), by using the participle "dancing" for the 1942 to 1947 action, blurs the distinction to be made from the 1948 action. (D) reverses the tenses required and so violates the time sense.

Section VI

1. **(D)** 40 percent of $2000, or $800, goes for business expenses. That leaves $1200. 10 percent of the remaining $1200, or $120, is reinvested.

2. **(B)** Since 8 is equal to 2^3, 8^4 is equal to $(2^3)^4$, which is equal to 2^{12}. (To raise a power to a power, you multiply the exponents together to get the new exponent.) 2^{12} divided by $2^{10} = 2^2$, or 4. In a division problem involving exponents on the same base (in this case the base is 2) you must subtract the exponents to obtain the answer.

3. **(A)** The base here is 2000, the percentage is 50; thus rate $= \dfrac{50}{2000} = .025 = 2.5\%$. Remember that in a "this is what percent of that?" problem, the number immediately following the "of" is the denominator of the fractional equivalent of the desired percentage.

4. **(C)** Multiplying the binomials together, using FOIL, and remembering that the square root of 5^2 is 5, we obtain $(4 + \sqrt{5})(4 - \sqrt{5}) = 16 + 4(\sqrt{5}) - 4(\sqrt{5}) - 5 = 11$. You may recognize the binomials as the factors of the difference of two squares, and thus see the answer more quickly.

5. **(E)** If the shorter piece is designated by x, then the longer piece must be x + 8. The two pieces added together must equal 32 feet, that is, x + (x + 8) = 32 or x = 12 and x + 8 = 20. Thus the ratio of the larger piece to the smaller piece is $\dfrac{20}{12}$ or $\dfrac{5}{3}$.

6. **(B)** If 3 people take $5\dfrac{1}{3}$ days, then one person would take 3 times as long, or 16 days. Thus one person can do $\dfrac{1}{16}$ of a job in a day. Two people can do twice as much of a job, or $\dfrac{1}{8}$, in a day. Alternatively, you may set up the equation (3) $(5\dfrac{1}{3}) = (2)(x)$, where x is the time it takes 2 workers to complete the job. x = 8 days, thus 2 people do $\dfrac{1}{8}$ of a job in 1 day.

7. **(D)** We simply want to find how long it will take to amass interest equal to 100 percent of the original amount saved. So we must divide 100 percent by the rate of interest per year, $6\dfrac{1}{4}$ percent, to get the number of years:
$$\frac{100}{6\dfrac{1}{4}} = 16$$

8. **(B)** The area of a rectangle is length times width: A = lw. For a rectangle with $\dfrac{1}{2}$ the length and 4 times the width of the original rectangle, the area can be expressed as $\dfrac{1}{2}(l)(4w)$ which equals 2(1w). The ratio of the original area to the new area would be $\dfrac{1(1w)}{2(1w)}$ or $\dfrac{1}{2}$. The fact that in the original rectangle the length is twice the width is irrelevant to the answer. The ratio would be $\dfrac{1}{2}$ no matter what the shape of the original rectangle.

9. **(A)** In the diagram, the angle opposite e is 80° so e must be 80°. a + e + d = 180 (since they sum to a straight angle) and a = 3d, so 3d + e + d = 180. Since e = 80, 3d + 80 + d = 180, or 4d = 100 and d = 25. Since b is opposite d, b also equals 25.

10. **(E)** In a problem such as this, which appears to involve considerable arithmetic, one should look for a shortcut. If you recognize that 3510 × 3508 is the same as (3508 + 2) (3508), which equals (3508 × 3508) + (3508 × 2), the problem becomes much easier. We then have $(3508)^2 -$ (3510 × 3508) = (3508 × 3508) − [(3508 × 3508) + (2 × 3508)] = −(2 × 3508) = −7016.

11. **(E)** First we need to find the cost of the berries. 2000 quarts × 80 cents per quart is $1600. The gross profit must be 20 percent of that amount, or (.20)($1600) = $320. The total selling price of the berries must be $1600 + $320 = $1920. One-quarter of the berries cannot be sold, that is, $\frac{3}{4}$ of the berries can be sold. $\frac{3}{4}$ of 2000 is 1500 quarts. The selling price per quart must be $1920/(1500 quarts), or $1.28 per quart.

12. **(B)** Let us call Charlene's income for January x. She spent $\frac{2}{5}$x on rent, leaving $\frac{3}{5}$x. $\frac{3}{4}$ of the remainder was spent on other expenses, leaving $(\frac{1}{4})(\frac{3}{5})$x or $\frac{3}{20}$x. That must equal the remaining $180, so $\frac{3}{20}$x = $180, and x = $1200.

13. **(B)** We first find the value of the taxable items. The tax rate is 6 percent and the tax is 30 cents, so .06x = $.30, where x is the taxable amount, and x = $5.00. At this point, we must be careful to find the cost of the tax-free items by subtracting the cost of the taxable items *and* the tax from the total:

$$\$25.00 - \$5.00 - \$.30 = \$19.70$$

14. **(D)** Triangle ABC is an equilateral triangle, since its third angle must also be 60°. If we can find the side of this triangle, we can then find its area. Triangle ACD is a 30-60-90 right triangle, so AC, which is the hypotenuse, must be twice as long as the shorter leg, DC; thus, it is 4. Now that we have the side, we may calculate the area of equilateral triangle ABC. The altitude a of the triangle makes two 30-60-90 triangles as illustrated in the diagram below, in which triangle ABC is shown alone and rotated 60°. Note that this altitude will bisect the base BC.

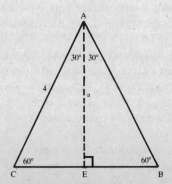

Triangle ACE is the 30-60-90 triangle which allows us to find the needed altitude. The small leg of triangle ACE (side CE) is half of AC, that is, 2. Thus the longer leg (side AE) is $\sqrt{3}$ times that, or 2 $\sqrt{3}$. The area of ABC can now be found to be $(\frac{1}{2})$(base)(height) = $(\frac{1}{2})$ (4) $(2\sqrt{3})$ = $4\sqrt{3}$.

15. **(A)** Let us for convenience call the original fraction $\frac{a}{b}$. Then the numerator of the new fraction (being decreased by 25 percent, which is .25a) must be a − .25a, or .75a. The new denominator, being increased by 25 percent, must be b + .25b, or 1.25b. The new fraction is, therefore, $\frac{.75a}{1.25b}$. Percentage decrease is found by taking the difference of the two fractions and dividing by the original fraction. In this case the difference is $\frac{a}{b}$ − $\frac{.75a}{1.25b}$. Factoring out the $\frac{a}{b}$ we have $\frac{a}{b}(1 - \frac{.75}{1.25})$ Since .75 is equal to $\frac{3}{4}$ and 1.25 is equal to $1\frac{1}{4}$, or $\frac{5}{4}$, the expression inside the parenthesis is $1 - \frac{\frac{3}{4}}{\frac{5}{4}}$ or $1 - \frac{3}{5}$, which equals $\frac{2}{5}$. So the difference is $(\frac{2}{5})(\frac{a}{b})$. The percentage increase is now found to be $(\frac{2}{5})(\frac{a}{b})$ divided by the old fraction, $\frac{a}{b}$, yielding an answer of $\frac{2}{5}$ = 40 percent.

Or, as a test-taking practice, you might pick any fraction, say, $\frac{1}{1}$. Then you perform the needed manipulations:

$$\frac{1 - (.25 \times 1)}{1 + (.25 \times 1)} = \frac{.75}{1.25} = \frac{3}{5}$$

So the decrease, expressed as a percent, was:

$$\frac{1 - \frac{3}{5}}{1} = \frac{2}{5} = 40 \text{ percent}$$

16. **(C)** We must first find the area of the racetrack, which we may then multiply by the depth of the asphalt layer to find the volume of asphalt needed. From the diagram below it should be clear that the area of the track is found by calculating the area of the large circle and the area of

the small circle, then subtracting the latter from the former.

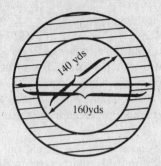

The larger circle has a diameter of 160 yards, thus a radius of 80 yards and an area of π times $(80)^2$, or 6400π square yards. The smaller has a diameter of 140 yards, thus a radius of 70 yards and an area of π times $(70)^2$, or 4900π square yards. Subtracting the smaller area from the larger, we obtain the $6400\pi - 4900\pi = 1500\pi$ as the area of the track. Since the asphalt layer is to be 1 foot, or $\frac{1}{3}$ yard, deep, we must multiply 1500π by $\frac{1}{3}$, getting 500π cubic yards as the answer.

17. **(E)** This problem is actually quite easy if one thinks to apply some backward reasoning to its solution. If the vat is full after one hour, then 2 minutes earlier it must have been half-full, since the cells double every 2 minutes. Two minutes earlier than an hour later is 58 minutes later. Note that the dimensions of the vat are irrelevant to the answer to this question. If the vat is full after 1 hour, it will be half-full after 58 minutes regardless of the capacity of the vat.

18. **(A)** To answer this question, we must follow the instructions given in the question about interpreting the symbol P and apply them by beginning inside the parentheses and working our way out. 2P3 must equal $\frac{2 \times 3}{(3 - 2)} = 6$ since 2 can be substituted for a and 3 substituted for b in the given formula. Now we can replace (2P3) with 6 in the expression we are to evaluate. This gives us 5P6, which, since a is now 5 and b is now 6, will equal $\frac{5 \times 6}{(6 - 5)} = 30$.

19. **(B)** It would be a mistake to assume that if Brown went 50 miles per hour going to city B and 30 miles per hour returning, he would average 40 miles per hour for the round trip. The reason that one simply cannot average the two speeds to get the overall average is that the trip at the lower speed takes a longer time. Let us call the distance between city A and city B d. Then the round-trip distance is 2d. Using the relation Time = Distance/Rate, we see that the total time must be $\frac{2d}{40} = \frac{d}{20}$ hours. The first half of the trip takes $\frac{d}{50}$ hours, so the second half must take $\frac{d}{20} - \frac{d}{50}$ hours. This is equal to $\frac{5d}{100} - \frac{2d}{100} = \frac{3d}{100}$ hours. Thus the average speed on the return trip, Distance / Time, must equal $\frac{d}{\frac{3d}{100}} = \frac{100}{3} = 33\frac{1}{3}$ miles per hour.

20. **(C)** Let x = original price of the item. The marked-down price would be $\frac{5}{6}x$. The coupon provides for a 20 percent, or $\frac{1}{5}$, further discount. So, the price paid by Joe was $(\frac{4}{5})(\frac{5}{6}x)$, which equals $\frac{2}{3}x$. This would have to be increased by $\frac{1}{3}x$ to equal the original price of x. The percentage increase is found by dividing $\frac{1}{3}x$ by $\frac{2}{3}x$, which yields $\frac{1}{2}$, or 50 percent.

Section VII

1. **(E)** Neither of the propositions is sufficient by itself. The issue then becomes whether a right triangle with hypotenuse of length 5 is fully determined, and thus can have its area determined. The triangle described by (1) and (2) together is not necessarily a 3-4-5 right triangle; for example, it could be an isosceles right triangle, and this triangle would have a different area from that of the 3-4-5 right triangle. Therefore, the area cannot be computed from even (1) and (2) together. The Pythagorean Theorem states that the sum of the squares of the two legs equals the square of the hypotenuse; thus, if the legs are AB and BC, $\overline{AB}^2 + \overline{BC}^2 = 5^2$. This makes it clear that AB can get longer and BC can get smaller, or vice versa. The unique aspect of a

3-4-5 right triangle is that it is the only INTEGER solution for a hypotenuse of length 5.

2. **(C)** Taking (1) and (2) together, we may set up a weighted average:

$$\frac{4(27) + 3(33)}{7} = \text{average age}$$

3. **(D)** If -2 times a is negative, then a must be positive because only a negative times a positive will yield a negative, so (1) is sufficient. If 5 times a is positive, then a must be positive, so (2) is sufficient.

4. **(B)** (1) is irrelevant since we do not need to know how many quarts George drinks. (2) allows us to figure out how many cartons George drinks per week, which is what we need to know.

5. **(E)** Knowing the range of weights does not give us the average weight, which is what we would need to obtain the number of riders from (1), by division. (2) is simply irrelevant.

6. **(A)** If each of the numbers is greater than 60, as (1) specifies, then their sum must be greater than 120. (2) is insufficient since the two numbers might both be negative.

7. **(E)** A quadrilateral that has four 90° angles is a rectangle, but not necessarily a square. Thus, even knowing both (1) and (2) is insufficient to obtain the perimeter of the quadrilateral, given only the length of side AB.

8. **(B)** Knowing the number of pounds of sand in the sandbox does not tell us the number of shovels of sand. Thus, (1) is not sufficient. (2) gives us the equation: $\frac{1}{3}$ (number of shovels of sand needed to fill the sandbox) = 50, and is therefore sufficient.

9. **(C)** The area of a rectangle is equal to its base times its height. The area of a triangle inscribed in that rectangle is $\frac{1}{2}$ times the same base times the same height, which is half the area of the rectangle. The area of triangle CDE, which is inscribed in rectangle ABCD, is thus half the area of that rectangle. Triangles ACE and BDE combined make up the other half, so the sum of their

areas equals the area of triangle CDE. Thus we need both (1) and (2).

10. **(D)** (1) is sufficient since $\frac{\$100}{(\$10 \text{ per sale})} = $ 10 sales, and 10 sales times $50 per sale = $500. (2) is also sufficient since 20 percent of the total collected would have to equal $100, again leading to a total of $500. (The question does not ask for the number of vacuums sold.)

11. **(E)** We do not know that the sections are equal in number of students, thus we cannot find the overall average even knowing both (1) and (2).

12. **(A)** (1) is sufficient, since it shows that $y = 4$ and $x = +3$ or $x = -3$ and the product of x and y in either case would be an integer. (2) is not sufficient; for example, with $x = \frac{1}{4}$ and $y = 2$, x^2y^4 would be an integer while xy would be a fraction.

13. **(B)** (1) is not sufficient because we do not know the number of bricks in the wall. If after 4 hours $\frac{2}{3}$ of the wall is erected, the whole wall would take 6 hours to finish, so (2) is sufficient.

14. **(E)** Even knowing both (1) and (2), we have no idea of how many players play all three games and so cannot determine how many players play backgammon and chess.

15. **(C)** If one-quarter of the marbles are milkies and there are twice as many cat's-eyes as milkies, then half the marbles are cat's-eyes, and $\frac{1}{2}$ is the required probability. Therefore, both (1) and (2) are needed.

16. **(C)** Using (1) and (2) together, the number of students taking only English would be 120 − (10 + 50). The total number of students taking English could then be found by adding the number taking both English and French to the number taking only English.

17. **(A)** (1) is sufficient since it tells us that not raining tomorrow means not raining today, but it will rain today, so it must also rain tomorrow. (2) is not sufficient since it leaves open the possibility that it will rain today and not rain tomorrow.

18. **(C)** (1) alone yields by substitution the quadratic equation $r^2 - r = 20$, which yields $r^2 - r - 20 = 0$, which factors into $(r - 5)(r + 4) = 0$; thus, $r = 5$ or -4. (2) alone implies that $r^2 = 16$ and r is the square root of 16, or $+4$ or -4. The two propositions together show that $r = -4$ and $p = 16$, and, thus, together they are sufficient.

19. **(B)** (2) is sufficient because the number of hours can be found by multiplying the number of days by 24. (1) is not sufficient since we do not know, and should not assume, that the two days mentioned are in the same week.

20. **(B)** (1) is not sufficient since we do not know anything about route Y. (2) would allow us to set up the equations: Distance = 60 hours times the average rate of the bus, and Distance = 80 hours times (the average rate of the bus − 10). Since this is a situation in which there are two equations and two variables or unknowns, the situation can be solved for both unknowns. The rate can be obtained, and then the distance can be calculated by multiplying by 60 hours.

21. **(A)** (1) tells us that the remainder would be 2 when y is divided by 6. All that (2) means is that y is divisible by 2 since $\frac{(3y)}{6} = \frac{y}{2}$. That is helpful, but not sufficient, since an even number could have a remainder of 0, 2, or 4 when divided by 6.

22. **(D)** If $c^2 - 1$ is odd, then c^2 is even. The square of a number is even only if the number is even, so c must be even. If the product of two integers is odd, the two integers must be odd, so (2) means that $c - 3$ is odd, and so c must be even. Thus either (1) or (2) is sufficient.

23. **(D)** The key point in this problem is the recognition that OA and OB, as radii of circle O, are equal to each other and equal 2. (1) tells us that triangle OAB is equilateral, since the base angles OAB and OBA must equal each other and thus 60°. By subtracting the area of the triangle

from $\frac{1}{6}$ of the area of the circle (60° worth) we could obtain the shaded area. (2) also implies that triangle OAB is equilateral, since AO = OB = AB, and is therefore also sufficient.

24. **(C)** When we first analyze this problem, we see that we either need to find the values of the three unknowns, x, y, and z, or we need to find the values of the two factors that are being multiplied together. (2) provides the value of the first factor in the multiplication, $x + y$. This is not sufficient by itself. (1) by itself does not even give that much help. The question then is what can be figured out from the two propositions taken together. Since we have one factor given to us directly, the logical thing to do would be to see whether there is some way of computing the other factor. As it happens, there is. Subtracting the entire equation given in (1) from that in (2) provides the value of the other part of the product, $x - z$. Therefore (1) and (2) together are sufficient.

25. **(E)** Profit = Income − Costs, so we need to know income and costs. Neither proposition by itself will allow us to compute the 1981 costs and income. The information in (1) and (2) together give us only percentage increases. Without the actual 1980 income and cost numbers, we cannot calculate 1981 income and costs. If the percentage increases for costs and income had been the same, then you could have computed the new profit. For example, if both costs and income had increased by 50 percent, then the profit would also have increased by 50 percent. With the given information, it is not enough. For example, if in 1980 income were $1,000,000 and the costs were $400,000 (for a 1980 profit of $600,000), the 1981 income would be $1,200,000 and the 1981 costs would be $500,000, for a 1981 profit of $700,000. If the 1980 figures were $10,000,000 − $9,400,000 = $600,000, then 1981 would be $12,000,000 − $11,750,000 = $250,000. This shows that you don't even know whether the profit is larger or smaller in 1981.

ANSWER SHEET—PRACTICE EXAMINATION 4

SECTION I

1 Ⓐ Ⓑ Ⓒ Ⓓ Ⓔ	6 Ⓐ Ⓑ Ⓒ Ⓓ Ⓔ	11 Ⓐ Ⓑ Ⓒ Ⓓ Ⓔ	16 Ⓐ Ⓑ Ⓒ Ⓓ Ⓔ	21 Ⓐ Ⓑ Ⓒ Ⓓ Ⓔ
2 Ⓐ Ⓑ Ⓒ Ⓓ Ⓔ	7 Ⓐ Ⓑ Ⓒ Ⓓ Ⓔ	12 Ⓐ Ⓑ Ⓒ Ⓓ Ⓔ	17 Ⓐ Ⓑ Ⓒ Ⓓ Ⓔ	22 Ⓐ Ⓑ Ⓒ Ⓓ Ⓔ
3 Ⓐ Ⓑ Ⓒ Ⓓ Ⓔ	8 Ⓐ Ⓑ Ⓒ Ⓓ Ⓔ	13 Ⓐ Ⓑ Ⓒ Ⓓ Ⓔ	18 Ⓐ Ⓑ Ⓒ Ⓓ Ⓔ	23 Ⓐ Ⓑ Ⓒ Ⓓ Ⓔ
4 Ⓐ Ⓑ Ⓒ Ⓓ Ⓔ	9 Ⓐ Ⓑ Ⓒ Ⓓ Ⓔ	14 Ⓐ Ⓑ Ⓒ Ⓓ Ⓔ	19 Ⓐ Ⓑ Ⓒ Ⓓ Ⓔ	24 Ⓐ Ⓑ Ⓒ Ⓓ Ⓔ
5 Ⓐ Ⓑ Ⓒ Ⓓ Ⓔ	10 Ⓐ Ⓑ Ⓒ Ⓓ Ⓔ	15 Ⓐ Ⓑ Ⓒ Ⓓ Ⓔ	20 Ⓐ Ⓑ Ⓒ Ⓓ Ⓔ	25 Ⓐ Ⓑ Ⓒ Ⓓ Ⓔ

SECTION II

1 Ⓐ Ⓑ Ⓒ Ⓓ Ⓔ	5 Ⓐ Ⓑ Ⓒ Ⓓ Ⓔ	9 Ⓐ Ⓑ Ⓒ Ⓓ Ⓔ	13 Ⓐ Ⓑ Ⓒ Ⓓ Ⓔ	17 Ⓐ Ⓑ Ⓒ Ⓓ Ⓔ
2 Ⓐ Ⓑ Ⓒ Ⓓ Ⓔ	6 Ⓐ Ⓑ Ⓒ Ⓓ Ⓔ	10 Ⓐ Ⓑ Ⓒ Ⓓ Ⓔ	14 Ⓐ Ⓑ Ⓒ Ⓓ Ⓔ	18 Ⓐ Ⓑ Ⓒ Ⓓ Ⓔ
3 Ⓐ Ⓑ Ⓒ Ⓓ Ⓔ	7 Ⓐ Ⓑ Ⓒ Ⓓ Ⓔ	11 Ⓐ Ⓑ Ⓒ Ⓓ Ⓔ	15 Ⓐ Ⓑ Ⓒ Ⓓ Ⓔ	19 Ⓐ Ⓑ Ⓒ Ⓓ Ⓔ
4 Ⓐ Ⓑ Ⓒ Ⓓ Ⓔ	8 Ⓐ Ⓑ Ⓒ Ⓓ Ⓔ	12 Ⓐ Ⓑ Ⓒ Ⓓ Ⓔ	16 Ⓐ Ⓑ Ⓒ Ⓓ Ⓔ	20 Ⓐ Ⓑ Ⓒ Ⓓ Ⓔ

SECTION III

1 Ⓐ Ⓑ Ⓒ Ⓓ Ⓔ	6 Ⓐ Ⓑ Ⓒ Ⓓ Ⓔ	11 Ⓐ Ⓑ Ⓒ Ⓓ Ⓔ	16 Ⓐ Ⓑ Ⓒ Ⓓ Ⓔ	21 Ⓐ Ⓑ Ⓒ Ⓓ Ⓔ
2 Ⓐ Ⓑ Ⓒ Ⓓ Ⓔ	7 Ⓐ Ⓑ Ⓒ Ⓓ Ⓔ	12 Ⓐ Ⓑ Ⓒ Ⓓ Ⓔ	17 Ⓐ Ⓑ Ⓒ Ⓓ Ⓔ	22 Ⓐ Ⓑ Ⓒ Ⓓ Ⓔ
3 Ⓐ Ⓑ Ⓒ Ⓓ Ⓔ	8 Ⓐ Ⓑ Ⓒ Ⓓ Ⓔ	13 Ⓐ Ⓑ Ⓒ Ⓓ Ⓔ	18 Ⓐ Ⓑ Ⓒ Ⓓ Ⓔ	23 Ⓐ Ⓑ Ⓒ Ⓓ Ⓔ
4 Ⓐ Ⓑ Ⓒ Ⓓ Ⓔ	9 Ⓐ Ⓑ Ⓒ Ⓓ Ⓔ	14 Ⓐ Ⓑ Ⓒ Ⓓ Ⓔ	19 Ⓐ Ⓑ Ⓒ Ⓓ Ⓔ	24 Ⓐ Ⓑ Ⓒ Ⓓ Ⓔ
5 Ⓐ Ⓑ Ⓒ Ⓓ Ⓔ	10 Ⓐ Ⓑ Ⓒ Ⓓ Ⓔ	15 Ⓐ Ⓑ Ⓒ Ⓓ Ⓔ	20 Ⓐ Ⓑ Ⓒ Ⓓ Ⓔ	25 Ⓐ Ⓑ Ⓒ Ⓓ Ⓔ

SECTION IV

1 Ⓐ Ⓑ Ⓒ Ⓓ Ⓔ	6 Ⓐ Ⓑ Ⓒ Ⓓ Ⓔ	11 Ⓐ Ⓑ Ⓒ Ⓓ Ⓔ	16 Ⓐ Ⓑ Ⓒ Ⓓ Ⓔ	21 Ⓐ Ⓑ Ⓒ Ⓓ Ⓔ
2 Ⓐ Ⓑ Ⓒ Ⓓ Ⓔ	7 Ⓐ Ⓑ Ⓒ Ⓓ Ⓔ	12 Ⓐ Ⓑ Ⓒ Ⓓ Ⓔ	17 Ⓐ Ⓑ Ⓒ Ⓓ Ⓔ	22 Ⓐ Ⓑ Ⓒ Ⓓ Ⓔ
3 Ⓐ Ⓑ Ⓒ Ⓓ Ⓔ	8 Ⓐ Ⓑ Ⓒ Ⓓ Ⓔ	13 Ⓐ Ⓑ Ⓒ Ⓓ Ⓔ	18 Ⓐ Ⓑ Ⓒ Ⓓ Ⓔ	23 Ⓐ Ⓑ Ⓒ Ⓓ Ⓔ
4 Ⓐ Ⓑ Ⓒ Ⓓ Ⓔ	9 Ⓐ Ⓑ Ⓒ Ⓓ Ⓔ	14 Ⓐ Ⓑ Ⓒ Ⓓ Ⓔ	19 Ⓐ Ⓑ Ⓒ Ⓓ Ⓔ	24 Ⓐ Ⓑ Ⓒ Ⓓ Ⓔ
5 Ⓐ Ⓑ Ⓒ Ⓓ Ⓔ	10 Ⓐ Ⓑ Ⓒ Ⓓ Ⓔ	15 Ⓐ Ⓑ Ⓒ Ⓓ Ⓔ	20 Ⓐ Ⓑ Ⓒ Ⓓ Ⓔ	25 Ⓐ Ⓑ Ⓒ Ⓓ Ⓔ

SECTION V

1 Ⓐ Ⓑ Ⓒ Ⓓ Ⓔ	6 Ⓐ Ⓑ Ⓒ Ⓓ Ⓔ	11 Ⓐ Ⓑ Ⓒ Ⓓ Ⓔ	16 Ⓐ Ⓑ Ⓒ Ⓓ Ⓔ	21 Ⓐ Ⓑ Ⓒ Ⓓ Ⓔ
2 Ⓐ Ⓑ Ⓒ Ⓓ Ⓔ	7 Ⓐ Ⓑ Ⓒ Ⓓ Ⓔ	12 Ⓐ Ⓑ Ⓒ Ⓓ Ⓔ	17 Ⓐ Ⓑ Ⓒ Ⓓ Ⓔ	22 Ⓐ Ⓑ Ⓒ Ⓓ Ⓔ
3 Ⓐ Ⓑ Ⓒ Ⓓ Ⓔ	8 Ⓐ Ⓑ Ⓒ Ⓓ Ⓔ	13 Ⓐ Ⓑ Ⓒ Ⓓ Ⓔ	18 Ⓐ Ⓑ Ⓒ Ⓓ Ⓔ	23 Ⓐ Ⓑ Ⓒ Ⓓ Ⓔ
4 Ⓐ Ⓑ Ⓒ Ⓓ Ⓔ	9 Ⓐ Ⓑ Ⓒ Ⓓ Ⓔ	14 Ⓐ Ⓑ Ⓒ Ⓓ Ⓔ	19 Ⓐ Ⓑ Ⓒ Ⓓ Ⓔ	24 Ⓐ Ⓑ Ⓒ Ⓓ Ⓔ
5 Ⓐ Ⓑ Ⓒ Ⓓ Ⓔ	10 Ⓐ Ⓑ Ⓒ Ⓓ Ⓔ	15 Ⓐ Ⓑ Ⓒ Ⓓ Ⓔ	20 Ⓐ Ⓑ Ⓒ Ⓓ Ⓔ	25 Ⓐ Ⓑ Ⓒ Ⓓ Ⓔ

SECTION VI

1 Ⓐ Ⓑ Ⓒ Ⓓ Ⓔ	5 Ⓐ Ⓑ Ⓒ Ⓓ Ⓔ	9 Ⓐ Ⓑ Ⓒ Ⓓ Ⓔ	13 Ⓐ Ⓑ Ⓒ Ⓓ Ⓔ	17 Ⓐ Ⓑ Ⓒ Ⓓ Ⓔ
2 Ⓐ Ⓑ Ⓒ Ⓓ Ⓔ	6 Ⓐ Ⓑ Ⓒ Ⓓ Ⓔ	10 Ⓐ Ⓑ Ⓒ Ⓓ Ⓔ	14 Ⓐ Ⓑ Ⓒ Ⓓ Ⓔ	18 Ⓐ Ⓑ Ⓒ Ⓓ Ⓔ
3 Ⓐ Ⓑ Ⓒ Ⓓ Ⓔ	7 Ⓐ Ⓑ Ⓒ Ⓓ Ⓔ	11 Ⓐ Ⓑ Ⓒ Ⓓ Ⓔ	15 Ⓐ Ⓑ Ⓒ Ⓓ Ⓔ	19 Ⓐ Ⓑ Ⓒ Ⓓ Ⓔ
4 Ⓐ Ⓑ Ⓒ Ⓓ Ⓔ	8 Ⓐ Ⓑ Ⓒ Ⓓ Ⓔ	12 Ⓐ Ⓑ Ⓒ Ⓓ Ⓔ	16 Ⓐ Ⓑ Ⓒ Ⓓ Ⓔ	20 Ⓐ Ⓑ Ⓒ Ⓓ Ⓔ

SECTION VII

1 Ⓐ Ⓑ Ⓒ Ⓓ Ⓔ	6 Ⓐ Ⓑ Ⓒ Ⓓ Ⓔ	11 Ⓐ Ⓑ Ⓒ Ⓓ Ⓔ	16 Ⓐ Ⓑ Ⓒ Ⓓ Ⓔ	21 Ⓐ Ⓑ Ⓒ Ⓓ Ⓔ
2 Ⓐ Ⓑ Ⓒ Ⓓ Ⓔ	7 Ⓐ Ⓑ Ⓒ Ⓓ Ⓔ	12 Ⓐ Ⓑ Ⓒ Ⓓ Ⓔ	17 Ⓐ Ⓑ Ⓒ Ⓓ Ⓔ	22 Ⓐ Ⓑ Ⓒ Ⓓ Ⓔ
3 Ⓐ Ⓑ Ⓒ Ⓓ Ⓔ	8 Ⓐ Ⓑ Ⓒ Ⓓ Ⓔ	13 Ⓐ Ⓑ Ⓒ Ⓓ Ⓔ	18 Ⓐ Ⓑ Ⓒ Ⓓ Ⓔ	23 Ⓐ Ⓑ Ⓒ Ⓓ Ⓔ
4 Ⓐ Ⓑ Ⓒ Ⓓ Ⓔ	9 Ⓐ Ⓑ Ⓒ Ⓓ Ⓔ	14 Ⓐ Ⓑ Ⓒ Ⓓ Ⓔ	19 Ⓐ Ⓑ Ⓒ Ⓓ Ⓔ	24 Ⓐ Ⓑ Ⓒ Ⓓ Ⓔ
5 Ⓐ Ⓑ Ⓒ Ⓓ Ⓔ	10 Ⓐ Ⓑ Ⓒ Ⓓ Ⓔ	15 Ⓐ Ⓑ Ⓒ Ⓓ Ⓔ	20 Ⓐ Ⓑ Ⓒ Ⓓ Ⓔ	25 Ⓐ Ⓑ Ⓒ Ⓓ Ⓔ

PRACTICE EXAMINATION 4

SECTION I

Time—30 Minutes
25 Questions

Directions: Below each of the following passages, you will find questions or incomplete statements about the passage. Each statement or question is followed by lettered words or expressions. Select the word or expression that most satisfactorily completes each statement or answers each question in accordance with the meaning of the passage. After you have chosen the best answer, blacken the corresponding space on the answer sheet.

In the art of the Middle Ages, we never encounter the personality of the artist as an individual; rather it is diffused through the artistic genius of centuries embodied in the rules of religious art. Art of the Middle Ages is first a sacred script, the symbols and meanings of which were well settled. The circular halo placed vertically behind the head signifies sainthood, while the halo impressed with a cross signifies divinity. By bare feet, we recognize God, the angels, Jesus Christ and the apostles, but for an artist to have depicted the Virgin Mary with bare feet would have been tantamount to heresy. Several concentric, wavy lines represent the sky, while parallel lines water or the sea. A tree, which is to say a single stalk with two or three stylized leaves, informs us that the scene is laid on earth. A tower with a window indicates a village, and, should an angel be watching from the battlements, that city is thereby identified as Jerusalem. Saint Peter is always depicted with curly hair, a short beard, and a tonsure, while Saint Paul has always a bald head and a long beard.

A second characteristic of this iconography is obedience to a sacred mathematics. "The Divine Wisdom," wrote Saint Augustine, "reveals itself everywhere in numbers," a doctrine attributable to the neo-Platonists who revived the genius of Pythagoras. Twelve is the master number of the Church and is the product of three, the number of the Trinity, and four, the number of material elements. The number seven, the most mysterious of all numbers, is the sum of four and three. There are the seven ages of man, seven virtues, seven planets. In the final analysis, the seven-tone scale of Gregorian music is the sensible embodiment of the order of the universe. Numbers require also a symmetry. At Chartres, a stained glass window shows the four prophets, Isaac, Ezekiel, Daniel, and Jeremiah, carrying on their shoulders the four evangelists, Matthew, Mark, Luke and John.

A third characteristic of this art is to be a symbolic language, showing us one thing and inviting us to see another. In this respect, the artist was called upon to imitate God, who had hidden a profound meaning behind the literal and wished nature itself to be a moral lesson to man. Thus, every painting is an allegory. In a scene of the final judgment, we see the foolish virgins at the left hand of Jesus and the wise at his right, and we understand that this symbolizes those who are lost and those who are saved. Even seemingly insignificant details carry hidden meaning: The lion in a stained glass window is the figure of the Resurrection.

These, then, are the defining characteristics of the art of the Middle Ages, a system within which even the most mediocre talent was elevated by the genius of the centuries. The artists of the early Renaissance broke with tradition at their own peril. When they are not outstanding, they are scarcely able to avoid insignificance and banality in their religious works, and, even when they are great, they are no more than the equals of the old masters who passively followed the sacred rules.

1. The primary purpose of the passage is to
   (A) theorize about the immediate influences on art of the Middle Ages
   (B) explain why artists of the Middle Ages followed the rules of a sacred script
   (C) discuss some of the important features of art of the Middle Ages
   (D) contrast the art of the Middle Ages with that of the Renaissance
   (E) explain why the Middle Ages had a passion for order and numbers

2. It can be inferred that a painting done in the Middle Ages is most likely to contain
   (A) elements representing the numbers three and four
   (B) a moral lesson hidden behind the literal figures
   (C) highly stylized buildings and trees
   (D) figures with halos and bare feet
   (E) a signature of the artist and the date of execution

3. Which of the following best describes the attitude of the author toward art of the Middle Ages?
   (A) He understands and admires it.
   (B) He regards it as the greatest art of all time.
   (C) He prefers music of the period to its painting.
   (D) He realizes the constraints placed on the artist and is disappointed that individuality is never evident.
   (E) He regards it generally as inferior to the works produced during the period preceding it.

4. The author refers to Saint Augustine in order to
   (A) refute a possible objection
   (B) ridicule a position
   (C) present a suggestive analogy
   (D) avoid a contradiction
   (E) provide proof by illustration

5. All of the following are mentioned in the passage as elements of the sacred script EXCEPT
   (A) abstract symbols such as lines to represent physical features
   (B) symbols such as halos and crosses
   (C) clothing used to characterize individuals
   (D) symmetrical juxtaposition of figures
   (E) use of figures to identify locations

6. The passage would most likely be found in a
   (A) sociological analysis of the Middle Ages
   (B) treatise on the influence of the Church in the Middle Ages
   (C) scholarly analysis of art in the Middle Ages
   (D) preface to a biography of Saint Augustine
   (E) pamphlet discussing religious beliefs

7. By the phrase "diffused through the artistic genius of centuries," the author most likely means
   (A) the individual artists of the Middle Ages did not have serious talent
   (B) great works of art from the Middle Ages have survived until now
   (C) an artist who faithfully followed the rules of religious art was not recognized during his lifetime
   (D) the rules of religious art, developed over time, left little freedom for the artist
   (E) religious art has greater value than the secular art of the Renaissance

8. The author of the passage employs which of the following techniques?

   I. referring to biographical data
   II. mentioning the features of works of art
   III. citing authorities on art of the Middle Ages

   (A) I only
   (B) II only
   (C) I and II only
   (D) II and III only
   (E) I, II, and III

The most damning thing that can be said about the world's best-endowed and richest country is that it is not only not the leader in health status, but that it is so low in the ranks of the nations. The United States ranks 18th among nations of the world in male life expectancy at birth, 9th in female life expectancy at birth, and 12th in infant mortality. More importantly, huge variations are evident in health status in the United states from one place to the next and from one group to the next.

The forces that affect health can be aggregated into four groupings that lend themselves to analysis of all health problems. Clearly the largest aggregate of forces resides in the person's environment. His own behavior, in part derived from his experiences with his environment, is the next greatest force affecting his health. Medical care services, treated as separate from other environmental factors because of the special interest we have in them, make a modest contribution to health status. Finally, the contributions of heredity to health are difficult to judge. We are templated at conception as to our basic weaknesses and strengths, but many hereditary attributes never become manifest because of environmental and behavioral forces that act before the genetic forces come to maturity and other hereditary attributes are increasingly being palliated by medical care.

No other country spends what we do per capita for medical care. The care available is among the best technically, even if used too lavishly and thus dangerously, but none of the countries which stand above us in health status have such a high proportion of medically disenfranchised persons. Given the evidence that medical care is not that valuable and access to care not that bad, it seems most unlikely that our bad showing is caused by the significant proportion who are poorly served. Other hypotheses have greater explanatory power: excessive poverty, both actual and relative, and excessive affluence.

Excessive poverty is probably more prevalent in the United States than in any of the countries that have a better infant mortality rate and female life expectancy at birth. This is probably true also for all but four or five of the countries with a longer male life expectancy. In the notably poor countries that exceed us in male survival, difficult living conditions are a more accepted way of life, and, in several of them, a good basic diet, basic medical care, basic education and lifelong employment opportunities are an everyday fact of life. In the United States a national unemployment level of 10 percent may be 40 percent in the ghetto, while less than 4 percent elsewhere. The countries that have surpassed us in health do not

have such severe or entrenched problems. Nor are such a high proportion of their people involved in them.

Excessive affluence is not so obvious a cause of ill health, but, at least until recently, few other nations could afford such unhealthful ways of living. Excessive intake of animal protein and fats, dangerous imbibing of alcohol, use of tobacco and drugs (prescribed and proscribed), and dangerous recreational sports and driving habits are all possible only because of affluence. Our heritage, desires, opportunities and our macho, combined with the relatively low cost of bad foods and speedy vehicles, make us particularly vulnerable to our affluence. And those who are not affluent try harder. Our unacceptable health status, then, will not be improved appreciably by expanded medical resources nor by their redistribution so much as a general attempt to improve the quality of life for all.

9. Which of the following would be the most logical continuation of the passage?
    (A) suggestions for specific proposals to improve the quality of life in America
    (B) a listing of the most common causes of death among male and female adults
    (C) an explanation of the causes of poverty in America, both absolute and relative
    (D) a proposal to ensure that residents of central cities receive more and better medical care
    (E) a study of the overcrowding in urban hospitals serving primarily the poor

10. All of the following are mentioned in the passage as factors affecting the health of the population EXCEPT
    (A) the availability of medical care services
    (B) the genetic endowment of individuals
    (C) overall environmental factors
    (D) the nation's relative position in health status
    (E) an individual's own behavior

11. The author is primarily concerned with
    (A) condemning the United States for its failure to provide better medical care to the poor
    (B) evaluating the relative significance of factors contributing to the poor health status in the United States.

(C) providing information which the reader can use to improve his or her personal health

(D) comparing the general health of the U.S. population with world averages

(E) advocating specific measures designed to improve the health of the U.S. population

12. The passage best supports which of the following conclusions about the relationship between per capita expenditures for medical care and the health of a population?

(A) The per capita expenditure for medical care has relatively little effect on the total amount of medical care available to a population.

(B) The genetic makeup of a population is a more powerful determinant of the health of a population than the per capita expenditure for medical care.

(C) A population may have very high per capita expenditures for medical care and yet have a lower health status than other populations with lower per capita expenditures.

(D) The higher the per capita expenditure on medical care, the more advanced is the medical technology; the more advanced the technology, the better is the health of the population.

(E) Per capita outlays for medical care devoted to adults are likely to have a greater effect on the status of the population than outlays devoted to infants.

13. The author refers to the excessive intake of alcohol and tobacco and drug use in order to

(A) show that some health problems cannot be attacked by better medical care

(B) demonstrate that use of tobacco and intoxicants is detrimental to health

(C) cite examples of individual behavior which have adverse consequence for health status

(D) refute the contention that poor health is related to access to medical care

(E) illustrate ways in which affluence may contribute to poor health status

14. The passage provides information to answer which of the following questions?

(A) What is the most powerful influence on the health status of a population?

(B) Which nation in the world leads in health status?

(C) Is the life expectancy of males in the United States longer than that of females?

(D) What are the most important genetic factors influencing the health of an individual?

(E) How can the United States reduce the incidence of unemployment in the ghetto?

15. In discussing the forces which influence health, the author implies that medical care services are

(A) the least important of all

(B) a special aspect of an individual's environment

(C) a function of an individual's behavior pattern

(D) becoming less important as technology improves

(E) too expensive for most people

16. Which of the following statements best describes the main point of the passage?

(A) The relative low health status of the United States is not primarily a result of a lack of medical care resources.

(B) The United States does not provide sufficient medical care to guarantee the health of most of its citizens.

(C) Despite the high quality of medical care in the United States, citizens of the United States are not as healthy as citizens of other countries.

(D) The health status of citizens in the United States could be drastically improved by increased expenditures of money on medical care.

(E) Factors such as environment are more important determinants of the health status of the individual than his or her income.

17. The author's attitude toward the health care status of the United States can best be described as

(A) approving

(B) critical
(C) supportive
(D) indifference
(E) rejection

Nitroglycerin has long been famous for its relief of angina pectoris attacks but ruled out for heart attacks on the theory that it harmfully lowers blood pressure and increases heart rate. A heart
5 attack, unlike an angina attack, always involves some localized, fairly rapid heart muscle death, or myocardial infarction. This acute emergency happens when the arteriosclerotic occlusive process in one of the coronary arterial branches culmi-
10 nates so suddenly and completely that the local myocardium—the muscle area that was fed by the occluded coronary—stops contracting and dies over a period of hours, to be replaced over a period of weeks by a scar, or "healed infarct."
15 In 1974, in experiments with dogs, it was discovered that administration of nitroglycerin during the acute stage of myocardial infarction consistently reduced the extent of myocardial injury, provided that the dogs' heart rate and
20 blood pressure were maintained in the normal range. Soon after, scientists made a preliminary confirmation of the clinical applicability of nitroglycerin in acute heart attack in human patients. Five of twelve human subjects developed some
25 degree of congestive heart failure. Curiously, the nitroglycerin alone was enough to reduce the magnitude of injury in these five patients, but the other seven patients, whose heart attacks were not complicated by any congestive heart failure,
30 were not consistently helped by the nitroglycerin until another drug, phenylephrine, was added to abolish the nitroglycerin-induced drop in blood pressure. One explanation for this is that the reflex responses in heart rate, mediated through
35 the autonomic nervous system, are so blunted in congestive heart failure that a fall in blood pressure prompts less of the cardiac acceleration which otherwise worsens the damage of acute myocardial infarction.
40 It appears that the size of the infarct that would otherwise result from a coronary occlusion might be greatly reduced, and vitally needed heart muscle thus saved, by the actions of certain drugs and other measures taken during the acute phase
45 of the heart attack. This is because the size of the myocardial infarct is not really determined at the

moment of the coronary occlusion as previously thought. The fate of the stricken myocardial segment remains largely undetermined, hanging on the balance of myocardial oxygen supply and 50 demand which can be favorably influenced for many hours after the coronary occlusion. So it is possible to reduce the myocardial ischemic injury during acute human heart attacks by means of nitroglycerin, either alone or in combination with 55 phenylephrine.

Other drugs are also being tested to reduce myocardial infarct size, particularly drugs presumed to affect myocardial oxygen supply and demand, including not only vessel dilators such as 60 nitroglycerin but also antihypertensives, which block the sympathetic nerve reflexes that increase heart rate and work in response to exertion and stress. Such measures are still experimental, and there is no proof of benefit with regard to the 65 great complications of heart attack such as cardiogenic shock, angina, or mortality. But the drugs for reducing infarct size now hold center stage in experimental frameworks.

18. According to the passage, the primary difference between a heart attack and an angina attack is that a heart attack
    (A) involves an acceleration of the heartbeat
    (B) cannot be treated with nitroglycerin
    (C) generally results in congestive heart failure
    (D) takes place within a relatively short period of time
    (E) always results in damage to muscle tissue of the heart

19. In the study referred to in lines 21–23, the patients who developed congestive heart failure did not experience cardiac acceleration because
    (A) the nitroglycerin was not administered soon enough after the onset of the heart attack
    (B) the severity of the heart attack blocked the autonomic response to the nitroglycerin-induced drop in blood pressure
    (C) administering phenylephrine mitigated the severity of the drop in blood pressure caused by nitroglycerin

(D) doctors were able to maintain blood pressure, and thus indirectly pulse rate, in those patients

(E) those patients did not experience a drop in blood pressure as a result of the heart attack

20. The passage provides information to answer all of the following questions EXCEPT:
(A) What are some of the physiological manifestations of a heart attack?
(B) What determines the size of a myocardial infarct following a heart attack?
(C) What effect does nitroglycerin have when administered to a patient experiencing a heart attack?
(D) What are the most important causes of heart attacks?
(E) What is the physiological effect of phenylephrine?

21. It can be inferred from the passage that nitroglycerin is of value in treating heart attacks because it
(A) lowers the blood pressure
(B) stimulates healing of an infarct
(C) causes cardiac acceleration
(D) dilates blood vessels
(E) counteracts hypertension

22. The author's attitude toward the use of nitroglycerin and other drugs to treat heart attack can best be described as one of
(A) concern
(B) resignation
(C) anxiety

(D) disinterest
(E) optimism

23. It can be inferred that the phenylephrine is administered in conjunction with nitroglycerin during heart attack in order to
(A) prevent the cardiac acceleration caused by a drop in blood pressure
(B) block sympathetic nerve reflexes that increase the pulse rate
(C) blunt the autonomic nervous system which accelerates the pulse rate
(D) reduce the size of a myocardial infarct by increasing oxygen supply
(E) prevent arteriosclerotic occlusion in the coronary arterial branches

24. The author is primarily concerned with
(A) explaining a predicament
(B) evaluating a study
(C) outlining a proposal
(D) countering an argument
(E) discussing a treatment

25. Which of the following would be the most appropriate title for the passage?
(A) Common Causes of Heart Attack in Human Patients
(B) Clinical Symptoms of Angina and Heart Attack
(C) Use of Nitroglycerin for Treatment of Congestive Heart Failure
(D) Nitroglycerin as a Possible Treatment for Heart Attack
(E) Laboratory Experiments Confirm Value of Nitroglycerin in Treating Heart Attack

STOP

END OF SECTION. IF YOU HAVE ANY TIME LEFT, GO OVER YOUR WORK IN THIS SECTION ONLY. DO NOT WORK IN ANY OTHER SECTION OF THE TEST.

SECTION II

Time—30 minutes
20 Questions

Directions: For each of the following questions, select the best of the answer choices and blacken the corresponding space on your answer sheet.
Numbers: All numbers used are real numbers.
Figures: The diagrams and figures that accompany these questions are for the purpose of providing information useful in answering the questions. Unless it is stated that a specific figure is not drawn to scale, the diagrams and figures are drawn as accurately as possible. All figures are in a plan unless otherwise indicated.

1. If the average of x, y, and 30 is 10, then the average of x and y is
   (A) 0
   (B) 5
   (C) $7\frac{1}{2}$
   (D) 10
   (E) 30

2. All of the 120 seniors in Coolidge High School are members of the chess club, the pep club, or both. If 90 seniors are in the pep club and 70 seniors are in the chess club, how many seniors are in both clubs?
   (A) 10
   (B) 20
   (C) 30
   (D) 40
   (E) 50

3. For which of the following can the area be found if the perimeter is given?
   (A) rectangle
   (B) circle
   (C) triangle
   (D) parallelogram
   (E) hexagon

4. If a and b are positive integers and $a^3 b^2 = 72$, then a + b =
   (A) 36
   (B) 17
   (C) 8
   (D) 6
   (E) 5

5. $\frac{.250}{.333}$ divided by $\frac{.125}{.167}$ is most nearly
   (A) 10
   (B) 5
   (C) 1
   (D) .667
   (E) .500

6. Which of the following fractions is closest to 1 given that a>b>1?
   (A) $\frac{a}{b}$
   (B) $\frac{(a + 2)}{(b + 2)}$
   (C) $\frac{(a + 1)}{(b + 1)}$
   (D) $\frac{(a + 1)}{b}$
   (E) $\frac{(a - 1)}{(b - 1)}$

7. In an office with 21 staff members, $\frac{1}{3}$ are men and $\frac{2}{3}$ are women. To obtain a staff in which $\frac{1}{4}$ are men, how many women should be hired?
   (A) 7
   (B) 5
   (C) 3
   (D) 2
   (E) 1

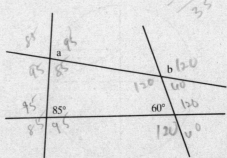

8. In the figure above, b − a =
   (A) 20

(B) 25
(C) 30
(D) 35
(E) 40

9. In college X, 40 percent of the women and 20 percent of the men are taking courses in mathematics. If 55 percent of the students at college X are women, what percent of all college X students take mathematics courses?
(A) 35
(B) 31
(C) 30
(D) 26
(E) 25

10. If cylinder A has three times the height and one-third the diameter of cylinder B, what is the ratio of the volume of A to the volume of B?
(A) 3:1
(B) 1:1
(C) 1:3
(D) 1:9
(E) 1:27

11. A jogger desires to run a certain course in $\frac{1}{4}$ less time than she usually takes. by what percent must she increase her average running speed to accomplish this goal?
(A) 20%
(B) 25%
(C) $33\frac{1}{3}\%$
(D) 50%
(E) 75%

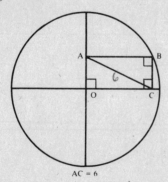

AC = 6

12. What is the area of circle O above?
(A) 24 π

(B) 36 π
(C) 48 π
(D) 64 π
(E) It cannot be determined from the information given.

13. A statistician squared a positive number and divided the result by 3 when he should have taken the square root of the number and multiplied the result by 9. The answer he obtained was 27. What was the correct answer?
(A) 1
(B) 3
(C) 9
(D) 27
(E) 81

14. A magazine costs $1.00 per copy to produce. If $20,000 was taken in for advertising in the magazine, how many copies at 75 cents per copy must be sold to make a profit of exactly $10,000?
(A) 10,000
(B) 20,000
(C) 25,000
(D) 35,000
(E) 40,000

15. If a is a positive integer and if remainders of 4 and 6 are obtained when 89 and 125, respectively, are divided by a, then a =
(A) 7
(B) 9
(C) 15
(D) 17
(E) 19

16. A pen-and-pencil set costs $12, the same as when the items are bought separately. If the pen costs $11 more than the pencil, what is the cost of the pencil?
(A) $0.50
(B) $1.00
(C) $1.50
(D) $6.00
(E) $11.00

17. A salesman makes a commission of x percent on the first $2,000 worth of sales in any given month and y percent on all further

sales during that month. If he makes $700 from $4,000 of sales in October and he makes $900 from $5,000 of sales in November, what is the value of x?

(A) 2%
(B) 5%
(C) 10%
(D) 15%
(E) 20%

18. 200 children came to the park last Sunday. All of the older children rode bicycles into the park and all of the younger children came on tricycles. 480 wheels rode into the park that day, all of them functioning on the children's bicycles or tricycles. How many younger children came to the park last Sunday?

(A) 120
(B) 100
(C) 80
(D) 75
(E) 60

$2o + 3y = 480$

$o + y = 200$

19. A magician wants to ship a magic wand to the location of his next show. The rectangular box he has available for this purpose measures 6 inches wide by 8 inches long by 10 inches high. What is the longest cylindrical wand of neglibile diameter that can be shipped in this box?

(A) 10 inches
(B) $8\sqrt{2}$ inches
(C) $8\sqrt{3}$ inches
(D) $10\sqrt{2}$ inches
(E) $10\sqrt{3}$ inches

20. The price of a left-handed widget increased 20 percent in 1981 and 10 percent in 1982. By approximately what percent would the price at the end of 1982 have to be decreased to restore the price of the widget to its pre-1981 price?

(A) 40%
(B) 35%
(C) 30%
(D) 26%
(E) 24%

STOP

END OF SECTION. IF YOU HAVE ANY TIME LEFT, GO OVER YOUR WORK IN THIS SECTION ONLY. DO NOT WORK ON ANY OTHER SECTION OF THE TEST

SECTION III

Time—30 minutes
25 Questions

Directions: Each question below is followed by two numbered facts. You are to determine whether the data given in the statements is sufficient for answering the question. Use the data given, plus your knowledge of math and everyday facts, to choose between the five possible answers.

(A) if statement 1 alone is sufficient to answer the question, but statement 2 alone is not sufficient

(B) is statement 2 alone is sufficient to answer the question, but statement 1 alone is not sufficient

(C) if both statements together are needed to answer the question, but neither statement alone is sufficient

(D) if either statement by itself is sufficient to answer the question

(E) if not enough facts are given to answer the question

1. Exactly how many pennies are there in Jean's piggy bank?
   (1) There are more than 7 pennies in the bank.
   (2) There are fewer than 9 pennies in the bank.

2. Joe bought a $2,400 microcomputer on a monthly payment plan. How much money does Joe still owe on the computer?
   (1) He has made six payments.
   (2) He still owes ten payments of $150 each.

3. Does x = 15?
   (1) The average of x, y, and z is 5.
   (2) y = −z

4. Which team, the Lions or the Tigers, scored more points and thus won the basketball game?
   (1) The Lions scored more points than the Tigers in three of the four quarters of the game.
   (2) The Tigers scored more points than the Lions in one of the four quarters of the game.

5. How far is gas station X from gas station Z?
   (1) Gas station Y is 5 miles from gas station Z.
   (2) Gas station X is 3 miles from gas station Y.

6. What was the annual interest earned on a savings account of $3,000?
   (1) The rate of interest on the account was $5\frac{1}{4}\%$ annual simple interest.
   (2) The account was maintained for 10 years.

7. Is Susan taller than Jill?
   (1) Susan is taller than Beth.
   (2) Beth is shorter than Jill.

8. Is a + b + c + d > 20?
   (1) The average of a, b, c, and d is 6.
   (2) a = b = c = 6.

9. What is the 57th number in a series of numbers?
   (1) Each number in the series is 3 more than the preceding number.
   (2) The tenth number in the series is 29.

10. John took a test composed of 125 questions. What percent of all the questions on the test did John answer correctly?
    (1) He left 20 of the questions blank.
    (2) He answered 53 of the questions correctly.

11. What percent of the selling price of item X was profit?
    (1) The profit was $20 less than the selling price of item X.
    (2) The cost of the item was $\frac{3}{4}$ of the selling price.

12. If a is a positive integer, what is the value of 75 percent of $\frac{b}{a}$?
    (1) a = 2
    (2) b = 4a

13. If r and s are integers, is r > 1?
    (1) r + s < 1
    (2) r − s > 1

14. What are the chances that a die will come up six on the fifth roll?
    (1) It is a normal six-sided die which is unbiased and always comes up either one, two, three, four, five, or six.
    (2) The first four rolls came up six.

15. How old is Robert now?
    (1) The product of his age now and his age five years from now is 24.
    (2) Six years from now he will be three times as old as he is now.

16. How many square floor tiles of size x will it take to cover a rectangular kitchen floor?
    (1) The width of the kitchen floor is 10x.
    (2) The length of the kitchen floor is 30x.

17. What is the height of a cylindrical condensed milk can with a diameter of 4 inches?
    (1) The number of cubic inches in the volume of the can is 10π times the radius of the can.
    (2) The can hold 2 pounds of milk.

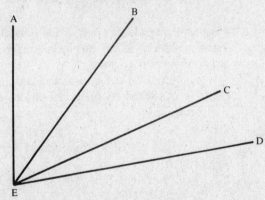

18. What is the measure of ∠ CED in the figure above?
    (1) ∠ BED = 60°
    (2) ∠ AEC = 60°

19. If a + b + c = 50, what is the value of a?
    (1) c = 4a − b.
    (2) The average of b and c is 2a.

20. If x is an integer, is x an odd number?
    (1) x^3 is not negative.
    (2) x is either a negative number or an odd number, but not both.

21. What is the average speed of an automobile as it travels the 300 miles between city A and city B?
    (1) The automobile averages 50 miles per hour for the first three hours.
    (2) The automobile averages 45 miles per hour for the last three hours.

22. If the ratio of boys to girls attending school S in 1980 was $\frac{1}{2}$, what was the ratio of boys to girls attending school S in 1981?
    (1) 50 more boys were attending school S in 1981 than in 1980.
    (2) 50 more girls were attending school S in 1981 than in 1980.

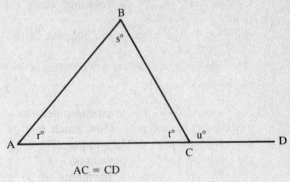

AC = CD

23. In the figure above, does r = t?
    (1) The length of AB plus the length of AC equals the length of BC plus the length of CD.
    (2) u = s + t.

24. A tiger at point A on the edge of a circular cage walks in a straight line until he encounters the edge again at point B. He then walks in another straight line until he once more encounters the edge of the cage at point C, which is directly opposite point A in the cage. How many paces in circumference is the cage?
    (1) In going from point A to point B, the tiger walked 5 paces.
    (2) In going from point B to point C, the tiger walked 12 paces.

25. How many of the three different positive integers a, b, and c are divisible by 7?
    (1) The product of a, b, and c is divisible by 3, but only c is divisible by 21.

    (2) Each of the three positive integers is divisible by 3, but only c is divisible by 21.

STOP

END OF SECTION. IF YOU HAVE ANY TIME LEFT, GO OVER YOUR WORK IN THIS SECTION ONLY. DO NOT WORK ON ANY OTHER SECTION OF THE TEST.

SECTION IV

Time—30 minutes
25 Questions

Directions: In each problem below, either part or all of the sentence is underlined. The sentence is followed by five ways of writing the underlined part. Answer choice (A) repeats the original; the other answer choices vary. If you think that the original phrasing is the best, choose (A). If you think one of the other answer choices is the best, select that choice.

This section tests the ability to recognize correct and effective expression. Follow the requirements of Standard Written English: grammar, choice of words, and sentence construction. Choose the answer which results in the clearest, most exact sentence, but do not change the meaning of the original sentence.

1. After reading two different poems, <u>she could not decide which poem was the most beautiful, since each had their own</u> unique features.
   (A) she could not decide which poem was the most beautiful, since each had their own
   (B) she could not decide which poem was the more beautiful, since each had their own
   (C) she could not decide which poem was the most beautiful, since each had its own
   (D) she could not decide which poems were the most beautiful, since each had their own
   (E) she could not decide which poem was the more beautiful, since each had its own

2. The exclusive French restaurant has been popular with business customers <u>because of its excellent service, responsive management, and because its parking facilities are extensive.</u>
   (A) because of its excellent service, responsive management, and because its parking facilities are extensive.
   (B) because of its excellent service, responsive management, and because their parking facilities are extensive.
   (C) because of its service, which is excellent, management, which is respon-

sive, and because of parking facilities which are extensive.
   (D) because of its excellent service, responsive management, and extensive parking facilities.
   (E) because of its excellent service, responsive management, and its extensive parking facilities.

3. <u>Men's interest in developing a cure for cancer have promoted</u> the rapid advances in the abstruse field now known as Genetic Engineering.
   (A) Men's interest in developing a cure for cancer have promoted
   (B) Men's interest in developing a cure for cancer has promoted
   (C) That men are interested in developing a cure for cancer have promoted
   (D) Interest in developing a cure for cancer has promoted
   (E) Men's interest in developing a cure for cancer has promoted

4. Delegates to the Republican Party convention <u>chose their candidate and was able</u> to ratify all aspects of his campaign platform at the convention in Denver.
   (A) chose their candidate and was able
   (B) chose their candidate and were able
   (C) chose its candidate and were able
   (D) chose its candidate and was able
   (E) had chosen their candidate and was able

5. <u>For the reason that</u> the university's senior tenured faculty is still quite young and therefore many years away from retirement, it seems unlikely that the junior faculty will be able to easily achieve tenure in the foreseeable future.
   (A) For the reason that
   (B) Because
   (C) Being that
   (D) On account of
   (E) In that

6. Just as William Shakespeare was the preeminent poet of England, so Robert Frost was the preeminent poet of the United States.
   (A) Just as William Shakespeare was the preeminent poet of England, so Robert Frost
   (B) Just like William Shakespeare was the preeminent poet of England, so Robert Frost
   (C) As William Shakespeare was the preeminent poet of England, Robert Frost
   (D) Just as England's preeminent poet was William Shakespeare, Robert Frost
   (E) As William Shakespeare was the preeminent poet of England, in the same manner Robert Frost

7. Jonas Salk, an American physician whose careful studies demonstrated a means of providing lasting immunity to polio.
   (A) Jonas Salk, an American physician whose careful studies demonstrated a means of providing lasting immunity to polio.
   (B) Providing lasting immunity to polio was demonstrated by Jonas Salk, an American physician with careful studies.
   (C) Jonas Salk was an American physician who had careful studies which demonstrated a means of providing lasting immunity to polio.
   (D) Jonas Salk was an American physician whose careful studies demonstrated a means of providing lasting immunity to polio.
   (E) Jonas Salk, whose careful studies demonstrated a means of providing lasting immunity to polio, an American physician.

8. The selection in the free-agent draft was based less on the player's availability and more on his willingness to accept a low salary.
   (A) and more on
   (B) than
   (C) but more on
   (D) as on
   (E) than on

9. The winding roads of San Jacinto Hill were less in number than El Capitan.
   (A) were less in number than El Capitan.
   (B) were less in number than those of El Capitan.
   (C) were fewer in number than that of El Capitan.
   (D) fewer in number than those of El Capitan
   (E) were less than El Capitan.

10. The nurse told me that the doctor's office closes at 5:00 P.M.
    (A) The nurse told me that the doctor's office closes at 5:00 P.M.
    (B) The nurse told me that the doctor's office closed at 5:00 P.M.
    (C) The nurse had told me that the doctor's office had closed at 5:00 P.M.
    (D) The nurse told me that the doctor's office had closed at 5:00 P.M.
    (E) The nurse told me that the doctor's office would have to close at 5:00 P.M.

11. It has been shown through extensive physical and statistical testing that domestic cars accelerate like foreign cars do.
    (A) accelerate like foreign cars do.
    (B) can accelerate like foreign cars do.
    (C) accelerate as foreign cars.
    (D) accelerate as foreign cars do.
    (E) will accelerate as foreign cars.

12. Results of the recent study make it mandatory that the Surgeon General rejects implementation of the experimental procedure.
    (A) rejects
    (B) should reject
    (C) reject
    (D) must reject
    (D) must reject
    (E) will reject

13. Fidel Castro found it simple to seize power, but maintaining it difficult.
    (A) maintaining it difficult.
    (B) its maintenance difficult.
    (C) difficult to maintain it.
    (D) difficulty was experienced in maintaining it.
    (E) difficult inasmuch as maintaining it was concerned.

14. In an unexpected move for a corporate executive, the chairman of the board's order mandated salary cuts for almost half of the company's employees.
    (A) the chairman of the board's order mandated salary cuts
    (B) the chairman of the board's order was to mandate salary cuts
    (C) the chairman of the board was successful in mandating cuts in salary
    (D) the chairman of the board's order instituted mandated salary cuts
    (E) the chairman of the board mandated salary cuts

15. The reason why the boxing commission refused to grant a license to the fighter was because it concluded he could not pass the required physical exam.
    (A) The reason why the boxing commission refused to grant a license to the fighter was because it concluded
    (B) The boxing commission's refusal to grant a license to the fighter was because it concluded
    (C) The boxing commission refused to grant a license to the fighter because it concluded
    (D) The reason the boxing commission refused to grant a license was because it concluded
    (E) The boxing commission refused to grant a license, the reason being that it concluded

16. The court order's requirement that each transit worker return to work was generally ignored.
    (A) that each transit worker return to work
    (B) that each transit worker would return to work
    (C) that each transit worker should return to work
    (D) for each transit worker to return to work
    (E) that each transit worker returns to work

17. Having been ordered by the judge to resume alimony payments, Ms. Jones was still not required by it to see her children on weekends.
    (A) Ms. Jones was still not required by it

(B) still had not been required by it
(C) still was not to be required
(D) was still not required
(E) was not sufficiently required

18. The police officers throughout the department were so distrustful of the new commissioner that they refused to carry out his orders.
    (A) were so distrustful of the new commissioner that they refused
    (B) was so distrustful of the new commissioner that they refused
    (C) were distrustful of the new commissioner to such an extent that they were to refuse
    (D) were so distrustful of the new commissioner that they had to refuse
    (E) were as distrustful of the new commissioner that they refused

19. To consider a diagnosis on the basis of inadequate or misleading evidence is neglecting years of specialized medical training.
    (A) To consider a diagnosis on the basis of inadequate or misleading evidence is neglecting
    (B) To consider a diagnosis on the basis of inadequate or misleading evidence is to neglect
    (C) In considering a diagnosis on the basis of inadequate or misleading evidence is neglecting
    (D) Considering a diagnosis on the basis of inadequate or misleading evidence is to neglect
    (E) Considering a diagnosis on the basis of inadequate or misleading evidence amounts to neglecting

20. Twenty years ago, on my graduation from law school, I would have liked to have had the chance to join the partnership, but the substantial investment required would have made such a move impossible.
    (A) I would have liked to have had the chance
    (B) I would like to have the chance
    (C) I like to have the chance
    (D) I will like to have had the chance
    (E) I would like to have had the chance

21. The recent discovery of Tutankhamen's tomb by Egyptologists has provided information which suggests that the wealth accumulated by ancient Egyptian pharaohs was greater than <u>believed</u>.
    (A) believed.
    (B) is believed.
    (C) was believed before.
    (D) they have believed before.
    (E) had been believed.

22. The accident victim was very grateful to the hospital that had saved his life, but viewed his insurance company with suspicion <u>out of fear that it will refuse</u> to pay his claim and very expensive medical bills.
    (A) out of fear that it will refuse
    (B) in fear that it will refuse
    (C) out of fear that it would refuse
    (D) out of fear that it is refusing
    (E) out of fear that they will refuse

23. The young spouse, concerned because her husband <u>has just been laid off, is likely to buy inferior clothing when forced to choose among price and value.</u>
    (A) has just been laid off, is likely to buy inferior clothing when forced to choose among price and value.
    (B) had just been laid off, is likely to buy inferior clothing when forced to choose among price and value.
    (C) has just been laid off, is likely to have bought inferior clothing when forced to choose among price and value.
    (D) had just been laid off, was unlikely to have bought inferior clothing when forced to choose among price and value.
    (E) has just been laid off, is likely to buy inferior clothing when forced to choose between price and value.

24. Accused of dishonesty, <u>his repeated lies caused his colleagues to distrust him intensely.</u>
    (A) his repeated lies caused his colleagues to distrust him intensely.
    (B) he was distrusted intensely by his colleagues because of his repeated lies.
    (C) he was intensely distrusted by his colleagues due to his repeated lies.
    (D) his repeated lies cause his colleagues to distrust him intensely.
    (E) his repeated lies have caused his colleagues to have distrusted him intensely.

25. For some children, <u>accepting parental discipline that they consider unfair constitute</u> a necessary accommodation.
    (A) accepting parental discipline that they consider unfair constitute
    (B) accepting parental discipline which they consider unfair constitute
    (C) accepting parental discipline that one considers unfair constitute
    (D) to accept parental discipline that they consider unfair constitute
    (E) accepting parental discipline which they consider unfair constitutes

STOP

END OF SECTION. IF YOU HAVE ANY TIME LEFT, GO OVER YOUR WORK IN THIS SECTION ONLY. DO NOT WORK ON ANY OTHER SECTION OF THE TEST.

SECTION V

Time—30 minutes
25 Questions

Directions: Each question below is followed by two numbered facts. You are to determine whether the data given in the statements is sufficient for answering the question. Use the data given, plus your knowledge of math and everyday facts, to choose between the five possible answer.

(A) if statement 1 alone is sufficient to answer the question, but statement 2 alone is not sufficient
(B) if statement 2 alone is sufficient to answer the question, but statement 1 alone is not sufficient
(C) if both statements together are needed to answer the question, but neither statement alone is sufficient
(D) if either statement by itself is sufficient to answer the question
(E) if not enough facts are given to answer the question

1. A stock returned what percent of its cost in a dividend at the end of the year?
   (1) The amount of the dividend was less than 10 percent of the cost of the stock.
   (2) The amount of dividened paid on each share was $1.20; and the stock cost $60 per share.

2. What is the average (arithmetic mean) of the ages of Mark, Paul, Edward, Maxine, and Linda?
   (1) The average (arithmetic mean) of the ages of Mark, Paul, and Edward is 20 years.
   (2) The average (arithmetic mean) of the ages of Maxine and Linda is 25 years.

3. Peter, Mary, and Edna took the same examination. Which of them received the highest score?
   (1) There was a 10-point gap between Peter's score and Mary's score.
   (2) There was an 8-point gap between Edna's score and Peter's score.

4. If a stationer sells his entire stock of 6 gross of pens for $4.50 per pen, what is his total profit on the pens?
   (1) The selling price of each pen was 120 percent of its cost.

(2) The cost to the stationer for his inventory of pens was $3,240.00.

5. Each of the figures above is a different color: green, red, blue, orange, or yellow. Which is the green figure?
   (1) The green figure is between the blue and the orange figures.
   (2) The green figure is between the red and the yellow figures.

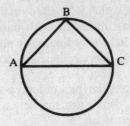

6. In the figure above, is angle ABC a right angle?
   (1) AC is the diameter of the circle.
   (2) AB = BC

7. If a car is driven 150 miles, the fuel tank is filled to what percent of capacity at the end of the trip?
   (1) The car averaged 15 miles per gallon for the trip.
   (2) The tank was filled to 75 percent of capacity at the start of the trip.

8. If Marsha, Deborah, and Wanda have a total of $240 among them, how much money does Wanda have?
   (1) Marsha has $20 more than Wanda, who has $40 less than Deborah.

(2) Wanda has $\frac{3}{4}$ as much as Marsha, who has $80.

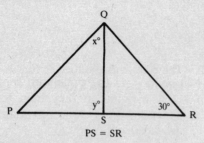

PS = SR

9. What is the measure of angle SQR?
   (1) x = 40°
   (2) y = 80°

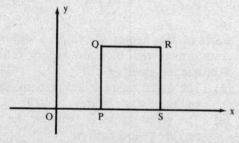

10. In the figure above, PQRS is a square the base of which is situated on the x-axis. What is the perimeter of the square?
    (1) The y-coordinate for point Q is 6.
    (2) The x-coordinate for point P is 4.

11. A rectangular plot of land is represented on a map. What are the actual dimensions of the plot of land?
    (1) The length of the rectangular figure on the map representing the actual plot of land is twice as long as the width.
    (2) The map is drawn so that each $\frac{1}{4}$ inch on the map represents an actual distance of 10 feet.

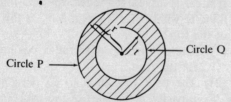

12. If circle P has radius r and circle Q has radius t, what is the area of the shaded region of the figure?
    (1) r − t = 3
    (2) r = 9 and t = 6.

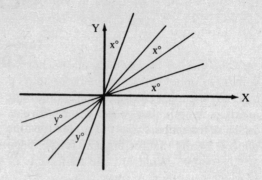

13. The figure above is a set of coordinate axes. What is the value of x?
    (1) x − y = 15
    (2) y = 9

14. Is $\frac{p}{4}$ an integer?

    (1) $\frac{p}{424}$ is an integer.

    (2) $\frac{p}{424,424}$ is an integer.

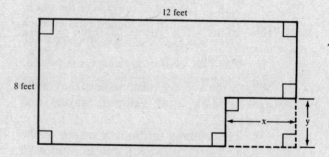

15. What is the area of the figure shown above?
    (1) x = 2 feet
    (2) y = 3 feet

16. P is a polygon. Is it possible to construct a circle such that each vertex of the polygon is a point on the circle?
    (1) All sides of the polygon are of equal length.
    (2) All angles of P have equal measure.

17. If p, q, r, and s are nonzero numbers, is $\left[-\frac{3q^2r^3}{5p^3s^4} \right]^3$ positive?
    (1) p = −15 and r = −2
    (2) q = −3 and s = −9

18. Is $(a + b)^2 - (a - b)^2$ equal to 56?
    (1) $ab = 14$
    (2) $a + b = 9$

19. Marlene has a card which allows her to withdraw money from her bank 24 hours a day, but she must enter her secret four-digit identification number, which she has forgotten. She remembers that the sum of the four digits is 24 and that the first and fourth digits are the same. What are the four digits of Marlene's number, in order?
    (1) The sum of the first and third digits is 13.
    (2) The sum of the second and fourth digits is 11.

20. Two runners, X and Y, competed in the 10,000-meter run. The race took place on an oval track 400 meters long. What is the ratio of X's time for the race to Y's time for the race?
    (1) Just as X crossed the finish line he lapped Y for the second time.
    (2) X averaged 60 seconds per lap, and Y averaged 62.4 seconds per lap.

21. How many of a group of three positive integers are even?
    (1) The sum of the three integers is odd.
    (2) The product of any two of the integers is even.

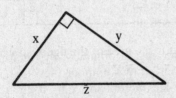

22. If A is the area of a triangle with sides of lengths x, y, and z, as shown, what is the value of A?
    (1) $x = 3$
    (2) $z = 5$

23. Is the point P on the circle with center O?
    (1) Q is a point on the circle and the distance from P to Q is equal to the distance from O to Q.
    (2) Q is on the circle and PQO is an equilateral triangle.

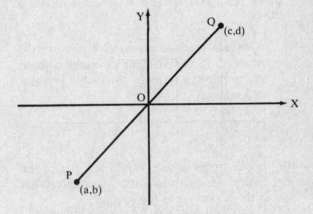

24. In the figure shown above, is the line segment PO equal to the line segment OQ?
    (1) $a^2 = c^2$ and $b^2 = d^2$
    (2) Line PQ bisects the angle formed by the x- and y-axes.

25. r, s, t, and u are integers such that r is greater than s, s is not greater than t, and u is less than r. Is u less than t?
    (1) t is greater than r.
    (2) u is less than s.

STOP

END OF SECTION. IF YOU HAVE ANY TIME LEFT, GO
OVER YOUR WORK IN THIS SECTION ONLY. DO NOT
WORK ON ANY OTHER SECTION OF THE TEST.

SECTION VI

20 Questions
Time–30 Minutes

Directions: For each of the following questions, select the best of the answer choices and blacken the corresponding space on your answer sheet.
Numbers: All numbers used are real numbers.
Figures: The diagrams and figures that accompany these questions are for the purpose of providing information useful in answering the questions. Unless it is stated that a specific figure is not drawn to scale, the diagrams and figures are drawn as accurately as possible. All figures are in a plane unless otherwise indicated.

1. A certain machine produces 8 toys every 4 seconds. If the machine operates without interruption, how many toys will it produce in 2 minutes?
   (A) 60
   (B) 120
   (C) 240
   (D) 480
   (E) 960

2. If the total sales for a business in a certain year were $150,000, what were sales in June, if June sales were half the monthly average?
   (A) $6,250
   (B) $12,500
   (C) $15,000
   (D) $25,000
   (E) $48,000

3. A flower bouquet contains red carnations, white carnations, and pink carnations. If the bouquet contains 12 red carnations, 18 white carnations and 24 pink carnations, then what percentage of the flowers in the bouquet are red carnations?
   (A) $22\frac{2}{9}\%$
   (B) $28\frac{4}{7}\%$
   (C) $33\frac{3}{9}\%$
   (D) 50 %
   (E) $66\frac{2}{3}\%$

4. If $(x - 2)^3 = 8$, then which of the following are possible real number values of x?

   I. -2
   II. 0
   III. $+4$

   (A) I only
   (B) III only
   (C) I and II only
   (D) I and III only
   (E) I, II, and III

5. In a certain school, 40% of the students are girls. If 120 students are boys, then how many students are in the school?
   (A) 48
   (B) 168
   (C) 200
   (D) 248
   (E) 300

6. A store sells five different kinds of nuts. If it is possible to buy x pounds of the most expensive nuts for $3.20 and x pounds of the cheapest nuts for $1.40, then which of the following could be the cost of purchasing a mixture containing x pounds of each type of nut?
   (A) $1.76
   (B) $2.84
   (C) $3.54
   (D) $13.60
   (E) $16.00

7. If the result obtained by multiplying a number, x, by a number 1 less than itself is 4 less than multiplying x by itself, then x =
   (A) 1
   (B) 2
   (C) 3
   (D) 4
   (E) 5

8. If the length of each edge of a rectangular solid is an integer, then the sum of the lengths of all the edges of the solid is necessarily divisible by which of the following numbers?
   (A) 3
   (B) 4

(C) 6
(D) 8
(E) 32

9. At a certain party attended by 32 people, 24 of them were students. If 12 of those in attendance were women, and if 6 of the women in attendance were students, then how many of the men who attended the party were not students?
(A) 2
(B) 4
(C) 8
(D) 12
(E) 18

10. Patricia invested a sum of money at an annual simple interest rate of $10\frac{1}{2}\%$. At the end of 4 years the amount invested plus interest earned was $781.00 What was the dollar amount of the original investment?
(A) $231.84
(B) $318.16
(C) $550.00
(D) $750.00
(E) $781.84

11. If a taxicab charges x cents for the first $\frac{1}{5}$ mile and $\frac{2}{5}$ cents for each additional $\frac{1}{5}$ mile or fraction thereof, what is the charge, in cents, for a ride of y miles, where y is a whole number?
(A) $x + \frac{xy - x}{45}$
(B) $x - \frac{xy - x}{45}$
(C) $\frac{2x + 9y}{5}$
(D) $x + \frac{9x - y}{5}$
(E) $x + \frac{9xy - x}{5}$

12. The formula for calculating the final velocity of a body, initially at rest, that undergoes a constant acceleration is $v^2 = 2ad$; where v is final velocity, a is acceleration and d is distance traveled. If a body initially at rest is subjected to a constant acceleration of 10 meters/second^2 until it reaches a velocity of 20 meters/second, how far, expressed in meters, has the body traveled?
(A) 200
(B) 100
(C) 40
(D) 20
(E) 10

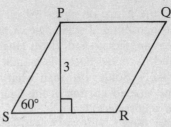

13. If all four sides of the quadrilateral shown above are equal, then what is the perimeter of PQRS?
(A) $2\sqrt{3}$
(B) $6\sqrt{3}$
(C) 9
(D) $8\sqrt{3}$
(E) 27

14. Two mail sorters, P and Q, work at constant rates. If P can sort x letters in 60 minutes and Q can sort x letters in 30 minutes, how long will it take (expressed in minutes) for both sorters, working together but independently, to sort x letters?
(A) 45
(B) 20
(C) 15
(D) 10
(E) 3

15. If 20 liters of chemical X are added to 80 liters of a mixture that is 10% chemical X and 90% chemical Y, then what percentage of the resulting mixture is chemical X?
(A) 15%
(B) 28%
(C) $33\frac{1}{3}\%$
(D) 40%
(E) 60%

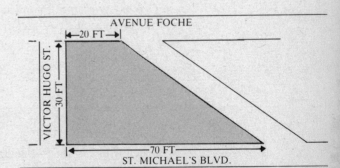

16. In the figure on page 399, all streets run in straight lines. If the angle of intersection of Avenue Foche and Victor Hugo Street is 90° and Avenue Foche is parallel to St. Michael's Boulevard, then what is the area of the shaded portion of the figure (expressed in square feet)?
    (A) 600
    (B) 750
    (C) 1350
    (D) 2400
    (E) 3750

17. The average of five numbers, x, 24, 96, 48, and 32 is what percentage of the sum of the five numbers?
    (A) 20%
    (B) 25%
    (C) 40%
    (D) 50%
    (E) It cannot be determined from the information given.

18. For a certain police precinct, the percentage of cases solved in January was 70% and the percentage of cases solved for February was 80%. If the percentage of cases solved for both months combined was 78%, what was the ratio of the number of cases in January to the number of cases in February?
    (A) $\frac{1}{5}$
    (B) $\frac{1}{4}$
    (C) $\frac{1}{2}$
    (D) $\frac{5}{4}$
    (E) $\frac{6}{5}$

19. A merchant wishes to price a certain item so that when it is placed on sale she still realizes a profit of 12.5% of the cost of the item. If the cost of the item is $32 and the sale price will be 25% less than the usual selling price of the item, then what should be the usual selling price of the item?
    (A) $48
    (B) $42
    (C) $40
    (D) $36
    (E) $34

20. If an isosceles right triangle is inscribed in a circle, what is the ratio of the area of the circle to the area of the triangle?
    (A) 1
    (B) $\frac{1}{2}$
    (C) $\frac{\pi}{2}$
    (D) π
    (E) 2π

STOP

END OF SECTION. IF YOU HAVE ANY TIME LEFT, GO OVER YOUR WORK IN THIS SECTION ONLY. DO NOT WORK IN ANY OTHER SECTION OF THE TEST.

SECTION VII

Time—30 Minutes
25 Questions

Directions: In this section, the questions ask you to analyze and evaluate the reasoning in short paragraphs or passages. For some questions, all of the answer choices may conceivably be answers to the question asked. You should select the *best* answer to the question, that is, an answer which does not require you to make assumptions which violate commonsense standards by being implausible, redundant, irrelevant or inconsistent. After choosing the best answer, blacken the corresponding space on the answer sheet.

1. There are no lower bus fares from Washington, D.C. to New York City than those of Flash Bus Line.

Which of the following is logically inconsistent with the above advertising claim?

   I. Long Lines Airways has a Washington, D.C. to New York City fare that is only one-half that charged by Flash.
   II. Rapid Transit Bus Company charges the same fare for a trip from Washington, D.C. to New York City as Flash charges.
   III. Cherokee Bus Corporation has a lower fare from New York City to Boston than does Flash.

  (A) I only
  (B) II only
  (C) I and II only
  (D) I, II, and III
  (E) None of the statements is inconsistent.

Questions 2 and 3

Roberts is accused of a crime, and Edwards is the prosecution's key witness.

   I. Roberts can be convicted on the basis of Edwards' testimony against him.
   II. Edwards' testimony would show that Edwards himself participated in Roberts' wrongdoing.
   III. The crime of which Roberts is accused can only be committed by a person acting alone.
   IV. If the jury learns that Edwards himself

committed some wrong, they will refuse to believe any part of his testimony.

2. If propositions I, II, and III are assumed to be true and IV false, which of the following best describes the outcome of the trial?
  (A) Both Edwards and Roberts will be convicted of the crime of which Roberts is accused.
  (B) Both Edwards and Roberts will be convicted of some crime other than the one with which Roberts is already charged.
  (C) Roberts will be convicted while Edwards will not be convicted.
  (D) Roberts will not be convicted.
  (E) Roberts will testify against Edwards.

3. If all four propositions are taken as a group, it can be pointed out that the scenario they describe is
  (A) a typical situation for a prosecutor
  (B) impossible because the propositions are logically inconsistent
  (C) unfair to Edwards, who may have to incriminate himself
  (D) unfair to Roberts, who may be convicted of the crime
  (E) one which Roberts' attorney has created

Questions 4 and 5

There is a curious, though nonetheless obvious, contradiction in the suggestion that one person ought to give up his life to save the life of the one other person who is not a more valuable member of the community. It is true that we glorify the sacrifice of the individual who throws herself in front of the attacker's bullets saving the life of her lover at the cost of her own. But here is the ____(4)____: Her life is as important as his. Nothing is gained in the transaction; not from the community's viewpoint, for one life was exchanged for another equally as important; not

from the heroine's viewpoint, for she is
____(5)____; and not from the rescued lover's
perspective, for he would willingly have exchanged places.

4. (A) beauty of human love
   (B) tragedy of life
   (C) inevitability of death
   (D) defining characteristic of human existence
   (E) paradox of self-sacrifice

5. (A) dying
   (B) in love
   (C) dead
   (D) a heroine
   (E) a faithful companion

6. It is a well-documented fact that for all teenage couples who marry, the marriages of those who do not have children in the first year of their marriage survive more than twice as long as the marriages of those teenage couples in which the wife does give birth within the first 12 months of marriage. Therefore, many divorces could be avoided if teenagers who marry were encouraged to seek counseling on birth control as soon after marriage as possible.

   The evidence regarding teenage marriages supports the author's conclusion only if
   (A) in those couples to which a child was born within the first 12 months, there is not a significant number in which the wife was pregnant at the time of marriage
   (B) the children born during the first year of marriage to those divorcing couples lived with the teenage couple
   (C) the child born into such a marriage did not die at birth
   (D) society actually has an interest in determining whether or not people should be divorced if there are not children involved
   (E) encouraging people to stay married when they do not plan to have any children is a good idea

7. CLARENCE: Mary is one of the most important executives at the Trendy Cola Company.

PETER: How can that be? I know for a fact that Mary drinks only Hobart Cola.

Peter's statement implies that
(A) Hobart Cola is a subsidiary of Trendy Cola
(B) Mary is an unimportant employee of Hobart Cola
(C) all cola drinks taste pretty much alike
(D) an executive uses only that company's products
(E) Hobart is a better-tasting cola than Trendy

8. ERIKA: Participation in intramural competitive sports teaches student the importance of teamwork, for no one wants to let his teammates down.

NICHOL: That is not correct. The real reason students play hard is that such programs place a premium on winning and no one wants to be a member of a losing team.

Which of the following comments can most reasonably be made about the exchange between Erika and Nichol?
(A) If fewer and fewer schools are sponsoring intramural sports programs now than a decade ago, Erika's position is undermined.
(B) If high schools and universities provide financial assistance for the purchase of sports equipment, Nichol's assertion about the importance of winning is weakened.
(C) If teamwork is essential to success in intramural competitive sports, Erika's position and Nichol's position are not necessarily incompatible.
(D) Since the argument is one about motivation, it should be possible to resolve the issue by taking a survey of deans at schools that have intramural sports programs.
(E) Since the question raised is about hidden psychological states, it is impossible to answer it.

9. Clark must have known that his sister Janet and not the governess pulled the trigger, but he silently stood by while the jury convicted the governess. Any person of clear conscience would have felt terrible for not having come forward with the information about his sister, and Clark lived with that information until his death 30 years later. Since he was an extremely happy man, however, I conclude that he must have helped Janet commit the crime.

Which of the following assumptions must underlie the author's conclusion of the last sentence?
(A) Loyalty to members of one's family is conducive to contentment.
(B) Servants are not to be treated with the same respect as members of the peerage.
(C) Clark never had a bad conscience over his silence because he was also guilty of the crime.
(D) It is better to be a virtuous man than a happy one.
(E) It is actually better to be content in life than to behave morally toward one's fellow humans.

10. Current motion pictures give children a distorted view of the world. Animated features depict animals as loyal friends, compassionate creatures, and tender souls, while "spaghetti Westerns" portray men and women as deceitful and treacherous, cruel and wanton, hard and uncaring. Thus, children are taught to value animals more highly than other human beings.

Which of the following, if true, would weaken the author's conclusion?

I. Children are not allowed to watch "spaghetti Westerns."
II. The producers of animated features do not want children to regard animals as higher than human beings.
III. Ancient fables, such as *Androcles and the Lion,* tell stories of the cooperation between humans and animals, and

they usually end with a moral about human virtue.

(A) I only
(B) II only
(C) I and II only
(D) III only
(E) I, II, and III

11. There is something irrational about our system of laws. The criminal law punishes a person more severely for having successfully committed a crime than it does a person who fails in his attempt to commit the same crime—even though the same evil intention is present in both cases. But under the civil law a person who attempts to defraud his victim but is unsucessful is not required to pay damages.

Which of the following, if true, would most weaken the author's argument?
(A) Most persons who are imprisoned for crimes will commit another crime if they are ever released from prison.
(B) A person is morally culpable for his evil thoughts as well as for his evil deeds.
(C) There are more criminal laws on the books than there are civil laws on the books.
(D) A criminal trial is considerably more costly to the state than a civil trial.
(E) The goal of the criminal law is to punish the criminal, but the goal of the civil law is to compensate the victim.

12. In his most recent speech, my opponent, Governor Smith, accused me of having distorted the facts, misrepresenting his own position, suppressing information, and deliberately lying to the people.

Which of the following possible responses by this speaker would be LEAST relevant to his dispute with Governor Smith?
(A) Governor Smith would not have begun to smear me if he did not sense that his own campaign was in serious trouble.
(B) Governor Smith apparently misunderstood my characterization of his position, so I will attempt to state more clearly my understanding of it.

(C) At the time I made those remarks, certain key facts were not available, but new information uncovered by my staff does support the position I took at that time.

(D) I can only wish Governor Smith had specified those points he considered to be lies so that I could have responded to them now.

(E) With regard to the allegedly distorted facts, the source of my information is a Department of Transportation publication entitled "Safe Driving."

13. Politicians are primarily concerned with their own survival; artists are concerned with revealing truth. Of course, the difference in their reactions is readily predictable. For example, while the governmental leaders wrote laws to ensure the triumph of industrialization in Western Europe, artists painted, wrote about, and composed music in response to the horrible conditions created by the Industrial Revolution. Only later did political leaders come to see what the artists had immediately perceived, and then only through a glass darkly. Experience teaches us that_____.

Which of the following represents the most logical continuation of the passage?

(A) artistic vision perceives in advance of political practice

(B) artists are utopian by nature while governmental leaders are practical

(C) throughout history political leaders have not been very responsive to the needs of their people

(D) the world would be a much better place to live if only artists would become kings

(E) history is the best judge of the progress of civilization

14. A parent must be constant and even-handed in the imposition of burdens and punishments and the distribution of liberties and rewards. In good times, a parent who too quickly bestows rewards creates an expectation of future rewards that he may be unable to fulfill during bad times. In bad times, a parent who waits too long to impose the punishment gives the impression that his response was forced, and the child may interpret this as_____.

Which of the following represents the most logical continuation of the passage?

(A) a signal from his parent that the parent is no longer interested in the child's welfare

(B) a sign of weakness in the parent that he can exploit

(C) indicating a willingness on the part of the parent to bargain away liberties in exchange for the child's assuming some new responsibilities.

(D) an open invitation to retaliate

(E) a symbol of his becoming an adult

15. As dietician for this 300-person school I am concerned about the sudden shortage of beef. It seems that we will have to begin to serve fish as our main source of protein. Even though beef costs more per pound than fish, I expect that the price I pay for protein will rise if I continue to serve the same amount of protein using fish as I did with beef.

The speaker makes which of the following assumptions?

(A) Fish is more expensive per pound than beef.

(B) Students will soon be paying more for their meals.

(C) Cattle ranchers make greater profits than fishermen.

(D) Per measure of protein, fish is more expensive than beef.

(E) Cattle are more costly to raise than fish.

Questions 16 and 17

New Weight Loss Salons invites all of you who are dissatisfied with your present build to join our Exercise for Lunch Bunch. Instead of putting on even more weight by eating lunch, you actually cut down on your daily caloric intake by exercising rather than eating. Every single one of us has the potential to be slim and fit, so take the initiative and begin losing excess pounds today. Don't eat! Exercise! You'll lose weight and feel stronger, happier, and more attractive.

16. Which of the following, if true, would weaken the logic of the argument made by the advertisement?

    I. Most people will experience increased desire for food as a result of the exercise and will lose little weight as a result of enrolling in the program.
    II. Nutritionists agree that skipping lunch is not a healthy practice.
    III. In our society, obesity is regarded as unattractive.
    IV. A person who is too thin is probably not in good health.

    (A) I only
    (B) I and II only
    (C) II and III only
    (D) III and IV only
    (E) I, II, and III

17. A person hearing this advertisement countered, "I know some people who are not overweight and are still unhappy and unattractive." The author of the advertisement could logically and consistently reply to this objection by pointing out that he never claimed that
    (A) being overweight is always caused by unhappiness
    (B) being overweight is the only cause of unhappiness and unattractiveness
    (C) unhappiness and unattractiveness can cause someone to be overweight
    (D) unhappiness necessarily leads to being overweight
    (E) unhappiness and unattractiveness are always found together

18. Since all swans that I have encountered have been white, it follows that the swans I will see when I visit the Bronx Zoo will also be white.

    Which of the following most closely parallels the reasoning of the preceding argument?
    (A) Some birds are incapable of flight; therefore, swans are probably incapable of flight.
    (B) Every ballet I have attended has failed to interest me; so a theatrical production that fails to interest me must be a ballet.

(C) Since all cases of severe depression I have encountered were susceptible to treatment by chlorpromazine, there must be something in the chlorpromazine that adjusts the patient's brain chemistry.
(D) Because every society has a word for *justice,* the concept of fair play must be inherent in the biological makeup of the human species.
(E) Since no medicine I have tried for my allergy has ever helped, this new product will probably not work either.

Questions 19 and 20

The blanks in the following paragraph mark deletions from the text. For each question, select the phrase that most appropriately completes the text.

Libertarians argue that laws making suicide a criminal act are both foolish and an unwarranted intrusion on individual conscience. With regard to the first, they point out that there is no penalty which the law can assess which inflicts greater injury than the crime itself. As for the second, they argue that it is no business of the state to prevent suicide, for whether it is right for a person to inflict fatal injury on himself as opposed to others is a matter between him and his God—one in which the state, by the terms of the Constitution, may not interfere. Such arguments, however, seem to me to be ill-conceived. In the first place, the libertarian makes the mistaken assumption that deterence is the only goal of the law. I maintain that the laws we have proscribing suicide are ____(19)____.

By making it a crime to take any life—even one's own—we make a public announcement of our shared conviction that each person is unique and valuable. In the second place, while it must be conceded that the doctrine of the separation of church and state is a useful one, it need not be admitted that suicide is a crime ____(20)____. And here we need not have recourse to the possibility that a potential suicide might, if given the opportunity, repent of his decision. Suicide inflicts a cost upon us all: the emotional cost on those close to the suicide;

an economic cost in the form of a loss of production of a mature and trained member of the society which falls on us all; and a cost to humanity at large for the loss of a member of our human community.

19. (A) drafted to make it more difficult to commit suicide.
    (B) passed by legislators in response to pressures by religious lobbying groups
    (C) written in an effort to protect our democratic liberties, not undermine them
    (D) important because they educate all to the value of human life
    (E) outdated because they belong to a time when church and state were not so clearly divided

20. (A) which does not necessarily lead to more serious crimes
    (B) without victim
    (C) as well as a sin
    (D) which cannot be prevented
    (E) without motive

21. All high-powered racing engines have stochastic fuel injection. Stochastic fuel injection is not a feature that is normally included in the engines of production-line vehicles. Passenger sedans are production-line vehicles.

    Which of the following conclusions can be drawn from these statements?
    (A) Passenger sedans do not usually have stochastic fuel injection.
    (B) Stochastic fuel injection is found only in high-powered racing cars.
    (C) Car manufacturers do not include stochastic fuel injection in passenger cars because they fear accidents.
    (D) Purchasers of passenger cars do not normally purchase stochastic fuel injection because it is expensive.
    (E) Some passenger sedans are high-powered racing vehicles.

22. During New York City's fiscal crisis of the late 1970's, governmental leaders debated whether to offer federal assistance to New York City. One economist who opposed the suggestion asked, "Are we supposed to help out New York City every time it gets into financial problems?"

    The economist's question can be criticized because it
    (A) uses ambiguous terms
    (B) assumes everyone else agrees New York City should be helped
    (C) appeals to emotions rather than using logic
    (D) relies on second-hand reports rather than first-hand accounts
    (E) completely ignores the issue at hand

23. Some philosophers have argued that there exist certain human or natural rights that belong to all human beings by virtue of their humanity. But a review of the laws of different societies shows that the rights accorded a person vary from society to society and even within a society over time. Since there is no right that is universally protected, there are no natural rights.

    A defender of the theory that natural rights do exist might respond to this objection by arguing that
    (A) some human beings do not have any natural rights
    (B) some human rights are natural, whereas others derive from a source such as a constitution
    (C) people in one society may have natural rights that people in another society lack
    (D) all societies have some institution that protects the rights of an individual in that society
    (E) natural rights may exist even though they are not protected by some societies

Questions 24 and 25

The single greatest weakness of American parties is their inability to achieve cohesion in the legislature. Although there is some measure of party unity, it is not uncommon for the majority party to be unable to implement important legislation. The unity is strongest during election campaigns; after the primary elections, the losing candidates all promise their support to the party nominee. By the time the Congress convenes, the unity has dissipated. This phenomenon is attributable to the fragmented nature of party politics. The national committees are no more than feudal lords who receive nominal fealty from their vassals. A congressman builds his own power on a local base. Consequently, a congressman is likely to be responsive to local special interest groups. Evidence of this is seen in the differences in voting patterns between the upper and lower houses. In the Senate where terms are longer, there is more party unity.

24. Which of the following, if true, would most strengthen the author's argument?
    (A) On 30 key issues, 18 of the 67 majority party members in the Senate voted against the party leaders.
    (B) On 30 key issues, 70 of the 305 majority party members in the House voted against the party leaders.
    (C) On 30 key issues, over half of the members of the minority party in both houses voted with the majority party against the leaders of the minority party.
    (D) Of 30 key legislative proposals introduced by the president, only eight passed both houses.
    (E) Of 30 key legislative proposals introduced by a president whose party controlled a majority in both houses, only four passed both houses.

25. Which of the following, if true, would most weaken the author's argument?
    (A) Congressmen receive funds from the national party committee.
    (B) Senators vote against the party leaders only two-thirds as often as members of the House.
    (C) The primary duty of an officeholder is to be responsive to his local constituency rather than party leaders.
    (D) There is more unity among minority party members than among majority party members.
    (E) Much legislation is passed each session despite party disunity.

STOP

END OF SECTION. IF YOU HAVE ANY TIME LEFT, GO OVER YOUR WORK IN THIS SECTION ONLY. DO NOT WORK ANY OTHER SECTION OF THE TEST.

ANSWER KEY—PRACTICE
EXAMINATION 4

SECTION I

1.	C	6.	C	11.	B	16.	A	21.	D
2.	B	7.	D	12.	C	17.	B	22.	E
3.	A	8.	B	13.	E	18.	E	23.	A
4.	E	9.	A	14.	A	19.	B	24.	E
5.	D	10.	D	15.	B	20.	D	25.	D

SECTION II

1.	A	5.	C	9.	B	13.	D	17.	D
2.	D	6.	B	10.	C	14.	E	18.	C
3.	B	7.	A	11.	C	15.	D	19.	D
4.	E	8.	D	12.	B	16.	A	20.	E

SECTION III

1.	C	6.	A	11.	B	16.	C	21.	E
2.	B	7.	E	12.	B	17.	A	22.	E
3.	C	8.	A	13.	E	18.	E	23.	D
4.	E	9.	C	14.	A	19.	D	24.	C
5.	E	10.	B	15.	D	20.	C	25.	B

SECTION IV

1.	E	6.	A	11.	D	16.	A	21.	E
2.	D	7.	D	12.	C	17.	D	22.	C
3.	D	8.	E	13.	C	18.	A	23.	E
4.	B	9.	D	14.	E	19.	B	24.	B
5.	B	10.	A	15.	C	20.	A	25.	E

SECTION V

1. B	6. A	11. E	16. D	21. C
2. C	7. E	12. B	17. A	22. C
3. E	8. D	13. D	18. A	23. B
4. D	9. B	14. D	19. E	24. A
5. C	10. A	15. C	20. B	25. D

SECTION VI

1. C	5. C	9. A	13. D	17. A
2. A	6. D	10. C	14. B	18. B
3. A	7. D	11. E	15. B	19. A
4. B	8. B	12. D	16. C	20. D

SECTION VII

1. E	6. A	11. E	16. B	21. A
2. D	7. D	12. A	17. B	22. E
3. B	8. C	13. A	18. E	23. E
4. E	9. C	14. B	19. D	24. E
5. C	10. A	15. D	20. B	25. C

EXPLANATORY ANSWERS

Section I

1. **(C)** This is obviously a main idea question. The author discusses three important characteristics of art of the Middle Ages—the sacred script, the sacred mathematics and sacred symbolic language. At the close of his remarks, the author mentions in passing the Renaissance, primarily as a way of praising the art of the Middle Ages. (C) does a fair job of describing this development. (A) can be eliminated because the discussion focuses on the art of the Middle Ages, not on the art preceding the Middle Ages. And to the extent that the author does mention what might be called influences, e.g., the revival of certain views of Pythagoras, he does so in passing. They do not constitute the focus of the passage. (D) is incorrect for the same sort of reason. The closing reference to art of the Renaissance cannot be considered the overall theme of the passage. Finally, (B) and (E) are incorrect because the author never takes on the "why."

2. **(B)** This is an inference question. In essence, the question is asking which of the five features listed was most likely to be found in a painting. (E) can be eliminated since that is inconsistent with the idea of the artist who recedes into the background of the sacred rules. As for (A), the author's only example of numbers was their use in music. This does not lead us to conclude that numbers might not be important in painting as well, but we cannot conclude on the other hand that every painting was likely to use the numbers three or four. (C) and (D) are mentioned as characteristics of certain subjects, but the author does not imply that the subjects were treated in every painting. (B), however, has the specific support of paragraph three. There the author states that

"every painting is an allegory." So, though the specific content of paintings of the period would vary from work to work, the technique of a literal image and a hidden meaning pervaded the work of the period.

3. **(A)** The tone of the passage is clearly one of appreciation—both in the sense that the author understands and in the sense that he admires what he understands. This is further supported by the contrast between art of the Middle Ages and religious art of the Renaissance at the end of the passage. (B) overstates the case. The author is only discussing the one period, with only casual reference to the period following it. We cannot conclude from the fact that he discusses art of the Middle Ages in this text that he considers this art the greatest of all art. (C) cannot be deduced from the passage, for the reference to music will not support such a judgment. (D) is inconsistent with the author's opening and closing remarks. Finally, (E), too, must be incorrect given the generally approving treatment of the passage.

4. **(E)** This is a question about a logical detail: Why does the author quote Saint Augustine? At that point, the author has just asserted that the art of the Middle Ages also is characterized by a passion for numbers. Then he quotes a statement from Augustine which makes that very point. The reason for the quotation must be to give an example of the general attitude toward numbers. Answer choice (E) describes this move. (A) is incorrect since no objection is mentioned. (B) is incorrect for the same reason, and for the further reason that "ridicule" is inconsistent with the tone of the passage. (C) is incorrect because the author is not attempting to demonstrate the similarities between two things. Finally, (D) is incorrect since it does not appear that the

author is in any danger of falling into a contradiction.

5. **(D)** This is an explicit idea question. Each of the incorrect answers is mentioned in the first paragraph as an element of the sacred script. As for (A), lines may be used to represent water or the sky. As for (B), these indicate sainthood or divinity. As for (C), shoes are mentioned as an identifying characteristic. And (E) also is mentioned (a tree represents earth). (D), however, is not mentioned as an element of the sacred script. Symmetry is discussed in conjunction with numbers, and that has to do with another characteristic altogether.

6. **(C)** This is an application question. Of course, we do not know where the passage actually appeared, and the task is to pick the most likely source. We stress this because it is always possible to make an argument for any of the answer choices to a question of this sort. But the fact that a justification is possible does not make that choice correct. The strongest possible justification makes the correct choice correct. (C) is the most likely source. The passage focuses on art and is scholarly in tone. (A) can be eliminated because the passage casts no light on social conditions of the period. (B) can be eliminated for a similar reason. The author treats art in and of itself, not as a social force. And certainly we cannot conclude that by discussing religious art the author wants to discuss the Church. (D) is incorrect because the reference to Saint Augustine is incidental and illustrative only. (E) is incorrect because it is inconsistent with the scholarly and objective tone of the passage.

7. **(D)** This is an inferred idea question, one asking for an interpretation of a phrase. The idea of the first paragraph is that the rules of art in the Middle Ages place constraints on the artist so that his artistic effort had to be made within certain conventions. As a result, painting was not individualistic. This is most clearly expressed by (D). (A) is incorrect since the author is saying that the artist's talent just did not show as individual talent. (B) is incorrect, for though this is a true

statement, it is not a response to the question. (C) is perhaps the second best answer because it at least hints at what (D) says more clearly. But the author does not mean to say the artist was not recognized in his lifetime. Perhaps he was. What the author means to say is that we do not now see the personality of the artist. Finally, (E) is just a confused reading of a part of the passage not relevant here.

8. **(B)** This is a fairly easy logical detail question. The author makes no mention of the biography of any person, so statement I is not part of the correct answer. Similarly, the author cites no authority (Augustine was cited as an example of someone who held the beliefs mentioned). So III is not part of the correct answer. II, however, is a technique used by the artist. The author does not illustrate arguments with references to works of art. So the correct answer is II only.

9. **(A)** This is an application question. As we have noted before, application questions tend to be difficult because the correct answer can be understood as correct only in context. With an explicit idea question, for example, an answer can be understood as right or wrong—either the author said it or he did not. With a question such as this, the *most logical continuation* depends on the choices available. Here the best answer is (A). The author concludes the discussion of the causes of our poor showing on the health status index by asserting that the best way to improve this showing is a general improvement in the quality of life. That is an intriguing suggestion, and an appropriate follow-up would be a list of proposals that might accomplish this. As for (B), this could be part of such a discussion, but a listing of the most common causes of death would not, in and of itself, represent an extension of the development of the argument. (C), too, has some merit. The author might want to talk about the causes of poverty as a way of learning how to improve the quality of life by eliminating the causes. But this argument actually cuts in favor of (A), for the justification for (C) then depends on (A)—that is, it

depends on the assumption that the author should discuss the idea raised in (A). (D) is incorrect because the author specifically states in his closing remarks that redistribution of medical resources is not a high priority. (E) can be eliminated on the same ground.

10. **(D)** This is an explicit idea question, and we find mention of (A), (B), (C), and (E) in the second paragraph. (D), too, is mentioned, but (D) is not a "factor affecting the health of the population." (D) is a measure of, or an effect of, the health of the population, not a factor causing it.

11. **(B)** This is a main idea question. (A) can be eliminated because the author actually minimizes the importance of medical care as a factor affecting the health of a population. (C) can be eliminated because this is not the author's objective. To be sure, an individual may use information supplied in the passage to improve in some way his or her health, but that is not why the author wrote the passage. (D) is incorrect because this is a small part of the argument, a part which is used to advance the major objective outlined in (B). Finally, (E) is incorrect since the author leaves us with a pregnant suggestion but no specific recommendations. (B), however, describes the development of the passage. The author wishes to explain the causes of the poor health status of the United States. It is not, he argues, lack of medical care or even poor distribution of medical care, hypotheses which, we can infer from the text, are often proposed. He then goes on to give two alternative explanations: affluence and poverty.

12. **(C)** This is an application question. (C) is strongly supported by the text. In the third paragraph, the author specifically states that we have the highest per capita expenditure for medical care in the world. Yet, as he notes in the first paragraph, we rank rather low in terms of health. (A) is not supported by the arguments given in the passage. Though medical care may not be the most important determinant of health, the author never suggests that expenditure is not corre-

lated with overall availability. (B) is incorrect and specifically contradicted by the second paragraph, where the author states that genetic problems may be covered over by medical care. (D) is incorrect since the author minimizes the importance of technology in improving health. Finally, (E) is simply not supported by any data or argument given in the passage.

13. **(E)** This is a logical detail question. The author refers to excess consumption to illustrate the way in which affluence, one of his two hypotheses, could undermine an individual's health. As for (A), while it is true that such problems may not be susceptible to medical treatment, the author does not introduce them to prove that. He introduces them at the particular point in the argument to prove that affluence can undermine health. (B) is incorrect for a similar reason. The author does not introduce the examples to prove that drinking and smoking are unhealthful activities; he presupposes his readers know that already. Then, on the assumption that the reader already believes that, the author can say, "See, affluence causes smoking and drinking, which we all know to be bad." (C) must fail for the same reason. Finally, (D) is incorrect since this is not the reason for introducing the examples. Although the author does argue that medical care and health are not as tightly linked as some people might think, this is not the point he is working on when he introduces smoking and drinking. With a logical detail question of this sort, we must be careful to select an answer that explains why the author makes the move he does at the particular juncture in the argument. Neither general reference to the overall idea of the passage (e.g., to prove his main point) nor a reference to a collateral argument will do the trick.

14. **(A)** The answer to the question posed in answer choice (A) is explicitly provided in the second paragraph, environment. As for (B), though some information is given about the health status of the United States, no other country is mentioned by name. As for (C), though some statistics are given about

life expectancies in the United States, no comparison of male and female life expectancies is given. As for (D), though genetic factors are mentioned generally in the second paragraph, no such factors are ever specified. Finally, the author offers no recommendations, so (E) must be incorrect.

15. **(B)** This is an inferred idea question based on a specific reference. In the second paragraph the author lists four groups of factors that influence health. In referring to medical services, he says they are treated separately from environmental factors because of our special interest in them. This implies that he would actually consider them to be just another, although important, factor in the environment. As for (A), the least important group of factors is specifically stated to be genetic factors. As for (C), there is no support for such a conclusion in that paragraph. The same reason allows us to eliminate both (D) and (E).

16. **(A)** This is a main idea question. As we have already discussed, the main idea of the passage is to explain the poor health status of the United States. The cause for this, the author argues, is not, as might seem, lack of medical care resources nor even their distribution. Rather it is what might be called "life-style." (A) makes this point. (B) is therefore contradictory to the main point of the passage. (C) is only a part of the main point and so cannot be the overall idea of the passage—and therefore cannot be the correct answer to a main idea question such as this. (D) suffers from the same defect as (B): It is in tension with the real main idea of the passage. As for (E), this might be a point the author could accept, but even setting that aside, this is surely not the theme point of the passage.

17. **(B)** This is a tone question. It should be fairly easy once the overall structure of the passage is understood. The author is critical of the performance of the United States particularly because the United States should have a very good health status. So we can eliminate any positive judgments, (A) and (C), and also any neutral judgments,

(D). The only question is whether (C) or (E) is the more appropriate description of the author's tone. The author cannot be said to "reject" the health status of the United States, though he can be said to be critical of it. Therefore, we prefer (B) to (E).

18. **(E)** This is an explicit idea question. The answer can be found in the first paragraph, where the author notes that a heart attack is unlike an angina attack because the heart attack always involves the death of heart muscle. As for (A), although a heart attack may involve acceleration of the heartbeat, this is not what distinguishes it from angina. (B) is incorrect since the author describes the way in which nitroglycerin may be used to treat heart attack. (C) is incorrect both because this is not a statement which can be justified by the text and because it is not the defining characteristic of a heart attack. Finally, (D) is incorrect, for though the heart attack involves rapid muscle death, it is the death of tissue and not the length of time of the attack that is the distinguishing feature.

19. **(B)** This, too, is an explicit idea question, but it is more difficult than the preceding one. The author cites the "curious" result that the nitroglycerin helped the most seriously stricken patients but did not help the less seriously stricken patients. He explains that in the more seriously stricken patients the ordinary automatic response to a drop in blood pressure, which would be a faster heart rate, did not occur. Apparently, the congestive heart failure effectively blocked this reaction. Consequently, the drop in blood pressure caused by the nitroglycerin did not invite the normal increase in heart rate. This explanation is presented by choice (B). (A) is incorrect since no mention is made of any delay in administering drugs. (C) is incorrect since phenylephrine was not available to the twelve patients at the time of the study. Phenlyephrine was later used to counter the drop in blood pressure caused by nitroglycerin. (D) is incorrect since the passage states that blood pressure did drop in those patients with congestive heart failure. The difference between those patients

and the less seriously stricken ones was that the drop in blood pressure did not cause an increase in heart rate. For the same reason, (E) must also be eliminated.

20. **(D)** This is an explicit idea question. As for (A), several results of heart attack are mentioned at various points in the text. The answer to (B) is explicitly provided in the third paragraph. As for (C), the author mentions the effect of nitroglycerin at various points, e.g., dilates blood vessels, reduces blood pressure. Finally, (E) is answered in the second paragraph. (D), however, is not answered in the passage. Though the author discusses the effects of heart attack, he does not discuss the causes of heart attack.

21. **(D)** The answer to this inference question can be found in the final paragraph. There the author states that research is being done on drugs that affect myocardial oxygen supply and demand "including . . . vessel dilators such as nitroglycerin." From this we can infer that nitroglycerin dilates blood vessels and this somehow affects the oxygen balance in the heart muscle. This is the value of the drug. (A) is incorrect because the lowering of blood presure is an unwanted side effect of nitroglycerin, not its medical value. (B) is incorrect since the value of nitroglycerin is to prevent damage, not to aid in healing. (C) is incorrect for the same reason that (A) is incorrect. Finally, (E) is incorrect because nitroglycerin is mentioned as a vessel dilator in the final paragraph, not as a drug that counters hypertension.

22. **(E)** This is a tone question. The author's attitude is best studied in the final paragraph. Having described the possibility of treating heart attack with nitroglycerin, he adds the disclaimer that there is no proof yet of the value of the treatment in very serious cases. From this we may infer, however, that the author believes it has some value in less serious cases. Moreover, since he refers to research being done, he apparently believes that the treatment may prove to have value in other cases as well. This attitude is best described as one of optimism. Since the

passage has, on balance, a positive tone, we can eliminate (B), (C), and (D). As for (A), though the author may be concerned about the treatment of heart attacks, the overall tone of the discussion is not concern or worry, but rather hope or optimism.

23. **(A)** This is an inference question the answer to which is found in the second paragraph. There it is stated that phenylephrine is used to maintain blood pressure, but that simple statement is not enough to answer the question. We must dig deeper. Why is it important to maintain blood pressure? The final sentence of the paragraph states that a drop in blood pressure causes the heart to speed up. It is this increase in heart rate that "worsens the damage." So the value of phenylephrine is that it prevents cardiac acceleration by maintaining blood pressure. This is the explanation given in choice (A). (B) and (C) make essentially the same statement using language drawn from different parts of the passage, but they describe something other than the effect of phenylephrine. (D) is incorrect since the phenylephrine has a particular use that complements nitroglycerin. Although the effect of both drugs taken together may be something like that described in (D), this is not an answer to the question asked. Finally, (E) is just language taken from the first paragraph and is not an answer to the question asked.

24. **(E)** This is a main idea question. The best way of describing the development of the passage is given in (E). The author is discussing a treatment for heart attack. As for (A), the only suggestions of a predicament is contained in the first paragraph, namely, that nitroglycerin has beneficial effects but it also lowers blood pressure. But once that has been stated, the author proceeds to explain how the dilemma has been resolved. So the passage, if anything, explains not a predicament, but how a predicament has been solved. As for (B), though the author does evaluate the results of a study, that evaluation is incidental to the larger goals of describing a treatment. As for (C), though the reader may see implicit in

the treatment some sort of proposal, it cannot be said that the author is concerned with outlining a proposal. Finally, (D) is the least effective choice since there is no argument presented.

25. **(D)** Here we have another main idea question, this one as a "best title" question. The technique for answering the question is the same as that for answering any main idea question. (A) can be eliminated since there is no discussion of the causes of heart attacks. (B) can be eliminated since any mention of clinical symptoms is incidental to the main idea. (C) is incorrect since the discussion of congestive heart failure is just one minor point of the passage (the second paragraph, the experiment with nitroglycerin). (E) is incorrect because it overstates the case made by the author. The value of the drug has not been firmly established in the case of heart attack. Thus, (D) is correct. You will notice that (D) also nicely expresses the element of doubt mentioned in our discussion of question 22.

Section II

1. **(A)** We may express the given information as $\dfrac{x + y + 30}{3} = 10$. Thus, $x + y + 30 = 30$, $x + y = 0$, and $\dfrac{x + y}{2} = 0$, so the average of x and y is 0. Since $x + y = 0$, $x = -y$ (and $y = -x$), which means that of x and y, one term must be positive and the other negative (e.g., +3 and −3).

2. *(D)** This is a problem of intersecting sets, and can be diagrammed with circles, as below. The total number of seniors is 120. Letting x be the number of seniors in both clubs, $70 - x$ seniors must be in the chess club only and $90 - x$ seniors must be in the pep club only. The sum of those three quantities must be the total number of

seniors. Thus, $x + (70 - x) + (90 - x) = 120$ and $x = 40$.

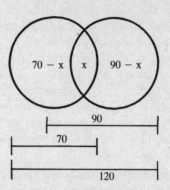

3. **(B)** The area of a circle can be found if the perimeter is given because the radius can be obtained from the perimeter (circumference) by using the formula radius = circumference/2π. The area may then be found by substituting the radius into the formula for the area of a circle, area = $(\pi)(\text{radius})^2$. None of the other figures' areas can be found from their perimeters since none of them are necessarily regular figures, that is, have all their sides equal, and only with regular figures can area be found from perimeter.

4. **(E)** This problem has a certain trial-and-error aspect to it. We need to find a pair of factors of 72 such that one of them is a perfect square and the other is a perfect cube. 72 is 9×8, and 9 is 3 squared and 8 is 2 cubed, so a is 3 and b is 2. Thus, a + b is 5.

5. **(C)** The solution to this problem is greatly facilitated if fractional equivalents of the decimal expressions are used, since there are convenient equivalents for each of the decimals in the problem. .250 is $\frac{1}{4}$, .333 is about $\frac{1}{3}$, .125 is $\frac{1}{8}$, and .167 is about $\frac{1}{6}$. (If you did not notice this immediately, a review of the percentage equivalents provided in the math refresher section is indicated.) The problem now becomes:

$$\dfrac{\frac{1}{4}}{\frac{1}{3}}\bigg/\dfrac{\frac{1}{8}}{\frac{1}{6}} = \frac{1}{4} \times \frac{3}{1} \bigg/ \frac{1}{8} \times \frac{6}{1} = \frac{3}{4} \bigg/ \frac{3}{4} = 1$$

6. **(B)** This is an example of a problem whose exact nature is not fully known until the answer choices are examined. Here, a simplifying approach is to choose convenient values for a and b and then evaluate the fractions, picking the fraction nearest to 1 as the answer. Let us work with a = 3 and b = 2, since a must be larger than b. Then answer choice (A) becomes $\frac{3}{2}$, or $1\frac{1}{2}$. (B) becomes $\frac{5}{4}$, or $1\frac{1}{4}$. (C) becomes $\frac{4}{3}$, or $1\frac{1}{3}$. (D) becomes $\frac{4}{2}$, or 2. Finally, (E) becomes $\frac{2}{1}$, or 2. All of the answer choices are greater than one, and (B), which is the smallest of them, is therefore closest to 1.

7. **(A)** If the office has 21 staff members and $\frac{1}{3}$ are men, then there are $21 \times \frac{1}{3}$ or 7 men on the staff. Since the problem does not specify the hiring of any more men, the 7 men must be $\frac{1}{4}$ of the new staff total. So $\frac{1}{4}x = 7$ where x is the total number of staff after hiring. Hence x = 28, and substracting from this total the 21 current staff members yields 7 women who must be hired.

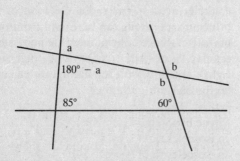

8. **(D)** From the diagram above, it can be seen that there is a quadrilateral whose angles can be expressed in terms of numerical quantities of b and a alone. The sum of the four angles must be 360°, so we have the equation (180 − a) + 60 + 85 + b = 360, or, transferring the numerical quantities to the right-hand side of the equation, b − a = 35. Note that it is impossible to solve for a or b individually since there is only one equation available to solve for two unknowns. However, the problem did not require us to do this.

9. **(B)** Answering this question involves finding percentages of percentages. If 40% of the women students take mathematics courses and 55% of the students are women, then 40% of 55% of the students are women enrolled in mathematics courses. This is (.40)(.55) = .22 = 22%. Similarly, since 100 − 55 = 45% of all students are men, then 20% of 45% of the students are men taking mathematics courses. This is equal to (.20)(.45) = .09 = 9%. The total percentage taking mathematics courses is found by adding the two computed percentages together: 22% + 9% = 31%.

10. **(C)** The volume of a cylinder is $\pi r^2 h$ where r is the radius of the base and h is the height of the cylinder. Letting this represent the volume of cylinder B, we can then find what the volume of cylinder A would be. If the height of cylinder B is h, then the height of cylinder A is 3h. If the radius of cylinder B is r, then the radius of cylinder A is $\frac{1}{3}$ r. Therefore, the volume of cylinder A must be $\pi(\frac{1}{3} r)^2 3h = \pi \times \frac{1}{9} r^2 \times 3h = \frac{1}{3} \pi r^2 h$. The ratio of the volume of A to that of B, which is what the question asks for, must be $\frac{1/3\ \pi r^2 h}{\pi r^2 h} = \frac{1}{3}$, by cancellation.

11. **(C)** Let us call the jogger's original rate r_1 and her increased rate r_2. If the original time is t, then the new time would be $\frac{3}{4}t$. Since the distance is the same in both cases, D = $r_1 t$ = $r_2 (\frac{3}{4}t)$, or $r_2 = \frac{4}{3} r_1$. The increase in speed would be $\frac{4}{3}r_1 − r_1 = \frac{1}{3} r_1$. Dividing this by the old total gives us the percentage increase: $\frac{1/3\ r_1}{r_1} = \frac{1}{3} = 33\frac{1}{3}\%$

12. **(B)** This question is basically an "insight" problem in the sense that solving it is quite easy if one sees a key relationship in the problem. Here we are given the length of a diagonal of ABCO, AC = 6. ABCO is a rectangle, so its diagonals are equal in length. The other diagonal of ABCO, OA, is also a radius of circle O, and also has a length of 6. Thus the area of circle O, π times radius squared, is π times 6^2 or 36π. If the "insight" escaped you, there was one further tactic you could have employed: measure. In this section, unless otherwise indicated, drawings are to scale. You could have used the edge of your answer sheet to measure the known quantity and then have compared that to the radius of the circle. The radius of the circle would have measured 6.

13. **(D)** If we designate the unknown number by x, then the statistician squared x and divided the result by 3, obtaining 27, that is, $\frac{x^2}{3} = 27$, $x^2 = 81$, and $x = 9$ since it is a positive number. The answer the statistician should have gotten is found by taking the square root of 9 (which is 3) and multiplying by 9, getting 27.

14. **(E)** Profit = Income − Cost = $10,000. Income is here made up of two parts, advertising income and sales income. Advertising income is $20,000, and sales income is the number of copies sold times the price per copy, or ($0.75)(x), where x is the number of copies sold. Income is thus (.75x + 20,000) dollars. Total cost is cost per copy times the number of copies, or (1.00x) dollars. So the desired equation is (.75x + 20.000) − 1.00x = 10,000 or −.25x = −10,000 or x = 40,000 copies.

15. **(D)** If a remainder of 4 is obtained when 89 is divided by a, then a must divide 89 − 4 = 85 evenly. Similarly, if a remainder of 6 is obtained when 125 is divided by a, then a must divide 125 − 6 = 119 evenly. 85 is 17 × 5 and 119 is 17 × 7. The only integer that divides both numbers evenly is 17, so that is the correct answer.

16. **(A)** It is easy to misread this problem. It states that the pen costs $11 more than the pencil, not that the pen costs $11. Letting x = the cost of the pen and y = the cost of the pencil, we can write two equations: x + y = 12 and x − y = 11. Subtracting the second equation from the first we get 2y = 1 and y = .50.

17. **(D)** The information given in this problem again allows us to set up two equations with two unknowns. The October commission can be expressed as $(\frac{x}{100})(2000) + \frac{y}{100})$ (4000 − 2000) which must equal 700. This simplifies to 20x + 20y = 700. The November commission can be written as $(\frac{x}{100})$ (2000) + $(\frac{y}{100})(5000 - 2000) = 900$, which simplifies to 20x + 30y = 900. Subtracting the first equation from the second, we get 10y = 200

or y = 20. Substituting for y in the first equation we get 20x + (20)(20) = 700, 20x = 300 or x = 15.

18. **(C)** Once again we have a problem that can be solved by simultaneous equations. Let x be the number of younger children and y the number of older children. Then x + y = 200. But we also know that each younger child rode on three wheels into the park and each older child rode on two wheels into the park. Thus, 3x + 2y = total numbers of wheels = 480. The easiest way to solve for x is to double the first equation, getting 2x + 2y = 400, and subtracting that from 3x + 2y = 480. This yields x = 80.

19. **(D)** The longest straight-line distance in a rectangular box is the diagonal of that box, that is, the distance from a bottom corner to the opposite upper corner. The diagonal of the box is the hypotenuse of a right triangle in which one leg is the height of the box and the other leg is the bottom of the box. The height of the box is 10 inches. The diagonal of the box bottom is the hypotenuse of a right triangle with legs of 6 inches and 8 inches. Thus, we have a triangle twice the size of a 3-4-5 right triangle, that is, a 6-8-10 right triangle. So the diagonal of the bottom of the box is 10 inches. Thus, both legs of the right triangle whose hypotenuse we seek are 10 inches; it is an isosceles right triangle. The hypotenuse of an isosceles right triangle is the square root of 2 multiplied by the length of a leg of that triangle. Therefore, the length of the hypotenuse, which is the diagonal of the box, is 10 times the square root of 2.

20. **(E)** An approach that seems useful to many problems of this sort is to select a convenient original price to work with. Suppose the widget was priced at $100 before 1981. After a 20% increase in 1981, the price rose to 100 + (.2)(100) = $120. After the 10% increase in 1982, the price rose to 120 + (.1)(120) = $132. This means that the price would have to be decreased by $32 to return it to the pre-1981 price of $100. Now the question becomes: What percentage of $132 is $32? This is $\frac{32}{132}$ times 100%, which is a little more than 24%.

Section III

1. **(C)** According to (1) there are more than 7 pennies in the bank, and according to (2) there are fewer than 9 pennies in the bank. The only integer greater than 7 but less than 9 is 8, and that must be the number of pennies in the bank. If this situation did not refer to pennies (or something else that had to occur in integral values), there would not be sufficient information to answer the question since 7.5, 8.6, etc., might then be acceptable.

2. **(B)** (1) does not tell us how much is still owed. It doesn't even tell us, by itself, how much Joe has paid since (1) does not tell us the amount of the monthly payments. (2), however, is sufficient by itself, since it allows us to compute his indebtedness: $150 × 10 = $1500.

3. **(C)** (1) tells us that $(\frac{x + y + z}{3}) = 5$, which is not sufficient by itself to determine x. However, if we also know (2), we may substitute $-z$ for y in the equation from (1), getting $[\frac{x + (-z) + z}{3}] = 5$, or $\frac{x}{3} = 5$ and x = 15.

4. **(E)** Even knowing both (1) and (2) together, that is, that the Lions scored more points than the Tigers in three of the four quarters and that the Tigers outscored the Lions in the other quarter, is not sufficient to determine who won since the Tigers could have more than made up the point deficit from the three quarters they "lost" in the one quarter they "won."

5. **(E)** We do not know how the three gas stations are ordered, or even if they all fall on the same straight line, so, even knowing (1) and (2), it is impossible to calculate the distance from gas station X to gas station Z.

6. **(A)** To find interest earned, we need to have the amount of principal, the rate of interest and the time period. The original information gives us the principal and the time period (annual). Thus (1), which gives the interest rate, is sufficient to obtain an answer (by finding $5\frac{1}{4}$% of $3000, which is .0525 × $3000 = $157.50). (2) is irrelevant since annual interest income, not total in-

come, is asked for. Also, (2) does not provide us with the interest rate for the period during which the account was maintained.

7. **(E)** Since both statements are merely comparative (*-er*) and they do not compare the two items we are asked to compare, neither is sufficient by itself. Combining both pieces of information tells us that Beth is shorter than either Susan or Jill (thus, she is the shortest), but we have no information relating Susan and Jill to each other and thus cannot tell who is the tallest.

8. **(A)** We need the sum of the four numbers. From (1) we can compute the sum of a, b, c, and d by multiplying the average of those four numbers, 6, by the number of numbers averaged, 4. This yields 24 as the answer. (2) gives us no information about the value of d and is therefore not sufficient by itself.

9. **(C)** (1) does give us a lot of information about the series, but it does not tell us where the series starts, and a series does not have to start with 1. Thus, (1) is not sufficient by itself. (2) clearly does not suffice by itself since there is no way to connect the 10th number in the series to the 57th. Knowing (1) and (2) together, we could count forward by threes from the 10th number, 29, to the 57th number. Alternatively, we could write an equation: 57th number in the series = 29 + (57 − 10)(3). This is a perfect example of a problem that you should absolutely *NOT* solve numerically. Once you know that there is enough information, that's the end of it.

10. **(B)** To compute the percentage asked for, we need the number correctly answered and the total number of questions. The total is given in the original information, so all that is needed is the number correctly answered. (1) reveals the number of questions left blank but says nothing about the number of questions answered correctly or incorrectly. (2) is sufficient since the required percentage would be $(\frac{53 \text{ correct}}{125}) × 100$.

11. **(B)** The requested percentage is a fraction in which the profit is the numerator and the selling price is the denominator. Another way to look at the question is that we need to be

able to link the profit and the selling price paid into a fraction or ratio or percentage. We might also be asked to use the everyday idea of profit as the difference between cost and selling price. (1) allows us to link the profit and selling price in the form: profit = selling price − $20. However, that is a linkage based on addition and subtraction and does not permit a firm conclusion about the ratio we have been asked to determine. For example, the selling price could be $520 and the profit $500, or the selling price could be $30 and the profit $10. (2) tells us that $\frac{1}{4}$ of the selling price is profit (since $\frac{3}{4}$ of the selling price was the cost of the item and the cost plus the profit equals the selling price). Don't confuse yourself by worrying about different types of costs.

12. **(B)** Since (1) tells us nothing about b, it cannot be sufficient. By dividing each side of the equation in (2) by a, we obtain $\frac{b}{a} = 4$, and 75 percent of 4 is 3, so (2) is sufficient. This is a good example of a question in which you could easily leap ahead to a (C) answer choice without sufficient consideration of each proposition by itself.

13. **(E)** An integer can be either positive, negative, or zero. If s is a sufficiently small negative number, r could be either negative or positive in either inequality presented. For example, suppose s = −3, then r could be +1, but it could also be −1 in either one of the inequalities presented in (1) and (2). Thus, (1) and (2) are not sufficient singly or together to answer the question asked. It is true that you can figure out that s is negative since adding 2s (going from r − s to r + s) makes the sum smaller (going from greater than 1 to less than 1), but that won't help you to answer the question.

14. **(A)** From (1) we know that there are six different, equally likely outcomes of any throw of the die. The probability of the die coming up six is thus one out of six. However, each roll is totally independent, and thus the fate of previous rolls does not affect the chances for the current roll. Thus (2) is irrelevant.

15. **(D)** (1) gives us the equation x(x + 5) = 24, were x is Robert's age now. This equation has a positive root, 3, and a negative root, −8.

Although you can find these roots by solving the quadratic equation $x^2 + 5x − 24 = 0$, it is quicker to just consider what the factors of 24 are and select the ones that satisfy the conditions. Even more efficient would be an approach of trying out potential ages and seeing which ones work. The only advantage to knowing the quadratic formulation is that you will more quickly appreciate that there is only one positive root; since Robert cannot be −8 years old, he must be 3 years old and thus (1) is sufficient. (2) yields the equation x + 6 = 3x, and again x = 3.

16. **(C)** We need the area of one tile and the area of the floor. A square floor tile of side x has an area of x^2. From (1) and (2) the area of the kitchen floor can be calculated as $(10x)(30x) = 300x^2$. The number of tiles needed to cover the floor must then be the area of the floor divided by the area per tile, that is, $\frac{300x^2}{x^2}$ or 300.

17. **(A)** The height of the can is asked for and the diameter is given. The likely connection will be the formula for volume of a cylinder or can, V = $(\pi)(radius)^2(height)$. Since the diameter is given, we know the radius. Since that leaves only one variable in the equation, the volume, in addition to the height, we might well find that one proposition is sufficient. (1) allows us to set up the equation Volume = $(\pi)(r)^2(h) = (10)(\pi)(r)$. The radius is 2 inches, so the equation can be solved for h, so (1) is sufficient. (2) is not sufficient, however. Even knowing the *volume* of the can's contents [as opposed to the *weight* as given by (2)] would not give us the volume of the can itself.

18. **(E)**

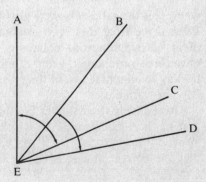

From (1) and (2) we know the measures of angles AEC and BED, but we cannot find the measure of the overlap of those angles (∠BEC), and therefore cannot find ∠CED either.

19. **(D)** To find the value of a, we need to establish the value of b and c. From (1), by substituting for c in the equation from the original information, we obtain a + b + 4a − b = 50, or 5a = 50 and a = 10. (2) means that $\frac{b + c}{2}$ = 2a or b + c = 4a. Substituting 4a for b + c in the original equation gives us a + 4a = 5a = 50 once again.

20. **(C)** (1) tells us that x must be positive or zero, since the cube of any negative number is negative. From (2) we know that x is negative or odd, but not both. Thus, given (1) and (2), x must be odd.

21. **(E)** In order to find the average speed for the whole trip, we will at least need to have information about all of the miles of the trip. Traveling at 50 miles per hour for the first three hours and 45 miles per hour for the last three hours, the car will have gone (50 × 3) + (45 × 3) = 285 miles. We do not know how long it took to travel the remaining 15 miles, and so cannot calculate the average speed for the entire trip.

22. **(E)** The question can be analyzed algebraically by expressing each statement as an equation. Letting x represent the number of boys attending S in 1980 and y the number of girls for the same year, we have:

$$\frac{1}{y} = \frac{1}{2}$$

$$\frac{x + 50}{y + 50} = z$$

where z is the ratio of boys to girls for 1981. Even if we treat these two algebraic statements as simultaneous equations, we still have three variables, x, y and z, and there is no way to eliminate two of three to solve for any one variable.

Alternatively, you should be able to see that neither statement alone is sufficient to answer the question. Then you can prove that the correct answer is (E) by using the test-taking tactic of picking concrete numbers. Assuming the numbers of boys in 1980 to be 25 and the numbers of girls in 1980 to be 50 (a ratio of 1:2), the ratio of boys to girls in 1981 would be:

$$\frac{25 + 50}{50 + 50} = \frac{75}{100} = \frac{3}{4}$$

But assuming the number of boys in 1980 to be 250 and the number of girls to be 500 (again, the 1:2 ratio stipulated by the question stem), the ratio for 1981 would be:

$$\frac{250 + 50}{500 + 50} = \frac{300}{550} = \frac{6}{11}$$

So the ratio for 1981 depends on the actual number of students attending S in 1980 and not just on the ratio for 1980. Neither statement, however, gives us any information about the actual number of students in attendance in 1980.

23. **(D)** Since AC and CD are equal, (1) means that AB = BC, triangle ABC is isosceles, and r = t. (2) tells us that u = s + t. u also equals s + r since it is an exterior angle to triangle ABC. Therefore, s + r = s + t or r = t.

24. **(C)** The line connecting points A and C is a diameter since A is directly opposite C in the circular cage. The two tiger walks, from A to B and B to C, are thus the two legs of an inscribed right triangle. (1) and (2) provide the lengths of the legs, from which the diameter could be found by the Pythagorean theorem. The circumference of the cage can then be obtained from the diameter by the formula Circumference = π × Diameter.

25. **(B)** (1) means that there is at least one factor of 3 in the three integers, but two or all three could be divisible by 3. The fact that only one of the three is divisible by 21 means that only one is divisible by *both* 3 and 7. However, the question concerns merely the divisibility of the three integers by 7 alone. It is certainly possible to be divisible by 7 and not by 21. For example, satisfying (1), the three integers could be 2, 5 and 21, in which case only one of the three is divisible by 7; but it is also possible that

the three integers are 2, 7 and 21, in which case two of the three are divisible by 7. Thus (1) is not sufficient. (2) is sufficient since any integer divisible by 3 and 7 is divisible by 21. Therefore, since only c is divisible by 21, only c can be divisible by 7.

Section IV

1. **(E)** The original sentence contains two errors. First, when comparing only two items, we must use the comparative degree of the adjective (the *-er* form for most adjectives). Thus the sentence should use "more" rather than "most." Second, the pronoun "their" is plural, but its antecedent or referent is "each," a singular pronoun. This error can be eliminated by changing "their" to "its." (B) and (C) each corrects one error but not both. (D) fails to make either correction and commits the additional sin of introducing an illogical change in the number of the subject. Only (E) makes the needed, and only the needed, changes.

2. **(D)** The error in this sentence is one of faulty parallelism. When presenting elements in a series, you should remember to make sure those elements are of similar type, e.g., all clauses, all phrases, all infinitives, all gerunds. Here, the first two elements are noun phrases (. . . service, . . .managment). To preserve the parallelism, the third element should have the same form: . . . service, . . . managment, . . . facilities. Both (D) and (E) make the required change. (D) is preferable to (E), however, because (E) includes a second, and gratuitous, "its," disrupting the parallelism.

3. **(D)** The sentence contains two errors. First, the phrasing "Men's interest . . ." is both awkward and incorrect. The sentence could be changed to read "Man's interest," but even that is unnecessary. The sentence can be more concisely written as rendered by (D)—and conciseness is important on the test. Second, there is a failure of agreement between subject and verb. The subject of the sentence is "interest," which must take a

singular verb; (D) does this by changing "have" to the singular "has."

4. **(B)** The error here is a failure of agreement between subject and verb. The subject of the sentence is "delegates," so the verb should be the plural "were." The pronoun "their" is correct as written, so any choice which fails to correct the error or gratuitously changes the number of "their" is incorrect.

5. **(B)** The construction "For the reason that" is just not acceptable usage. (C), (D) and (E) are also unacceptable constructions in Standard Written English. In general, as a matter of test-taking tactics, choose a simple and direct construction.

6. **(A)** The sentence contains no error. (B) introduces an error by changing "as" to "like," substituting a preposition for a conjunction, but the sentence needs a conjunction to join the two clauses. (D) introduces an error in parallelism by changing the order of the subject and the predicate complement. (E) introduces an awkward phrasing in the main clause. (C) is a bit more subtle. First, the changes made by (C) alter slightly the meaning of the sentence. Second, (C) makes changes which are not required, and, as a matter of tactics, you should make no change unless you have a justification for that change. The justification need not be couched in formal terms, but it should be more than "I just don't like it." You should be able to pinpoint an error, explain in informal terms why it is an error, and then find a sentence that corrects the error before you make any change.

7. **(D)** The sentence is not really a sentence at all, only a sentence fragment, for the original phrasing contains no verb for which "Jonas Salk" is the subject. (E) suffers from the same defect. (B) and (C) have the merit of introducing a verb, but both (B) and (C) are incorrect because of awkward and, in (C)s case, incorrect structure.

8. **(E)** The error in the sentence is an illogical construction. As written, the sentence reads

"less on . . . and more on. . . ." The sentence means to say "less on . . . than on. . . ." (E) makes the needed change.

9. **(D)** The sentence contains two errors. First, there is a faulty comparison. As constructed, the sentence makes an attempt to compare the number of winding roads of San Jacinto Hill with El Capitan. But the comparison should be between "roads" and "roads." Second, when referring to discrete quantities, items that can be counted, we use the words "fewer" and "fewest" rather than "less" and "least."

10. **(A)** The sentence is correct as written. The only question is whether the present tense of the verb is correct. In this case, the sentence uses the present tense, "closes," to assert that this is the usual practice of the doctor. Each alternative answer choice changes the meaning of the sentence. Thus, each alternative choice is incorrect, because it makes a gratuitous change from the original and, in so doing changes the intent of the original sentence.

11. **(D)** The error in the sentence is its use of the preposition "like." Since "like" is intended to join a clause, we need a conjunction such as "as." (C) and (E) make the needed correction, but (C) introduces a slight ambiguity through its needless change and (E) alters the meaning of the sentence somewhat.

12. **(C)** Without getting involved in the intricacies of the subjunctive, we can explain this question by appealing to the "ear." Your ear should tell you that with a construction of the type "it is necessary that," "it is required that," or "it is mandatory that," we use what would otherwise be considered the plural form of the verb: "reject" rather than "rejects." Here the sentence should read, in essence, "it is necessary that he reject. . . ."

13. **(C)** Here the sentence suffers from faulty parallelism. The sentence should read "to seize power, . . . to maintain it."

14. **(E)** The error in this sentence is related to the notorious dangling modifier. The sentence opens with a modifier that because of its placement, is intended to modify the subject of the sentence. But the subject of the sentence is "order." How could an order make a move? The sentence means to say that the chairman of the board made a move, but, to convey that accurately, it is necessary to clarify the subject. (E) does this by making "the chairman of the board" the subject of the sentence.

15. **(C)** As originally written, the sentence is a mess. First, we have the unacceptable construction "The reason why. . . ." Second, "because" should not be used to introduce a noun clause; that is, you should not use the structure "is because." (C) corrects the sentence by eliminating unnecessary words and stating directly the meaning of the sentence.

16. **(A)** Here we have a problem similar to that discussed in question 12. The sentence, with the verb "return," is correct as written. (B), (C) and (D) make unneeded changes that introduce errors into the otherwise correct construction. (E) is guilty on the same count for the reasons advanced in our justification for the correct answer to question 12.

17. **(D)** The difficulty with the sentence is the needless verbiage "by it." (C) and (E) also make the needed correction, but they are incorrect because they add something to the sentence to make it awkward.

18. **(A)** The sentence is correct as rendered. (B) changes a properly plural verb to a singular verb, introducing a new error. (C) adds unneeded words, making the sentence awkward. (D) changes the meaning of the sentence slightly. Finally, (E) introduces a new error in usage by changing "so" to "as."

19. **(B)** The difficulty with the sentence is a failure of parallelism. The subject of the sentence is the infinitive "to consider," but the complement is the gerund "is neglecting." One or the other must be changed so that they both have the same form. (B) does this. (D) changes both, so it commits the mirror image of the original error. (C)

introduces wording that makes the sentence illogical. (E) introduces a new error, the unacceptable usage of "amounts to."

20. **(A)** The sentence is correct as written. Since the time frame refers to something which occurred in the past and is now over, the verb "would have liked" is correct.

21. **(E)** There is a problem here with verb tense. To express correctly the thought of the sentence, it must be made clear that the erroneous belief preceded the discovery of the new information and that it was ended by that discovery. (E), by using the past perfect "had," correctly places the "belief" as a completed act in the past.

22. **(C)** Again, without getting involved in the intricacies of the subjunctive, because the refusal is not a certainty, to express the doubt we require the "would." Every other choice is wrong because it does not capture the element of doubt expressed by the phrase "out of fear that."

23. **(E)** The verb tenses, though at first seemingly awkward, are correct. Think of this as a report in an economic journal. The present tense is correct because it is used to describe the typical "young spouse": she *does* this, she *does* that. The only error in the original is the use of "among." We should use "among" when we are referring to more than two elements. When referring to only two elements, we should use "between."

24. **(B)** This question illustrates the error of the dangling modifier. The introductory phrase, "Accused of dishonesty," will refer to the nearest element of the sentence, which is the subject. But the subject of the sentence is "lies," and it is the liar, not the lies, who is accused of the dishonesty. Both (B) and (C) make the appropriate correction by changing the subject of the sentence, but (C) introduces a new error: "due to." "Due to" is not an appropriate substitute for "because."

25. **(E)** The error in the sentence is a failure of subject-verb agreement. The subject of the

sentence is the gerund "accepting," a singular subject (it refers to *one* general action). We need a singular verb: "constitutes." Only (E) makes the needed change. In (D), the use of "to accept" also requires "constitutes," for the same reason.

Section V

1. **(B)** Proposition (1) only gives a limit on the percentage the question asks about. (2) does give the information needed to compute the percentage of the stock's cost which the dividend represents.

2. **(C)** In order to determine the average of all five of the persons mentioned in the problem, the total of the five ages is needed. Knowing the averages of the three men and of the two women will permit this calculation. The only thing that you need to check carefully is that all of the persons are included in the two averages and that there is no overlap.

3. **(E)** The key to this problem is the insight that there is no information given about which of the scores is at the higher end of the gap and which at the lower end of the gap. Thus, neither of the propositions gives adequate, or indeed helpful, information.

4. **(D)** Even if you do not know the exact definition of a gross (a dozen dozen or 144), you can conclude that the original information gives you the selling price of the pens. In order to compute the profit, you need to know the cost or make a connection between the selling price and the profit. (1) does the latter and (2) does the former. Thus, either is sufficient to permit the calculation of the profit.

5. **(C)** This is really a logic problem, not a mathematics problem. Whatever is being asked for, the answer will be found by ordinary reasoning rather than some esoteric formula. Each proposition by itself merely establishes that the green figure is not at the ends since it must be between two other figures. Taking them together shows

that the green figure must be the central figure; there must be two figures to the left of the green figure and two figures to the right of it.

6. **(A)** Angle ABC is an angle inscribed in a semicircle. An inscribed angle cuts off an arc with twice the degree measure of the angle. If the angle cuts off a semicircle, whose arc measures 180°, the angle is a right angle. Thus, (1) is sufficient. That (2) is not sufficient is shown by the following figures:

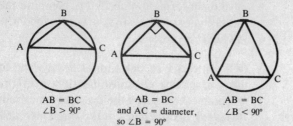

AB = BC	AB = BC	AB = BC
∠B > 90°	and AC = diameter,	∠B < 90°
	so ∠B = 90°	

7. **(E)** This is the sort of problem in which it is particularly important to analyze what sort of information would be required to answer the question before doing any computation or detailed analysis. Since the original information gives data about the length of the trip and asks about the percentage of capacity to which the tank is filled, you will need to link these two ideas in order to answer the question. In order to know what percentage of the tank is full, you will need to know the amount of gas in the tank and the total capacity of the tank. Nowhere in the problem is there the slightest information that gives you the total capacity of the tank. Nor is there any information that would allow you to deduce the final percentage of the starting percentage, though (2) does take one step along that path. (1) allows the calculation that the tank contains 10 gallons less $(\frac{150}{15})$ at the end of the trip than at the beginning, but since the original amount of gas is unknown, the answer to final percentage filled is unobtainable.

8. **(D)** The original information gives one equation: The total of the three is $240. There are three unknowns, so the addition of two more equations in a situation where the variables are not cross-multiplied or

raised to a power will give three equations and three unknowns, which can be solved. Propositions (1) and (2) each give the required two additional equations. As long as the equations are different, this will be sufficient.

9. **(B)** In order to find angle SQR, either the whole of angle PQR must be found so that x can be substracted from it to give the desired answer, or the angle QSR must be found so that the three angles of the right-hand triangle can be added together to make 180°, thus permitting the calculation of angle SQR. Although PS = SR, there is no reason to believe that QS is perpendicular to PR. Point Q could be moved up and down line QR (QR could be lengthened or shortened) without affecting the fact that PS = SR. However, once (2) tells you what y is, angle QSR can be found by substracting y from 180°, since those two angles together make up a straight line. Once QSR is found (it is 100°, though you wouldn't even need to compute it), SQR can be found from ∠QSR + ∠SQR + 30° = 180°. Thus, (2) is sufficient by itself. (1) by itself does not address either of the two issues identified at the beginning of this discussion. Knowing just a part of angle PQR does not permit the calculation of the other part without further information. Thus, (1) is not sufficient by itself. Identifying at the beginning the kind of information that is most likely to help would direct your attention to (2) first and reduce your chances of mistakenly calling this a (C).

10. **(A)** In order to find the perimeter of a square, you need to know the length of a side. In a coordinate geometry situation, some information is known from the conventions of the graph. For instance, the x-axis, part of which forms one of the sides of the square, has a y-coordinate of 0. Furthermore, since the figure is a square, the line QP is perpendicular to the x-axis. As a vertical line, every point on it will have the same x-coordinate, and the distance along the line can be found directly from the y-coordinate. (1) is sufficient because knowing that the y-coordinate of P is 0 from the

diagram and the y-coordinate of Q is 6 from the proposition permits the deduction that the length of PQ is 6. PQRS is then a square with a side of 6, whose perimeter would be (6)(4) or 24. (2) is not sufficient because knowing how far the square is from the y-axis is of no help in determining the length of a side.

11. **(E)** The question asks for the actual dimensions of the land itself. Given that the land is rectangular, knowing the width and length would be sufficient to answer the question. Neither statement alone nor both statements together provide this information. (1) is clearly insufficient since it does not give us the actual measurement of either the length or the width. (2) alone is insufficient since it does not tell us the legnth or width of the figure on the map. Even using both together, we are still lacking a critical piece of information: the length and width (either of the figure or the plot of land).

12. **(B)** Like most shaded-area problems, this one shows a shaded area that must be understood as the difference between two other areas, in this case, the difference between the two circles. The area of a circle depends on the radius of the circle; thus, you need information about the two radii. (2) is clearly sufficient by itself since knowing the radii of the circles will give you the means to compute their areas and the difference in the areas. Proposition (1) is a little trickier. Knowing the width of the shaded area might seem helpful, but it is not sufficient. Imagine the area of a 3-foot edge running around a circular field 100 yards across. Compare that to the area of a 3-foot edge running around a circular garden 10 feet across. The areas of the two edges are clearly not the same, even though they are the same width.

13. **(D)** In this particular problem, the fact that you are shown a set of coordinate axes is *almost* besides the point. The fact that helps is that the angle between the two axes is 90°. Using the rule about vertical or opposite angles being equal, all the x's and y's can be put in the same quadrant.

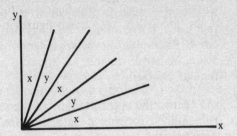

Thus 3x + 2y = 90. One further equation, such as given by either proposition, will permit the solution for the value of x, though you would not actually need to compute it.

14. **(D)** Asking whether $\frac{p}{4}$ is an integer is the same as asking whether p has a factor of 4. In proposition (1), saying that $\frac{p}{424}$ *is* an integer is saying that p *does* have a factor of 424. The only remaining question is whether having a factor of 424 implies having a factor of 4. Since (106)(4) = 424, the answer is yes. Thus (1) does prove that $\frac{p}{4}$ is an integer. (2) works exactly the same way since (106,106) (4) = 424,424.

15. **(C)** Since all of the angles in the figure are right angles, you do know that the larger figure is a larger rectangle with a smaller rectangular chunk taken out of it. You are given the dimensions of the larger rectangle in the diagram, and (1) and (2) together give the dimensions of the smaller rectangle. You have no reason to suppose that the dimensions of the two rectangles are proportional to each other, unless the propositions happen to say so. Therefore, both propositions taken together are needed.

16. **(D)** The essence of a circle is that all of the points on the circle are the same distance from the circle's center. In order for a polygon to have all of its vertices lying on a circle, there must be enough symmetry in the polygon for all of the vertices to be equally distant from some point, the center of the circle. While it is true that there are many types of polygons that can be inscribed in a circle, you are not actually being asked for a general description of all those polygons. Both propositions describe a situation

in which polygon P is totally regular and thus totally symmetrical. This leads to the insight that such polygons can be inscribed in a circle. Examples of regular polygons include an equilateral triangle, a square, and a regular pentagon.

17. **(A)** Since the problem involves exponents, you will be concerned with the effects of positive and negative bases, and with the rule that a base raised to an even exponent is definitely positive if the base is not zero. Since the bases are not zero, the first step is to see if there are any even exponents. The q and s terms have even exponents and thus they will be positive no matter what the bases are. This means that you do not need any further information about q and s. Thus (2) is unnecessary and insufficient. (1) does give you information about the signs of the two remaining variables and is sufficient. It is worth noting that this is one of the few problems you will see in which the final answer to a yes/no question is no. According to (1), p and r are negative. Thus, the top and bottom of the fraction shown will each be negative, and the overall fraction will therefore be positive until the negative sign in front of the fraction is taken into account. This makes that total number inside the brackets negative, and a negative to an odd-numbered exponent will be negative.

18. **(A)** Using the general rule that when you see algebraic expressions of this type in factors you should expand them (unless there is an obvious way to use them as they are), you find that the original question becomes:

$$(a^2 + 2ab + b^2) - (a^2 - 2ab + b^2)$$
$$= a^2 + 2ab + b^2 - a^2 + 2ab - b^2$$
$$= 4ab.$$

This makes it clear that (1) is sufficient. (2) is not sufficient because knowing the sum of two numbers does not tell you their product or the difference between them. If $a + b = 9$, there are still many possible pairs of a and b which satisfy the equation, all of which give different results to $a - b$.

19. **(E)** This is a problem that could easily use up a lot of your time if you let it. Your

original information is that there are three numbers, x, a, and b, each being an integer from 0 through 9 and satisfying the following conditions.:

$$x + a + b + x = 24$$
$$x + b = 13$$
$$x + a = 11$$

At first there seem to be three equations and three unknowns, which would be sufficient. However, the bottom two equations together amount to a restatement of the first equation. Thus there are not really three different equations The only remaining hope for a solution would be some effect of limiting the situation because the digits must be between 0 and 9. If $x + b$ had equalled 18, for instance, this would have permitted only one solution, $x = 9$ and $b = 9$. However, since the sums are ones that permit many solutions, and indeed many overlapping solutions, there is no definite final answer. For example:

$x + b = 13$		$X + a = 11$	
7	7	7	4
8	6	8	3,
etc.		etc.	

20. **(B)** Since the original question is about the ratio of the runners' times, (2) will suffice. The total time for each runner can be computed from the number of laps run times the average speed per lap. You know the number of laps from the original information: total distance divided by distance per lap. (1) will not suffice because it leaves open the issue of how long it takes Y to complete the final two laps. If there were additional information to the effect that Y had run the final two laps at the same average pace as the first part of the race, then a ratio of times could be inferred. But the actual situation is not sufficient.

21. **(C)** The simple properties of odd and even addition and multiplication are needed for this problem. There is no original information, so the starting possibilities are that none, one, two, or three of the numbers may be even. (1) can only work if there are no even numbers or two even numbers. (2) means that in each possible pairing of the

three numbers there is at least one even number. That means that there are either two or three even numbers. Neither proposition is sufficient by itself, but between them they only permit the possibility that there are two even numbers and one odd number.

22. **(C)** Knowing only one side of a right triangle does not permit the calculation of the other sides of the triangle unless the angle are in a special ratio (e.g., 30-60-90- or 90-45-45). This is true even when the side that is known is the hypotenuse. Thus, knowing the hypotenuse to be 5 does *not* mean that the only possible values for the other two sides are 3 and 4. For example, x and y could equal $\sqrt{15}$ and $\sqrt{10}$, respectively. This would satisfy the Pythagorean equation $(\sqrt{15})^2 + (\sqrt{10})^2 = 5^2$; $15 + 10 = 25$. The special virtue of the 3-4-5 right triangle is that it is the only *integral* solution when the hypotenuse is 5.

23. **(B)** In order to determine whether a point is on a circle, you will need to determine whether its distance from the center of the circle equals the length of the radius. In a plane, which we can assume here, all of the points that are 1 radius from the center of the circle must lie on the circle. (1) tells you that the distance from P to Q is equal to a radius. However, Q is not the center of the circle, so this does not help. The situation could be like this:

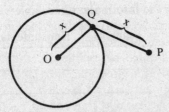

(2) is more powerful. If PQO is an equilateral triangle, PQ = PO = QO. Since Q is on the circle and O is the center of the circle, QO is a radius. Thus, PO is also a radius and P is one radius in distance from the center of the circle, which is all that was needed to answer the original question.

24. **(A)** Since the diagram shows point Q to lie in the upper right-hand quadrant, both c

and d must be positive numbers. Similarly, point P, being in the lower left-hand quadrant, implies that both a and b must be negative numbers. (1) gives the information that $a^2 = c^2$ and $b^2 = d^2$. Taking the square root of both sides means that $a = \pm c$ and $b = \pm d$. Since we know the actual signs from the diagram, we can limit that further and deduce that $a = -c$ and $b = -d$. This makes P and Q symmetrical points in relation to the origin, and thus the distance from P to O is equal to the distance from O to Q. You could also use the distance formula for coordinate geometry to determine the lengths of the two line segments, but that is unnecessary computational work. (2) does not address the problem of the lengths of the two segments and thus is insufficient.

25. **(D)** This problem is largely a matter of getting the original information sorted out correctly. The original sentences are equivalent to saying:

$$s < r, u < r, s \leqslant t$$

Adding (1) tells us that u is less than t because it establishes the relationships:

$$u < r < t$$

(2) is also sufficient because it establishes the relationships:

$$u < s \leqslant t$$

Section VI

1. **(C)** This question asks about rate: given a certain rate of operation, how many units will be produced during a certain period? The machine operates at the rate of 8 toys every 4 seconds, or 2 toys every second, which is equal to 120 per minute. Therefore, in 2 minutes, the machine will produce twice that number or 240 toys.

2. **(A)** This question asks about an average. If yearly sales for the business were $150,000, then the monthly average was $150,000 divided by 12, or $12,500. The question then

asks for the June sales, given that sales that month were half the monthly average for the year. Since the monthly average for the year was $12,500 and since June sales were half that, June sales must have been $6,250.

3. **(A)** To answer the question you need to create the fraction: red carnations/total flowers. Substituting the numbers provided, the fraction becomes: $\frac{12}{54} = \frac{2}{9}$. And $\frac{2}{9}$ is equal to $22\frac{2}{9}\%$.

4. **(B)** Perhaps the easiest way to solve this question is to substitute the values given in the Roman-numeraled statements back into the equation given in the question stem. As for I, -2 does not work as a value for x because $-2 - 2 = -4$, which when cubed is not equal to 8. As for II, $0 - 2$, when cubed is -8 not $+8$. III, however, is a possible value. $+4 - 2 = 2$, and 2 to the third power is 8. So the correct answer is III only.

5. **(C)** Here is a question that can be solved in relatively easy fashion by setting the given information into algebraic form. The question stem states that 40% of the total number of students are girls, which means that 60% of the students are boys. Then, given that there are 120 boys, we can write: .60 of Total = 120 or

$$.60T = 120$$
$$T = \frac{120}{.60}$$
$$T = 200$$

So there are 200 students in the school.

6. **(D)** This question can be solved with a little common sense. We know the cost of the most expensive and the least expensive types of nuts. The cost of the other three must be between $1.40 and $3.20 for x pounds. What is the least we could expect to pay for x pounds of each type? Well, assume that the other three cost $1.41 per x pounds: $1.40 + $1.41 + $1.41 + $1.41 + $3.20 = $8.83. This shows that (A), (B) and (C) are incorrect. Next, what is the most you could expect to pay for x pounds of each type? Now assume that the other three cost $3.19 per x pounds:

$3.20 + $3.19 + $3.19 + $3.19 + $1.40 = $14.17. Thus, we eliminate (E). The correct choice is (D) since $13.60 is in the range between $8.83 and $14.17.

7. **(D)** Translated into algebra, the question reads:

$$x(x) - x(x - 1) = 4$$
$$x^2 - x^2 + x = 4$$
$$x = 4$$

8. **(B)** The following picture of a rectangular solid may help you understand the solution:

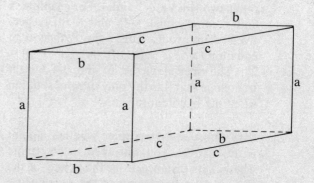

Notice that the solid has 4 edges labeled a, 4 labeled b, and 4 labeled c. The total is 4a + 4b + 4c. If we factor out 4, we can rewrite this as 4(a + b + c), and this can be read as saying that the total is always a multiple of 4.

9. **(A)** This question can be solved by organizing the information in a table:

	Students	Nonstudents	Total
Women			
Men			
Total			

Entering information:

	Students	Nonstudents	Total
Women	6		12
Men			
Total	24		32

Deducing our further conclusions:

	Students	Nonstudents	Total
Women	6	6	12
Men	18	2	20
Total	24	8	32

The table shows that 2 of the persons at the party were men who were not students.

10. **(C)** This question can be solved algebraically. We know that the original investment plus interest earned equals $781.00:

Original Investment + Interest = $781.00

But how much interest was earned? We know that the money earned 4 years of interest at 10.5%, which is $4 \times 10.5 = 42\%$ total interest. So Interest = .42 × Original Investment. Using this, we rewrite our original equation:

Original Investment + 42% of Original Investment = $781
Original Investment + .42 × Original Investment = $781
$$1.42 \text{ OI} = \$781$$
$$\text{OI} = \tfrac{\$781}{1.42}$$
$$\text{OI} = \$550$$

11. **(E)** We calculate the charges as follows. The first $\tfrac{1}{9}$ mile costs x cents. Every additional $\tfrac{1}{9}$ miles costs $\tfrac{x}{5}$ cents. In y miles there are 9y $\tfrac{1}{9}$'s of a mile, but we take away the first $\tfrac{1}{9}$ (which costs x cents) to find how much the additional mileage will cost:

$$9y - 1(\tfrac{x}{5}) = \frac{9xy - x}{5}$$

This is the cost of the additional mileage after the first $\tfrac{1}{9}$ mile. Now we add in the x cents for the first $\tfrac{1}{9}$ mile:

$$x + \frac{9xy - x}{5}$$

12. **(D)** Although the subject matter of this question involves physics, no knowledge of physics is needed to answer it. Instead, you need only to substitute the numbers into the formula provided and solve for the missing variable:

$$v^2 = 2ad$$
$$(20)^2 = 2\,(10)\,d$$
$$400 = 20d$$
$$d = 20$$

So the object traveled 20 meters.

13. **(D)** The key to this question is the peculiar interrelationships of the 30-60-90 triangle. In such a triangle, the side opposite the 60° angle is equal to $\frac{\sqrt{3}}{2}$ times the length of the hypotenuse:

$$h \times \frac{\sqrt{3}}{2} = 3$$
$$h = 3 \times \frac{2}{\sqrt{3}}$$
$$h = \frac{6}{\sqrt{3}} = 2\sqrt{3}$$

So each side of the quadrilateral had a length of $2\sqrt{3}$, so the perimeter of the figure is $4 \times 2\sqrt{3} = 8\sqrt{3}$.

14. **(B)** This question asks you to combine two work rates:

Rate 1 + Rate 2 = Combined Rate

Using the rates provided in the question stem:

$$\frac{x}{30} \text{ minutes} + \frac{x}{60} \text{ minutes} = \frac{x}{k} \text{ minutes}$$

(where the unknown k is the solution to the problem.) Finding a common denominator and adding the fractions on the left:

$$\frac{2x + x}{60} = \frac{x}{k}$$

Cross-multiplying:

$$k = \frac{60x}{3x} = 20$$

So together the two machines will sort x letters in 20 minutes.

15. **(B)** You don't need any fancy formulas to attack this problem. If we start with 80 liters

of a mixture that is 10% X and 90% Y, we have 8 liters of X and 72 liters of Y. If we add 20 liters of X, we end up with 28 liters of X and 72 liters of Y, for a total of 100 liters of the mixture. Since 28 out of the 100 liters of mixture are X, we have a mixture that is $\frac{28}{100}$ or 28% X.

16. **(C)** The best way to attack this question is to see that the shaded area of the figure can be analyzed into two figures—a rectangle and a triangle:

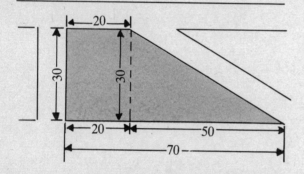

The area of the rectangle is $30 \times 20 = 600$, and the area of the triangle is $\frac{1}{2}(30)(50) = 750$. So the area of the composite figure is 1350.

17. **(A)** Perhaps the easiest way to attack this question is to write out in math what is said in English. The average of the five numbers is their sum divided by 5:

$$\frac{x + 24 + 96 + 48 + 32}{5} = \text{Average}$$

$$\frac{x + 200}{5} = \text{Average}$$

But the question asks: average/sum is equal to what? So we make a fraction with the average as the numerator and the sum as the denominator:

$$\frac{\frac{x + 200}{5}}{x + 200} = \frac{x + 200}{5} \cdot \frac{1}{x + 200} = \frac{1}{5}$$

And $\frac{1}{5}$ is equal to 20%.

Another way of attacking the question is to reason that the average is $\frac{1}{5}$ of the sum of the numbers, or 20%.

18. **(B)** This question is really a question about how to weight the two numbers. And to answer the question we need only a ratio, not the actual numbers involved. We are told that 70% of a number and 80% of a number, when averaged, is equal to 78% of the two numbers combined:

$$.70x + .80y = .78(x + y)$$
$$.70x + .80y = .78x + .78y$$
$$.02y = .08x$$
$$\frac{.02}{.08} = \frac{x}{y}$$
$$\frac{x}{y} = \frac{1}{4}$$

19. **(A)** Perhaps the "slickest" way to answer this question is just to test answer choices. Start with choice (C). Assume that the usual selling price is $40. On that assumption, a discount of 25% would yield a sale price of $40 − .25($40) = $40 − $10 = $30. But that is a loss—not a profit at all. This proves that (C) is incorrect, but which choice should we test next: (B) or (D)? Since an assumed price of $40 resulted in a loss, our initial assumption was too low. So we try a higher number, or (B). Assuming that the usual price is $42, the sale price will be $42 − .25($42) = $42 − $10.50 = $31.50. Again a loss rather than a profit. So (A) must, by the process of elimination, be correct. And you do not even need to test (A)—unless you are still not persuaded: $48 − .25($48) = $48 − $12 = $36. And that would be a $4 profit, or expressed as a percentage of cost, $\frac{\$4}{\$32} = \frac{1}{8} = .125 = 12.5\%$.

20. **(D)** A picture should make this question more manageable:

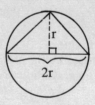

Here we have an isoceles right triangle inscribed in a circle. Notice that the height of the triangle is also the radius of the circle. So using r as the radius, we have:

$$\frac{\text{Area Circle}}{\text{Area Triangle}} = \frac{\pi r^2}{\frac{1}{2}(r)(2r)} = \frac{\pi r^2}{r^2} = \pi$$

Section VII

1. **(E)** This question is primarily a matter of careful reading. The phrase "no lower bus fares" must not be read to mean that Flash uniquely has the lowest fare; it means only that no one else has a fare lower than that of Flash. It is conceivable that several companies share the lowest fare. So II is not inconsistent with the claim made in the advertisement. III is not inconsistent since it mentions the New York City to Boston route, and it is the Washington, D.C. to New York City route that is the subject of the ad's claim. Finally, I is not inconsistent since it speaks of an *air* fare and the ad's language carefully restricts the claim to *bus* fares.

2. **(D)** We take the first three propositions together and ignore the fourth since we are to assume it is false. Roberts cannot be convicted without Edwards' testimony (I), but that testimony will show that Edwards participated in the crime (II). But if Edwards participated in the crime, Roberts cannot be convicted of it because he is accused of a crime that can be committed only by a person acting alone (III). Either Edwards will testify or Edwards will not testify—that is a tautology (logically true). If Edwards testifies, according to our reasoning, Roberts cannot be convicted. If Edwards does not testify, Roberts cannot be convicted (I). Either way, Roberts will not be convicted. (E) cannot be correct since we have no way of knowing, as a matter of logic, whether Edwards will or will not testify. We know only that *if* he does, certain consequences will follow, and *if* he does not, other consequences will follow. (A) can be disregarded since the crime is one that only a solo actor can commit (III). (C) is incorrect because we have proved that, regardless of Edwards' course of action, Roberts cannot be convicted. Finally, (B) is a logical *possibility*, which is not precluded by the given information, but we cannot logically deduce it from the information given.

3. **(B)** Examine carefully the connection between II and IV. Suppose Edwards testifies. His testimony will show he too has committed some wrong (II); but when the jury learns this, they will not believe any part of that testimony (IV), which means that they will not believe Edwards committed the wrong—a contradiction. Since II and IV cannot both be true at the same time, the scenario they describe is an impossible one—like saying a circle is a square. The remaining answers are all distractions.

4. **(E)** In the very first sentence, the author remarks that this is "curious" and a "contradiction," so the only correct answer choice will be one that follows up on this idea as (E) does when it speaks of *paradox*. Nothing that precedes the blank suggests that the author is speaking of "beauty" or "tragedy," so (A) and (B) can be disregarded. As for (C), the passage does speak about death, but not of death's inevitability; rather it dwells on death under certain circumstances that may not be inevitable. As for (D), while death may characterize human existence, the kind of death mentioned—self-sacrifice—is not indicated to be an inherent part of all human life.

5. **(C)** The author is explaining why the sacrifice is meaningless. From three different perspectives, he shows that it can have no value. The community does not win, because both lives were equally important. The lover who is saved does not profit, and that is shown by the fact that he would be perfectly willing to do the transaction the other way. If he has no preference (or even prefers the alternative outcome, his death), it cannot be said that he benefited from the exchange of lives. Finally, the need to prove that the action has no value to the heroine: He says she does not benefit because she is not in a position to enjoy or savor, or whatever, her heroism. The reason for that is that she is *dead* (C), not dying (A), for dying would leave open the possibility that her sacrifice would bring her joy in her last minutes, and then the author's contention that the transaction has *no* value would be weakened. (D) is wrong, for it is specifically stated that she is a heroine, so it is an inappropriate *completion* of the sentence.

(B) and (E) may both be true, but they do not explain why the action has no value to anyone.

6. **(A)** The main point of the passage is that pregnancy and a child put strain on a young marriage, and so such marriages would have a higher survival rate without the strain of children. It would seem, then, that encouraging such couples not to have children would help them stay married; but that will be possible only if they have not already committed themselves, so to speak, to having a child. If the wife is already pregnant at the time of marriage, the commitment has already been made, so the advice is too late. (B) and (C) are wrong for similar reasons. It is not only the continued presence of the child in the marriage that causes the stress but the very pregnancy and birth. So (B) and (C) do not address themselves to the *birth* of the child, and that is the factor to which the author attributes the dissolution of the marriage. (D) is wide of the mark. Whether society does or does not have such an interest, the author has shown us a causal linkage, that is, a mere fact of the matter. He states: If this, then fewer divorces. He may or may not believe there should be fewer divorces. (E) is wrong for this reason also, and for the further reason that it says "do not *plan*" to have children. The author's concern is with children during the early part of the marriage. He does not suggest that couples should never have children.

7. **(D)** Peter's surprise is over the fact that an important executive of a company would use a competitor's product, hence (D). (B) is wrong because Peter's surprise is not that Mary is unimportant; rather he knows Mary is important, and that is the reason for surprise. (E) is irrelevant to the exchange, for Peter imagines that regardless of taste, Mary ought to consume the product she is responsible in part for producing. The same reasoning can be applied to (C). Finally, (A) is a business distraction. It has business overtones, but it is important to always keep in mind that this section, like all sections of the GMAT, tests reasoning and reading abilities—not knowledge of business.

8. **(C)** The dispute here is over the motivation to compete seriously in intramural sports. Erika claims it is a sense of responsibility to one's fellows; Nichol argues it is a desire to win. But the two may actually support one another. In what way could one possibly let his fellows down? If the sport was not competitive, it would seem there would be no opportunity to disappoint them. So the desire to win contributes to the desire to be an effective member of the team. Nothing in the exchange presupposes anything about the structure of such programs beyond the fact that they are competitive, that is, that they have winners and losers. How many such programs exist, how they are funded, and similar questions are irrelevant, so both (A) and (B) are incorrect. (D) is close to being correct, but it calls for a survey of *deans*. The dean is probably not in a position to describe the motivation of the *participants*. Had (D) specified participants, it too would have been a correct answer. Of course, only one answer can be correct on the GMAT. Finally, (E) must be wrong for the reason cited in explaining (D); it should be possible to find out about the motivation.

9. **(C)** Clark was unhappy if he had a clear conscience but knew, or Clark was happy if he knew but had an unclear conscience. It is not the case that Clark was unhappy, so he must have been happy. Since he knew, however, his happiness must stem from an unclear conscience. (A), (D), and (E) are incorrect because they make irrelevant value judgments. As was just shown, the author's point can be analyzed as a purely logical one. (B) is just distraction, playing on the connection between "governess" and "servant," which, of course, are not the same thing.

10. **(A)** The author's point depends on the *assumption* that children see both animated features and "spaghetti Westerns." Obviously, if that assumption is untrue, he cannot claim that his conclusion follows. It may be true that children get a distorted picture of the world from other causes, but the author has not claimed that. He claims only that it comes from their seeing ani-

mated features and "spaghetti Westerns." Presumably, the two different treatments cause the inversion of values. The intention of the producers in making the films is irrelevant since an action may have an effect not intended by the actor. Hence, II would not touch the author's point. Further, that there are other sources of information that present a proper view of the world does not prove that the problem cited by the author does not produce an inverted view of the world. So III would not weaken his point.

11. **(E)** The point of the passage is that there is a seeming contradiction in our body of laws. Sometimes a person pays for his attempted misdeeds, and other times he does not pay for them. If there could be found a good reason for this difference, then the contradiction could be explained away. This is just what (E) does. It points out that the law treats the situations differently because it has different goals: Sometimes we drive fast because we are in a hurry; other times we drive slowly because we want to enjoy the scenery. (B) would not weaken the argument, for it only intensifies the contradiction. (D) makes an attempt to reconcile the seemingly conflicting positions by hinting at a possible goal of one action that is not a goal of the other. But, if anything, it intensifies the contradiction because one might infer that we should not try persons for attempted crimes because criminal trials are expensive, yet we should allow compensation for attempted frauds because civil trials are less expensive. (C) and (A) are just distractions. Whether there are more of one kind of law than another on the books has nothing to do with the seeming contradiction. And whether persons are more likely to commit a second crime after they are released from prison does not speak to the issue of whether an unsuccessful attempt to commit a crime should be a crime in the first place.

12. **(A)** The question stem asks us to focus on the "dispute" between the two opponents. What will be relevant to it will be those items that affect the merits of the issues, or perhaps those that affect the credibility of the parties. (C) and (E) both mention items—facts and their sources—that would be relevant to the substantive issues. (B) and (D) are legitimate attempts to clarify the issues and so are relevant. (A) is not relevant to the issues, nor is it relevant to the credibility (e.g., where did the facts come from) of the debaters. (A) is the least relevant because it is an ad hominem attack (an attack on the person and not on an argument).

13. **(A)** The point of the passage is that artists see things as they really are, whereas politicians see things as they want them to be. (B) is wrong, for, if anything, it is the politicians who see things through rose-colored glasses, whereas the artists see the truth of a stark reality. (C) can be overruled, for the passage implies that political leaders are responsive to the needs of people—it is just that they are a little late. Moreover, the point of the passage is to draw a contrast between artists and politicians; and even if the conclusion expressed in (C) is arguably correct, it is not as good an answer choice as (A), which *completes* the comparison. (D) has no ground in the passage. Be careful not to move from an analysis of facts—artists saw the problems earlier than the politicians did—to a conclusion of value or policy—therefore we should turn out the politicians. The author may very well believe that as sad as these circumstances are, nothing can be done about them, e.g., things are bad enough with the politicians in charge, but they would be much worse with artists running things. (E) also finds no ground in the passage.

14. **(B)** The argument for consistency is that it avoids the danger that actions will be misinterpreted. If a parent is overly generous, a child will think the parent will always be generous, even when generosity is inappropriate. By the same token, if a parent does not draw the line until he is pushed to do so, the child will believe that he *forced* the parent's response. A parent, so goes the argument, should play it safe and leave himself a cushion. (D) makes an attempt to capture this thought but overstates the case.

The author implies only that this may show weakness, not that the child will necessarily exploit that weakness and certainly not that the child will exploit it violently. And if the author had intended that thought he surely would not have used the word *retaliate,* which implies a *quid pro quo.* Both (A) and (E) have no basis in the passage, and neither is relevant to the idea of rewards and punishments. (C) does treat the general idea of the passage, but if confuses the idea of weakness with the more specific notion of willingness to bargain.

15. **(D)** The key phrase in this paragraph is "beef costs more per pound than fish." A careful reading would show that (A) is in direct contradiction to the explicit wording of the passage. (B) cannot be inferred since the dietitian merely says, "I pay." Perhaps he intends to keep the price of a meal stable by cutting back in other areas. In any event, this is another example of not going beyond a mere factual analysis to generate policy recommendations (see #13) unless the question stem specifically invites such an extension, e.g., which of the following courses of action would the author recommend? (C) makes an unwarranted inference. From the fact that beef is more costly one would not want to conclude that it is more profitable. (E) is wrong for this reason also. (D) is correct because it focuses on the "per measure of protein," which explains why a fish meal will cost the dietitian more than a beef meal, even though fish is less expensive per pound.

16. **(B)** I would undermine the advertisement considerably. Since the point of the ad is that you will lose weight, any unforeseen effects that would make it impossible to lose weight would defeat the purposes of the program. II is less obvious, but it does weaken the ad somewhat. Although the ad does not specifically say you will be healthier for having enrolled in the program, surely the advantages of the program are less significant if you have to pay an additional, hidden cost, i.e., health. III, if anything, supports the advertisement. IV is irrelevant since the ad does not claim you will become too thin.

17. **(B)** This question is like one of those simple conversation questions: "X: All bats are mammals. Y: Not true, whales are mammals too." In this little exchange, Y misunderstands X to have said that "all mammals are bats." In the question, the objection must be based on a misunderstanding. The objector must think that the ad has claimed that the only cause of unhappiness, etc., is being overweight; otherwise he would not have offered his counterexample. (A) is wrong because the ad never takes a stand on the *causes* of overweight conditions—only on a possible cure. This reasoning invalidates (C) and (D) as well. (E) makes a similar error but about effects, not about causes. The ad does not say everyone who is unhappy in unattractive, or vice versa.

18. **(E)** The sample argument is a straightforward generalization: All observed S are P. X is an S. Therefore, X is P. Only (E) replicates this form. The reasoning in (A) is: "Some S are P. All M are S. (All swans are birds, which is a suppressed assumption.) Therefore, all M are P." That is like saying: "Some children are not well behaved. All little girls are children. Therefore, all little girls are not well behaved." (B), too, contains a suppressed premise. Its structure is: "All S are P. All S are M. (All ballets are theatrical productions, which is suppressed.) Therefore, all M are P." That is like saying "All little girls are human. Therefore, all humans are little girls." (C) is not a generalization at all. It takes a generalization and attempts to explain it by uncovering a causal linkage. (D) is simply a non sequitur. It moves from the universality of the *concept* of justice to the conclusion that justice is a *physical* trait of man.

19. **(D)** The author is attempting to argue that laws against suicide are legitimate. He argues against a simplistic libertarian position that says suicide hurts only the victim. The goal of the law, he argues, is not just to protect the victim from himself. A society passes such a law because it wants to underscore the importance of human life. Reading beyond the blank in the second

paragraph makes clear the author's views on the value of human life. (A) flies in the face of the explicit language of the passage. The author does not defend the law as being a deterrent to suicide. (B) might be something the author believes, but it is not something he develops in the passage. He is not concerned here with explaining how the laws came to be on the books; he is concerned only with defending them. If anything, (B) would be more appropriate in the context of an argument against such laws. (C) also is something the author may believe, but his defense of the suicide law is not that it protects liberties—only that it serves a function and does not interfere with constitutional liberties any more than laws that prohibit doing violence to others. (E) is wrong for the same reasons that (B) is wrong. It seems to belong more in the context of an argument against suicide laws.

20. **(B)** With the comments in #19 in mind, it is clear that (B) must be correct. The author wants to make the point that suicide is not a victimless crime; it affects a great many people—even, he claims, some who were never personally acquainted with the suicide. Again, reading the whole passage is helpful. (A) is a joke—obviously suicide does not lead to more serious crimes. That is like saying the death penalty is designed to rehabilitate the criminal. (C) simply focuses on the superficial content of the sentence: One, it's talking about church and state, so (C), which mentions sin, must be correct. (D) is wrong because the author is not concerned to defend the laws as deterrents to suicide, as we discussed in #19. Finally, (E) is irrelevant to the point that the entire community is affected by the death of any one of its members.

21. **(A)** (C) and (D) are wrong because they extrapolate without sufficient information. These are very much like answers (C) and (E) in #15. (E) contradicts the last given statement and so cannot be a conclusion of it. That would be like trying to infer "all men are mortal" from the premise that "no men are mortal." (B) commits an error by moving from "all S are P" to "all P are S."

Just because all racing engines have SFI does not mean that all SFIs are in racing engines. Some may be found in tractors and heavy-duty machinery.

27. **(E)** This is a very sticky question. The key here is to keep in mind that you are to pick the BEST answer, and sometimes you will not be very satisfied with any of them. Here (E) is correct by default of the others. (A) has some merit. After all, the economist really isn't very careful in his statement of his claim. He says "here we go again" when there is no evidence that we have ever been there before. But there is no particular term he uses that we could call ambiguous. (B) is wrong because, although the economist assumes some poeple take that position (otherwise, against whom he would be arguing), he does not imply that he alone thinks differently. (C) is like (A), a possible answer, but this interpretation requires additional information. You would have to have said to yourself. "Oh, I see that he is against it. He is probably saying this in an exasperated tone and in the context of a diatribe." If there were such additional information, you would be right, and (C) would be a good answer. But there isn't. (E) does not require this additional speculation and so is truer to the given information. (D) also would require speculation. (E) is not perfect, just BEST by comparison.

23. **(E)** The argument assumes that a right cannot exist unless it is recognized by the positive law of a society. Against this assumption, it can be argued that a right may exist even though there is no mechanism for protecting or enforcing it. That this is at least plausible has been illustrated by our own history, e.g., minority groups have often been denied rights. These rights, however, existed all the while—they were just not protected by the government. (A) is incorrect, for the proponent of the theory of natural rights cannot deny that some human beings do not have them. That would contradict the very definition of natural right on which he bases his claim. (B) is incorrect because it is not responsive to the argument. Even if (B) is true, the attacker of natural

rights still has his argument that there are no universally recognized rights, so there are no universal (natural) rights at all. (C), like (A), is inconsistent with the very idea of a "natural" right. (D) is incorrect because it does not respond to the attacker's claim that no one right is protected universally. Consistency or universality within one society does not amount to consistency or universality across all societies.

24. **(E)** The author is arguing that political parties in America are weak because there is no party unity. Because of this lack of unity, the party is unable to pass legislation. (E) would strengthen this contention. (E) provides an example of a government dominated by a single party (control of the presidency and both houses), yet the party is unable to pass its own legislation. (A) provides little, if any, support for the argument. If there are only 18 defectors out of a total of 67 party members, that does not show tremendous fragmentation. (B) is even weaker by the same analysis: 70 defectors out of a total of 305 party members. (C) is weak because it focuses on the minority party. (D) strengthens the argument less clearly than (E) because there are many possible explanations for the failure, e.g., a different party controlled the legislature.

25. **(C)** Here we are looking for the argument that will undermine the position taken by the paragraph. Remember that the ultimate conclusion of the paragraph is that this disunity is a weakness and that this prevents legislation from being passed. One very good way of attacking this argument is to attack the value judgment on which the conclusion is based: Is it good to pass the legislation? The author assumes that it would be better to pass the legislation. We could argue, as in (C), that members of the Congress should not pass legislation simply because it is proposed by the party leadership. Rather, the members should represent the views of their constituents. Then, if the legislation fails, it must be the people who did not want it. In that case, it is better not to pass the legislation. (A) does not undermine the argument. That members receive funding proves nothing about unity after elections. As for (B), this seems to strengthen rather than weaken the argument. The author's thesis argues that there is greater unity in the Senate than in the House. (D) would undermine the argument only if we had some additional information to make it relevant. Finally, (E) does not weaken the argument greatly. That some legislation is passed is not a denial of the argument that more should be passed.

ANSWER SHEET—PRACTICE EXAMINATION 5

SECTION I

1 Ⓐ Ⓑ Ⓒ Ⓓ Ⓔ	6 Ⓐ Ⓑ Ⓒ Ⓓ Ⓔ	11 Ⓐ Ⓑ Ⓒ Ⓓ Ⓔ	16 Ⓐ Ⓑ Ⓒ Ⓓ Ⓔ	21 Ⓐ Ⓑ Ⓒ Ⓓ Ⓔ
2 Ⓐ Ⓑ Ⓒ Ⓓ Ⓔ	7 Ⓐ Ⓑ Ⓒ Ⓓ Ⓔ	12 Ⓐ Ⓑ Ⓒ Ⓓ Ⓔ	17 Ⓐ Ⓑ Ⓒ Ⓓ Ⓔ	22 Ⓐ Ⓑ Ⓒ Ⓓ Ⓔ
3 Ⓐ Ⓑ Ⓒ Ⓓ Ⓔ	8 Ⓐ Ⓑ Ⓒ Ⓓ Ⓔ	13 Ⓐ Ⓑ Ⓒ Ⓓ Ⓔ	18 Ⓐ Ⓑ Ⓒ Ⓓ Ⓔ	23 Ⓐ Ⓑ Ⓒ Ⓓ Ⓔ
4 Ⓐ Ⓑ Ⓒ Ⓓ Ⓔ	9 Ⓐ Ⓑ Ⓒ Ⓓ Ⓔ	14 Ⓐ Ⓑ Ⓒ Ⓓ Ⓔ	19 Ⓐ Ⓑ Ⓒ Ⓓ Ⓔ	24 Ⓐ Ⓑ Ⓒ Ⓓ Ⓔ
5 Ⓐ Ⓑ Ⓒ Ⓓ Ⓔ	10 Ⓐ Ⓑ Ⓒ Ⓓ Ⓔ	15 Ⓐ Ⓑ Ⓒ Ⓓ Ⓔ	20 Ⓐ Ⓑ Ⓒ Ⓓ Ⓔ	25 Ⓐ Ⓑ Ⓒ Ⓓ Ⓔ

SECTION II

1 Ⓐ Ⓑ Ⓒ Ⓓ Ⓔ	5 Ⓐ Ⓑ Ⓒ Ⓓ Ⓔ	9 Ⓐ Ⓑ Ⓒ Ⓓ Ⓔ	13 Ⓐ Ⓑ Ⓒ Ⓓ Ⓔ	17 Ⓐ Ⓑ Ⓒ Ⓓ Ⓔ
2 Ⓐ Ⓑ Ⓒ Ⓓ Ⓔ	6 Ⓐ Ⓑ Ⓒ Ⓓ Ⓔ	10 Ⓐ Ⓑ Ⓒ Ⓓ Ⓔ	14 Ⓐ Ⓑ Ⓒ Ⓓ Ⓔ	18 Ⓐ Ⓑ Ⓒ Ⓓ Ⓔ
3 Ⓐ Ⓑ Ⓒ Ⓓ Ⓔ	7 Ⓐ Ⓑ Ⓒ Ⓓ Ⓔ	11 Ⓐ Ⓑ Ⓒ Ⓓ Ⓔ	15 Ⓐ Ⓑ Ⓒ Ⓓ Ⓔ	19 Ⓐ Ⓑ Ⓒ Ⓓ Ⓔ
4 Ⓐ Ⓑ Ⓒ Ⓓ Ⓔ	8 Ⓐ Ⓑ Ⓒ Ⓓ Ⓔ	12 Ⓐ Ⓑ Ⓒ Ⓓ Ⓔ	16 Ⓐ Ⓑ Ⓒ Ⓓ Ⓔ	20 Ⓐ Ⓑ Ⓒ Ⓓ Ⓔ

SECTION III

1 Ⓐ Ⓑ Ⓒ Ⓓ Ⓔ	6 Ⓐ Ⓑ Ⓒ Ⓓ Ⓔ	11 Ⓐ Ⓑ Ⓒ Ⓓ Ⓔ	16 Ⓐ Ⓑ Ⓒ Ⓓ Ⓔ	21 Ⓐ Ⓑ Ⓒ Ⓓ Ⓔ
2 Ⓐ Ⓑ Ⓒ Ⓓ Ⓔ	7 Ⓐ Ⓑ Ⓒ Ⓓ Ⓔ	12 Ⓐ Ⓑ Ⓒ Ⓓ Ⓔ	17 Ⓐ Ⓑ Ⓒ Ⓓ Ⓔ	22 Ⓐ Ⓑ Ⓒ Ⓓ Ⓔ
3 Ⓐ Ⓑ Ⓒ Ⓓ Ⓔ	8 Ⓐ Ⓑ Ⓒ Ⓓ Ⓔ	13 Ⓐ Ⓑ Ⓒ Ⓓ Ⓔ	18 Ⓐ Ⓑ Ⓒ Ⓓ Ⓔ	23 Ⓐ Ⓑ Ⓒ Ⓓ Ⓔ
4 Ⓐ Ⓑ Ⓒ Ⓓ Ⓔ	9 Ⓐ Ⓑ Ⓒ Ⓓ Ⓔ	14 Ⓐ Ⓑ Ⓒ Ⓓ Ⓔ	19 Ⓐ Ⓑ Ⓒ Ⓓ Ⓔ	24 Ⓐ Ⓑ Ⓒ Ⓓ Ⓔ
5 Ⓐ Ⓑ Ⓒ Ⓓ Ⓔ	10 Ⓐ Ⓑ Ⓒ Ⓓ Ⓔ	15 Ⓐ Ⓑ Ⓒ Ⓓ Ⓔ	20 Ⓐ Ⓑ Ⓒ Ⓓ Ⓔ	25 Ⓐ Ⓑ Ⓒ Ⓓ Ⓔ

SECTION IV

1 Ⓐ Ⓑ Ⓒ Ⓓ Ⓔ	6 Ⓐ Ⓑ Ⓒ Ⓓ Ⓔ	11 Ⓐ Ⓑ Ⓒ Ⓓ Ⓔ	16 Ⓐ Ⓑ Ⓒ Ⓓ Ⓔ	21 Ⓐ Ⓑ Ⓒ Ⓓ Ⓔ
2 Ⓐ Ⓑ Ⓒ Ⓓ Ⓔ	7 Ⓐ Ⓑ Ⓒ Ⓓ Ⓔ	12 Ⓐ Ⓑ Ⓒ Ⓓ Ⓔ	17 Ⓐ Ⓑ Ⓒ Ⓓ Ⓔ	22 Ⓐ Ⓑ Ⓒ Ⓓ Ⓔ
3 Ⓐ Ⓑ Ⓒ Ⓓ Ⓔ	8 Ⓐ Ⓑ Ⓒ Ⓓ Ⓔ	13 Ⓐ Ⓑ Ⓒ Ⓓ Ⓔ	18 Ⓐ Ⓑ Ⓒ Ⓓ Ⓔ	23 Ⓐ Ⓑ Ⓒ Ⓓ Ⓔ
4 Ⓐ Ⓑ Ⓒ Ⓓ Ⓔ	9 Ⓐ Ⓑ Ⓒ Ⓓ Ⓔ	14 Ⓐ Ⓑ Ⓒ Ⓓ Ⓔ	19 Ⓐ Ⓑ Ⓒ Ⓓ Ⓔ	24 Ⓐ Ⓑ Ⓒ Ⓓ Ⓔ
5 Ⓐ Ⓑ Ⓒ Ⓓ Ⓔ	10 Ⓐ Ⓑ Ⓒ Ⓓ Ⓔ	15 Ⓐ Ⓑ Ⓒ Ⓓ Ⓔ	20 Ⓐ Ⓑ Ⓒ Ⓓ Ⓔ	25 Ⓐ Ⓑ Ⓒ Ⓓ Ⓔ

SECTION V

1 Ⓐ Ⓑ Ⓒ Ⓓ Ⓔ	5 Ⓐ Ⓑ Ⓒ Ⓓ Ⓔ	9 Ⓐ Ⓑ Ⓒ Ⓓ Ⓔ	13 Ⓐ Ⓑ Ⓒ Ⓓ Ⓔ	17 Ⓐ Ⓑ Ⓒ Ⓓ Ⓔ
2 Ⓐ Ⓑ Ⓒ Ⓓ Ⓔ	6 Ⓐ Ⓑ Ⓒ Ⓓ Ⓔ	10 Ⓐ Ⓑ Ⓒ Ⓓ Ⓔ	14 Ⓐ Ⓑ Ⓒ Ⓓ Ⓔ	18 Ⓐ Ⓑ Ⓒ Ⓓ Ⓔ
3 Ⓐ Ⓑ Ⓒ Ⓓ Ⓔ	7 Ⓐ Ⓑ Ⓒ Ⓓ Ⓔ	11 Ⓐ Ⓑ Ⓒ Ⓓ Ⓔ	15 Ⓐ Ⓑ Ⓒ Ⓓ Ⓔ	19 Ⓐ Ⓑ Ⓒ Ⓓ Ⓔ
4 Ⓐ Ⓑ Ⓒ Ⓓ Ⓔ	8 Ⓐ Ⓑ Ⓒ Ⓓ Ⓔ	12 Ⓐ Ⓑ Ⓒ Ⓓ Ⓔ	16 Ⓐ Ⓑ Ⓒ Ⓓ Ⓔ	20 Ⓐ Ⓑ Ⓒ Ⓓ Ⓔ

SECTION VI

1 Ⓐ Ⓑ Ⓒ Ⓓ Ⓔ	6 Ⓐ Ⓑ Ⓒ Ⓓ Ⓔ	11 Ⓐ Ⓑ Ⓒ Ⓓ Ⓔ	16 Ⓐ Ⓑ Ⓒ Ⓓ Ⓔ	21 Ⓐ Ⓑ Ⓒ Ⓓ Ⓔ
2 Ⓐ Ⓑ Ⓒ Ⓓ Ⓔ	7 Ⓐ Ⓑ Ⓒ Ⓓ Ⓔ	12 Ⓐ Ⓑ Ⓒ Ⓓ Ⓔ	17 Ⓐ Ⓑ Ⓒ Ⓓ Ⓔ	22 Ⓐ Ⓑ Ⓒ Ⓓ Ⓔ
3 Ⓐ Ⓑ Ⓒ Ⓓ Ⓔ	8 Ⓐ Ⓑ Ⓒ Ⓓ Ⓔ	13 Ⓐ Ⓑ Ⓒ Ⓓ Ⓔ	18 Ⓐ Ⓑ Ⓒ Ⓓ Ⓔ	23 Ⓐ Ⓑ Ⓒ Ⓓ Ⓔ
4 Ⓐ Ⓑ Ⓒ Ⓓ Ⓔ	9 Ⓐ Ⓑ Ⓒ Ⓓ Ⓔ	14 Ⓐ Ⓑ Ⓒ Ⓓ Ⓔ	19 Ⓐ Ⓑ Ⓒ Ⓓ Ⓔ	24 Ⓐ Ⓑ Ⓒ Ⓓ Ⓔ
5 Ⓐ Ⓑ Ⓒ Ⓓ Ⓔ	10 Ⓐ Ⓑ Ⓒ Ⓓ Ⓔ	15 Ⓐ Ⓑ Ⓒ Ⓓ Ⓔ	20 Ⓐ Ⓑ Ⓒ Ⓓ Ⓔ	25 Ⓐ Ⓑ Ⓒ Ⓓ Ⓔ

SECTION VII

1 Ⓐ Ⓑ Ⓒ Ⓓ Ⓔ	6 Ⓐ Ⓑ Ⓒ Ⓓ Ⓔ	11 Ⓐ Ⓑ Ⓒ Ⓓ Ⓔ	16 Ⓐ Ⓑ Ⓒ Ⓓ Ⓔ	21 Ⓐ Ⓑ Ⓒ Ⓓ Ⓔ
2 Ⓐ Ⓑ Ⓒ Ⓓ Ⓔ	7 Ⓐ Ⓑ Ⓒ Ⓓ Ⓔ	12 Ⓐ Ⓑ Ⓒ Ⓓ Ⓔ	17 Ⓐ Ⓑ Ⓒ Ⓓ Ⓔ	22 Ⓐ Ⓑ Ⓒ Ⓓ Ⓔ
3 Ⓐ Ⓑ Ⓒ Ⓓ Ⓔ	8 Ⓐ Ⓑ Ⓒ Ⓓ Ⓔ	13 Ⓐ Ⓑ Ⓒ Ⓓ Ⓔ	18 Ⓐ Ⓑ Ⓒ Ⓓ Ⓔ	23 Ⓐ Ⓑ Ⓒ Ⓓ Ⓔ
4 Ⓐ Ⓑ Ⓒ Ⓓ Ⓔ	9 Ⓐ Ⓑ Ⓒ Ⓓ Ⓔ	14 Ⓐ Ⓑ Ⓒ Ⓓ Ⓔ	19 Ⓐ Ⓑ Ⓒ Ⓓ Ⓔ	24 Ⓐ Ⓑ Ⓒ Ⓓ Ⓔ
5 Ⓐ Ⓑ Ⓒ Ⓓ Ⓔ	10 Ⓐ Ⓑ Ⓒ Ⓓ Ⓔ	15 Ⓐ Ⓑ Ⓒ Ⓓ Ⓔ	20 Ⓐ Ⓑ Ⓒ Ⓓ Ⓔ	25 Ⓐ Ⓑ Ⓒ Ⓓ Ⓔ

PRACTICE EXAMINATION 5

SECTION I

Time—30 Minutes
25 Questions

Directions: Each question below is followed by two numbered facts. You are to determine whether the data given in the statements is sufficient for answering the question. Use the data given, plus your knowledge of math and everyday facts, to choose between the five possible answers.

(A) if statement 1 alone is sufficient to answer the question, but statement 2 alone is not sufficient
(B) if statement 2 alone is sufficient to answer the question, but statement 1 alone is not sufficient
(C) if both statements together are needed to answer the question, but neither statement alone is sufficient
(D) if either statement by itself is sufficient to answer the question
(E) if not enough facts are given to answer the question

1. Exactly how many of the 18 persons on a college's debating team are seniors?
   (1) There are more than 14 seniors on the debating team.
   (2) The number of persons on the debating team who are not seniors is 3.

2. What percent is x of y?
   (1) 3x = 5y
   (2) y is 60% of x.

3. Which point, point P or point Q, is farther from the center of circle O?
   (1) Point P is inside circle O.
   (2) Point Q is outside circle O.

4. In the figure, **what is the value of x?**
   (1) y + z = 7
   (2) y = 5

5. The population of county X was 25,000 on January 1, 1976. During what year did its population reach 250,000?
   (1) The population doubled each year.
   (2) The population was 800,000 on January 1, 1981.

6. Marshall bought a set of encyclopedias on the installment plan. How much money does he still owe on the encyclopedias?
   (1) He has already paid $384.
   (2) He still owes 12 monthly payments of $36 dollars each.

7. What time will a watch show at noon on Wednesday if it loses x seconds every y hours?
   (1) x = 6
   (2) y = 24

8. At a graduation ceremony, 15 students received a total of 22 awards. How many students received exactly two awards?
   (1) Each of the students received at least one award.
   (2) Exactly three students received three awards each.

9. What is the value of the integer x?
   (1) x is an integral multiple of 3, 4, and 5
   (2) 50 < x < 70

10. A sealed tank is constructed so that liquid can be added to the tank only through pipe

X and taken from the tank only through pipe Y. If the tank contains 10,000 gallons of liquid, how long will it take to reduce the amount of liquid to 1200 gallons?
 (1) Pipe Y removes liquid from the tank 8 times faster than pipe X adds liquid to the tank.
 (2) Pipe X adds 50 gallons of liquid to the tank per minute while pipe Y removes 400 gallons of liquid from the tank per minute.

11. How long will it take machine M to fill an order for x widgets if the machine operates at a constant rate and operation is not interrupted?
 (1) The machine produces 150 widgets per minute.
 (2) At the end of 2 hours, the machine has produced 40% of the widgets needed to fill the order.

12. What is the total weight of four crates?
 (1) The average weight of each crate is 200 pounds.
 (2) The total weight of two of the crates is exactly three times the total weight of the other two crates.

13. Is x an integer?
 (1) $x > 0$
 (2) $x^2 - 1 = 0$

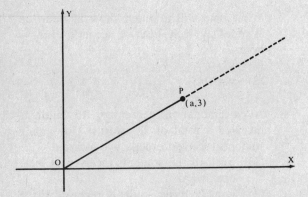

14. Line OP is drawn on the coordinate axes as shown. What is the value of a?
 (1) $OP = 6$
 (2) The angle formed by OP and the x-axis is 30°.

15. A rectangular piece of carpet of 200 square yards is cut into two pieces, and the smaller

piece is sold. What is the perimeter of the remaining piece?
 (1) The area of the remaining piece is 120 square yards.
 (2) The following figure is a diagram of the remaining piece

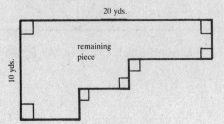

16. What is the value of $\frac{1}{x} + \frac{1}{y} + \frac{1}{z}$?
 (1) $\frac{xy + xz + yz}{xyz} = 4$
 (2) $x + y = 3$

17. How many times does Mary get paid in a certain year X?
 (1) Mary is paid every Friday.
 (2) The year X is a leap year.

18. How long did it take machine X to produce 1000 units?
 (1) Machine X produced the first 650 units in 2 hours and 30 minutes.
 (2) Machine X produced the last 650 units in 2 hours and 30 minutes.

19. How many of the 60 applicants for a job passed neither the physical nor the written exam?
 (1) Of the 60 applicants, exactly 10% passed both the physical and the written exams.
 (2) Of the 60 applicants, exactly 50% passed the physical exam, and exactly 20% passed the written exam.

20. The area of a circle is A and the circumference is C. What is the radius of the circle?
 (1) $\frac{A}{C} = \frac{3}{2}$
 (2) $A - C = 3\pi$

21. If polygons P and Q are each equilateral and equiangular, which has the greater area?
 (1) One side of P is equal in length to one side of Q.

(2) The sum of the interior angles of P is greater than the sum of the interior angles of Q.

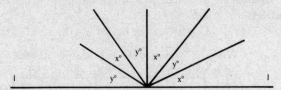

22. What is the value of x in the figure?
    (1) y = 30°
    (2) x + y = 60°

23. A piece of rectangular property with 750 feet of frontage along a road was subdivided. Into how many lots was the property subdivided?

(1) The original piece of property was 100 feet deep.
(2) Each resulting lot has a frontage along the road of 125 feet.

24. Can a circle be drawn so that its circumference includes all four vertices of quadrilateral Q?
    (1) Each angle of Q is 90°.
    (2) All four sides of Q are equal in length.

25. How many rigid rectangular boxes with a height of 8 inches and a width of 6 inches can be packed into a crate?
    (1) The inside dimensions of the crate are 6 feet by 8 feet by 4 feet.
    (2) The height of the crate is one-half the length and 2 feet less than the width.

STOP

END OF SECTION. IF YOU HAVE ANY TIME LEFT, GO OVER YOUR WORK IN THIS SECTION ONLY. DO NOT WORK IN ANY OTHER SECTION OF THE TEST.

SECTION II

Time—30 Minutes
20 Questions

Directions: For each of the following questions, select the best of the answer choices and blacken the corresponding space on your answer sheet.
Numbers: All numbers used are real numbers.
Figures: The diagrams and figures that accompany these questions are for the purpose of providing information useful in answering the questions. Unless it is stated that a specific figure is not drawn to scale, the diagrams and figures are drawn as accurately as possible. All figures are in a plane unless otherwise indicated.

1. Which of the following could be the measures of the sides of a single triangle?

    I.   3, 4, 5
    II. 5, 12, 18
    III. 3, 3, 3

    (A) I only
    (B) II only
    (C) III only
    (D) I and II only
    (E) I and III only

2. A deck of cards is 1.5 centimeters thick. If each of the cards is 0.03 centimeters thick, how many cards are in the deck?
    (A) 45
    (B) 50
    (C) 450
    (D) 500
    (E) 1500

3. A certain candy assortment contains only chocolates and caramels. If there are four times as many chocolates as caramels in the assortment, what fraction of the assortment is caramels?
    (A) $\frac{1}{5}$
    (B) $\frac{1}{4}$
    (C) $\frac{1}{2}$
    (D) $\frac{3}{4}$
    (E) $\frac{4}{5}$

4. Of a certain group of 100 people, 40 graduated from High School X, 65 graduated from College Y, and 30 live in City Z.

What is the greatest possible number of people in this group who did *not* graduate from High School X, did *not* graduate from College Y, *and* do *not* live in City Z?
    (A) 5
    (B) 15
    (C) 35
    (D) 65
    (E) 85

5. If $(x - 6)(2x + 1) = 0$, and $x > 0$, then $x =$
    (A) 6
    (B) 3
    (C) 2
    (D) $\frac{1}{2}$
    (E) $\frac{1}{6}$

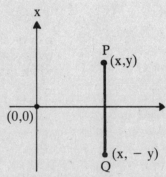

6. In the figure above, what are the coordinates of the midpoint of PQ?
    (A) (x,y)
    (B) (x,0)
    (C) (0,0)
    (D) (0,y)
    (E) (−x,−y)

7. At the beginning of a certain job, the counter on a photocopy machine read 1254. At the end of the job, the counter read 2334. If the running time for the job was 30 minutes, then what was the average operating speed of the machine in copies per *second*?
    (A) .6
    (B) 1.1
    (C) 6

(D) 36
(E) 2160

8. An elementary school had a total enrollment of 612 students on the first day of the school year. During the school year 31 students transferred out of the school. If on the last day of the school year the school had a total enrollment of 654 students, then how many new students enrolled in the school during the school year?
    (A) 11
    (B) 42
    (C) 73
    (D) 84
    (E) 115

9. A merchant makes a profit of $10 on a certain item. If the dollar cost of the item is a whole number, then which of the following could NOT represent her profit as a percentage of her cost?
    (A) 10%
    (B) 20%
    (C) 25%
    (D) 40%
    (E) 80%

10. If x is an even number, which of the following must be odd?

     I. $3x + 1$
     II. $5x^2 + 2$
     III. $(x + 1)^2$

     (A) I only
     (B) III only
     (C) I and II only
     (D) I and III only
     (E) I, II, and III

11. A salesclerk is paid a minimum weekly salary of $210 plus a commission equal to 10% of the value of sales she makes in excess of $3000 for the week. If the salesclerk wishes to earn at least $370 for a week, what is the minimum value of sales she must make for that week?
     (A) $1600
     (B) $3700
     (C) $4600
     (D) $6700
     (E) $6910

12. On Monday, a depositor withdraws funds from his savings account equal to 10% of the amount on deposit, and on Friday he deposits $140. If there were no other transactions, and if the amount in the account following Friday's transaction was 125% of the original amount, how much money was originally in the account?
     (A) $125
     (B) $175
     (C) $400
     (D) $500
     (E) $540

13. In a certain population, x of every y persons are found to have characteristic ϕ. If 200 persons were found to have characteristic ϕ, what is the total number of persons in the population?
     (A) 200x
     (B) 200y
     (C) $\dfrac{200x}{y}$
     (D) $\dfrac{200y}{x}$
     (E) $200(x - y)$

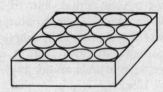

14. Sixteen cylindrical cans, each with a radius of 1 inch, are placed inside a rectangular cardboard box as shown above. If the cans touch adjacent cans and/or the walls of the box as shown, which of the following could be the interior area of the bottom of the box, expressed in square inches?
     (A) 16
     (B) 32
     (C) 64
     (D) 128
     (E) 256

15. In a certain shipment of 120 new cars, $\frac{2}{3}$ of the cars are equipped with radios and $\frac{2}{5}$ are equipped with air conditioners. If 20 of the cars are equipped with neither a radio nor with an air conditioner, how many cars in

the shipment are equipped with both a radio and an air conditioner?

(A) 20
(B) 28
(C) 32
(D) 58
(E) 76

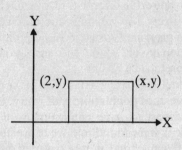

16. If the figure above is a rectangle, then what is the area of the figure, expressed in terms of x and y?

(A) xy
(B) 4xy
(C) xy²
(D) y(x − 2)
(E) x(y − 2)

17. Mr. Williams invested a total of $12,000 for a one-year period. Part of the money was invested at 5% simple interest, and the rest was invested at 12% simple interest. If he earned a total of $880 in interest for the year, how much of the money was invested at 12%?

(A) $1920
(B) $4000
(C) $4800
(D) $7200
(E) $8000

18. If xy = 10, what is the value of $(x + y)^2 - (x - y)^2$?

(A) 10

(B) 20
(C) 40
(D) 60
(E) It cannot be determined from the information given.

19. A candy bar originally costs x cents per y ounces. If the size of the candy bar is reduced by 1 ounce and the price is increased by 10%, what is the new cost of the candy bar, expressed in cents per ounce?

(A) $\dfrac{x - y}{10}$

(B) $\dfrac{11(x - y)}{10}$

(C) $\dfrac{11x}{10y}$

(D) $\dfrac{11x}{10(y-1)}$

(E) $\dfrac{11x}{1 - y}$

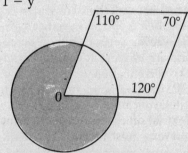

20. In the figure above, the circle O has a radius of 6. What is the area of the shaded portion of the figure?

(A) $\dfrac{\pi}{2}$

(B) $\dfrac{5\pi}{2}$

(C) 12π
(D) 18π
(E) 30π

STOP

END OF SECTION. IF YOU HAVE ANY TIME LEFT, GO
OVER YOUR WORK IN THIS SECTION ONLY. DO NOT
WORK IN ANY OTHER SECTION OF THE TEST.

SECTION III

Time—30 Minutes
25 Questions

Directions: Below each of the following passages, you will find questions or incomplete statements about the passage. Each statement or question is followed by lettered words or expressions. Select the word or expression that most satisfactorily completes each statement or answers each question in accordance with the meaning of the passage. After you have chosen the best answer, blacken the corresponding space on the answer sheet.

Desertification in the arid United States is flagrant. Groundwater supplies beneath vast stretches of land are dropping precipitously. Whole river systems have dried up; others are
5 choked with sediment washed from denuded land. Hundreds of thousands of acres of previously irrigated cropland have been abandoned to wind or weeds. Several million acres of natural grassland are eroding at unnaturally high rates as
10 a result of cultivation or overgrazing. All told, about 225 million acres of land are undergoing severe desertification.

Federal subsidies encourage the exploitation of arid land resources. Low-interest loans for irriga-
15 tion and other water delivery systems encourage farmers, industry, and municipalities to mine groundwater. Federal disaster relief and commodity programs encourage arid-land farmers to plow up natural grassland to plant crops such as
20 wheat and, especially, cotton. Federal grazing fees that are well below the free-market price encourage overgrazing of the commons. The market, too, provides powerful incentives to exploit arid land resources beyond their carrying
25 capacity. When commodity prices are high relative to the farmer's or rancher's operating costs, the return on a production-enhancing investment is invariably greater than the return on a conservation investment. And when commodity prices
30 are relatively low, arid land ranchers and farmers often have to use all of their available financial resources to stay solvent.

The incentives to exploit arid land resources are greater today than ever. The government is now
35 offering huge new subsidies to produce synfuel from coal or oil shale as well as alcohol fuel from

crops. Moreover, commodity prices are on the rise; and they will provide farmers and agribusiness with powerful incentive to overexploit arid
40 land resources. The existing federal government cost-share programs designed to help finance the conservation of soil, water, and vegetation pale in comparison to such incentives.

In the final analysis, when viewed in the national
45 perspective, the effects on agriculture are the most troublesome aspect of desertification in the United States, for it comes at a time when we are losing over a million acres of rain-watered crop and pasture land per year to "higher uses"—shopping
50 centers, industrial parks, housing developments, and waste dumps—heedless of the economic need of the United States to export agricultural products or of the world's need for U.S. food and fiber. Today the arid West accounts for 20% of the
55 nation's total agricultural output. If the United States is, as it appears, well on its way toward overdrawing the arid land resources, then the policy choice is simply to pay now for the appropriate remedies or pay far more later, when
60 productive benefits from arid land resources have been both realized and largely terminated.

1. The author is primarily concerned with
   (A) discussing a solution
   (B) describing a problem
   (C) replying to a detractor
   (D) finding a contradiction
   (E) defining a term

2. The passage mentions all of the following as effects of desertification EXCEPT
   (A) increased sediment in rivers
   (B) erosion of land
   (C) overcultivation of arid land
   (D) decreasing groundwater supplies
   (E) loss of land to wind or weeds

3. The author most likely encloses the phrase "higher uses" (line 49) in quotations marks in order to
   (A) alert the reader to the fact that the term is very important

(B) minimize the importance of desertification in non-arid land

(C) voice his support for expansion of such programs

(D) express concern over the extent of desertification

(E) indicate disagreement that such uses are more important

4. The passage mentions which of the following as tending to encourage desertification?

   I. High prices for certain commodities that provide incentives for farmers to use arid lands

   II. Low government fees for grazing on public lands

   III. The world's need for food and fiber produced by the United States

(A) I only

(B) II only

(C) III only

(D) I and II only

(E) I, II, and III

5. According to the passage, the most serious long-term effect of desertification would be the reduced ability of

(A) the United States to continue to export agricultural products

(B) municipalities to supply water to meet the needs of residents

(C) farmers to cover the cost of producing crops

(D) the United States to meet the food needs of its own people

(E) the United States to produce sufficient fuel for energy from domestic sources

6. The passage leads most logically to discussion of a proposal for

(A) reduced agricultural output in the United States

(B) direct government aid to farmers affected by desertification

(C) curtailing the conversion of land to shopping centers and housing

(D) government assistance to develop improved farming methods to increase exploitation of arid land

(E) increased government assistance to finance the conservation of arid land

7. The author's attitude toward desertification can best be described as one of

(A) alarm

(B) optimism

(C) understanding

(D) conciliation

(E) concern

8. The author implies that when commodity prices are low, ranchers and farmers do not invest in conservation because

(A) low prices discourage the cultivation of arid land

(B) they anticipate that prices will soon return to higher levels

(C) they lack the funds to make such investments when prices are low

(D) they are reluctant to make any investment that does not increase production

(E) the availability of government loans for conservation fluctuates with commodity prices

9. It can be inferred from the passage that the federal government could control overgrazing of public lands by

(A) reducing the fee charged for grazing

(B) fixing a permanent fee for grazing that would not change with economic conditions

(C) allowing ranchers and farmers to use public grazing lands free of charge

(D) setting the fee for grazing on public lands at a level that would be set by the free market

(E) providing financial incentives to livestock owners to expand their breeding operations

According to legend, Aesculapius bore two daughters, Panacea and Hyegeia, who gave rise to dynasties of healers and hygienists. The schism remains today, in clinical training and in practice; (5) and because of the imperative nature of medical care and the subtlety of health care, the former has tended to dominate. Preventive medicine has as its primary objective the maintenance and promotion of health. It accomplishes this by controlling or (10) manipulating environmental factors that affect health and disease. For example, in California presently there is serious suffering and substantial economic loss because of the failure to introduce

controlled fluoridation of public water supplies.
15 Additionally, preventive medicine applies prophylactic measures against disease by such actions as immunization and specific nutritional measures. Third, it attempts to motivate people to adopt healthful life-styles through education.

20   For the most part, curative medicine has as its primary objective the removal of disease from the patient. It provides diagnostic techniques to identify the presence and nature of the disease process. While these may be applied on a mass
25 basis in an attempt to "screen" out persons with preclinical disease, they are usually applied after the patient appears with a complaint. Second, it applies treatment to the sick patient. In every case, this is, or should be, individualized accord-
30 ing to the particular need of each patient. Third, it utilizes rehabilitation methodologies to return the treated patient to the best possible level of functioning.

    While it is true that both preventive medicine
35 and curative medicine require cadres of similarly trained personnel such as planners, administrators, and educators, the underlying delivery systems depend on quite distinctive professional personnel. The requirements for curative medi-
40 cine call for clinically trained individuals who deal with patients on a one-to-one basis and whose training is based primarily on an understanding of the biological, pathological, and psychological processes that determine an individual's health
45 and disease status. The locus for this training is the laboratory and clinic. Preventive medicine, on the other hand, calls for a very broad spectrum of professional personnel, few of whom require clinical expertise. Since their actions apply either
50 to environmental situations or to population groups, their training takes place in a different type of laboratory or in a community not necessarily associated with the clinical locus.

    The economic differences between preventive
55 medicine and curative medicine have been extensively discussed, perhaps most convincingly by Winslow in the monograph *The Cost of Sickness and the Price of Health*. Sickness is almost always a negative, nonproductive and harmful state. All
60 resources expended to deal with sickness are therefore fundamentally economically unproductive. Health, on the other hand, has a very high value in our culture. To the extent that healthy members of the population are replaced by sick
65 members, the economy is doubly burdened.

Nevertheless, the per capita cost of preventive measures for specific diseases is generally far lower than the per capita cost of curative medicine applied to treatment of the same disease.
70 Prominent examples are dental caries, poliomyelitis and phenylketonuria.

    There is an imperative need to provide care for the sick person within a single medical care system, but there is no overriding reason why a
75 linkage is necessary between the two components of a health care system, prevention and treatment. A national health and medical care program composed of semiautonomous systems for personal health care and medical care would have
80 the advantage of clarifying objectives and strategies and of permitting a more equitable division of resources between prevention and cure.

10.   The author is primarily concerned to
      (A)   refute a counterargument
      (B)   draw a distinction
      (C)   discuss a dilemma
      (D)   isolate causes
      (E)   describe new research

11.   The author mentions which of the following as differences between curative and preventive medicine?

      I.   Curative medicine is aimed primarily at people who are already ill, whereas preventive medicine is aimed at healthy people.
      II.   Curative medicine is focused on an individual patient, whereas preventive medicine is applied to larger populations.
      III. The per capita cost of curative medicine is generally much higher than the per capita cost of preventive medicine.

      (A)   I only
      (B)   II only
      (C)   I and II
      (D)   II and III only
      (E)   I, II, and III

12.   It can be inferred that the author regards a program of controlled fluoridation of public water supplies as
      (A)   an unnecessary government program that wastes economic resources

(B) a potentially valuable strategy of preventive medicine

(C) a government policy that has relatively little effect on the health of a population

(D) an important element of curative medicine

(E) an experimental program the health value of which has not been proved

13. Which of the following best explains the author's use of the phrase "doubly burdened" (line 65)?

(A) A person who is ill not only does not contribute to production, but his treatment consumes economic resources.

(B) The per capita cost of preventive measures is only one-half of the per capita cost of treatment.

3,13/(C) The division between preventive medicine and curative medicine requires duplication of administrative expenses.

(D) The individual who is ill must be rehabilitated after the cure has been successful.

(E) The person who is ill uses economic resources that could be used to finance prevention rather than treatment programs.

14. It can be inferred that the author regards Winslow's monograph (line 57) as

(A) ill-conceived

(B) incomplete

(C) authoritative

(D) well organized

(E) highly original

15. The author cites dental caries, poliomyelitis, and phenylketonuria in order to prove that

(A) some diseases can be treated by preventive medicine

(B) some diseases have serious consequences if not treated

(C) preventive medicine need not be linked to treatment

(D) the cost of preventing some diseases is less than the cost for treatment

(E) less money is allocated to prevention of some diseases than to treating them

16. The main reason the author advocates separating authority for preventive medicine from that for curative medicine is

(A) the urgency of treatment encourages administrators to devote more resources to treatment than to prevention

(B) the cost of treating a disease is often much greater than the cost of programs to prevent the disease

(C) the professionals who administer preventive health care programs must be more highly trained than ordinary doctors

(D) curative medicine deals primarily with individuals who are ill, whereas preventive medicine is applied to healthy people

(E) preventive medicine is a relatively recent development, whereas curative medicine has a long history

17. The tone of the passage can best be described as

(A) analytical and concerned

(B) objective and disinterested

(C) tentative and unsure

(D) critical and alarmed

(E) conciliatory and discouraged

From the time they were first proposed, the 1962 Amendments to the Food, Drug and Cosmetic Act have been the subject of controversy among some elements of the health community and the pharmaceutical industry. The Amendments added a new requirement for Food and Drug Administration approval of any new drug: The drug must be demonstrated to be effective by substantial evidence consisting of adequate and well-controlled investigations. To meet this effectiveness requirement, a pharmaceutical company must spend considerable time and effort in clinical research before it can market a new product in the United States. Only then can it begin to recoup its investment. Critics of the requirement argue that the added expense of the research to establish effectiveness is reflected in higher drug costs, decreased profits, or both, and that this has resulted in a "drug lag."

The term drug lag has been used in several different ways. It has been argued that the research required to prove effectiveness creates a lag between the time when a drug could theoretically be marketed without proving effectiveness and the time when it is actually marketed. Drug lag has also been used to refer to the difference between the number of new drugs introduced annually before 1962 and the number of new drugs introduced each year after that date. It is also argued that the Amendments resulted in a lag between the time when new drugs are available in other countries and the time when the same drugs are available in the United States. And drug lag has also been used to refer to a difference in the number of new drugs introduced per year in other advanced nations and the number introduced in the same year in the United States.

Some critics have used drug lag arguments in an attempt to prove that the 1962 Amendments have actually reduced the quality of health care in the United States and that, on balance, they have done more harm than good. These critics recommend that the effectiveness requirements be drastically modified or even scrapped. Most of the specific claims of the drug lag theoreticians, however, have been refuted. The drop in new drugs approved annually, for example, began at least as early as 1959, perhaps five years before the new law was fully effective. In most instances, when a new drug was available in a foreign country but not in the United States, other effective drugs for the condition were available in this country and sometimes not available in the foreign country used for comparison. Further, although the number of new chemical entities introduced annually dropped from more than 50 in 1959 to about 12 to 18 in the 1960's and 1970's, the number of these that can be termed important—some of them of "breakthrough" caliber—has remained reasonably close to 5 or 6 per year. Few, if any, specific examples have actually been offered to show how the effectiveness requirements have done significant harm to the health of Americans. The requirement does ensure that a patient exposed to a drug has the likelihood of benefitting from it, an assessment that is most important, considering the possibility, always present, that adverse effects will be discovered later.

18. The author is primarily concerned with
    (A) outlining a proposal
    (B) evaluating studies
    (C) posing a question

(D) countering arguments
(E) discussing a law

19. The passage states that the phrase "drug lag" has been used to refer to all of the following situations EXCEPT
    (A) a lag between the time when a new drug becomes available in a foreign country and its availability in the United States
    (B) the time period between which a new drug would be marketed if no effectiveness research were required and the time it is actually marketed
    (C) the increased cost of drugs to the consumer and the decreased profit margins of the pharmaceutical industry
    (D) the difference between the number of drugs introduced annually before 1962 and the number introduced after 1962
    (E) the difference between the number of new drugs introduced in a foreign country and the number introduced in the United States

20. The author would most likely agree with which of the following statements?
    (A) Whatever "drug lag" may exist because of the 1962 Amendments is justified by the benefit of effectiveness studies.
    (B) The 1962 Amendments have been beneficial in detecting adverse effects of new drugs before they are released on the market.
    (C) Because of the requirement of effectiveness studies, drug consumers in the United States pay higher prices than consumers in foreign countries.
    (D) The United States should limit the number of new drugs which can be introduced into this country from foreign countries.
    (E) Effectiveness studies do not require a significant investment of time or money on the part of the pharmaceutical industry.

21. The author points out the drop in new drugs approved annually before 1959 in order to
    (A) draw an analogy between two situations

(B) suggest an alternative causal explanation

(C) attack the credibility of an opponent

(D) justify the introduction of statistics

(E) show an opponent misquoted statistics

22. The author implies that the nonavailability of a drug in the United States and its availability in a foreign country is not necessarily proof of a drug lag because this comparison fails to take into account

(A) the number of new drugs introduced annually before 1959

(B) the amount of research done on the effectiveness of drugs in the United States

(C) the possible availability of another drug to treat the same condition

(D) the seriousness of possible unwanted side effects from untested drugs

(E) the length of time needed to accumulate effectiveness research

23. The author attempts to respond to the claim that the number of new chemical entities introduced annually since the Amendments has dropped by

(A) denying that the total number of new chemical entities has actually dropped

(B) analyzing the economic factors responsible for the drop

(C) refining terminology to distinguish important from non-important chemical entities

(D) proposing that further studies be done to determine the effectiveness of new chemical entities

(E) listing the myriad uses to which each new chemical entity can be put

24. The comparisons made by proponents of the "drug lag" theory between the availability of drugs in foreign countries and their availability in the United States logically depend upon which of the following presuppositions?

I. The pharmaceutical industry in the foreign country is roughly as sophisticated as that in the United States.

II. The pharmaceutical industry in the foreign country is more profitable than that of the United States.

III. New drugs in the United States are subject to a more rigorous testing requirement than new drugs in the foreign country.

(A) I only

(B) II only

(C) III only

(D) I and III only

(E) I, II, and III

25. The author apparently believes that "drug lag" is

(A) not a serious problem

(B) more important in Europe than in the United States

(C) a pressing problem that requires an immediate solution

(D) an urgent problem that cannot be easily solved

(E) a serious problem that requires further study

STOP

END OF SECTION. IF YOU HAVE ANY TIME LEFT, GO
OVER YOUR WORK IN THIS SECTION ONLY. DO NOT
WORK IN ANY OTHER SECTION OF THE TEST.

SECTION IV

Time—30 Minutes
25 Questions

Directions: In this section, the questions ask you to analyze and evaluate the reasoning in short paragraphs or passages. For some questions, all of the answer choices may conceivably be answers to the question asked. You should select the *best* answer to the question, that is, an answer which does not require you to make assumptions which violate commonsense standards by being implausible, redundant, irrelevant or inconsistent. After choosing the best answer, blacken the corresponding space on the answer sheet.

1. All effective administrators are concerned about the welfare of their employees, and all administrators who are concerned about the welfare of their employees are liberal in granting time off for personal needs; therefore, all administrators who are not liberal in granting time off for their employees' personal needs are not effective administrators.

   If the argument above is valid, then it must be true that
   (A) no ineffective administrators are liberal in granting time off for their employees' personal needs
   (B) no ineffective administrators are concerned about the welfare of their employees
   (C) some effective administrators are not liberal in granting time off for their employees' personal needs
   (D) all effective administrators are liberal in granting time off for their employees' personal needs
   (E) all time off for personal needs is granted by effective administrators

2. CLYDE: You shouldn't drink so much wine. Alcohol really isn't good for you.

   GERRY: You're wrong about that. I have been drinking the same amount of white wine for 15 years, and I never get drunk.

   Which of the following responses would best strengthen and explain Clyde's argument?
   (A) Many people who drink as much white wine as Gerry does get very drunk.

   (B) Alcohol does not always make a person drunk.
   (C) Getting drunk is not the only reason alcohol is not good for a person.
   (D) If you keep drinking white wine, you may find in the future that you are drinking more and more.
   (E) White wine is not the only drink that contains alcohol.

3. In considering the transportation needs of our sales personnel, the question of the relative cost of each of our options is very important. The initial purchase outlay required for a fleet of diesel autos is fairly high, though the operating costs for them will be low. This is the mirror image of the cost picture for a fleet of gasoline-powered cars. The only way, then, of making a valid cost comparison is on the basis of _____.

   Which of the following best completes the above paragraph?
   (A) projected operating costs for both diesel- and gasoline-powered autos
   (B) the average costs of both fleets over the life of each fleet
   (C) the purchase cost for both diesel-powered and gasoline-powered autos
   (D) the present difference in the operating costs of the two fleets
   (E) the relative amount of air pollution that would be created by the one type of car compared with the other

4. The Dormitory Canteen Committee decided that the prices of snacks in the Canteen vending machines were already high enough, so they told Vendo Inc., the company holding the vending machine concession for the Canteen, either to maintain prices at the then current levels or to forfeit the concession. Vendo, however, managed to thwart the intent of the Committee's instructions without actually violating the letter of those instructions.

Which of the following is probably the action taken by Vendo referred to in the above paragraph?

(A) The president of Vendo met with the University's administration, and they ordered the Committee to rescind its instructions.

(B) Vendo continued prices at the prescribed levels but reduced the size of the snacks vended in the machines.

(C) Vendo ignored the Committee's instructions and continued to raise prices.

(D) Vendo decided it could not make a fair return on its investment if it held the line on prices, so it removed its machines from the Dormitory Canteen.

(E) Representatives of Vendo met with members of the Dormitory Canteen Committee and offered them free snacks to influence other members to change the Committee's decision.

5. The president of the University tells us that a tuition increase is needed to offset rising costs. That is simply not true. Weston University is an institution approximately the same size as our own University, but the president of Weston University has announced that they will not impose a tuition increase on their students.

The author makes his point primarily by
(A) citing new evidence
(B) proposing an alternative solution
(C) pointing out a logical contradiction
(D) drawing an analogy
(E) clarifying an ambiguity

6. Only White Bear gives you all-day deodorant protection and the unique White Bear scent.

If this advertising claim is true, which of the following cannot also be true?

I. Red Flag deodorant gives you all-day deodorant protection.
II. Open Sea deodorant is a more popular deodorant than White Bear.

III. White Bear after-shave lotion uses the White Bear scent.

(A) I only
(B) II only
(C) III only
(D) I and III only
(E) All of the propositions could be true.

7. Clara prefers English Literature to Introductory Physics. She likes English Literature, however, less than she likes Basic Economics. She actually finds Basic Economics preferable to any other college course, and she dislikes Physical Education more than she dislikes Introductory Physics.

All of the following statements can be inferred from the information given above EXCEPT

(A) Clara prefers Basic Economics to English Literature.
(B) Clara likes English Literature better than she likes Physical Education.
(C) Clara prefers Basic Economics to Advanced Calculus.
(D) Clara likes World History better than she likes Introductory Physics.
(E) Clara likes Physical Education less than she likes English Literature.

8. In *The Adventure of the Bruce-Partingon Plans*, Sherlock Holmes explained to Dr. Watson that the body had been placed on the top of the train while the train paused at a signal.

"It seems most improbable," remarked Watson.

"We must fall back upon the old axiom," continued Holmes, "that when all other contingencies fail, whatever remains, however improbable, must be the truth."

Which of the following is the most effective criticism of the logic contained in Holmes' response to Watson?

(A) You will never be able to obtain a conviction in a court of law.
(B) You can never be sure you have accounted for all other contingencies.
(C) You will need further evidence to satisfy the police.

(D) The very idea of putting a dead body on top of a train seems preposterous.

(E) You still have to find the person responsible for putting the body on top of the train.

9. PROFESSOR: Under the rule of primogeniture, the first male child born to a man's first wife is always first in line to inherit the family estate.

    STUDENT: That can't be true; the Duchess of Warburton was her father's only surviving child by his only wife and she inherited his entire estate.

The student has misinterpreted the professor's remark to mean which of the following?

(A) Only men can father male children.

(B) A daughter cannot be a first-born child.

(C) Only sons can inherit the family estate.

(D) Illegitimate children cannot inherit their fathers' property.

(E) A woman cannot inherit her mother's property.

10. All of the following conclusions are based upon accurate expense vouchers submitted by employees to department heads of a certain corporation in 1982. Which of them is LEAST likely to be weakened by the discovery of additional 1982 expense vouchers?

(A) The accounting department had only 15 employees and claimed expenses of at least $500.

(B) The sales department had at least 25 employees and claimed expenses of at least $35,000.

(C) The legal department had at least 2 employees and claimed no more than $3,000 in expenses.

(D) The public relations department had no more than 1 employee and claimed no more than $200 in expenses.

(E) The production department had no more than 500 employees and claimed no more than $350 in expenses.

11. Mr. Mayor, when is the city government going to stop discriminating against its His-

panic residents in the delivery of critical municipal services?

The form of the question above is most nearly paralleled by which of the following?

(A) Mr. Congressman, when is the Congress finally going to realize that defense spending is out of hand?

(B) Madam Chairperson, do you anticipate the committee will take luncheon recess?

(C) Dr. Greentree, what do you expect to be the impact of the Governor's proposals on the economically disadvantaged counties of our state?

(D) Gladys, since you're going to the grocery store anyway, would you mind picking up a quart of milk for me?

(E) Counselor, does the company you represent find that its affirmative action program is successful in recruiting qualified minority employees?

12. The main ingredient in this bottle of Dr. John's Milk of Magnesia is used by nine out of ten hospitals across the country as an antacid and laxative.

If this advertising claim is true, which of the following statements must also be true?

  I. Nine out of ten hospitals across the country use Dr. John's Milk of Magnesia for some ailments.

 II. Only one out of ten hospitals in the country do not treat acid indigestion and constipation.

III. Only one out of ten hospitals across the country do not recommend Dr. John's Milk of Magnesia for patients who need a milk of magnesia.

(A) I only

(B) II only

(C) I and III only

(D) I, II, and III

(E) None of the statements is necessarily true.

Questions 13 and 14

  I. All wheeled conveyances that travel on the highway are polluters.

 II. Bicycles are not polluters.

III. Whenever I drive my car on the highway, it rains.

IV. It is raining.

13. If the above statements are all true, which of the following statements must also be true?
    (A) Bicycles do not travel on the highway.
    (B) Bicycles travel on the highway only if it is raining.
    (C) If my car is not polluting, then it is not raining.
    (D) I am now driving on the highway.
    (E) My car is not a polluter.

14. The conclusion "my car is not polluting" could be logically deduced from statements I–IV if statement
    (A) II were changed to: "Bicycles are polluters."
    (B) II were changed to: "My car is a polluter."
    (C) III were changed to: "If bicycles were polluters, I would be driving my car on the highway."
    (D) IV were changed to: "Rainwater is polluted."
    (E) IV were changed to: "It is not raining."

15. Statistics published by the U.S. Department of Transportation show that nearly 80% of all traffic fatalities occur at speeds of under 50 miles per hour and within 25 miles of home. Therefore, you are safer in a car if you are driving at a speed over 50 miles per hour and not within a 25-mile radius of your home.

    Which of the following, if true, most weakens the conclusion of the argument above?
    (A) Teenage drivers are involved in 75% of all traffic accidents resulting in fatalities.
    (B) 80% of all persons arrested for driving at a speed over the posted speed limit are intoxicated.
    (C) 50% of the nation's annual traffic fatalities occur on six weekends which are considered high-risk weekends because they contain holidays.
    (D) The Department of Transportation statistics were based on police reports compiled by the 50 states.

    (E) 90% of all driving time is registered within a 25-mile radius of the driver's home and at speeds less than 50 miles per hour.

16. Usually when we have had an inch or more of rain in a single day, my backyard immediately has mushrooms and other forms of fungus growing in it. There are no mushrooms or fungus growing in my backyard.

    Which of the following would logically complete an argument with the premises given above?

    I. Therefore, there has been no rain here in the past day.
    II. Therefore, there probably has been no rain here in the past day.
    III. Therefore, we have not had more than an inch of rain here in the past day.
    IV. Therefore, we probably have not had more than an inch of rain here in the past day.

    (A) I only
    (B) II only
    (C) III only
    (D) IV only
    (E) II and IV only

Questions 17 and 18

Can you really have that body you want without a monotonous program of daily exercise? Is there really an exercise routine that will help you to shed that fat quickly and painlessly? Now, a university study shows that this is possible. Surely, you would not want to miss a chance to find out whether you can have that body once again. Try the new Jack Remain's twice-a-week workout—and judge for yourself.

17. Which of the following conclusions can be completely justified assuming that the statements made are true?
    (A) Only Jack Remain's program offers the possibility for effortless weight loss.
    (B) Exercise experts have developed a program to help people of all ages lose weight.
    (C) Following Jack Remain's twice-a-week

workout program might help you to lose weight.

(D) If you follow Jack Remain's twice-a-week workout program, you will lose weight.

(E) Most people must exercise in order to lose weight.

18. The method of persuasion used by the advertisement can be described as
(A) providing evidence and allowing the listener to arrive at his or her own conclusions
(B) presenting the reader with a logical set of premises and inviting the reader to draw his or her own conclusion
(C) presenting both sides of an issue while carefully avoiding influencing the reader's decision
(D) asking that the reader provide evidence to test the truth of the claims made in the advertisement
(E) attempting to convince the reader that similar claims made by others are false

19. I recently read a book by an author who insists that everything man does is economically motivated. Leaders launch wars of conquest in order to capture the wealth of other nations. Scientists do research in order to receive grants or find marketable processes. Students go to college to get better jobs. He even maintains that people go to museums to become better informed on the off-chance that some day they will be able to turn that knowledge to their advantage. So persuaded was I by the author's evidence that, applying his theory on my own, I was able to conclude that he had written the book ──────.

Which of the following provides the most logical completion of the above paragraph?
(A) as a labor of love
(B) in order to make money
(C) as a means of reforming the world by calling man's attention to his greed
(D) as an exercise in scientific research
(E) in response to a creative urge to be a novelist

20. In our investigation of this murder, we are guided by our previous experience with the Eastend Killer. You will recall that in that case, the victims were also carrying a great deal of money when they were killed but the money was not taken. As in this case, the murder weapon was a pistol. Finally, in that case also, the murders were committed between six in the evening and twelve midnight. So we are probably after someone who looks very much like the Eastend Killer, who was finally tried, convicted, and executed: 5 feet 11 inches tall, a mustache, short, brown hair, walks with a slight limp.

The author makes which of the following assumptions?

I. Crimes similar in detail are likely to be committed by perpetrators who are similar in physical appearance.

II. The Eastend Killer has apparently escaped from prison and has resumed his criminal activities.

III. The man first convicted as the Eastend Killer was actually innocent, and the real Eastend Killer is still loose.

(A) I only
(B) II only
(C) III only
(D) I and II only
(E) I and III only

21. I. Everyone who has not read the report either has no opinion in the matter or holds a wrong opinion about it.

II. Everyone who holds no opinion in the matter has not read the report.

Which of the following best describes the relationship between the two above propositions?
(A) If II is true, I may be either false or true.
(B) If II is true, I must also be true.
(C) If II is true, I is likely to be true.
(D) If I is true, II must also be true.
(E) If I is false, II must also be false.

22. The idea that women should be police officers is absurd. After all, women are on the average three to five inches shorter than men and weigh 20 to 50 pounds less. It is clear that a woman would be less effective than a man in a situation requiring force.

Which of the following, if true, would most weaken the above argument?

(A) Some of the female applicants for the police force are larger than some of the male officers presently on the force.

(B) Police officers are required to go through an intensive 18-month training program.

(C) Police officers are required to carry pistols and are trained in the use of their weapons.

(D) There are a significant number of desk jobs in the police force which women could fill.

(E) Many criminals are women.

23. No sophomores were selected for Rho Rho Phi. Some sophomores are members of the Debating Society. Therefore, some members of the Debating Society were not selected for Rho Rho Phi.

Which of the following is logically most similar to the argument given above?

(A) Everyone who exercises in the heat will get ill. I never exercise in the heat, so I will probably never be ill.

(B) Drivers who wish to avoid expensive automobile repairs will have their cars tuned up regularly. My uncle refuses to have his car tuned up regularly. Therefore, he enjoys paying for major repairs.

(C) Some books that are beautiful were written in French, and French literature is well respected. Therefore, any book that is beautiful is well respected.

(D) All pets are excluded from this apartment complex. But many pets are valuable. Therefore, some valuable animals are excluded from this apartment complex.

(E) St. Paul is a long way from London. Minneapolis is a long way from Lon-

don. Therefore, St. Paul is a long, long way from Minneapolis.

24. If the batteries in my electric razor are dead, the razor will not function. My razor is not functioning. Therefore, the batteries must be dead.

Which of the following arguments is most similar to that presented above?

(A) If Elroy attends the meeting, Ms. Barker will be elected club president. Ms. Barker was not elected club president; therefore, Elroy did not attend the meeting.

(B) All evidence is admissible unless it is tainted. This evidence is inadmissible. Therefore, it is tainted.

(C) If John committed the crime, his fingerprints will be found at the scene. John's fingerprints were found at the scene; therefore, John committed the crime.

(D) Grant is my uncle. Sophie is Grant's niece. Therefore, Sophie is my sister.

(E) Jonathan will wear his dark glasses if the coast is clear. The coast is clear. Therefore, Jonathan will wear his dark glasses.

25. All general statements are based solely on observed instances of a phenomenon. That the statement has held true up to a certain point in time is no guarantee that it will remain unexceptionless. Therefore, no generalization can be considered free from possible exception.

The logic of the above argument can best be described as

(A) self-defeating
(B) circular
(C) ill defined
(D) valid
(E) inductive

STOP

END OF SECTION. IF YOU HAVE ANY TIME LEFT, GO OVER YOUR WORK IN THIS SECTION ONLY. DO NOT WORK ON ANY OTHER SECTION IN THE TEST.

SECTION V

Time—30 Minutes
20 Questions

Directions: For each of the following questions, select the best of the answer choices and blacken the corresponding space on your answer sheet.
Numbers: All numbers used are real numbers.
Figures: The diagrams and figures that accompany these questions are for the purpose of providing information useful in answering the question. Unless it is stated that a specific figure is not drawn to scale, the diagrams and figures are drawn as accurately as possible. All figures are in a plane unless otherwise indicated.

1. If $x = 5$, $y = 3$, and $z = 2$, then
   $$\frac{x(y - z)}{y(x + y + z)} =$$
   (A) $\frac{1}{30}$
   (B) $\frac{1}{6}$
   (C) 1
   (D) 5
   (E) 10

2. What is 200% of 0.010?
   (A) 0.0002
   (B) 0.0005
   (C) 0.020
   (D) 0.050
   (E) 0.20

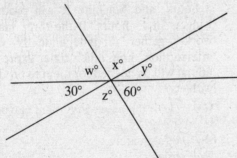

3. In the figure above, $x =$
   (A) 30
   (B) 60
   (C) 75
   (D) 90
   (E) 100

4. If the average (arithmetic mean) of five different integers is 1, which of the following must be true?

   I. 1 is one of the integers.
   II. At least one of the integers is negative.
   III. 0 is not one of the integers.

   (A) I only
   (B) II only
   (C) I and II only
   (D) II and III only
   (E) I, II, and III

5. In a certain school library, 60% of the books are clothbound books. If 30% of those are works of fiction, then what percentage of all books in the library are clothbound works of fiction?
   (A) 90%
   (B) 30%
   (C) 20%
   (D) 18%
   (E) 2%

6. A traveler has booked a vacation plan with agent X for a total cost of $1200 and has already paid agent X a nonrefundable deposit equal to 10% of the cost of the vacation plan. She learns that she can purchase the same vacation plan from agent Y for 20% less. If these are the only costs involved, what will be the net result of breaking the contract with agent X, thereby forfeiting the deposit, and then purchasing the plan through agent Y?
   (A) An increase in the cost of the vacation of $240
   (B) An increase in the cost of the vacation of $120
   (C) No change in the cost of the vacation
   (D) A decrease in the cost of the vacation of $120
   (E) A decrease in the cost of the vacation of $240

7. A gymnast's score for a routine is the average of the scores awarded by ten judges on a scale ranging from 0 to 10. If the first seven judges have awarded the gymnast

scores of 7, 8, 7.5, 9, 8.2, 8.5, and 7.8, and she does not receive a score lower than 6 from any of the other judges, then her final score for the routine will be
(A) greater than 8.0
(B) greater than 7.8
(C) greater than or equal to 7.8
(D) between 7.0 and 7.4
(E) greater than or equal to 7.4

8. A certain experiment involves repeatedly subjecting a chemical sample to the same procedure, with the result that the sample loses $\frac{1}{2}$ its weight after each repetition. If the weight after the sixth repetition is 16 grams, then what is the weight, in grams, after the third repetition?
(A) 8
(B) 32
(C) 128
(D) 256
(E) 512

9. During a sale, a certain item is sold at a price 40% below its usual selling price. If the dollar savings on the item is $12, then what is its *sale* price?
(A) $30
(B) $24
(C) $18
(D) $15
(E) $6

10. If $\frac{1}{x} = 6$ and $\frac{1}{y} = \frac{1}{3}$, then $\frac{x}{y} =$
(A) $\frac{1}{18}$
(B) $\frac{1}{2}$
(C) 1
(D) 2
(E) 18

11. If during a one-year period, the dividend paid on a certain share of stock was equal to $8\frac{3}{8}\%$ of the par value of the stock, then the dividend paid was what fraction of the par value of the stock?
(A) $\frac{32}{800}$
(B) $\frac{67}{800}$
(C) $\frac{32}{100}$
(D) $\frac{67}{100}$
(E) $\frac{72}{100}$

12. From March 1 to March 31 the price of a certain commodity fell by $\frac{1}{4}$, and from April

1 to April 30 the price fell by $\frac{1}{3}$. By what percentage would the price of the commodity have to increase during the month of May to bring it back up to the level of March 1?
(A) $14\frac{2}{7}\%$
(B) 25%
(C) 50%
(D) $66\frac{2}{3}\%$
(E) 100%

13. If the assessed value of a piece of property is increased by 25% while the tax rate is decreased by 25%, what is the net effect on the taxes on the property?
(A) An increase of 18.75%
(B) An increase of 6.25%
(C) No net change
(D) A decrease of 6.25%
(E) A decrease of 18.75%

14. If a machine consumes $\frac{k}{5}$ kilowatts of power every t hours, how much power will three such machines consume in 10 hours?
(A) $\frac{6t}{k}$
(B) $\frac{t}{k}$
(C) 30kt
(D) $\frac{k}{t}$
(E) $\frac{6k}{t}$

15. Machine P can produce x widgets in 10 hours, Machine Q can produce x widgets in 6 hours, and Machine R can produce 2x widgets in 15 hours. If the three machines work together but independently, without interruption, how much time, expressed in hours, will be needed for them to produce 5x widgets?
(A) $7\frac{2}{3}$
(B) 8
(C) $10\frac{2}{3}$
(D) $12\frac{1}{2}$
(E) $23\frac{1}{2}$

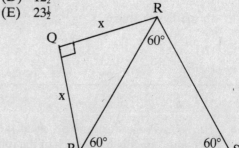

16. If QR = 2, then what is the perimeter of quadrilateral PQRS?
    (A) 6 √2 + 4
    (B) 4 √2 + 4
    (C) 4 √2 + 2
    (D) 2 √2 + 2
    (E) 3 √2

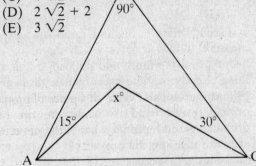

note: Figure not drawn to scale.

17. In the figure above, if angle ADC = 90°, then what is the size of angle x?
    (A) 150°
    (B) 135°
    (C) 120°
    (D) 110°
    (E) 105°

18. A study of a city's water-use patterns shows that for every 8q% increase in the price of water, usage drops by q%. If the price charged for water is currently $1.05 per 1000 cubic feet, by how much should the price per 1000 cubic feet be raised in order to obtain an immediate reduction in usage of 2%?
    (A) $0.042

(B) $0.105
(C) $0.168
(D) $0.225
(E) It cannot be determined from the information given.

19. A experimental car traveled the first half of a 120-mile test course at an average speed of 40 miles per hour. What average speed must be maintained over the second half of the course in order to average 60 miles per hour for the entire test course?
    (A) 50 miles/hour
    (B) 75 miles/hour
    (C) 90 miles/hour
    (D) 120 miles/hour
    (E) 150 miles/hour

20. A group of investors purchased an apartment building that returned total net income over a 10-year period equal to the original $414,000 investment. If expenses consumed 25% of the annual gross income from the building, what was the average annual gross income from the building over the 10-year period?
    (A) $10,350
    (B) $41,400
    (C) $51,750
    (D) $55,200
    (E) $103,500

STOP

END OF SECTION. IF YOU HAVE ANY TIME LEFT, GO OVER YOUR WORK IN THIS SECTION ONLY. DO NOT WORK IN ANY OTHER SECTION OF THE TEST.

SECTION VI

Time—30 Minutes
25 Questions

Directions: Below each of the following passages, you will find questions or incomplete statements about the passage. Each statement or question is followed by lettered words or expressions. Select the word or expression that most satisfactorily completes each statement, or answers each question in accordance with the meaning of the passage. After you have chosen the best answer, blacken the corresponding space on the answer sheet.

Like our political society, the university is under severe attack today and perhaps for the same reason; namely, that we have accomplished much of what we have set out to do in this generation, that we have done so imperfectly, and while we have been doing so, we have said a lot of things that simply are not true. For example, we have earnestly declared that full equality of opportunity in universities exists for everyone, regardless of economic circumstance, race or religion. This has never been true. When it was least true, the assertion was not attacked. Now that it is nearly true, not only the assertion but the university itself is locked in mortal combat with the seekers of perfection.

In another sense the university has failed. It has stored great quantities of knowledge; it teaches more people; and despite its failures, it teaches them better. It is in the application of this knowledge that the failure has come. Of the great branches of knowledge—the sciences, the social sciences and humanities—the sciences are applied, sometimes almost as soon as they are learned. Strenuous and occasionally successful efforts are made to apply the social sciences, but almost never are the humanities well applied. We do not use philosophy in defining our conduct. We do not use literature as a source of real and vicarious experience to save us the trouble of living every life again in our own.

The great tasks of the university in the next generation are to search the past to form the future, to begin an earnest search for a new and relevant set of values, and to learn to use the knowledge we have for the questions that come before us. The university should use one-fourth of

a student's time in his undergraduate years and organize it into courses which might be called history, and literature and philosophy, and anything else appropriate and organize these around primary problems. The difference between a primary problem and a secondary or even tertiary problem is that primary problems tend to be around for a long time, whereas the less important ones get solved.

One primary problem is that of interfering with what some call human destiny and others call biological development, which is partly the result of genetic circumstance and partly the result of accidental environmental conditions. It is anticipated that the next generation, and perhaps this one, will be able to interfere chemically with the actual development of an individual and perhaps biologically by interfering with his genes. Obviously, there are benefits both to individuals and to society from eliminating, or at least improving, mentally and physically deformed persons. On the other hand, there could be very serious consequences if this knowledge were used with premeditation to produce superior and subordinate classes, each genetically prepared to carry out a predetermined mission. This can be done, but what happens to free will and the rights of the individual? Here we have a primary problem that will still exist when we are all dead.

Of course, the traditional faculty members would say, "But the students won't learn enough to go to graduate school." And certainly they would not learn everything we are in the habit of making them learn, but they would learn some other things. Surely, in the other three-quarters of their time, they would learn what they usually do, and they might even learn to think about it by carrying new habits into their more conventional courses. The advantages would be overwhelmingly greater than the disadvantages. After all, the purpose of education is not only to impart knowledge but to teach students to use the knowledge that they either have or will find, to teach them to ask and seek answers for important questions.

1. The author suggests that the university's greatest shortcoming is its failure to
   (A) attempt to provide equal opportunity for all
   (B) offer courses in philosophy and the humanities
   (C) prepare students adequately for professional studies
   (D) help students see the relevance of the humanities to real problems
   (E) require students to include in their curricula liberal arts courses

2. It can be inferred that the author presupposes that the reader will regard a course in literature as a course
   (A) with little or no practical value
   (B) of interest only to academic scholars
   (C) required by most universities for graduation
   (D) uniquely relevant to today's primary problems
   (E) used to teach students good writing skills

3. Which of the following questions does the author answer in the passage?
   (A) What are some of the secondary problems faced by the past generation?
   (B) How can we improve the performance of our political society?
   (C) Has any particular educational institution tried the proposal introduced by the author?
   (D) What is a possible objection to the proposal offered in the passage?
   (E) Why is the university of today a better imparter of knowledge than the university of the past?

4. Which of the following questions would the author most likely consider a primary question?
   (A) Should Congress increase the level of Social Security benefits?
   (B) Is it appropriate for the state to use capital punishment?
   (C) Who is the best candidate for president in the next presidential election?
   (D) At what month can the fetus be considered medically viable outside the mother's womb?
   (E) What measures should be taken to solve the problem of world hunger?

5. With which of the following statements about the use of scientific techniques to change an individual's genetic makeup would the author LEAST likely agree?
   (A) Society has no right to use such techniques without the informed consent of the individual.
   (B) Such techniques can have a positive benefit for the individual in some cases.
   (C) Use of such techniques may be appropriate even though society, but not the individual, benefits.
   (D) The question of the use of such techniques must be placed in a philosophical as well as a scientific context.
   (E) The answers to questions about the use of such techniques will have important implications for the structure of our society.

6. The primary purpose of the passage is to
   (A) discuss a problem and propose a solution
   (B) analyze a system and defend it
   (C) present both sides of an issue and allow the reader to draw a conclusion
   (D) outline a new idea and criticize it
   (E) raise several questions and provide answers to them

7. The development discussed in the passage is primarily a problem of
   (A) political philosophy
   (B) educational philosophy
   (C) scientific philosophy
   (D) practical science
   (E) practical politics

8. The tone of the passage can best be described as
   (!) concerned but hopeful
   (B) sincere but complaisant
   (C) alarmed and confused
   (D) satisfied and unconcerned
   (E) judgmental and skeptical

The high unemployment rates of the early 1960's occasioned a spirited debate within the economics profession. One group found the primary cause of unemployment in slow growth and the solution in economic expansion. The other found the major explanation in changes that had occurred in the supply and demand for labor and stressed measures for matching demand with supply.

The expansionist school of thought, with the Council of Economic Advisers as its leading advocates, attributed the persistently high unemployment level to a slow rate of economic growth resulting from a deficiency of aggregate demand for goods and services. The majority of this school endorsed the position of the Council that tax reduction would eventually reduce the unemployment level to 4% of the labor force with no other assistance. At 4%, bottlenecks in skilled labor, middle-level manpower and professional personnel were expected to retard growth and generate wage-price pressures. To go beyond 4%, the interim goal of the Council, it was recognized that improved education, training and retraining and other structural measures would be required. Some expansionists insisted that the demand for goods and services was nearly satiated and that it was impossible for the private sector to absorb a significant increase in output. In their estimate, only the lower-income fifth of the population and the public sector offered sufficient outlets for the productive efforts of the potential labor force. The fact that the needs of the poor and the many unmet demands for public services held higher priority than the demands of the marketplace in the value structure of this group no doubt influenced their economic judgments.

Those who found the major cause of unemployment in structural features were primarily labor economists, concerned professionally with efficient functioning of labor markets through programs to develop skills and place individual workers. They maintained that increased aggregate demand was a necessary but not sufficient condition for reaching either the CEA's 4% target or their own preferred 3%. This pessimism was based, in part, on the conclusion that unemployment among the young, the unskilled, minority groups and depressed geographical areas is not easily attacked by increasing general demand. Further, their estimate of the numbers of potential members of the labor force who had withdrawn or not entered because of lack of employment opportunity was substantially higher than that of the CEA. They also projected that increased demand would put added pressure on skills already in short supply rather than employ the unemployed, and that because of technological change, which was replacing manpower, much higher levels of demand would be necessary to create the same number of jobs.

The structural school, too, had its hyperenthusiasts: fiscal conservatives who, as an alternative to expansionary policies, argued the not very plausible position that a job was available for every person, provided only that he or she had the requisite skills or would relocate. Such extremist positions aside, there was actually considerable agreement between two main groups, though this was not recognized at the time. Both realized the advisability of a tax cut to increase demand, and both realized that reduction of structural rigidities would be needed to reduce unemployment below a point around 4%. In either case, the policy implications differed in emphasis and not in content.

9. The primary purpose of the passage is to
(A) suggest some ways in which tools to manipulate aggregate demand and eliminate structural deficiencies can be used to reduce the level of unemployment
(B) demonstrate that there was a good deal of agreement between the expansionist and structuralist theories on how to reduce unemployment in the 1960s
(C) explain the way in which structural inefficiencies prevent the achievement of a low rate of unemployment without wage-price pressures
(D) discuss the disunity within the expansionist and structuralist schools to show its relationship to the inability of the government to reduce unemployment to 4%
(E) describe the role of the Council of Economic Advisers in advocating expansionist policies to reduce unemployment to 4%

10. Which of the following is *not* mentioned in the passage as a possible barrier to achieving

a 4% unemployment rate through increased aggregate demand?

(A) Technological innovation reduces the need for workers, so larger increases in demand are needed to employ the same number of workers.

(B) The increase in output necessary to meet an increase in aggregate demand requires skilled labor, which is already in short supply, rather than unskilled labor, which is available.

(C) An increase in aggregate demand will not create jobs for certain subgroups of unemployed persons such as minority groups and young and unskilled workers.

(D) Even if the tax reduction increases aggregate demand, many unemployed workers will be unwilling to relocate to jobs located in areas where there is a shortage of labor.

(E) An increase in the number of available jobs will encourage people not in the labor market to enter it, which in turn will keep the unemployment rate high.

11. The author's treatment of the "hyperenthusiasts" (lines 62–67) can best be described as one of
(A) strong approval
(B) lighthearted appreciation
(C) summary dismissal
(D) contemptuous sarcasm
(E) malicious rebuke

12. Which of the following best describes the difference between the position taken by the Council of Economic Advisers and that taken by dissenting expansionists (lines 26–28)?
(A) Whereas the Council of Economic Advisers emphasized the need for a tax cut to stimulate general demand, the dissenters stressed the importance of structural measures such as education and training.
(B) Although the dissenters agreed that an increase in demand was necessary to reduce unemployment, they argued government spending to increase demand should fund programs for lower income groups and public services.

(C) The Council of Economic Advisers set a 4% unemployment rate as its goal, and dissenting expansionists advocated a goal of 3%.

(D) The Council of Economic Advisers rejected the contention, advanced by the dissenting expansionists, that a tax cut would help to create increased demand.

(E) The dissenting expansionists were critical of the Council of Economic Advisers because members of the Council advocated politically conservative policies.

13. The passage contains information that helps to explain which of the following?

I. The fact that the economy did not expand rapidly in the early 1960s.
II. The start of wage-price pressures as the employment rate approaches 4%.
III. The harmful effects of unemployment on an individual worker.

(A) I only
(B) II only
(C) I and II only
(D) I and III only
(E) I, II, and III

14. Which of the following best describes the author's attitude toward the expansionists mentioned in line 10?
(A) The author doubts the validity of their conclusions because they were not trained economists.
(B) The author discounts the value of their judgment because it was colored by their political viewpoint.
(C) The author refuses to evaluate the value of their contention because he lacks sufficient information.
(D) The author accepts their viewpoint until it can be demonstrated that it is incorrect.
(E) The author endorses the principles on which their conclusions are based but believes their proposal to be impractical.

15. It can be inferred from the passage that the hyperenthusiasts (lines 62–67) contended that
    (A) the problem of unemployment could be solved without government retraining and education programs
    (B) the number of persons unemployed was greatly overestimated by the Council of Economic Advisers
    (C) a goal of 3% unemployment could not be reached unless the government enacted retraining and education programs
    (D) the poor had a greater need for expanded government services than the more affluent portion of the population
    (E) fiscal policies alone were powerful enough to reduce the unemployment rate to 4% of the work force

16. The author's primary concern is to
    (A) compare two theories
    (B) defend one theory against another
    (C) disprove two theories
    (D) advance a new theory
    (E) pose a question and then answer it

An assumption that underlies most discussions of electric facility siting is that the initial selection of a site is the responsibility of the utility concerned—subject to governmental review and approval only after the site has been chosen. This assumption must be changed so that site selection becomes a joint responsibility of the utilities and the appropriate governmental authorities from the outset. Siting decisions would be made in accordance with either of two strategies. The metropolitan strategy takes the existing distribution of population and supporting facilities as given. An attempt is then made to choose between dispersed or concentrated siting and to locate generating facilities in accordance with some economic principle. For example, the economic objectives of least-cost construction and rapid start-up may be achieved, in part, by a metropolitan strategy that takes advantage of existing elements of social and physical infrastructure in the big cities. Under the frontier strategy, the energy park may be taken as an independent variable, subject to manipulation by policymakers as a means of achieving desired demographic or social goals, e.g., rural-town-city mix. Thus,

population distribution is taken as a goal of national social policy, not as a given of a national energy policy. In the frontier strategy, the option of dispersed siting is irrelevant from the standpoint of community impact because there is no preexisting community of any size.

Traditionally, the resource endowment of a location—and especially its situation relative to the primary industry of the hinterland—has had a special importance in American history. In the early agricultural period, the most valued natural endowment was arable land with good climate and available water. America's oldest cities were mercantile outposts of such agricultural areas. Deepwater ports developed to serve the agricultural hinterlands, which produced staple commodities in demand on the world market. From the 1840's onward, the juxtaposition of coal, iron ore and markets afforded the impetus for manufacturing growth in the northeastern United States. The American manufacturing heartland developed westward to encompass Lake Superior iron ores, the Pennsylvania coalfields, and the Northeast's financial, entrepreneurial and manufacturing roles. Subsequent metropolitan growth has been organized around this national core.

Against the theory of urban development, it is essential to bear in mind the unprecedented dimensions of an energy park. The existing electric power plant at Four Corners in the southwest United States—the only human artifact visible to orbiting astronauts—generates only 4000 megawatts electric. The smallest energy parks will concentrate five times the thermal energy represented by the Four Corners plant. An energy park, then, would seem every bit as formidable as the natural harbor conditions or coal deposits that underwrote the growth of the great cities of the past—with a crucial difference. The founders of past settlements could not choose the geographic locations of their natural advantages.

The frontier strategy implements the principle of man-made opportunity; and this helps explain why some environmentalists perceive the energy park idea as a threat to nature. But the problems of modern society, with or without energy parks, require ever more comprehensive planning. And energy parks are a means of advancing American social history rather than merely responding to power needs in an unplanned, ad hoc manner.

17. Which of the following statements best describes the main point of the passage?
    (A) Government regulatory authorities should participate in electric facility site selection to further social goals.
    (B) Energy parks will have a significant influence on the demographic features of the American population.
    (C) Urban growth in the United States was largely the result of economic forces rather than conscientious planning.
    (D) Under the frontier siting strategy for energy parks, siting decisions are influenced by the natural features of the land.
    (E) America needs larger power-producing facilities in urban and rural areas to meet the increased demand for energy.

18. All of the following are mentioned in the passage as characteristics of energy parks EXCEPT
    (A) energy parks will be built on previously undeveloped sites
    (B) energy parks will be built in areas remote from major population centers
    (C) energy parks will produce considerably more thermal energy than existing facilities
    (D) energy parks will be built at sites that are near fuel sources such as coal
    (E) energy parks may have considerable effects on population distribution

19. According to the passage, which of the following are characteristics of past siting decisions for electric facilities?

    I. Government authority exercised only a review function.
    II. Decisions were made without regard to the effect the facility would have on people.
    III. Sites selected by utilities were often opposed by environmental groups.

    (A) I only
    (B) II only
    (C) I and II only
    (D) I and III only
    (E) I, II, and III

20. Which of the following, if true, would most seriously *weaken* the author's position?
    (A) The first settlements in America were established in order to provide trading posts with Native Americans.
    (B) The cost of constructing an electric power plant in an urban area is not significantly greater than that for a rural area.
    (C) An energy park will be so large that it will be impossible to predict the demographic consequences of its construction.
    (D) Cities in European countries grew up in response to political pressures during the feudal period rather than economic pressures.
    (E) The United States is presently in a period of population migration that will change the rural-town-city mix.

21. With which one of the following statements would the author most likely agree?
    (A) Decisions about the locations for power plant construction should be left in the hands of the utilities.
    (B) Government leaders in the nineteenth century were irresponsible in not supervising urban growth more closely.
    (C) Natural features of a region such as cultivatable land and water supply are no longer important to urban growth.
    (D) Modern society is so complex that governments must take greater responsibility for decisions such as power plant siting.
    (E) The electric power plant at Four Corners should not have been built because of its mammoth size.

22. According to the passage, the most important difference between the natural advantages of early cities and the features of an energy park is
    (A) the features of an energy park will be located where the builders choose
    (B) natural advantages are no longer as important as they once were
    (C) natural features cannot be observed from outer space but energy parks can
    (D) early cities grew up close to agricul-

tural areas, but energy parks will be located in mountains

(E) policy planners have learned to minimize the effects of energy parks on nature

23. The author's attitude toward energy parks can best be described as
    (A) cautious uncertainty
    (B) circumspect skepticism
    (C) studied indifference
    (D) qualified endorsement
    (E) unrestrained enthusiasm

24. The author mentions the Four Corners facility in order to
    (A) give an example of a poor electric facility siting decision
    (B) help the reader understand how large energy parks might be
    (C) illustrate the process of governmental review of siting decision
    (D) underscore the need for locating en-

ergy parks away from larger urban centers

(E) focus attention on the need for additional energy-producing facilities

25. Which of the following best describes the author's treatment of the environmentalists' position mentioned in the final paragraph?
    (A) He regards their objection as serious but defers giving a response until a later time.
    (B) He doesn't understand their objection but is confident that it is not well founded.
    (C) He treats the objection as a serious one and is willing to reconsider his position on energy parks.
    (D) He states that the objection is not unique to energy parks and dismisses it without further discussion.
    (E) He believes that the objection contains a logical contradiction and is therefore invalid.

STOP

END OF SECTION. IF YOU HAVE ANY TIME LEFT, GO OVER YOUR WORK IN THIS SECTION ONLY. DO NOT WORK IN ANY OTHER SECTION OF THE TEST.

SECTION VII

Time—30 minutes
25 Questions

Directions: In each problem below, either part or all of the sentence is underlined. The sentence is followed by five ways of writing the underlined part. Answer choice (A) repeats the original; the other answer choices vary. If you think that the original phrasing is the best, choose (A). If you think one of the other answer choices is the best, select that choice.

This section tests the ability to recognize correct and effective expression. Follow the requirements of Standard Written English: grammar, choice of words, and sentence construction. Choose the answer that results in the clearest, most exact sentence, but do not change the meaning of the original sentence.

1. The former First Lady continued her efforts on behalf of the mentally retarded, raising funds, visiting hospitals, <u>and she was speaking out for their rights.</u>
   (A) and she was speaking out for their rights.
   (B) and their rights were spoken out for by her.
   (C) and to speak out for their rights.
   (D) also in speaking out for their rights.
   (E) and speaking out for their rights.

2. The number of adults in the United States who are illiterate is <u>rising, but it is probably only temporary.</u>
   (A) rising, but it is probably only temporary.
   (B) rising, but it is only temporary.
   (C) rising, but it is temporary only.
   (D) rising, but the increase is probably only a temporary one.
   (E) rising, although the increase may only be temporarily.

3. Although most physicians agree that exercise is necessary for physical and mental well-being, <u>they caution against doing too much too soon.</u>
   (A) they caution against doing too much too soon.
   (B) doing too much too soon is cautioned against by them.
   (C) but cautioning against doing too much too soon.
   (D) yet caution against doing too much too soon.
   (E) it is cautioned against to do too much too soon.

4. Transcendentalism was seen as a somewhat pantheistic philosophy <u>and opposed by orthodox Christians.</u>
   (A) and opposed by orthodox Christians.
   (B) and orthodox Christians opposed them.
   (C) that orthodox Christians opposed it.
   (D) being opposed by orthodox Christians.
   (E) and orthodox Christians oppose it.

5. Although the consensus reaction to initial marketing surveys was not favorable, the growing acceptance by consumers <u>seem to indicate that the product will ultimately be very popular.</u>
   (A) seem to indicate that the product will ultimately be very popular.
   (B) seems to indicate the ultimate popularity of the product.
   (C) seems to indicate that the product will ultimately be very popular.
   (D) are indicating that the product will ultimately be very popular.
   (E) seems to be an indication as to the ultimately popularity of the product.

6. Unlike <u>Edgar Allen Poe, whose works were ignored in his native country, the</u> works of Hawthorne were read and appreciated by the public and by contemporary critics.
   (A) Edgar Allen Poe, whose works were ignored in his native country, the
   (B) Edgar Allen Poe whose native country ignored his work, the
   (C) the works of Edgar Allen Poe, ignored in his native country, the
   (D) the works of Edgar Allen Poe which were ignored in his native country, the
   (E) the works of Edgar Allen Poe having been ignored in his native country, the

7. Jockeys at most racetracks <u>become familiar with the horses by riding them in early</u>

morning workouts which keeps both the jockeys and the horses in good condition.

(A) become familiar with the horses by riding them in early morning workouts which

(B) become familiar with the horses and also ride them in early morning workouts which

(C) become familiar with the horses by riding them in early morning workouts, a practice which

(D) ride horses to become familiar with them in early morning workouts which

(E) ride horses in early morning workouts and become familiar with them which

8. In addition to the revised curriculum requested last semester, the students are now demanding that a new grading system be instituted.

(A) In addition to the revised curriculum requested last semester, the students are now demanding that a new grading system be instituted.

(B) In addition to the revised curriculum that had been requested last semester, the students are now demanding that a new grading system be instituted.

(C) The students are now demanding that a new grading system be instituted in addition to the revised curriculum they requested last semester.

(D) Added to the revised curriculum that was requested last semester by the students, they are now demanding the institution of a new grading system.

(E) Added to the new curriculum requested last semester, the students have now demanded the institution of a new grading system.

9. Her lecture was unsuccessful not so much because of her lack of preparation but instead because of her inability to organize her material.

(A) but instead because of
(B) as
(C) so much as
(D) than
(E) rather than

10. A private house in New York City is a building owned by an individual or individu-

als having less than eight units and no commercial space.

(A) a building owned by an individual or individuals having less than eight units and no commercial space.

(B) one that an individual or individuals own with fewer than eight units and no commercial space.

(C) a building with fewer than eight units, no commercial space, and is owned by an individual or individuals.

(D) one that has fewer than eight units, no commercial space and it is owned by an individual or individuals.

(E) one that has fewer than eight units, is owned by an individual or individuals, and has no commercial space.

11. Kate Chopin, an American writer of the last century, and a feminist, writing about strong independent women before such a movement existed.

(A) and a feminist writing about strong independent women before such a movement existed.

(B) was a feminist before such a movement existed, and she wrote about strong independent women.

(C) wrote about strong, independent women and was a feminist before such a movement existed.

(D) was writing about strong independent women and was feminist before the existence of such a movement.

(E) a feminist before such a movement existed and writing about strong independent women before such a movement existed.

12. Although severely damaged by the collision and already sinking, the coast guard arrived at the freighter in time to save the crew.

(A) Although severely damaged by the collision and already sinking,

(B) Although it had been severely damaged by the collision and was already sinking,

(C) Although the freighter had been severely damaged in the collision and was already sinking,

(D) Although the freighter was severely damaged in the collision and it was also already sinking,

(E) Severely damaged in the collision, and although sinking,

13. According to recent studies, <u>the median income of women is still only equal to two thirds of men.</u>
    (A) the median income of women is still only equal to two thirds of men.
    (B) women's median income is still two-thirds of men only.
    (C) the median income of women is still only two-thirds that of men.
    (D) women's median income is still two-thirds of only that of men.
    (E) the median income of women is still only two-thirds of a man's.

14. The new advances in the field of genetic <u>engineering hopefully will enable scientists to prevent most crippling birth defects.</u>
    (A) engineering hopefully will enable scientists to prevent most crippling birth defects.
    (B) engineering will, it is hoped, enable scientists to prevent most crippling birth defects.
    (C) engineering hopefully will enable the prevention of most crippling birth defects by scientists.
    (D) engineering, it is hoped, would enable scientists to prevent most crippling birth defects.
    (E) engineering, it is hoped, will enable the scientists' preventing most crippling birth defects.

15. A panel from the World Health Organization concluded that malnutrition is the most serious health problem facing the third world countries, <u>but it could or will</u> be eradicated with the assistance of developed countries.
    (A) but it could or will
    (B) but they could or will
    (C) but that it would be or could
    (D) but that it can and will be
    (E) but it would and should

16. <u>Having discovered the Roman aristocrats to be suffering from lead poisoning,</u> it is now thought that this was a major cause of their inability to reproduce.

(A) Having discovered the Roman aristocrats to be suffering from lead poisoning,
(B) To have discovered the Roman aristocrats to be suffering from lead poisoning,
(C) Since scientists have discovered that the Roman aristocrats suffered from lead poisoning,
(D) Since the suffering of lead poisoning by Roman aristocrats was discovered by scientists,
(E) Due to the fact Roman aristocrats were suffering from lead poisoning was discovered by scientists,

17. Henry Wadsworth Longfellow was a professor of Modern Languages at *Harvard*, <u>at the same time also one of America's greatest poets.</u>
    (A) Harvard, at the same time also one of America's greatest poets.
    (B) Harvard, and, at the same time was also one of America's greatest poets.
    (C) Harvard, at the same time as he was one of America's greatest poets.
    (D) Harvard, at the same time that he had been one of America's greatest poets.
    (E) Harvard, being one of America's greatest poets at the same time.

18. <u>Despite her harsh criticism of the competition,</u> the actress was at the ceremony to accept her award.
    (A) Despite her harsh criticism of the competition,
    (B) Always harshly criticizing such competitions,
    (C) Any competition was criticized, yet
    (D) Saying that all competitions should be harshly criticized,
    (E) In spite of criticizing all such competitions,

19. While many citizens feel powerless to influence national policy, <u>it is actually effective to write to a Congressperson with an opinion.</u>
    (A) it is actually effective to write to a Congressperson with an opinion.
    (B) writing to your Congressperson with your opinion is actually effective.

(C) to write to a Congressperson with an opinion is effective.

(D) that writing your opinion to your Congressperson is effective.

(E) the writing of an opinion to a Congressperson may be effective.

20. In light of the increasing evidence of the complexity of the body's immune system, they now realize that their approach to finding a cure for cancer has been too simplistic.

(A) they now realize that their approach to finding a cure for cancer has been too simplistic.

(B) scientists now realize that their approach to finding a cure for cancer has been too simplistic.

(C) it is now realized that the approach at curing cancer was too simplistic in their approach.

(D) approaches by them at curing cancer have been too simplistic.

(E) they now realize that their approaches to curing cancer has been too simplistic.

21. It is characteristic of the Metropolitan Opera, as of every major international company, that the casting is based more on the availability of singers as it is on the tastes of the music director and the public.

(A) as of every major international company, that the casting is based more on the availability of singers as it is

(B) as it is of every major international company, that the casting is based more on the availability of singers than it is

(C) as it is of every major international company, that the casting had been based more on the availability of singers as

(D) as about every major international company, that casting is based more on the availability of singers than it was

(E) as it is of every major international company, where the casting is based more on the availability of singers than it is

22. Although all dogs are descended from the wolf and the jackal, the various breeds of dog are so different from one another that it hardly seems possible that they had a common ancestry.

(A) are so different from one another that it hardly seems possible that they had a common ancester.

(B) are so different from each other that it hardly seems possible that they have a common ancestry.

(C) are so different, one from another, that their having a common ancestor hardly seems possible.

(D) being so different from one another makes it hard to believe that they had a common ancestry.

(E) that having a common ancestry hardly seem possible in that they are so different from one another.

23. Having lived in the Orient, the works of both Perse and Claudel were greatly influenced by oriental philosophy and landscape.

(A) the works of both Perse and Claudel were greatly influenced by oriental philosophy and landscape.

(B) both Perse and Claudel were influenced by oriental philosophy and landscape.

(C) oriental philosophy and landscape influenced Perse and Claudel both.

(D) both Perse and Claudel were influenced by oriental philosophy and landscape in their work.

(E) both Perse and Claudel were influenced in their work by not only oriental philosophy, but oriental landscape as well.

24. The relationship of smoking and lung cancer have been firmly established, yet people continue to ignore warnings, jeopardizing their health and that of others.

(A) The relationship of smoking and lung cancer have been firmly established, yet people continue to ignore warnings, jeopardizing their health and that of others.

(B) The relationship of smoking to lung cancer has been firmly established, yet people continue ignoring the warnings, jeopardizing their health and that of others.

(C) The relationship of smoking to lung

cancer has been firmly established, yet people continually ignore the warnings which jeopardize their own health and that of others

(D) The relationship between smoking and lung cancer has been firmly established, yet people continue to ignore warnings, jeopardizing their own health and that of others.

(E) The relationship of smoking with lung cancer has been firmly established, with people continuing to ignore the warnings and jeopardizing their own health and others.

25. To protest their being underpaid in comparison to other city agencies, a strike was called by the sanitation workers.

(A) To protest their being underpaid in comparison to other city agencies, a strike was called by the sanitation workers.

(B) To protest them being underpaid in comparison with other city agencies, the sanitation workers called a strike.

(C) To protest their being comparatively underpaid with other city agencies, a strike was called by the sanitation workers.

(D) To protest their being underpaid in comparison with workers of other city agencies, the sanitation workers called a strike.

(E) The sanitation workers called a strike to protest them being underpaid in comparison with other city workers.

STOP

END OF SECTION. IF YOU HAVE ANY TIME LEFT, GO OVER YOUR WORK IN THIS SECTION ONLY. DO NOT WORK IN ANY OTHER SECTION OF THE TEST.

ANSWER KEY—PRACTICE EXAMINATION 5

SECTION I

1.	B	6.	B	11.	B	16.	A	21.	C
2.	D	7.	E	12.	A	17.	E	22.	A
3.	C	8.	C	13.	B	18.	E	23.	B
4.	C	9.	C	14.	D	19.	C	24.	A
5.	A	10.	B	15.	B	20.	D	25.	E

SECTION II

1.	E	6.	B	11.	C	16.	D
2.	B	7.	A	12.	C	17.	B
3.	A	8.	C	13.	D	18.	C
4.	C	9.	E	14.	C	19.	D
5.	A	10.	D	15.	B	20.	E

SECTION III

1.	B	6.	E	11.	E	16.	A	21.	B
2.	C	7.	E	12.	B	17.	A	22.	C
3.	E	8.	C	13.	A	18.	D	23.	C
4.	D	9.	D	14.	C	19.	C	24.	D
5.	A	10.	B	15.	D	20.	A	25.	A

SECTION IV

1.	D	6.	E	11.	A	16.	D	21.	A
2.	C	7.	D	12.	E	17.	C	22.	A
3.	B	8.	B	13.	A	18.	D	23.	D
4.	B	9.	C	14.	E	19.	B	24.	C
5.	D	10.	B	15.	E	20.	A	25.	A

SECTION V

1.	B	6.	D	11.	B	16.	B
2.	E	7.	E	12.	E	17.	B
3.	D	8.	C	13.	D	18.	C
4.	B	9.	C	14.	E	19.	D
5.	D	10.	A	15.	D	20.	D

SECTION VI

1.	D	6.	A	11.	C	16.	A	21.	D
2.	A	7.	B	12.	B	17.	A	22.	A
3.	D	8.	A	13.	B	18.	D	23.	E
4.	B	9.	B	14.	B	19.	C	24.	B
5.	A	10.	D	15.	A	20.	C	25.	D

SECTION VII

1.	E	6.	D	11.	C	16.	C	21.	B
2.	D	7.	C	12.	C	17.	B	22.	A
3.	A	8.	A	13.	C	18.	A	23.	B
4.	A	9.	B	14.	B	19.	B	24.	B
5.	C	10.	E	15.	D	20.	B	25.	D

EXPLANATORY ANSWERS

Section I

1. **(B)** (1) is not sufficient, even with the information provided by the question stem. Although we learn from the stem that there are 18 persons on the team, (1) leaves us with the possibilities of 15, 16, 17 or 18 seniors. (2), however, is sufficient. The dichotomy seniors–not-seniors is exhaustive; that is, a member must fall into one of the two categories. Therefore, knowing that the number of not-seniors is 3, coupled with the information provided in the stem that the total is 18, tells us that the number of seniors is 15. Of course, it was not necessary to carry the analysis to this final step. It was sufficient to recognize that sufficient information is provided by (2).

2. **(D)** A percentage is nothing but a fraction expressed in a special way, e.g., $\frac{1}{5}$ = .20 = 20%, or $\frac{1}{2}$ = .50 = 50%. So if we can find the appropriate fraction, i.e., the appropriate ratio, then we can convert that fraction or ratio to a percentage. So this question really asks, "What is $\frac{x}{y}$?" (1), by manipulation, gives $\frac{x}{y} = \frac{5}{3}$. Though we do not need to carry through the calculation, this tells us that x is $166\frac{2}{3}$ percent of y. Similarly, (2) is expressed mathematically as: y = .6x, which can be rewritten as, $\frac{x}{y} = \frac{1}{.6} = 166\frac{2}{3}$ percent. But we stress that there is no reason to do the conversion. Once you see that you have the ratio of $\frac{x}{y}$, you can stop.

3. **(C)** The question stem provides no information other than that there are two points and a circle. The question is whether P or Q is farther from the center. (1) establishes that P is in the circle, but where is Q? (2) establishes that Q is outside the circle, but where is P? This shows that neither alone is sufficient. Both (1) and (2) together are sufficient. Since a circle is defined as the location of all points equidistant from the center (take a fixed length of string, tie a crayon to one end and nail down the other end, then draw a circle), the point inside the circle must be closer to the center than any point either on the circle or, in this case, outside the circle.

4. **(C)** Here is a case for the Pythagorean theorem. As a matter of test tactics, any time you see a right triangle you should think $a^2 + b^2 = c^2$ (the square of the hypotenuse, c, is equal to the sum of the squares of the other two sides, a and b). So to find x, we must have $y^2 + z^2 = x^2$. If we know y and z, that will be sufficient. (Since distances are always positive, if we know that $3^2 + 4^2 = c^2$, we know that c is the positive value, 5, not +5 or −5.) (1), however, is not sufficient. y + z is not necessarily equal to $y^2 + z^2$ (try some numbers). Nor is (2) sufficient, for this gives us only one of the three variables needed for the Pythagorean equation. Both (1) and (2) together give us values for x and y. Treating the two statements as simultaneous equations, we can determine the value of z as well as y. Then, substituting into the Pythagorean theorem, we could compute the value of x.

5. **(A)** This question reminds us of the importance of considering each statement independently of the other. (1) is sufficient. If we know the starting date and the population on that date, since (1) gives us the rate of growth, we know when the population reaches a certain mark. (2) alone will not do

the trick. This proves that the correct choice is (A). You may also have noted that (2) is actually deducible from (1) coupled with the question stem. As we have pointed out in our instructional overview, the two statements will never contradict each other. In this case, (2) is a conclusion that could be reached on the basis of the other information given in the problem. (2) presents information that could be obtained from (1), so the answer must be either (A) or (D).

6. **(B)** This question is slightly different from the preceding question. In the preceding question the second statement was redundant, that is, already contained in the stem and (1). So there the choice had to be either (A) or (D). Here, however, (1) not only cannot establish an answer, in and of itself, but it is also irrelevant to the question since the total price is not given. (2), on the other hand, is sufficient to answer the question, since it tells us how much is owed.

7. **(E)** (1) and (2) are interesting in that they tell us how much time the watch will lose every hour, but what does the question ask? Not how much time will be lost but what the watch will read. For that we would need to know the reading at the starting point of the relevant period and also the length of the relevant period. As it is, the watch could read anything.

8. **(C)** This is one of those questions for which it is necessary to check the interaction between the two statements. Now, it should have been clear to you that neither (1) nor (2) is, in and of itself, sufficient. The only question can be whether the two together are sufficient or not, that is, whether the correct answer is (C) or (E). The answer will depend on whether, by counting, we establish the number who received one award each. We can! There are 22 awards. Proposition (2) establishes that three students received a total of 9 awards, leaving a total of 13 awards to be distributed among the remaining 12 students. Since we know by (1) that each student received at least one award, this establishes that only one student received exactly two awards. In a way, then,

this question is an exception to the general injunction that you should not calculate an exact answer. If we change the number of awards to 25 or 26, then the answer must be (E) for the numbers do not work out precisely. We hope that you can see the difference between a question such as this, where to distinguish between (C) and (E) answers you must determine whether the numbers *work out,* and a question such as question 2, where no such calculation is needed.

9. **(C)** This question will reinforce the point made by question 8. It should be obvious that neither (1) nor (2), in and of itself, is sufficient. The question, then, is whether we have a (C) or an (E) question. We can only have a (C) answer if both statements serve to define a single precise value for x. This must be checked by calculation. The lowest common multiple of x will be $3 \times 4 \times 5 = 60$. The next largest multiple of x will be 120. So (2), with (1), proves that $x = 60$.

10. **(B)** For this question, it is important to pay attention to the question and to observe that (1) is redundant of (2). First, the question asks *how long* it will take to reduce the amount of liquid to 1200 gallons. Since we are given the total in the tank at the start, (2) is sufficient; you just take the difference between the two rates to find how much liquid will disappear during a certain time. Then (1) is not sufficient, since it does not give an absolute number—for example, one could fill at the rate of 1 gallon a minute and the other empty at the rate of 8 gallons a minute.

11. **(B)** (2) is sufficient. If we know that the machine produces 40% of x in 2 hours, then, assuming a constant rate of production (as stipulated by the question stem), the machine will produce x (or the entire order) in 5 hours. (1) is not sufficient by itself, nor is it needed for this calculation.

12. **(A)** If we know the average of a group and the number of items or members in the group, then we must also know the total for the group. So statement (1) tells us that the total weight is $200 \times 4 = 800$. Statement (2)

is not sufficient by itself since for it to be sufficient we would need some other numbers (for example, the weight of two smaller crates).

13. **(B)** The question asks, "Is x an integer?" That is a yes or no question. Does (1) answer that question? Obviously not, so we must consider (2) in isolation. What does (2) establish? It says that x is either +1 or −1. This can be shown mathematically in either of two ways:

Alternative 1:

$$x^2 - 1 = 0$$
$$x^2 = 1$$
$$x = \sqrt{1}$$
$$x = \pm 1$$

Alternative 2:

$$x^2 - = 0$$
$$(x + 1)(x - 1) = 0$$

So either $x + 1 = 0$ or $x - 1 = 0$ and either $x = -1$ or $x = +1$. But either way you do the algebra, (2) establishes that *x is an integer*—and that is an answer to the question.

14. **(D)** Here we must see the possibility of using the Pythagorean theorem. Since we are dealing with a coordinate system, we can add the following line to make a right triangle:

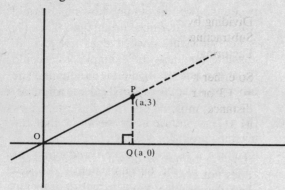

Since line PQ is parallel to the y-axis, point Q must have the same x-coordinate as point P. And since Q is on the x-axis, it has a y-coordinate of 0. This means that PQ = 3. The conclusion can be reached either by common reasoning or by the distance formula. By common reasoning, the only distance covered from P to Q is the vertical

distance from 0 on the y-axis to a value of 3 on the y-axis. So the line is 3 units long. For those who prefer to use the distance formula:

$$d = \sqrt{(x_2 - x_1)^2 + (y_2 - y_1)^2}$$

which is really nothing but a special case of the Pythagorean theorem. So:

$$d = \sqrt{(a - a)^2 + (3 - 0)^2}$$
$$d = \sqrt{(3)^2} = 3$$

Thus, (1) is sufficient, for we have one leg of the right triangle as 3 (PQ), and the hypotenuse as 6 [by (1)], so we could use the Pythagorean theorem to find the length of OQ. And that length will be equal to the x-coordinate, a. Similarly, (2) allows us to determine that OPQ is a 30°-60°-90° triangle, and, using the special properties of that triangle, we can also determine the length of OP and the value of a.

15. **(B)** (1) is not sufficient as shown by the following drawings.

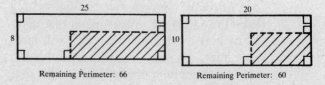

Remaining Perimeter: 66   Remaining Perimeter: 60

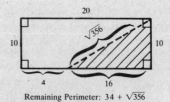

Remaining Perimeter: $34 + \sqrt{356}$

(1) does not assert that the cut used right angles. (2), however, does assert it, and that is sufficient to answer the question regarding the perimeter:

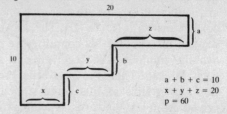

$$a + b + c = 10$$
$$x + y + z = 20$$
$$p = 60$$

16. **(A)** 1) is sufficient. The expression $\frac{1}{x} + \frac{1}{y} + \frac{1}{z} = \frac{y + x}{xy} + \frac{1}{z} = \frac{xy + xz + yz}{xyz}$ and (1) establishes that this has the value of 4, answering the question. (2) is not sufficient.

Breaking into the addition (at the point where we have $\frac{y + x}{xy} + \frac{1}{z}$) with the information that $x + y = 3$, gives the expression $\frac{3}{xy} + \frac{1}{z}$, but that is insufficient to establish a value for the expression.

17. **(E)** (1) is not sufficient to answer the question because it does not establish how many Fridays are in the year, Nor is (2) sufficient, for it does not give Mary's pay schedule. Finally, even taking both together we cannot answer the question, for they do not establish how many Fridays there are in the particular leap year. $\frac{366}{4} = 91$ with remainder 2. So there could be be 91 or 92 paydays for Mary.

18. **(E)** Neither statement by itself will answer the question. Will both taken together solve the problem? No, as can be shown by a diagram:

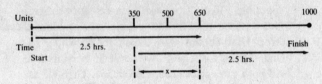

How long did it take to produce the 300 units in the overlap, that is, how long was x? We do not know because we cannot assume that the machine operated at the constant rate.

19. **(C).** That (1) is insufficient to answer the question can be shown by a diagram:

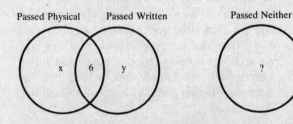

(1) does not tell us how many persons are in x and y. That (2) is not sufficient can be shown by a similar diagram:

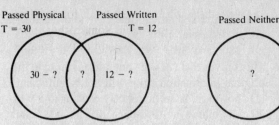

Total Passed Both Exams = ?

(2) does not establish how many applicants passed both exams, and that is needed; the question stem asks how many passed neither. Both taken together will do the trick:

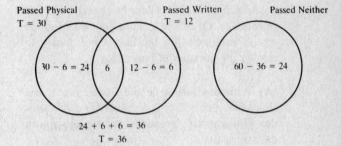

$$24 + 6 + 6 = 36$$
$$T = 36$$

20. **(D)** Statement (1) provides the following information:

$$\frac{\pi r^2}{2\pi r} = \frac{3}{2} \text{ and } \frac{r}{2} = \frac{3}{2} \text{ so } r = 3$$

(1), therefore, is sufficient. Similarly, (2) is sufficient:

$$\pi r^2 - 2\pi r = 3\pi$$

Dividing by π: $\qquad\qquad r^2 - 2r = 3$
Subtracting 3: $\qquad\qquad r^2 - 2r - 3 = 0$
Factoring: $\qquad\qquad (r - 3)(r + 1) = 0$

So either $r - 3 = 0$ or $r + 1 = 0$, and either $r = +3$ or $r = -1$; but since a radius, as a distance, must be positive, this establishes r as 3.

21. **(C)** (1) is not sufficient by itself since it does not establish which of the two figures has the greater number of sides. (2) is insufficient since it establishes only that P has more sides than Q, but it does not give information about the length of those sides. Both together, however, establish that P has more sides of the same length as those of Q, so P must be larger; that is, P has the greater area.

22. **(A)** Since 1 is a straight line, we know that the six angles equal 180°. So $y + x + y + x + y + x = 180°$ and $3y + 3x = 180°$, so $x + y = 60°$. This proves that (2) does not add anything to the original information, so it will not be sufficient. (1), however, is sufficient. By establishing y as 30°, (1) allows us to deduce that $3x = 90°$ and $x = 30°$.

23. **(B)** (1) will allow us to compute the area, but it will not by itself tell us how many lots resulted from the subdivision. (2), however, establishes that there must have been $\frac{750}{125} = 6$ lots. Otherwise, each lot could not have had exactly 125 feet of frontage. Of course, (2) does not establish the *size* of each new lot, but that is not needed to answer the question of how many.

24. **(A)** Without resorting to an elaborate proof, you should be able to recognize that (1) establishes that Q is a rectangle and answer the question in the affirmative.

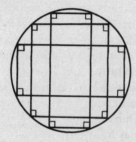

(2) however, leaves open the possibility that Q is a square (in which case it *is* possible to draw the circle) or a rhombus (in which case it is not).

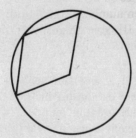

25. **(E)** Even using both statements, one crucial piece of information, the remaining dimension of the boxes, is missing.

Section II

1. **(E)** As for I, a triangle could have sides of 3, 4, and 5 and would be the special case of the right

triangle. And the numbers given in III could also form a triangle, an equilateral triangle. But no triangle could have the sides given in II, for the largest side would be longer than the sum of the other two sides.

2. **(B)** This problem is solved simply by division——but make sure you keep track of your decimal point: $1.5 \div 0.03 = 50$.

3. **(A)** Notice that the question asks "what fraction of the assortment is caramels?" This means we want the ratio:

caramels/total NOT caramels/chocolates

Since there are five parts (caramels are 1 of the total of 5 and chocolates are 4 of the total of 5), the caramels are $\frac{1}{5}$ of the total.

4. **(C)** We want the greatest possible number of people who do not fall into at least one of the three categories. We find the theoretical maximum by concentrating as many persons as possible in the three categories, leaving as many as possible "free" from the three categories. So if we assume that the 40 people who graduated from High School X are among the 65 who graduated from College Y, we leave 35 persons free of both categories ($100 - 65 = 35$). Then we assume that the 30 who live in City Z also belong to the group of 65, though just what other characteristics they share does not concern us. We are still left with a maximum of 35 people who fall into none of the three categories.

5. **(A)** This question shows an equation in the stage just prior to solving for the two roots (the two possible values of x). The equation can be read as saying either $(x - 6)$ is equal to 0 or $(2x + 1) = 0$. This means the two possible values of x are $+6$ and $-\frac{1}{2}$. Since the question stem stipulates that $x > 0$, we want the positive root, which is $+6$. As an alternative to this reasoning, you might simply have substituted choices back into the equation, starting with (A), until you found one that worked:

$$(+6 - 6)(2(6) + 1) = 0 \ (13) = 0$$

which demonstrates that $+6$ works. So (A) must be the correct choice.

into the equation, starting with (A), until you found one that worked:

$$(+6 - 6) (2(6) + 1) = 0 (13) = 0$$

which demonstrates that +6 works. So (A) must be the correct choice.

6. **(B)** This questions tests your familiarity with the coordinate system, and I suppose a basic problem many people have is remembering which is the up-down axis and which is the side-to-side axis. The first number given in the pair is always the x-coordinate and represents location from side to side; the second number is the y-coordinate and represents location on the up-and-down axis. The line shown on the graph runs in an up-down direction, with no change from side to side. This means that the x-coordinate is the same for every point on that line. So the correct solution will look like this: (x,?). Then, if we look for a point that is midway between y and −y, that will have to be 0, and the coordinates of the midpoint are (x,0).

7. **(A)** This is a fairly straightforward problem asking you to compute rate. The only trick is to make sure your final choice is expressed in copies per second. You find the total number of copies produced by subtracting: 2334 − 1254 = 1080. That number was produced in 30 minutes, or 1800 seconds (30 × 60 = 1800). So the rate per second is $\frac{1080}{1800}$ = 0.6 copies per second.

8. **(C)** There are two changes mentioned in the question. Some students leave and others enter. The number of entering students is equal to the number who left (31) *plus* a number great enough to increase the total enrollment to 654. The increase from the beginning to the end of the year is 42. And 42 + 31 = 73.

9. **(E)** Notice the presence of the word *NOT* in the question. We are looking for the one choice that is not possible, given that the dollar cost of the item is a whole number. To express profit as a percentage of cost, you would create a fraction profit/cost, which would then be converted to a percentage. So

profit/cost × 100 gives profit as a percentage of cost. Since profit is $10, the calculation for this particular question must be $10/cost × 100 is equal to percent profit:

$$\$10/cost \times 100 = x\%$$

This we can rewrite as:

$$\$10(100)/x\% = cost$$

Or as: $$\$10/x = cost$$

where x now represents the decimal equivalent of a percentage. So to determine whether an answer choice is possible, you need only substitute the decimal equivalent in for x. For example, (A):

$$\$10/.10 = \$100$$

Which says that a profit of $10 on top of a cost of $100 would be a 10% profit. Since the $100 is a whole dollar amount, (A) is possible.

The correct choice is (E):

$$\frac{\$10}{.80} = \$12.50$$

But $12.50 is not a whole dollar value.

10. **(D)** This question tests properties of odd and even numbers and can be solved either by substituting some values for x into each statement or by thinking about the characteristics of such numbers in a more abstract way. Thinking in the more general way, we reason as follows.

As for I, since x is even, 3x must also be even, and 3x + 1 an odd number.

As for II, since x is even, 5x must be even; and since 5x is even, 5x times 5x is even, and an even number plus 2 is still even.

As for III, since x is even, x + 1 is odd and x + 1 times x + 1 is also an odd number.

11. **(C)** The main trick here is to figure out how the accounting procedure takes account of the specific numbers. First, if the clerk wishes to earn at least $370 for a week, then in addition to her base salary of $210, she must earn at least $160 in commissions. Since her commission is 10% of sales, sales of $1600 will earn her the $160. But (!) she earns commissions only on those sales in excess of $3000, so she must sell $1600 more than $3,000, or at least $4,600.

12. **(C)** The transactions can be described algebraically as follows:

$$OT - .1OT + \$140 = 1.25OT$$

where OT represents "original total." Translated into ordinary English, the algebra reads "The original total minus 10% of the original total plus another 140 dollars is equal to 125% of the original total." Solving for OT:

$$OT - .10T + 140 = 1.25OT$$
$$.90T + 140 = 1.25OT$$
$$140 = .35OT$$
$$OT = \frac{140}{.35}$$
$$OT = 400$$

You can check the result of this algebraic manipulation by using $400 as the original total. Take away 10% of that, or $40, leaving $360 in the account. Then add back in $140, bringing the total to $500. And $500 is 25% more than $400.

13. **(D)** This question can be solved easily by the use of a direct proportion:

$$\frac{x}{y} = \frac{200}{Total}$$

Cross-multiplying: (x)Total = 200y

Divide by x: $Total = 200\frac{y}{x}$

14. **(C)** A picture should make clear the solution to the problem:

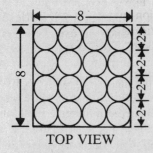

TOP VIEW

The box has inside dimensions of 8 and 8, so the area is 8 × 8 = 64 square inches

15. **(B)** The solution to this question requires you to see the relationship between two, overlapping categories or sets:

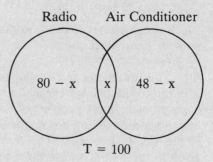

Radio   Air Conditioner

T = 100

The x in the overlapping area indicates that we do not know how many cars belong to both categories. Then, the part of the circle labeled "Radio" that does not belong to the overlap has 80 − x cars ($\frac{2}{3}$ of the 120 cars have radios). Similarly, the part of the circle labeled "Air Conditioner" that does not belong to the overlap has 48 − x cars ($\frac{2}{5}$ of the 120 cars have air conditioners). And the total of all three areas is 100 (since 20 cars have no radio or air conditioner, 120 − 20 = 100). So we add the three areas together:

$$(80 - x) + x + (48 - x) = 100$$
$$128 - x = 100$$
$$x = 28$$

So the number of cars with both radios and air conditioners is 28.

16. **(D)** Here is another question testing your understanding of the coordinate graph. To find the area of the rectangle, we must express the dimensions using x and y. The width of the rectangle is simply y, because the point (x,y) is located y units above the x-axis. The length of the rectangle is x − 2 because it runs from point 2 to point x, parallel to the x-axis. Since width is y and length is x − 2, the area must be y(x − 2).

17. **(B)** This question can be solved using simultaneous equations. For example, let x be the amount of money invested at 5% and let y be the amount of money invested at 12%. Using those symbols, since the total amount invested was $12,000, we write:

$$x + y = \$12,000$$

Next, we know that the interest earned on x (at the rate of 5% per year) plus the interest earned on y (at the rate of 12%) per year was a total of $880 in interest:

$$x(.05) + y(.12) = \$880$$

So we have two equations:

$$x + y = 12,000$$
$$.05 + .12y = 880$$

We can solve for each variable by the following method. First, since $x + y = 12,000$, $x = 12,000 - y$. We substitute that value of x into the second equation:

$$.05(12,000 - y) + .12y = 880$$
$$600 - .05y + .12y = 880$$
$$.07y = 280$$
$$y = 4,000$$

So the amount invested at 12% was $4000.

18. **(C)** This question can be answered by multiplying the expression given and simplifying:

$$(x + y)^2 - (x - y)^2 =$$
$$x^2 + 2xy + y^2 - (x - y)^2 =$$
$$x^2 + 2xy + y^2 - (x^2 - 2xy + y^2) =$$
$$2xy + 2xy = 4xy$$

Then given that $xy = 10$, the entire expression is 4 times 10 or 40.

19. **(D)** This question asks that you express the changes described in an algebraic formula. The original cost per ounce is x cents per ounce. One change is the increase in price of 10%, from x cents to $\frac{11}{10}$x cents. But the size of the candy bar is reduced by 1 ounce. So instead of the new price being $\frac{11}{10}$x cents per ounce, it is now $\frac{11}{10}$x cents per $y - 1$ ounces. So the correct formula is $\frac{11x}{10(y-1)}$.

20. **(E)** The key here is to see that the shaded area is what is left over after the unshaded portion of the circle is taken away from the entire area of the circle:

Shaded Area = Area of Circle minus Unshaded Wedge

First, the area of the entire circle is πr^2 or 36π. Next, the angle at the center of the circle belongs to the quadrilateral. The sum of the interior angles of a quadrilateral is 360°, so the missing angle must be 60°. And 60° is $\frac{1}{6}$ of the total number of degrees in a circle, so the unshaded wedge is $\frac{1}{6}$ the area of the circle, or $\frac{1}{6}$ of 36π, which is 6π. Substituting into our solution statement:

Shaded Area = 36π minus $6\pi = 30\pi$

Section III

1. **(B)** This is a main-idea question. The author's primary concern is to discuss the problem of desertification. So choice (B) is correct. A natural extension of the discussion would be a proposal to slow the process of desertification, but that is not included in the passage as written, so (A) must be incorrect. (C), (D), and (E) are each incorrect because we find no elements in the passage to support those choices. Even admitting that the author intends to define, implicitly, the term "desertification," that is surely not the main point of the passage. The author also dwells at length on the causes of the problem.

2. **(C)** This is an explicit-idea question. In the first paragraph, the author mentions (A), (B), (D), and (E) as features of desertification. (C), however, is one of the *causes* of desertification mentioned in the second paragraph.

3. **(E)** This is an inference question. The author places the phrase "higher uses" in quotation marks. In essence, this is similar to prefacing the phrase with the disclaimer "so called." This impression is reinforced by the final entry in the list of examples of "higher uses": waste dumps. This is not to say that the author would argue that such uses are not important. Rather, this is to say that the author does not believe that those uses are more important than agricultural uses. (A) is incorrect since this term is no more important than other terms used in the passage. (B) is incorrect since the author is talking about the conversion of non-arid land to higher uses. (C) is incorrect since the author is clearly opposed to such expansion.

Finally, (D) is a sentiment expressed in the passage, but that is not the reason for placing this phrase in quotation marks.

4. **(D)** This is an explicit-idea question. In the second paragraph, the author mentions that high commodity prices encourage farmers to expand production of arid lands, so statement I is part of the correct answer. Also, relatively low government fees for grazing on common lands is mentioned in that same paragraph, so statement II is part of the correct answer. The world's need for U.S. agricultural exports, however, is not mentioned as a factor encouraging desertification. It is mentioned in the final paragraph as being connected with the ultimate danger of desertification. To be sure, it is possible to argue that the demand creates the need to produce, but that is an argument that demand creates production—not that demand creates desertification. Indeed, the author believes it is possible to meet that demand without sacrificing land. So statement III is not part of the correct answer. Moreover, as a matter of test-taking wisdom, since this is an explicit idea question, it is better to prefer a fairly obvious answer, something stated on the face of the text, and not to dig for some possible connection.

5. **(A)** This is an explicit-idea question, and the answer is found in the last paragraph. There the author states that the most serious long-term effect of desertification will be on the United States' ability to export agricultural products. This will be harmful to the United States economically and to the rest of the world in terms of meeting the demand for food and fiber. As for (B) and (C), though these are plausible as effects of desertification, the author does not mention them specifically, and he certainly does not describe them as the most serious effects of desertification. (D) is incorrect because the author's concern is over the ability of the United States to continue to export agricultural products, not the ability of the United States to meet domestic demand. Finally, (E) fails for the same reason that (B) and (C) are incorrect. Though it might arguably be one result of desertification (and that is

an issue we need not address), the author never mentions it as a possible effect.

6. **(E)** This is an application question. In the passage the author indicates that government programs which encourage exploitation of arid land are in large measure responsible for the rapid rate of desertification. A natural extension of the discussion would be a proposal for government spending to conserve arid lands. And this receives specific support in the third paragraph, where the author mentions that government conservation incentives are inadequate. With regard to (A), the author seems to believe that it is necessary for the United States to continue to export agricultural products to meet the world demand; he favors conserving arid land while meeting this demand. (B) is surely incorrect, for the author argues that aid to farmers is one cause of the rapid rate of desertification. (D) is incorrect for the same reason. As for (C), the conversion of land to "higher uses" is mentioned as a factor complicating the process of desertification. It is not a cause of desertification. The most natural extension of the passage would be a discussion of how to combat desertification.

7. **(E)** This is a tone question. We can surely eliminate (B), (C), and (D) as not expressing the appropriate element of worry. Then, between (A) and (E), (A) overstates the case. The author says we solve the problem now or we solve it later (at a higher cost). But that is an expression of concern, not alarm.

8. **(C)** This is an inferred-idea question. In the second paragraph, the author states that when prices are high, ranchers and farmers put their money into strategies to expand production rather than into conservation. And when prices are low, they don't have any extra money. We may infer that when prices are low, farmers might be willing to invest in strategies to conserve resources and cut costs, but they lack the funds for such investments.

As for (A), this may be true, but it is not responsive to the question asked (why do farmers not invest in conservation when prices are low?). As for (B), this is possibly true, but there is no support for such a conclusion in the passage. (D) represents a confusion of the two situations, high commodity and low commodity prices. Finally, (E) has no support at all in the selection.

9. **(D)** This is an inference question. In the second paragraph the author states that government fees are low compared to those set by the free market, and the *difference* between them causes overgrazing. We can infer, therefore, that overgrazing could be solved by ensuring that government fees reflect conditions in the market place. (A), (B), and (C) will not solve the problem, for they don't peg the fee for the use of public lands to the free-market price. Finally, (E) has no direct connection to the use of public grazing lands.

10. **(B)** This is a main-idea question. The author draws a distinction between preventive health care and curative health care. Using this distinction, he suggests that there should be established separate authorities for each. So the primary method of developing the argument is the drawing of a distinction, as correctly stated by (B). (A) is incorrect since the author does not cite any counterarguments to his position. (C) is incorrect, for a dilemma is a "damned if you do and damned if you don't" argument. To draw a distinction is not necessarily to set up a dilemma. (D) is incorrect, for whatever causes of poor health are discussed in the passage are not the main focus of the discussion. (E) is incorrect for a similar reason. Whatever new research we may try to read into the passage, e.g., the Winslow monograph, is surely not the main point of the passage.

11. **(E)** This is an explicit-idea question. In the first sentence of the second paragraph, the author notes that treatment is aimed at a patient already ill, but we have been told in the first paragraph that preventive care is just that, aimed at people who are healthy in order to keep them that way. So statement I is part of the correct answer. Similarly,

statement II is supported by the first two paragraphs, particularly the sentence of the second paragraph that reads, "While these may be applied on a mass basis . . . , they are usually applied after the patient appears with a complaint," thus distinguishing preventive care from curative care. Finally, per capita differences in cost care are discussed in paragraph 4.

12. **(B)** This is an inference question. In the first paragraph, the author is discussing the basic strategy of preventive medicine. He then states that in California there is needless suffering and economic harm due to the failure of authorities to implement controlled fluoridation. The development of the argument leads us to conclude that the author regards the failure of the authorities to fluoridate water as a failure to implement a preventive health care program. (B) explains this reasoning. (A) is incorrect since the author holds a positive attitude about fluoridation. (C) is incorrect because the author cites the failure to fluoridate as an example of a failure to adopt a potentially valuable preventive strategy. (D) is incorrect because fluoridation is a preventive, rather than a treatment, strategy. Finally, (E) is incorrect since the author recommends the fluoridation of water as a valuable preventive strategy.

13. **(A)** This is an inference question. In paragraph 4, the author remarks that expenditure of resources on treatment is an expenditure that is lost, that is, produces nothing positive (eliminating the negative is not regarded as producing a positive result). Then, the sick person is also not contributing anything positive while he or she is sick. So the economy is doubly disadvantaged because of the burden on or drain on resources to cure an ill person and because production is lost. (A) neatly captures this idea. (B) is incorrect because the author never quantifies the cost difference between the two types of care. He says only that prevention is less costly than treatment. (C) is incorrect because the author eventually will support such a division on the ground that the two activities are sufficiently dis-

similar to warrant a division of authority. (D) is incorrect since both rehabilitation and cure belong to curative medicine, so that will not explain why the economy is doubly burdened. Finally, (E) is attractive because it is at least consistent with the general theme of the passage. But (E) is not responsive to the question. It does not explain why the economy is doubly burdened by the person who requires treatment.

14. **(C)** This is an attitude, or tone, question. Two clues support answer choice (C). First, the author refers to the monograph and then continues to make points made by Winslow. This indicates he agrees with Winslow. Second the author refers to the analysis by Winslow as "convincing." (A) and (B) can be eliminated because of the negative connotations associated with both terms. (D) can be eliminated because style is not relevant to the point under discussion. Finally, (E) is the second best answer. We eliminate (E) because the author states that the economics of prevention have been widely discussed, indicating that the uniqueness of Winslow's contribution is not necessarily originality. Further, the reference to the persuasiveness of Winslow's analysis makes (C) a better descriptive phrase to apply to the author's attitude than (E).

15. **(D)** This is a logical detail question. The author introduces these three diseases in the paragraph discussing the economics of prevention, and following the statement that the cost of prevention is less than the cost of treatment when averaged out on a per capita basis. (D) makes this point. (A) is incorrect, for while this is a statement the author would surely accept, it is not the reason for introducing the examples. (B) is incorrect for a similar reason. This may very well be true, but it is not an answer to the question. (C) must be wrong, for though this is one of the main points of the discussion, it will not answer this particular question. Finally, (E) is also a statement which the author could accept, but it is not responsive to the question.

16. **(A)** This is a question about the logical structure of the argument. The author mentions several differences between preventive and curative medicines: cost, personnel, persons addressed. But these differences are not compelling reasons for creating a division of authority. The need to separate authority for the two strategies is discussed in the first and last paragraphs. The value of the division will be to clarify objectives and redress the inequitable division of resources. These are problems, so says the first paragraph, because "the imperative nature of medical care" will allow it to dominate health care. In other words, the urgency of treatment attracts attention. This is the explanation provided in (A). And for this reason it is not cost, (B), personnel, (C), or persons addressed, (D), which is the important difference. Finally, (E) is directly contradicted by the opening sentences of the passage.

17. **(A)** This is a tone question. The author evidences a sincere interest in the topic he discusses. He analyzes a situation and makes recommendations. Thus, the best description of the tone of the passage is provided by (A). You can eliminate (B) because the author is not disinterested. You can eliminate (C) as inconsistent with the confident tone of the passage. (D), however, overstates the case. There is no element of alarm in the selection. Finally, (E) is inconsistent with the confidence expressed in the selection.

18. **(D)** This is a main-idea question. The author cites several arguments in favor of the "drug lag" theory, then offers refutations of at least some of them. He concludes that the arguments for "drug lag" are not conclusive and that, contrary to the view of the "drug lag" theoreticians, the 1962 Amendments are not, on balance, harmful. The main technique of development is refutation of arguments cited. (D) is therefore the best answer to this question. (A) can be eliminated since the author does not outline a proposal. Discussing the effectiveness of some past action is not outlining a proposal. (B) has some merit because the author does analyze the evidence presented by the "drug lag" theoreticians. This analysis, however, is not the final objective of the passage. It is

presented in order to further the goal of refuting the general position of that group. (C) is incorrect since the author poses no question, and indeed seems to answer any question that might be implicit in the passage regarding the value of the Amendments. (E) has some merit since the focus of the passage is a law. But the intent of the author is not to discuss the law per se. Rather, the intent of the passage is to refute objections to the law. On balance, (D) more precisely describes the main idea than the other choices.

19. **(C)** (A), (B), (D), and (E) are all mentioned as "drug lag" arguments in the second paragraph. As for (C), the argument that effectiveness studies cost money is mentioned in the first paragraph. But "drug lag" results from the time and cost of effectiveness studies. "Drug lag" is not the increased cost itself.

20. **(A)** This is an application question. Support for (A) is found in the closing sentences of the passage. In the final paragraph, the author insists that there are few, if any, examples of harm done by the requirements of effectiveness studies. Then he says that we are at least assured that the drug, which might actually prove harmful, does have some benefit. The qualified nature of the claim suggests that the author would acknowledge that some "drug lag" does exist but that, on balance, it is justified. This thought is captured by choice (A). (B) is incorrect because the author never states the effectiveness studies are designed to determine whether the drug has unwanted effects. Apparently, effectiveness studies, as the name implies, are designed to test the value of the drug. This is not to say that such studies may not, in fact, uncover unwanted side effects, but given the information in the passage, (B) is a more tenuous inference than (A). (C) is incorrect for two reasons. First, the passage never states that the cost of drugs is higher in the United States than in other countries. The passage states only that the proponents of the "drug lag" theory argue that the effectiveness study requirement increases the cost of drugs here. That

makes no comparison with a foreign country. Second, the author seems to discount the significance of the increased cost. (D) is incorrect because there is no basis for such a recommendation in the passage. Finally, (E) is incorrect because the passage never states that the studies do not cost money or time. The author only doubts whether the cost or time create profit pressures serious enough to cause "drug lag."

21. **(B)** This is a logical structure question. In the final paragraph the author states that the drop in new drugs introduced annually began before the Amendments took effect. He does not deny that the drop occurred; rather, he points out that it predated the supposed cause. In other words, the author is suggesting that there must be some other reason for the drop. Answer (B) correctly describes the author's logical move. (E) is directly contradicted by this analysis. The author does not deny that there was a drop in the number of new drugs introduced every year. As for (A), the author does not point to any similarity between two situations. He says only that the situation being studied existed even before the Amendments took effect. (C) is incorrect because the author never questions the credibility of an opponent, only the value of his opponent's arguments. Finally, (D) is incorrect because the author's use of statistics is not an attempt to justify his use of those statistics. He uses statistics to prove some further conclusion.

22. **(C)** This is a logical-structure question. In the second paragraph, the author cites, as one argument for the existence of "drug lag," the nonavailability in the United States of a drug that is available in a foreign country. In the third paragraph, he offers a refutation of this argument. The simple availability–nonavailability comparison is not valid because consumers may not suffer from the nonavailability of that particular drug if another drug is available to treat the same condition. Answer (C) correctly describes the structure of this argument. The remaining answer choices are in various ways related to the overall argument of the

passage, but they are not answers to this particular question.

23. **(C)** Again, we have a logical-structure question. We have already noted that the author does not deny that fewer drugs were introduced each year after the Amendments than before the Amendments. But he argues that the total number of new chemical entities is not necessarily a measure of the value of new drugs introduced. By redefining terms so that we speak not just of new chemical entities but of unimportant, important, and breakthrough chemical entities, he minimizes the significance of the argument. The relevant comparison, he claims, is between important and breakthrough chemical entities, not total new chemical entities introduced. Answer (C) correctly points out that the essence of this logical move is redefining terminology. (A) is incorrect because the author does not deny that the total number had dropped. (B) is incorrect because the author does not explain why that number has dropped. (D) is incorrect because the author makes no such proposal. Finally, (E) is only remotely related to the correct answer. While it may be true that an important or breakthrough chemical has many more uses than an unimportant chemical entity, the author does not list the uses of any chemical.

24. **(D)** This is an application question. What are the logical underpinnings of the comparison? Notice that the author's description of the arguments he attacks includes reference to "advanced" nations. Apparently, the proponents of the "drug lag" theory realize that a comparison between the United States and a non-advanced country would not be relevant. They want a situation in which the only important difference is the strictness of the laws on new drugs. For this reason both I and III are presuppositions of the argument. II is not a presupposition of the argument since proponents of the theory do not have to make any assumption about profitability. The opponents of the Amendments claim only that the testing required increases the cost of drugs in the U.S., not that it makes drugs more costly in the U.S. than elsewhere, nor that the pharmaceutical industry here is less profitable than elsewhere.

25. **(A)** This is an attitude question. The author's main concern is to demonstrate that the arguments adduced to prove the existence of a "drug lag" fail. They don't prove that such a problem exists. So (A) is the best description of the author's attitude.

Section IV

1. **(D)** Let us use letters to represent the categories. "All effective administrators" will be A. "Concerned about welfare" will be C. "Are liberal" will be L. The three propositions can now be represented as:

1. All A are W.
2. All W are L.
3. All non-L are not A.

Proposition # 3 is equivalent to "all A are not non-L," and that is in turn equivalent to "all A are L." Thus, (D) follows fairly directly as a matter of logic. (A) is incorrect, for while we know that "all A are L," we would not want to conclude that "No L are A"—there might be some ineffective administrators who grant time off. They could be ineffective for other reasons. (B) is incorrect for the same reason. Even though all effective administrators are concerned about their employees' welfare, this does not mean that an ineffective administrator could not be concerned. He might be concerned but ineffective for another reason. (C) is clearly false given our propositions; we know that all effective administrators are liberal. Finally, (E) is not inferable. Just because all effective administrators grant time off does not mean that all the time granted off is granted by effective administrators.

2. **(C)** The weakness in Gerry's argument is that he assumes, incorrectly, that getting drunk is the only harm Clyde has in mind. Clyde could respond very effectively by pointing to some other harms of alcohol. (A) would not be a good response for Clyde since he is concerned with Gerry's welfare.

The fact is that other people get drunk when Gerry does not is hardly a reason for Gerry to stop drinking. (B) is also incorrect. That other people do or do not get drunk is not going to strengthen Clyde's argument against Gerry. He needs an argument that will impress Clyde, who apparently does not get drunk. (D) is perhaps the second best answer, but the explicit wording of the paragraph makes it unacceptable. Gerry has been drinking the same quantity for 15 years. Now, admittedly, it is possible he will begin to drink more heavily, but that *possibility* would not be nearly so strong a point in Clyde's favor as the *present* existence of harm (other than inebriation). Finally, (E) is irrelevant, since it is white wine that Gerry does drink.

3. **(B)** The point of the passage is that a meaningful comparison between the two systems is going to be difficult since the one is cheap in the short run but expensive in the long run, while the other is expensive in the short run and cheap in the long run. The only appropriate way of doing the cost comparison is by taking account of both costs—which is what (B) does. To take just the long-run costs would be to ignore the short-run costs involved, so (A) is wrong; and taking the short-run costs while ignoring the long-run costs is no better, so (C) is wrong. If (A) is wrong, then (D) also has to be wrong, and the more so because it is not even projecting operating costs. Finally, (E) is a distraction—the connection between diesel fuel and air pollution is irrelevant in a paragraph which is concerned with a cost comparison.

4. **(B)** One way of "making more money" other than raising the price of a product is to lower the size or quality of the product. This is what Vendo must have done. By doing so, they accomplished the equivalent of a price increase without actually raising the price. (C) contradicts the paragraph which states that Vendo did not violate the letter of the instructions—that is, the literal meaning—though they did violate the intention. (D) also contradicts the paragraph. Had Vendo forfeited the franchise, that would have

been within the letter of the "either-or" wording of the instructions. (A) and (E) require much speculation beyond the information given, and you should not indulge yourself in imaginative thinking when there is an obvious answer such as (B) available.

5. **(D)** The author's argument seems fairly weak. He introduces the example of the second university without explaining why we should consider that case similar to the one we are arguing about (except for size). This shows that the author is introducing an analogy—though not a very strong one. (A) is perhaps the second best answer. But it would be correct only if there were a *contention* that the author had introduced new evidence in support of the argument. He does not articulate a contention and then adduce evidence for it. (B) is wrong because the author really has no solution to the problem—he wants to argue that the problem does not exist. Finally, (C) and (E) must be wrong because the author never mentions a logical contradiction nor does he point to any ambiguity in his opponent's argument.

6. **(E)** Careful reading of the ad shows that all three propositions could be true even if the ad is correct. First, another deodorant might also give all-day protection. The ad claims that White Bear is the only deodorant that gives you *both* protection and scent—a vacuous enough claim since White Bear is probably the only deodorant with the White Bear scent. Of course, III is not affected by this point, since the White Bear Company may put its unique scent into many of its products. Finally, II is also not inconsistent with the ad—that another product is more popular does not say that it has the features the ad claims for the White Bear deodorant.

7. **(D)** The easiest way to set this problem up is to draw a relational line:

Dislikes ————————→ Likes
 PE   IP   EL   BE

We note that Clara likes Basic Economics better than anything else, which means she must like it better than Advanced Calculus. So even though Advanced Calculus does not appear on our line, since we know that Basic Economics is the maximum, Clara must like Advanced Calculus less than Basic Economics. So (C) can be inferred. But we do not know where World History ranks on the preference line, and since Introductory Physics is not a maximal or a minimal value, we can make no judgment regarding it and an unplaced course. Quick reference to the line will show that (A), (B), and (E) are inferable.

8. **(B)** We have seen examples before of the form of argument Holmes has in mind: "P or Q; not-P; therefore, Q." Here, however, the first premise of Holmes' argument is more complex: "P or Q or R . . . S," with as many possibilities as he can conceive. He eliminates them one by one until no single possibility is left. The logic of the argument is perfect, but the weakness in the form is that it is impossible to guarantee that all contingencies have been taken into account. Maybe one was overlooked. Thus, (B) is the correct answer. (A), (C), and (E) are wrong for the same reason. Holmes' method is designed to answer a particular question—in this case, "Where did the body come from?" Perhaps the next step is to apply the method to the question of the identity of the murderer, as (E) suggests, but at this juncture he is concerned with the preliminary matter of how the murder was committed. In any event, it would be wrong to assail the logic of Holmes' deduction by complaining that it does not prove enough. Since (A) and (C) are even more removed from the particular question raised, they, too, must be wrong. Finally, (D) is nothing more than a reiteration of Watson's original comment, and Holmes has already responded to it.

9. **(C)** Notice that the student responds to the professor's comment by saying, "That can't be true," and then uses the Duchess of Warburton as a counterexample. The Duchess would only be a counterexample to the professor's statement had the professor said that women cannot inherit the estates of their families. Thus, (C) must capture the student's misinterpretation of the profes-

sor's statement. What has misled the student is that he has attributed too much to the professor. The professor has cited the general rule of primogeniture—the eldest male child inherits—but he has not discussed the special problems that arise when no male child is born. In those cases, presumably a non-male child will have to inherit. (E) incorrectly refers to inheriting from a mother in discussing a case in which the woman inherited her father's estate. (D) is wrong, for the student specifically mentions the conditions that make a child legitimate: born to the wife of her father. (A) was inserted as a bit of levity: Of course, only men can *father* children of either sex. Finally, first-born or not, a daughter cannot inherit as long as there is any male child to inherit, so (B) must be incorrect.

10. **(B)** This question requires careful attention to the quantifiers in each claim. An additional expense voucher might indicate additional expenses for an already identified employee or expenses incurred by an additional employee. A claim that states only that there are "at least so many employees" and that they incurred "at least this in expenses" cannot be contradicted by a revision upward in any number. A claim that states "there were exactly so many employees" or that states "there were at most so many employees" is contradicted by the discovery of another employee. The same reasoning applies to expenses. An "at least" claim is not contradicted by an upward revision, but the other claims are. (A) can be contradicted by an upward revision in the number of employees. (C) can be contradicted by an upward revision in the amount of expenses claimed. (D) and (E) can be contradicted on both grounds. (B) cannot be contradicted by any new finding.

11. **(A)** The question stem contains a hidden assumption: It is a loaded question. It presupposes that the person questioned agrees that the city is discriminating against its Hispanic residents. (A) is a pretty nice parallel. The questioner assumes that the Congressman agrees that defense spending is out of hand, which may or may not be

true. (B) makes no such assumption. It can be answered with a simple yes if the chairperson plans to take a luncheon recess; otherwise a no will do the job. (C) requires more than a yes or no answer, but it still contains no presuppositions. Since the question asks "what," the speaker may respond by saying much, little, or none at all. (D) may be said to make a presupposition—Gladys is going to the store—but here the presupposition is not concealed. It is made an explicit condition of the answer. Finally, (E) is a little like (B) in that a simple yes or no can communicate the counselor's opinion. It might be objected that (E) presupposes that the company has an affirmative action program, and that this makes it similar to the question stem. Two responses can be made. First, (E) is in this way like (D): The assumption—if there is one—is fairly explicit. Second, (E) does not have the same loaded tone as (A) does, so by comparison (A) is a better choice.

12. **(E)** The ad is a little deceptive. It tries to create the impression that if hospitals are using Dr. John's Milk of Magnesia, people will believe it is a good product. But what the ad actually says is that Dr. John uses the same *ingredient* that hospitals use (milk of magnesia is a simple suspension of magnesium hydroxide in water). The ad is something like an ad for John's Vinegar which claims it has "acetic acid," which is vinegar. I falls into the trap of the ad and is therefore wrong. II is not inferable since there may be treatments other than milk of magnesia for these disorders. Finally, since I is incorrect, III must certainly also be incorrect. Even if I had been true, III might still be questionable since use and recommendation are not identical.

13. **(A)** Statements I and II combine to give us (A). If all wheeled conveyances that travel on the highway are polluters, and a bicycle does not travel on the highway, then a bicycle cannot be a polluter. If (A) is then correct, (B) must be incorrect because bicycles do not travel on the highways at all. (C) and (D) make the same mistake. III must be read to say, "If I am driving, it is raining,"

not "If it is raining, I am driving." (E) is clearly false since my car is driven on the highway. Don't make the problem harder that it is.

14. **(E)** Picking up on our discussion of (C) and (D) in the previous question, III must read, "If I am driving, then it is raining." Let that be: "If P, then Q." If we then had not-Q, we could deduce not-P. (E) gives us not-Q by changing IV to "It is not raining." Changing I or II or even both is not going to do the trick, for they don't touch the relationship between my driving my car and rain—they deal only with pollution and we need the car to be connected. Similarly, if we change III to make it deal with pollution, we have not adjusted the connection between my driving and rain, so (C) must be wrong. (D) is the worst of all the answers. Whether rainwater is polluted or not has nothing to do with the connection between my driving and rain. Granted, there is the unstated assumption that my car only pollutes when I drive it, but this is OK.

15. **(E)** The reasoning in the argument is representative of the fallacy of false cause. Common sense tells you that you are not necessarily safer driving at higher speeds. Moreover, the distance you are from your home does not necessarily make you more or less safe. And it will not do to engage in wild speculation, e.g., people suddenly become more attentive at speeds over 45 miles per hour. The exam is just not that subtle. Rather we should look for a fairly obvious alternative explanation, and we find it in (E). The real reason there are fewer fatalities at speeds over 50 miles per hour and at a distance greater than 25 miles from home is that less driving time is logged under such conditions. Most driving originates at home and proceeds at speeds set for residential areas. (A), (B), and (C) all seem to make plausible statements, but they are irrelevant to the claim made in the stem paragraph. It is difficult to see how they could either weaken or strengthen the argument. (D) has the merit of addressing the statistics used to support the argument, but without further information (D) does not weaken the argu-

ment—it merely makes an observation. To be sure, if we knew that states were notoriously bad at gathering statistics, (D) could weaken the argument. But that requires speculation, and we always prefer an obvious answer such as (E).

16. **(D)** The author states that a certain amount of rain in a given time *usually* results in mushrooms growing in his backyard. Both I and II are wrong for the same reason. From the fact that there has not been the requisite minimum rainfall required for mushrooms, we would not want to conclude that there has been *no* rain at all. III overstates the author's case and is for that reason wrong. The author specifically qualifies his claim by saying it "usually" happens this way. Thus, he would not want to say that the absence of mushrooms and fungus definitely means that the requisite amount of rain has not fallen—only that it seems likely or probable that there has not been enough rain.

17. **(C)** Given the fairly "soft" information provided in the paragraph, any conclusion that is to be "completely justified" on the basis of that information will have to be a fairly minimal claim. We can eliminate (A) since the paragraph asserts something about the effect of Jack Remain's program but never claims that the Jack Remain program is unique in this respect. (B) goes beyond the scope of the argument by asserting the program is effective for all ages. The paragraph actually makes only a minimal claim, namely, this is possible. Even if the program is effective only for persons 20 to 25, the claim is not false—it is true though only for that limited age group. (D) overstates the case. The paragraph claims that weight loss is possible—not that it is certain. (E) cannot be justified, for that would be to move from the premise "weight loss is possible" to the conclusion "most people need exercise to lose weight." But the conclusion does not follow from the premise. (C), however, can be justified. If it is true, as the stem asks us to assume, that a study shows weight loss is possible, then it must be true that the program is effective for some—even if only

for one person. This is all (C) claims: You might be one of the lucky ones.

18. **(D)** In essence, the advertisement attempts to shift the burden of proof to the reader. It is possible—you try it and find out whether it is possible for you. (E) is incorrect since no other claims are cited. (C) is incorrect since the ad is clearly an attempt to influence the reader's decision. (B) should be eliminated in favor of (A) since the paragraph is not a logical set of premises. This leaves (A) as the second best answer. And it can be argued that the paragraph does provide evidence (the study) and, further, that it does allow the reader to reach a conclusion. But what would that conclusion be? If the conclusion mentioned in (A) is to try or not to try the product, then (A) is incorrect since the ad reaches the conclusion that the reader should try it. But if the conclusion is whether or not the product works, then (D) is better because it more accurately describes the attempt to shift the burden of proof.

19. **(B)** The author's claim is self-referential—it refers to itself or includes itself in its own description. The author says that *every* action is economically motivated; therefore, we may conclude that his own motivation in making such a claim and in writing a book about it is also economically motivated. The speaker in our passage says he is going to apply the author's theory to his (the author's) own actions. This is why (B) is correct. Neither (A) nor (E) can be correct inasmuch as the author of the book claims that there are no such motivations. Ultimately, he says, all motivations can be reduced to one, economics. (C) has to be wrong, since the author of the book claims that everything done is economically motivated. His examples make it clear that even a reformer with some seemingly noneconomic motive would be "pure" only on the surface, with a deeper, economic motivation for reforming. Finally, (D) can be rejected since it conflicts with one of the examples given by the author of the book.

20. **(A)** The argument makes the rather outlandish assumption that the physical charac-

teristics of the criminal dictate the kind of crime he will commit. But as unreasonable as that may seem in light of common sense, it *is* an assumption made by the speaker. (We did not make the assumption, he did.) II is not an assumption of the argument, since the paragraph specifically states that the killer was executed—he cannot have escaped. III does not commit the blatant error committed by II, but it is still wrong. Although III might be a better explanation for the crimes now being committed than that proposed by our speaker, our speaker advances the explanation supported by I, not III. In fact, the speaker uses phrases such as "looks very much like" which tell us that he assumes there are two killers.

21. **(A)** The form of the argument can be represented using letters as:

    I.   All R are either O or W. (All non-Readers are non-Opinion holders or Wrong.)
    II. All O are R.

    If II is true, I might be either false or true, since it is possible that there are some who have not read the report who hold right opinions. That is, even if II is true and all O are R, that does not tell us anything about all the R's, only about all the O's. The rest of the R's might be W's (wrong-opinion holders) or something else altogether (right-opinion holders). By this reasoning we see that we cannot conclude that I is definitely true, so (B) must be wrong. Moreover, we have no ground for believing I to be more or less likely true, so (C) can be rejected. As for (D), even if we assume that all the R's are *either* O or W, we are not entitled to conclude that all O's are R's. There may be someone without an opinion who has not read the report. Finally (E), if it is false that all the O's (non-opinion holders) are not R's, this tells us nothing about all R's and their distribution among O and W.

22. **(A)** The fallacy in the author's argument is that he takes a group term ("the average size of women") and applies it to the individual. (A) calls attention to this fallacy. The average size of women is irrelevant in the case of those women who are of sufficient

size. (D) concedes too much to the author. We do not have to settle for the conclusion that some women may be suitable for desk jobs. We can win the larger claim that some women may be suitable to be police officers—or at least as suitable as their male counterparts. (B), (C), and (E) are possible arguments to be used against the author's general position. We might want to claim, for example, that training or weapons will compensate for want of size, but again there is no reason even to grant the author that much. We do not even have to concede that the *average* size is relevant. Finally, (E) also gives away too much. Although the use of pistols is sometimes called "deadly force," the author's linkage of size to force specifies force as being a strength or size idea.

23. **(D)** We can use our capital letters to see why (D) is the correct answer. The structure of the stem argument is:

    No S are R.
    Some S are D.
    Therefore, Some D are not R.

    (D) shares this form:

    All pets are excluded: No P are A.   (A = allowed)
    Many = Some: Some P are V.
    Therefore, some V are not A.

    (A) has a very different form since it is presented as a probabilistic, not a deductive or logical, argument. (B)'s conclusion goes beyond the information given in the premises. We cannot conclude that uncle *enjoys* paying the bills, even though he may incur them. (C) has the form:

    Some BB are F.
    All F is WR.
    Therefore, All BB are WR.

    This does not parallel our question stem for two reasons. First, our stem argument is valid, while the argument in (C) is not. Second, (D) is more nearly parallel to the stem arrangement than (C); for even if we rearrange the assumptions in (C) to put the "all" proposition first and the "some" proposition second, the "all's" and the "some's" of (C) do not parallel those of the question stem. (E) does not share the stem form. First, it is not the same argument form (all, some, etc.). Second, (E) is clearly not a proper logical argument.

24. **(C)** The stem argument has the form: "If P, then Q. Q. Therefore, P." The argument is invalid. There may be other reasons that the razor is not functioning, e.g., the switch is not on, it is broken, etc. (C) has this form also. John's fingerprints might have been found at the scene, yet he may not have committed the crime. (A) has the form: "If P, then Q. Not Q. Therefore, not P," which not only is not parallel to the question stem, but is valid and thus a poor parallel to the invalid original argument as well. (B) has the form: "P or Q. Not P. Therefore, Q." This, too, does not parallel the stem argument, and like (B), is valid. (D) is invalid, but the fallacy is not the same as what we find in the stem argument. The stem argument is set up using "if, then" statements. (D) does not parallel this form. (E) does use "if, then" statements, but its form is: "If P, then Q. P. Therefore, P." This argument is clearly valid.

25. **(A)** The author's statement is self-contradictory or paradoxical. It says, in effect, "No statement is always correct," but then that statement itself must be false—since it attempts to make a claim about "always." The author's statement is inductive, that is, a generalization; but (E) is not as good an answer as (A) because it fails to pick up on the fact that the statement is internally contradictory. The statement cannot be valid, (D), since the author tries to pass it off as a generalization. Generalizations can be strong or weak, well founded or ill founded, but they cannot be valid or invalid. (C) is incorrect for there is nothing ambiguous or poorly defined in the argument. Finally, the argument is not circular, (B), because the author does not seek to establish his conclusion by assuming it. As we have noted, the statement is self-contradictory, so it could not possibly be circular.

Section V

1. **(B)** This question requires that you evaluate the expression using the numbers given:

$$\frac{x(y - z)}{y(x + y + z)} = \frac{5(3 - 2)}{3(5 + 3 + 2)} = \frac{5}{30} = \frac{1}{6}$$

2. **(C)** One way of solving this problem is to multiply 0.010 by 200% which is just 2.0. Or you might recognize that 200% of any number is twice that number, so 200% of 0.010 must be 0.020.

3. **(D)** The opposite angles in the figure are equal to one another. So angle y is 30°, and angle w is 60°. And, angles w, x and y form a straight line and their measures must total 180°. This means that x must be 90°.

4. **(B)** As for I, although the average of the five integers is 1, 1 need not be one of the five. For example, the average of −3, −2, 2, 3 and 5 is 1. As for III, 0 could be one of the integers, e.g., the average of −3, −2, −1, 0 and 11 is 1. II, however, is true. Since the five numbers are different integers, at least one of them must be negative in order to "pull down" the average to 1.

5. **(D)** This question is answered by taking a percentage of a percent. 60% of the books are clothbound, and 30% of those are works of fiction. So, 30% of 60%, or .30 × .60 = .18 or 18% are clothbound works of fiction.

6. **(D)** Here we have a bookkeeping problem. If the traveler breaks her present contract, forfeiting the deposit, she loses 10% of the $1200 price, or $120. She will then buy the other trip for a cost of 20% less than $1200: $1200 − .20($1200) = $1,200 − $240 = $960. So the total cost will be $960 plus the forfeited deposit of $120: $960 + $120 = $1080. Still, $1080 is $120 less than the original price of $1200.

7. **(E)** The first seven judges have awarded the gymnast a total of 56 points. If she receives nothing lower than a 6 from the other three judges, she will earn from them at least another 18 points, for a total of 74. This means that her average score will be at least 7.4, and it might (or might not) be higher.

8. **(C)** This question can be answered by following the change in the sample's weight

step by step, from the sixth repetition back to the third:

After test:

6	5	4	3
16	32	64	128

9. **(C)** If the item is sold at a 40% discount, then the dollar savings is equal to 40% of the usual price:

$$.40 \times \text{Usual Price} = \$12$$

Usual Price =
$$\frac{\$12}{.40} = \$30$$

This is the usual selling price. The sale price is $12 less, or $18.

10. **(A)** A quick way to answer the question is to recognize that each of the equations can be turned upside down. In other words, $\frac{1}{x}$ = 6, then x = $\frac{1}{6}$. And $\frac{1}{y} = \frac{1}{3}$, then y = 3. So $\frac{x}{y} = \frac{1/6}{3} = \frac{1}{18}$.

11. **(B)** For all of the distracting business about stock and par value and so on, this question really just requires that you convert a mixed fraction to an improper fraction. The question asks "the dividend was what fraction of the par value?" We are told that the dividend was $8\frac{3}{8}\%$ of the par value. So we set up a fraction:

$$8\frac{3}{8}\% = \frac{8\frac{3}{8}}{100} = \frac{\frac{67}{8}}{100} = \frac{67}{800}$$

12. **(E)** One way of answering the question is to assign an arbitrary number to represent the price of the commodity on March 1. Let us assume it was $100. First, the price falls by $\frac{1}{4}$, from $100 to $75. Then it falls another $\frac{1}{3}$ to $50. To return to its original level, the price must increase by $50, and $50 is 100% of $50.

13. **(D)** Again, let's attack the question by assuming arbitrary numbers. Let's assume that the assessed value of the property is $10,000 and that the tax rate is 100% of the assessed value. Admittedly these are unrealistic assumptions, but they do not have to be realistic, just convenient. On these assumptions, the tax on the property would be 100% of $10,000, or $10,000. Now, we manipulate the numbers according to in-

structions. The assessed value is increased by 25%: $10,000 + (.25 × $10,000) = $12,500. And the tax rate goes down by 25%: 100% − (.25 × 100%) = 75%. So the new tax is 75% of $12,500 = $9,375, a drop of $625. Finally, to find what that represents as a percentage of the original tax, we create a fraction $\frac{625}{10,000} = 0.0625 = 6.25\%$. So there was a net decrease of 6.25%.

14. **(E)** Here we are asked to express a relationship using an algebraic formula. We reason as follows. First, a single machine consumes $\frac{k}{5}$ kilowatts every t hours, which is a rate of $\frac{k/5}{t}$, or $\frac{k}{5t}$. Next, we have three such machines, and they will consume at three times the rate of one machine: $\frac{3k}{5t}$. Finally, a direct proportion will show us how much is consumed in 10 hours:

$$\frac{3k}{5t} = \frac{x}{10}$$

Cross-multiply: $30k = (x)5t$

Divide by 5t: $\frac{30k}{5t} = x$

$$\frac{6k}{t} = x$$

So three such machines operating for 10 hours will consume $\frac{6k}{t}$.

15. **(D)** Here we have a problem asking us to calculate a combined rate of operation—with the additional twist that the rates are expressed in terms of an x. We proceed in the usual fashion:

Rate (1) + Rate (2) + Rate (3) = Rate Combined

Amount: $\frac{x}{10} + \frac{x}{6} + \frac{2x}{15} = \frac{5x}{y}$
Time:

(where y is the unknown time needed to answer the question.)

Add Fractions: $\frac{3x + 5x + 4x}{30} = \frac{5x}{y}$

$$\frac{12x}{30} = \frac{5x}{y}$$

Cross-multiply: $y(12x) = 150x$

Divide by 12x: $y = \frac{150x}{12x} = 12.5$ hours

16. **(B)** Notice that PQR is an isosceles right triangle of known sides, 2. This allows us to compute the length of PR which is both the hypotenuse of PQR and the side of equilateral triangle PRS. In an isosceles right triangle, the hypotenuse is equal to the side multiplied by $\sqrt{2}$. So PR = $2\sqrt{2}$, and RS and SP have the same length. So the entire perimeter is:

$$PQ + QR + RS + SP = \text{Perimeter PQRS}$$
$$2 + 2 + 2\sqrt{2} + 2\sqrt{2} = \text{Perimeter PQRS}$$
$$4 + 2(2\sqrt{2}) = \text{Perimeter PQRS}$$
$$4 + 4\sqrt{2} = \text{Perimeter PQRS}$$

17. **(B)** For clarity, let us begin by labeling the unlabeled angles in the drawing:

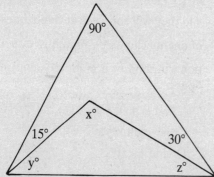

Notice that x + y + z, the interior angles of a triangle, must total 180 degrees. To find x, however, we need only the *sum* of y and z—not their actual measures. If you look at the position y and z occupy in the larger triangle, you will see that

$$(15 + y) + (30 + z) + 90 = 180$$
$$(15 + y) + (30 + z) = 90$$
$$45 + y + z = 90$$
$$y + z = 45$$

So the sum of y and z is 45, and

$$x + y + z = 180$$
$$x + 45 = 180$$
$$x = 135$$

18. **(C)** This question is really not as complicated as it might at first seem. We are told that an increase of 8q% in the price results in a drop in consumption of q%. So if we want a decrease in consumption of 2%, we must increase the price $8 \times 2 = 16\%$. And 16% of $1.05 = $0.168.

19. **(D)** The most likely error here is the urge to reason that the average of 40 and 80 is 60, so the car should travel the second half of the course at 80 miles per hour. Notice, however, that the array of answer choices does not include that as a possible choice. This should have alerted you to the fact that the inclination to average is an error. The reason it is an error is that the time spent traveling at 40 miles per hour will not be equal to the time spent traveling at 60 miles per hour, so you cannot weight the two equally.

The correct solution is to recognize that if the car is to cover the entire 120 miles at an average of 60 miles per hour, it will have to cover the entire course in exactly 2 hours. Since it traveled the first 60 miles at only 40 miles per hour, it has already been traveling for 1.5 hours, so it must cover the second half in only .5 hours. So the second half must be traveled at the rate of 60 miles in .5 hours, which is 120 miles per hour.

20. **(D)** This question can be solved algebraically, but a "neater" approach is to test answer choices until you find one that works. Ordinarily, we would suggest you start in the middle with choice (C), but a quick preview of the choices and a little common sense can make the task even simpler. Look at choice (B). What does it mean? The question tells us that *net* after 10 years repaid the investment. But if the gross is only $41,400 per year, the gross for 10 years would be $414,000, equal to the investment. But that means net would be less. This tells you (B) (and with it choice A) is too small.

So we are left with (C), (D), and (E). Pick the middle value, (D), and one calculation will give you the correct choice. If (D) is the gross income, $55,200, then the net income would be:

$$\$55,200 - 25\%(\$55,200) = \$55,200 - \$13,800 = \$41,400$$

And that, when multiplied by 10 equals the investment. So (D) is correct.

Had the choices been arranged differently, so that (D) turned out to be too small, this would have proved the correctness of the next larger choice. Conversely, had (D) proved too large, this would have proved the correctness of the next smaller number.

Section VI

1. **(D)** This is a fairly easy inference question. We are asked to determine which of the problems mentioned by the author is the most important. (B) can be eliminated because the author's criticism is not that such courses are not offered, nor even that such courses are not required. So we eliminate (E) as well. The most important shortcoming, according to the author, is that students have not been encouraged to apply the principles learned in the humanities. The support for this conclusion is to be found at the end of the second paragraph. As for (C), this is not mentioned by the author as a weakness in the present curriculum structure. Rather, he anticipates that this is a possible objection to his proposal to require students to devote part of their time to the study of primary problems. (A) is indeed a weakness of the university, and the author does admit that the university has not yet achieved equal opportunity for all. But this he discusses in the first paragraph, where he is outlining the university's successes. Only in the second paragraph does he begin the discussion of the university's failure. This indicates that the author does not regard the university's failure to achieve complete equality of opportunity as a serious problem.

2. **(A)** This is an inference question as well, though of a greater degree of difficulty. It seems possible to eliminate (C) and (E) as fairly implausible. The author's remarks about literature (at the end of the second paragraph), addressed to us as readers, do not suggest that we believe literature is required, nor that it is used to teach writing. As for (D), the author apparently presupposes that we, the readers, do not see the relevance of literature to real problems, for that it is relevant is at least part of the burden of his argument. (B) is perhaps the second best answer. It may very well be that most people regard literature as something scholarly, but that does not prove that (B) is a presupposition of the argument. When the author mentions literature, he states that it is a source of real and vicarious experience. What is the value of that? The author states that it relieves us of the necessity of living everyone else's life. He is trying to show that literature has a real, practical value. The crucial question, then, is why the author is attempting to prove that literature has real value. The answer is, because he presupposes that we disagree with this conclusion. There is a subtle but important difference between a presupposition that literature is scholarly and a presupposition that literature has no practical value. After all, there are many nonscholarly undertakings that may lack practical value.

3. **(D)** This is an explicit-idea question. It is important to keep in mind that an explicit idea question is almost always answerable on the basis of information actually stated in the text. With a format of this sort, this means that the question should be readily answerable without speculation, and that this answer should be fairly complete. (D) is correct because the author himself raises a possible objection in the final paragraph. (A) is incorrect because the author never gives any such examples. (B) is incorrect because the author never addresses the issue of political society. That is mentioned only as a point of reference in his introductory remarks. (C) is not answered since no university is ever named. And (E) is incorrect since the author makes the assertion, without elaborating, that the university is a better teacher today than in the past. There is a further point to be made. It is possible to argue that (B) is partially answered. After all, if we improve our students' ability to pose and answer questions, is this not also a way to improve the performance of our political society? But that is clearly more attenuated than the answer we find to question (D). The same reasoning may be applied to other incorrect answers as well. It may be possible to construct arguments in their favor, but this is a standardized exam. And there is a clear, easy answer to (D) in the text, indicating that this is the answer the test-writer is looking for.

4. **(B)** This is an application question. The author uses the term "primary problems" to refer to questions of grave importance that are not susceptible to an easy answer. Each of

the incorrect answers poses a question that can be answered with a short answer. (A) can be answered with a yes or no. (C) can be answered with a name. (D) can be answered with a date. (E) can be answered with a series of proposals. And even if the answers are not absolutely indisputable, the questions will soon become dead issues. The only problem that is likely to still be around after "we are all dead" is the one of capital punishment.

5. **(A)** This is an application question—with a thought reverser. The question asks us to identify the statement with which the author would be *least* likely to agree. In the fourth paragraph, the author introduces an example of a primary problem. What makes this a primary problem is that there are competing arguments on both sides of the issue: There are benefits to the individual and to society, but there are dangers as well. (A) is not likely to get the author's agreement since he acknowledges that the question is an open one. He implies that society may have such a right, but he points out also that the use of such measures must be studied very carefully. That same paragraph strongly suggests that the author would accept statements (B) and (C). As for (D) and (E), these are strands which are woven into the text at several points.

6. **(A)** This is a main-idea question. The author does describe a problem, and he does propose a solution. (B) is incorrect since the analysis of the system leads the author to propose a reform. (C) is incorrect since the author makes a definite recommendation. (D) is incorrect since the new idea the author outlines is defended in the text, not criticized. (E) is incorrect since the author does not develop the passage by raising questions.

7. **(B)** This too is a main-idea question in that the question asks, what is the general topic? (B) is the best answer since the author is speaking about the university and he is addressing fundamental questions of educational philosophy. (A) and (C) are incorrect since politics and science are only tangentially related to the argument. (D) and (E) can be eliminated on the same ground and

on the additional ground that though the author wants to make education practical, the decision to do that will be a decision based on philosophical concerns.

8. **(A)** This is a tone question. You can eliminate both (B) and (D) since the author does talk about a problem and in such a way that he makes it his problem. He does not, however, express alarm or confusion, so (C) is wrong. Finally, (E) overstates the case. Though the author makes some critical comments, he is not judgmental.

9. **(B)** This is a main-idea question presented in the format of a sentence completion. We are looking for the answer choice that, when added to the question stem, produces a sentence that summarizes the main thesis of the passage. Insofar as the verbs are concerned, that is, the first words of each choice, each choice seems acceptable. One could say that the author is concerned to "suggest," "demonstrate," "explain," "discuss," or "describe." So we must look at the fuller content of each choice. The author begins the passage by noting that there were two schools of thought on how to reduce unemployment, and then proceeds to describe the main ideas of both schools of thought. Finally, the author concludes by noting that, for all of their avowed differences, both schools share considerable common ground. This development is captured very well by (B). (A) is perhaps the second best choice. It is true that the author does mention some economic tools that can be used to control unemployment, but the main thesis is not that such ways exist. Rather, the main thesis, as pointed out by (B), is that the two groups, during the 1960s, had seemingly different yet ultimately similar views on how the tools could best be used. (C) is incorrect since the discussion of structural inefficiencies is only a minor part of the development. (D) is incorrect because the discussion of disunity is included simply to give a more complete picture of the debate and not to show that this prevented the achievement of full employment. Finally, the CEA is mentioned as a matter of historical interest, but its role is not the central focus of the passage.

10. **(D)** This is an explicit-idea question. Each of the incorrect answers is mentioned as a possible barrier to achieving 4% unemployment in the discussion of structural inefficiencies of the third paragraph. There reference is made to the effect of technological innovation, the shortage of skilled labor, the problem of minority and unskilled labor, and the reserve of workers not yet counted as being in the labor force. There is no mention, however, of the need to relocate workers to areas of labor shortage. The only reference to relocation is in the final paragraph. Since (D) is never mentioned as a possible barrier to achieving the 4% goal, it is the correct answer.

11. **(C)** This is an attitude or tone question. The author refers to the position of the hyperenthusiasts as "not very plausible," which indicates he does not endorse the position. On this ground we can eliminate (A). (B) can be eliminated on the same ground, and on the further ground that "lighthearted" is not a good description of the tone of the passage. (D) and (E), however, are overstatements. Though the author obviously rejects the position of the hyperenthusiasts, there is no evidence that he holds so negative an attitude as those suggested by (D) and (E). (C) describes well the author's mood. He mentions the position and then does not even bother to discuss it.

12. **(B)** This is an explicit-idea question. The needed reference is found in the second paragraph. The difference between the CEA and the dissenting expansionists grew out of the question of where to spend the money that would be used to stimulate the economy. The dissenting faction wanted to target the expansionary spending for public services and low-income groups. (B) presents this difference very well. (A) is incorrect and conflates the dissenting expansionists (paragraph 2) and the structuralists (paragraph 3). (C) commits the same error. (D) represents a misreading of the second paragraph: The CEA were expansionists. (E) is incorrect since the passage does not state that the CEA were conservatives.

13. **(B)** This is an explicit-idea question. Information that would bear on the issue raised by statement II is included in the third paragraph. As for statement I, there is no such information in the passage. In the first paragraph, the author mentions that the economy failed to expand rapidly in the early 1960's, but he offers no explanation for that phenomenon. And III is never mentioned at any point in the text. So our correct answer must be II only.

14. **(B)** The author mentions a dissenting group of expansionists in the closing lines of paragraph 2. This question asks about his attitude toward those economists. The author remarks of their arguments that their commitment to certain political ideals likely interfered with their economic judgments. For this reason he places very little faith in their arguments. (B) nicely brings out this point. (A) is incorrect. Though the author does discount the value of their conclusions, he does not do so because they were not trained as economists. As for (C), there is nothing that suggests that the author lacks information. Rather, it seems from the passage that the author has what he believes is sufficient information to discount the position. (D) is clearly in contradiction to this analysis and must be incorrect, and (E) can be eliminated on the same ground.

15. **(A)** Here we have a relatively easy inference question. The hyperenthusiasts used structuralist-type arguments to contend that jobs were already available. That being the case, the hyperenthusiasts dissented from both the positions of the expansionists and the structuralists who believed unemployment to be a problem. We may infer, then, that the essence of the hyperenthusiasts' position was that no government action was needed at all—at least no government action of the sort being discussed by the main camps described by the author. As for (B), nowhere in the passage does the author state or even hint that anyone overestimated the number of people out of work. As for (C), this represents a reading which confuses the hyperenthusiasts (paragraph 4) with the main-line structuralists (paragraph 3). (D) is

incorrect and conflates the hyperenthusiasts of the expansionary school of thought with those of the structuralist school. Finally, (E) is incorrect since it describes the position of the main group of expansionists.

16. **(A)** This is a main-idea question that asks about the overall development of the selection. The author describes two economic theories and shows that they were actually much closer in substance than their proponents originally imagined. This development is described by (A). You can eliminate (D) because the author does not advance a theory of his own. Finally, you can eliminate (E) because the author never explicitly raises any question.

17. **(A)** Here we have a main-idea question. The structure of the passage is first to explain that previous siting decisions have been made by regulatory agencies with only a review function exercised by government. The author then explains that in the past the most important features affecting the demographic characteristics of the population were natural ones. Then he argues that, given the effect siting decisions will have in the future, the government ought to take an active role in making those decisions, and that the government ought to take social considerations into account in making such decisions. Given this brief synopsis of the argument, we can see that (A) neatly restates this thesis. Further, we can see that (B) constitutes only a part, not the entirety, of the argument. (C), too, forms only one subpart of the whole analysis. (D) can be eliminated since the author believes that future siting decisions need not be governed by only natural features. Finally, (E) may very well be true, but it surely is not the main point of the argument presented.

18. **(D)** This is an explicit-idea question. (A) is mentioned in the final sentence of the first paragraph along with (B). (E) is a theme which runs generally through that paragraph, and (C) is specifically mentioned in the third paragraph. Nowhere does the author suggest that proximity to fuel sources needs to be taken into the siting decision.

19. **(C)** Again we have an explicit-idea question. In the opening remarks, the author specifically supports statement I. Then, this remark, taken in conjunction with the point made at the end of the first paragraph, tells us that II also is a characteristic of past siting decisions. As for III, the passage states in the final paragraph that environmentalists may oppose the construction of energy parks, but this is in opposition to future siting decisions—not to past siting decisions.

20. **(C)** This is a logical-structure question. The author's analysis and recommendation depend on the assumption that it will be possible to predict the demographic consequences of an energy park. Without this assumption, the recommendation that the government use electric facility siting decisions to effect social goals loses much of its persuasiveness. As for (A) and (D), the historical explanation is in large part expository only, that is, background information which is not, strictly speaking, essential to the argument supporting the recommendation. To the extent, then, that either (A) or (D) does weaken the historical analysis, and that is doubtful, the damage to the overall argument would not be great. As for (B) and (E), these are both irrelevant, and the proof is that whether (B) and (E) are true or false does not affect the argument.

21. **(D)** The correct answer to this application question is clearly supported by the concluding remarks of the passage. (A) is contradicted by these remarks and must be incorrect. (B) goes beyond the scope of the passage. We cannot attribute such a critical judgment ("were irresponsible") to the author. In fact, the passage at least implies that decisions during the nineteenth century were made in a natural (no pun intended) way. (C) overstates the case. Though the author believes that siting decisions for power plants need not depend on natural features, there is no support in the text for such a broad conclusion as that given in (C). Finally, as for (E), there is no evidence that the author would make such a judgment.

22. **(A)** This is an explicit-idea question the answer to which is found at the end of the

third paragraph. The most important feature of an energy park is that the place in which the massive effects will be manifested can be chosen. So, unlike the harbor, a natural feature located without regard to human desires, the energy park can be located where it will serve goals other than the production of energy. As for (B), even to the extent that (B) makes an accurate statement, the statement is not responsive to the question. This is not an important difference between the natural advantages of an early city and the man-made features of the energy park. A similar argument invalidates (D). As for (C), this is obviously irrelevant to the question asked. Finally, (E) is incorrect for two reasons. First, such a conclusion is not supported by the passage. Second, it is not a response to the question asked.

23. **(E)** There can be little doubt that the author is an advocate of energy parks. What criticism he notes in passing in the final paragraph, he simply dismisses. Thus, we can conclude that his attitude is one of whole-hearted support, as indicated by answer (E). We can eliminate (D) because the author in no way qualifies his recommendation. (A), (B), and (C) can be eliminated because of the author's positive attitude.

24. **(B)** The author introduces that paragraph with the statement that the size of energy parks is unprecedented. He then states that the power plant at Four Corners is large by today's standards (it was the only man-made object that was visible to the astronauts), but energy parks will be several times larger than the Four Corners facility. So the author mentions the facility in order to give the reader an idea of the magnitude of an energy park.

25. **(D)** In the final paragraph the author mentions the objection of environmentalists. He then states that with or without energy parks social problems must be addressed by adequate planning. (D) is the best description of this treatment. He acknowledges the objection, says that it is not unique to energy parks, and says nothing more about it.

Section VII

1. **(E)** The original sentence contains an error of faulty parallelism. You need a form to parallel raising funds and visiting hospitals. (B) and (C) fail to correct the error. (D) has the merit of using the *-ing* form of to speak (making it parallel in that respect), but the gratuitous "in" is not idiomatic and also destroys the parallelism.

2. **(D)** The problem is that the "it" has no clear antecedent. Only (D) and (E) correct the error. (E) is incorrect, however, because it introduces a new error—"temporarily" is an adverb and cannot describe "increase."

3. **(A)** is correct. (B) is wrong because it uses a clumsy indirect expression (the passive voice). (C) is wrong because it is a fragment without a main verb. (D) is incorrect because the additional conjunction (yet) is not needed, and because the resulting clause lacks a subject. (E) is incorrect because "it" is singular and cannot have as its antecedent, "physicians."

4. **(A)** The original sentence contains a correct elliptical construction. The second verb, "opposed," implicitly relies on the verb "was." (B) introduces a new error. "Them" is a plural pronoun and cannot be used to refer to "Transcendentalism," which is singular. (C) and (D) disrupt the parallel construction of the sentence. (E) introduces a new error (the illogical choice of verb tense).

5. **(C)** The original sentence is incorrect because the verb "seem" does not agree with its subject "acceptance." (D) changes the verb but fails to correct the error. (B) and (E) correct the error in the original but use unidiomatic phrases ("indicate the popularity" and "as to").

6. **(D)** This sentence is wrong because it incorrectly compares Edgar Allen Poe (the person) with the works of Hawthorne. (B) contains the same error. (C) contains an ambiguity. It is not clear whether it was Poe

or his works that were ignored. (E) uses an incorrect verb tense "having been."

7. **(C)** The original sentence is wrong because "which" has no antecedent. Only (C) solves the problem (by adding a noun, "practice"). In addition, (B) changes the meaning of the sentence because it no longer says that the jockey rides in order to become familiar with the horses. (E) commits the same error.

8. **(A)** is correct. (B) uses an incorrect verb tense "had been requested." (C) is wordy and also changes the logic of the sentence by saying that the grading system is somehow to be added to the curriculum. (E) commits the same error. (D) is awkward and needlessly uses the passive voice.

9. **(B)** (A) is incorrect because it is unidiomatic to say "not so much as x but instead because of y." The correct idiom is "not so much x as y."

10. **(E)** The original sentence commits an error of logic. It actually says that it is the individual or individuals who have eight units and no commercial space. (B) runs together several logically separate ideas. (C) and (D) do separate the ideas, but the ideas are not rendered in parallel forms.

11. **(C)** The sentence has no main verb. (E) fails to correct the error. (B) is incorrect because (by using a new independent clause) it changes the logic of the sentence. (D) uses an incorrect verb tense, "was writing."

12. **(C)** The original sentence contains a misplaced modifier. It says that the coast guard was severely damaged and already sinking. (B) fails to correct the error. The "it" still "wants" to refer to the coast guard because of the proximity of the modifier to that noun. (E) too fails to correct the error. (D) corrects the problem of the misplaced modifier but makes an error of faulty parallelism.

13. **(C)** This sentence contains a logical error. It compares the median income of women to men and not to the income of men. (B) and

(D) contain the same error. (E) is wrong because it changes the logic of the original sentence. (E) makes a comparison between the median income of women and the median income of *a* man (which man?).

14. **(B)** is wrong because "hopefully" is not idiomatic English. (C) contains the same error. (D) is incorrect because although it corrects the error by using the expression "it is hoped," it introduces an incorrect verb tense. There is no reason to use the conditional "would" in this sentence. (E) also corrects the original error but introduces a new error. The *-ing* form (the gerund) is not idiomatic here. The *to* form (the infinitive) should be used.

15. **(D)** The original choice of verbs is not logical. The pairing of "could" and "will" in this context doesn't make a meaningful statement. (E) makes an attempt to correct the error but the pairing "would" and "should" is no better than the original.

16. **(C)** The original sentence contains an error that might best be described as the mirror image of the error of the dangling modifier. The introductory phrase is properly placed to modify a subject that is the person or persons who made the discovery. Unfortunately, the impersonal "it" is the wrong subject. (C) corrects this error. (B) fails to correct the original mistake and compounds the problem by substituting an illogical verb tense. (D) is awkward. Finally, (E) uses the phrase "due to" which cannot be used as a conjunction in standard written English.

17. **(B)** The original sentence runs together two distinct ideas. (B) separates the two ideas and does so in such a way that it gives equal weight to both. (C) attempts to separate the ideas, but the resulting sentence does not give them equal weight. (D) makes the same error as (C), plus (D) contains the additional mistake of an inappropriate verb. Finally, (E) subordinates the second idea to the first, but the two ideas should be given equal weight.

18. **(A)** is correct. Each of the other choices in some way changes the logical structure or meaning of the original.

19. **(B)** The original sentence is illogical. As written, it implies that one should write to a Congressperson who has an opinion. (B) eliminates this ambiguity. (C) fails to eliminate the ambiguity. (D) is incorrect because the resulting sentence lacks a main clause. (E) is incorrect because it changes the logic of the original sentence (from "is" to "may be") and because it is awkward ("the writing").

20. **(B)** The original sentence is wrong because "they" has no antecedent. (C) is wrong because it is not idiomatic to say "the approaches at curing." (D) contains the same error and makes the additional mistake of using an awkward indirect construction ("by them"). (E) repeats the original mistake and compounds it by using a plural subject "approaches" with a singular verb form "has."

21. **(B)** (A) is incorrect. It is not idiomatic English to say "more on x as on y." (B) uses the correct idiom, "more on x than on y." (C) repeats the original error and adds an incorrect verb form, "had been based." (D) corrects the original error but does not follow the sequence of events. It switches from the present tense (is) to the past tense (was). (E) repeats the original error and introduces a new one, using "where" to mean "in which."

22. **(A)** The sentence is correct as written. (B) makes a slight change in the original, but one that changes the meaning of the original. "Each other" implies that there are only two breeds of dog; "one another" implies that there are several. (C), (D), and (E) make gratuitous changes that result in awkward constructions.

23. **(B)** The original is incorrect because it has a misplaced modifier; the original states that the works of Perse and Claudel lived in the Orient. (C) makes a similar error, implying that Oriental philosophy and landscape lived in the Orient. (D) is needlessly wordy. Compare it to the correct answer for clarity and conciseness. (E) is hopelessly wordy and awkward.

24. **(B)** The original sentence is incorrect because it is not idiomatic to say "the relationship of x and y." The correct expression is "the relationship of x to y." (C) corrects that mistake but introduces a logical error. It now says that the warnings jeopardize health. (D) is unidiomatic, and (E) is both wordy and unidiomatic.

25. **(D)** (A) is incorrect because it is illogical. It compares sanitation workers to other city agencies instead of to other city workers. (B) repeats this error and adds a new one. The possessive case is needed when a pronoun modifies the *-ing* form of verb (the gerund). Therefore, "their being underpaid," not "them being underpaid" is correct. (E) repeats this error. (C) repeats the illogical comparison.

ANSWER SHEET—PRACTICE EXAMINATION 6

SECTION I

1 Ⓐ Ⓑ Ⓒ Ⓓ Ⓔ   5 Ⓐ Ⓑ Ⓒ Ⓓ Ⓔ   9 Ⓐ Ⓑ Ⓒ Ⓓ Ⓔ   13 Ⓐ Ⓑ Ⓒ Ⓓ Ⓔ   17 Ⓐ Ⓑ Ⓒ Ⓓ Ⓔ

2 Ⓐ Ⓑ Ⓒ Ⓓ Ⓔ   6 Ⓐ Ⓑ Ⓒ Ⓓ Ⓔ   10 Ⓐ Ⓑ Ⓒ Ⓓ Ⓔ   14 Ⓐ Ⓑ Ⓒ Ⓓ Ⓔ   18 Ⓐ Ⓑ Ⓒ Ⓓ Ⓔ

3 Ⓐ Ⓑ Ⓒ Ⓓ Ⓔ   7 Ⓐ Ⓑ Ⓒ Ⓓ Ⓔ   11 Ⓐ Ⓑ Ⓒ Ⓓ Ⓔ   15 Ⓐ Ⓑ Ⓒ Ⓓ Ⓔ   19 Ⓐ Ⓑ Ⓒ Ⓓ Ⓔ

4 Ⓐ Ⓑ Ⓒ Ⓓ Ⓔ   8 Ⓐ Ⓑ Ⓒ Ⓓ Ⓔ   12 Ⓐ Ⓑ Ⓒ Ⓓ Ⓔ   16 Ⓐ Ⓑ Ⓒ Ⓓ Ⓔ   20 Ⓐ Ⓑ Ⓒ Ⓓ Ⓔ

SECTION II

1 Ⓐ Ⓑ Ⓒ Ⓓ Ⓔ   6 Ⓐ Ⓑ Ⓒ Ⓓ Ⓔ   11 Ⓐ Ⓑ Ⓒ Ⓓ Ⓔ   16 Ⓐ Ⓑ Ⓒ Ⓓ Ⓔ   21 Ⓐ Ⓑ Ⓒ Ⓓ Ⓔ

2 Ⓐ Ⓑ Ⓒ Ⓓ Ⓔ   7 Ⓐ Ⓑ Ⓒ Ⓓ Ⓔ   12 Ⓐ Ⓑ Ⓒ Ⓓ Ⓔ   17 Ⓐ Ⓑ Ⓒ Ⓓ Ⓔ   22 Ⓐ Ⓑ Ⓒ Ⓓ Ⓔ

3 Ⓐ Ⓑ Ⓒ Ⓓ Ⓔ   8 Ⓐ Ⓑ Ⓒ Ⓓ Ⓔ   13 Ⓐ Ⓑ Ⓒ Ⓓ Ⓔ   18 Ⓐ Ⓑ Ⓒ Ⓓ Ⓔ   23 Ⓐ Ⓑ Ⓒ Ⓓ Ⓔ

4 Ⓐ Ⓑ Ⓒ Ⓓ Ⓔ   9 Ⓐ Ⓑ Ⓒ Ⓓ Ⓔ   14 Ⓐ Ⓑ Ⓒ Ⓓ Ⓔ   19 Ⓐ Ⓑ Ⓒ Ⓓ Ⓔ   24 Ⓐ Ⓑ Ⓒ Ⓓ Ⓔ

5 Ⓐ Ⓑ Ⓒ Ⓓ Ⓔ   10 Ⓐ Ⓑ Ⓒ Ⓓ Ⓔ   15 Ⓐ Ⓑ Ⓒ Ⓓ Ⓔ   20 Ⓐ Ⓑ Ⓒ Ⓓ Ⓔ   25 Ⓐ Ⓑ Ⓒ Ⓓ Ⓔ

SECTION III

1 Ⓐ Ⓑ Ⓒ Ⓓ Ⓔ   6 Ⓐ Ⓑ Ⓒ Ⓓ Ⓔ   11 Ⓐ Ⓑ Ⓒ Ⓓ Ⓔ   16 Ⓐ Ⓑ Ⓒ Ⓓ Ⓔ   21 Ⓐ Ⓑ Ⓒ Ⓓ Ⓔ

2 Ⓐ Ⓑ Ⓒ Ⓓ Ⓔ   7 Ⓐ Ⓑ Ⓒ Ⓓ Ⓔ   12 Ⓐ Ⓑ Ⓒ Ⓓ Ⓔ   17 Ⓐ Ⓑ Ⓒ Ⓓ Ⓔ   22 Ⓐ Ⓑ Ⓒ Ⓓ Ⓔ

3 Ⓐ Ⓑ Ⓒ Ⓓ Ⓔ   8 Ⓐ Ⓑ Ⓒ Ⓓ Ⓔ   13 Ⓐ Ⓑ Ⓒ Ⓓ Ⓔ   18 Ⓐ Ⓑ Ⓒ Ⓓ Ⓔ   23 Ⓐ Ⓑ Ⓒ Ⓓ Ⓔ

4 Ⓐ Ⓑ Ⓒ Ⓓ Ⓔ   9 Ⓐ Ⓑ Ⓒ Ⓓ Ⓔ   14 Ⓐ Ⓑ Ⓒ Ⓓ Ⓔ   19 Ⓐ Ⓑ Ⓒ Ⓓ Ⓔ   24 Ⓐ Ⓑ Ⓒ Ⓓ Ⓔ

5 Ⓐ Ⓑ Ⓒ Ⓓ Ⓔ   10 Ⓐ Ⓑ Ⓒ Ⓓ Ⓔ   15 Ⓐ Ⓑ Ⓒ Ⓓ Ⓔ   20 Ⓐ Ⓑ Ⓒ Ⓓ Ⓔ   25 Ⓐ Ⓑ Ⓒ Ⓓ Ⓔ

SECTION IV

1 Ⓐ Ⓑ Ⓒ Ⓓ Ⓔ   6 Ⓐ Ⓑ Ⓒ Ⓓ Ⓔ   11 Ⓐ Ⓑ Ⓒ Ⓓ Ⓔ   16 Ⓐ Ⓑ Ⓒ Ⓓ Ⓔ   21 Ⓐ Ⓑ Ⓒ Ⓓ Ⓔ

2 Ⓐ Ⓑ Ⓒ Ⓓ Ⓔ   7 Ⓐ Ⓑ Ⓒ Ⓓ Ⓔ   12 Ⓐ Ⓑ Ⓒ Ⓓ Ⓔ   17 Ⓐ Ⓑ Ⓒ Ⓓ Ⓔ   22 Ⓐ Ⓑ Ⓒ Ⓓ Ⓔ

3 Ⓐ Ⓑ Ⓒ Ⓓ Ⓔ   8 Ⓐ Ⓑ Ⓒ Ⓓ Ⓔ   13 Ⓐ Ⓑ Ⓒ Ⓓ Ⓔ   18 Ⓐ Ⓑ Ⓒ Ⓓ Ⓔ   23 Ⓐ Ⓑ Ⓒ Ⓓ Ⓔ

4 Ⓐ Ⓑ Ⓒ Ⓓ Ⓔ   9 Ⓐ Ⓑ Ⓒ Ⓓ Ⓔ   14 Ⓐ Ⓑ Ⓒ Ⓓ Ⓔ   19 Ⓐ Ⓑ Ⓒ Ⓓ Ⓔ   24 Ⓐ Ⓑ Ⓒ Ⓓ Ⓔ

5 Ⓐ Ⓑ Ⓒ Ⓓ Ⓔ   10 Ⓐ Ⓑ Ⓒ Ⓓ Ⓔ   15 Ⓐ Ⓑ Ⓒ Ⓓ Ⓔ   20 Ⓐ Ⓑ Ⓒ Ⓓ Ⓔ   25 Ⓐ Ⓑ Ⓒ Ⓓ Ⓔ

SECTION V

1 Ⓐ Ⓑ Ⓒ Ⓓ Ⓔ	6 Ⓐ Ⓑ Ⓒ Ⓓ Ⓔ	11 Ⓐ Ⓑ Ⓒ Ⓓ Ⓔ	16 Ⓐ Ⓑ Ⓒ Ⓓ Ⓔ	21 Ⓐ Ⓑ Ⓒ Ⓓ Ⓔ
2 Ⓐ Ⓑ Ⓒ Ⓓ Ⓔ	7 Ⓐ Ⓑ Ⓒ Ⓓ Ⓔ	12 Ⓐ Ⓑ Ⓒ Ⓓ Ⓔ	17 Ⓐ Ⓑ Ⓒ Ⓓ Ⓔ	22 Ⓐ Ⓑ Ⓒ Ⓓ Ⓔ
3 Ⓐ Ⓑ Ⓒ Ⓓ Ⓔ	8 Ⓐ Ⓑ Ⓒ Ⓓ Ⓔ	13 Ⓐ Ⓑ Ⓒ Ⓓ Ⓔ	18 Ⓐ Ⓑ Ⓒ Ⓓ Ⓔ	23 Ⓐ Ⓑ Ⓒ Ⓓ Ⓔ
4 Ⓐ Ⓑ Ⓒ Ⓓ Ⓔ	9 Ⓐ Ⓑ Ⓒ Ⓓ Ⓔ	14 Ⓐ Ⓑ Ⓒ Ⓓ Ⓔ	19 Ⓐ Ⓑ Ⓒ Ⓓ Ⓔ	24 Ⓐ Ⓑ Ⓒ Ⓓ Ⓔ
5 Ⓐ Ⓑ Ⓒ Ⓓ Ⓔ	10 Ⓐ Ⓑ Ⓒ Ⓓ Ⓔ	15 Ⓐ Ⓑ Ⓒ Ⓓ Ⓔ	20 Ⓐ Ⓑ Ⓒ Ⓓ Ⓔ	25 Ⓐ Ⓑ Ⓒ Ⓓ Ⓔ

SECTION VI

1 Ⓐ Ⓑ Ⓒ Ⓓ Ⓔ	5 Ⓐ Ⓑ Ⓒ Ⓓ Ⓔ	9 Ⓐ Ⓑ Ⓒ Ⓓ Ⓔ	13 Ⓐ Ⓑ Ⓒ Ⓓ Ⓔ	17 Ⓐ Ⓑ Ⓒ Ⓓ Ⓔ
2 Ⓐ Ⓑ Ⓒ Ⓓ Ⓔ	6 Ⓐ Ⓑ Ⓒ Ⓓ Ⓔ	10 Ⓐ Ⓑ Ⓒ Ⓓ Ⓔ	14 Ⓐ Ⓑ Ⓒ Ⓓ Ⓔ	18 Ⓐ Ⓑ Ⓒ Ⓓ Ⓔ
3 Ⓐ Ⓑ Ⓒ Ⓓ Ⓔ	7 Ⓐ Ⓑ Ⓒ Ⓓ Ⓔ	11 Ⓐ Ⓑ Ⓒ Ⓓ Ⓔ	15 Ⓐ Ⓑ Ⓒ Ⓓ Ⓔ	19 Ⓐ Ⓑ Ⓒ Ⓓ Ⓔ
4 Ⓐ Ⓑ Ⓒ Ⓓ Ⓔ	8 Ⓐ Ⓑ Ⓒ Ⓓ Ⓔ	12 Ⓐ Ⓑ Ⓒ Ⓓ Ⓔ	16 Ⓐ Ⓑ Ⓒ Ⓓ Ⓔ	20 Ⓐ Ⓑ Ⓒ Ⓓ Ⓔ

SECTION VII

1 Ⓐ Ⓑ Ⓒ Ⓓ Ⓔ	6 Ⓐ Ⓑ Ⓒ Ⓓ Ⓔ	11 Ⓐ Ⓑ Ⓒ Ⓓ Ⓔ	16 Ⓐ Ⓑ Ⓒ Ⓓ Ⓕ	21 Ⓐ Ⓑ Ⓒ Ⓓ Ⓔ
2 Ⓐ Ⓑ Ⓒ Ⓓ Ⓔ	7 Ⓐ Ⓑ Ⓒ Ⓓ Ⓔ	12 Ⓐ Ⓑ Ⓒ Ⓓ Ⓔ	17 Ⓐ Ⓑ Ⓒ Ⓓ Ⓔ	22 Ⓐ Ⓑ Ⓒ Ⓓ Ⓔ
3 Ⓐ Ⓑ Ⓒ Ⓓ Ⓔ	8 Ⓐ Ⓑ Ⓒ Ⓓ Ⓔ	13 Ⓐ Ⓑ Ⓒ Ⓓ Ⓔ	18 Ⓐ Ⓑ Ⓒ Ⓓ Ⓔ	23 Ⓐ Ⓑ Ⓒ Ⓓ Ⓔ
4 Ⓐ Ⓑ Ⓒ Ⓓ Ⓔ	9 Ⓐ Ⓑ Ⓒ Ⓓ Ⓔ	14 Ⓐ Ⓑ Ⓒ Ⓓ Ⓔ	19 Ⓐ Ⓑ Ⓒ Ⓓ Ⓔ	24 Ⓐ Ⓑ Ⓒ Ⓓ Ⓔ
5 Ⓐ Ⓑ Ⓒ Ⓓ Ⓔ	10 Ⓐ Ⓑ Ⓒ Ⓓ Ⓔ	15 Ⓐ Ⓑ Ⓒ Ⓓ Ⓔ	20 Ⓐ Ⓑ Ⓒ Ⓓ Ⓔ	25 Ⓐ Ⓑ Ⓒ Ⓓ Ⓔ

PRACTICE EXAMINATION 6

SECTION I

Time—30 Minutes
20 Questions

Directions: For each of the following questions, select the best of the answer choices and blacken the corresponding space on your answer sheet.
Numbers: All numbers used are real numbers.
Figures: The diagrams and figures that accompany these questions are for the purpose of providing information useful in answering the questions. Unless it is stated that a specific figure is not drawn to scale, the diagrams and figures are drawn as accurately as possible. All figures are in a plane unless otherwise indicated.

1. If $x + 5 = 4x - 10$, then $x =$
   (A) -15
   (B) -5
   (C) -3
   (D) 3
   (E) 5

2. $\dfrac{2^6 - 8^2}{4^3}$
   (A) 0
   (B) 1
   (C) 2
   (D) 4
   (E) 8

3. $\frac{8}{5}$ is equal to
   (A) .625
   (B) 1.5
   (C) 1.6
   (D) 2.8
   (E) 8.5

4. A square floor with side of 3 meters is to be covered with square tiles. If each tile has a perimeter of 1 meter, what is the minimum number of tiles needed to cover the floor?
   (A) 3

   (B) 9
   (C) 12
   (D) 36
   (E) 144

5. In a certain city, the average income for a family of four rose from $12,200 in 1980 to $16,300 in 1986. This represents an increase of *approximately*
   (A) 4%
   (B) 25%
   (C) $33\frac{1}{3}$%
   (D) 40%
   (E) 60%

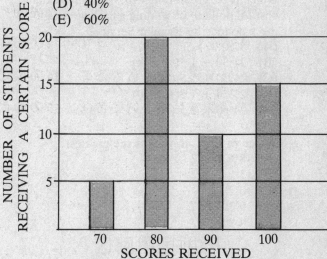

6. The graph above shows the distribution of test scores for a certain class. What was the average (arithmetic mean) score?
   (A) 87
   (B) 81
   (C) 80
   (D) 78
   (E) 75

Questions 7 and 8 refer to the following table.

Shipping Rates

	Regular Service	Express Service
First Pound	$5.10	$17.50
Each additional pound or fraction of a pound up to 10 pounds	$1.80	$2.60
Each additional pound or fraction of a pound over 10 pounds	$1.50	$1.20

7. How much does it cost to send a package weighing 23.5 pounds by Express Service?
   (A) $22.50
   (B) $42.50
   (C) $67.50
   (D) $64.30
   (E) $66.20

8. If the weight of a package is x pounds and x is an integer greater than 10, then what is the cost (in dollars) of sending a package weighing x pounds by Regular Service?
   (A) $5.10 + 1.5(x + 10)$
   (B) $21.30 + 1.5(10 - x)$
   (C) $21.30 + 1.5 (10 + x)$
   (D) $21.30 + 1.5(x - 10)$
   (E) $24.60 + 1.5 (10 + x)$

9. Which of the following is the greatest?
   (A) 8×0.012
   (B) 3×0.122
   (C) 0.7^5
   (D) 0.3% of 7
   (E) 0.98×3

   ⟦C⟧ ⟦B⟧ ⟦E⟧ ⟦F⟧ ⟦D⟧ ⟦A⟧

10. Six blocks shown above are to be rearranged so that the letters are in alphabetical order, reading from left to right. What is the minimum number of blocks that must be moved to arrive at the desired arrangement?
    (A) 2
    (B) 3
    (C) 4

(D) 5
(E) 6

11. In a certain company, 55% of the workers are men. If 30% of the workers are full-time employees and 60% of these are women, what percentage of the full-time workers in the company are men?
    (A) 12%
    (B) 40%
    (C) 60%
    (D) $66\frac{2}{3}$%
    (E) $77\frac{7}{9}$%

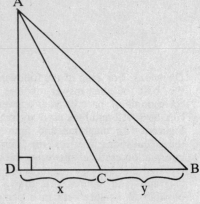

12. In the figure above, x = y, what is the ratio area △ ABC/area △ADC?
    (A) $\frac{1}{2}(x + y)$
    (B) $x + y$
    (C) xy
    (D) $\frac{1}{2}$
    (E) 1

13. In a certain direct mail center, each of E employees addresses L letters every M minutes. If every employee works without interruption, how many hours are required for the center to address 10,000 letters?
    (A) $\dfrac{10,000E}{60LM}$
    (B) $\dfrac{10,000EL}{60M}$
    (C) $\dfrac{10,000M}{60EL}$
    (D) $\dfrac{60EL}{10,000M}$
    (E) $\dfrac{60L}{10,000EM}$

14. If in a certain shipment of new cars, the cost of car X is twice the average of the other 11 cars in the shipment, what fraction of the total cost of 12 cars is the cost of car X?
    (A) $\frac{1}{12}$
    (B) $\frac{1}{11}$

(C) $\frac{2}{13}$

(D) $\frac{2}{11}$

(E) $\frac{1}{6}$

15. The weight of a glass jar is 20% of the weight of the jar filled with coffee beans. After some of the beans have been removed, the weight of the jar and the remaining beans is 60% of the original total weight. What fractional part of the beans remain in the jar?

(A) $\frac{1}{5}$

(B) $\frac{1}{3}$

(C) $\frac{2}{5}$

(D) $\frac{1}{2}$

(E) $\frac{2}{3}$

16. If x is an integer such that $2 < x < 12$, $4 < x < 21$, $9 > x > -1$, $8 > x > 0$, and $x + 1 < 7$, then x is

(A) 3

(B) 5

(C) 6

(D) 8

(E) It cannot be determined

$$
\begin{array}{r}
7\,29 \\
5X3 \\
+\ 9X1 \\
\hline
2{,}2X3
\end{array}
$$

17. In the addition calculation above, the number X must be

(A) 0

(B) 2

(C) 3

(D) 7

(E) 9

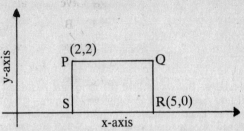

18. If the figure above is a rectangle, what is the area of PQRS?

(A) 2

(B) 4

(C) 5

(D) 6

(E) 10

19. The value of a share of stock P and the value of a share of stock Q each increased by 16%. If the value of a share of stock P increased by 16 cents and the value of a share of stock Q increased by $1.68, what is the difference between the value of stock Q and the value of stock P *before* the increases?

(A) $8.00

(B) $9.50

(C) $10.00

(D) $10.50

(E) $11.02

20. An express train traveled at an average speed of 100 kilometers per hour, stopping for 3 minutes after every 75 kilometers. A local train traveled at an average speed of 50 kilometers, stopping for 1 minute after every 25 kilometers. If the trains began traveling at the same time, how many kilometers did the local train travel in the time it took the express train to travel 600 kilometers?

(A) 300

(B) 305

(C) 307.5

(D) 1200

(E) 1236

STOP

END OF SECTION. IF YOU HAVE ANY TIME LEFT, GO OVER YOUR WORK IN THIS SECTION ONLY. DO NOT WORK IN ANY OTHER SECTION OF THE TEST.

SECTION II

Time—30 minutes
25 Questions

Directions: Below each of the following passages, you will find questions or incomplete statements about the passage. Each statement or question is followed by lettered words or expressions. Select the word or expression that most satisfactorily completes each statement or answers each question in accordance with the meaning of the passage. After you have chosen the best answer, blacken the corresponding space on the answer sheet.

At the present time, 98% of the world energy consumption comes from stored sources, such as fossil fuels or nuclear fuel. Only hydroelectric and wood energy represent completely renewable
5 sources on ordinary time scales. Discovery of large additional fossil fuel reserves, solution of the nuclear safety and waste disposal problems, or the development of controlled thermonuclear fusion will provide only a short-term solution to
10 the world's energy crisis. Within about 100 years, the thermal pollution resulting from our increased energy consumption will make solar energy a necessity at any cost.

Man's energy consumption is currently about
15 one part in ten thousand that of the energy we receive from the sun. However, it is growing at a 5% rate, of which about 2% represents a population growth and 3% a per capita energy increase. If this growth continues, within 100 years our
20 energy consumption will be about 1 percent of the absorbed solar energy, enough to increase the average temperature of the earth by about one degree centigrade if stored energy continues to be our predominant source. This will be the point at
25 which there will be significant effects in our climate, including the melting of the polar ice caps, a phenomenon that will raise the level of the oceans and flood parts of our major cities. There is positive feedback associated with this process,
30 since the polar ice cap contributes to the partial reflectivity of the energy arriving from the sun: As the ice caps begin to melt, the reflectivity will decrease, thus heating the earth still further.

It is often stated that the growth rate will
35 decline or that energy conservation measures will preclude any long-range problem. Instead, this only postpones the problem by a few years. Conservation by a factor of 2, together with a maintenance of the 5% growth rate, delays the
40 problem by only 14 years. Reduction of the growth rate to 4% postpones the problem by only 25 years; in addition, the inequities in standards of living throughout the world will provide pressure toward an increase in growth
45 rate, particularly if cheap energy is available. The problem of a changing climate will not be evident until perhaps 10 years before it becomes critical due to the nature of an exponential growth rate together with the normal annual
50 weather variations. This may be too short a period to circumvent the problem by converting to other energy sources, so advance planning is a necessity.

The only practical means of avoiding the
55 problem of thermal pollution appears to be the use of solar energy. (Schemes to "air-condition" the earth do not appear to be feasible before the twenty-second century.) Using the solar energy before it is dissipated to heat does not increase
60 the earth's energy balance. The cost of solar energy is extremely favorable now, particularly when compared to the cost of relocating many of our major cities.

1. The author is primarily concerned with
   (A) describing a phenomenon and explaining its causes
   (B) outlining a position and supporting it with statistics
   (C) isolating an ambiguity and clarifying it by definition
   (D) presenting a problem and advocating a solution for it
   (E) citing a counter-argument and refuting it

2. According to the passage, all of the following are factors which will tend to increase thermal pollution EXCEPT
   (A) the earth's increasing population
   (B) melting of the polar ice caps

(C) increase in per capita energy consumption

(D) pressure to redress standard of living inequities by increasing energy consumption

(E) expected anomalies in weather patterns

3. The positive feedback mentioned in lines 29–30 means that the melting of the polar ice caps will
   (A) reduce per capita energy consumption
   (B) accelerate the transition to solar energy
   (C) intensify the effects of thermal pollution
   (D) necessitate a shift to alternative energy sources
   (E) result in the inundations of major cities

4. The author mentions the possibility of energy conservation (lines 35–37) in order to
   (A) preempt and refute a possible objection to his position
   (B) support directly the central thesis of the passage
   (C) minimize the significance of a contradiction in the passage
   (D) prove that such measures are ineffective and counterproductive
   (E) supply the reader with additional background information

5. It can be inferred that the "airconditioning" of the earth (lines 56–58) refers to proposals to
   (A) distribute frigid air from the polar ice caps to coastal cities as the temperature increases due to thermal pollution
   (B) dissipate the surplus of the release of stored solar energy over absorbed solar energy into space
   (C) conserve completely renewable energy sources by requiring that industry replace these resources
   (D) avoid further thermal pollution by converting to solar energy as opposed to conventional and nuclear sources
   (E) utilize hydroelectric and wood energy to replace nonconventional energy sources such as nuclear energy

6. The tone of the passage is best described as one of
   (A) unmitigated outrage
   (B) cautious optimism
   (C) reckless abandon
   (D) smug self-assurance
   (E) pronounced alarm

7. Which of the following would be the most logical topic for the author to address in a succeeding paragraph?
   (A) the problems of nuclear safety and waste disposal
   (B) a history of the development of solar energy
   (C) the availability and cost of solar energy technology
   (D) the practical effects of flooding of coastal cities
   (E) the feasibility of geothermal energy

8. The phrase "energy balance" (line 60) means the
   (A) total amount of energy produced by all energy sources
   (B) ratio of the amount of energy produced as solar energy to the amount produced by all other sources
   (C) excess of energy produced from non-solar sources over that derived from the sun
   (D) number of years remaining before thermal pollution reaches an irreversible point
   (E) difference between the rate at which energy is received from the sun and the rate at which it is lost into space

It would be enormously convenient to have a single, generally accepted index of the economic and social welfare of the people of the United States. A glance at it would tell us how much better or worse off we had become each year, and we would judge the desirability of any proposed action by asking whether it would raise or lower this index. Some recent discussion implies that such an index could be constructed. Articles in the popular press even criticize the Gross National Production (GNP) because it is not such a complete index of welfare, ignoring, on the one hand, that it was never intended to be, and suggesting, on the other, that with appropriate changes it could be converted into one.

The output available to satisfy our wants and needs is one important determinant of welfare. Whatever want, need, or social problem engages our attention, we ordinarily can more easily find resources to deal with it when output is large and growing than when it is not. GNP measures output fairly well, but to evaluate welfare we would need additional measures which would be far more difficult to construct. We would need an index of real costs incurred in production, because we are better off if we get the same output at less cost. Use of just man-hours for welfare evaluation would unreasonably imply that to increase total hours by raising the hours of eight women from 60 to 65 a week imposes no more burden that raising the hours of eight men from 40 to 45 a week, or even than hiring one involuntarily unemployed person for 40 hours a week. A measure of real costs of labor would also have to consider working conditions. Most of us spend almost half of our waking hours on the job and our welfare is vitally affected by the circumstances in which we spend those hours.

To measure welfare we would need a measure of changes in the need our output must satisfy. One aspect, population change, is now handled by converting output to a per capita basis on the assumption that, other things equal, twice as many people need twice as many goods and service to be equally well off. But an index of needs would also account for differences in the requirements for living as the population becomes more urbanized and suburbanized; for the changes in national defense requirements; and for changes in the effect of weather on our needs. The index would have to tell us the cost of meeting our needs in a base year compared with the cost of meeting them equally well under the circumstances prevailing in every other year.

Measures of "needs" shade into measures of the human and physical environment in which we live. We all are enormously affected by the people around us. Can we go where we like without fear of attack? We are also affected by the physical environment—purity of water and air, accessibility of parkland and other conditions. To measure this requires accurate data, but such data are generally deficient. Moreover, weighting is required: to combine robberies and murders in a crime index; to combine pollution of the

Potomac and pollution of Lake Erie into a water pollution index; and then to combine crime and water pollution into some general index. But there is no basis for weighting these beyond individual preference.

There are further problems. To measure welfare we would need an index of the "goodness" of the distribution of income. There is surely consensus that given the same total income and output, a distribution with fewer families in poverty would be better, but what is the ideal distribution? Even if we could construct indexes of output, real costs, needs, state of the environment, we could not compute a welfare index because we have no system of weights to combine them.

9. The author is primarily concerned to
   (A) refute arguments for a position
   (B) make a proposal and defend it
   (C) attack the sincerity of an opponent
   (D) show defects in a proposal
   (E) review literature relevant to a problem

10. The author implies that man-hours is not an appropriate measure of real cost because it
   (A) ignores the conditions under which the output is generated
   (B) fails to take into consideration the environmental costs of production
   (C) overemphasizes the output of real goods as opposed to services
   (D) is not an effective method for reducing unemployment
   (E) was never intended to be a general measure of welfare

11. It can be inferred from the passage that the most important reason a single index of welfare cannot be designed is
   (A) the cost associated with producing the index would be prohibitive
   (B) considerable empirical research would have to be done regarding output and needs
   (C) any weighting of various measures into a general index would be inherently subjective and arbitrary
   (D) production of the relevant data would require time, thus the index would be only a reflection of past welfare
   (E) accurate statistics on crime and pollution are not yet available

12. The author regards the idea of a general index of welfare as
    (A) an unrealistic dream
    (B) a scientific reality
    (C) an important contribution
    (D) a future necessity
    (E) a desirable change

13. According to the passage, the GNP is
    (A) a fairly accurate measure of output
    (B) a reliable estimate of needs
    (C) an accurate forecaster of welfare
    (D) a precise measure of welfare
    (E) a potential measure of general welfare

14. According to the passage, an adequate measure of need must take into account all of the following EXCEPT
    (A) changing size of the population
    (B) changing effects on people of the weather
    (C) differences in needs of urban and suburban populations
    (D) changing requirements for governmental programs such as defense
    (E) accessibility of parkland and other amenities

15. The passage is most likely
    (A) an address to a symposium on public policy decisions
    (B) a chapter in a general introduction to statistics
    (C) a pamphlet on government programs to aid the poor
    (D) the introduction to a treatise on the foundations of government
    (E) a speech by a university president to a graduating class

16. The passage relies heavily on which of the following?
    (A) Chains of deductive reasoning to draw further conclusions
    (B) Attempts to discredit other authors
    (C) Use of examples to illustrates contentions
    (D) Statistics to describe a phenomenon in quantitative terms
    (E) Extrapolation to construct a picture of a future situation

17. The tone of the passage can best be described as
    (A) critical and sarcastic
    (B) diffident and self-effacing
    (C) neutral and detached
    (D) analytical and confident
    (E) contentious and sardonic

Our current system of unemployment compensation has increased nearly all sources of adult unemployment: season and cyclical variations in the demand for labor, weak labor force attach-
5 ment and unnecessarily long durations of unemployment. First, for those who are already unemployed, the system greatly reduces the cost of extending the period of unemployment. Second, for all types of unsteady work—seasonal, cyclical
10 and casual—it raises the net wage to the employee, relative to the cost of the employer.

As for the first, consider a worker who earns $500 per month or $6000 per year if she experiences no unemployment. If she is unemployed for
15 one month, she loses $500 in gross earnings but only $116 in net income. How does this occur? A reduction of $500 in annual earnings reduces her federal, payroll and state tax liability by $134. Unemployment compensation consists of 50% of
20 her wage or $250. Her net income therefore falls from $366 if she is employed, to $250 paid as unemployment compensation. Moreover, part of the higher income from employment is offset by the cost of transportation to work and other
25 expenses associated with employment; and in some industries, the cost of unemployment is reduced further or even made negative by the supplementary unemployment benefits paid by employers under collective bargaining agree-
30 ments. The overall effect is to increase the duration of a typical spell of unemployment and to increase the frequency with which individuals lose jobs and become unemployed.

The more general effect of unemployment
35 compensation is to increase the seasonal and cyclical fluctuations in the demand for labor and the relative number of short-lived casual jobs. A worker who accepts such work knows she will be laid off when the season ends. If there were no
40 unemployment compensation, workers could be induced to accept such unstable jobs only if the wage rate were sufficiently higher in those jobs than in the more stable alternative. The higher cost of labor, then, would induce employers to

45 reduce the instability of employment by smoothing production through increased variation in inventories and delivery lags, by additional development of off-season work and by the introduction of new production techniques, e.g., new
50 methods of outdoor work in bad weather.

Employers contribute to the state unemployment compensation fund on the basis of the unemployment experience of their own previous employees. Within limits, the more benefits that
55 those former employees draw, the higher is the employer's tax rate. The theory of experience rating is clear. If an employer paid the full cost of the unemployment benefits that his former employees received, unemployment compensation
60 would provide no incentive to an excess use of unstable employment. In practice, however, experience rating is limited by a maximum rate of employer contribution. For any firm that pays the maximum rate, there is no cost for additional
65 unemployment and no gain from a small reduction in unemployment.

The challenge at this time is to restructure the unemployment system in a way that strengthens its good features while reducing the harmful
70 disincentive effects. Some gains can be achieved by removing the ceiling on the employer's rate of contribution and by lowering the minimum rate to zero. Employers would then pay the full price of unemployment insurance benefits and this would
75 encourage employers to stabilize employment and production. Further improvement could be achieved if unemployment insurance benefits were taxed in the same way as other earnings. This would eliminate the anomalous situations in
80 which a worker's net income is actually reduced when he returns to work.

18. The author is primarily concerned to
   (A) defend the system of unemployment compensation against criticism
   (B) advocate expanding the benefits and scope of coverage of unemployment compensation
   (C) point to weaknesses inherent in government programs that subsidize individuals
   (D) suggest reforms to eliminate inefficiencies in unemployment compensation
   (E) propose methods of increasing the effectiveness of government programs to reduce unemployment

19. The author cites the example of a worker earning $500 per month (lines 12–22) in order to
   (A) show the disincentive created by unemployment compensation for that worker to return to work
   (B) demonstrate that employers do not bear the full cost of worker compensation
   (C) prove that unemployed workers would not be able to survive without unemployment compensation
   (D) explain why employers prefer to hire seasonal workers instead of permanent workers for short-term jobs
   (E) condemn workers who prefer to live on unemployment compensation to taking a job

20. The author recommends which of the following changes be made in the unemployment compensation?
   I. taxing unemployment compensation to lower net benefits received by workers
   II. shortening the length of time during which a worker is eligible to receive benefits to force the worker to seek work
   III. eliminating any maximum rate of employer contribution to increase the amount of money paid by employers into the unemployment compensation fund

   (A) I only
   (B) I and II only
   (C) I and III only
   (D) II and III only
   (E) I, II, and III

21. The author mentions all of the following as ways by which employers might reduce seasonal and cyclical unemployment EXCEPT
   (A) developing new techniques of production not affected by weather
   (B) slowing delivery schedules to provide work during a slow seasons
   (C) adopting a system of supplementary benefits for workers laid off in slow periods

(D) manipulating inventory supplies to require year-round rather than short-term employment

(E) finding new jobs to be done by workers during the off-season

22. With which of the following statements about experience rating (lines 56–57) would the author most likely agree?

(A) Experience rating is theoretically sound, but its effectiveness in practice is undermined by maximum contribution ceilings.

(B) Experience rating is an inefficient method of computing employer contribution because an employer has no control over the length of an employee's unemployment.

(C) Experience rating is theoretically invalid and should be replaced by a system in which the employee contributes the full amount of benefits he will later receive.

(D) Experience rating is basically fair, but its performance could be improved by requiring large firms to pay more than small firms.

(E) Experience rating requires an employer to pay a contribution that is completely unrelated to the amount his employees draw in unemployment compensation benefits.

23. The author makes which of the following criticisms of the unemployment compensation system?

I. It places an unfair burden on firms whose production is cyclical or seasonal.

II. It encourages out-of-work employees to extend the length of time they are unemployed.

III. It constitutes a drain on state treasuries, which must subsidize unemployment compensation funds.

(A) I only
(B) II only
(C) III only
(D) I and II only
(E) II and III only

24. It can be inferred that the author regards the unemployment compensation system as

(A) socially necessary
(B) economically efficient
(C) inherently wasteful
(D) completely unnecessary
(E) seriously outdated

25. In discussing the example of the worker in lines 12–22, the author makes which of the following assumptions?

(A) Her unemployment compensation is not taxed.

(B) She is not actively seeking employment.

(C) She quit a job in order to receive unemployment compensation.

(D) She is receiving supplemental unemployment benefits from her previous employer.

(E) She is unwilling to work at the same wage she earned before she became unemployed.

STOP

END OF SECTION. IF YOU HAVE ANY TIME LEFT, GO OVER YOUR WORK IN THIS SECTION ONLY. DO NOT WORK IN ANY OTHER SECTION OF THE TEST.

SECTION III

Time—30 Minutes
25 Questions

Directions: In this section, the questions ask you to analyze and evaluate the reasoning in short paragraphs or passages. For some questions, all of the answer choices may conceivably be answers to the question asked. You should select the *best* answer to the question, that is, an answer that does not require you to make assumptions that violate commonsense standards by being implausible, redundant, irrelevant or inconsistent. After choosing the best answer, blacken the corresponding space on the answer sheet.

1. MME. CHARPENTIER: Research has demonstrated that the United States, which has the most extensive health care industry in the world, has only the 17th lowest infant mortality rate in the world. This forces me to conclude that medical technology causes babies to die.

   M. ADAMANTE: That is ludicrous. We know that medical care is not equally available to all. Infant mortality is more likely a function of low income than of medical technology.

   M. Adamante attacks Mme. Charpentier's reasoning in which way?
   (A) by questioning the validity of her supporting data
   (B) by offering an alternative explanation of the data
   (C) by suggesting that her argument is circular
   (D) by defining an intermediate cause
   (E) by implying that her data leads to the opposite conclusion

2. When this proposal to reduce welfare benefits is brought up for debate, we are sure to hear claims by the liberal Congressmen that the bill will be detrimental to poor people. These politicians fail to understand, however, that budget reductions are accompanied by tax cuts—so everyone will have more money to spend, not less.

   Which of the following, if true, would undermine the author's position?

   I. Poor people tend to vote for liberal Congressmen who promise to raise welfare benefits.

   II. Poor people pay little or no taxes so that a tax cut would be of little advantage to them.

   III. Any tax advantage the poor will receive will be more than offset by cuts in the government services they now receive.

   (A) I only
   (B) II only
   (C) II and III only
   (D) III only
   (E) I, II, and III

3. Many people ask, "How effective is Painaway?" So to find out we have been checking the medicine cabinets of the apartments in this typical building. As it turns out, eight out of ten contain a bottle of Painaway. Doesn't it stand to reason that you too should have the most effective pain-reliever on the market?

   The appeal of this advertisement would be most weakened by which of the following pieces of evidence?
   (A) Painaway distributed complimentary bottles of medicine to most apartments in the building two days before the advertisement was made.
   (B) The actor who made the advertisement takes a pain-reliever manufactured by a competitor of Painaway.
   (C) Most people want a fast, effective pain-reliever.
   (D) Many people take the advice of their neighborhood druggists about pain-relievers.
   (E) A government survey shows that many people take a pain-reliever before it is really needed.

Questions 4 and 5

An artist must suffer for his art say these successful entrepreneurs who attempt to pass themselves off as artists. They auction off to the highest bidder, usually a fool in his own right, the most mediocre of drawings; and then, from their well-laid tables, they have the unmitigated gall to imply that they themselves——(4)——.

4. Choose the answer that best completes the paragraph.
   (A) are connoisseurs of art
   (B) suffer deprivation for the sake of their work
   (C) are artists
   (D) know art better than the art critics do
   (E) do not enjoy a good meal

5. Which of the following must underlie the author's position?

   I. One must actually suffer to do great art.
   II. Financial deprivation is the only suffering an artist undergoes.
   III. Art critics have little real expertise and are consequently easily deceived.

   (A) I only
   (B) II only
   (C) I and II only
   (D) II and III only
   (E) I, II, and III

Questions 6 and 7

Stock market analysts always attribute a sudden drop in the market to some domestic or international political crisis. I maintain, however, that these declines are attributable to the phases of the moon, which also cause periodic political upheavals and increases in tension in world affairs.

6. Which of the following best describes the author's method of questioning the claim of market analysts?
   (A) He presents a counterexample.
   (B) He presents statistical evidence.
   (C) He suggests an alternative causal linkage.
   (D) He appeals to generally accepted beliefs.
   (E) He demonstrates that market analysts' reports are unreliable.

7. It can be inferred that the author is critical of the stock analysts because he
   (A) believes that they have oversimplified the connection between political crisis and fluctuations of the market.
   (B) knows that the stock market generally shows more gains than losses
   (C) suspects that stock analysts have a vested interest in the stock market, and are therefore likely to distort their explanations
   (D) anticipates making large profits in the market himself
   (E) is worried that if the connection between political events and stock market prices becomes well-known, unscrupulous investors will take advantage of the information

8. This piece of pottery must surely date from the late Minoan period. The dress of the female figures, particularly the bare and emphasized breasts, and the activities of the people depicted—note especially the importance of the bull—are both highly suggestive of this period. These factors, when coupled with the black, semigloss glaze that results from firing the pot in a sealed kiln at a low temperature, makes the conclusion a virtual certainty.

Which of the following is a basic assumption made by the author of this explanation?
   (A) Black, semigloss glazed pottery was made only during the late Minoan period.
   (B) The bull is an animal that was important to most ancient cultures.
   (C) Throughout the long history of the Minoan people, their artisans decorated pottery with seminude women and bulls.
   (D) By analyzing the style and materials of any work of art, an expert can pinpoint the date of its creation.
   (E) There are key characteristics of works of art that can be shown to be typical of a particular period.

9. Most radicals who argue for violent revolution and complete overthrow of our existing society have no clear idea of what will emerge from the destruction. They just assert that things are so bad now that any change would have to be a change for the

better. But surely this is mistaken, for things might actually turn out to be worse.

The most effective point that can be raised against this argument is that the author says nothing about

(A) the manner in which the radicals might foment their revolution

(B) the specific results of the revolution, which would be changes for the worse

(C) the economic arguments the radicals use to persuade people to join in their cause

(D) the fact that most people are really satisfied with the present system so that the chance of total revolution is very small

(E) the loss of life and property that is likely to accompany total destruction of a society

Questions 10 and 11

Having just completed Introductory Logic 9, I feel competent to instruct others in the intricacies of this wonderful discipline. Logic is concerned with correct reasoning in the form of syllogisms. A syllogism consists of three statements, two of which are premises, the third of which is the conclusion. Here is an example:

MAJOR PREMISE: The American buffalo is disappearing.
MINOR PREMISE: This animal is an American buffalo.
CONCLUSION: Therefore, this animal is disappearing.

Once one has been indoctrinated into the mysteries of this arcane science, there is no statement he may not assert with complete confidence.

10. The reasoning of the author's example is most similar to that contained in which of the following arguments?

(A) Any endangered species must be protected; this species is endangered; therefore, it should be protected.

(B) All whales are mammals; this animal is a whale; therefore, this animal is a mammal.

(C) Engaging in sexual intercourse with a person to whom one is not married is a sin; and since premarital intercourse

is, by definition, without the institution of marriage, it is, therefore, a sin.

(D) There are 60 seconds in a minute; there are 60 minutes in an hour; therefore, there are 3600 seconds in an hour.

(E) Wealthy people pay most of the taxes; this man is wealthy; therefore, this man pays most of the taxes.

11. The main purpose of the author's argument is to

(A) provide instruction in logic

(B) supply a definition

(C) cast doubt on the value of formal logic

(D) present an argument for the protection of the American buffalo

(E) show the precise relationship between the premises and the conclusion of his example

Questions 12 and 13

On a recent trip to the Mediterranean, I made the acquaintance of a young man who warned me against trusting Cretans. "Everything they say is a lie," he told me, "and I should know because I come from Crete myself." I thanked the fellow for his advice but told him in light of what he had said I had no intention of believing it.

12. Which of the following best describes the author's behavior?

(A) It was unwarranted because the young man was merely trying to be helpful to a stranger.

(B) It was paradoxical, for in discounting the advice he implicitly relied on it.

(C) It was understandable inasmuch as the young man, by his own admission, could not possibly be telling the truth.

(D) It was high-handed and just the sort of thing that gives American tourists a bad name.

(E) It was overly cautious, for not everyone in a foreign country will try to take advantage of a tourist.

13. Which of the following is most nearly analogous to the warning issued by the young man?

(A) An admission by a witness under cross-examination that he has lied.

(B) A sign put up by the Chamber of Commerce of a large city alerting visitors to the dangers of pickpockets.

(C) The command of a military leader to his marching troops to do an about-face.

(D) A sentence written in chalk on a blackboard that says, "This sentence is false."

(E) The advice of a veteran worker to a newly hired person: "You don't actually have to work hard so long as you look like you're working hard."

14. Doctors, in seeking a cure for *aphroditis melancholias,* are guided by their research into the causes of *metaeritocas polymanias* because the symptoms of the two diseases occur in populations of similar ages, manifesting symptoms in both cases of high fever, swollen glands, and lack of appetite. Moreover, the incubation period for both diseases is virtually identical. So these medical researchers are convinced that the virus responsible for *aphroditis melancholias* is very similar to that responsible for *metaeritocas polymanias.*

The conclusion of the author rests on the presupposition that

(A) *metaeritocas polymanias* is a more serious public health hazard than *aphroditis melancholias*

(B) for every disease, modern medical science will eventually find a cure

(C) saving human life is the single most important goal of modern technology

(D) *aphroditis melancholias* is a disease that occurs only in human beings

(E) diseases with similar symptoms will have similar causes

15. I. Whenever some of the runners are leading off and all of the infielders are playing in, all of the batters attempt to bunt.

II. Some of the runners are leading off but some of the batters are not attempting to bunt.

Which of the following conclusions can be deduced from the two statements above?

(A) Some of the runners are not leading off.

(B) Some of the batters are attempting to bunt.

(C) None of the infielders is playing in.

(D) All of the infielders are playing in.

(E) Some of the infielders are not playing in.

Questions 16 and 17

The federal bankruptcy laws illustrate the folly of do-good protectionism at its most extreme. At the debtor's own request, the judge will list all of his debts, take what money the debtor has, which will be very little, and divide that small amount among his creditors. Then the judge declares that those debts are thereby satisfied, and the debtor is free from those creditors. Why, a person could take his credit card and buy a car, a stereo, and a new wardrobe and then declare himself bankrupt! In effect, he will have conned his creditors into giving him all those things for nothing.

16. Which of the following adages best describes the author's attitude about a bankrupt debtor?

(A) "A penny saved is a penny earned."

(B) "You've made your bed, now lie in it."

(C) "Absolute power corrupts absolutely."

(D) "He that governs least governs best."

(E) "Millions for defense, but not one cent for tribute."

17. Which of the following does the author imply?

(A) A judge will not use all of a debtor's assets, including personal possessions, to pay his creditors.

(B) Most persons who own credit cards are financially irresponsible.

(C) A bankrupt debtor ought to be imprisoned until he is able to raise the money to pay all of his debts.

(D) Most personal bankruptcy proceedings are initiated at the request of the creditors.

(E) Borrowing money is immoral.

18. Either you punish a child severely when he is bad or he will grow up to be a criminal. Your child has just been bad. Therefore, you should punish him severely.

All EXCEPT which of the following would be appropriate objection to the argument?
(A) What do you consider to be a severe punishment?
(B) What do you mean by the term "bad"?
(C) Isn't your "either-or" premise an oversimplification?
(D) Don't your first and second premises contradict one another?
(E) In what way has this child been bad?

19. The Supreme Court's recent decision is unfair. It treats nonresident aliens as a special group when it denies them some rights ordinary citizens have. This treatment is discriminatory, and we all know that discrimination is unfair.

Which of the following arguments is most nearly similar in its reasoning to the above argument?
(A) Doing good would be our highest duty under the moral law, and that duty would be irrational unless we had the ability to discharge it; but since a finite, sensate creature could never discharge that duty in his lifetime, we must conclude that if there is moral law, the soul is immortal.
(B) Required core courses are a good idea because students just entering college do not have as good an idea about what constitutes a good education as do the professional educators; therefore, students should not be left complete freedom to select coursework.
(C) This country is the freest nation on earth largely as a result of the fact that the founding fathers had the foresight to include a Bill of Rights in the Constitution.
(D) Whiskey and beer do not mix well; every evening that I have drunk both whiskey and beer together, the following morning I have had a hangover.
(E) I know that this is a beautiful painting because Picasso created only beautiful works of art, and this painting was done by Picasso.

20. Creativity must be cultivated. Artists, musicians, and writers all practice, consciously or unconsciously, interpreting the world from new and interesting viewpoints. A teacher can encourage his pupils to be creative by showing them different perspectives for viewing the significance of events in their daily lives.

Which of the following, if true, would most undermine the author's claim?
(A) In a well-ordered society, it is important to have some people who are not artists, musicians, or writers.
(B) A teacher's efforts to show a pupil different perspectives may actually inhibit development of the student's own creative process.
(C) Public education should stress practical skills, which will help a person get a good job, instead of creative thinking.
(D) Not all pupils have the same capacity for creative thought.
(E) Some artists, musicians, and writers "burn themselves out" at a very early age, producing a flurry of great works and then nothing after that.

21. Opponents to the mayor's plan for express bus lanes on the city's major commuter arteries objected that people could not be lured out of their automobiles in that way. The opponents were proved wrong; following implementation of the plan, bus ridership rose dramatically, and there was a corresponding drop in automobile traffic. Nonetheless, the plan failed to achieve its stated objective of reducing average commuting time.

Which of the following sentences would be the most logical continuation of this argument?
(A) The plan's opponents failed to realize that many people would take advantage of improved bus transportation.
(B) Unfortunately, politically attractive solutions do not always get results.
(C) The number of people a vehicle can transport varies directly with the size of the passenger compartment of the vehicle.
(D) Opponents cited an independent survey of city commuters showing that before the plan's adoption only one

out of every seven used commuter bus lanes.

(E) With the express lanes closed to private automobile traffic, the remaining cars were forced to use too few lanes and this created gigantic traffic tie-ups.

22. Last year, Gambia received $2.5 billion in loans from the International Third World Banking Fund, and its Gross National Product grew by 5%. This year Gambia has requested twice as much money from the ITWBF, and its leaders expect that Gambia's GNP will rise by a full 10%.

Which of the following, if true, would undermine the expectations of Gambia's leaders?

I. The large 5% increase of last year is attributable to extraordinary harvests due to unusually good weather conditions.

II. Gambia's economy is not strong enough to absorb more than $3 billion in outside capital each year.

III. Gambia does not have sufficient heavy industry to fuel an increase in its GNP of more than 6% per year.

(A) I only
(B) II only
(C) I and II only
(D) II and III only
(E) I, II, and III

23. Efficiency experts will attempt to improve the productivity of an office by analyzing production procedures into discrete work tasks. They then study the organization of those tasks and advise managers on techniques to speed production, such as rescheduling of employee breaks or relocating various equipment such as the copying machines. I have found a way to accomplish increases in efficiency with much less to do. Office workers grow increasingly productive as the temperature drops, so long as it does not fall below 68°F.

The passage leads most naturally to which of the following conclusions?
(A) Some efficiency gains will be short-term only.

(B) To maintain peak efficiency, an office manager must occasionally restructure office tasks.
(C) Employees are most efficient when the temperature is 68°F.
(D) The temperature-efficiency formula is applicable to all kinds of work.
(E) Office workers will be equally efficient at 67°F and 69°F.

Questions 24 and 25

PROABORTION SPEAKER: Those who oppose abortion on demand make the foundation of their arguments the sanctity of human life, but this seeming bedrock assumption is actually as weak as shifting sand. And it is not necessary to involve the red herring that many antiabortion speakers would allow that human life must sometimes be sacrificed for a great good, as in the fighting of a just war. There are counterexamples to the principle of sanctity of life that are even more embarrassing to prolife advocates. It would be possible to reduce the annual number of traffic fatalities to virtually zero by passing federal legislation mandating a nationwide fifteen-mile-per-hour speed limit on *all* roads. You see, implicitly we have always been willing to trade off quantity of human life for quality.

ANTIABORTION SPEAKER: The analogy my opponent draws between abortion and traffic fatalities is weak. No one would propose such a speed limit. Imagine people trying to get to and from work under such a law, or imagine them trying to visit a friend or relatives outside their own neighborhoods, or taking in a sports center or a movie. Obviously such a law would be a disaster.

24. Which of the following best characterizes the antiabortion speaker's response to the proabortion speaker?
(A) His analysis of the traffic fatalities case actually supports the argument of the proabortion speaker.
(B) His analysis of the traffic fatalities case is an effective rebuttal of the proabortion argument.
(C) His response provides a strong affirmative statement of the antiabortionist position.
(D) His response is totally irrelevant to the

issue raised by the proabortion speaker.

(E) His counterargument attacks the character of the proabortion speaker instead of the merits of his argument.

25. In his argument, the proabortionist makes which of the following assumptions?

  I. It is not a proper goal of a society to protect human life.

  II. The human fetus is not a human life.
  III. The trade-off between the number of human lives and the quality of those lives is appropriately decided by society.

(A) I only
(B) II only
(C) I and II only
(D) III only
(E) I, II, and III

STOP

END OF SECTION. IF YOU HAVE ANY TIME LEFT, GO OVER YOUR WORK THIS SECTION ONLY. DO NOT WORK IN ANY OTHER SECTION OF THE TEST.

SECTION IV

Time—30 Minutes
25 Questions

Directions: Each question below is followed by two numbered facts. You are to determine whether the data given in the statements is sufficient for answering the question. Use the data given, plus your knowledge of math and everyday facts, to choose between the five possible answers.

(A) If statement 1 alone is sufficient to answer the question, but statement 2 alone is not sufficient

(B) if statement 2 alone is sufficient to answer the question, but statement 1 alone is not sufficient

(C) if both statements together are needed to answer the question, but neither statement alone is sufficient

(D) if either statement by itself is sufficient to answer the question

(E) if not enough facts are given to answer the question

1. Attendance at a certain play was 8% higher on Saturday night than it was on Friday night. What was the attendance on Saturday night?
   (1) Friday night's attendance was 200.
   (2) Attendance increased from Friday night to Saturday night by 16 people.

2. At a street fair, a concessionaire sold both bracelets and necklaces. How much money did she take in on the sale of the bracelets?
   (1) She took in a total of $540 on the sale of bracelets and necklaces.
   (2) She took in $12 for each of the 25 necklaces she sold.

3. How many people visited a certain museum in 1985?
   (1) In 1985, four times as many people visited the museum as in 1984.
   (2) In its first year of operation, 3000 people visited the museum.

4. Three persons, Jack, Jill, and Jerry, are sitting in a boat. Which of the three weighs the most?
   (1) Jack's weight is $\frac{5}{4}$ of Jill's weight.
   (2) Jill's weight is $\frac{2}{3}$ of Jerry's weight.

5. A box is filled with cookies ranging in weight from 3.2 grams to 3.8 grams. How many cookies are in the box?
   (1) The gross weight of the box and the cookies is 130 grams.
   (2) The net weight of the cookies is 112 grams.

6. Is $x + 3 > 0$?
   (1) $x + 5 > 0$
   (2) $x < 0$

7. What is the area of Circle O?
   (1) The diameter of Circle O is 4.
   (2) The circumference of Circle O is 4π.

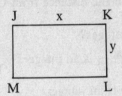

8. Is the area of rectangle JLKM, above, an integer?
   (1) y is an integer
   (2) $\frac{x}{y}$ is an integer.

9. Is it cheaper to buy bagels by the dozen rather than singly?
   (1) A single bagel costs 30 cents.
   (2) A dozen bagels cost ten times as much as a single bagel.

10. What was the greatest difference between the high and low test scores of any student in the third grade at PS 11?
    (1) The highest test score earned by any student in the third grade at PS 11 was 98.
    (2) The lowest test score earned by any student in the third grade at PS 11 was 44.

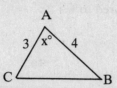

11. What is the area of the triangle shown above?
    (1) $AB^2 = BC^2 - AC^2$
    (2) $x = 90$

12. An airplane took off from airport P and later landed at airport R at the same time that another airplane landed at airport R, completing its flight from airport Q. If both flights were nonstop flights, which airplane flew at the faster average speed?
    (1) The first plane took off a half hour before the second plane.
    (2) The distance from P to R is greater than the distance from Q to R.

13. Is $\frac{x}{7}$ an integer?
    (1) $\dfrac{x}{787,787}$ is an integer.
    (2) $\dfrac{x}{784}$ is an integer.

14. Is x a positive number?
    (1) $2x - 5 > 0$
    (2) $2x + 1 > 2$

15. A container manufactured for the transport of liquids is a right circular cylinder. If it has a diameter of 40 inches, what is its volume?
    (1) The surface area of the container, excluding the top and the bottom, is 1200π square inches.
    (2) The entire surface area of the container is 2000π square inches.

16. Edna has exactly 73 cents in her pocket, in dimes and nickels and pennies. How many nickels does she have in her pocket?
    (1) She has twice as many dimes as she has pennies.
    (2) She has three pennies.

17. In 1985, the Party Time Catering Hall spent a total of $1200 for metered water. How much did it spend for metered water in 1986?
    (1) In 1986, Party Time Catering Hall purchased 10% more metered water than it did in 1985.
    (2) The average price per gallon of metered water purchased by Party Time Catering Hall in 1986 was 5% more than that for 1985.

18. What is the value of the two-digit number N?
    (1) The sum of its digits is 15.
    (2) The product of its digits is 54.

19. What is the value of x + y?
    (1) $x + y + z = x + y - z + 1$
    (2) $x - y + z = 0$

20. How many rectangular cereal boxes can be shipped in a certain cardboard carton?
    (1) Each cereal box has a volume of 120 cubic centimeters.
    (2) The cardboard carton has a volume of 2400 cubic centimeters.

21. How many hours long is time period T?
    (1) T begins at 12:01 a.m. on Friday and ends at 12:01 a.m. on Wednesday.
    (2) T is exactly 5 days long.

22. A shipment of 70 items is to be divided into three lots. How many pieces are in the largest of the three lots?
    (1) The number of items in the largest lot is equal to the sum of the number of items of the other two lots.
    (2) The smallest lot contains 10 items.

23. If N > 0, is N a whole number?
    (1) $3 \times N$ is an odd number.
    (2) $2 \times N$ is an even number.

24. How long did a round trip journey take?
    (1) The return trip took 2 hours longer than the outbound trip.
    (2) The entire round trip covered 210 miles, and the average speed of the trip was 30 miles per hour.

25. A swimming pool is supplied water by two pipes, P and Q. If pipe P operating alone can fill the pool in 12 hours, how long will it take pipe Q operating alone to fill the pool?
    (1) Operating together, pipes P and Q can fill the pool in 4 hours.
    (2) Pipe P supplies water at the rate of 520 gallons per hour, and 6240 gallons are required to fill the pool.

STOP

END OF SECTION. IF YOU HAVE ANY TIME LEFT, GO OVER YOUR WORK IN THIS SECTION ONLY. DO NOT WORK IN ANY OTHER SECTION OF THE TEST.

SECTION V

Time—30 minutes
25 Questions

Directions: In each problem below, either part or all of the sentence is underlined. The sentence is followed by five ways of writing the underlined part. Answer choice (A) repeats the original; the other answer choices vary. If you think that the original phrasing is the best, choose (A). If you think one of the other answer choices is the best, select that choice.

This section tests the ability to recognize correct and effective expression. Follow the requirements of Standard Written English: grammar, choice of words, and sentence construction. Choose the answer that results in the clearest, most exact sentence, but do not change the meaning of the original sentence.

1. Because of the accident, toxic fumes were released into the atmosphere, and the inhabitants of several communities had to be relocated to an army base from their homes 20 miles away.
   - (A) had to be relocated to an army base from their homes 20 miles away.
   - (B) have to be relocated to an army base 20 miles away from their homes.
   - (C) had to be relocated 20 miles away from their homes to an army base.
   - (D) had to be relocated to an army base, 20 miles away from their homes.
   - (E) has to be relocated to an army base, 20 miles away from their house.

2. The numerous constraints placed on the members of the First Family has made it difficult for them to engage in normal social activities such as going to the movies.
   - (A) has made it difficult for them to engage in normal social activities such as going to the movies.
   - (B) have made it difficult engaging in normal social activities such as going to the movies.
   - (C) has made the engagement in normal social activities such as going to the movies difficult.
   - (D) have made it difficult to engage in normal social activities such as going to the movies.
   - (E) has made their engagement in normal social activities such as going to the movies difficult.

3. Like their counterparts in other countries, the student movement in the United States in the 1960s was a powerful one and probably helped to bring the war in Vietnam to an end.
   - (A) Like their counterparts in other countries, the student movement in the United States in the 1960s
   - (B) As in other countries, the student movement in the United States in the 1960s,
   - (C) Just as the student movements in other countries, the student movement in the United States in the 1960s,
   - (D) Like its counterparts in other countries, the student movement in the United States in the 1960s
   - (E) The student movement in the United States in the 1960s, like in other countries,

4. The Metropolitan Museum of Art will soon add a wing devoted entirely to modern art, whereas before other museums exhibited modern art while the Met ignored it.
   - (A) art, whereas before other museums exhibited modern art while the Met ignored it.
   - (B) art, while before other museums exhibited modern art while the Met ignored it.
   - (C) art, meanwhile before the other museums had exhibited the art while the Met ignored it.
   - (D) art, other museums exhibited the art before with the Met ignoring it.
   - (E) art: until now, other museums exhibited modern art, but the Met ignored it.

5. Deregulated in 1984, the researchers at AT&T continue to produce new and important ideas and products such as undersea fiberoptic cable.
   - (A) Deregulated in 1984, the researchers at AT&T continue to produce
   - (B) Having been deregulated in 1984, the

researchers at AT&T are continuing to produce

(C) The researchers at AT&T, even though it was deregulated in 1984, continues to produce

(D) Although AT&T was deregulated in 1984, its researchers continue to produce

(E) Despite its being deregulated in 1984, the researchers for AT&T continue to produce

6. The success scientists have had developing treatments for once incurable types of cancer have led to a host of patent lawsuits which will effect the prices individuals will pay for the cure.

(A) The success scientists have had developing treatments for once incurable types of cancer have led to a host of patent lawsuits which will effect the prices individuals will pay for the cure.

(B) The success scientists have had in developing treatments for once incurable types of cancer has led to a host of patent lawsuits which will affect the prices individuals will pay for the cure.

(C) The success scientists has had in the development of treatments for once incurable types of cancer have led to a host of patent lawsuits which affect the prices individuals will pay for the cure.

(D) The success scientists had had in the development of treatments for once incurable types of cancer have led to a host of patent lawsuits which would affect the prices individuals would pay for a cure.

(E) Scientists have had success in the development of treatments for once incurable types of cancer which have led to a host of patent lawsuits which will effect the prices individuals will pay for the cure.

7. The senator was so popular that she was reelected with as wide of a margin as any candidate in the state's history.

(A) she was reelected with as wide of a margin as any candidate in the state's history.

(B) she had been relected with as wide of a margin as any candidate in the state's history.

(C) having been reelected with as wide a margin as any candidate in the state's history.

(D) she was reelected with as wide a margin as any candidate in the state's history.

(E) she was reelected with as wide a margin than any candidate in the state's history.

8. Like Andy Warhol, the "pop art" of Roy Lichtenstein is full of familiar images such as cartoon characters.

(A) Like Andy Warhol, the "pop art" of Roy Lichtenstein

(B) As with that of Andy Warhol, the "pop art" of Roy Lichtensten

(C) Like the work of Andy Warhol, the "pop art" of Roy Lichtenstein

(D) The "pop art" of Roy Lichtenstein similar to Andy Warhol

(E) It being similar to Andy Warhol's, the "pop art" of Roy Lichtenstein

9. The New England community was one of the most literate in history, with that the Puritans had to be able to read the Bible in order to maintain their relationship with God.

(A) with that the Puritans had to be able to read the Bible in order to maintain

(B) due to the fact that the Puritans have to be able to read the Bible in order to maintain

(C) since the Puritans had to be able to read the Bible maintaining

(D) because the Puritans had to be able to read the Bible in order to maintain

(E) because Puritans had to be able to read the Bible and also to maintain

10. The smoking of cigarettes being injurious to nonsmokers is rapidly becoming a major concern of public health officials.

(A) The smoking of cigarettes being injurious to nonsmokers is

(B) Cigarette smoking being injurious to nonsmokers is

(C) The fact that cigarette smoking is injurious to nonsmokers are

(D) It being injurious to nonsmokers, cigarette smoking is

(E) The fact that cigarette smoking is injurious to nonsmokers is

11. A substance from the licorice plant, 50 times sweeter than sucrose, was recently discovered, is not only a natural sweetener but also prevents tooth decay.

   (A) A substance from the licorice plant, 50 times sweeter than sucrose, was recently discovered,

   (B) A substance, which was recently discovered, from the licorice plant, 50 times sweeter than sucrose,

   (C) A substance from the licorice plant, which was recently discovered to be 50 times sweeter than sucrose,

   (D) A substance from the licorice plant, 50 times sweeter than sucrose, which was recently discovered,

   (E) A recently discovered substance, 50 times sweeter than sucrose from the licorice plant,

12. It is widely accepted by scientists that chlorofluorocarbons released into the atmosphere as a result of industrial refrigeration and insulation is the main cause of the huge gaps in the earth's ozone layer.

   (A) released into the atmosphere as a result of industrial refrigeration and insulation is

   (B) released into the atmosphere as a result of industrial refrigeration and insulation are

   (C) resulting from industrial refrigeration and insulation released into the atmosphere are

   (D) being released into the atmosphere as a result of industrial refrigeration and insulation is

   (E) having been released into the atmosphere and resulting from industrrial refrigeration and insulation are

13. There are over 110 million dogs and cats in the United States, which is more than the population of any Western European country.

   (A) which is more than the population of any Western European country.

   (B) which are more than the population of any Western European country.

   (C) being more than the population of any Western European country.

   (D) more than any Western European country in population.

   (E) more than in any Western European country by population.

14. Autism, where a child may be severely retarded, have problems speaking, and exhibit bizarre behavior, occur in 5 of every 10,000 children.

   (A) Autism, where a child may be severely retarded, have problems speaking, and exhibit bizarre behavior, occur

   (B) Autism, which manifests itself in children in severe retardation, speech problems and bizarre behavior, occurs

   (C) Autism is a disease in which a child may be severely retarded, have problems speaking and also bizarre behavior and it occurs

   (D) A disease causing severe retardation, speech problems, and behavior may be bizarre, is autism which occurs

   (E) Autism, causing severe retardation, speech problems and bizarre behavior, and occurring

15. Despite the repeated warnings against drug abuse and the numerous fatalities, drug use is equally as prevalent, if not more so than, a decade ago.

   (A) is equally as prevalent, if not more so than, a decade ago.

   (B) is equally as prevalent, if not more so than, it was a decade ago.

   (C) is as prevalent, if not more than a decade ago.

   (D) is as prevalent as, if not more prevalent than, it was a decade ago.

   (E) is as prevalent, if not more so than a decade ago.

16. A career in the medical profession, which requires an enormous investment of time and money, do not guarantee success as there is so much competition.

   (A) which requires an enormous investment of time and money, do not guarantee success as there is so much competition.

(B) which requires an enormous investment of time and money, does not guarantee success since there is so much competition.

(C) requiring an enormous investment of time and money, without guarantee because there is so much competition.

(D) requires an enormous investment of time and money, and it cannot guarantee success because there is so much competition.

(E) requires that an enormous investment of time and money be made and success cannot be guaranteed due to the competition.

17. It was believed that a thorough knowledge of Latin would not only enable students to read the classics, also enabling them to think clearly and precisely.

(A) It was believed that a thorough knowledge of Latin would not only enable students to read the classics, also enabling them to think clearly and precisely.

(B) It had been believed that a thorough knowledge of Latin would not only enable students to read the classics but rather enable them to think clearly and precisely.

(C) It was believed that a thorough knowledge of Latin would not only enable students to read the classics but also enabling them to think clearly and precisely.

(D) It used to be believed that a thorough knowledge of Latin would enable a student to be able to read the classics but also enable them to think clearly and precisely.

(E) It was believed that a thorough knowledge of Latin would not only enable students to read the classics, but would also enable them to think clearly and precisely.

18. Most adolescents struggle to be free both of parental domination but also from peer pressure.

(A) both of parental domination but also from peer pressure.

(B) both of parental domination and also from peer pressure.

(C) both of parental domination and also of peer pressure.

(D) both of parental domination and of peer pressure as well.

(E) of parental domination and their peer pressure as well.

19. The president of the block association tried to convince her neighbors they should join forces to prevent crime in the neighborhood rather than continuing to be victimized.

(A) they should join forces to prevent crime in the neighborhood rather than continuing to be victimized.

(B) that they should join forces to prevent crime in the neighborhood rather than continue to be victimized.

(C) about joining forces to prevent crime in the neighborhood instead of continuing to be victimized.

(D) for the joining of forces to prevent crime in the neighborhood rather than continue to be victimized.

(E) to join forces to prevent crime in the neighborhood rather than continuing to be victimized.

20. Although he is as gifted as, if not more gifted than, many of his colleagues, he is extremely modest and his poetry is unpublished.

(A) Although he is as gifted as, if not more gifted than, many of his colleagues, he is extremely modest and his poetry is unpublished.

(B) Although he is as gifted, if not more gifted, than many of his colleagues, he is extremely modest with his poetry remaining unpublished.

(C) Although he is as gifted as, if not more gifted than, many of his colleagues, he is extremely modest and will not publish his poetry.

(D) Despite his being gifted, if not more gifted than his colleagues, he is extremely modest and will not publish his poetry.

(E) Being as gifted as, or more gifted than, many of his colleagues, he is extremely modest and his poetry is unpublished.

21. Although the manager agreed to a more flexible work schedule, he said that it must be posted on the bulletin board so that both management and labor will know what everyone is assigned to do.
    (A) he said that it must be posted on the bulletin board so that both management and labor will know what everyone is
    (B) he said it had to be posted on the bulletin board so that both management and labor knows what everyone is
    (C) he said that they would have to post the assignments on the bulletin board so that management and labor knew what everyone was
    (D) he said that the schedule would have to be posted on the bulletin board so that both management and labor would know what everyone was
    (E) saying that the schedule had to be posted on the bulletin board so that both management and labor would know what everyone had been

22. With just several quick strokes of the pen, the monkeys were drawn by the artist, capturing their antics.
    (A) the monkeys were drawn by the artist, capturing their antics.
    (B) the artist sketched the monkeys, capturing their antics.
    (C) the artist captured the antics of the monkeys, sketching them.
    (D) the artist sketched the monkeys and also capturing their antics.
    (E) the monkeys and their antics were sketched by the artist.

23. The paintings of Gustav Klimt are different from the painters he inspired who were more interested in exploring the unconscious than him.
    (A) from the painters he inspired who were more interested in exploring the unconscious than him.
    (B) from those of the painters he inspired who were more interested in exploring the unconscious than he.
    (C) than those of the painters he inspired who were more interested in the exploration of the unconscious than he.
    (D) than the painters he inspired because they were more interested in exploring the unconscious than he was.
    (E) from those of the painters he inspired being more interested in the exploration of the unconscious than he.

24. Both Samuel Beckett and Joseph Conrad were brought up speaking one language and then they wrote in another language when they wrote novels.
    (A) and then they wrote in another language when they wrote novels.
    (B) having written novels in another language altogether.
    (C) but wrote their novels in another language.
    (D) yet when they wrote novels, they wrote them in another language.
    (E) with their novels being written in a different language.

25. To lack self-discipline is to lack any true commitment to the goals one has set for himself.
    (A) To lack self-discipline is to lack
    (B) To be lacking in self-discipline is to lack
    (C) To lack self-discipline must be to lack
    (D) Lacking self-discipline is to be lacking
    (E) Lacking self-discipline is the lack of

STOP

END OF SECTION. IF YOU HAVE ANY TIME LEFT, GO OVER YOUR WORK IN THIS SECTION ONLY. DO NOT WORK IN ANY OTHER SECTION OF THE TEST.

SECTION VI

Time—30 Minutes
20 Questions

Directions: For each of the following questions, select the best of the answer choices and blacken the corresponding space on your answer sheet.
Numbers: All numbers used are real numbers.
Figures: The diagrams and figures that accompany these questions are for the purpose of providing information useful in answering the questions. Unless it is stated that a specific figure is not drawn to scale, the diagrams and figures are drawn as accurately as possible. All figures are in a plane unless otherwise indicated.

1. The number 45 is what percentage of 9,000?
   (A) 0.05%
   (B) 0.405%
   (C) 0.5%
   (D) 4.05%
   (E) 5%

2. If $3x = 6$ and $x - y = 0$, then $y =$
   (A) -2
   (B) 0
   (C) 2
   (D) 6
   (E) 12

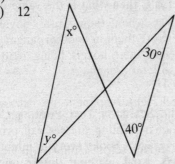

3. In the figure above, $x + y =$
   (A) 40
   (B) 70
   (C) 90
   (D) 110
   (E) It cannot be determined from the information given.

4. A demographic survey of 100 families in which two parents were present revealed that the average age, A, of the oldest child is 20 years less than $\frac{1}{2}$ the sum of the ages of the two parents. If F represents the age of one parent and M the age of the other

parent, then which of the following is equivalent to A?
   (A) $\dfrac{F+M-20}{2}$
   (B) $\dfrac{F+M}{2} + 20$
   (C) $\dfrac{F+M}{2} - 20$
   (D) $F + M - 10$
   (E) $F + M + 10$

5. A professional athlete was offered a three-year contract to play with team K that provided for an annual salary of $100,000 in the first year, an increase in annual salary of 20% over the previous year for the next two years, and a bonus of $50,000 on signing. Team L offered a three-year contract providing for an annual salary of $150,000 in the first year, an increase in annual salary of 10% over the previous year for the next two years, and no signing bonus. If he accepts the offer of Team L and fulfills the three-year contract terms, the athlete will receive how much more money by choosing Team L over Team K?
   (A) $32,500
   (B) $50,000
   (C) $82,500
   (D) $92,000
   (C) $100,000

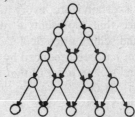

6. The figure above illustrates a managerial table of organization in which each person, except those on the lowest level, supervises exactly two persons on the next lower level. If each lower level contains exactly one person more than the next higher level, which of the following could be the total

number of persons in an organization built on such a pattern?
(A) 7
(B) 16
(C) 21
(D) 28
(E) 35

7. If $2x^2 + x - 2 = 1$ and $x > 0$, then $x =$
(A) 1
(B) $\frac{3}{2}$
(C) 3
(D) 6
(E) 9

8. On a certain three-dimensional drawing, an actual dimension of 1.5 meters is represented by 5 centimeters. If a cube is shown on the drawing with a side of 10 centimeters, what is its actual volume (in cubic meters)?
(A) 4.5
(B) 9
(C) 27
(D) 900
(E) 1500

9. If x is a positive integer, which of the following statements must be true?

I. $2x - 1$ is positive
II. $2x^2$ is an odd number
III. $2x + 1$ is an even number

(A) I only
(B) II only
(C) I and II only
(D) I and III only
(E) I, II and III

10. In a certain store, every item is on sale for a price that represents a reduction from the usual selling price of 30%. If the price of an item has been reduced by $2.40, what is the usual selling price of that item?
(A) $5.60
(B) $7.20
(C) $8.00
(D) $10.40
(E) $15.00

11. In a list of numbers, each number after the first is exactly $\frac{1}{3}$ the number immediately preceding it. If the fifth number in the list is 3, what is the second number in the sequence?
(A) $\frac{1}{9}$

(B) $\frac{1}{3}$
(C) 1
(D) 27
(E) 81

12. A merchant sells a certain item for a price that is a whole number of dollars. If the cost of the item to her is $50, then which of the following could be her profit as a percentage of her cost?
(A) 15%
(B) 25%
(C) $33\frac{1}{3}$%
(D) 40%
(E) 75%

13. If N is an even number, then N* is equal to N. If N is an odd number, then N* is equal to $N + 1$. For example, $2^* = 2$ and $3^* = 4$. What is the value of $1^* (4^* + 5^*)$?
(A) 9
(B) 10
(C) 16
(D) 20
(E) 22

14. The ratio of x to y is $\frac{1}{2}$. If the ratio of $x + 2$ to $y + 1$ is $\frac{2}{3}$, then what is the value of x?
(A) 6
(B) 4
(C) 3
(D) 2
(E) 1

15. At the Scholarly Text Printing Company, each of n printing presses can produce on the average t books every m minutes. If all presses work without interruption, how many hours will be required to produce a run of 10,000 books?
(A) 10,000 (60) mn/t
(B) 10,000 (60) tm/n
(C) 10,000mn/60t
(D) 10,000m/60nt
(E) 10,000/60mnt

16. If $\dfrac{(x - y)^2}{x^2 - y^2} = 9$, then $\dfrac{x + y}{x - y} =$
(A) $\frac{1}{9}$
(B) $\frac{1}{3}$
(C) 1
(D) 3
(E) 9

17. A certain manufacturer has three machines producing the same item. If Machine X produces $\frac{1}{4}$ as many of the item as Machine Y produces in the same time, and Machine Y produces twice as many of the item as Machine Z in the same time, then during a fixed period Machine Z produces what fraction of the total number of items produced?

(A) $\frac{1}{14}$
(B) $\frac{2}{7}$
(C) $\frac{1}{3}$
(D) $\frac{1}{2}$
(E) $\frac{4}{7}$

18. A car rental company charges a fee of $35 for each 24-hour period for the first 72 hours plus $5 for each 6 hours or every fraction thereof after 72 hours. If a car is taken at 8:00 a.m. on a Monday morning and returned at 9:45 p.m. on Thursday of the same week, what should be the total rental charge?

(A) $45
(B) $50
(C) $115
(D) $120
(E) $560

19. In a certain community, property is assessed at 60% of its appraised value and taxed at the rate of $4.00 per $100 of assessed value. If a taxpayer is assessed $240 per quarter in property taxes, what is the appraised value of the property?

(A) $6000
(B) $22,500
(C) $24,000
(B) $40,000
(E) $60,000

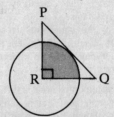

R is the center of the circle.

20. In the figure above, if isosceles right triangle PQR has an area of 4, what is the area of the shaded portion of the figure?

(A) π
(B) 2π
(C) $2\sqrt{2}\,\pi$
(D) 4π
(E) 8π

STOP

END OF SECTION. IF YOU HAVE ANY TIME LEFT, GO OVER YOUR WORK IN THIS SECTION ONLY. DO NOT WORK IN ANY OTHER SECTION OF THE TEST.

Section VII

Time—30 minutes
25 Questions

Directions: Each question below is followed by two numbered facts. You are to determine whether the data given in the statements is sufficient for answering the question. Use the data given, plus your knowledge of math and everyday facts, to choose between the five possible answers.

(A) if statement 1 alone is sufficient to answer the question, but statement 2 alone is not sufficient

(B) if statement 2 alone is sufficient to answer the question, but statement 1 alone is not sufficient

(C) if both statements together are needed to answer the question, but neither statement alone is sufficient

(D) if either statement by itself is sufficient to answer the question

(E) if not enough facts are given to answer the question

1. Is x divisible by 70?
   (1) x is divisible by 2 and 5.
   (2) x is divisible by 2 and 7.

2. Does Bob have more records in his record collection than Linda has in hers?
   (1) Christina has more records in her collection than Linda.
   (2) Bob has fewer records in his collection than Christina.

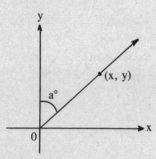

3. In the diagram above, what is the value of a?
   (1) x = 3
   (2) y = 3

4. A class of 30 children took a test. What was the average test score of the students in the class?
   (1) The highest score was 40.
   (2) The lowest score was 10.

5. Allen and Chris founded a company in 1980. In which year did the company's profits first exceed $100,000?
   (1) In 1980, the company had profits of $15,000, and in every year after that profits

were double those of the previous year.
   (2) In 1982, the company had profits of $60,000.

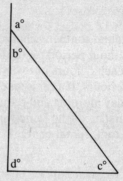

6. In the figure above, what is the value of d?
   (1) b + c = 90
   (2) c + a = 180

7. Is x an integer?
   (1) x > 0
   (2) $3^2 + 4^2 = x^2$

8. Is xy > 0?
   (1) $x^3y^3 > 0$
   (2) $x^2y^2 > 0$

9. What is the volume of cube C?
   (1) The total surface area of C is 54 square inches.
   (2) The area of each face of C is 9 square inches.

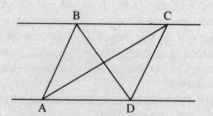

10. In the figure above, what is the ratio
$$\frac{\text{Area of Triangle ABD}}{\text{Area of Triangle ACD}}?$$
   (1) AB ∥ CD
   (2) BC ∥ AD

BUDGET FOR DAY SCHOOL D

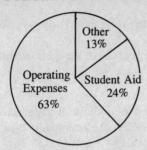

11. How much money did Day School D spend on operating expenses?
    (1) The total budget for the school was $9 million.
    (2) The school spent $2,160,000 on student aid.

12. What is the value of the integer N?
    (1) N is an integer multiple of 2, 3, and 6.
    (2) $30 < N < 70$

13. What is the total number of students in the six grades of a certain grammar school?
    (1) Each grade except the first has six more students than the grade immediately below it.
    (2) There is an average of 75 students in each grade.

14. How much money is saved by buying a box of a dozen donuts instead of 12 donuts singly?
    (1) When purchased in a box of 12, the cost of each donut is $0.05 less than if purchased singly.
    (2) The price of a box of a dozen donuts is $2.40.

15. What is the value of $a^4 - b^4$?
    (1) $a^2 + b^2 = 24$
    (2) $a^2 - b^2 = 0$

16. Daniel invested a total of $10,000 for a period of one year. Part of the money he put into an investment that earned 6 percent simple interest, and the rest of the money into an investment that earned 8 percent simple interest. How much money did he put into the investment that earned 6 percent?
    (1) The total interest earned on the $10,000 for the year was $640.
    (2) The dollar value of the investment that earned 6 percent was only one-fourth the dollar value of the investment that earned 8 percent.

17. Is x greater than y?
    (1) $3x = 4y$
    (2) $x = \frac{k}{3}$, $y = \frac{k}{4}$, and $k > 0$

18. What is the ratio $\dfrac{\text{Area of Circular Region X}}{\text{Area of Circular Region Y}}$?
    (1) The ratio of the circumference of region X to the circumference of region Y is $3:2$.
    (2) The circumference of region X is 6π.

19. Is the perimeter of a rectangular yard greater than 60 meters?
    (1) The two shorter sides of the yard are each 15 meters long.
    (2) The length of the yard is 3 meters longer than the width of the yard.

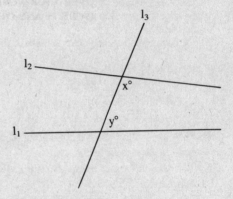

20. In the figure above, l_1 and l_2 intersect l_3. Do l_1 and l_2 intersect to the right of l_3?
    (1) $x > y$
    (2) $x + y < 180$

21. What is the value of $(p + q)(r + s)$?
    (1) $p(r + s) = 5$ and $q(r + s) = 3$
    (2) $(p + q) = (r + s)$

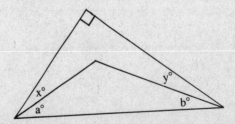

22. In the figure above, what is the value of $x + y$?
    (1) $a = 2b$
    (2) $a + b = 45$

23. Can a circle be drawn so that its circumference includes all four vertices of quadrilateral Q?

(1) All four sides of Q are equal in length.
(2) Each of the interior angles of Q measures 90°.

24. What is the sum of three consecutive integers?
    (1) The ratio of the least of the three integers to the greatest is 2.
    (2) The sum of the three integers is less than the average of the three integers.

25. If Patty is five years older than Rod, how old is Rod?
    (1) Fifteen years ago, Patty was twice as old as Rod.
    (2) Five years ago, the sum of Patty's age and Rod's age was 35.

STOP

END OF SECTION. IF YOU HAVE ANY TIME LEFT, GO OVER YOUR WORK IN THIS SECTION ONLY. DO NOT WORK IN ANY OTHER SECTION OF THE TEST.

ANSWER KEY—PRACTICE EXAMINATION 6

SECTION I

1. E	6. A	11. B	16. B
2. A	7. C	12. E	17. D
3. C	8. D	13. C	18. D
4. E	9. E	14. C	19. B
5. C	10. B	15. D	20. C

SECTION II

1. D	6. B	11. C	16. C	21. C
2. E	7. C	12. A	17. D	22. A
3. C	8. E	13. A	18. D	23. B
4. A	9. D	14. E	19. A	24. A
5. B	10. A	15. A	20. C	25. A

SECTION III

1. B	6. C	11. C	16. B	21. E
2. C	7. A	12. B	17. A	22. E
3. A	8. E	13. D	18. D	23. C
4. B	9. B	14. E	19. E	24. A
5. B	10. E	15. E	20. B	25. D

SECTION IV

1. D	6. E	11. D	16. A	21. B
2. C	7. D	12. E	17. C	22. A
3. E	8. C	13. D	18. E	23. B
4. C	9. B	14. D	19. E	24. B
5. E	10. E	15. D	20. E	25. A

SECTION V

1.	D	6.	B	11.	C	16.	B	21.	A
2.	D	7.	D	12.	B	17.	E	22.	B
3.	D	8.	C	13.	A	18.	D	23.	B
4.	E	9.	D	14.	B	19.	B	24.	C
5.	D	10.	E	15.	D	20.	C	25.	A

SECTION VI

1.	C	6.	D	11.	E	16.	A
2.	C	7.	A	12.	D	17.	B
3.	B	8.	C	13.	D	18.	D
4.	C	9.	A	14.	B	19.	D
5.	C	10.	C	15.	D	20.	A

SECTION VII

1.	C	6.	A	11.	D	16.	D	21.	A
2.	E	7.	B	12.	E	17.	B	22.	B
3.	C	8.	A	13.	B	18.	A	23.	B
4.	E	9.	D	14.	A	19.	A	24.	A
5.	A	10.	B	15.	B	20.	B	25.	D

EXPLANATORY ANSWERS

Section I

1. **(E)** This question is easily solved by manipulating the equation to find the value of x:

   Subtract x from both sides:
   $$x + 5 = 4x - 10$$
   $$\underline{-x \qquad\quad -x}$$
   $$5 = 3x - 10$$

   Add 10 to each side:
   $$\underline{+10 \qquad +10}$$
   $$15 = 3x$$

   Rearrange if you wish:
   $$3x = 15$$

   Divide both sides by 3:
   $$\frac{3x}{3} = \frac{15}{3}$$
   $$x = 5$$

2. **(A)** This question is most easily solved by manipulating exponents rather than by a complicated and lengthy series of multiplications. Since 8 is equal to 2 to the third power, we can substitute 2^3 for 8:

   $$\frac{2^6 - (2^3)^2}{4^3}$$

   The second term of the numerator indicates that 2 to the third power is being raised to the second power. The rules of exponents require that we multiply in this situation:

   $$(2^3)^2 = 2^6$$

   Now it becomes clear that the value of the numerator is 0, so the value of the entire expression is 0.

3. **(C)** This question can be answered directly by converting the fraction to its decimal equivalent:

   $$\frac{8}{5} = 1.6$$

4. **(E)** Obviously, to answer the question you must know the length of the side of a piece of tile. Since each tile is square and has a perimeter of 1 meter, each side is 1 divided by 4, or $\frac{1}{4}$ meters in length. Then, the length of the side of the square to be tiled is 3 meters, and 3 divided by $\frac{1}{4}$ is 12. So you would need 12 such tiles laid side by side to cover one edge of the area. Finally, since the area to be covered is 3 meters by 3 meters, you would need at least 12 times 12, or 144 tiles.

5. **(C)** This question involves the computation of a percentage increase. The formula for finding a percentage change is Increase/Original Total. Notice also that the question specifically allows you to use an approximation:

   $$\frac{16,300 - 12,200}{12,200} = \frac{4,100}{12,200} \cong \frac{1}{3} = 33\frac{1}{3}\%$$

   So the closest approximation is (C).

6. **(A)** The information for this question is presented in graphic form. The solution requires the computation of a weighted average; that is, to find the overall class average, we must make sure we give proper weight to each score according to the number of students who achieved that score:

5	×	70	=	350
20	×	80	=	1600
10	×	90	=	900
15	×	100	=	1500
Totals:	50 students			4350 points

   To find the average, we divide the total number of points by the total number of students:

   $$\frac{4350}{50} = 87$$

7. **(C)** This question tests nothing more than your ability to do some simple, if tedious, bookkeeping. To find the cost of sending a 23.5 pound package by express service, we must use all three express rates:

First lb.		$17.50
Next 9 lbs:	9 × $2.60 =	23.40
Additional 13.5 lbs:	14 × $1.20 =	16.80
Total:		$57.90

8. **(D)** This question is a little trickier because it requires that you express your calculation in terms of an unknown. Still, the procedure is similar. First, since the package weighs more than 10 pounds, we can calculate the cost of the first 10 pounds using the rate schedule for Regular Service:

First lb.	$ 5.10
Next 9 lbs:	$9 \times \$1.80 = 16.20$
Cost of 10 lbs:	21.30

Now we must express the cost of the excess weight in terms of x. The total weight of the package is x pounds, but we have already calculated the cost of the first 10 pounds. So all that remains is the cost of the *excess*. That is, the excess is x less the first 10 pounds, or $x - 10$: $\$1.50(x - 10)$. The total cost, therefore (expressed in dollars), is $21.30 + 1.5(x - 10)$.

9. **(E)** This question is more easily solved by using common sense than by doing the operations indicated. Without making a final decision about (A) and (B), you can see that they are similar, so don't try to compare them at first. Then, (C) involves raising a fraction to the fifth power, and as you do that, the numbers get smaller and smaller. So (C) is going to be much smaller than either (A) or (B). (D), however, when rewritten as 0.003×7, looks very much like (A) and (B). So go on to (E). (E) is somewhat like (A), (B) and (D), *except* that the decimal number in (E) is much larger than those of the other choices. Consequently, (E) will be correspondingly larger than any of the others. And you can reach this conclusion without actually doing any multiplication.

10. **(B)** To a certain extent, answering this question is a matter of trial and error. One way of arriving at the desired arrangement is:

	C	B	E	F	D	A
STEP 1:	A	C	B	E	F	D
STEP 2:	A	B	C	E	F	D
STEP 3:	A	B	C	D	E	F

While this is not the only way of doing it, a little experimentation will show you that it cannot be done in fewer steps.

Further, we can offer a sort of informal proof that it is not possible to do the job in fewer steps. Given the arrangement:

C B E F D A

We know that we must move A to the left of B, C to the right of B and D to the left of E. That will require a minimum of three steps.

11. **(B)** This question can be solved using a table:

	Full-Time	Part-Time	Total
Men			
Women			
Total			

The table or matrix shows the possibilities. We begin to fill in the individual squares, or cells, by using the information provided:

	Full-Time	Part-Time	Total
Men			55%
Women			
Total	30%		

But we know that the total labor force is 100%, and this means that the percentages for Full-Time and Part-Time must equal 100 and that the percentages for Men and Women must equal 100. So we can fill in some further information:

	Full-Time	Part-Time	Total
Men			55%
Women			45%
Total	30%	70%	100%

Next we reason that 60% of the 30% who are Full-Time employees are women. In other words, Full-Time women workers account for 60% of 30% of the work force:

	Full-Time	Part-Time	Total
Men			55%
Women	18%		45%
Total	30%	70%	100%

Now, since we have totals indicated, we can use arithmetic to find the missing information:

	Full-Time	Part-Time	Total
Men	12%	43%	55%
Women	18%	27%	45%
Total	30%	70%	100%

Notice that all totals check out.

The final step is to use the information to answer the question:

$$\frac{\text{Men Full-Time}}{\text{Total Full-Time}} = \frac{.12}{.30} = \frac{2}{5} = 40\%$$

12. **(E)** The trick here is to recognize that both triangles, ADC and ABC, have the same altitude, AD:

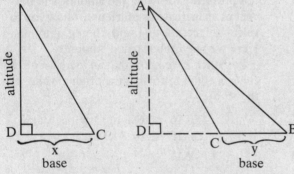

Now you use the standard formula ($\frac{1}{2} \times$ altitude $\times$ base) to find the area of each triangle. For $\triangle$ ADC it is $\frac{1}{2}(x)$ (AD) and for $\triangle$ ABC it is $\frac{1}{2}(y)$ (ABD). Then you set up your ratio:

$$\frac{\frac{1}{2}(x) \, (AD)}{\frac{1}{2}(y) \, (AD)} = \frac{x}{y}$$

But since x and y are equal, the ratio is just 1.

13. **(C)** Here we are looking for the appropriate formula to express the relationship described in the problem. Now, without worrying at first too much about symbols, try to formulate the solution in words. You might reason that to find the time required to produce a certain number of units, you need to divide the number of units by the rate at which the people (or whatever) work. (Already, then, you know that the correct choice must be 10,000 divided by the rate of

work—and that allows you to eliminate both (D) and (E) because the choices show 10,000 in the denominator and not in the numerator.) The group works at the rate of L letters every M minutes, so your solution is the total number of letters to be addressed divided by the rate:

$$\frac{10,000}{L/M}$$

And L/M is just a fraction, so when you divide you invert and multiply:

$$\frac{10,000}{L/M} = 10,000 \times M/L = \frac{10,000M}{L}$$

Next, you must divide this expression by E, since the number of workers reduces the time required to do the job. (Think how long it will take to do 10,000 letters with E people working.)

$$\frac{10,000M}{EL}$$

Finally, you must take into account that there are 60 minutes in each hour. You will want to divide by 60 because it takes fewer hours than minutes to produce the same number of units:

$$\frac{10,000M}{60EL}$$

14. **(C)** A good approach to this question is to try to express the information given in English in algebraic terms. We are told that the cost of car X is twice the average of the other 11 cars. To express the average cost of the other 11 cars we can use the letter T to represent their total cost (all 11 combined), and so the average will be $\frac{T}{11}$. Then we are told that the cost of X is twice this, or $\frac{2T}{11}$. We now have all costs represented in terms of T, and we can address ourselves to the question asked: "what fraction of total is car X?" Expressed with symbols:

$$\frac{\text{Cost of Car X}}{\text{Total of All}}$$

The total cost of the cars in the shipment will be the cost of the 11 cars plus the cost of car X: Total Cost $= T + \frac{2T}{11} = \frac{13T}{18}$ Now we substitute this into the fraction above:

$$\frac{\dfrac{2T}{11}}{\dfrac{13T}{11}} = \frac{2T}{11} \times \frac{11}{13T} = \frac{2}{13}$$

15. **(D)** Above, we solved the problem using "official" algebraic unknowns, but in other situations we have used actual numbers. Question 14 could also have been handled in such a way. For this question, let us use the alternative method rather than the "official" algebraic approach.

We are not told the weight of the jar or its contents, so we can arbitrarily supply our own numbers. Let us pick a number that is not too large nor too small—something convenient to work with, say 10 pounds. If the total weight of the jar and its contents is 10 pounds, then the jar alone weights 20% of 10 pounds, or 2 pounds, and the coffee therefore weighs 8 pounds. Now if we remove beans so that the combined weight of the jar and the remaining beans is 60% of the original total, the new combined weight is only 6 pounds, of which 2 pounds is glass jar and 4 pounds is coffee. So we have only 4 pounds of coffee remaining out of an original total of 8 pounds. Therefore, we have removed 4 out of 8 pounds or exactly $\frac{1}{2}$ of the coffee.

16. **(B)** A simple approach to this question is to combine the information given in an informal way, rather than trying to perform precise manipulations by the rules. First, on the lower end, we know that x must be larger than 2, larger than 4, larger than −1, and larger than 0, which means simply that x is bigger than 4. On the other side, x is less than 12, less than 21, less than 9, less than 8, and less than 6 (if x + 1 < 7 then x < 6). Therefore, x (which is said to be an integer) is bigger than 4 and less than 6, so x must be 5.

17. **(D)** Perhaps the very best way to solve this question is just to test each answer choice to find out which one works. If you test each choice by substitution into the calculation for X, you will find that only 7 works:

$$\begin{array}{r} 729 \\ 573 \\ +\ 971 \\ \hline 2,273 \end{array}$$

18. **(D)** This question tests your knowledge of coordinate geometry. Given the coordinates of the two points indicated, it is possible to find both the length and the width of the rectangle. First, the width is easily found, since it is the distance from the horizontal axis (the x-axis) to point P. Since the y-coordinate of P is 2, the point is two units above the horizontal axis. Second, the length is found by finding the distance from point P to point Q. Since line QR is parallel to the y-axis (straight up and down), point Q will have the same x coordinate as R. So the x coordinate for Q is 5, and line PQ runs from 2 to 5, for a length of 3. Now the final step is easy. A rectangle with a length of 3 and a width of 2 has an area of 2 × 3, or 6.

19. **(B)** Here we have a percentage question that involves several manipulations. Only one basic insight, however, is needed to handle the problem. Knowing the amount and percent of an increase is sufficient to allow you to calculate the starting and ending amounts. Here we need the starting amounts.

For stock P we know that an increase of 16 cents is equal to 16% of the original value of the stock:

$$\$0.16 = 16\% \text{ of Original Value}$$
$$\$0.16 = .16 \times \text{OV}$$
$$\frac{\$0.16}{.16} = \text{OV}$$

Original Value = $1.00

For stock Q we know that an increase of $1.68 is equal to 16% of the original value of the stock:

$$\$1.68 = 16\% \text{ of Original Value}$$
$$\$1.68 = .16 \times \text{OV}$$
$$\frac{\$1.68}{.16} = \text{OV}$$

Original Value = $10.50
Now we find the difference between the original values:

$$\$10.50 - \$1.00 = \$9.50$$

20. **(C)** This problem is rather tedious because it requires calculating the times for these two trains that stop and start. How long does it take the express train to travel 600 kilometers? Since it travels at the rate of 100 kilometers per hour, the total time while actually moving will be:

$$\frac{600 \text{ kilometers}}{100 \text{ kilometers}} \text{ per hour} = 6 \text{ hours}$$

Now we calculate the non-moving time:

75 kilometers, total traveled of 75, then first stop

75 kilometers, total traveled of 150, then second stop

75 kilometers, total traveled of 225, then third stop

75 kilometers, total traveled of 300, then fourth stop

75 kilometers, total traveled of 375, then fifth stop

75 kilometers, total traveled of 450, then sixth stop

75 kilometers, total traveled of 525, then seventh stop

75 kilometers, total traveled of 600

Note that when the train reaches 600 kilometers, you do not add in another stop. The question requires that you calculate the time needed to *travel* 600 kilometers. So the total time is 6 hours plus 7 × 3 minutes, or 6 hours and 21 minutes.

Now how far can the local train travel in that length of time? Since the local train travels at 50 kilometers per hour, it will cover 25 kilometers in 30 minutes:

$$25 \text{ kilometers}/50 \text{ kilometers per hour} = .5 \text{ hours, or } 30 \text{ minutes}$$

This means that the train will travel 12 × 25 = 300 kilometers in exactly 6 hours, but that includes 12 1-minute stops. So in 6 hours and 12 minutes the local train travels 300 kilometers and completes its final stop. Now the train starts up again and runs for another 9 minutes, to give our total of 6 hours and 21 minutes. How far does it travel in 9 minutes?

$$50 \text{ kilometers per hour} \times \frac{9}{60} \text{ hours} = 7.5 \text{ k}$$

The local train travels a total of 307.5 kilometers in the same time it takes the express train to travel 600 kilometers.

Section II

1. **(D)** This is a main idea question. The author does two things in the passage: He describes the problem of increasing thermal pollution and he suggests that solar energy will solve the problem. (D) neatly describes this double development. (A) is incorrect, for though the author does describe the phenomenon of thermal pollution and its causes, he also proposes a solution. (B) is incorrect since it fails to make reference to the fact that an important part of the passage is the description of a problem. It must be admitted that it can be argued that (B) does make an attempt to describe the development of the passage, but it does not do as nicely as (D) does. (C) is easily eliminated since no ambiguity is mentioned. Finally, (E) is incorrect since whatever objection the author may implicitly try to refute (opponents of solar energy), he never cites and then refuses a counterargument.

2. **(E)** This is an explicit-idea question. (A), (B), and (C) are mentioned in the second paragraph as factors contributing to thermal pollution. (D) is mentioned in the third paragraph as a pressure increasing thermal pollution. (E) is mentioned in the third paragraph—but not as a factor contributing to thermal pollution. Unpredictable weather patterns make it difficult to predict when the thermal pollution problem will reach the critical stage, but the patterns do not contribute to thermal pollution.

3. **(C)** This is an inference question. In discussing the melting of the polar ice caps, the author notes that there is a positive feedback mechanism: Since the ice caps reflect sunlight and therefore dissipate solar energy which would otherwise be absorbed by the earth, the melting of the ice caps increases the amount of energy captured by the earth, which in turn contributes to the melting of the ice caps, and so on. (C) correctly describes this as intensifying the effects of thermal pollution. (A) is easily eliminated since this feedback mechanism has nothing to do with a possible reduction in per capita energy consumption. (B) is incorrect, for though this feedback loop increases the problem, and thereby the urgency for the changeover to solar energy, the loop itself will not cause a change in policy. (D) is incorrect for the same reason. Finally, though the melting of the polar ice caps will result in flooding, this flooding is not an explanation of the feedback loop. Rather it is the result of the general phenomenon of the melting of the ice caps.

4. **(A)** This is a logical-detail question. Why does the author discuss energy conservation? Conservation may appear as a possible alternative to solar energy. The author argues, however, that a closer examination shows that conservation cannot avert but only postpone the crisis. In terms of tactics, the author's move is to raise a possible objection and give an answer to it—as stated in (A). (B) is incorrect, for the refutation of a possible objection does not support the central thesis directly, only indirectly by eliminating a possible counterargument. (C) is incorrect since the author never acknowledges he has fallen into any contradiction. (D) is incorrect since it overstates the case. The author admits that conservation has a beneficial effect, but he denies that conservation obviates the need for solar energy. Finally, (E) is incorrect since the point is argumentative and not merely informational.

5. **(B)** This is an inference question. In the final paragraph the author makes references to the possibility of "air-conditioning" the earth, a word placed in quotation marks, which indicates that he is using it in nonstandard way. Ordinarily, we use the word "air-condition" to mean to cool, say, a room or an entire building. Obviously, the author is not referring to some gigantic Carrier air-conditioning unit mounted, say, on top of the earth. But the general idea of removing heat seems to be what the term means in this context. This is consonant with the passage as well. Thermal pollution is the buildup of energy, and we are showing a positive buildup because fossil fuel and other sources of energy release energy which was only stored. So this, coupled with the sun's energy which comes in each moment, gives us a positive (though not desirable) balance of energy retention over loss. The idea of air-conditioning the earth, though not feasible to the passage, must refer to schemes to get rid of this energy, say, into outer space. This is the idea presented in (B). As for (A), redistribution of thermal energy within the earth's energy system will not solve the problem of accumulated energy, so that cannot be what proponents of "air conditioning" have in mind. (C) is a

good definition of conservation, but not "air conditioning." (D) is the recommendation given by the author, but that is not a response to this question. Finally, (E) is incorrect for the reason that burning wood is not going to cool the earth.

6. **(B)** This is a tone question. The author describes a very dangerous situation, but he also shows the way to solve the problem. The author does not necessarily believe that the battle for solar energy has been won; otherwise, he would not be advocating a shift to solar energy. On balance, the tone of the passage is hope or optimism, qualified by the realization that solar energy is not yet a high priority. This qualified hope is best described by (B). (A) is incorrect since this is not the tone of the passage. Though the author may be distressed at what he perceives to be the short-sightedness of policy makers, this distress does not color the writing in the passage. (C) is totally inappropriate since the author is analytical. (D) is inconsistent with the author's concern. Finally, (E) overstates the case. Though the author is concerned, he is not in a panic.

7. **(C)** This is an application question. We are looking for the *most* logical continuation. Since the author has urged us to adopt solar energy, an appropriate continuation would be a discussion of how to implement solar energy. And (C) would be a part of this discussion. (B) can be eliminated since the proposal depends upon the cost and feasibility of solar energy, not on its history. (A) and (E) can be eliminated since the author has explicitly asserted that *only* solar energy will solve the problem of thermal pollution. Finally, (D) is incorrect since the author need not regale us with the gory details of this situation. He has already made the point. As readers, we will want to see the practical details of his plan to avoid disaster.

8. **(E)** This is an inference question. The author does not specifically define the phrase in question, but we can infer from the passage what is meant by it. The phrase appears just after the reference to schemes to "air-condition" the earth. (See the discus-

sion of question 5, above.) Since that is not possible, the author says that solar energy is the only alternative to disaster, for the use of solar energy doesn't increase the energy balance. Thus, the balance referred to must be the one that, when upset, creates thermal pollution. So the balance is the difference between the rate at which energy is added to the system (both through natural addition of solar energy and the release of stored solar energy) and the rate at which energy can be exhausted into space.

9. **(D)** This is a main-idea question. The author begins by stating that it would be useful to have a general index to measure welfare and notes that some have even suggested the GNP might be adapted for that purpose. He then proceeds to demonstrate why such an index cannot be constructed. Generally, then, the author shows the defects in a proposal for a general index of welfare, and (D) nicely describes this development. (A) is incorrect for the author never produces any arguments for the position he is attacking. And even when the author raises points such as the suggestion that hours worked might be a measure of cost of production, he is not citing arguments for that position; he is only mentioning the position to attack it. (B) is incorrect since the author is attacking and not defending the proposal discussed. (C) is easily eliminated because the author never attacks the sincerity of those he opposes. Finally, (E) is wrong, for the author never reviews any literature on the subject he is discussing.

10. **(A)** This is an inference question. We turn to the second paragraph. There the author mentions that a general index of welfare would have to include some measure of the cost of producing the output. He suggests that someone might think hours worked would do the trick. He rejects that position by noting that hours worked, as a statistic, does not take account of the quality of the work-time, e.g., long hours versus short hours, working conditions, satisfaction of workers. Answer (A) best describes this argument. (B) is incorrect, for the author discusses environmental costs in connection with another aspect of a general index. (C) is incorrect since this distinction is never used by the author. (D) is incorrect since this is not mentioned as a goal of such a measure. Finally, (E) confuses the GNP, mentioned in the first part of the paragraph, with the index to measure real costs.

11. **(C)** This is an inference question that asks about the main point of the passage. The author adduces several objections to the idea of a general index of welfare. Then the final blow is delivered in the last paragraph: Even if you could devise measures for these various components of a general index, any combination or weighting of the individual measures would reflect only the judgment (personal preference) of the weighter. For this reason alone, argues the author, the entire idea is unworkable. (C) makes this point. (A) and (D) can be eliminated since the author never uses cost or time as arguments against the index. (B) can be eliminated on similar ground. The author may recognize that considerable research would be needed to attempt such measures, yet he does not bother to use that as an objection. (E) can be eliminated for a similar reason. The author may have some arguments against the way such statistics are gathered now, but he does not bother to make them. His argument has the structure: Even assuming there are such data, we cannot combine these statistics to get a general measure of the quality of the environment.

12. **(A)** This is a tone question, and the justification for (A) is already implicit in the discussion thus far. The author sees fatal theoretical weaknesses inherent in the idea of an index of welfare. So we might say that he regards such a notion as an unrealistic, that is, unachievable, dream. (B) is incorrect because the author does not believe the idea can ever be implemented. (C), (D), and (E) can be eliminated on substantially the same ground.

13. **(A)** This is an explicit-idea question. In the second paragraph, the author acknowledges that the GNP is a fairly accurate measure of output. He never suggests that the GNP can

estimate needs, predict welfare, or measure welfare generally. So we can eliminate the remaining choices.

14. **(E)** This is an explicit-idea question, with a thought reverser. (A), (B), (C) and (D) are all mentioned in the third paragraph as aspects of a needs index. The fourth paragraph does not treat the idea of a needs index but the idea of a physical environment index. That is where the author discusses the items mentioned in (E). So the author does mention the items covered by (E), but not as part of a needs index.

15. **(A)** This is an application question. We are looking for the most likely place for the passage. To be sure, it is possible that the passage might appear in any of the five suggested locations, but the most likely place is that suggested by (A). This could easily be one of a series of papers addressed to a group meeting to discuss public policy decisions. As for (B), it is not likely that the passage would be an introduction to a general text on statistics. It is too firmly dedicated to a particular idea, and the use of statistics is in a way subordinate to the theoretical discussion. (C) is inappropriate since the discussion bears only remotely on programs to aid the poor. (D) is even less likely since the passage does not discuss the foundations of government. Finally, (E) is to a certain extent plausible, but (A) is more closely connected to the content of the passage.

16. **(C)** This is a logical detail question. One of the striking features about the development of the selection is the author's extensive use of examples to illustrate his contentions. For example, when he mentions environmental problems, he gives several illustrations.

17. **(D)** This is a tone question. The author confidently asserts several contentions and then, as was just noted, backs them up with particular examples. So the one is both analytical and confident.

18. **(D)** This is a main-idea question. The main idea of the passage is fairly clear: suggest reforms to correct the problems discussed. Choice (D) is a very good description of this development. (A) is incorrect since the author himself criticizes the system. (B) is incorrect since no recommendation for expanding benefits and scope is made by the author. (C) overstates the case. The author limits his indictment to unemployment compensation, and even then he believes that the shortcomings of the system can be remedied. (E) is incorrect because the author is discussing unemployment compensation, not government programs designed to achieve full employment generally. We may infer from the passage that unemployment compensation is not a program designed to achieve full employment, but a program designed to alleviate the hardship of unemployment. On balance, (D) is the most precise description given of the development of the passage.

19. **(A)** This is a logical-detail question. In the second paragraph the author introduces the example of a worker who loses surprisingly little by being unemployed. The author does this to show that unemployment encourages people to remain unemployed by reducing the net cost of unemployment. (A) makes this point. (B) is incorrect, for the author does not discuss the problem of employer contribution until the fourth paragraph. (C) is incorrect, for this is not the reason that the author introduces the point. (D) is incorrect because the topic is not taken up until the third paragraph. Finally, (E) is incorrect since the author analyzes the situation in a neutral fashion; there is no hint of condemnation.

20. **(C)** This is an explicit-idea question. Statement I contains a recommendation made by the author in the final paragraph. Statement III is also recommended in that paragraph. As for statement II, the author never suggests shortening the time an out-of-work person may receive benefits. Though such a change might encourage people to limit the length of their unemployment, this was not mentioned in the passage. And the question is an explicit idea question that asks what recommendations were made by the author.

21. **(C)** Here, too, we have an explicit-idea question. (A), (B), (D), and (E) are all mentioned in the third paragraph as ways by which an employer might reduce seasonal and cyclical fluctuations in labor needs. (C), however, was not mentioned as a way to minimize unemployment. Indeed, we may infer from other information supplied by the passage that supplementary benefits actually increase unemployment.

22. **(A)** This is an application question. We are asked to apply the author's analysis of the rating system to conclusions given in the answer choices. The author is critical of the rating system because it does not place the full burden of unemployment on the employer. This is because there is a maximum contribution limit, and in the final paragraph the author recommends the ceiling be eliminated. From these remarks, we may infer that the author believes the rating system is, in theory, sound, but that practically it needs to be adjusted. Choice (A) neatly describes this judgment. (B) can be eliminated since the author implies that the system is, in principle, sound. Moreover, the author implies that the employer does have some control over the time his former employees remain out of work. The maximum limit on employer contribution allows the employer to exploit this control. As for (C), this is contradicted by our analysis thus far and for the further reason that the passage never suggests employee contribution should replace employer contribution. Indeed, the author implies that he regards the system as serving a useful and necessary social function. (D) can be eliminated because the author never draws a distinction between contributions by large firms and contributions by small firms. Finally, (E) is incorrect since the experience rating system is theoretically tied to the amount drawn by employees. The difficulty is not with the theory of the system, but with its implementation.

23. **(B)** This is an explicit detail question. We are looking for criticisms which are made in the passage. Statement II is such a criticism, and it can be found in the very opening sentence. As for statement I, the author actually states the opposite: The system allows firms of this sort to use the unemployment compensation system as a subsidy for their employees, reducing their own costs of production. As for statement III, the author only states that employers contribute to the fund from which benefits are paid. No mention is ever made of a state contribution. So the correct answer is II only.

24. **(A)** This is a tone question. In the final paragraph, as he makes his recommendations, the author states that we must reform the system, preserving its good aspects and correcting its bad effects. (A) describes this judgment. (B) is incorrect since much of the discussion in the passage is an indictment of the system's economic inefficiency. (C) is wrong because the author makes recommendations which, he states, will correct the wasteful effects. (D) is incorrect, for the author implies that the system has usefulness. Finally, though the author criticizes the system, his objection is that the system is inefficient, not that it is outdated.

25. **(A)** This is an inference question. In making his calculation, the author compares the worker's take-home pay from employment with the unemployment compensation she receives in order to illustrate the point that the difference is small enough to provide little incentive for a worker to return to work. Since he does not adjust the worker's unemployment compensation for taxes, we can infer that the author believes such compensation is not taxed (and whether at this time such compensation is taxable is irrelevant to the logical structure of the argument). As for (C), the reason the worker is unemployed is really irrelevant to the point the author makes (whether she has an incentive to return to work). As for (B) and (E), it is not the actions or motivations of any particular worker that are relevant, but the general nature of the economic incentive created by unemployment compensation. Finally, as for (D), if there were such additional compensation, it would make the author's point even stronger. We may infer from his failure to mention it, that the hypothetical worker does not receive supplemental benefits.

Section III

1. **(B)** The basic move by M. Adamante is to offer a competing explanation for the phenomenon. That is, he seems to agree that the United States has the 17th lowest infant mortality rate, but he attributes this to distributional factors rather than to medical technology itself. (D) is the second most attractive answer. But Adamante does not introduce any intervening variables, e.g., technology allows more pregnancies that would otherwise abort to go to term, which in turn means that weaker infants are born, and so more die. (A) is incorrect since Adamante seems to accept the validity of the data and to contest the explanation. (E) is incorrect for the same reason. Finally, (C) is incorrect since Adamante does not suggest that the first speaker has made a logical error—only a factual one.

2. **(C)** The author is arguing that the budget cuts will not ultimately be detrimental to the poor since the adverse effects will be more than offset by beneficial ones. II and III attack both elements of this reasoning. II points out that there will be no beneficial effects to offset the harmful ones, and III notes that the harmful effects will be so harmful that they will outweigh any beneficial ones that might result. I, however, is not relevant to the author's point. The author is arguing a point of economics. How the Congressmen get themselves elected has no bearing on that point.

3. **(A)** The author reasons from the premise "there are bottles of this product in the apartments" to the conclusion "therefore, these people believe the product is effective." The ad obviously wants the hearer to infer that the residents of the apartments decided themselves to purchase the product because they believed it to be effective. (A) directly attacks this linkage. If it were true that the company gave away bottles of the product, this would sever that link. (B) does weaken the ad, but only marginally. To be sure, we might say to ourselves, "Well, a person who touts a product and does not use

it himself is not fully to be trusted." But (B) does not aim at the very structure of the argument as (A) does. (C) can hardly weaken the argument, since it appears to be a premise on which the argument itself is built. (C), therefore, actually strengthens the appeal of the advertisement. It also does not link to Painaway's effectiveness. (D) seems to be irrelevant to the *appeal* of the ad. The ad is designed to *change* the hearer's mind, so the fact that he does not now accept the conclusion of the ad is not an argument against the ability of the ad to accomplish its stated objective. Finally, (E) is irrelevant to the purpose of the ad for reasons very similar to those cited for (D).

4. **(B)** The author is accusing the artists of being inconsistent. He claims they give lip service to the idea that an artist must suffer, but that they then live in material comfort—so they do not themselves suffer. Only (B) completes the paragraph in a way so that this inconsistency comes out. (A) and (D) can be dismissed because the author is concerned with those whom he attacks as *artists*, not as connoisseurs or purchasers of art, nor as critics of art. (C) is inadequate for it does not reveal the inconsistency. The author apparently allows that these people are, after a fashion, artists; what he objects to is their claiming that it is necessary to suffer while they do not themselves suffer. (E) is the second best answer, but it fails, too. The difficulty with (E) is that the author's point is that there is a contradiction between the actions and the words of those he accuses: They claim to suffer but they do not. But the claimed suffering goes beyond matters of eating and has to do with deprivation generally.

5. **(B)** II is an assumption of the author because the inconsistency of which he accuses others would disappear if, though they were not poor, they nonetheless endured great suffering, e.g., emotional pain or poor health. I is not an assumption of the author. He is trying to prove that he has uncovered a contradiction in another's words and actions: It is the others who insist suffering is necessary. The author himself never says

one way or the other whether he considers that suffering is necessary to produce art—only that these others claim it is, and then eat well. Finally, III incorrectly construes the author's reference to purchasers of art. He never mentions the role of the critic.

6. **(C)** Take careful note of the exact position the author ascribes to the analysis: They *always* attribute a sudden drop to a crisis. The author then attacks this simple causal explanation by explaining that, though a crisis is followed by a market drop, the reason is not that the crisis causes the drop but that both are the effects of some common cause, the changing of the moon. Of course, the argument seems implausible, but our task is not to grade the argument, only to describe its structure. (A) is not a proper characterization of that structure since the author never provides a specific example. (B), too, is inapplicable since no statistics are produced. (D) can be rejected since the author is attacking generally accepted beliefs rather than appealing to them to support his position. Finally, though the author concedes the reliability of the reports in question, he wants to draw a different conclusion from the data, (E).

7. **(A)** Given the implausibility of the author's alternative explanation, he is probably speaking tongue-in-cheek, that is, he is ridiculing the analysts for *always* attributing a drop in the market to a political crisis. But whether you took the argument in this way or as a serious attempt to explain the fluctuations of the stock market, (A) will be the correct answer. (E) surely goes beyond the mere factual description at which the author is aiming, as does (D) as well. The author is concerned with the *causes* of fluctuations; nothing suggests that he or anyone else is in a position to exploit those fluctuations. (C) finds no support in the paragraph for nothing suggests that he wishes to attack the credibility of the source rather than the argument itself. Finally, (B) is inappropriate to the main point of the passage. Whether the market ultimately evens itself out has nothing to do with the causes of the fluctuations.

8. **(E)** The assumption necessary to the author's reasoning is the fairly abstract or minimal one that there is a connection between the characteristics of a work of art and the period during which it was produced. If there were no such connection, that is, if there were not styles of art that lasted for some time but only randomly produced works unrelated to one another by medium, content, or detail, the argument would fail. Every other answer, however, attributes too much to the author. (D) for example states that the expert can *pinpoint* the date of the work, but this goes far beyond the author's attempt to date generally the piece of pottery he is examining. (C) says more than the author does. He mentions that the details of seminude women and bulls are characteristic of the *late* Minoan period, not that they generally characterize the entire history of that people. (B) also goes far beyond the details offered. The author connects the bull with a period of *Minoan* civilization—not ancient civilizations in general. Finally, (A) fails because, while the author apparently believes that Minoan pottery of this period was made in a certain way, he does not claim that all such pottery came from this period. He uses a group of characteristics in combination to date the pottery: It is the combination that is unique to the period, not each individual characteristic taken in isolation.

9. **(B)** The weakness in the argument is that it makes an assertion without any supporting argumentation. The author states that things might turn out to be worse, but he never mentions any specific way in which the result might be considered less desirable than what presently exists. As for (A), the author might have chosen to attack the radicals in this way, but that he did not adopt a particular line of attack available to him is not nearly so severe a criticism as that expressed by (B)—that the line of attack he did adopt is defective, or at least incomplete. The same reasoning applies to both (C) and (E). It is true the author might have taken the attack proposed by (C), but that he chose not to is not nearly so serious a weakness as that pointed out by (B). (E)

comes perhaps the closest to expressing what (B) says more explicitly. (E) hints at the specific consequences that might occur, but it is restricted to the *transition* period. It is not really detailing the bad results which might finally come out of a revolution, only the disadvantages of undertaking the change. Finally, (D) describes existing conditions, but it does not treat the question whether there *should* be a revolution; and, in any event, to defend against the question whether there *should* be a revolution by arguing there *will not be* one would itself be weak, had the author used the argument.

10. **(E)**   The sample syllogism uses its terms in an ambiguous way. In the first premise the category "American buffalo" is used to refer to the group as a whole, but in the second premise it is used to denote a particular member of that group. In the first premise, "disappearing" refers to extinction of a group, but in the second premise "disappearing" apparently means fading from view. (E) is fraught with similar ambiguities. The argument there moves from wealthy people as a group to a particular wealthy person, an illegitimate shifting of terminology. (A) is a distraction. It mentions subject matter similar to that of the question stem, but our task is to parallel the *form* of the argument, not to find an argument on a similar topic. (A), incidentally, is an unambiguous and valid argument. So too is (B), and a moment's reflection will reveal that it is very similar to (A). (C) is not similar to (A) and (B), but then again it is not parallel to the question stem. (C) contains circular reasoning—the very thing to be proved had to be assumed in the first place—but while circular reasoning is incorrect reasoning, it does not parallel the error committed by the question stem: ambiguity. (D) is clearly a correct argument, so it cannot be parallel to the question stem, which contains a fallacious argument.

11. **(C)**   The tone of the paragraph is tongue-in-cheek. The author uses phrases such as "mysteries of this arcane science" and "wonderful discipline," but then gives a silly example of the utility of logic. Obviously, he

means to be ironic. The real point he wants to make is that formal logic has little utility and that it may even lead one to make foolish errors. (A) cannot be correct because the example is clearly not an illustration of correct reasoning. (B) can be rejected since the author does not attempt to define the term "logic"; he only gives an example of its use. (D) is a distraction. The author's particular illustration does mention the American buffalo, but he could as easily have taken another species of animal or any other group term that would lend itself to the ambiguous treatment of his syllogism. (E) is incorrect since the author never examines the relationship between the premises and the conclusion. He gives the example and lets it speak for itself.

12. **(B)**   The author's behavior is paradoxical because he is going along with the young man's paradoxical statement. He concludes the young man is lying because the young man told him so, but that depends on believing what the young man told him is true. So he accepts the content of the young man's statement in order to reject the statement. Once it is seen that there is a logical twist to this problem, the other answer choices can easily be rejected. (A), of course, overlooks the paradoxical nature of the tourist's behavior. The stranger may have been trying to be helpful, but what is curious about the tourist's behavior is not that he rejected the stranger's offer of advice, *but* that he relied on that very advice at the moment he rejected it! (C) also overlooks the paradox. It is true the tourist rejects the advice, but his rejection is not *understandable;* if anything it is self-contradictory, and therefore completely incomprehensible. (D) is the poorest possible choice since it makes a value judgment totally unrelated to the point of the passage. Finally, (E) would have been correct only if the tourist were possibly being victimized.

13. **(D)**   As we explained in the previous question, the tourist's behavior is self-contradictory. So, too, the sentence mentioned in (D) in self-contradictory. For if the sentence is taken to be true, what it asserts

must be the case, so the sentence turns out to be false. On the other hand, if the sentence is taken to be false, then what it says is correct, so the sentence must be true. In other words, the sentence is true only if it is false, and false only if it is true: a paradox. (A) is not paradoxical. The witness *later* admits that he lied in the first instance. Thus, though his later testimony contradicts his earlier testimony, the statements taken as a group are not paradoxical, since he is not claiming that the first and the second are true *at the same time*. (B) and (C) do not have even the flavor of paradox. They are just straightforward statements. Do not be deceived by the fact that (C) refers to an about-face. To change directions, or even one's testimony, is not self-contradictory—see (A). Finally, (E) is a straightforward, self-consistent statement. Although the worker is advised to dissemble, he does not claim that he is both telling the truth and presenting a false image at the same time.

14. **(E)** The author cites a series of similarities between the two diseases, and then in his last sentence he writes, "So . . . ," indicating that his conclusion that the causes of the two diseases are similar rests upon the other similarities he has listed. Answer (E) correctly describes the basis of the argument. (A) is incorrect, for nothing in the passage indicates that either disease is a public health hazard, much less that one disease is a greater hazard than the other. (B) is unwarranted, for the author states only that the scientists are looking for a cure for *aphroditis melancholias*. He does not state that they will be successful; and even if there is a hint of that in the argument, we surely would not want to conclude on that basis that scientists will eventually find a cure for *every* disease. (C), like (A), is unrelated to the conclusion the author seeks to establish. All he wants to maintain is that similarities in the symptoms suggest that scientists should look for similarities in the causes of these diseases. He offers no opinion of the ultimate goal of modern technology, nor does he need to do so. His argument is complete without any such addition. (D) is probably the second best answer, but it is

still completely wrong. The author's argument based on the assumption that similarity of effect depends upon similarity of cause would neither gain nor lose persuasive force if (D) were true. After all, many diseases occur in both man and other animals, but at least (D) has the merit—which (A), (B), and (C) all lack—of trying to say something about the connection between the causes and effects of disease.

15. **(E)** This item tests logical deduction. Statement I establishes that all batters bunt whenever two conditions are met: Some runners lead off and all infielders play in. Statement II establishes that one of the two conditions is met (some runners are leading off), but denies that all batters are bunting. This can only be because the other condition is not met: It is false that "All infielders are playing in." Recalling our discussion of direct inferences in the instructional overview, we know that this means "Some infielders are not playing in," or answer (E). We cannot conclude (C), that none of the infielders are playing in, only that some are not. Nor can we deduce (D), that all are playing in—for that is logically impossible. Then, recalling our discussion of the meaning of *some* in the Instructional Overview, we eliminate both (A) and (B). Some means "at least one" without regard to the remaining population. That some runners are leading off does not imply that some are not leading off (B). And that some batters are not bunting does not imply that some are bunting.

16. **(B)** The author's attitude toward the bankruptcy law is expressed by his choice of the terms "folly," "protectionism," "conned." He apparently believes that the debtor who has incurred these debts ought to bear the responsibility for them and that the government should not help him get off the hook. (B) properly expresses this attitude: You have created for yourself a situation by your own actions; now you must accept it. The author may share (A) as well, but (A) is not a judgment he would make about the bankrupt, that is, a person who does not have a penny to save. (C) is completely

unrelated to the question at hand; the bankrupt has no power to wield. The author may believe (D)—in fact, he opposes at least this one instance of governmental interference and hints that he is, in general, opposed to government interference for the protection of people from themselves—but the question stem asks for the author's attitude about the bankrupt debtor, not the government. (D) would be appropriate to the latter, but it has no bearing on the question at hand. Finally, (E) would be applicable if the government were giving money to pay a ransom to terrorists or some similar situation. The assistance it provides to the bankrupt debtor is not such a program. It does not pay tribute to the debtor.

17. **(A)** For the author's conclusion to follow from his premises—the debtor will make out like a bandit with the goods he procured with credit—it must be the case that after the proceedings are completed the debtor will be left with those goods. At least the author leads us to believe this is the way the law works. As a matter of fact, that implication is incorrect (in part) and is a serious defect in the author's position; but for present purposes we do not need to worry what the "real" law is nor whether the suggestion is *mis*leading or not—only that the author does lead in that direction. (B) is incorrect because it attributes more to the author than he actually claims. He is making an argument about people who abuse credit; he never even hints that most persons who can obtain credit through use of a card abuse their credit. (C), too, takes us far beyond what the author has specifically claimed. The author argues only that the bankruptcy laws are too favorable to the debtor; he never extends his argument to say what sort of substitute he would advocate. And we certainly do not, without evidence, want to attribute to the author anything so drastic as imprisonment of the debtor as an appropriate remedy. (D) fails for it is highly speculative. Such a conclusion finds no support in the passage because the author is silent about how many debtors take advantage of the law; and, in any event, if there is such an implication in the paragraph, it must surely

be that the debtors and not the creditors are the ones to initiate the proceedings. (E) fails for the same reasons that (B) and (C) fail. The author never even hints at such a position.

18. **(D)** The argument commits several errors. One obvious point is that the first premise is very much an oversimplification. Complicated questions about punishment and child rearing are hardly ever easily reduced to "either-or" propositions. Thus, (C) is a good objection. Beyond that, the terms "severely punish" and "bad" are highly ambiguous. It would be legitimate to ask the speaker just what he considered to be bad behavior, (B) and severe punishment, (A). Also, since the speaker has alleged the child has been "bad," and since the term is ambiguous, we can also demand clarification on that score, (E). The one objection it makes no sense to raise is (D). The premises have the very simple logical structure: If child is bad and not punished, then he becomes a criminal. Child X is bad. There is absolutely no inconsistency between those two statements.

19. **(E)** The argument given in the question stem is circular, that is, it begs the question. It tries to prove that the decision is unfair by claiming that it singles out a group, which is the same thing as discriminatory, and then concludes that *since* all discrimination is unfair, so too is the court's decision unfair. Of course, the real issue is whether singling out this particular group is unfair. After all, we do make distinctions, e.g., adults are treated differently from children, businesses differently from persons, soldiers different from executives. The question of fairness cannot be solved by simply noting that the decision singles out some persons. (E) also is circular: It tries to prove this is a beautiful painting because all paintings of this sort are beautiful. (A) is perhaps the second best answer, but notice that it is purely hypothetical in its form: *If* this were true, *then* that would be true. As a consequence, it is not as similar to the question stem as (E), which is phrased in categorical assertions rather than hypothetical state-

ments. (B) moves from the premise that students are not good judges of their needs to a conclusion about the responsibility for planning course work. The conclusion and the premises are not the same so the argument is not circular. (C) is not, technically speaking, even an argument. Remember from our instructional material at the beginning of the book, an argument has premises and a conclusion. These are separate statements. (C) is one long statement, not two short ones. It reads: "A because B"; not "A; therefore B." For example, the statement "I am late because the car broke down" is not an inference but a causal statement. In (D), since the premise (everything after the semicolon) is not the same as the conclusion (the statement before the semicolon), the argument is not a circular argument and so does not parallel the stem argument.

20. **(B)** The author's claim depends in a very important way on the assumption that the assistance he advocates will be successful. After all, any proposed course of action which just won't work clearly ought to be rejected. (B) is just this kind of argument: Whatever else you say, your proposed plan will not work; therefore, we must reject it. (A) opens an entirely new line of argument. The author has said only that there is a certain connection between guidance and creativity; he never claims that everyone can or should be a professional artist. Thus, (A) is wrong, as is (E) for the same reason. (C) is wrong for a similar reason. The author never suggests that all students should be professional artists; and, in fact, he may want to encourage students to be creative no matter which practical careers they may choose. (E) is probably the second best answer; it does, to a certain extent, try to attack the workability of the proposal. Unfortunately, it does not address the general connection the author says exists between training and creativity. In other words, (E) does not say the proposal will not work at all; it merely says it may work too well. Further, (E) is wrong because it does not attribute the "burn out" to the training of the sort proposed by the author.

21. **(E)** What we are looking for here is an intervening causal link that caused the plan to be unsuccessful. The projected train of events was: (1) Adopt express lanes, (2) fewer cars, and (3) faster traffic flow. Between the first and the third steps, however, something went wrong. (E) alone supplies that unforeseen side effect. Since the cars backed up on too few lanes, total flow of traffic was actually slowed, not speeded up. (A) is irrelevant since it does not explain what went wrong *after* the plan was adopted. (B) does not even attempt to address the sequence of events which we have just outlined. Although (C) is probably true and was something the planners likely considered in their projections, it does not explain the plan's failure. Finally, (D) might have been relevant in deciding whether or not to adopt the plan, but given that the plan was adopted, (D) cannot explain why it then failed.

22. **(E)** We have all seen arguments of this sort in our daily lives, and perhaps if we have not been very careful, we have even made the same mistakes made by the leaders of Gambia. For example, last semester, which was fall, I made a lot of money selling peanuts at football games. Therefore, this spring semester I will make even more money. All three propositions point out weaknesses in the projections made by Gambia's leaders. I: Of course, if the tremendous increase in GNP is due to some unique event (my personal income increased last semester when I inherited $2000 from my aunt), it would be foolish to project a similar increase for a time period during which that event cannot repeat itself. II: This is a bit less obvious, but the projection is based on the assumption that Gambia will receive additional aid, and will be able to put that aid to use. If they are not in a position to use that aid (I cannot work twice as many hours in the spring), they cannot expect the aid to generate increases in GNP. Finally, III also is a weakness in the leaders' projections. If there are physical limitations on the possible increases, then the leaders have made an error. Their projections are premised on the existence of physical re-

sources which are greater than those they actually have.

23. **(C)** The conclusion of the paragraph is so obvious that it is almost difficult to find. The author says office workers work better the cooler the temperature—provided the temperature does not drop below 68°. Therefore, we can conclude, the temperature at which workers will be most efficient will be precisely 68°. Notice that the author does not say what happens once the temperature drops below 68° except that workers are no longer as efficient. For all we know, efficiency may drop off slowly or quickly compared with improvements in efficiency as the temperature drops to 68°. So (E) goes beyond the information supplied in the passage. (D) also goes far beyond the scope of the author's claim. His formula is specifically applicable to *office* workers. We have no reason to believe the author would extend his formula to non-office workers. (B) is probably not a conclusion the author would endorse since he claims to have found a way of achieving improvements in efficiency in a different and seemingly permanent way. Finally, (A) is not a conclusion the author seems likely to reach since nothing indicates that his formula yields only short-term gains which last as long as the temperature is kept constant. To be sure, the gains will not be repeatable, but then they will not be short-run either.

24. **(A)** The antiabortion speaker unwittingly plays right into the hands of the proabortion speaker. The "pro" speaker tries to show that there are many decisions regarding human life in which we allow that an increase in the quality of life justifies an increase in the danger to human life. All that the "anti" speaker does is to help prove this point. He says the quality of life would suffer if we lowered the speed limits to protect human life. Given this analysis, (B) must be incorrect, for the "anti" speaker's position is completely ineffective as a rebuttal. Moreover, (C) must be incorrect, for his response is not a strong statement of an antiabortion position. (D) is incorrect, for while his response is of no value to the

position he seeks to defend, it cannot be said that it is irrelevant. In fact, as we have just shown, his position is very relevant to that of the "pro" speaker's because it supports that position. Finally, (E) is not an appropriate characterization of the "anti" speaker's position, for he tries, however ineptly, to attack the merits of the "pro" speaker's position, not the character of that speaker.

25. **(D)** This is a very difficult question. That III is an assumption the author makes requires careful reading. The author's attitude about the just war tips us off. He implies that this is an appropriate function of government and, further, that there are even clearer cases. Implicit in his defense of abortion is that a trade-off must be made and that it is appropriately a collective decision. I is not an assumption of the argument. Indeed, the author seems to assume, as we have just maintained, that the trade-off is an appropriate goal of society. Finally, the author does not assume II; if anything, he almost states that he accepts that the fetus is a life but it may be traded off in exchange for an increase in the quality in the lives of others.

Section IV

1. **(D)** Statement (1) coupled with the information supplied in the question stem is sufficient to answer the question asked. An increase of 8% over Friday night's attendance would be an increase of 16 persons (8% of 200 = 16), so 216 persons attended Saturday night.

   Statement (2), when coupled with the information supplied in the stem, is also sufficient to answer the question asked. The increase of 16 persons is equal to an increase of 8%:

$$8\% \text{ of Friday night's attendance} = 16 \text{ persons}$$

So   Friday night's attendance $= \dfrac{16}{.08}$

Friday night's attendance = 200 persons

Given that, plus the information about the increase, we establish that Saturday night's attendance was 216.

2. **(C)** Statement (1) is clearly not sufficient to answer the question, for it does not break down the receipts between the two categories.

Statement (2) is alone not sufficient to answer the question, for it gives you only the receipts derived from the sale of necklaces—not bracelets.

The two statements taken together, however, do answer the question. You can use statement (2) to find the money taken in from the sale of necklaces and subtract that total from $540, the amount specified in statement (1), to find the money taken in from the sale of bracelets.

3. **(E)** Statement (1) does nothing to establish the *number* of people who visited the museum in 1985, and statement (2) does nothing to establish the number of people who visited the museum in *1985*. So we eliminate choices (A), (B) and (D), and check for a possible interaction between (1) and (2). As it turns out, there is no way of relating the information given in one to that given in another, so the correct choice is (E).

4. **(C)** Notice that the question asks for the *identity* of the person with the greatest weight, not the actual weight of the person. Statement (1) establishes that Jack weighs more than Jill, but that alone does not answer the question. Statement (2) establishes that Jill weights less than Jerry, and that by itself is insufficient. But statement (2) can be reworded:

$$\text{Jill} = \frac{2}{3} \text{ of Jerry, so Jerry} = \frac{3}{2} \text{ of Jill}$$

Now we have

(1) $\text{Jack} = \frac{5}{4} \text{ of Jill}$

(2) $\text{Jerry} = \frac{3}{2} \text{of Jill}$

So both Jack and Jerry weigh more than Jill, and Jerry weighs more than Jack. Both statements taken together do answer the question.

5. **(E)** Statement (1) is insufficient since it does not even allow us to determine the weight of the cookies in the container. Statement (2) has the merit of overcoming

this by establishing directly the weight of the cookies, but even that is not sufficient to establish the *number* of cookies in the box because of the variation in weight. Using extreme cases to illustrate the possibilities, if only one cookie weighs 3.8 grams and all others weigh 3.2 (or as close to 3.2 as possible), then the box would contain 1 cookie weighing 3.8 grams plus $(112 - 3.8) \div 3.2(+) = 1 + 33 = 34$ cookies. But if the opposite were true, then the box would contain 1 cookie weighing 3.2 grams plus $(112 - 3.2) \div 3.8(-) = 1 + 28 = 29$ cookies.

So the box could contain anywhere from 29 to 34 cookies.

6. **(E)** Statement (1) is not sufficient to answer the question, for it establishes only that $x > -5$. If x is -4, then $x + 3$ is not more than 0, but if x is -1, then $x + 3$ is greater than 0.

Statement (2) is also insufficient for the same reason. Are they suficient when taken together? No. Taken together they establish only that x is greater than -5 and less than 0:

$$-5 < x < 0$$

But given that range, it is impossible to determine whether $x + 3$ is greater than 0.

7. **(D)** Statement (1) is sufficient to establish the area of the circle. The radius of a circle is one-half its diameter, and the formula for computing the area of a circle is $A = \pi r^2$.

Statement (2) is also sufficient. The formula for finding the circumference of a circle is $C = 2\pi r$. Given the circumference, it is possible to find the radius, and with that the area.

8. **(C)** Although this problem uses a geometric figure, it really has more to do with the properties of fractions and whole numbers than it does with geometry. Since the formula for calculating the area of a rectangle is width times length, the question is really asking whether x time y is an integer. Statement (1) is not, in and of itself, sufficient to answer this question. Even though y is an integer, xy might or might not be an integer depending on the value of x.

Similarly, statement (2) alone is not sufficient. Although $\frac{x}{y}$ is an integer, this does not determine whether x or y individually is an integer. For example, if $x = \frac{1}{4}$ and $y = \frac{1}{8}$, then, $\frac{x}{y} = 2$, but xy is not an integer. On the other hand, x and y might be integers, say x = 8 and y = 4, in which case xy would be an integer.

So neither alone is sufficient. Are they sufficient when taken together? Yes. If y is an integer, as established by statement (1), and if $\frac{x}{y}$ is an integer also, as established by statement (2), then x must also be an integer. (Otherwise, $\frac{x}{y}$ would be a fraction.) If both x and y are integers, then x times y is also an integer. If both statements are used, this establishes that xy is an integer, and the area of the rectangle is an integer.

9. **(B)** Statement (1) is not sufficient because it does not supply the comparison between the cost of a single bagel and the cost of a dozen bagels.

Statement (2), however, is by itself sufficient. If 12 bagels cost only 10 times as much as one bagel, then bagels are cheaper by the dozen. If the cost were the same, then a dozen bagels would cost 12 times as much as a single bagel.

Be careful, however, not to assume that you need statement (1) as well. Once you know that a dozen bagels cost only 10 times what one bagel purchased singly costs, you can answer the question. Yes, they are cheaper by the dozen. You do not need the actual unit cost to reach that conclusion.

10. **(E)** Here you must read the question carefully. The question asks for the greatest difference for any *student*—not the greatest difference between the lowest score recorded (of all students) and the highest score recorded (of all students). It is true that the statements, taken together, establish that the range among all students was 44 to 98, or 54 points. But nothing establishes that this was the range of a particular student. And the question asks for the greatest range of scores for a single student.

11. **(D)** Statement (1) is enough to establish that this is a right triangle. We usually think of the Pythagorean theorem as saying that in a right triangle the square of the longest side

(the hypotenuse) is equal to the sum of the squares of the other two sides. But the converse is also true. Any triangle in which the square of the longest side is equal to the sum of the squares of the other two sides *is necessarily* a right triangle. Statement (1), when rewritten as $AB^2 + AC^2 = BC^2$, says that this triangle fits the Pythagorean theorem.

Once we know that angle A is a right angle, then we can calculate the area of the triangle. We can use CA as an altitude and BA as a base, and the area is $\frac{1}{2} \times$ altitude $\times$ base, or 6.

Statement (2) is also sufficient and operates in an even more direct fashion. If x = 90 degrees, then, as described above, we can use CA as an altitude and BA as the base for purposes of computing the area.

12. **(E)** Statement (1) does not establish the relative speeds, for it makes a statement about time only, saying nothing about distance.

Statement (2) suffers from the opposite deficiency, making a statement about distance but not about time.

So neither statement alone can be sufficient. But even together they fail to answer the question. They establish that the first plane flew farther and flew for a longer period of time, but that does not determine whether it flew faster than the second plane.

13. **(D)** The trick to this question is to see that the numbers in the two statements are divisible by 7. As for statement (1), 787,787 is evenly divisible by 7. This means that if $\frac{x}{787,787}$ is an integer, then x is also evenly divisible by 7, and $\frac{x}{7}$ must be an integer. The same reasoning applies to statement (2). Since 784 is evenly divisible by 7, x is also evenly divisible by 7.

14. **(D)** At first glance you might think we need both statements, using them together in a manner similar to simultaneous equations. In fact, each statement is by itself sufficient to answer the question asked. The question is whether x is greater than 0. We can rewrite each of the statements.

$$(1) \quad 2x - 5 > 0$$
$$2x > 5$$
$$x > \frac{5}{2}$$

So x is more than $\frac{5}{2}$ and therefore greater than 0.

$$(2) \quad 2x + 1 > 2$$
$$2x > 1$$
$$x > \frac{1}{2}$$

So x is greater than $\frac{1}{2}$ and therefore greater than 0.

15. **(D)** The key to this question is the technique for finding the surface area of a cylinder. Notice we say "technique" and not "formula." There really is no point in trying to memorize such a rule, for the surface area of a cylinder can be analyzed into three components:

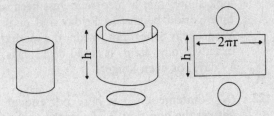

As the exploded view shows, the surface area consists of the top and the bottom and the wraparound side. As the diagram shows, the top and the bottom are both circles, whereas the wraparound area is really a rectangle wrapped into a cylindrical shape. The width of the wraparound rectangle is the same as the circumference of the circle.

To find the entire surface area you need only two dimensions: the radius of the top or bottom and the height. The radius of the top and bottom is given in the question stem, so any information that provides the height is all that is required answer the question.

Statement (1) gives the information. If the rectangular wrap around has an area of $1,200\pi$ square inches, and if one side (as we know) is equal to the circumference of a circle of known radius, then we can find the other side of the rectangular wraparound. And that is the height of the cylinder.

Statement (2) also provides the needed information. We know from the question stem the areas of the top and bottom. Then given the total surface area of the cylinder, we simply subtract the top and the bottom and are left with the area of the rectangular wrap-around. After that, we find the height in the method just described.

16. **(A)** Statement (2) is not sufficient to answer the question because it does not fix the number of nickels or dimes. For example, she might have 6 dimes, 2 nickels, and 3 pennies. Or she might have 1 dime, 12 nickels, and 3 pennies.

Statement (1), however, is sufficient to answer the question. Try the various possibilities. The minimum number of pennies Edna might have is 3. If she has 3 pennies, then she would have 6 dimes, for a total of 63 cents, and therefore 2 nickels. Then try the next possibility. Could Edna have exactly 8 pennies? No, for if she has twice as many dimes as pennies, 8 pennies would mean 16 dimes, for a total of 168 cents. But that is more than stipulated by the question. So if Edna has twice as many dimes as pennies, then she must have exactly 3 pennies and 6 dimes and 2 nickels. And that is sufficient to answer the question asked.

17. **(C)** This question requires only that you see that to find a total cost you need the per unit price and the number of items purchased. In this case, the information is supplied in a somewhat indirect fashion, for the question stem does not give us the unit price of the earlier year.

Since no unit price is given, it is unknown and we can call it x. In other words, the per gallon price for metered water in 1985 was $x per gallon. Also we do not know the number of gallons purchased in 1985, so we can call that y. We do know, however, that the price multiplied by the number of gallons gives the total amount spent: $x/gallons times y gallons = $1200. Or put in official algebra:

$$xy = 1200$$

Notice that both numbered statements give some information related to this equation. Statement (1) gives information that relates 1986 to x, and statement (2) gives information that relates 1986 to y. But neither alone is sufficient.

Taken together, however, they are sufficient. Statement (1) establishes the 1986 price as 10% more than x, or 1.1x. And statement (2) establishes that 1986 consumption was 5% more than y, or 1.05y. Combining the two, 1986 consumption was 1.1x (1.05y) = 1.115xy. This means that 1986 charges were 11.5% more than the $1200 spent in 1985, and that is enough to answer the question.

Of course, there is no reason to work out the final numbers. We are concerned only to determine when information is sufficient, not to arrive at final numerical solutions.

18. **(E)** Statement (1) is not sufficient to establish the digits of the number N, for the pairs 6,9 and 7,8 will satisfy the statement. Statement (2) is more powerful, for only one pair of numbers will satisfy this statement: 6 and 9. No other pair of single digits, when multiplied together, yield the product 54. Still, statement (2) fails to answer the question, for the number N might be 69 or 96.

19. **(E)** The numbered statements here are two equations. To determine the sufficiency of the data provided we need to simplify each equation.

As for statement (1):

$$x + y + z = x + y - z + 1$$
$$x + z = x - z + 1$$
$$z = -z + 1$$
$$2z = 1$$
$$\text{so } z = \frac{1}{2}$$

As for statement (2), although the equation can be rewritten, it cannot be further simplified. That is, we cannot eliminate any of the three variables. Thus, neither statement alone is sufficient.

But can they work together to provide a solution? Substituting our result from the manipulation of statement (1) into the equation in statement (2), we have:

$$x - y + \frac{1}{2} = 0$$
$$x - y = -\frac{1}{2}$$

Even that, however, is not enough. For knowing only the value of x *minus* y is not sufficient to determine the value of x *plus* y.

20. **(E)** To answer the question we need to know the volume of the overall container and the volume of the individual packages to be placed in the larger container. But that is not enough. We must also know the dimensions of each, that is the shape of each. Even using both numbered statements, we have no information about the shape of either the larger carton or the individual boxes.

21. **(B)** Statement (2) is quite clearly enough to answer the question. A time period that is exactly 5 days long is 120 hours long.

The tricky part of the question is statement (1). At first glance, it might seem that statement (1) provides essentially the same information as statement (2), but a closer look shows that is incorrect. Just because a time period begins on Friday and ends on Wednesday does not mean the period is exactly 5 days long. It could be 12 days, or 19 days, or even longer.

22. **(A)** Statement (2) is here not enough to answer the question. To know the size of the smallest lot is not enough to fix the size of the largest lot.

Statement (1), however, does fix the size of the largest lot. What statement (1) is really saying is that the largest lot is exactly $\frac{1}{2}$ of the total shipment. (It is equal to the sum of the other two, so it must be half.) Since it is half of the shipment, and since the shipment contains 70 items, the largest lot contains 35 items.

Of course, statement (1) alone does not fix the size of each of the other two lots, but that is not important. The question asks only for the number of items in the largest lot.

23. **(B)** This question illustrates the importance of considering all possibilities. At first, you might think that statement (1) is sufficient, reasoning (erroneously) that for 3N to be an odd number N must be an integer. But this is incorrect. If $N = \frac{1}{3}$, then $3N = 1$, and N is in that case a fraction, not a whole number. So statement (1) is not enough.

Statement (2), however, is sufficient to establish that N is a whole number. The smallest even (positive) number is 2. So the least N could be, given statement (2), is 1—a whole number. And for any even number larger than 2, N would still have to be a whole number.

24. **(B)** To find the traveling time for a journey, we need the distance traveled and the speed for the trip. Statement (2) provides both pieces of information.

As for statement (1), it makes an attempt to provide information about time, but fails even there, for it does not give total time. Moreover, it provides no information about distance.

25. **(A)** Statement (1), when coupled with the information given in the stem, is sufficient to answer the question. The stem establishes that pipe P operates at the rate of 1 pool/12 hours. Statement (1) establishes that P and Q operate together at the rate of 1 pool/4 hours. Combining the two pieces of information:

$$\frac{1 \text{ pool}}{12 \text{ hours}} + Q\text{'s rate} = \frac{1 \text{ pool}}{4 \text{ hours}}$$

Then you could solve for Q. (Note: It is not necessary to do so, but for practice here is how it is done.)

$$\frac{1}{12} + \frac{1}{x} = \frac{1}{4}$$

$$\frac{1}{x} = \frac{1}{4} - \frac{1}{12}$$

$$\frac{1}{x} = \frac{2}{12} = \frac{1}{6}$$

$$x = 6$$

In other words, pipe Q could do the job in 6 hours.

Statement (2) is neither sufficient nor necessary to the solution just given.

Section V

1. **(D)** The original is incorrect because the order of the phrases "to an army base," "from their homes," and "20 miles away" does not correctly reflect the logic of the underlying thought of the sentence. (D) represents the best ordering of those phrases. Although (E) also uses the correct order, (E) introduces a error in its use of "has." "Has" fails to agree with the subject, and is the wrong verb tense.

2. **(D)** The original sentence is wrong because the subject "constraints" is plural and the verb "has made" is singular. (C) and (E) fail to correct the error. (B) corrects that error but introduces a new problem by using the -*ing* verb form instead of the infinitive.

3. **(D)** The "their" is intended to refer to "movement." But "movement" is singular. (D) corrects this error by using "its." (B) does correct the original error but introduces a new error, a faulty comparison. (B) implies a comparison between "countries" and "student movement." (E) commits a similar error. Finally, (C) is wrong because "Just as the student movements in other countries" doesn't express a complete thought. Ordinarily, that kind of phrasing would be used in the following situation: "Just as their parents did, many adults today are. . . ."

4. **(E)** The original sentence suffers from two defects. First, the phrasing is very awkward. Additionally, the "before" does not pinpoint the time frame intended. Does it mean before the moment at which the speaker is speaking or the time when the museum will open its new wing? Only (E), with its change in phrasing and punctuation, corrects these errors.

5. **(D)** (A) is incorrect because of a misplaced modifier. The sentence actually says that the researchers were deregulated. (B) repeats this error. (C) is grammatically incorrect (the verb does not agree with the subject), and it is needlessly wordy and awkward. (E) is incorrect because "its" does not have a clear referent.

6. **(B)** The original sentence fails on two counts. First, "success" is singular and requires a singular verb form. The original sentence says that "success . . . have led." There is also a mistake in diction. The correct word is the verb "affect" not "effect." (B) corrects these two errors without introducing new ones. (C) repeats one of the

errors; (D) introduces an incorrect verb tense; and (E) repeats the second error.

7. **(D)** The original sentence makes a mistake of diction. "As wide of a" is not standard English. Both (B) and (C) introduce incorrect verb tenses. (E) introduces a new error: "as wide than" is not idiomatic.

8. **(C)** This sentence makes an incorrect comparison between Andy Warhol and the work of Roy Lichtenstein. (B) makes a correct comparison of the art of Lichtenstein and that of Warhol but uses "as with" to make the comparison, which is incorrect. (D) repeats the incorrect comparison. (E) is incorrect because the "it being similar" is not acceptable in standard written English.

9. **(D)** (A) is wrong because "with that" cannot be used in standard English for "because." (B) introduces a new and illogical verb tense. (C) creates an unidiomatic construction by using "maintaining" instead of the infinitive "to maintain." (E) changes the meaning of the sentence by eliminating the sense that the Puritans did something in order to gain something else.

10. **(E)** The original sentence commits a grammatical mistake. The phrase modifying the gerund "being" should be in the possessive case. But the resulting phrase "smoking of cigarette's being injurious" is very awkward. The best course of action is to eliminate that phrase altogether, as (C) and (E) both do. (C), however, is wrong because the verb "are" does not agree with the new subject, "fact."

11. **(C)** The original sentence runs several ideas together. (C) correctly separates them, and places them in a logical order.

12. **(B)** The original sentence is wrong because the subject "chlorofluorocarbons," which is plural, cannot have the singular verb "is." (B) corrects this error without introducing new ones. (C) is not logical because it says that insulation and refrigeration are released into the atmosphere. (D) uses an incorrect verb form "being released" and repeats the

error of subject/verb agreement. (E) is awkward and wordy.

13. **(A)** is correct. (B) is incorrect because of the plural verb form "are." (C) is incorrect because a clause, not an adjective phrase, is needed to express the complete thought underlined in the original sentence. (D) changes the meaning of the original by making an illogical comparison. And (E) is not idiomatic.

14. **(B)** The original sentence is incorrect on two counts. The "where" cannot refer to autism ("where" cannot introduce an adjective clause). The original also fails because the subject, "autism," needs a singular verb—"occurs," not "occur." (B) corrects both of the problems. (C) and (D) both fail because their elements are not in parallel form. (E) is incorrect since the resulting sentences lack a main verb.

15. **(D)** The original sentence is incorrect because it illogically compares drug use to a decade ago. It also uses an unidiomatic construction for the comparison. The correct construction is "as . . . as x if not more than. . . ." Only (D) completes the comparison properly.

16. **(B)** The original sentence is incorrect because the subject and verb do not agree. Further, it is incorrect to use "as" to mean "because." (C) is incorrect because the resulting sentence lacks a main verb. (D) is incorrect because the "it" has no antecedent. (E) is not technically wrong, but it is too wordy.

17. **(E)** The correct construction for this sentence is "not only x but y." (B) introduces an incorrect verb tense, "it had been believed," and a construction, "not x but rather y," which is incorrect. (C) uses the proper construction but fails to make the verbs parallel. (D) is illogical because there is no reason for the "but" since there is no comparison made.

18. **(D)** The phrase "but also" implies a contrast between two ideas, but no such con-

trast is supported by the original. (D), by using the simple conjunction "and," makes it clear that the two ideas are parallel. The other choices include a superfluous "also."

19. **(B)** The original sentence commits the error of faulty parallelism. The "this rather than that" construction requires two elements of the same form: "join rather than continue." (D) and (E) fail on the grounds of parallelism. As for (C), the phrase "convince about" is not idiomatic English.

20. **(C)** The first part of the original sentence (from "although" to "colleagues") is correct. The comparison is logical and properly completed. So (B), (D), and (E), which makes changes in that part of the original, are incorrect. The second part of the original, however, contains a logical error. The "and" fails to specify the nature of the connection between the person's modesty and the fact that the poetry is unpublished. (C) correctly supplies the connection.

21. **(A)** The original sentence contains no error. (B) makes two errors. First, in changing the present tense "must" to "had," it introduces an error of logic. The requirement of posting is ongoing, not contained in the past. Second, the verb "knows" does not agree with the plural subject "both management and labor." (C) is incorrect because the verb "knew" does not correctly reflect the fact that the requirement of posting is an ongoing one. (D) and (E) are both incorrect because the use of the verb "would" implies a condition that is not mentioned or suggested by the sentence.

22. **(B)** The original sentence contains a misplaced modifier. As a rule, a modifier should be placed as close to the element modified as possible. (B), therefore, is better than the original. (C), (D), and (E) all make unneeded changes and result in awkward sentences.

23. **(B)** The original sentence contains two errors. First, there is an illogical comparison (paintings versus painters). Second, the phrase "than him" is actually an elliptical expression for "than him did," so the correct pronoun is "he." (B) corrects both of these errors. (C) and (D) correct the errors just discussed but introduce a new mistake. The construction "different than" is not acceptable English. Finally, (E) is incorrect because "being" cannot introduce a clause.

24. **(C)** The original sentence runs together two ideas and is needlessly wordy. (C) correctly contrasts the two ideas (brought up in one language but wrote in another) and eliminates the excess verbiage. (B) is incorrect (at least) because it introduces an illogical verb tense. (D) is needlessly wordy. Finally, (E) makes the mistake of using "being."

25. **(A)** The sentence is correct as written. The subject of the sentence (to lack) is correctly paralleled by the predicate nominative (to lack). Each of the wrong choices destroys this parallelism.

Section VI

1. **(C)** This is a fairly straightforward calculation problem. To answer a question of the sort "x is what percent of y," you create a fraction using the y term (the object of the preposition "of") as the denominator and using the x term as the numerator: $\frac{45}{9,000} = 0.005$. (Be sure to keep track of your decimal point!) Then convert that decimal to a percentage by moving the decimal two places to the right: $0.005 = 0.5\%$

2. **(C)** You can solve for y by treating the information as simultaneous equations. First solve for x in the equation $3x = 6$: $x = \frac{6}{3} = 2$. Then substitute that value for x in the other equation: $2 - y = 0$, so $2 = y$.

3. **(B)** Here is a fairly simple geometry question. You might answer the question by finding the value of the unlabeled angle in the triangle to the right. That would be 110 degrees. Then you would reason that the value of the unlabeled angle in the left-hand triangle must be the same. Given that, since

(x + y) plus the 110° angle must equal 180°, x + y must be 70.

Or, more abstractly, you might have seen that the two unlabeled angles have to be equal, so the *sum* of the remaining two angles must also be equal. This means that x + y must be equal to 30 + 40.

4. **(C)** Here is a question that asks you to translate English into "algabrese." We are told that A is equal to 20 years less than $\frac{1}{2}$ the sum of the ages of the two parents. Since F and M designate the ages of the two parents, the sum of the ages of the two parents is just F + M. And the $\frac{1}{2}$ of that is just F + M divided by 2. So we render that as

$$\frac{F + M}{2}$$

Next, A is 20 years less than that, so the formula is:

$$\frac{F + M}{2} - 20$$

5. **(C)** This question is pretty much just a matter of bookkeeping, even though it does get a little complicated because of the mass of information. In the end, we want to know how much more the athlete will receive in the package offered by Team L than in the package offered by Team K. What does each offer?

First, K offers $100,000 for the first year, $100,000 + 20% of 100,000 = $120,000 in the second year, and $120,000 + 20% of $120,000 = $144,000 in the third year, plus the signing bonus of $50,000:

$100,000 + $120,000 + $144,000 + $50,000
= $414,000

L offers a salary of $150,000 in the first year, $150,000 + 10% of $150,000 = $165,000 in the second year, and $165,000 + 10% of $165,000 = $181,500 in the third year:

$150,000 + $165,000 + $181,500
= $496,500

So L pays more than K: $496,500 − $414,000 = $82,500

6. **(D)** To answer this question you do not need any advanced mathematics, just some good common sense. The pyramid structure shown in the drawing looks like the pin setup in bowling (ten pins). And the principle is the same. Each subsequent row contains one more member than the earlier row. So the progression is 1, 2, 3, 4, 5, etc. And the total number of members goes, 1, 3, 6, 10, 15, 21, 28, etc. So to answer the question you just need to count until you find one of the "magic" numbers in the choices.

7. **(A)** This question tests whether you remember how to manipulate an equation with an x-squared term to find the possible values of x. You can solve for the roots of the equation:

$$2x^2 + x - 2 = 1$$
$$2x^2 + x - 3 = 0$$
$$(2x + 3)(x - 1) = 0$$

So either $2x + 3 = 0$, $2x = -3$
and $x = -\frac{3}{2}$

Or $x - 1 = 0$, and $x = 1$
Since we are told that $x > 0$, the correct choice must be 1, or (A).

In the alternative, you can answer the question simply by substituting values back into the equation. For example, (A):

$$2(1^2) + 1 - 2 = 1$$
$$2(1) + 1 - 2 = 1$$
$$2 + 1 - 2 = 1$$
$$1 = 1$$

Since 1 = 1, we know that (A) is the correct substitution.

8. **(C)** First, determine the actual length of the side of the cube. Since each 5 centimeters in the drawing represents an actual length of 1.5 meters, a line 10 centimeters long in the drawing represents an actual length of 3 meters. So we have a cube with an edge of 3 meters, and its volume is $3 \times 3 \times 3 = 27$ cubic meters.

9. **(A)** The question treats properties of integers. As for I, the smallest positive integer is +1, and when that is substituted for x, the result is still positive. And, of course,

integers larger than 1 will also give a positive result. So I is true. As for II, any integer when multiplied by 2 yields an even product. So 2x is always even, and 2x times 2x is also even, and II is false. As for III, since 2x is always even, 2x + 1 must always be odd, and III is false.

10. **(C)** $2.40 is equal to 30% of the usual selling price:

$$2.40 = .30 \text{ Usual Selling Price}$$

$$\frac{2.40}{.30} = 8.00 = \text{Usual Selling Price}$$

11. **(E)** To answer this question, you must work out the sequence, but make sure you work in the correct direction. We know the fifth term, and we want to know the second term. Since each term is $\frac{1}{3}$ the number preceding it in the sequence, the numbers get smaller as the sequence progresses. We are moving backwards, however, so our numbers get larger:

5th	4th	3rd	2nd
3	9	27	81

12. **(D)** Since the question stem has the form "which of the following could be . . .?", the proper approach is to test choices until you find one that works. Since her cost is $50, we test (A):

$$\frac{x}{\$50} = .15$$
$$x = \$7.50$$

But a dollar profit or markup of $7.50 would generate a selling price of $57.50—not a whole number. (B), (C), and (E) also yield fractional amounts. (D), however, yields a markup of $20 for a whole dollar selling price of $70.

13. **(D)** This question centers on a defined operation. The trick is just to follow the directions. An even number remains itself, whereas an odd number is converted to the next higher even number. Now we evaluate the expression 1* (4* + 5*). Even numbers remain themselves: 1 * (4 + 5*). But odd numbers are changed:

$$2(4 + 6) = 2(10) = 20$$

14. **(B)** This question is answered by manipulating simultaneous equations:

$$\frac{x}{y} = \frac{1}{2}$$

So $$y = 2x$$
And $$\frac{x + 2}{y + 1} = \frac{2}{3}$$

Substituting: $$\frac{x + 2}{2x + 1} = \frac{2}{3}$$

Cross-multiplying: $$3(x + 2) = 2(2x + 1)$$
$$3x + 6 = 4x + 2$$
Solving for x: $$x = 4$$

15. **(D)** This question asks you to express a certain relationship in algebraic notation. Each machine operates at the rate of t books per m minutes or $\frac{t}{m}$. But there are n such machines, so the overall rate of operation will be n times $\frac{t}{m}$ which is $\frac{nt}{m}$. To find the time it will take to produce 10,000 books, we divide that number by the rate of operation:

$$\frac{10,000}{\frac{nt}{m}} = 10,000 \times \frac{m}{nt} = \frac{10,000m}{nt}$$

Finally, we divide that by 60 since there are 60 minutes in every hour: $$\frac{10,000m}{60nt}$$

16. **(A)** This question tests manipulation of expressions. Begin by factoring the denominator (which is the difference of two squares): $x^2 - y^2 = (x + y)(x - y)$. Since the numerator is $(x - y)(x - y)$, we can cancel one $x - y$ with the $x - y$ in the denominator, leaving $\frac{x - y}{x + y}$ so $\frac{x - y}{x + y}$, its reciprocal, is equal to $\frac{1}{9}$.

17. **(B)** Obviously, one way to attack this question is to assign a variable to represent the unknown quantity. But another approach is to assume a concrete value. Let's assume that X produces 100 units in any time period. Machine Y would produce four times that, or 400 units, and Machine Z would produce half of that, or 200 units. On that assumption, the three machines would produce a total of 700 units, of which 200 are produced by Z: $\frac{200}{700} = \frac{2}{7}$.

18. **(D)** Another bookkeeping problem (sigh)! How long is the rental period? First, from 8:00 a.m. on Monday to 9:45 p.m. the following Thursday would be 85.75 hours. What are the charges?

$35 × 3 for the first 3 24-hour
   periods = $105
$5 × 2 for the next 12 hours
   (2 6-hour periods) = $10
$5 for the next fraction
   of 6 hours = $5
Total charges = $120

19. **(D)** First, we find the annual tax bill: $240 × 4 = $960. And the rate of taxation is $4.00/$100. = 4.0%. So $960 is equal to 4.0% of the assessed value:

$$\$960 = 4.0\% \text{ of assessed value}$$
$$\$960 = 0.04 \text{ AV}$$
$$AV = \frac{\$960}{0.04} = \$24,000$$

So the assessed value of the property is $24,000, but that is only 60% of the appraised value:

$$\text{Appraised Value} = \$24,000/0.60 = \$40,000$$

20. **(A)** The shaded area in the question is just a sector of the circle, and since angle R is 90°, the sector is $\frac{1}{4}$ of the whole circle. Once we find the area of the entire circle, we can find the area of the shaded sector, and we can find the area of the circle by determining the length of the radius. How? All we know is that the area of the triangle is 4. Since PR and RQ form a right angle, we can treat them as altitude and base:

$$\frac{1}{2} (PR) (RQ) = 4$$

But they are equal, so

$$\frac{1}{2} (PR) (PR) = 4$$
$$PR^2 = 8$$
$$PR = 2\sqrt{2}$$

Now we add a radius and see that it forms a new isosceles right triangle:

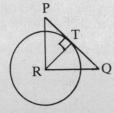

With this type of triangle, the two shorter sides are always equal to half the hypotenuse times $\sqrt{2}$:

$$RT = \frac{1}{2}(2\sqrt{2})\,(\sqrt{2}) = 2$$

Now we have the radius. The area of the entire circle is:

$$\pi r^2 = \pi(2)^2 = 4\pi$$

And the shade area is $\frac{1}{4}$ of that, or just π.

Section VII

1. **(C)** Statement (1) alone is not sufficient to answer the question. Statement (1) implies that x is divisible by 10 (2 × 5 = 10), but a number can be divisible by 10 without being divisible by 70. Similarly, (2) alone is insufficient. (2) implies that x is divisible by 14 (2 × 7 = 14), but a number can be divisible by 14 without being divisible by 70. Both statements taken together are sufficient to answer the question, for together they imply that x is divisible by 70 (2 × 5 × 7 = 70).

2. **(E)** Neither (1) nor (2) alone can be sufficient, because neither provides a basis for comparing the number of records in Bob's collection with the number in Linda's collection. Nor are the two together sufficient. Although the two statements establish that both Bob and Linda have fewer records than Christina, that information is not sufficient to answer the question asked.

3. **(C)** Neither statement alone is sufficient to determine the angle at which the line intersects the y axis, but both taken together contain sufficient information to determine that the angle is 45°:

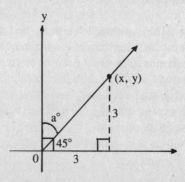

4. **(E)** Neither (1) nor (2) is sufficient to answer the question. And even taken together the statements

are insufficient, because they do not provide any information about the scores of the other 28 children.

5. **(A)** Statement (1) is sufficient to answer the question. In 1981, profits were $30,000; in 1982, $60,000; and in 1983, $120,000. Therefore, it was in 1983 that profits first exceeded $100,000. Statement (2), however, is not sufficient to answer the question. Since (1) alone is sufficient to answer but (2) is not, this item should be classified as (A).

6. **(A)** Statement (1) alone is sufficient. Since the sum of the degree measures of the interior angles of a triangle is 180°, $b° + c° + d° = 180°$. Then, given that $b° + c° = 90°$,

$$(b° + c°) + d° = 180°$$
$$90° + d° = 180°$$
$$d° = 90°$$

(2), however, is not sufficient to answer the question. $a + b = 180$, so $b = 180 - a$. This in turn implies

$$d + c + (180 - a) = 180$$
$$c - a + d = 180$$

But $c° - a°$ is not equal to $c° + a°$, so information about $c° + a°$ does not answer the question.

7. **(B)** (1) alone is not sufficient to answer the question, for (1) implies only that x is a positive number, not that x is an integer. (2) alone, however, is sufficient to answer the question.

8. **(A)** Statement (1) alone is sufficient to answer the question. That $x^3 y^3$ is positive implies that x^3 and y^3 both have the same sign. If x^3 and y^3 are positive, x and y are also positive, and $xy > 0$. If x^3 and y^3 are negative, x and y are both negative, and $xy > 0$. (2), however, is not sufficient to answer the question, for x and y could have the same or different signs and still satisfy the condition contained in (2).

9. **(D)** Statement (1) alone is sufficient to answer the question. The surface area of a cube is composed of six equal faces, and each of those faces is a square. (1) implies that the edge of the cube has a length of 3:

$$54 = 6 \times edge \times edge$$
$$9 = edge^2$$
$$edge = 3$$

(2) also is sufficient, for it too implies that the length of the edge is 3:

$$area = edge \times edge$$
$$9 = edge^2$$
$$edge = 3$$

10. **(B)** Since the triangles share a common base, they will have the same area if, and only if, they have altitudes of equal length. That (1) alone is not sufficient to answer the question can be demonstrated by distorting the figure:

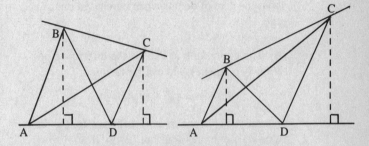

Even though AB ∥ CD in each of the figures, the lengths of the altitudes of the two triangles may or may not be equal. (2), however, is sufficient to answer the question, for (2) implies that the two altitudes have the same length:

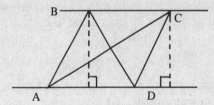

11. **(D)** Statement (1) alone is sufficient to answer the question. Operating expenses were 63% of $9,000,000 = $5,670,000. Statement (2) is also sufficient, for (2) implies that the total budget was $9,000,000:

$$63\% \text{ of Total} = \$5,670,000$$
$$0.63T = \$5,670,000$$
$$T = \$9,000,000$$

And as shown above, that information, when coupled with the data provided by the chart, is sufficient to answer the question.

12. **(E)** Neither (1) nor (2) alone is sufficient to answer the question, and even taken together they do not provide enough information to answer it. Although (1) implies that N must be a multiple of 6, there are six numbers between 30 and 70 that are divisible by 6.

13. **(B)** (1) alone is not sufficient to answer the question, for it provides no information about the number of students in any one grade. (2) alone is sufficient to answer the question, for (2) implies that the total number of students in the school is $6 \times 75 = 450$.

14. **(A)** Statement (1) alone is sufficient to answer the question. (1) implies that buying a box of a dozen donuts results in a cost savings of $12 \times \$0.05 = \$0.60$. Statement (2), however, is not sufficient, because (2) provides no information about the cost of donuts when purchased one at a time.

15. **(B)** The expression $a^4 - b^4$ is the difference between two squares and can be factored:

$$a^4 - b^4 = (a^2 + b^2)(a^2 - b^2)$$

Statement (1) alone is not sufficient to fix the value of the expression, but (2) is. If $a^2 - b^2 = 0$:

$$a^4 - b^4 = (a^2 + b^2)(0) = 0$$

16. **(D)** Statement (1) alone is sufficient to answer the question, for you can set up simultaneous equations. Let x stand for the amount invested at 6 percent and y for the amount invested at 8 percent. Since a total of $10,000 was invested at both rates,

$$x + y = \$10,000$$

Then, $(x)(0.06)$ plus $(y)(0.08)$ is the total amount of interest earned:

$$0.06x + 0.08y = \$640$$

Using the first equation, redefine y in terms of x:

$$y = \$10,000 - x$$

And substitute this value for y in the second equation:

$$0.06x + 0.08(\$10,000 - x) = \$640$$
$$0.06x + \$800 - 0.08x = \$640$$
$$0.02x = \$160$$
$$x = \$8,000$$

Statement (2) is also sufficient. Again, let x stand for the amount that earned 6 percent and y for the amount that earned 8 percent. (2) implies

$$x = 4y$$

Given that $x + y = \$10,000$,

$$4y + y = \$10,000$$
$$5y = \$10,000$$
$$y = \$2,000$$

So $x = \$10,000 - \$2,000 = \$8,000$

17. **(B)** Statement (1) alone is not sufficient. If x and y are positive, then given that $3x = 4y$, x is larger than y. But if x and y are negative, then given that $3x = 4y$, y is larger than x. (For example, x might be -4 and y, -3.) Statement (2), however, is sufficient to answer the question. Since x = k/3, $3x = k$; and since y = k/4, $4y = k$. This implies that $3x = 4y$. And here it is stipulated that k is positive, which means that both x and y must also be positive. Therefore, (2) implies that x is greater than y.

18. **(A)** Statement (1) is sufficient to answer the question that is asked (even though it is not sufficient to determine the actual area of either region). If we let x and y stand for the radii of regions X and Y, respectively, (1) implies:

$$\frac{2\pi(x)}{2\pi(y)} = \frac{3}{2}$$
$$\frac{x}{y} = \frac{3}{2}$$
$$x = \frac{3y}{2}$$

Thus, the area of region Y in terms of y is simply $\pi(y)^2$, and the area of region X in terms of y is $(3y/2)^2\pi = 9\pi y^2/4$. The ratio of the area of region X to the area of region Y is

$$\frac{\frac{9\pi y^2}{4}}{\pi y^2} = \frac{9}{4}$$

19. **(A)** Statement (1) is sufficient to answer the question. The sum of the lengths of the two shorter sides must be less than half of the perimeter of the rectangle. Since $15 + 15 = 30$, the total perimeter of the yard must be more than twice 30. (2), however, is not sufficient to answer the question, for (2) provides no information about the actual length of either side.

20. **(B)** Statement (1) is not sufficient, as the following figures make clear:

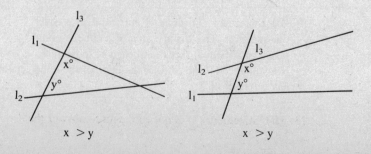

x > y   x > y

Statement (2) however, is sufficient. If x + y were equal to 180, l₁ and l₂ would be parallel and would not meet. Since x + y is less than 180, l₁ and l₂ must eventually intersect to the right of l₃:

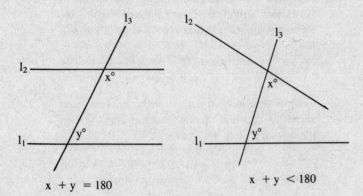

$$x + y = 180 \qquad x + y < 180$$

21. **(A)** First, perform the indicated operation:
$$(p + q)(r + s) = pr + ps + qr + qs$$
Statement (1) alone is sufficient to answer the question:
$$p(r + s) = pr + ps$$
$$q(r + s) = qr + qs$$

So the value of the expression in the question stem is $5 + 3 = 8$. Statement (2), however, is not sufficient to answer the question. The fact that the two terms are equal implies nothing about the product of those terms.

22. **(B)** Statement (1) is not sufficient to answer the question, for (1) provides no information about the size of x and y. Statement (2), however, is sufficient. Since the figure is a triangle,

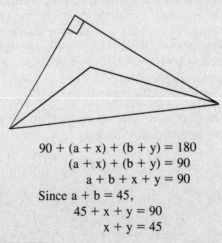

$$90 + (a + x) + (b + y) = 180$$
$$(a + x) + (b + y) = 90$$
$$a + b + x + y = 90$$
Since $a + b = 45$,
$$45 + x + y = 90$$
$$x + y = 45$$

23. **(B)** Statement (1) is not sufficient to answer the

question. If Q is a square, it can be inscribed in a circle:

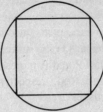

But a quadrilateral with four equal sides need not be a square:

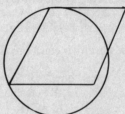

Statement (2), however, is sufficient to answer the question. A quadrilateral with four 90° angles is a rectangle. The diagonal of a rectangle creates two right triangles, and any right triangle can be inscribed in a semicircle:

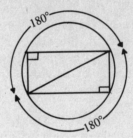

24. **(A)** Statement (1) alone is sufficient to answer the question. Let n represent the smallest of the three integers. Since these are consecutive integers, the second and third integers in the sequence can be defined as $n + 1$ and $n + 2$, respectively. Given that the ratio of the least to the greatest of the three is 2,
$$\frac{n}{(n + 2)} = 2$$
$$n = 2(n + 2)$$
$$n = 2n + 4$$
$$-n = 4$$
$$n = -4$$

So the smallest of the integers is -4, and the other two integers are -3 and -2. Therefore, the sum of the three is -9. Statement (2), however, is not sufficient to answer the question. The sum of any three consecutive, negative integers is less than the average of the three integers. For example, the sum of -3, -2, and -1 is -6; the average is -2; and $-6 < -2$.

25. **(D)** Statement (1) is sufficient to answer the question. Let P and R represent the present ages of Patty and Rod, respectively. The question stem establishes

$$P = R + 5$$

And statement (1) establishes

$$P - 15 = 2(R - 15)$$

We now have two equations and only two variables:

$$P = R + 5$$
$$P - 15 = 2(R - 15)$$

Solve for R:

$$(R + 5) - 15 = 2(R - 15)$$
$$R - 10 = 2R - 30$$
$$R = 20$$

A similar line of reasoning shows that statement (2) is also sufficient. Using P and R again, we represent the information provided by (2) as follows:

$$(P - 5) + (R - 5) = 35$$
$$P + R = 45$$

Couple this new equation with the one used above to describe the information contained in the question stem and solve for R:

$$P + R = 45$$
$$(R + 5) + R = 45$$
$$2R = 40$$
$$R = 20$$